PRACTICING LAW IN THE SHARING ECONOMY

PRACTICING LAW IN THE SHARING ECONOMY

HELPING PEOPLE BUILD COOPERATIVES, SOCIAL ENTERPRISE, AND LOCAL SUSTAINABLE ECONOMIES

JANELLE ORSI

ADVANCE PRAISE FOR *PRACTICING LAW IN THE SHARING ECONOMY*

"A unique and indispensable handbook for anyone working in the field of alternative ownership design. We've long needed this book, and at last it's here."

—Marjorie Kelly, fellow, Tellus Institute, and Director of Ownership Strategy, Cutting Edge Capital; author of *Owning Our Future: The Emerging Ownership Revolution*

"As Orsi notes in this invaluable book, lawyers often 'work for firms that grease the wheels of the very economic system that is causing the widespread ecological and social distress.' But this does not have to be the case! In *Practicing Law in the Sharing Economy*, she and her contributing co-authors provide an impressive roadmap to a range of innovative legal forms that can help communities build wealth and create the building blocks of a new economy."

—Gar Alperovitz, author of *America Beyond* Capitalism, and Lionel R. Bauman Professor of Political Economy, University of Maryland

"What William Blackstone did for the common law in the 18th century, Janelle Orsi has done for Sharing Economy Law in the 21st. This monumental treatise defines, legitimates, and elaborates the key legal challenges facing U.S. new economy advocates, and in terms that even non-lawyers can understand and deploy in their day-to-day work. Whatever your angle—cooperatives, cohousing, alternative currencies,

CSAs, social enterprise, crowdfunding—this book belongs front and center on your desk."

—Michael Shuman, JD, author of Local Dollars, *Local Sense* and *The Small-Mart Revolution*

"Every once in a while someone sees the emerging pattern of a new order of things and is able to bring conceptual clarity and useful tools to it, thus defining a new field. That is what Janelle Orsi has done in her remarkable book on the sharing economy. Collaborative consumption, credit unions, co-ops, community enterprises, and other features of the sharing economy require laws that work for them. In *Practicing Law in the Sharing Economy*, Orsi shows how it can be done."

—James Gustave Speth, JD, author of *America the Possible: Manifesto for a New Economy* (Yale Press, 2012).

"This is a book for those who have hoped and dreamed of a way to practice law that was good for lawyers, clients and the planet."

—J. Kim Wright, JD, Founder of Cutting Edge Law & Author of *Lawyers as Peacemakers: Practicing Holistic, Problem-Solving Law*

"Can a sharing economy emerge from and transform capitalism? Janelle Orsi's brilliant exegesis argues it can. Her book is a welcome clarion call to lawyers to learn and apply the rules that can support new forms of sharing and cooperation and to identify and change the rules that could inhibit or even endanger their continued growth."

—David Morris, co-founder of the Institute for Local Self-Reliance, author of *Self Reliant Cities: Energy and the Transformation of Urban America*, and *Seeing the Light: Regaining Control of Our Electricity System*

"This book breaks new ground by taking conventional legal practice and turning it on its head. Orsi provides concrete examples of practicing law through a paradigm of cooperation and sharing, rather than competition. At a time of significant economic and environmental breakdowns, Orsi courageously presents a set of lawyering principles that promote sustainable communities and advance the common good. What an opportunity, especially for young, unemployed attorneys: to consider a legal practice that contributes to a sharing economy and environmental sustainability."

—Patricia Siemen, OP, JD, Director of the Center for Earth Jurisprudence, Barry University School of Law

"Janelle Orsi's *Practicing Law in the Sharing Economy* offers a detailed and expansive vision of the role lawyers play in the new economy, and how the new economy can affect the practice of law. This book contains a wealth of substantive information and practical advice for any lawyer interested in participating in and creating more collaborative communities and a more sharing world."

—Emily Doskow, JD, co-author of *Making It Legal: A Guide to Same-Sex Marriage, Domestic Partnership & Civil Unions*, and *The Sharing Solution: How to Save Money, Simplify Your Life & Build Community*

Cover by Kelly Book/ABA Publishing.

Printed in the United States of America

16 15 14 13 5 4 3 2

Library of Congress Cataloging-in-Publication Data

Orsi, Janelle, 1979-
Practicing law in the sharing economy : helping people build cooperatives, social enterprise, and local sustainable economies / by Janelle Orsi.
p. cm.
Includes bibliographical references and index.
ISBN 978-1-61438-546-2 (print : alk. paper)
1. Cooperative societies—Law and legislation—United States. I. Title.
KF1470.O77 2012
346.73'0668—dc23

2012026990

Discounts are available for books ordered in bulk. Special consideration is given to state bars, CLE programs, and other bar-related organizations. Inquire at Book Publishing, ABA Publishing, American Bar Association, 321 North Clark Street, Chicago, Illinois 60654-7598.

www.ShopABA.org

DEDICATION

This book is dedicated to:
Everybody.
The sharing economy is for you.

All royalties for this book go to the nonprofit Sustainable Economies Law Center.

CONTENTS

ACKNOWLEDGMENTS

To My Sharing Economy Law Muse

First, I want to express enormous gratitude to Jenny Kassan, the attorney, leader, and visionary who co-founded the Sustainable Economies Law Center with me. Thank you for teaching me so much and for bringing to light so many puzzles and problems in the legal system. Thank you, also, for pouring an incredible amount of energy and thought into this book and into the work of creating a more sustainable and equitable world.

Whose Idea Was This Anyway?

Thank you to Erin Nevius, this book's editor and the person who persuaded me to write this book in the first place. You've been wonderful to work with!

To the Chapter Editing Superstars

Thank you to everyone who read, edited, or commented on book chapters: Jenny Kassan, Sarah Hoskinson, Christen Lee, Thomas Beckett, Linda Alvarez, Cynthia Hawley, Corinne Calfee, Emily Bolt, Ashlee Albies, Debra Butler, Shae Irving, and Cameron Holland. And an extra special thank-you goes to my mom, Jackie Orsi, who read and edited nearly every chapter, usually on a moment's notice.

To the Topical Gurus

Thank you to all the people who know more than I do about so many things and who contributed ideas, feedback, research, and writing to this book:

- **Law Practice and Ethics Gurus:** Christen Lee, Emily Doskow, Eileen Barker, Jenny Kassan, Brendan Conley

- **Contracts Guru:** Linda Alvarez
- **Legal Structure Gurus:** Jenny Kassan, Marjorie Kelly, Brian Howe, Daniel Fireside, Loren Rodgers, Christen Lee, and Clementine Blazy
- **Credit Union Gurus:** Mike Leung, Wesley Roe, William G. Sommers, Marjorie Lakin Erickson
- **Governance Gurus:** Tree Bressen, Gaya Erlandson
- **Barter, Time Bank, and Local Currency Gurus:** Edgar S. Cahn, Janelle J. Smith, Erin Byers, Jose Rivera, and Gordon Ng
- **Employment Law Gurus:** Emily Bolt, Ashlee Albies, and Tony LoPresti
- **Securities Law Gurus:** Jenny Kassan, Karan Singh Dhadialla, Aroma Sharma, Janelle J. Smith, Daniel Fireside, and Kathleen Kenney
- **Energy Law Gurus:** Linda Barrera and Rachel Gold
- **Intellectual Property Guru:** Inder Comar
- **Real Estate and Land Use Gurus:** Corinne Calfee, Cynthia Hawley, and Julie Pennington
- **Risk Management Guru:** Debra Butler

Other Legal Research Extraordinaires

Thank you to other Sustainable Economies Law Center volunteers who contributed to the research and knowledge base on which this book was built: Nicole Bartolomucci, Kelly Densmore, Christina Oatfield, Sean Betouliere, Christopher Curran, Esperanza Pallana, Kristen McArdle, Yassi Eskandari, Elizabeth Spellman, Eva Seidelman, and Allison Clark.

For Incredible Kindness and Support

A gargantuan thank-you goes to my wife, Catherine Shaffer, who is pretty much the kindest person on the planet. I cannot thank you enough for your support and patience while I was secluded in the office writing a gigantic book.

Whoever Washed the Dishes

A special thank-you goes to whoever did the dishes while I was writing this book. It most certainly wasn't I.

CHAPTER ONE

THE LEGAL LANDSCAPE OF THE SHARING ECONOMY

Part 1: Introduction

To most public interest–minded law students and lawyers, practicing transactional law isn't an obvious path to saving the world. After all, the majority of transactional lawyers work for firms that grease the wheels of the very economic system that is causing widespread ecological and social distress.

Now transactional lawyers are needed, en masse, to aid in an epic reinvention of our economic system. The world's economic and ecological meltdowns demand that we now redesign our livelihoods, our enterprises, our communities, our organizations, our food system, our housing, and much more. This glorious reinvention has already begun, and many refer to it as the "sharing economy," the "relationship economy," the "cooperative economy," the "grassroots economy," or just the "new economy."

Transactional lawyers manage economic activity and relationships, which puts them in a good position to work on the reinvention of our economy. Transactional lawyers write contracts, form business entities, structure transactions, manage and allocate risks, and navigate the world of tax, business regulations, land use, and labor laws. Sharing economy lawyers do all of these things, but we do them for the exploding numbers of social enterprises, cooperatives, urban farms, cohousing

Seeking 500,000 Sharing Economy Lawyers

Every community in the United States will soon need sharing economy lawyers, grassroots transactional lawyers, or whatever you may prefer to call these new legal specialists. With around 30,000 incorporated towns and cities in the United States, we will soon need at least 100,000 sharing economy lawyers. And as the sharing economy becomes the predominant economic force in our society, then all transactional lawyers in the United States (approximately 500,000) should consider transforming the focus of their practices to smooth the way toward a more sustainable economy. No matter how you do the math, the sharing economy offers a huge opportunity to new and experienced lawyers alike.

communities, time banks, local currencies, and the vast array of unique organizations arising from the sharing economy.

The work and legal questions faced by sharing economy lawyers are uniquely challenging, and they tell us some important things about both our economic system and our legal system. To understand what's unique about the practice of sharing economy law, it's important to first understand what is unique about the sharing economy.

Part 2: The Sharing Economy

Although it is hard to encapsulate the qualities of this new economy, it generally facilitates community ownership, localized production, sharing, cooperation, small-scale enterprise, and the regeneration of economic and natural abundance. To achieve this, the new economy involves different ways of meeting our needs, participating in production, and transacting with each other.

Sometimes, the best way to picture the sharing economy is to list the phenomena and practices that are beginning to comprise it:

- Cohousing communities
- Community gardens
- Social enterprise
- Community-owned enterprises
- Shared commercial kitchens
- Car-sharing groups

- Ecovillages
- Local currencies
- Barter networks
- Time banks
- Gift economies
- Community land trusts
- Grocery cooperatives
- Worker cooperatives
- Community-supported agriculture
- Community-supported kitchens
- Credit unions
- Creative commons licensing
- Housing cooperatives
- Childcare cooperatives
- Renewable energy cooperatives
- Tool lending libraries
- Coworking spaces
- Collaborative consumption

The sharing economy is not a top-down solution, meaning that it will not be imposed by a set of legislated policies. We also don't need to wait for a large organization or company to offer the solution to us. The sharing economy is being built, from the ground up, by every individual and group that chooses to begin consuming, transacting, and/or making a livelihood in a new way.

For each of us, individually, it means a very different plan for our lives. Most of us had a plan for our lives that looked something like the American Dream. We expected to grow up, get a good job, and make money to buy all the things we need. Usually, this involved owning one or two cars and a house full of every appliance, tool, and item we might need. If we needed something, we would go to the store and buy it. If we accumulated too much, we would rent a storage unit. We would try to max out our contribution to our retirement account so we could accumulate a big enough pile of cash to be comfortable when we retire.

Now we know that our original vision was based on the flawed assumption that the economy could grow continuously. The reality is that we have already used the planet's resources faster than they can be replenished, and we have built our current economic system by creating an ever-widening gap between the rich and the poor. That means that the new economy that we build must not just be *sustainable*, it must now *regenerate* the economic and ecological abundance necessary for everyone to thrive again.

It means that every single one of us must adopt a new plan for our futures. In fact, the sooner we can let go of our original plans, the greater the likelihood that we will transition gracefully to a viable new economy.

One way to understand how the new economy works is to look at three components separately: consumption, production, and exchange.

Consumption

Our Needs: The Explosion of an Access Economy

In the future, we might look back and gently laugh at the way we live now. The way we presently participate in consumption is by attempting to *buy* and *own* everything we need. We work long hours because we strive to *own* a car, *own* a house, and so on. But from the standpoint of wise resource use, individual ownership is not the most efficient or easiest way to meet our needs.

The sharing economy presents us with a viable and necessary alternative: we can have *access* to many things that we need without having to *own* them all by ourselves. Our right to access something will derive from a variety of new relationships—we may have an agreement to borrow or share an item; we may be a member of a group of friends, a cooperative, a nonprofit, or a service that gives us access to that item. Tool lending libraries, borrowing and lending, car-sharing clubs, and shared ownership will be the new norm.

In 2008, with co-author Emily Doskow, I wrote my first book, *The Sharing Solution: How to Save Money, Simplify Your Life & Build Community* (Nolo, 2009). The book surveyed ways that sharing can viably meet our needs and provided practical and legal tools for sharing in realms such as housing, food, work, household goods, transportation, and family care. Little did I know how quickly sharing would become a key component in society's effort to rebuild a resilient economy.

On the heels of *The Sharing Solution* came the launch of Shareable .net, a true hub of information about what is happening in the sharing economy, in the realm of consumption and far beyond. Then came

Rachel Botsman and Roo Rogers's book *What's Mine Is Yours: How Collaborative Consumption Is Changing the Way We Live* (Harper Collins, 2010), and Lisa Gansky's *The Mesh: Why the Future of Business Is Sharing* (Portfolio Hardcover, 2010). Both books looked at the explosion of businesses and organizations allowing us to meet our needs through sharing, with a particular focus on the power of technology to enable this revolution in consumption.

It has since become nearly impossible to keep up with what is happening in the realm of the access economy, collaborative consumption, and the peer-to-peer or P2P economy. Countless groups, communities, organizations, businesses, and websites are designed to facilitate sharing. Needless to say, sharing is rapidly being embraced as a way to meet our needs.

Our Land: Toward Collective Management

This shift from an economy of *ownership* to an economy of *access* is particularly powerful in how it will change our relationship with a "commodity" like land. Today, land and housing tend to be expensive, and they are treated just like any other investment—something to buy and to extract the maximum value out of as quickly as possible. Many individuals build their financial security around their investment in real property, and the market creates an incentive to exploit and degrade land—we develop it to its most marketable use, not to its most socially or environmentally beneficial use.

The shift to an access economy will not only lower what individuals pay for housing and land, but it will also likely create more sustainable structures for managing land and housing. We might gain the right to long-term use of land, but not the right to sell it and extract all equity from that sale. Land would be managed by cooperatives and land trusts that ensure that the land is used for the benefit of nature and communities.

Production

Our Work: Toward a Post-Jobs Economy

In many respects, it's easier to reimagine how we take part in consumption than to rethink how we take part in production, particularly when it comes to our labor. Rethinking our participation in labor is scary because it relates to our jobs, something we are fearful of losing. But the reality of our changing world is that jobs may no longer be the way that the majority of us make our productive contribution to the world. Jobs can be nice, on one hand; they create a somewhat reliable structure through which we can be productive and earn sustenance (usually in the form of money). Unfortunately, jobs are reliable only until the moment they disappear, and they are often prone to becoming scarce.

Our society's reaction to the scarcity of jobs is even more disempowering. Governments and nonprofits spend millions on setting up job fairs and resume writing workshops, as if that could somehow address the fact that there are not enough jobs to go around. If anything, it makes things worse by making people feel that a personal flaw prevents them from getting work.

The inherent problem with a focus on jobs is that jobs entail relying on *someone else* to create the work opportunities for us. We must fit ourselves into the requirements of whichever job we are lucky enough to get, whether or not that job is how we'd like to use our time and skills, and whether or not we subscribe to the mission of the company we are serving. That *someone else* who is providing our job does not necessarily have our or our community's interests in mind, and providing a sustainable livelihood for us is not likely his/her primary goal.

As described further below, in the new economy, we will shift away from our reliance on jobs that others create for us toward livelihoods that *we create for ourselves.*

Our Capital: Toward a Post–Wall Street Economy

Another way that people participate in production is with their capital. Many things we do require a lot of investment of resources up front—starting farms, building homes, installing solar, and so on. The current economy generally offers us only one way of contributing capital to projects and enterprises, and this is through a speculative casino known as Wall Street. Investing our money in Wall Street generally means that our wealth and resources fly out of our community and contribute to the oftentimes destructive work of large companies.

In the new economy, we will develop ways to keep our resources local, using our capital to support projects that benefit us and our community. As described below, the primary barrier to using resources locally tends to derive from securities law.

The Sharing Economy and the Blossoming of New Enterprises

Sharing is the key to an economy where everyone can make a livelihood through a combination of their own endeavors and cooperative enterprises. Many people might react to such a statement by thinking, "yes, but ... not everyone is cut out to be an entrepreneur." This is true only if you are thinking that entrepreneurs are rare individuals capable of tireless work, fierce competition, and the ability to impress venture capitalists. In our highly competitive economy, dominated by large businesses, this certainly *is* true of most successful entrepreneurs.

But it is not true in an economy based on sharing and relationships. In the new economy, entrepreneurs will be successful based on the *relationships they build with* others, not based on their ability to *compete with* others.

To fully envision how this works, it helps to adopt a more expansive concept of *enterprise*. Think of an enterprise as *any* productive activity that could bring us sustenance—either directly or through cooperation or exchange with other people. In the new economy, each person will likely be involved in multiple enterprises, many of which will not look like a typical business:

- **Sharing enterprise:** A sharing enterprise is aimed at sharing and offsetting the costs of ownership and maintenance of an item; it is not aimed at making a profit. For example, a group of residents in an apartment building may form an association to share ownership of a few cars.
- **Nano-enterprise:** Anything we do for others could be considered a nano-enterprise if the result is that the activity ends up providing for us in some way. These days, many people are finding little ways to casually swap with friends and neighbors, do favors for money, and so on. A woman lets her neighbors use her washer and dryer, in exchange for food and other favors. A jam enthusiast makes 30 jars of jam and sells them to her friends, or uses them as a currency for exchange. The first woman hasn't started a laundromat and the second hasn't exactly started a full-blown jam factory; yet, because of the valuable relationships they maintain, these nano-enterprises do provide for the women.
- **Producer cooperative enterprise:** Producer cooperatives can harness the nano-entrepreneur in all of us by aggregating and marketing the products of multiple small producers. For example,

a bread producers' cooperative could purchase bread from 20 home bakers (in states where home baking businesses are legal), and sell the bread at a local farmers' market. The baker-members can take turns staffing the farmers' market booth, and in this way, each one's business can become viable through the joint marketing and selling efforts.

- **Worker cooperative enterprise:** Worker cooperatives are businesses owned and governed by their workers. In many ways, worker cooperatives are like producer cooperatives, in that they give their members an opportunity to work and contribute to a fruitful enterprise. The difference is the relationship between the members and the cooperative; in the case of a worker cooperative, the members are regular employees, as opposed to independent sellers or contractors. And in a producer cooperative, the members themselves may be businesses as opposed to individuals.
- **Consumer cooperative enterprise:** Consumer cooperatives could take many forms and sizes: a group of friends pools money to buy pet food in bulk, or a much larger group forms a grocery buying cooperative that looks, on the surface, like a regular grocery store. In either case, the cooperative provides for its members by providing goods or services at cost and may keep costs especially low by involving members in the day-to-day work of the cooperative.
- **Social enterprise:** A social enterprise is an activity aimed at creating a social or environmental good and, in doing so, also generates income or sustenance for those engaged in the activity.
- **Community-supported enterprise:** The community-supported enterprise model is well established in the realm of agriculture and makes increasing sense for many kinds of businesses in an economy based on relationships. In the community-supported agriculture (CSA) model, a farmer and a group of customers form a relationship and agree to share a handful of things, including, to varying extents, the financing, the bounty, and the potential risks of farming. In a CSA's purest form, a CSA member generally pays the farm money at planting time, which gives the farmer operating capital throughout the year. In exchange, the CSA member gets a share of the harvest, which could mean a lot of vegetables in a good year, or fewer during a bad harvest year. Creating such a relationship with many local businesses is a wonderful way for

consumers to consciously involve themselves in creating a thriving local economy.

- **Community-owned enterprise:** Imagine that having a "diversified investment portfolio" could mean that we own shares of 50 or more local businesses. What better way for a business to finance itself than to give local community members ownership shares? And what better way for each of us to grow our wealth—both financially and by contributing to the wealth and vitality of our local communities?

What makes all of these enterprises work, and how can they truly provide for us? The answer is: relationships. All of these enterprises can engage us in productive activity, and they provide for us in meaningful ways because of the relationships and agreements we have made with other people.

Exchange

The sharing economy opens the doors to a wide variety of exchange mechanisms. Currently, we rely almost entirely on dollars to transact with each other, which means that we are relatively helpless when we don't have access to dollars. For growing numbers of people, dollars are scarce, which leaves our communities feeling increasingly helpless.

But the fact is that our communities have a wealth of resources—people, skills, and tangible items—which we could use to provide for ourselves. We simply need an incentive system to promote the sharing of these resources. Dollars are basically an incentive system; I'll weed your garden if you give me dollars. Dollars are a good incentive because I know that other people will be equally excited to accept those dollars in exchange for other favors.

Since dollars are essentially an incentive system, with no inherent value other than their exchangeability, the question becomes: what other systems could we adopt to share and exchange things of value? I met a man who, somewhat unintentionally, created a currency used among his friends. He made certificates that his friends could give back to him in exchange for a massage. He'd give them as gifts, or give them to a friend in exchange for a ride to the airport, for example.

At what point does such an incentive system become a currency? The answer is in the word itself: when it began to run or flow, like a *current.* His friends began to trade the certificates among each other, in exchange for other favors. Unlike dollars, the certificates are actually *backed* by something: a massage. (The U.S. Dollar, by the way, is no longer backed by anything.) The certificates have value not only because they can be exchanged for a massage, but also because they gained currency among a community willing to accept them as payment.

What this means is that dollars can be easily replaced. They will be replaced by casually created currencies like the massage certificates, by more formal local currency systems, by online barter networks, by time banks, and by a general culture of giving, sharing, swapping, and bartering.

The Four Platforms for the New Economy

Now, how do we make all of it happen? How can we more fully adopt these new ways of meeting our needs, new kinds of enterprises, and new forms of exchange? The answer lies in the platforms we build, and as demonstrated below, *everyone* has a role to play in building these platforms.

One way of looking at the platforms is to break them into four levels. The following levels are not stages in a progression; rather they are activities that must all take place simultaneously, in order to build firm grounding for a sharing economy:

Level 1: Building Relationships for Casual, Spontaneous, and One-Time Transactions

At the first level of the sharing economy, we begin to build relationships with each other, resulting in casual and spontaneous transactions. These transactions can include things like

- Borrowing a shovel,
- Lending someone your car,
- Running an errand for someone, or
- Giving a neighbor extra cucumbers from your garden.

These things sound relatively simple, but we currently live in a world where people don't do these enough. Such transactions take place naturally within communities of people that know and care for each other. These things take place naturally among the neighbors in my apartment building, now that we all know each other and have spent time together.

Generally, we live in a society where we tend not to know our neighbors, much less think of them when we need a favor or have something extra to share. The challenge for all of us, now, is to build community in ways that will catalyze such transactions. A goal for everyone should be to dramatically increase the ways we share, borrow, and lend among friends and neighbors.

Level 2: Building Agreements

Casual and spontaneous favors and sharing will only go so far in meeting our needs, which is why we need to build *agreements* for sharing and transacting. Agreements create a relationship that we can *rely* on to meet our needs. Rather than casually borrowing a neighbor's vacuum, you and your neighbor might agree to regularly share a vacuum. That way, you can rely on the availability of the vacuum when you need one. In the sharing economy, we will all be parties to many more agreements. We may

- Make an agreement to exchange child care,
- Make an agreement to co-own or regularly borrow a car,
- Make an agreement to share office space, or
- Agree to barter for goods or services.

Level 3: Building Organizations

Building organizations is a key component of the sharing economy because organizations generally endure even when individuals come and go from them. In that respect, organizations become lasting institutions in our communities. This is especially important in creating a resilient economy in a world where people are highly mobile.

An example of an organization is a neighborhood organization formed for the purpose of sharing cars. The organization can make provisions for people to join and leave the organization, as needed. Other examples of organizations might be

- Cohousing communities,
- Food cooperatives,
- Coworking spaces,

- Tool lending libraries, and
- Time banks, which create an hour-for-hour currency used to track favors exchanged in a community.

Level 4: Building Larger-Scale Infrastructure

At the fourth level, we build platforms for the sharing economy into the infrastructure of our cities, towns, and regions, which usually involves cooperation of multiple stakeholders and leadership by our local governments. For example, we might require that all new neighborhoods be physically designed to facilitate interaction among residents, by ensuring walkability or creating central gathering spaces. Other examples include

- Community-wide car-sharing programs,
- Community-wide bike sharing programs, and
- City- or state-owned banks.

The New American Dream

The four platforms described above are, essentially, the new American Dream. Envisioning the sharing economy in this way makes it much easier to let go of the original American Dream—the desire to own a house, own a car, and accumulate a large amount of wealth. If we live in a world where all four levels are thriving in our community and in communities around the world, then we can feel assured that we, too, will thrive.

Part 3: Legal Conundrums in the Sharing Economy

Now comes the interesting part: how do these platforms fit into our current legal framework? The sharing economy and the platforms on which it will operate can be built by individuals, groups, and local governments within communities. The creation of these platforms, especially at the second, third, and fourth levels described above, will be greatly facilitated by transactional lawyers with expertise in agreements, organizations, regulations, and so on.

Practicing law in this new economy comes with unique challenges, which also point to the shortcomings of our legal system. Clients approach their lawyers with incredibly innovative ideas for making their communities better. It is the lawyers' job to help them navigate the laws to improve their chances for success and sustainability.

A Hopeful Conundrum!

Although the legal gray areas encountered by the sharing economy can be bewildering, the very fact that activities in the sharing economy cannot be put into traditional legal boxes tells us something very powerful and hopeful: these activities are radically different from what we have been doing for the past century. What a relief! The unraveling of our economic and ecological systems has sent us a clear message that our society needs to do something radically different. By eluding most traditional legal categories, the sharing economy has shown us that it is, truly, a *new* economy.

But the process can be baffling to an attorney. The relationships, transactions, and organizations of the new economy are sometimes so unique that they cannot be classified within existing legal frameworks.

At the core of it is the fact that our laws were designed to regulate relationships in a competitive economy, not a collaborative economy. Our legal system has not foreseen the trend toward a more sharing economy.

Laws That Didn't Foresee Collaborative Relationships

Many of our laws developed over the last century to manage economic relationships that were becoming increasingly polarized or exploitative. These relationships include

- Employer/employee,
- Landlord/tenant,
- Developer/homebuyer,
- Business/investor, and
- Producer/consumer.

Due to the collaborative nature of relationships in the sharing economy, it is often very difficult for an attorney to determine:

- In a worker cooperative, whether an employer/employee relationship exists;
- In a housing cooperative, whether a landlord/tenant relationship exists;

- In a resident-developed cohousing community, whether a developer/homebuyer relationship exists;
- In a community-supported agriculture program, whether a business/investor relationship exists; or
- In a food cooperative, whether a producer/consumer relationship exists.

The fact is that, in the sharing economy, many of these relationships either overlap, are highly collaborative, or involve actors with a close and accountable relationship. Because it lacks many of the same power dynamics of the old economy, some have described the new economy as one with primarily horizontal, rather than vertical, relationships. This means that it can be very difficult to determine whether certain labor, real estate, securities, commercial, and other regulations even apply to activities in the sharing economy. And when such regulations do apply, they can be unduly burdensome given that they are designed to protect the powerless against the powerful, and such protections are often unnecessary when relationships are horizontal.

Laws That Didn't Take into Account the Varied Motivations Behind Our Activities/Enterprises

There is an assumption embedded in our legal system that we do things with three different and separate motivations: personal, commercial, and charitable. Take food-growing as an example:

1. **Personal:** Home gardeners grow food for personal consumption.
2. **Commercial:** Farmers grow food for commercial sale.
3. **Charitable:** Nonprofits run gardens to feed the poor or educate communities.

Each of these three activities is subject to different zoning regulations, different agricultural regulations, different types of insurance coverage, and different labor and tax laws. Furthermore, if these food growers form an organization for their activity, they will each likely choose a different legal entity structure and tax status. So long as activities fit neatly into the categories of personal, commercial, and charitable, the work of a lawyer is fairly uncomplicated.

Nothing is so perfectly segmented in the sharing economy. Sharing economy lawyers constantly meet clients engaging in activities that

1. **Straddle the line between personal and commercial:** A home gardener that sells backyard produce to neighbors.
2. **Straddle the line between commercial and charitable:** A nonprofit educational farm that sells a large amount of produce.
3. **Straddle the line between charitable and personal:** A nonprofit farm that "pays" its volunteers in food.

From social, environmental, economic, and practical perspectives, each of those three examples makes wonderful sense! After all, people are growing food in ways that nourish themselves and their communities and that contribute to the economic sustainability of the activity.

From a legal perspective, however, there may well be some difficult news to break. The home gardener may be told that her activity violates zoning regulations and will not be covered by homeowners insurance. The educational farm may be told that the Internal Revenue Service (IRS) will not consider the sale of large amounts of produce a tax-exempt activity. The other nonprofit farm may be told that "paying" volunteers in food violates rules against nonprofits distributing assets to private individuals, or brings up labor law problems, since volunteers are generally supposed to work without expectation of compensation.

Laws That Didn't Foresee Diverse Forms of Exchange

Our society is captivated by dollars, and so is our legal system. Taxes must be paid in dollars. Minimum wage must be paid in dollars. Most income is difficult to recognize and quantify unless it comes in the form of dollars. The application of many rules and regulations is determined by dollar volume of a business, and so on.

What is a sharing economy lawyer to do when complimentary currencies, barter, time banks, work-trade arrangements, and "sweat-equity" arrangements become a significant means by which value is exchanged in our economy? The primary challenges for a sharing economy lawyer are (1) to determine whether a regulated relationship has arisen from such an exchange (such as an employee/employer or investor/business relationship) and (2) to determine how to account for and advise on tax reporting for a transaction.

To Do: Change Our Laws

Sharing economy lawyers and community activists have a great deal of work ahead to bring our laws into sync with the realities of the sharing economy. Certain employment laws, securities regulations, commercial regulations, and zoning ordinances create incredibly difficult legal barriers, such that we should change them sooner rather than later. In other legal realms the sharing economy will forge ahead, *in spite of* the legal barriers and inconveniences that remain. In the meantime, sharing economy lawyers are well positioned to collect stories and examples, and to develop best practices and policy recommendations to adapt our laws to the needs of a changing economy.

For example, let's say that a kitchen is set up where customers come in, help out in the kitchen for 30 minutes, and then get a free meal in exchange for their time. How do you characterize such an exchange? Can you say that the volunteers are simply a group of people collaboratively cooking a meal for themselves, and no exchange has taken place? Or are these volunteers, in reality, doing work that should afford them the protection of labor laws and therefore requires that they be paid in dollars, rather than food? If payment in food is allowed, is the value of the meal taxable as income to the volunteers? Given the incredible variation in the pricing of foods, how would you even determine the fair market value of the meal? Our legal and tax systems are simply not set up for non-dollar forms of exchange to become a significant portion of our economy.

Part 4: Practicing Law in the Sharing Economy

What does the work of a sharing economy lawyer look like? The nine primary areas of work of a sharing economy lawyer serve as the basis for Chapters 3 through 11 of this book. These primary areas are described briefly here:

- **Designing and Drafting Agreements**: Agreements are the roadmaps to relationships in the sharing economy. Every person will likely be party to many agreements in the sharing economy, such as car-sharing agreements, agreements to share housing, and agreements to participate in a community-supported agriculture program. The work of a sharing economy lawyer in drafting agreements will need to be creative, since such agreements will structure highly collaborative, possibly complex, and long-term relationships. And, notwithstanding the fact that lawyers are expected to write like this, we hereby declare that the aforementioned contracts in the sharing economy shall henceforth be much more readable than this sentence!

- **Choosing, Forming, and Structuring Entities**: Entities provide a legal structure in which groups of people work together, manage assets, engage in cooperative activities, and operate social enterprises. The sharing economy offers endless opportunities for sharing economy lawyers to get creative in choosing and structuring entities. Our usual menu of entity choices—C Corporations, 501(c)(3) nonprofits, limited liability companies (LLCs), and so on—does not always meet the unique needs of organizations in the new economy. Sharing economy lawyers often look beyond the usual options to low-profit limited liability companies (L3Cs), Benefit Corporations, 501(c)(4) or 501(c)(7) nonprofits, cooperative corporations, and other less common entities and tax statuses. After choosing an entity, a sharing economy lawyer then works with clients to iron out questions related to governance, profit sharing, protection of social purpose, accountability to stakeholders, tax, and many more.
- **Advising on the Legalities and Taxation of Exchange**: Barter transactions, barter networks, community currencies, time banks, and other non-dollar modes of exchange bring up interesting questions for lawyers, not the least of which is: what is taxable income? Gifts and casual nontaxable exchanges generally do not result in taxable income, but more formal barter transactions do result in taxable income. The question becomes: what's the difference? In the sharing economy, people provide valuables, goods, and services to each other through a variety of relationships, and gray areas abound. As new currency systems develop, sharing economy lawyers must also grapple with a handful of questions to determine whether the currency is even legal.
- **Navigating Securities Regulations**: In a world where enterprises and housing will ideally be financed and owned by members of our local communities, securities law compliance will keep sharing

economy lawyers busy. By developing proficiency in securities laws, a sharing economy lawyer can help a grocery cooperative finance its start-up with member loans; a movie theater to sell ownership shares to its clients; or a cohousing community to purchase land with loans from friends and neighbors without risking lawsuits, fines, and other penalties for securities law violations. Yet again, unique legal gray areas abound; if 30 people put in $200 each to launch their small food-buying cooperative, is that a security? If members of a community-supported farm pay $500 to a farmer to receive a share of the year's harvest, is that a security?

- **Navigating Employment Regulations**: As communities adopt diverse and collaborative ways of making livelihoods, the labor and employment laws will need to be applied in some unexplored territory. If members of a grocery cooperative volunteer three hours per month to help receive and distribute bulk orders, must they be treated and paid as employees? Can residents of a housing cooperative put in work hours in exchange for lower rent, without violating employment laws? Can an employer pay an employee partially in a local currency, and if so, how does that payment get reported on taxes, and get factored into the calculation of the payment of overtime? Is it possible to volunteer or intern on a farm? Sharing economy lawyers frequently have to advise clients on how to structure their relationships and how to manage work and compensation in order to comply with or avoid application of employment laws.
- **Navigating Regulations on Production and Commerce**: Health and safety regulations, food and agricultural regulations, childcare center licensing, public utilities regulations, regulations on taxi cabs, regulations on the hotel industry—these are all topics that a lawyer may need to be familiar with when advising commercial clients. But how do these regulations apply to activities that are not clearly commercial, such as food-swapping events, community gardens, babysitting cooperatives, energy cooperatives, paid ride-sharing arrangements, or renting out a room to tourists? Are these activities subject to all of the same regulations as their commercial counterparts, and are there special exemptions for small-scale or collaborative arrangements? Regulations

on commercial activities have been largely developed to manage transactions between producers and consumers that have little or no relationship, and that are clearly in the commercial, impersonal realm. The sharing economy is built on a very different set of relationships, which makes it tricky to determine which regulations may or may not apply.

- **Managing Relationships with and Use of Land**: Land is an incredibly important resource, and the resilience of our economy and ecosystems demand that we find new ways to structure ownership of land, manage uses of land, finance the acquisition and development of land, and so on. For a sharing economy lawyer, this means developing creative new agreements and entities as well as navigating real estate, subdivision, and land use regulations that do not necessarily fit well with the ways we will structure relationships with land in the sharing economy.
- **Managing Intellectual Property**: Sharing of intellectual property, arguably, brought us some of the earliest innovations in sharing and the law, with the creation of open source software licenses and Creative Commons licenses. IP lawyers and creative people continue to break new ground, such as with the recent development of "humanitarian licenses" and other tools to make patented inventions available to use for the public good. With every new book, photograph, musical track, software program, and invention, the creators may ask themselves the question: do I want to share this, how, where, when, with whom, and for what purposes? By developing expertise in creative licensing, IP lawyers can help their clients navigate the array of options for shareability.
- **Managing Risk**: Since fear of liability and loss can be a barrier to sharing and collaboration, sharing economy lawyers spend a lot of time drafting agreements that clarify responsibilities, allocate risk, waive liability for certain activities, indemnify members of a group from others' liabilities, and create other ways to ensure that communities can remedy a loss, resolve disputes outside of litigation, and reduce risks of loss. The topic of insurance creates interesting challenges for attorneys, since, for example, traditional car insurance policies may not cover car sharing, and traditional

homeowners' policies may not cover backyard community gardening activities.

In sum, the work of a sharing economy lawyer will often be challenging but will always remain interesting and demand creativity. Perhaps best of all, the work of a sharing economy lawyer will contribute importantly to the creation of a world in which innumerable people have now decided they want to live.

CHAPTER TWO

PRACTICING LAW IN THE SHARING ECONOMY

Part 1: Lawyers in a Sharing World

Who Serves the 70 Percent?

There's something awry in the world when I have clients that earn $600 *per week* and lawyer friends that charge $600 *per hour.* Are some people really 40 times more valuable than others? Or is our economy truly that divided?

Of course, the entire Occupy movement has concluded that it's the latter, and I tend to agree. The question now is: Where will lawyers fit in a society that strives to replace scarcities with sharing and abundance? For a start, we need to acknowledge two artificially created scarcities holding the legal world captive: the artificial scarcity of legal job opportunities and the artificial scarcity of accessible legal services.

I'm not afraid of artificial scarcities. Unlike the *real* scarcities—such as the current scarcities of clean water, clean air, and fertile soil—*artificial* scarcities can be immediately remedied by a change in behavior. As lawyers, the way we practice law and structure our law practices could remedy scarcities in the legal system and far beyond.

The ABA acknowledged in the 1970s that the "middle 70% of our population is not being reached or served adequately by the legal profession."[1] Since then, lawyers have only gotten more expensive, funding for legal services has been cut, the rich have gotten richer, and the poor have become more numerous.

Yet, we don't have a shortage of trained legal minds. In 2011, the *ABA Journal*[2] reported that 32 percent of the prior year's law grads were without legal jobs.

Underserved Clients + Underemployed Attorneys = Artificial Scarcity

Put two and two together and you can see the artificially created scarcity. We should not have a scarcity of law jobs AND a scarcity of legal services. When supply fails to meet demand, something else is going on. If law firms were to hire more attorneys, provide more legal services at a lower cost, lower everyone's pay, and cut back on extravagant cocktail parties, then we could begin to remedy the scarcity. To do so, however, would begin to cut away at the elite status that lawyers have carved out for themselves in society. To protect that status, law firms have chosen, instead, to lay off lawyers and continue to accept only high-paying clients.

There are other factors contributing to the artificial scarcities of legal jobs and legal services:

Lawyers Keep Themselves Artificially Busy

Lawyers work in ways that force clients to return over and over again for pointless work. Lawyers write documents that are so complicated that a client must rehire the lawyer to explain what the document says, figure out how to apply it, and help with necessary changes. Clients have hired me simply to help them figure out what their bylaws mean, which shows me that the drafting attorney has done a disservice for his/her clients.

The Legal Profession's Culture of NOT Sharing

When I became a lawyer, I invited other solo attorneys to lunch to learn about their work. One lawyer somewhat reluctantly agreed to

---

1. Statistic cited by the Supreme Court in *Bates v. State Bar of Ariz*,. 433 U.S. 350 (1977).

2. Debra Cassens Weiss, *A Record Low for 2010 Law Grads: Only 68% Have Jobs Requiring Bar Passage*, ABA JOURNAL (June 1, 2011, 7:57 AM), http://www.abajournal.com/news/article/a_record_low_for_2010_law_grads_only_68_have_jobs_requiring_bar_passage/.

have lunch with me, but said he "wouldn't share any trade secrets." Lawyers have *trade secrets*? Maybe I shouldn't be so surprised, because plenty of people have advised me: "Don't write too many legal guides and share too much information or you will put yourself out of business." This has apparently become the generally accepted "wisdom" about how to be a lawyer.

When this kind of "wisdom" becomes so generally accepted, it's a dangerous thing. I simply cannot mesh the "wisdom" of keeping secrets with what I feel is lawyers' responsibility to do just the opposite.

I need only read the Preamble[3] of the ABA Model Rules of Professional Conduct to be reminded that I am an "officer of the legal system and a public citizen having special responsibility for the quality of justice." Furthermore, "[a]s a public citizen, a lawyer should seek improvement of the law, access to the legal system, the administration of justice and the quality of service rendered by the legal profession." Since I am an officer of the legal system and responsible for improving access to the legal system, I interpret this to mean that I have a responsibility to *share* information, rather than withhold it. (Plus, I do hope one day to stop hearing the joke: "'Sharing lawyer,' isn't that an oxymoron? Nyuck, nyuck.")

Lawyers' Real Stock in Trade

When I say that it is lawyers' duty to share information, I should clarify that *information* means something very different than *advice*. Abraham Lincoln said that "a lawyer's time and advice are [her] stock in trade." Advice is the work I do; it is the carefully crafted, individually tailored guidance that I give a client. Giving advice takes thought and time, even sweat and sleepless nights. This is what clients pay me for, and it feels like a good exchange. I have done something valuable for them, and they pay me in return.

What does not feel good is using *information* as a stock in trade, because to do so simply exploits a marketplace where clients are desperate for and do not have access to information. Lawyers do this all the time. Take, for example, a standard set of Conditions, Covenants & Restrictions (CC&Rs) for a two-unit condo property. The going rate

3. Model Rules of Prof'l Conduct, Preamble and Scope, http://www.americanbar.org/groups/professional_responsibility/publications/model_rules_of_professional_conduct/model_rules_of_professional_conduct_preamble_scope.html.

to have an attorney prepare such a document is around $4,000. Yet, depending on the templates available, this can sometimes take a lawyer only a few hours to prepare. Charging such a high fee to prepare a document that a lawyer *barely* has to do any work on is exploitative and contributes to the scarcity problem. However, if a lawyer charges for his/her actual time and efforts, then lawyers' place in the world will become a more balanced part of our natural economic ecosystem.

The Sustainability of Lawyers

The sustainability of lawyers, themselves, is dangerously threatened. The position of lawyers in our society is fraught with problems that not only hurt clients and communities but also do terrible damage to lawyers' health and happiness. A lawyer is nearly twice as likely as the average person to suffer from substance abuse and mental illness.

I believe the problems originate with the status that lawyers strive so hard to maintain. There is crushing pressure associated with the notion that your productive time is worth ten or more times others' productive time. To hold such status, lawyers can be highly prone to pretending they know things, when they are actually uncertain. Insincerity is stressful, and it feeds on itself.

Another problem is that too many lawyers do work that is not aligned with their values. Lawyers that act as cogs in the wheels of large firms or government entities may not even believe in the value of their work. There is nothing sustainable about spending the majority of your working hours feeling that you are not contributing to the world you want to live in.

One of the most powerful and freeing things that a lawyer can do is resolve to be uncompromisingly genuine and humble. An enormous burden lifts the moment you realize that you will be safe to let down the airs of superior knowledge, to stop being so protective of information and your status, to do work that matters to you, and to know you never again need to feel the guilt and stress of being insincere.

There is a deep connection between that which is humble and that which is sustainable. To be humble is to make a productive and creative contribution to the world without caving to the pressures to compete, withhold resources, and attain a status above others. Those pressures prevent us from sharing the wealth and resources that surround us, and thereby contribute to the basic unsustainability of everything.

Be the Change/Be a Sharing Economy Lawyer

Choosing to be a sharing economy lawyer means choosing a path that is intrinsically different from the usual routes that lawyers take. Big firms are unlikely to offer you a job as a sharing economy lawyer, but communities will embrace you as a precious resource because you make important work possible. A sharing economy law practice is a path that lawyers will carve out in response to the needs of their burgeoning local sharing economies. The law practice will be roughly as humble as the community and economy it seeks to create. The work will necessarily be collaborative, as it serves the clients that are creatively breaking new ground. There will rarely be cookie-cutter solutions for lawyers to hand their clients; rather, clients and lawyers will work together in creating and empowering communities with new legal solutions.

The agreements and organizations that a sharing economy lawyer crafts in partnership with her clients will become the replicable blueprints for a new economy. Those blueprints are a resource too valuable to be written in legalese that communities cannot understand. More importantly, those blueprints are too valuable not to be shared.

To borrow again from the Preamble of the ABA Model Rules: "Lawyers play a vital role in the preservation of society."[4] Society is in a tough spot right now. We have destroyed vital resources while creating artificial scarcities of other resources. Lawyers played a powerful role in getting us into this mess, and lawyers can play a powerful role in getting us out. What we do and how we do it matters immensely. How we structure our law practices, who we serve, how we assist clients, and how we charge for our work—these questions are what the rest of this chapter is about.

Part 2: Becoming a Sharing Economy Lawyer

Skills and Practices

A sharing economy lawyer is essentially a transactional lawyer that focuses on the needs of communities and enterprises developing within the new economy. In that respect, becoming a sharing economy lawyer is much like becoming a transactional lawyer for most practical purposes. It generally demands knowledge of topics such as

4. *Id.*

contracts, business entities, tax, risk management, and so on. It also means cultivating relationships and collaborations with other professionals, such as realtors, title companies, insurance brokers, mortgage brokers, bookkeepers, accountants, architects, contractors, mediators, facilitators, and business planners.

At the same time, sharing economy law practice has some unique demands.

Thinking Outside the Box

Too often, clients tell us about wonderful projects then say things like, "I'm so glad I talked to you—the other lawyer I spoke to said I shouldn't do this at all!" The reality of most activities in the sharing economy is that they don't fit into traditional legal boxes and categories. Many lawyers are unwilling to think outside of those traditional boxes, and the resulting advice is: your project is impossible. But most of this book is about solutions that fall outside of the box, and there are innumerable creative solutions we still haven't thought of. Everyone entering into the field of sharing economy law will become part of a greater effort to expand on creative solutions.

Helping Clients Navigate Gray Areas

Sometimes a client's activity will fall squarely in a legal gray area. In those cases there are two options: either encourage the client to reshape its activities and move closer to a clearer, more defined legal category; or let the client know that it is breaking new ground which could involve some risks. It will be necessary to train clients to be constantly mindful of the gray areas, and to empower clients to weigh the legal factors each time they make a decision or implement a new project. If a client chooses to take a risk by undertaking an activity with no clear precedent, it will need to prepare to be challenged. This can be an opportunity to make new laws that could be beneficial for future participants in the sharing economy.

For example, if your client is a 501(c)(3) with multiple "related" business activities, it could constantly be in danger of overstepping the bounds of what the Internal Revenue Service (IRS) considers "related." Even minor decisions about hiring and marketing could result in attention from the IRS. It's important to advise a client on the possibilities and limitations of activities, especially when they fall so close to or within a gray area.

Breaking the Reliance on Boilerplate and Standard Forms

Legal practice guides are full of standard form operating agreements, partnership agreements, corporate bylaws, and other forms. Such forms, though tempting to rely on, may in fact make a sharing economy lawyer's job harder. Due to the distinctiveness of our clients' projects and the collaborative nature of their relationships, drafting a contract from scratch will often be the best way to ensure that it makes sense to the client and applies well to his/her situation.

I have wasted time trying to adapt a standard limited liability company (LLC) Operating Agreement for clients forming a cohousing community and found that my edits and adaptations resulted in a contract that simply did not flow. When I abandoned that draft and started from scratch, I was able to craft an agreement that read more like a story of how they wanted their relationship to play out.

At the same time, there will always be a balance to strike between using language we know a client will understand and using language we know a court will understand. To ensure that our contracts will be appropriately interpreted if ever taken to court, there is good reason to use a certain number of standard provisions and commonly defined terms. For that reason, it's not the end of the world to sometimes use words and phrases that will make a client glaze over, like "severability," or that will make a client slightly curious or amused, like "time is of the essence." Even in those cases, we can add language that will explain the meaning of these time-worn boilerplate phrases.

Cultivating Mediation and Facilitation Skills

The success of most organizations, enterprises, and relationships depends less on the legal agreements that bind and govern them and more on the skillful communication and emotional intelligence of the participants. In that respect, a sharing economy lawyer who studies communication, mediation, and facilitation will be best equipped to guide clients toward a workable sharing agreement or governing document.

Sharing economy lawyers, more so than other attorneys, are likely to represent *groups* of people in their collective endeavors (the ethical issues that arise in multiple representation are discussed below). Even when they represent only one party to a transaction, sharing economy lawyers may still find themselves helping to facilitate a meeting involving multiple people in a collaborative relationship. Facilitating

Sharing Economy Law Meets Collaborative Law

The field of sharing economy law has much to learn from collaborative law, and collaborative lawyers, of whom there are now many thousands, could easily step into sharing economy law practice. Collaborative law, described in more detail below, has primarily been applied in divorce cases and sometimes in domestic relationship formation, such as in the process of adopting a pre-nuptial agreement. Recently, the International Academy of Collaborative Professionals (IACP) has begun to explore how collaborative law could be applied in civil and commercial matters, both in transactional matters and in disputes. In the same way that the collaborative approach has been used in negotiating pre-nuptial agreements, it could be applied when parties enter into co-ownership agreements, partnership agreements, and other situations where parties must balance concern for their own interests with the desire to come together and collaborate. Collaborative law should especially be used when sharing relationships dissolve, such as when a cooperative or cohousing community parts ways with a member under difficult circumstances.

In the collaborative model, each party is represented by an attorney to assert that party's interests. Typically, the attorneys are also trained mediators, and the parties are expected to come to the negotiating table in an open and cooperative spirit. Parties agree to make their best efforts at resolving the matter outside of litigation, and agree to fully disclose all of the information necessary to coming to a workable solution. In states that have adopted laws defining the procedures of collaborative law, the communications that take place during a collaborative negotiation are considered privileged. To add to the incentive to resolve the matter collaboratively, the attorneys involved agree to withdraw in the event that the matter does have to go to litigation.

In some sharing economy law cases, it is necessary or preferable for each party to be represented by separate counsel. A key resource for every sharing economy lawyer will be a list of other lawyers who are available and willing to undertake collaborative representation of other parties to a transaction or dispute. To learn more about the procedures and agreements that are core to collaborative law practice, visit IACP's website (www.collaborativepractice.com) and read the Uniform Collaborative Law Act (UCLA), written by the National Conference of Commissioners on Uniform State Laws (NCCUSL) and recently adopted in a handful of states.

the growth of an open and trusting relationship among parties could ultimately be just as important as lobbying for favorable contract terms for a single party. Each client's project usually involves risks, financial commitments, responsibilities to allocate, and other difficult decisions.

Helping clients talk through options, and make difficult choices, and testing for consensus on the resolutions are important steps for a lawyer to take with clients prior to memorializing an agreement in writing. When things get tense, a lawyer can borrow from her mediator's toolbox to help clients talk compassionately through tough topics.

Keeping a Toe in the Litigation World

We generally describe sharing economy law as a transactional area of practice, though it's important to acknowledge that the enterprises and activities of the sharing economy can and will lead to litigation (as mentioned above, this can happen when a client chooses to operate in a gray area). When they do reach the courts, it will be critical to ensure that sharing contracts are interpreted as they are designed, and that casual sharing relationships do not become subject to burdensome regulations. Otherwise, we risk creation of problematic precedent.

Litigation, of course, is not the ideal method for resolving disputes in the sharing economy. This is not only due to courts' lack of familiarity with the activities of the sharing economy, but also due to the high costs of litigation, the significant amount of time it takes, the stress it induces, and the relationships it tends to destroy. The activities of the sharing economy, by nature, will be small scale, will take place among groups of people that have ongoing relationships, and will likely be important to the livelihoods of those involved. For that reason, disputes are best resolved in less formal settings, such a mediation, which is quicker, cheaper, and usually helps to preserve relationships between parties. Furthermore, a resolution reached in mediation need not be based on an application of the law, but rather on the needs and desires of the parties.

Many prospective clients come to me when they have reached a point of frustration. Rather than asking me to help them share, they ask me to help them *un-share*. By the time they talk to me, they may be so fearful and fed up that they are ready to sue. In such cases, I have advised clients that I would be willing to play only one of two roles in such a matter: either as a mediator for the dispute or as an advisor to one side, but *only* so long as the dispute or dissolution of the sharing relationship is taking place outside of litigation. In the latter scenario, it would be preferable for the other party or parties to be represented by an attorney with a similarly non-adversarial approach. Better yet, following the model of collaborative law (which is primarily used in divorce and partnership dissolution cases but is also appropriate for sharing economy law), all parties and their lawyers could agree to make their best efforts to resolve the matter outside of litigation. Should the parties fail to reach a resolution and turn to litigation as a last resort, the agreement will provide that the original attorneys must withdraw and that the clients must seek other attorneys willing to litigate.

Even when it's possible to resolve a matter collaboratively, it is still important for a sharing economy lawyer to advise a client of his/her options and rights with regard to litigation, and to appropriately help the client weigh the benefits and disadvantages of taking the litigation route. It's also important to note that a lawyer should not attempt to sort out all "un-sharing" cases outside of court, primarily due to deadlines and statutes of limitations related to certain actions. For example, if a tenant in a shared housing arrangement has received a notice of unlawful detainer or other eviction-related notice, it may be critical that the tenant timely file the appropriate response with the court in order to successfully fight the action.

Training the Next Generation of Sharing Economy Lawyers

Law Schools and the Sharing Economy Law Imperative

Being a sharing economy lawyer, in all likelihood, means paving our own way. Most law schools and law professors, unfortunately, do not prepare us to be pavers of new ways. Our law schools' career offices generally prepare law students for the path of employment, and graduates have few options: struggle to get one of the scarce public interest law jobs, work for the government, or get a job at a private firm. Law students are trained well to take advantage of the opportunities our current infrastructure offers them. But if all we do is fit into the current infrastructure, then we are not doing much to create new paradigms.

Sharing economy law currently offers a viable and important opportunity for tens or even hundreds of thousands of lawyers, and law schools would be negligent to not prepare law students for this. There are at least four things that law schools could offer their students to help them in their careers as sharing economy lawyers:

1. Courses in the substantive areas of law as they apply to the sharing economy (in other words, the topics covered in the rest of this book);

2. Hands-on experience in a sharing economy law practice, through practicum courses and clinics;
3. Training in the skills that are valuable to a sharing economy lawyer's toolbox, including communication, mediation, facilitation, and clear document drafting; and
4. Preparation and resources to help new lawyers launch their own private practices or nonprofits.

Or, Never Mind Law School: Apprenticeships as a Path to Becoming a Sharing Economy Lawyer

Becoming a lawyer without attending law school may very well be an excellent option for becoming a sharing economy lawyer in the states where bar associations continue to make this possible. Since law schools may not provide students with the skills necessary to becoming a sharing economy lawyer, apprenticing with a sharing economy lawyer could be a far more effective way to learn how to practice.

There are innumerable leaders, organizers, and activists who could be even more effective in their work if they were able to practice law, but going to law school is not a realistic option for them because it would mean putting their work on hold for three years and incurring up to $200,000 of debt, a burden that can prevent new lawyers from dedicating their time to less lucrative practices. Furthermore, these leaders would make themselves vulnerable to the dangerous set of expectations that the culture of law school imposes on students. This is the culture that tells us to follow the path of prestige and to graduate feeling entitled to make a six-figure salary. This is the culture that swallows up the plans of most idealistic and progressive-minded new law students.

California, Vermont, Virginia, Washington, and Wyoming all allow people to become lawyers by "reading the law," meaning they study and apprentice in the office of a lawyer or judge, in lieu of going to law school.[5] New York and Maine also allow this, but they require at least one or two years of law study in addition to the apprenticeship.

In California, a person can become a lawyer by working and studying in the office of a lawyer or judge for 18 hours per week for four years.[6] The supervising attorney must provide five hours of direct supervision

5. G. Jeffrey MacDonald, *The Self-Made Lawyer*, Christian Sci. Monitor (June 3, 2003) http://www.csmonitor.com/2003/0603/p13s01-lecs.html.

6. Rules of the State Bar of Cal. tit. 4, div. 1, ch. 3, R. 4.29.

per week, and must administer exams to the apprentice to test his or her learning. The apprentice and supervising attorney must register with and regularly send progress reports to the State Bar of California, describing such things as the study materials used. The apprentice must pass the First-Year Law Students exam, in addition to the regular bar exam.

Note that distance learning courses are also a viable option for future lawyers that want to work in the field of sharing economy law while they study. Bar associations in California, New Mexico, and Washington, D.C., allow people to take the bar exam after doing a distance learning course.

Mini-Internships as a Strategy for Growing the Sharing Economy Law Movement

Short-term internships offer another opportunity to train sharing economy lawyers, but some barriers arise. While I was awaiting bar results and looking for learning opportunities, I asked many attorneys if I could intern temporarily in their offices or observe legal advice sessions. Many declined, for fear that my involvement could violate employment laws related to unpaid internships, and/or that my presence could destroy attorney–client privilege. What follows are some suggestions for overcoming both of these barriers.

The internship issue: When for-profit businesses take on unpaid interns, they must meet a rigorous six-part test[7] applied to internships under federal employment law (described more fully in Chapter 7). This test requires, among other things, that the involvement of an intern be for the purpose of educating the intern and not to benefit the business and that the intern's work does not replace work that would normally be done by an employee. In fact, courts have said that interns should really be a burden on the business that hosts them. Because this can be a strict test, it can be risky for a for-profit business to have unpaid interns. On the other hand, a charitable or educational organization is generally permitted to have volunteers without running afoul of employment law.[8]

7. Walling v. Portland Terminal Co., 330 U.S. 148 (1947).

8. Generally, individuals may work for charitable, civic, or religious nonprofit enterprises without expectation of compensation and be considered a volunteer. Op. U.S. Dep't of Labor, FLSA 2001-18 (2001), *available at* http://www.dol.gov/whd/opinion/flsa.htm#ftnt1.

At the same time, it is worth finding ways to involve interns in private law practice, since it's important to expose new lawyers to the "behind-the-scenes" work of sharing economy law. I have, in the context of my own law practice, on occasion, taken on an "intern for a day," or more accurately, a "3-hour intern." Allowing interns to observe a one-time legal advice session with a client is a great way to expose interns to the substantive work of a lawyer. Because the intern was there for the primary purpose of observing and learning, this most likely met the legal test for internships.

The privilege issue: However, involving interns for the primary purpose of observation brings up another problem: if an intern observes a client advice session, is the information still protected by attorney–client privilege? Attorney–client privilege generally only extends to communications that the client intends to be confidential. If an unnecessary third party is in the room, the third party's presence demonstrates that the communication is not intended to be confidential, and could therefore destroy the privilege.

Here is one solution to preserving the privilege: rather than have the intern idly observe, have the intern be the note-taker for the advice session and prepare a set of notes to send to the client. If the third party's presence is necessary to facilitate the communication between attorney and client, the attorney–client privilege is generally preserved. Courts have applied attorney–client privilege in the context of client communications in the presence of employees such as clerks, secretaries, language interpreters, transcript recorders, and other employees.[9] If an attorney can establish that the intern is acting as the attorney's "employee" or "agent," courts are likely to recognize attorney–client privilege.[10] Courts have defined employee in this context as "any person whose intervention is necessary to secure and facilitate the communication between attorney and client."[11]

That is why it is important that the intern/observer take notes for the client's benefit. If the intern were simply listening, it may be more difficult to argue that the intern's presence is "necessary to … facilitate the communication." Most clients take notes furiously during advice

9. Bulow *ex rel.* Auersperg v. von Bulow, 811 F.2d 136, 146 (2d Cir. 1987).
10. People v. Doe, 99 Misc. 2d 411, 415 (N.Y. App. Div. 1979).
11. *Id.* (citing Mileski v. Locker, 178 N.Y.S.2d 911, 916 (Sup. Ct. 1958)).

sessions, so having an assistant take notes could greatly facilitate the client's ability to listen to and absorb the information.

It's important to acknowledge that the application of attorney–client privilege in this scenario is not certain, as at least one prosecutor subpoenaed law student volunteers to serve as witnesses in a criminal matter being defended by a law school clinic. This matter sent shock waves through law school clinics, many of which assumed that attorney–client privilege extends to law students assisting on cases.[12]

If you would like to involve interns as observers/note-takers, to play it safe, you can (1) disclose to clients that there is a *slight* chance that the attorney–client privilege could be tested and have them acknowledge that in writing, (2) have the intern sign an agreement acknowledging that he/she is there to take notes both for the client's benefit and to learn about the practice of sharing economy law, and that he/she agrees to keep all information confidential, and (3) make sure not to involve intern/observers in consultations where the subject matter is the potential subject of litigation.

Case Studies as a Strategy for Building the Sharing Economy Law Movement

Many sharing economy law clients feel strongly that they want their model to be replicable; they have put a great deal of time and money into developing a project, and they would like the impact of their work to go far beyond their own community. By creating a case study of work done for a particular client, sharing economy lawyers can promote the replication of creative projects, at the same time that they accomplish an important goal of training other sharing economy lawyers to handle similar scenarios. For example, if the lawyer writes up a detailed explanation of the legal model of a cohousing community, this case study will be helpful to other cohousing communities *and* to other lawyers.

Note, however, that if a client does not ask you to turn its matter into a legal case study, it might be better to wait until your work with them has been completed before you ask for their permission to use their project as a case study. This will help to preserve clients' trust in the confidentiality of the representation. Note also that ABA Model

12. For more information, *see* Patrick C. Brayer, *Opposition to Law School Clinics Tests Attorney-Client Privilege*, Nat'l L.J., Sept. 6, 2010, http://www.law.com/jsp/nlj/PubArticleNLJ.jsp?id=1202471561457.

Going Viral: Open Sourcing the Field of Sharing Economy Law

I have called for sharing economy lawyers to share their documents, but here I'd like to mention the possibility of taking it to yet another level: open sourcing. Sharing documents serves as a way to grow the sharing economy law movement, and it empowers non-lawyers to take a self-help approach to meeting their legal needs. Open sourcing our documents means sharing them with a license that asks users to "share it forward." For example, if I make a sample Tenancy-in-Common (TIC) Agreement available to download, I can ask users to upload a redacted version (removing confidential info) of their own TIC Agreement, once they have adapted mine to their purposes. (I would of course advise anyone using my TIC Agreement to have an attorney review it prior to implementation.)

Open sourcing generally has a viral effect. The result of attaching open source licenses to our TIC Agreements will be the creation of a diverse online library of sample TIC Agreements. Each agreement will be specially adapted to a particular situation and jurisdiction, and over time, the agreements will be built upon and improved.

There will, of course, be an "honor system" element to the open source licenses we attach to our agreements. We can't enforce on users an obligation to upload their agreements when they have completed them. However, we can create a culture of sharing and ask users to make a good faith effort to share it forward. See Chapter 10 for more information about open source licensing.

Note that one difficulty with freely posting legal documents with an open source license is that the forms on which they are based may have originated from a copyrighted legal practice guide. These practice guides usually allow us to use the documents for our practices, but not to redistribute them publicly. To avoid problems related to lifting from such documents, the best practice for sharing economy lawyers will be to write new documents from scratch.

Rule of Professional Conduct 1.8(d) provides that "Prior to the conclusion of representation of a client, a lawyer shall not make or negotiate an agreement giving the lawyer literary or media rights to a portrayal or account based in substantial part on information relating to the representation." This rule was likely not written with an educational case study in mind (think major murder trial book rights); nevertheless, it's important to note that it's probably better not to muddle the representation process with a request to write about a client's case.

Part 3: Structuring a Sharing Economy Law Practice

The structure of a law practice matters, as it can affect the way attorneys work, the way they bill, their motivations, the way they interact with clients, and the quality of service.

Compare, for example, what happens at large hierarchical law firms to what happens in solo law practices. Three of my lawyer friends have told me that it's common at their large law firms for firm partners to pressure associates to "pad their hours." A friend was told that she should generally bill at least four or five minutes for each email she writes, even if it's a one-sentence email that only takes her two minutes. Other large firm lawyers have told me that they spend expensive billable hours doing menial tasks of the sort that other people get paid $20 per hour to do.

It is telling that my solo attorney friends make statements to the opposite effect. They say things like, "Oh, I never charge for all the hours I work. I worked 20 hours on this project, but only billed my client for 5 hours." These solos generally recognize that charging $350 for every hour spent on a project could result in a bill that is nowhere near the true value of a service provided. A solo attorney's billing decisions balance the attorney's needs with the client's, whereas larger firms tilt dramatically toward the pressures imposed by supervising law partners.

The irony of all this is that large law firms are practicing what our professional ethics rules were designed to prevent. For example, lawyers are not allowed to form firms and share fees with non-lawyers, for fear that non-lawyers could pressure an attorney to make decisions based on what earns the most money and not necessarily based on what best serves the client. Yet, this is exactly what is happening in many large hierarchical law firms.

A sharing economy law practice need not be a solo practice in order to maintain its integrity and be effective. In fact, lawyers that collaborate with other lawyers can be more effective than a lawyer working alone, and the collaboration can take place among solos or within a small firm. Below is an examination of some of the pros and cons of various structures.

Solo Practice

A solo practice affords the lawyer the greatest flexibility: you can choose clients that you like and that you want to work with. You have the ability to charge what you want, not charge at all, or accept car tune-ups or other types of payment in exchange for your services. The decisions you make derive from your own values and your own standards of quality and integrity.

Many people have a difficult time picturing themselves running their own law practice, and this makes me wonder what they picture. Some people that open new law firms immediately rent a sleek-looking office space, hire someone to sit at a receptionist desk, and install a fancy phone system. They start dressing nicer, giving firm handshakes, and work hard to make it sound like they already know a lot about everything.

But the reality is that starting a solo law practice can be almost as easy as falling off a log. These days, you don't even need an office, dedicated phone line, fax machine, or fancy pre-printed letterhead. Malpractice insurance is a good idea—it protects you and gives your clients a form of compensation if you mess up—but it's not mandatory. Really, the main thing you have to do to start a solo practice is to adopt some procedures for client engagement and start representing a client. In fact, the lower you keep your overhead, the more you can ensure that clients are paying for a lawyer's real "stock in trade"—your time and advice—and not for your fancy nameplate.

Contrary to the sound of it, a solo lawyer is, most likely, not alone. It is very difficult to develop the requisite competence in enough areas of law to meet every client's needs. Solo lawyers will often need to draw on the expertise of others and to collaborate or co-counsel with other attorneys. It's very helpful for solo attorneys to make intentionally collaborative arrangements with other attorneys, such as to share resources and document templates or to have regular check-in calls to bounce ideas off each other and work through problems.

Sharing economy lawyers are even more prone to collaboration, due to the fact that they are often called upon to represent *groups* of people. To avoid conflicts of interest and ethical violations associated with multiple representation, it's often better to represent only one party and to have other lawyers advise the other parties. The representation process is not necessarily adversarial, of course, and multiple sharing economy lawyers working on one transaction generally means a better transaction all around.

Small Firms

A small firm can be the site of wonderful collaboration. Lawyers come together to complement each other's topical expertise or to offer different strengths to the management of the practice. A sharing economy law practice can benefit greatly from the addition of an attorney who specializes in tax law or securities law, for example. At least, in my own firm, these are the two topics for which I most likely have to seek out assistance of a specialized attorney. A good partnership can also arise when one lawyer is skilled at connecting with prospective clients and another is good at focusing on the deliverables. In truth, it can be challenging for a solo to juggle both, since the former involves a lot of communication and interaction, and the latter requires such focused and sustained attention.

Even in a firm with multiple attorneys, it is still possible to keep overhead low. This is increasingly true with the growth of coworking and other shared workspaces and with technologies that enable lawyers within a firm to easily share information and documents without working in the same place. The firm may not even need a main office or special phone system. Operating a "virtual firm" is an ever more popular option, and this has been a successful model for Jenny Kassan's firm, Katovich & Kassan Law Group, which started out as completely virtual and now is semi-virtual (there is a small office, but most of the attorneys work off-site).

Law Cooperatives and Collectives

What it means to be a law cooperative or collective is an intriguing yet difficult to answer question. There is a tradition of law collectives in the United States, many of which arose out of activism in the 1960s. "Law collective" is nowhere officially defined, but we describe the common characteristics and some history of law collectives below. There are very few firms or organizations that have identified themselves as law cooperatives. But it is worth mentioning them here to explore what they could look like, especially since many sharing-minded lawyers have wondered about such a possibility. "Lawyer cooperative" could mean at least two different things, depending on the lawyers' relationships to the cooperative. The lawyers could be service providers in a cooperative law firm, or they could be customers of a cooperative entity that provides support and services to them (in a consumer cooperative model). Let's look at these two more closely.

A Cooperative Law Firm

A law cooperative could be owned by attorneys who work for it full-time, or it could be owned by multiple independent attorneys who provide services through the cooperative on a more intermittent and "of counsel" basis.

Either way, a key question is how to structure the firm. As we describe in Chapter 4, the word "cooperative," in the legal world, generally refers to a type of corporation or unincorporated association with special rules related to democratic governance and distribution of profits. Due to rules about the types of entities that professionals may form, it's quite possible that a group of lawyers would be unable to form an entity under a cooperative statute for their work. However, lawyers can still adopt the values, practices, and structure of a cooperative under the umbrella of another type of corporation or partnership. For example, the partnership agreement of a limited liability partnership (LLP) could include provisions allowing each lawyer to participate equally in decision-making (or in electing decision-makers). Another "essence" of cooperatives is the manner in which they distribute profits. Operating like a cooperative means that no lawyer in the firm will be skimming profits off the top; rather, any profits that are available to distribute at the end of the year would be paid to each of the lawyers on the basis of the quantity or value of the work that each did (this is the concept of patronage, discussed further in the section on cooperatives in Chapter 4).

A law cooperative owned by multiple independent attorneys could, potentially, serve as the site of valuable collaboration. For example, attorneys throughout the country and world could form a cooperative in order to collaborate on an as-needed basis in serving large clients of a particular type, like large social enterprises dealing in fair trade products (which, of course, should one day be the *only* kind of traded products). For the social enterprise, this could be a socially responsible alternative to hiring a large multi-national law firm. For the attorneys, it is a nice opportunity to step outside of working solely for small, local clients, and to collaborate and combine expertise for the purpose of serving a large client that operates in multiple jurisdictions.

Note that it would be incredibly difficult to include non-lawyers as owners in the cooperative, due to the prohibitions on lawyers sharing fees with non-lawyers. However, the partners can still endeavor to make internal operations cooperative, in the sense of involving all staff, including non-lawyers, in planning and decisions, and can strive to pay non-lawyers a wage close to that of the lawyers. Keep in mind that paying bonuses to non-lawyers, or raising and lowering a non-lawyer's salary in conjunction with law firm profits, could be seen as improper fee-sharing.

Lawyer Cooperative

A group of lawyers could form a cooperative in order to more effectively obtain services for themselves. For example, a group of sharing economy lawyers could form a sharing economy law cooperative that provides the following services to members:

- **Insurance:** Provides or collectively bargains for malpractice insurance tailored to sharing economy law practice.
- **CLE:** Offers inexpensive continuing legal education courses on sharing economy law.
- **Resources:** Offers members access to research tools and resources.
- **Services:** Through collective purchasing, offers members inexpensive access to services such as web design, business card printing, bookkeeping, and accounting.
- **Networking:** Provides sharing economy lawyers opportunities to meet, network, and share information with each other.
- **Advertising:** Provides group advertising and publishes a sharing economy lawyer directory.
- **Referral service**: The cooperative could even provide a referral service, matching clients to attorneys. Attorneys may even be able to pay referral fees to the cooperative, so long as the service complies with the state's rules regarding the operation of lawyer referral services,[13] in order to not run afoul of rules similar to ABA Model Rule 7.2(b) regarding the payment of referral fees.
- **Facilitating collaboration:** The cooperative's referral service could go one step further, by matching lawyers with each other to co-counsel on matters. Section 1.5(e) of the ABA Model Rules provides that lawyers in different firms can sometimes split fees, so long as they get written permission from the client, and as long as the fee is truly split based on each lawyer's contribution of services (i.e., one lawyer isn't collecting a premium from having found the client, for example). Thus, any sort of legal service cooperative

13. *See, e.g.*, Rules and Regulations of the State Bar of California Pertaining to Lawyer Referral Services, http://www.calbar.ca.gov/LinkClick.aspx?fileticket=RgHEKBl9POQ%3d&tabid=2660; Model Rules of Prof'l Conduct R. 7.2(b).

would need to ensure that the lawyers are being compensated on the basis of the time and efforts they put in.

Each member lawyer would pay the cooperative for the use of these services. At the end of the year, if the cooperative has extra income that it does not need to re-invest into the cooperative, it can distribute that money back to members as patronage refunds, determined on the basis of the value of the services that each member purchased from the cooperative. Therefore, the lawyer who purchased the most services would receive the largest patronage refund, and the result is that no single individual or investor is profiting from success of the cooperative.

A Note About Business Leagues

Note that another sort of association that could serve some, but not all, functions of the sharing economy law cooperative described above could be a mutual benefit nonprofit organization, tax-exempt under 501(c)(6), which is the form of exemption used by many professional organizations, bar associations, and chambers of commerce. The benefit here, of course, is that the entity is exempt from payment of income taxes and from payment of minimum franchise taxes in states that require corporations to pay such taxes. However, 501(c)(6)s can be limited in the ways that they can provide direct services to members. According to the IRS technical instruction publication on this topic, a 501(c)(6) business league is "an association of persons having a common business interest, whose purpose is to promote the common business interest and not to engage in a regular business of a kind ordinarily carried on for profit. Its activities are directed to the improvement of business conditions of one or more lines of business rather than the performance of particular services for individual persons."[14]

It is not necessarily easy to figure out the difference between what is an individual service and an activity directed at general improvement of the profession, since 501(c)(6)s are still able to provide certain benefits at a fee to the members receiving them (fees to take part in events and classes, for example). Anyone interested in forming a business league for sharing economy lawyers should carefully read the IRS publications and

14. John Francis Reilly, Carter C. Hull, & Barbara A. Braig Allen, IRC 501(c)(6) Organizations 3 (EO CPE 2003), http://www.irs.gov/pub/irs-tege/eotopick03.pdf.

revenue rulings on 501(c)(6)s to determine whether such a structure can meet their needs.[15]

Law Collectives

The phrase "law collective," although nowhere officially defined, is most often used to refer to an organization or law firm that is formed to support progressive activists and community organizers. Common characteristics of law collectives are:

- They are non-hierarchical and members make decisions collectively and democratically; however, note that lawyers still have a professional duty to exercise independent professional judgment in representation of clients.[16]
- They work very closely with community activists to set priorities and make decisions.
- They involve both non-lawyers and lawyers in the work.
- They work to empower non-lawyer members of the community to understand legal rights and issues.
- They often pay the same wage to lawyers and non-lawyers. Although, note that lawyers must exercise care in such an arrangement to ensure that this does not violate rules against lawyers splitting fees with non-lawyers; to avoid problems, wages should not be raised or lowered in conjunction with the profits of the collective.[17]

Most law collectives have focused on litigation efforts to defend and support activists in civil and criminal proceedings. However, law collectives could play an important role in the transition to a sharing economy, by empowering community members with information and tools to form and operate community-based enterprises.

To learn more about law collectives, see Brendan Conley's piece here, and an article entitled "Wrenching the Bench: People's Law

---

15. *Id.*
16. *See* Model Rules of Prof'l Conduct R. 2.1.
17. *See* Model Rules of Prof'l Conduct R. 5.4.

LAW COLLECTIVES

By Brendan Conley, Activist, writer, and attorney

What Is a Law Collective?

A law collective is a non-hierarchical, democratic way of organizing a law practice or legal services organization. Law collectives reject the notion that attorneys are superior to other legal services providers, or to their clients. A law collective may have a legal structure similar to a traditional firm or a nonprofit organization, but the members may organize their work internally on a more democratic basis. Some collectives do not have attorneys as members, and others strive to treat all members as equal, whether they are lawyers or not. Critics of the U.S. legal system point out that the high cost of law school and the standards of the bar exam have served to create an anti-competitive marketplace for legal services, in which attorneys dominate. Having attended law school or passed a bar exam is no guarantee against incompetence or malpractice, and many non-attorneys are more qualified to provide certain legal services than some lawyers. Collectives recognize this imbalance and attempt to subvert it by treating clients, attorneys, and other legal workers as equals.

Law collectives came into existence in the United States in the 1960s, as part of the cultural and political upheaval of that era. The activist-lawyers of that time considered themselves one branch of the general movement for social justice, often representing political protesters and providing legal support to organizations working for change. Today, attorneys from a new generation are choosing to organize themselves along the collective model.

Law Collectives in Action

Perhaps the best way to understand what law collectives are and how they differ from traditional firms is to look at specific examples. Collectives in the United States represent a diversity of forms and focuses.

The People's Law Office in Chicago is a prominent example of a legal collective that began as part of the social movements of the 1960s and has stayed true to its roots. In the aftermath of the 1968

Democratic National Convention protests, a group of five young lawyers came together to discuss a new type of legal practice, a "collective" that would not just represent members of the social justice movement, but be a part of it. The People's Law Office provided legal support for the Black Panther Party, the Attica prison protesters, and the Puerto Rican independence movement. The office continues its justice work today, taking on death penalty cases and prison work.

A younger generation of attorneys came together to form the Portland Law Collective (www.portlandlawcollective.com). Though organized legally as a limited liability partnership, the organization is collectively run. The office focuses on civil rights, employment law, and criminal defense. This group of advocates, all of whom have been attorneys for fewer than ten years, works together in a democratic model to provide support for activists and citizens.

Despite the conservatism of the legal world and the prevailing capitalist business model, attorneys striving to create an alternative have shown that it is possible to form sustainable legal structures that are inclusive and democratic.

Collectives and the Movement," by Phaedra Travis, Sarah Coffey, and Paul Marini, members of the Midnight Special Law Collective.[18]

Practicing Sharing Economy Law as a 501(c)(3) Nonprofit

Given that the heart of sharing economy law focuses on making the world a better place, the question inevitably arises: can lawyers form a 501(c)(3) nonprofit under which to practice sharing economy law? The short answer is yes, but the longer answer is that doing so may end up imposing too many limitations on the way the sharing economy lawyers choose and accept clients, charge fees, and fund their work. Furthermore, this is somewhat new territory for the IRS, and any sharing economy lawyer wishing to go this route should become very familiar with the Revenue Rulings that tell us what can and cannot be done under a

18. The article, published by *Earth First! Journal*, can be found at http://www.earthfirstjournal.org/article.php?id=123, and more information about the Midnight Special Law Collective (now disbanded) can be found at http://www.midnightspecial.net.

501(c)(3) tax exemption. See below for an analysis of the issue by attorney Christen Lee.

For attorneys with significant student loan debt, there is at least one very good reason to practice law in the context of a nonprofit: under the federal Public Service Loan Forgiveness (PSLF) program established in October of 2007, student loan debt will be forgiven for lawyers who work 30+ hours per week for a 501(c)(3) nonprofit for ten years. Also, many recent law graduates have opportunities to participate in a loan repayment assistance program (LRAP) at their law school if they are working for a 501(c)(3) nonprofit. In the case of Berkeley Law School, working "greater than half time" for a 501(c)(3) makes a graduate eligible to receive up to $9,000 per year in payments from the law school toward student loan debt. Unfortunately, the lawyer must be paid—*volunteering* for a nonprofit more than half time does not make a graduate eligible. Thus, even a nonprofit operating on a shoestring must find the budget to pay lawyers who want to take advantage of an LRAP at least minimum wage. Nevertheless, LRAPs offer an important subsidy to the sharing economy law movement because they make it more feasible for a lawyer to dedicate a significant amount of time to public interest work.

Creating a Sharing Economy Law Program Within an Existing Organization

Rather than starting a new nonprofit, one option for aspiring sharing economy lawyers is to find an existing organization that would be interested in adding a sharing economy law practice to its offerings. For example, in 2011, Berkeley Law School graduate Sushil Jacob received a two-year Skadden Fellowship to create the Green-Collar Communities Clinic (GC3) within the East Bay Community Law Center in Berkeley, California. This clinic provides transactional assistance to start-up businesses focusing on sustainable industries, with a particular emphasis on the development of worker cooperatives.

Similarly, established law centers and legal service organizations around the country could create programs that focus on sharing economy law, social enterprise law, cooperatives, and other grassroots community-economic development work.

Fiscal sponsorship is also a good option for launching a sharing economy law center. For example, the Sustainable Economies Law

STRUCTURING A SHARING ECONOMY LAW PRACTICE: CAN IT BE A 501(C)(3)?

By Attorney Christen Lee,
Director of Legal Education, Sustainable Economies Law Center

The 501(c)(3) organization is the most common type of nonprofit tax-exempt organization, and most nonprofits that offer legal services use the 501(c)(3) structure. You might consider structuring your sharing economy law practice as a 501(c)(3) for the following reasons: federal income tax exemption, ability to accept grants and tax-deductible donations, and ability to create positive public perception of the values driving your firm. The ability to accept grants and donations could help subsidize the costs of providing services to your clients, many of whom might otherwise not have the resources to hire a private lawyer. Also, lawyers who work for a 501(c)(3) organization can qualify for various loan repayment assistance programs sponsored by law schools and the federal government.

Operating as a 501(c)(3), however, does restrict your activities, legal fees, and types of clients served. Your legal fees will have to be lower than what you could collect as a for-profit practice, and you must limit the kinds of clients you could accept so as not to risk losing your tax-exempt status. For example, you might not be able to accept too many clients who are not low-income. There may be other trade-offs, including the requirement that major decisions be made by an independent board of directors. Due to rules against distributing nonprofit assets to private individuals, nonprofits are also limited in their ability to make barter a meaningful part of how they accept fees.

The question of whether a sharing economy law practice can obtain tax exemption under 501(c)(3) is actually fairly complicated, and the IRS has not addressed this question directly. Any lawyers that consider this route should look carefully at the relevant tax rulings or even seek guidance from the IRS. Providing legal services is not considered to be a tax-exempt purpose, in and of itself. However, if the primary purpose of the legal service provision is to further legitimate charitable purposes, then it is more likely to be considered within the 501(c)(3) guidelines.

Based on our research, we believe that a sharing economy law practice can implement some key practices to show that it is organized and operated exclusively for exempt purposes. The discussion below is not exhaustive, but is based on some of the main practices that tax-exempt legal services organizations and public interest law firms have put into place.

Client Fees

A 501(c)(3) sharing economy law practice must structure its legal fees in a charitable manner and serve clients who are part of a charitable class. A good way to structure your legal fees would be a sliding scale based on your client's ability to pay.[1] The sliding scale should be capped at a fee equal to at-cost, which includes the salaries, overhead, and other costs fairly allocable to each case.[2] However, if most of the fees that you collect are on the higher end of the sliding scale (i.e., at-cost), your sharing economy law practice might look more like a for-profit private law practice, and thus jeopardize your tax exemption.[3] Therefore, your sharing economy law practice should follow the guidelines set forth for public interest law firms: the total amount of all attorneys' fees should not exceed 50 percent of the total cost of operation of the organization's legal functions, calculated over a five-year period, unless the IRS gives an exception to the organization.[4] If your client is part of a charitable class, you may also have to agree to continue representation after the client is no longer able to pay.[5]

1. *See, e.g.*, Rev. Rul. 78-428, 1978-2 C.B. 177 (hourly legal fee based on client's hourly income); Special Ruling, Jan. 1978, C.C.H. ¶ 6418 (hourly legal fee based on client's hourly income plus 25 percent).

2. Rev. Proc. 92-59, 1992-2 C.B. 411 (client-paid fees for public interest law firms may not exceed actual cost, including salary/overhead/filing costs, although costs may be charged against a retainer with remaining balance to be refunded to client).

3. *See, e.g.*, *B.S.W. Grp. v. Comm'r*, 70 T.C. 352 (1978) (providing at-cost consulting services to nonprofits and entrepreneurial development programs lacks the donative element necessary to establish charitability).

4. Rev. Proc. 92-59, 1992-2 C.B. 411.

5. *Id.*

Types of Clients

Your clients should be part of a charitable class. The common thread among legal services organizations that receive tax exemption is that they not only limit their fees, but also meet the needs of one or more charitable classes.[6] These classes include but are not limited to low-income people, victims of prejudice and discrimination, the elderly, individuals with disabilities, other 501(c)(3) organizations, disadvantaged businesses operated by members of a charitable class, or other businesses or organizations serving primarily charitable or educational purposes. One question that arises is, what is "low-income"? Note that, in determining what constitutes charitable provision of housing, the IRS has adopted the definition used by the Department of Housing and Urban Development (HUD), which is 80 percent of an area's median income (adjusted for family size).[7]

Unrelated Business Income

If you accept clients that are not part of a charitable class, you would likely need to pay unrelated business income tax on that portion of your income. The organization will not jeopardize exemption if only an insubstantial part of its activities further non-exempt purposes.[8] Whether or not an activity is insubstantial depends on the facts and circumstances of the case, and may look at any of the following factors: income derived from the activity, expenditures for the activity, and time devoted to the activity.[9]

Donations

Donations must not be expressly tied, either directly or indirectly, to particular cases or clients.[10]

6. *See, e.g.*, Rev. Rul. 69-161, 1969-1 C.B. 149; Rev. Rul. 78-428, 1978-2 C.B. 177.

7. *See* Announcement 95-37, 1995-20 I.R.B. 18 (May 1, 1995).

8. *See, e.g.*, Ky. Bar Fed'n v. Comm'r, 78 T.C. 921 (1983), and for a discussion on unrelated business income tax, *see* CARLA NEELY FREITAG, PORTFOLIO 462: UNRELATED BUSINESS INCOME TAX (BNA Tax Management 2009).

9. For further discussion, *see* STEVEN D. SIMPSON, PORTFOLIO 869: TAX-EXEMPT ORGANIZATIONS: ORGANIZATIONAL AND OPERATIONAL REQUIREMENTS, at A-96 (BNA Tax Management 2010).

10. Rev. Proc. 92-59, 1992-2 C.B. 411, § 3-07 (there may be no arrangement to provide a deduction for litigation costs that is for the private benefit of the donor).

Attorney Compensation

All attorneys' fees should be paid to the organization, rather than to individual staff attorneys. All staff attorneys and other employees should be compensated on a straight salary basis, not exceeding reasonable salary levels and not established by reference to any fees received in connection with the cases they have handled.[11] Note that if clients make in-kind gifts to the law firm, the firm will likely not be able to distribute those gifts to the attorneys and employees, due to rules against distributing the assets of a nonprofit to private individuals.

Avoiding Private Benefit

Your organization's operations must not result in more than incidental benefits to private persons or entities, including disinterested private persons or entities.[12] A nonprofit sharing economy law practice must therefore be careful to avoid regularly and exclusively funneling clients to certain private attorneys or other service providers. Note, however, that referring clients to private providers is fine so long as doing so provides a benefit to the client, and that the benefit to the private provider is both qualitatively and quantitatively incidental.[13] The benefit is qualitatively incidental if it is a necessary circumstance of the activity that benefits the public; the activity can be accomplished only by benefiting certain private individuals.[14] The benefit is quantitatively incidental if it is not substantial after considering the overall public benefit conferred by the activity.[15]

Governance

A board or committee that is representative of the public interest should supervise and monitor the policies and programs of your

11. Rev. Proc. 92-59, 1992-2 C.B. 411, § 4-07.
12. *Id.*
13. I.R.S. Gen. Couns. Mem. 37,789 (Dec. 18, 1979).
14. Rev. Rul. 70-186, 1970-1 C.B. 128; *cf.* Ginsberg v. Comm'r, 46 T.C. 47 (1966).
15. Rev. Rul. 70-186, 1970-1 C.B. 128; *cf.* Ginsberg v. Comm'r, 46 T.C. 47 (1966).

sharing economy law practice, including fee schedules and attorney compensation.[16]

No Confusion with a Private Firm

If your sharing economy law practice is a 501(c)(3), it should not be operated in a manner so as to create identification or confusion with a particular private law firm.[17] For this reason, a nonprofit law firm should be very careful to distinguish itself when sharing office space with a private law firm, for example.

More Info

For a helpful publication on this topic of fee-for-service legal nonprofits, see "Fee-For-Service Activities: Tax Law and Other Considerations for Legal Service Programs," by Brad Caftel, 1995, published by the Insight Center for Community and Economies Development, available at: http://www.insightcced.org/uploads/publications/legal/fee-for-service%20article.pdf.

16. Rev. Proc. 92-59, 1992-2 C.B. 411, § 3-05 (committee not controlled by employees, nor by any organization that is not itself an organization described in section 501(c)(3) of the Code). Professional responsibility rules require attorneys to exercise their professional judgment solely on behalf of their client and not at the direction of third parties. However, courts have permitted this limited form of third party oversight for nonprofits that provide legal services. *See* Dennis G. Katz, *The Public's Interest in the Ethics of the Public Interest Lawyer*, 13 Ariz. L. Rev. 886 (1971).

17. Rev. Proc. 92-59, 1992-2 C.B. 411, § 3-06.

Center (SELC) is a fiscally sponsored program of a larger nonprofit called Community Ventures, which serves as an umbrella organization for a handful of projects devoted to community economic development. By choosing to go the fiscal sponsorship route, SELC is able to focus on its work while letting its fiscal sponsor handle administrative tasks and reporting to the IRS. Most fiscal sponsorship arrangements require that a percentage of the funds raised for the project (between 7 percent and 10 percent) is to be used by the fiscal sponsor to cover administrative costs.

Practicing Sharing Economy Law Under Both a Nonprofit and a For-Profit Firm

Doing legal work under both a nonprofit and a for-profit requires careful navigation, not only to avoid violations of 501(c)(3) rules but also to avoid violating rules of professional responsibility. I have navigated this particular territory; my colleague Jenny Kassan practices law under Katovich & Kassan Law Group, I practice under the Law Office of Janelle Orsi, and both of us work with the Sustainable Economies Law Center (SELC), which we co-founded. There are a few things we have kept careful tabs on to avoid running afoul of the rules:

- **Avoiding improper private benefit:** As discussed in Christen Lee's piece above, a 501(c)(3) nonprofit cannot operate for the benefit of private interests. Thus, a 501(c)(3) that routinely funnels clients to particular private attorneys would violate this rule, particularly if those private attorneys are insiders in the nonprofit. So if you practice out of both a nonprofit and a for-profit, it is essential that you do nothing to benefit the for-profit when you are wearing the nonprofit hat.
- **Taking care to prevent confusion of firms:** It's very important that clients fully understand which entity is responsible for representing them. It's also important to be clear about which entity you are representing at any given time. I typically tell people that I have a private law practice and that, *separately*, I direct the Sustainable Economies Law Center. A 2010 posting in the ABA Journal reported that a member of the Washington Bar had been suspended for 2.5 years for, among other things, misleading clients about what hat he was wearing when representing them.[19] He had a double-sided business card that listed his private law practice on one side, and his role as head of the Seattle office of the NAACP on the other.
- **Avoiding conflicts:** A lawyer that practices law under both a for-profit and a nonprofit umbrella should also keep in mind the potential for conflicts across entities. This could include conflicts due to

19. Debra Cassens Weiss, *Two-Sided Business Card, Potential Client Confusion Cited in Lawyer's Suspension* ABA Journal (Apr. 29, 2010, 7:51 AM), http://www.abajournal.com/weekly/article/two-sided_business_card_among_ethics_problems_leading_to_lawyers_suspension.

clients with adverse interests and conflicts that arise from advocating for an action that could adversely affect a client. For example, Rule 6.3 of the ABA Model Rules of Professional Conduct provides:

> A lawyer may serve as a director, officer or member of a legal services organization, apart from the law firm in which the lawyer practices, notwithstanding that the organization serves persons having interests adverse to a client of the lawyer. The lawyer shall not knowingly participate in a decision or action of the organization:
>
> > (a) if participating in the decision or action would be incompatible with the lawyer's obligations to a client under Rule 1.7; or
> > (b) where the decision or action could have a material adverse effect on the representation of a client of the organization whose interests are adverse to a client of the lawyer.

Part 4: Developing a Niche and Finding Clients

When I founded my law practice, I believed I had discovered a niche: sharing economy law. To the extent that I was, at the time, the only attorney calling myself a sharing economy lawyer, it was a niche, of sorts. It turned out that sharing economy law, as a field of practice, can be quite broad, with many potential niches within it. There can be many benefits to identifying a niche within sharing economy law: it means you don't have to learn a bafflingly large number of legal topics in order to meet clients' needs. It also means that you can narrow and concentrate your outreach efforts to particular groups, which can be a more effective way to find clients.

Four years after opening my sharing economy law office, I have more than enough prospective clients, and have carved out a niche by narrowing the category of clients I accept. These days, I usually say yes to ecovillages, cohousing communities, worker cooperatives, and urban farms. More and more, I say no to international nonprofits, web-based sharing services, and start-up social enterprises, since my work is less complicated if I don't have to stay on top of the specialized legal knowledge that these clients demand. I have also kept my practice intentionally humble, turning away a few "big clients" (potentially high-paying large companies, housing developments, or organizations), for the purpose of keeping my workload manageable and my stress levels low.

The important lesson in all of this is that there is a lot of room and need for more sharing economy lawyers, and that there are many angles to take. Below are some thoughts on how a sharing economy lawyer might develop and communicate a niche and find clients.

How to Frame Your Practice and Find a Niche

So long as the field of sharing economy law is new, deciding how to frame and communicate about a sharing economy law practice poses a creative challenge for attorneys. What do you tell people you meet at parties? What do you put on your website and business cards? Do you choose a sub-specialty or offer general services for sharing and social enterprise?

If you plan to start a sharing economy law practice in a small town, my recommendation is to keep your practice somewhat broad at first, to capture a range of clients. The Law Office of Janelle Orsi website header and business cards contain the tag line: Legal Services and Mediation for a Sustainable, Equitable, and Sharing World. The tag line is broad enough that farmers' markets, dance companies, plant nurseries, motorcycle clubs, and preschools have all felt like they fit within my description, which gives me a broad range of prospective clients to choose from. Yet, there is a common denominator among these prospective clients, which is that they share my concern for sustainability and justice.

In a flooded marketplace like the San Francisco Bay Area, however, I could have done well to start with a smaller niche and seek clients in that specialty area. Here is a menu of possible specialties that a sharing economy lawyer may want to adopt:

- **Shared housing law:** A practice that primarily focuses on small shared housing arrangements (between one and four units) would largely involve contract drafting and small real estate transactions.
- **Cohousing law:** A practice that focuses on the development of larger shared housing communities (five or more units) will typically involve larger real estate transactions, more difficult land use problems, financing challenges, common interest development (CID) law, structuring of homeowners associations, and so on.
- **Collaborative consumption law:** There are now thousands of web-based services set up to help people share—cars, rides, housing,

garden space, household goods, surplus food, and so on. There is a huge need for attorneys who specialize in serving the companies that provide these services, sometimes called collaborative consumption businesses[20] or mesh businesses.[21] This work includes drafting terms of service (TOS), sample agreements for program participants to use (a sample car-sharing agreement, for example); advising the business on limiting liability; managing intellectual property; and advising on commercial regulations.

- **Small social enterprise law:** Socially and environmentally focused enterprises can be a niche, especially if work is limited to smaller businesses with uncomplicated financing needs. In this case, an attorney can help with entity formation, contracts, and regulatory hurdles, but may not get caught up in complicated financing deals.
- **Large social enterprise law:** Representing larger social enterprises can require more specialized expertise, especially if the client needs to raise a few hundred thousand or a few million dollars. The securities compliance work and contracts involved require specialized knowledge. Furthermore, if it's a company planning to engage in commerce in multiple states or even multiple countries, navigating regulations can become more difficult.
- **Community-owned enterprise law:** To create more sustainable local economies, we believe that businesses should be owned by members of the local community they serve. However, due to securities regulations, this can be easier said than done. Jenny Kassan has carved out a niche for herself by learning the ins and outs of securities law, specifically for the purpose of helping businesses raise local capital.
- **Cooperative law:** Representing cooperatives generally requires familiarity with the particular cooperative corporation statutes of the state, with Subchapter T of the Internal Revenue Code (as well as other sections of the tax code), and with the unique structure and governance models that cooperatives tend to adopt.

---

20. *See* Rachel Botsman & Roo Rogers, What's Mine is Yours: How Collaborative Consumption Is Changing the Way We Live (Harper Collins, 2010).

21. *See* Lisa Gansky, The Mesh: Why the Future of Business Is Sharing (Portfolio Hardcover 2010).

- **Nonprofit law:** The rules that govern 501(c)(3)s and other tax-exempt categories are enough to keep one attorney busy for a whole career. Furthermore, the nonprofit sector is growing in relation to other sectors, so it's a good time to develop a specialty in nonprofits. Even within nonprofit law, there are many subspecialties. For example, a sharing economy lawyer might want to specialize in the legal issues raised when a nonprofit decides to operate a revenue generating activity for the purpose of furthering its mission.
- **Community food law:** I know of six attorneys who have started food law practices in recent years and appear to have done quite well. The slow food and locavore movements have meant that, even in a tough economy, start-up food enterprises continue to appear and thrive. Focusing on community-based food businesses (small-scale, community-owned, locally sourced) and sustainable food businesses can be a great niche. It requires knowing about health and safety regulations, food and agricultural regulations, organic certification, land use laws, and the usual transactional skills necessary to advise small businesses.
- **Community education and childcare law:** Focusing on cooperative and community-based preschools, K-12 schools, and child care centers could also be a good niche. It requires an understanding of child care regulations, zoning, educational codes, and nonprofit law.
- **Community health care law:** Developing health care cooperatives and other community-based health care providers could become an area of specialty. It requires an understanding of the federal and state health care laws, nonprofit and cooperative law, and rules relating to the health care professions.
- **Community energy law:** With the growth of community-based alternative energy projects, this could also become a specialty. It requires an understanding of public utilities regulations, specialized incentives, entity structures, and finance.
- **Shared intellectual property law:** Many people have creative works and inventions that they simultaneously want to protect and share; thus, there is a need for lawyers who specialize in drafting creative licenses for the sharing of intellectual property and

protecting it from being used by those whose purposes are inconsistent with the creator's mission.

Finding Clients

Word of mouth and a strong web presence—these tend to be what most successful attorneys will tell you are the keys to getting good clients. The question for sharing economy lawyers, then, is how to get people to talk about you in a positive way and build a strong web presence. Here are some tips:

Showing Up in All the Right Places

Simply showing up at workshops, mixers, conferences, and other events is a great way to build connections in the community. Although business mixer events have never felt like the most natural habitat for my personality, I made a concerted effort to show up at them in the early days of my law practice. Looking back, nearly every event I went to ultimately brought me a prospective client, even if they kept my card and called me three years later. I chose events carefully, primarily events focused on green business and sustainability, and generally found that attendees were happy to learn of an attorney focusing on sustainability issues.

Of course, a lawyer who goes to a networking event for the purpose of meeting prospective clients should always keep in mind his/her state's rules around solicitation by direct contact with prospective clients. See ABA Model Rules of Professional Conduct, Rule 7.3, and your applicable state law. What the rules generally point to is that it's a good idea to be subtle in the realm of self-promotion. At green business networking events, I've been aggressively solicited by insurance brokers and personal coaches promoting their services. Lawyers, most likely, should not do that!

Joining Communities and Organizations

Simply being a part of a community is an effective way to grow the visibility of your law practice. I was a member of a sustainable foods cooperative grocery for about a year and a half. Although I joined it for other reasons (the food and the people), it turned out to be a hotbed of prospective clients and good contacts. Other organizations that could

Story of the Rather Unconventional Business Cards

After I opened my sharing economy law practice in Berkeley, California, one of the ways that I began to find clients was by showing up at events and festivals with my rather unusual business cards. I initially printed 20,000 business cards, and if you can believe it, ran out within a year and a half. I printed 20 different cards, each on a different colored recycled card stock. On one side was information about my law firm, and on the other side were tips about living more sustainably, plus a cartoon drawing. Topics included things like: guide to seasonal vegetables, ways to share, ways to reduce waste, and communication tips.

At festivals and street fairs, such as the San Francisco Green Festival and Berkeley Earth Day, I would display the 20 colorful cards in stacks, and people would come and take the ones that interested them. The cards were so popular that people asked me if they could take stacks to hand out at other events. From time to time I get phone calls from people who say "I don't know how I got your card, but it has been on my refrigerator, and I need a lawyer to help with something." A PDF file showing most of my cards is available at: http://janelleorsi.com/files/Sustainability%20Cards%202010.pdf

be fruitful sources of clients are local chapters of the Business Alliance for Local Living Economies (BALLE), American Independent Business Alliance (AMIBA), Transition Town groups, the Green Chamber of Commerce, the Sierra Club, Occupy-related groups and gatherings, and the National Lawyers Guild.

Teaching Workshops and Other Public Speaking

Giving presentations and workshops to community groups is a great way to build visibility. A workshop I taught on housing co-ownership six months ago has already resulted in two clients. In conjunction with one workshop, I handed out a detailed booklet on co-ownership, which made it into the hands of other prospective clients.

The other benefit of teaching workshops is that there is no better way to ensure that you know and understand a topic than to commit to presenting about it. Once I've presented a topic in front of a group, I am far better and efficient at explaining it in a client meeting.

Here are some suggestions for workshops that a sharing economy lawyer can offer to communities:

- Legal 101 for Social Entrepreneurs
- Legal Workshop on Shared Housing
- Legal 101 for Urban Farmers
- Legal Workshop for Cooperatives
- The Legalities of Financing Your Community Enterprise

Web Presence

Web presence is an important supplement to word of mouth, as it allows clients to learn more about you and your firm before taking the leap to hire you. Furthermore, the web is how many clients will find you.

If you are a cooperatives lawyer in Kansas, clients could ideally find you by doing a web search for "Kansas cooperative lawyer." If this is the case, then you probably have good search engine optimization (SEO).

Blogging is an incredibly good way to build up SEO. If a client is looking to form a 501(c)(7) nonprofit, and they google "how to form a 501(c)(7)," and find a blog that you have written, then you are doing a good job with SEO. I knew that Jenny Kassan was doing a good job with SEO when I searched for "California nonprofit mutual benefit corporation," and found her law firm among the first few results, thanks to a blog post Jenny has written.

There is no shortage of topics on which a sharing economy lawyer can blog. There are so many unresolved questions, unexplored laws and legal entities, and innovative new ideas to write about. Researching and writing about all of this is a great way for a sharing economy lawyer to break into the SEO scene. If you find yourself researching a topic that no one else has written much about, that's a perfect opportunity to be the first to blog about it.

There are also more passive ways to build SEO. I have never worked very hard on my own web presence; nevertheless, a handful of clients have found me by googling things like "California cohousing attorney." I have learned that when I write articles, teach workshops, or take part in conference sessions, my information and bio end up on someone else's website, which has brought me clients. Some clients have called and said, "we found you when we did a search and saw that you are a workshop presenter at XYZ conference."

There are, of course, many technical tricks to building SEO, such as strategic use of tags and links. However, since I am a lawyer, not a techie, I won't even begin to describe those.

Part 5: Representing Clients

In this section, I'll walk through the process of representing a client. In some ways, the process of representing clients in a sharing economy law practice is very similar to that of any transactional practice. However, due to the fact that many clients are venturing into uncharted territory, it's often a good idea for a sharing economy lawyer to get involved in a project planning process earlier than usual. With traditional and mainstream enterprises, it is common for clients to complete a full business plan prior to meeting with an attorney. In the new economy, clients that wait until this point may meet with an attorney only to learn that a key component of their plan presents a large or even insurmountable barrier. Perhaps they planned to involve a large amount of volunteer labor in violation of employment laws, or they planned to solicit micro-investments in violation of securities laws. If there is a fatal legal flaw with a client's idea, it's much better to discover this early.

First Contact with Prospective Clients

My first contact with clients generally involves a short email exchange or a 10- to 20-minute phone call. My intention with this short exchange is to determine whether the client and I are a good fit for each other. For this, I do not charge. During this initial contact, I have been known to dispense a good amount of helpful information, and to point a client in the direction of resources. Sharing information and resources at this phase means that I end up with better-informed clients, and it also creates goodwill and a climate of sharing and generosity with the prospective client.

During this first contact, I usually offer clients the opportunity to schedule a thorough consultation. At this point, I try not to commit to the full scope of representation, since the first consultation could bring to the surface other issues that will affect whether I am willing to provide full representation.

Preparing to Meet with a Client

With every client consultation, it's important to come prepared, ready to explore and spot issues. To this end, first of all, I've found that it's good to have a surface level knowledge of a lot of different legal topics. This surface level knowledge will help you dredge up issues for further research. My favorite tool for developing a basic knowledge of many topics has been Nolo Press books, of which I have around 40—on divorce, patents, trademarks, landlord-tenant, employment law, and more.

Each time I meet with a client, I make a list of all of the issues that I should ask about. To remind myself of common issues, I'm still looking for the perfect mnemonic or acrostic device. In the meantime, I fall back on MICE EAT RICE.[22] The small problem with MICE EAT RICE is that it starts with the least common issue (marital property) and addresses the topics somewhat out of order from how I would normally bring them up. Nevertheless, for anyone else that may find it helpful, here it is:

- **Marital Property:** In the case of shared housing, how do marital property laws come into play to affect property co-ownership?
- **Insurance and Risk Management:** How should the client manage risk and insure against loss and liability?
- **Capital:** How will the client raise capital for the project? What securities compliance issues apply?
- **Entity:** What entity, if any, is appropriate for the client?
- **Employment Law:** Will the client [intentionally or inadvertently] create a relationship subject to employment laws?
- **Agreements/Contracts:** What contracts and leases might the client need?
- **Tax:** What are the income and property tax implications of a client's activity? What tax status or tax exemption will the client be eligible for?
- **Regulations and Licenses:** What regulations are imposed on client's activities? Will the client need any additional business licenses, permits, or approvals?

22. I created MICE EAT RICE after being inspired by Professor Bill Kell of UC Berkeley Law, who teaches his students to remember BECOME (Business planning, Entities, Capitalization and tax, Operational relationships, Managing risk, and Extra permits).

- **Intellectual Property:** Is the client producing intellectual property? How would they like to manage it?
- **City Land Use/Zoning:** Will this activity require zoning approval?
- **Estate Planning:** What role can estate planning play in the clients' vision for a property or business?

The First Full Consultation

With very few exceptions, after my first contact with a prospective client, my next step is to schedule the first full consultation, which generally lasts between one and three hours (although, in advance, I tell my clients to expect around 90 minutes). For this, I charge a flat fee of $200, no matter how long the session goes. I see this as the time to build a relationship with the client, learn about him/her, and gather all of the relevant information about the project the client has come to me to discuss. When I have charged by the hour for such meetings, clients tend to feel rushed and anxious and fail to talk about things they feel may not be relevant.

During this first meeting, as much as possible, I try to get through the entire MICE EAT RICE list of topics (see above). The result is that the first one or two hours with a client tend to be the most informative and the most helpful to the client. Knowing the incredible value of this time, I have contemplated charging a larger fee for the first consultation. However, because I believe it's important for everyone to have at least one issue-spotting consultation with a lawyer, it's more important for me to keep the consultation reasonably priced so that almost anyone can afford it.

For some clients, my representation only goes this far. Sometimes, the information I provide in such a consultation turns out to be enough for them to proceed on their own. Or, because this first consultation often occurs with groups in the very early stages of planning for their project, I do end up advising a good number of projects that never get off the ground. This is not necessarily due to legal barriers, but due to the difficulty of obtaining financing, land, time, or consensus for a project.

When I do represent the client further, we usually iron out the tasks and fee agreement during the first meeting. Other times, we sort these matters out via email following the first consultation.

A Note for New Lawyers

During my first year of law practice, the value of my initial consultations was, admittedly, much lower, due to my lack of knowledge and experience. In those days, with more than half of my clients, I gave the initial consultation for free. I got very good at responding to questions with: "That is a very good question! That is the kind of thing I would want to research further before answering." Now, I have memorized enough rules, cases, procedures, examples, and information that I can generally dispense advice and analysis on the spot. I note this because a lawyer in his/her first year of practice may want to consider offering a reduced price or free first consultation.

Who Is the Client During the First Consultation?

Since most of my clients are groups of people that are contemplating forming, but have not yet formed, an agreement or organization, it can be tricky to determine who is my client during the initial meeting versus who will be my client after that point. Generally, if the group is going to form an entity, I represent them jointly, as agents of a soon-to-be formed entity. After the entity is formed, I represent the entity.

The situation is somewhat more difficult with clients who are simply making an agreement with each other to share a car or home. At times, I have advised both parties simultaneously. However during the course of the first meeting, I may determine that it would be prudent, due to potential conflicts between the parties, to represent only one party, or neither. At this point, I talk to the parties about their willingness to each be advised by a separate attorney. If they are amenable, I agree to represent one party, and ask that the other party sign a waiver of any conflicts of interest that may have arisen as a result of my initial undertaking to advise both during the first meeting. The last section of this chapter includes further discussion on the ethical issues related to multiple party representation.

The Follow-up Memo

After most initial consultations, I send a follow-up email to clients with resources I may have mentioned during the meeting, but generally do not endeavor to give additional advice unless my clients have specifically asked me to. Sometimes, I have offered (for an additional fee) to send a fairly detailed summary memo to clients following the first consultation. Many clients appreciate this, since the quantity of information and advice discussed during an initial consultation can be difficult for clients to absorb. Even more difficult for clients is the task of explaining the information to other members of a group who weren't at the meeting. As a result, a summary memo can be an important resource for clients.

Entering into an Agreement for Legal Services

Following the initial consultation, provided that I continue to represent the client, my next step is usually to enter into a more detailed agreement for legal services. This defines the scope of my representation and the fee. At this point, depending on who I am representing, I may also need to obtain a written waiver of conflicts of interest. It is also at this point that I decide whether to set a flat fee, hourly fee, barter arrangement, sliding scale fee, or pro bono arrangement. My choice varies depending on a range of factors, which I discuss below in Part 6 on compensation for services.

Providing Legal Services

My clients typically engage me for one of two arrangements: either I prepare one or more documents, lead clients through a few necessary steps for their project, and then disengage; or I provide advice, support, and documents on an ongoing and as-needed basis, guiding them through the legal steps for starting and continued operation of their project. The majority of clients fall into the first category: I prepare formation document for an entity, a tax-exemption application, a zoning application, a co-ownership agreement, or some other type of contract.

Part 6: Compensation for Services

Decisions about how to structure compensation are important—they affect not only how much money you make, but also the quality of the work you do and the kinds of clients you can serve. Furthermore, as I discussed at the beginning of this chapter, this also affects the overall scarcity or abundance of legal jobs and legal services, and it affects the place of legal services and lawyers in the economic system a whole. Needless to say, I'm not about to explain how to get rich, but how to make a livelihood while doing good work and creating valuable relationships with clients.

THE VALUE OF CONSULTATION CLINICS AND LEGAL WORKSHOPS FOR THE SHARING ECONOMY

In 2011, the University of California Sustainable Agriculture Research and Education Program (SAREP) gave the Sustainable Economies Law Center (SELC) a grant to support free legal-advice clinics to advise 36 farm and food enterprise clients. The clinics were quite successful and clearly valuable to participants. Nearly all participants were low-income or unemployed, such that paying even for a regular legal consultation would have been difficult. The clinic sessions were planned in conjunction with three-hour workshops, which helped many clients spot issues and do independent research prior to sitting down with an attorney.

The model of providing workshops and one-time advice clinics has been so effective that I am going to summarize it here, so that others may consider replicating the model.

The Workshops

To date, we have offered three workshops in conjunction with legal-advice clinics. One of our workshops was called "Law Slaw," named by one of our clever interns, and reflective of the fact that the workshop was a "salad" of legal topics that a farm or food entrepreneur may need to know about. The workshops consisted of a series of action-packed five-minute presentations, all using a series of PowerPoint slides that consisted primarily of graphics rather than text. The topics were:

1. Business Formation and Entity Choice
2. Social Enterprise
3. Cooperatives
4. Nonprofits
5. Community-Supported Enterprise
6. Private Food Clubs
7. Accessing Land
8. Leasing
9. Zoning
10. Selling Food
11. Bartering with and Donating Food

12. Tax
13. Building Codes
14. Health & Safety Regulations
15. Food and Agricultural Regulations
16. Livestock Raising
17. Employment Law
18. Risk Management
19. Financing and Securities Law
20. Contracts
21. Accounting and Bookkeeping

All workshop participants received a 60-page booklet, which included a detailed section on every topic. Even though it's hard to thoroughly explain any topic in five minutes (we nevertheless tried), the handout served to provide additional information so that attendees could go deeper into topics relevant to their work. The workshops were an excellent opportunity to involve law students, lawyers, and other community volunteers. Each of the three workshops put on by SELC was prepared and presented by a different group of volunteers. Nearly every presentation was scripted in advance (between 700 and 900 words), to enable future volunteers to present the same topic, and also to aid in translation into other languages. With each successive workshop, we have improved upon the handouts, slides, and presentation scripts.

The Clinics

Running a legal clinic is an excellent way to expose law students and other interns to the experience of advising a client. For each clinic, interns and law student volunteers were responsible for handling intake of clients—interviewing or administering a questionnaire to the client to collect information about his/her project or enterprise. As the supervising attorney, I met with the interns to do a little issue spotting, based on the intake information, prior to the clinic session. We shared the intake information and issue-spotting notes with the volunteer attorneys taking part in the advice sessions, so that the advice attorneys could know in advance about the clients they would advise.

We had every client sign an acknowledgment that the advice session was a limited one-time representation, and that we would not be undertaking ongoing representation. We also had clients acknowledge that, due to the short-term nature of the consultation, we were not fully capable of checking all potential conflicts of interest for the client. Clients were also asked to fill out an evaluation form following the session.

For some clinic sessions, we brought in a handful of volunteer attorneys from the community. We paired them based on their expertise, seeking a balance of expertise in each session. Most attorneys were pleased with the opportunity to use their transactional lawyering skills for the public interest, and to do so on a one-time basis, without any necessary follow-up work.

The role of interns during the advice session was quite valuable. One intern recorded information on a whiteboard, while the other furiously typed notes on the conversation, to later serve as the basis for a summary memo. This freed up the attorney to listen and advise, and it freed up the client to listen and ask questions, which made the sessions unusually effective. Interns also helped by asking clarifying questions and offering ideas.

Following each clinic session, the interns typed up memos that summarized: (1) matters discussed and advice given, (2) unresolved questions, and (3) additional resources. Each memo began with a disclaimer that the memo was not meant to serve as thorough legal advice and that it only covered what was discussed during the clinic session. As supervising attorney, I reviewed and edited every memo prior to sending it to the clients. This was especially important for memos summarizing advice sessions with other volunteer attorneys because the review process let me ensure that information and advice given were reasonably accurate and sound.

Charging a Flat Fee

When I am to provide a fixed and somewhat predictable set of services for a client, I typically offer a flat fee. Most commonly, I have done this when I've drafted a Tenancy-in-Common (TIC) Agreement for a shared housing arrangement or applied for tax exemption on behalf of a nonprofit. When I offer a flat fee to clients, I usually feel that my relationship with, and attitude toward, my clients changes in a good way. For clients, the relationship is helpful because they can budget for their legal costs and don't have to worry that I'm racking up billable hours. On my end, I don't have a client that is pressuring me to cut corners and save time. I feel more like I have adopted my client and committed to doing whatever is necessary to doing a good job for them. Usually this means that I spend a good amount of time perfecting every sentence of their document, and that I am quite happy with my job well done.

The problem is that with sharing economy law clients, most things are not routine enough to attach a flat fee. A few times, I've arranged a flat fee with clients but then felt that they overstayed their welcome, asking for too many revisions, asking too many side questions, expecting multiple meetings and phone calls, and so on. Foreseeing this level of unpredictability and building it into a fee agreement is difficult. The best I have done is to carefully define the scope of my services, then put a cap on the number of hours I will spend on them, which necessitates that I keep track of my time despite the flat fee agreement.

As I noted at the beginning of the chapter, I think that many lawyers exploit flat fees as a way to capitalize off the general public's lack of access to legal information. For example, many real estate lawyers will charge a flat fee of $4,000 to prepare a set of Conditions, Covenants & Restrictions, even if the document they prepare is virtually identical to a document they've prepared in the past. In this respect, charging an hourly fee seems like a more honest way to charge for such services.

Charging an Hourly Fee

I charge an hourly fee to most clients, since sharing economy law matters are rarely routine or simple. If a client comes to me wanting to form a land trust and intentional community, it's usually next to impossible for me to foresee the amount of work that would be involved, even if I try to break it into small pieces (formation of entity, lease agreement, etc). Many unforeseen questions can come up, which makes it difficult to set a flat fee.

When I choose to charge an hourly fee, the challenge is to decide what to charge. Many of my clients are low-income individuals or nonprofits, and when I tell them I charge $200 per hour (my advertised rate), I can see the panic in my clients' faces. When they learn my fee, they sometimes go back to the drawing board and spend weeks or months trying to figure out how they can do the legal work themselves. Or they will ask me to do the minimum amount of work, so that they can keep their fees low. The problem with this is that I really don't feel happy when I do an incomplete job on things, and this can be more harmful than helpful to clients. I also don't like it when clients call me on the phone and talk extremely fast because they are worried about the cost of the conversation.

Recently, my solution has been to dramatically lower my fee for certain clients, and I'm quite pleased with the results. For some very low-income clients, I now charge $50 per hour and have found that they have been more relaxed about asking for my help, having me take part in long mediations, and so on. I appreciate the feeling that I can put in the time and do a good job for them. For some small nonprofits, I now charge about $75–$100 per hour, and for newly forming cohousing communities, I've been charging in the lower $100s. This brings my fees much closer to that of many other professionals (therapists, chiropractors, accountants, etc.), and I feel happy with this.

Concierge Lawyers or Community-Supported Lawyering

I have been inspired by a story on Minnesota Public Radio that examined how some doctors have responded to the ridiculously high cost of health care services.[23] The story cited an interesting phenomenon:

> A small but growing number of physicians practice "concierge medicine," charging patients annual retainers for basic medical care. A 2010 nationwide survey commissioned by a congressional agency pegged the number of concierge doctors at 756, up from 146 in 2005.[24]

Of course this raises the question: what about concierge lawyers? In some respects, concierge lawyers exist all over the place—they are called in-house attorneys, and they work for companies and organizations that require substantial and ongoing legal services. The relationship between a salaried in-house attorney and the company he/she works for tends to be mutually beneficial, in that the attorney can dedicate time and do a more thorough job for the company, and the

23. Jennifer Vogel, *Doctor as Renegade—Accepts Cash, Checks, Eggs or Pie, Not Insurance*, Minn. Pub. Radio (June 20, 2011), http://minnesota.publicradio.org/display/web/2011/06/20/ground-level-rural-health-care-renegade-rural-doctor/.

24. *Id.*

company has regular legal support without worrying about continuously mounting legal fees.

A concierge lawyer could do something similar with a group of clients. For example, an attorney could enter into an agreement with ten different cohousing communities to provide most necessary legal services (up to a limit of, say, 200 hours), for a total of $5,000 per year, per community. For the client, this could bring a great deal of peace of mind, necessary assistance, and the ability to budget for legal costs. For the attorney, it means having a guaranteed income, and a set of ten clients to whom you can direct your focused and thorough attention.

This approach could also be called "community-supported lawyering." This is very much like community-supported agriculture (CSA), which is now a widespread model for creating relationships between farmers and their customers.[25] In this model, customers pay a fixed amount to a farmer at the beginning of the planting season; in exchange, the customers each receive a share of the entire harvest. In this way, the customers share the risk that it will be a low-yielding harvest year, and they share in the benefits when there is a bountiful harvest.

Six Ways to Not Charge a Client

Because I became a sharing economy lawyer with the motivation to create economic opportunities for people in need, it would be counterproductive for me to turn away clients because they cannot pay me in dollars. Barter is an option, as I describe below. So, too, is the possibility of providing services without charging.

Believe it or not, there are multiple ways to *not* charge a client. If you do not charge your client money, the question is: what kind of expectation or relationship do you want to come of that? How you frame it is important. Think about the differences in the following ways to offer your services:

- **"Free legal services."** Giving something away for free may make it sound like a marketing tactic or like a program that clients can take advantage of, without any expectation of return or gratitude. "Free" sounds like something you can take and run, like the free

25. For more information about community-supported agriculture, see the USDA's resources on the topic at http://www.nal.usda.gov/afsic/pubs/csa/csa.shtml.

samples in a grocery store. For this reason, I generally avoid using the word "free" in conjunction with my offerings of services.

- **"I'll provide services pro bono."** ABA Model Rule 6.1 urges lawyers to do at least 50 hours of pro bono legal services per year. In this respect, a pro bono client becomes the beneficiary of a lawyer's commitment to public service, which creates a more significant relationship than "free services."
- **"I'm providing my services as a gift to you."** When people that I appreciate, love, and/or care about ask me for help on a legal matter, I often tell them that my services are a gift to them. This sends a different message than "free" or "pro bono." In this case, my services aren't part of a marketing tactic ("free"), and they aren't part of my duty of public service ("pro bono"). Rather, I provide them because I care about and appreciate the person. In all likelihood, I do this because I have a relationship with the person who provides for me in other ways. The person likely has done or will do something kind for me at some point, so I feel perfectly happy to gift my services.
- **"I will not charge you for my services, but I do ask that, on the honor system, you pay it forward."** Asking a client to "pay it forward" simply means asking them to do something helpful for someone else. I have done this on many occasions and find that clients appreciate this opportunity immensely. This approach is especially useful when people call and ask to "pick my brain for a little bit." I never know how long a conversation like that will last, so it's hard to know whether to charge for them to begin with. In the end, clients likely receive valuable information, they express a great deal of gratitude, and chances are, they do pay it forward. Sometimes, I'll mention that donating to my favorite nonprofit, which happens to be the Sustainable Economies Law Center, is a good way to express their gratitude. This has resulted in at least five donations to SELC, to date.
- **"I will not charge you for my services, but I would appreciate getting paid if you have the means to in the future."** I have done this with two clients, and one of them has paid me. In both cases, they are clients who I believe would normally have the capacity to pay me, but who did not, at the time, have the resources.

- **"I will not charge you for my services and will leave it up to you if, how, or when you either compensate me or pay it forward."** I have done this a couple times, but actually find that clients aren't entirely sure how to respond to something so open-ended. On one hand, it's nice to offer clients the freedom to decide, but they are probably wondering whether I will be disappointed if they do not offer to pay me.

Another Option: "You Can Pay Me on a Sliding Scale."

There are at least a couple ways to do this: you can give clients a range and let them choose within the range (usually, I'll leave a blank space on their fee agreement for them to choose the amount). Or you can indicate the normal cost of legal services and require only that they pay what they can when you bill them.

Bartering with Clients

Receiving all or part of your fee through a barter arrangement can be a wonderful way to set up a fee arrangement with a client. A client who has limited access to cash may still have abundant access to goods or services that he/she could provide as payment. Through barter arrangements with clients, I have received thousands of dollars worth of food, classes, clothing, and artwork. Coincidentally, my barter clients are some of my favorite clients, and I am grateful that the fact that they could not pay in cash was not a barrier to my representing them.

Bartering with clients is simply an alternative form of payment for services; it does not violate the ethical rules against soliciting gifts from clients,[26] so long as the arrangement is fair and does not constitute unreasonable or excessive fees.

The primary downside to bartering is that you must pay taxes in cash on the fair market value of something you did not receive in cash. It's especially sticky when you don't know the fair market value of something. I was delighted to receive "$1,200" worth of beautiful artwork from a client, but less excited to pay the IRS a few hundred dollars as a result. The $1,200 is what my client normally would have charged for

26. Model Rule 1.8(c) provides: "A lawyer shall not solicit any substantial gift from a client, including a testamentary gift, or prepare on behalf of a client an instrument giving the lawyer or a person related to the lawyer any substantial gift unless the lawyer or other recipient of the gift is related to the client."

her work, and she gave me an "invoice" for the work, which was paid in legal services. If I were to have declared a value different than the invoice, the IRS (if I were to be audited) would have expected me to provide a reasonable basis for my valuation, which is difficult, especially in the case of art.

Another tricky thing with bartering is knowing when you need to claim something as income. The IRS generally doesn't tax true gifts,[27] and the difficulty is sorting out the difference between a gift and a payment. If you receive something very small in exchange for your work, the next question is whether it could be considered a "de minimis" fringe benefit, of the sort the IRS does not expect you to report.[28] For example, once I spent about two hours advising a wonderful community organization and urban farm, and I did not charge for this advice. The next day, the person I met with returned unexpectedly to deliver a large bag of collard greens (so fresh, there were still at least 10 garden slugs riding along). Was this a gift? Was it "payment" for the advice I had given? All I knew was that this is probably not the kind of green the IRS wants me to count and report on my taxes. Had the gift been any more significant, I likely would have reported it on my taxes, since it came in conjunction with services I provided, and therefore looked more like income than a true gift. I explain this because a lawyer who routinely provides services without charging is likely to encounter this situation often. The intricacies of tax on barter income, gifts, and everything in between is discussed more fully in Chapter 5.

Lawyers Using Barter Exchanges

Directly bartering with clients may not always be convenient. If your client offers to paint your house in exchange for legal services, this won't be useful until your house needs painting. This is why it may sometimes be more convenient to take part in a barter network, where multi-party

27. I.R.C. § 102.

28. Although it applies to employment scenarios, the IRS's Taxable Fringe Benefit Guide (http://www.irs.gov/pub/irs-tege/fringe_benefit_fslg.pdf) provides helpful guidance in determining what kinds of payments would be considered "de minimis." The Guide provides: "De minimis fringe benefits include property or services, provided by an employer for an employee, with a value so small that accounting for it is unreasonable or administratively impracticable. The value of the benefit is determined by the frequency it is provided to each individual employee, or, if this is not administratively practical, by the frequency provided by that employer to the workforce as a whole." I.R.C. § 132(e); Reg. § 1.132-6(b).

barter transactions can take place. Participation in a barter network could mean that your client pays you in "points" that you can redeem for goods and services from someone else in the network. Your client will earn back the points by painting someone else's house.

It is interesting to note that, until recently, many state bar associations declared that it was unethical for lawyers to participate in barter exchanges. This was due, in part, to the now-abandoned rules prohibiting lawyers from advertising their services. In addition, the bar associations expressed disapproval of the arrangement between the lawyer and barter exchange, which sometimes resembled fee-splitting. Since the issue has yet to be re-examined in many states, I'll examine it here in more detail and explain why I believe participation in online barter networks is no longer prohibited per se.

In a recent ethics opinion,[29] the North Carolina State Bar confirmed that a lawyer may participate in a barter exchange, so long as participation doesn't result in any ethical violations (related to reasonable fees, solicitations, misleading advertising, lawyer referral services, etc.). The primary issue that the state bar grappled with was whether the 10 percent cash fee that the barter exchange took constituted fee sharing with a non-lawyer. The bar ultimately concluded that the 10 percent fee does not resemble fee-sharing, but is more similar to the type of fee that a credit card company might charge to process a payment:

> [P]aying for services of a nonlawyer based upon a percentage of a legal fee is not *per se* fee sharing. The use of credit cards to pay for legal services has long been allowed, although credit card banks routinely charge a "discount fee" that is a percentage of the legal fee charged to the credit card. [...] Paying a percentage fee to a barter exchange manager is no different than paying a discount fee to a credit card bank. The fee is a surcharge on the transaction and is not fee sharing with a nonlawyer. *See* ABA Formal Opinion 88-356 (1988) (lawyer placement agency's fee based on the amount of the legal fee is not fee splitting).

To further elucidate their position, the opinion authors cite a New York State Bar ethics opinion[30] that also addresses barter exchanges:

---

29. N.C. State Bar 2010, Formal Ethics Op. 4 (Oct. 29, 2010), http://www.ncbar.gov/ethics/ethics.asp?page=6&keywords=credit+card.

30. N.Y. State Bar Ass'n Comm. on Prof'l Ethics, Op. 665 (1994).

> There are a number of rationales for the prohibition against sharing legal fees with non-lawyers: (1) to avoid the possibility of a nonlawyer interfering with the exercise of the lawyer's professional judgment in representing a client, (2) to ensure that the total fee paid by the client is not unreasonably high, and (3) to ensure that the nonlawyer is not motivated to engage in improper solicitation of business for the lawyer. [Citations omitted.] We do not believe that the proposed barter exchange implicates these concerns so long as the barter exchange exercises no influence over the professional judgment of the lawyer, the lawyer's legal fee complies with [the reasonableness requirement of] DR 2-106(A) of the [New York] Code [of Professional Responsibility], and the exchange sponsor does not engage in in-person solicitation of customers or use written advertising materials that the lawyer/participant could not use.

Florida came to a different conclusion in a 1984 ethics opinion,[31] stating that a lawyer may participate in a barter exchange where there is a flat membership fee, as opposed to a fee based on a percentage of a legal fee.

Texas is yet another story. It is interesting to contrast North Carolina's and New York's approaches to the approach that Texas took in its 1986 ethics opinion[32] (which, we'll note, was before the internet age):

> The essence of an attorney's membership in a barter exchange is a transfer of value by an attorney to the exchange (in the form of membership fees and/or in the form of a percentage of trade credits paid by the attorney to other members to the exchange) in return for the exchange's making the attorney's name available to other exchange members and facilitating payments through barter for the attorney's legal services. A lawyer's participation in such an arrangement therefore violates Disciplinary Rule ("DR")DR 2-103(C): A lawyer shall not compensate or give anything of value to a person or organization to recommend or secure his employment by a client, or as a reward for having made a recommendation resulting in his employment by a client.

Although this ethics opinion has not been superseded by a subsequent opinion on barter exchanges in Texas, in all likelihood, Texas lawyers could now participate in online barter exchanges, due to the

31. Fla. Ethics Op. 84-2.
32. Tex. Comm. on Prof'l Ethics, Op. 435, 49 Tex. B.J. 1015 (1986).

fact that most barter exchange operators do not actively promote the attorneys or solicit clients. Most barter exchanges allow members to set up profiles for themselves and don't act as active match makers. As a result, the Texas opinion probably does not fully hold up in the age of online barter exchanges.

It is important to note that other states (like Utah[33]) that have recently examined the ethics of attorneys using barter exchanges have ultimately determined that there is nothing, per se, wrong with it. In the end, the problems that arise, if any, relate to the terms of payment between the lawyer and the barter exchange. This also points to the fact that a lawyer's participation in a time bank or a barter network that does not take a fee would be no problem under any ethics rulings that I know of.

Lawyers Using Time Banks

What follows is a piece by law professor and TimeBanks USA founder Edgar S. Cahn, describing the implementation of a time bank system by a legal service organization in Oregon. This system allows the organization's clients to "pay it forward" by doing favors for others through a time bank. It also allows pro bono attorneys to get "paid" in time dollars, which they can "spend" to receive other services. A time bank is similar to a barter network, in that people earn "points," "hours," or "time dollars" for the services they provide to people, and those points can be spent to receive services provided by others. What is different is that all points in a time bank are earned on an hour-for-hour basis. No matter what kind of work you do, it is measured by the time you put in, and you earn one point per hour.

It is important to note that many of the favors people do for each other through time banks are not of the sort that the IRS seeks to tax as income—cooking a meal, walking a dog, giving someone a ride, and so on. However, if a lawyer were to provide regular legal services through a time bank, I do believe that the value of the services that the lawyer receives in return would be taxable income, and it is up to the lawyer to measure and report that. Unlike barter exchanges, which are required to report taxable barter transactions, time banks have been specifically exempted from the requirement to report their members' transactions.

33. Utah State Bar Ethics Advisory Opinion Comm., Op. 97-05 (approved Apr. 25, 1997), http://www.utahbar.org/rules_ops_pols/ethics_opinions/op_97_05.html.

The IRS has not directly addressed the issue of which time bank transactions are taxable, perhaps in recognition that this should remain an uncharted gray area. I will discuss this gray area in greater depth in Chapter 5.

FROM CONSUMERS OF LEGAL SERVICES TO CO-PRODUCERS OF JUSTICE: THE PARADIGM SHIFT

By Edgar S. Cahn, Creator of Time Dollars, founder of TimeBanks USA, and co-founder of the National Legal Services Program and the Antioch School of Law (now the David A. Clarke School of Law at the University of the District of Columbia)

It is one thing to call for a paradigm shift. It is something else to see the paradigm shift actually taking place. The changes that are underway at the Roseberg office of Legal Aid Services of Oregon (LASO) represent nothing less than a paradigm shift in legal services: the plan is for clients to be asked to match the staff hours spent by LASO on their case by enrolling in a TimeBank that was set up jointly with the League of Women Voters and the United Way.

In doing so, this LASO office is undertaking to transform the clients it serves from consumers of legal services to co-producers of justice. A paradigm is defined as a map, a world view, a model that one uses to chart a course to get A to B. When the legal service program was launched as part of the Johnson administration's War on Poverty in the 1960s, effective legal representation was regarded as a key to enfranchisement. Lawyers would be the advocates needed to amplify the voices of those who were disenfranchised. It was hoped that providing that voice would break down barriers to opportunity, would hold officials accountable to the rule of law, and would thereby expand access to those "inalienable rights to life, liberty and the pursuit of happiness."

Five years ago, the Legal Services Corporation released a study that for every client seen by a legal service program, one was turned away. Other studies confirm that the gap in availability of counsel was far greater, that fewer than one-fifth of those who needed legal services could get them. Now, with the need greater than ever, with unprecedented demand for government benefits and with a vast backlog, Congress has cut federal funding for legal services by one-fifth. Given the shortage of resources and the magnitude of unmet demand, Sharon Lee Schwartz of LASO decided to do something that legal service lawyers are not used to doing: ask for client's help to address the critical social problems that so often give rise to legal problems.

Legal Aid Services of Oregon went to the United Way and the League of Women Voters to establish an independent TimeBank. Then, they linked their pro bono program to the TimeBank, whereby local lawyers offering pro bono assistance could be rewarded for their time by earning time dollars. The lawyers or their firm could accept and utilize those time credits for themselves (or their families) or donate those time credits to advance a worthy cause. The hope is that eventually that will stimulate more pro bono work.

At the same time, LASO is asking its own clients to participate in a "pay it forward" pilot program, through which clients agree to do a certain number of hours of work and favors for other community members and, in turn, earn time dollars they can use to receive help and favors from others. This partnership has been constructed in a way that conforms to Legal Service Corporation requirements. Furthermore, the effort to incorporate a time bank into the work of a legal services organization has the support of the primary national funder of legal services, the Legal Services Corporation. In October of 2010, Victor M. Fortuno, the president of Legal Services Corporation, wrote a letter to TimeBanks USA in support of this project, where he stated: "Given the potential TimeBanks holds for the legal service community (and the nation as a whole), LSC supports your efforts to introduce it to our grantees for integration with and enhancement of their programs of advancing equal access to justice."

A TimeBank is simply an arrangement where people come together to give their time to help others. You give an hour of help; you earn one time credit. The person receiving the help owes one time credit; he/she pays it back by helping someone else. Records of hours earned and spent are kept in the computer system. One uses hours when needed or one can give them to someone else or to an organization that serves the community. To date, in Roseberg, a rural office, the TimeBank has enrolled 250 members and several organizations.

In LASO's case, clients receive help from LASO attorneys; in return, they are asked to pay it forward by helping someone else. Participation is not required. Regardless of whether clients choose to join the TimeBank, they will be referred to the normal case conference. But the establishment of the TimeBank, the perception that clients can do things that advance the mission of legal services, and the arrangement of a vehicle to enlist client capacity all represent a major break with the past.

In 2009, the Legal Service Corporation reported that it served nearly one million clients. LASO is asking: what would it mean to enlist one million persons to build community, advance health, promote education, reduce substance abuse, make neighborhoods safer, care for the elderly, strengthen families, and bridge lines of race and national origin?

First, it means that clients are far more than the sum of their legal problems. They have capacities that have often gone unknown, unnoted, and underutilized.

Second, by referring clients to the TimeBank, LASO has chosen to enlist them in addressing critical social problems to value their contribution, and at the same time to provide clients with a way to enhance their own well-being by exchanges that can address and alleviate critical personal needs.

Third, it means that the legal services are no longer delivered as a one-way transaction. A pay-it-forward reciprocity changes the message from "how can I help you?" to "how can we help each other?"

Fourth, it brings clients together, ending isolation that can inadvertently be perpetuated by canons of confidentiality and privacy. Creating social networks and building community does not breach confidentiality.

Finally, when clients are redefined as contributors, their voices are amplified. A feedback loop providing a measure of effectiveness is created. When the governed become the actual workforce needed to address critical social problems, officials can be held accountable in a new way.

Charles Houston, architect of the path that led to *Brown v. Board of Education*, was renowned for declaring "A lawyer is either a social engineer or a parasite on society." LASO is teaching us what being a social engineer could mean.

More information about time banks can be found at www.timebanks.org.

PART 7: COMMON ETHICAL ISSUES IN SHARING ECONOMY LAW

There are a few professional ethics issues that sharing economy lawyers commonly encounter, and these issues arise from one primary source: sharing economy lawyers often work with groups of people, rather than simply representing single individuals. The three primary ethical concerns I will discuss here are:

- **Multiple Representation:** A sharing economy lawyer may be asked to represent a group of people entering into an agreement to govern their relationship. The lawyer must assess the conflicts of interest, determine whether multiple representation is appropriate, and properly obtain clients' informed consent.
- **Representing Parties to Collaborative Transactions:** In other cases, the lawyer may represent only one party to a transaction but find himself or herself communicating and collaborating frequently with the other parties. This brings up the need to communicate clearly who is the client, inform clients of attorney–client privilege issues, and determine if and how you can communicate with other parties.
- **Moving Between the Role of Lawyer and Mediator:** When can a mediator provide legal services, and when can an attorney offer mediation services? Attorney–mediators in sharing economy law will sometimes find it useful to employ both lawyering and mediation skills in a single matter; yet this brings up ethical dilemmas due to the conflicting responsibilities of lawyers and mediators.

A fourth and common ethical concern for sharing economy lawyers arises when representing an organization or business entity. Much has been written about a lawyer's responsibilities to a client when the client is an entity such as a corporation or limited liability company. Since this issue is quite common outside of sharing economy law and has been written about in business law practice guides, I will not explore this issue here.

Note that here and throughout this chapter, I have made reference primarily to the ABA Model Rules, even though each state's rules are the ones that truly bind lawyers.

Multiple Representation

Inevitably, clients who come to you for assistance in a sharing arrangement will sometimes ask you to represent two or more people simultaneously. I most commonly encounter this situation when two families purchase a home together and ask me to draft a co-ownership agreement. Oftentimes, it doesn't even occur to clients to seek multiple attorneys, and they may assume that it is possible for the lawyer to provide assistance to everyone simultaneously. The idea of involving multiple attorneys is unattractive to clients who do not want to spend a lot of money on legal fees or who want to maintain the spirit of collaboration in their arrangement.

At the same time, lawyers' professional ethics rules favor, but do not absolutely mandate, having each party represented by independent counsel. This is to ensure that each party is fully advised of his/her rights, responsibilities, and risks entering into an agreement, and that, when the interests of parties are in conflict, each party's attorney can advocate for an ideal outcome for the client.

The dilemma for a sharing economy lawyer is: when two or more people ask you to represent them simultaneously, how do you proceed? Some lawyers have a strict policy against multiple representation, arguing that there is too much risk that it could come back and bite when one client realizes that he or she wasn't adequately advised of his or her rights, responsibilities, or risks. I have never been willing to take such a hard and fast stance against multiple representation. In fact, I believe that when two people work together with one lawyer and communicate openly about their different interests, it can lay a strong groundwork for their ongoing collaborative relationship. If each party seeks his or her own attorney, there is a risk that the relationship could start out on a slightly adversarial foot, depending on how each party's attorney chooses to communicate the client's interests.

Approximately half the time that prospective clients ask me to do multiple representation, I agree to it, but only after looking carefully at the situation and the potential conflicts of interest. What follows is a description of the various factors that I weigh in the decision, and how I proceed during multiple representation.

First of all, every lawyer should read his/her state's rules around conflicts of interest and any state ethics decisions pertaining to multiple and simultaneous representation. Here is the relevant section, Rule 1.7, of the ABA Model Rules of Professional Conduct:

> **Rule 1.7 Conflict of Interest: Current Clients**
>
> (a) Except as provided in paragraph (b), a lawyer shall not represent a client if the representation involves a concurrent conflict of interest. A concurrent conflict of interest exists if:
>
> (1) the representation of one client will be directly adverse to another client; or
>
> (2) there is a significant risk that the representation of one or more clients will be materially limited by the lawyer's responsibilities to another client, a former client or a third person or by a personal interest of the lawyer.
>
> (b) Notwithstanding the existence of a concurrent conflict of interest under paragraph (a), a lawyer may represent a client if:
>
> (1) the lawyer reasonably believes that the lawyer will be able to provide competent and diligent representation to each affected client;
>
> (2) the representation is not prohibited by law;
>
> (3) the representation does not involve the assertion of a claim by one client against another client represented by the lawyer in the same litigation or other proceeding before a tribunal; and
>
> (4) each affected client gives informed consent, confirmed in writing.

The first question is, is there a conflict of interest? When an attorney represents two parties to the same transaction, I believe the answer will almost always be yes. One California ethics opinion, which examines what constitutes a conflict of interest in multiple representation, explains that a conflict exists when there are "conflicting objectives of the clients in which the lawyer cannot effectively advance one client's objective without detrimentally affecting another client's objective."[34]

34. State Bar of Cal., Standing Comm. on Prof'l Responsibility and Conduct, Formal Op. 1999-153.

It would be rare or miraculous for two people to be in agreement about *everything*. And when two clients are in disagreement about something, I may not be able to advance once client's objectives without detrimentally affecting the other's. Thus, my assumption in any multiple representation is that there will be conflicts of interest.

With that in mind, I typically follow a two-step process in deciding whether to represent both parties. First, I look at the situation and determine whether I can adequately advise each client, despite their conflicting interests. According to ABA Model Rule 1.7, above, a lawyer may not represent both clients if the lawyer will not "be able to provide competent and diligent representation to each affected client."[35] My second step is to communicate with clients about the conflict issues and obtain their written informed consent to the simultaneous representation. Here are details about how I navigate each step.

Determining Whether I Can Provide Competent and Diligent Representation to All Clients Involved

Providing competent and diligent representation includes advising each client of the rights, responsibilities, and risks that he or she is assuming. When clients have substantially different goals from each other, I find it more difficult to adequately advise each one. I am more likely to conclude that I can provide competent and diligent representation to multiple clients if (1) the transaction between clients is fairly symmetrical, (2) the goals of clients are fairly aligned, and (3) the financial positions of clients are fairly similar.

An example of a symmetrical co-ownership agreement between two parties, for example, is one where each client purchases approximately 50 percent of a property, and all rights and responsibilities are allocated on a roughly 50/50 basis. However, if one party were to assume a substantially greater share of ownership, rights, and responsibilities, I would question whether I could effectively advise both parties of their rights and risks without appearing to be siding with one party or another. Likewise, if one client intends to use the property as a long-term residence, and the other party thinks of it as an investment property, it might be more difficult to simultaneously advise each client on how to achieve his or her goals. Finally, if one party has a significantly

35. MODEL RULES OF PROF'L CONDUCT R. 1.7(b)(1).

less stable financial position than the other, it may be difficult for me to advise on the financial provisions of an agreement in a way that balances the needs and risks of each party. For example, I could add a provision that requires that each party contribute $100 per month to a reserve fund. This additional financial responsibility protects both parties in the event of unexpected costs or one party's default; however, the additional burden could put one party at a much greater risk of default if they can't contribute to the reserve fund.

At the same time, even when such asymmetries exist, I may still conclude that I can provide competent and diligent representation if I feel that both clients are willing and able to thoroughly explore the implications of the asymmetries and to work toward an agreement that balances their interests. This calls for good communication on everyone's part. The important thing is that I feel able to listen to the needs of each client, and speak openly about clients' differences. My role is to help each client feel fully informed of the issues, which won't always be easy for everyone to hear. For example, I would need to inform one client of how another client's proposal could put him or her at risk.

Sometimes the personalities of and power dynamics between clients clue me in to whether I will be able to effectively communicate with all clients. I once had an initial meeting with two clients planning to purchase a house together, and I noticed that one of them did most of the talking and even seemed mildly irritated and interrupted when the other voiced her concerns. Due to the difficulty of hearing the concerns of the other client, this was an immediate clue that I would have a difficult time providing proper representation to both. Clients with more open communication are better candidates for multiple representation.

Obtaining Informed Consent

If I do decide to represent multiple parties simultaneously, my next step is to determine the best way to communicate the actual and potential conflicts so that clients will be fully informed in giving consent. For this reason, my written waivers of conflicts of interest are typically long and give details about how a conflict could arise in the client's particular case. Writing a thorough waiver requires that I already know enough about the clients' planned transaction to tell them what aspects of the arrangement could or already bring up conflicts. For example, if I learn that one client has a pending lawsuit against him or her, I should inform all clients that a conflict could arise if the lawsuit affects a client's ability to carry out financial commitments. The text of one of my consent forms follows.

Even after obtaining initial informed consent, a lawyer to a multiple representation must continue to point out new conflicts when they arise and obtain clients' consent to continued representation. The fact is that small conflicts will arise naturally throughout the negotiation process, as clients iron out the details of their agreement. Most clients will work through these details and come to a workable agreement.

Creating an Additional Record of the Informed Consent

If you are drafting an agreement between multiple clients, it's also a good idea to acknowledge in the text of the agreement that you represented everyone jointly after they gave informed consent. This is to protect you and the parties in the event that there is later litigation in connection with the agreement and one party claims that he/she didn't have the opportunity to consult with independent counsel. If you are drafting a co-ownership agreement, for example, you could add the following language:

> This Agreement was drafted by attorney ____________ [your name], who represented both parties in the preparation of this Agreement. On ____________ [date], each party waived, in writing, all real and potential conflicts of interest associated with having one attorney simultaneously represent both parties. The parties have been advised that they should each seek the counsel of an independent attorney to review the agreement prior to signing and each party acknowledges that he/she has been given opportunity to do so.

Representing Clients in Collaborative Transactions with Non-clients

Another common scenario for a sharing economy lawyer is to represent one party to a transaction but to communicate frequently with non-client parties to the transaction. For example, a client hired me to draft a co-ownership agreement for her and a friend. Although I did not take the friend on as a client, he attended both meetings I had with my client and took part in many email conversations as we refined the points of the draft agreement. I advised the friend that he should seek the advice

SAMPLE LANGUAGE TO OBTAIN INFORMED CONSENT FOR MULTIPLE REPRESENTATION

This is sample language that I add to my engagement letter when I represent multiple clients. At the end is the consent statement that I ask clients to sign.

Joint Representation: Generally, professional ethics rules require that attorneys represent only one party to a transaction, so that each party may have his or her own advisor and advocate. However, exceptions can be made when the interests of parties are closely aligned. For example, it is typical for an attorney to jointly represent domestic partners and/or married couples when they purchase a home together. In your case, I believe the three of you have a similar vision and goals, which makes joint representation possible. Nevertheless, I must advise you that having separate attorneys is traditionally considered the most effective way to ensure that each party's interests are protected. At any time, if you feel that you would benefit from having your own attorneys, you may end our attorney–client relationship and seek separate representation. In the meantime, it is important for me to explain a couple of matters that come up when an attorney represents multiple parties:

a. **Confidentiality:** In representing all of you, matters that one of you might discuss with me would not be protected from disclosure to the others. While anything that anyone of you discusses with me is confidential with respect to third parties, I am prohibited from agreeing with any of you to withhold information from the others.
b. **Conflicts of interest:** In addition, ethical rules require that I obtain a written waiver of actual or potential conflicts that may arise out of my simultaneous representation of two or more clients in the same matter. To work with potential conflicts and for your co-ownership arrangement to be successful, it is important to openly discuss any imbalances in your transaction, and to acknowledge how decisions you make could affect each of you differently.

For example, if applicable, we should examine the implications of

i. Any situation where one party is contributing substantially more money than the others, or receiving property of substantially different value;
ii. Any significant differences in your financial statuses or credit ratings;
iii. Any situation in which one of you has different financial goals than the other (an example would be a situation in which one of you is thinking of this purchase as a short-term investment, whereas another is envisioning this as a permanent residence);
iv. Any situation where joint ownership may subject one party to risk as a result of the other party's liabilities (such as a pending lawsuit against one party); and
v. Any other situation that demonstrates that your goals are significantly divergent.

In your particular case, I have already noted at least two potential conflicts that are important to be aware of. First of all, Irene has indicated that she plans to do a significant amount of work on her portion of the property, much more so than Mark or Ravi. Irene's additional investment of time and resources in the property means that you have important decisions to make about how to compensate co-owners for their improvements, and the decision you make will likely have different impacts on each of you. Second, you have acknowledged that Mark has a poor credit rating, which could affect your ability to get ideal loan terms. Thus, you will have some decisions to make regarding your approach to obtaining a loan, and the decision you make could affect each of you differently.

As potential conflicts such as these come to the surface, I can point out the pros and cons of such differing opinions and help you determine how your course of action will affect each of you. However, as the attorney for all of you, I cannot advocate one of your positions over those of the others.

If significant conflicts arise among the three of you, and those conflicts are not resolved through our discussion process, it would become necessary for me to withdraw as your joint attorney, at which point I would advise each of you to obtain another attorney.

Agreement, Consent, and Waiver of Conflicts of Interest

We hereby agree and consent to representation by Janelle Orsi for the purposes and on the terms set forth above. In particular, we understand the discussion of conflicts of interest and confidentiality in the letter. We acknowledge that although the interests of Irene, Mark, and Ravi are generally aligned in this matter, it is recognized and understood that differences already exist and that others may become evident during the course of our representation. Despite these possibilities, we have determined that it is in our individual and mutual interests to have a single attorney represent us jointly in connection with our co-ownership agreement. We further agree that Janelle may withdraw her representation should she determine that conflicts of interests prevent her from providing competent and diligent representation to each of us.

of his own attorney (although he never did) and reminded him that my role was to consider the interests of my client, and not his interests. Nevertheless, his participation was a natural part of the process because he was entering into an important agreement with my client.

In such collaborative scenarios, a lawyer representing only one party should be aware of a few potential ethical problems:

1. **Informing and reminding the unrepresented party of your role:** When unrepresented parties take part in conversations related to the representation of your client, it's important to communicate to the other parties that you are not representing them, and that your duty is to your client. ABA Model Rule 4.3 states that "In dealing on behalf of a client with a person who is not represented by counsel, a lawyer shall not state or imply that the lawyer is disinterested." It is also important to remind non-clients of this periodically because the collaborative nature of the conversations

could lead the non-client to *feel* that you are looking out for his/her interests, even though it is not your job to do so.

2. **Informing your client when attorney–client privilege may not apply:** When you involve non-clients in meetings or copy them on emails, does the attorney-client privilege still apply to the communication? Attorney–client privilege generally only extends to communications that the client intends to be confidential. If a third party is in the room, the third-party's presence may demonstrate that the communication is not intended to be confidential and could therefore destroy the privilege. In non-adversarial sharing economy law cases, most clients will not be bothered by the fact that they are waiving the privilege by involving others in the conversation. It is nevertheless important to let the client know that the information may no longer be protected by attorney–client privilege, which would matter in the event that you or the third party are subpoenaed to testify about the information.

   Note, however, that the privilege could be preserved if the other party is represented by counsel and all parties and lawyers have entered into an agreement to carry out the matter in accordance with the procedures of collaborative law, in states that have specifically recognized such procedures. See the box above entitled "Sharing Economy Law Meets Collaborative Law" for more information.

3. **Communicating with other parties when they are represented by counsel:** Another important rule to keep in mind is ABA Model Rule 4.2 regarding communication with parties represented by counsel: "In representing a client, a lawyer shall not communicate about the subject of the representation with a person the lawyer knows to be represented by another lawyer in the matter, unless the lawyer has the consent of the other lawyer or is authorized to do so by law or a court order." This could come up, for example, if I draft a co-ownership agreement and my client asks me to email it to her and forward a copy to her co-owner. If I know the co-owner was intending to hire an attorney to advise him on the matter, I should probably ask that he (or his attorney) let me know when he enters into an attorney–client relationship. Once the other party is represented by counsel, it is still possible

to communicate directly with the other party, so long as I obtain permission from the other attorney to do so. Many times, at the request of my client and with the other side's consent, I send each communication to everyone—my client, the other party, and the other party's attorney—and most conversations proceed with everyone's involvement.

Moving Between the Roles of Mediator and Attorney

Because I am both an attorney and mediator, there are at least two common situations in which I have found myself awkwardly moving between the role of a mediator and an attorney:

1. **Mediator turns into attorney:** Clients hire me to mediate a dispute related to their co-ownership of property. During the mediation, they ask me for advice on how a proposed transaction will affect their taxes. Can I answer their question and give legal advice during the course of the mediation? Following the mediation, they ask me to take their resolutions and incorporate them into a thorough co-ownership agreement. Again, they are essentially asking me to step into the role that I normally play as an attorney. Is this allowed?
2. **Attorney turns into mediator:** Two clients hire me to represent them simultaneously for the purpose of a co-ownership agreement. During our meetings, clients find themselves in disagreement with each other over a particular agreement term. Because it is not my role to impose a solution, I generally ask questions and lead a discussion about the issue, until clients come to an agreement about how to move forward. The fact is that lawyers do this all the time, whether or not they are trained as mediators. The question is, although this *feels* a little like mediation, is it mediation, or at what point does this become mediation? What if clients *explicitly* ask me to mediate the conversation? Can I move into this role while I'm still an attorney for both parties?

In truth, the professional ethics rules and guidance about how to proceed in these scenarios are somewhat muddy and difficult to apply to real-life scenarios. I will describe my approach and provide some of those rules here. First, let's look at the relevant ABA Model Rule 2.4(b):

> (b) A lawyer serving as a third-party neutral shall inform unrepresented parties that the lawyer is not representing them. When the lawyer knows or reasonably should know that a party does not understand the lawyer's role in the matter, the lawyer shall explain the difference between the lawyer's role as a third-party neutral and a lawyer's role as one who represents a client.

Rule 2.4(b) emphasizes that serving as a mediator is different from serving as a lawyer. Putting that principle into practice is quite difficult! In the course of mediation, parties frequently ask me legal questions, and it's hard to know whether and how I can answer them. The ABA Section on Dispute Resolution adopted the following principle in a 2002 Resolution:[36]

> Mediation is a process in which an impartial individual assists the parties in reaching a voluntary settlement. Such assistance does not constitute the practice of law. The parties to the mediation are not represented by the mediator. [...] In disputes where the parties' legal rights or obligations are at issue, the mediator's discussions with the parties may involve legal issues. Such discussions do not create an attorney–client relationship, and do not constitute legal advice, whether or not the mediator is an attorney.

This Resolution seems to be saying that I can give legal information and discuss legal issues, but not give *advice*. In truth, when a client asks me how their proposed agreement will impact their taxes, it's very hard to answer the question in a way that does not constitute giving advice. In sum, I find the above principle somewhat difficult to apply, but I nevertheless try my best. During the course of the mediation, I have tried to answer legal questions in the following way: "As you know, I'm not in my role as an attorney right now, and I can't give you legal advice. What I *can* give you is a little information about how real estate transactions generally affect taxes. However, please do not rely on this as advice. It would be better for you to seek the advice of an independent attorney for questions like this."

But what happens after mediation when the parties ask me to write a detailed contract? The Resolution quoted above offers this guidance:[37]

36. ABA Section on Dispute Resolution, Resolution on Mediation and the Unauthorized Practice of Law (adopted Feb. 2, 2002).

37. *Id.*

> When an agreement is reached in a mediation, the parties often request assistance from the mediator in memorializing their agreement. The preparation of a memorandum of understanding or settlement agreement by a mediator, incorporating the terms of settlement specified by the parties, does not constitute the practice of law. If the mediator drafts an agreement that goes beyond the terms specified by the parties, he or she may be engaged in the practice of law. However, in such a case, a mediator shall not be engaged in the practice of law if (a) all parties are represented by counsel and (b) the mediator discloses that any proposal that he or she makes with respect to the terms of settlement is informational as opposed to the practice of law, and that the parties should not view or rely upon such proposals as advice of counsel, but merely consider them in consultation with their own attorneys.

I find it quite difficult to adhere to this guidance. Almost every agreement that I draft requires that I add terms that are beyond those discussed by the parties, even if it's just boilerplate contract language. It would be disingenuous to call such additions "informational," since I am essentially *advising* clients to include them. One solution is to simply act as a "scribe," write down the basic components of the parties' resolution, and then send them to other attorneys to draft the full agreement.[38] This is not always practical, since clients often feel strongly that they want me to write the full agreement. My solution has been to enter into a second agreement with clients after mediation, whereby I end my role as a mediator and the parties agree that I may act as an attorney representing them simultaneously for the limited purpose of putting their mediation resolution into a binding contract. I also have the parties waive any conflicts of interests that may exist as a result of the fact that I am jointly representing them after mediating their dispute. For example, during the mediation, one party may have shared information with me that they intended to be confidential with regard to the other party. I will keep that information confidential, but both parties should acknowledge that I have information about one party that has not been disclosed to the other party.

An important note of caution: My own approach may not be acceptable in every state! One Utah ethics opinion stated that

38. Note that many divorce/dissolution mediator-attorneys will draft and even file a full marital settlement agreement for clients, so long as the agreement does not go beyond issues discussed in mediation. Most mediator-attorneys require that parties have the agreement reviewed by independent counsel prior to filing.

> When a lawyer–mediator, after a successful mediation, drafts the settlement agreement, complaint and other pleadings to implement the settlement and obtain a divorce for the parties, the lawyer–mediator is engaged in the practice of law and attempting to represent opposing parties in litigation. A lawyer may not represent both parties following a mediation to obtain a divorce for the parties.[39]

It is not clear whether the Utah opinion applies to non-divorce or non-litigation matters. It's also important to note that the Utah opinion had a strong dissent, which argued that an attorney–mediator "in limited circumstances [may] undertake the subsequent joint representation of the mediating parties in obtaining final judicial approval of a fully successful settlement." In sum, this matter seems slightly unsettled in Utah, and an attorney–mediator should tread carefully in deciding how to proceed if clients ask her to draft agreements after mediation. Generally, every lawyer should read his/her state's rules on multiple representation along with any relevant ethics opinions.

To summarize my approach to the "mediator turns into attorney" scenario: during the course of the mediation, I tell clients that I am not acting as an attorney, and I provide legal *information*, rather than *advice*. Following the mediation, I either send clients to other attorneys to draft the agreement, I act as a mere "scribe" and create a contract that does not go beyond the subjects discussed in mediation, or I sometimes obtain consent from my clients to switch roles and act as their joint attorney for the purposes of putting their agreement into writing.

What the above rules and guidance tell me is that I should never try to be a lawyer and mediator simultaneously, because of the potential to mislead clients about my role, and because I cannot provide legal advice when I'm in my role as a mediator. Now, what happens in the second scenario, where I am serving as an attorney for clients who have a disagreement with one another? If I mediate the conversation, I do run the risk of improperly straddling the line between attorney and mediator, especially if the clients explicitly ask me to mediate.

At the same time, I do believe that it's possible for me to assist with the conversation without having it officially become mediation.

---

39. Utah State Bar Bd. of Bar Comm'rs, Op. 05-03, http://www.utahbar.org/rules_ops_pols/ethics_opinions/op_05_03.html.

The question is: when does something officially become mediation? The Uniform Mediation Act adopted by the National Conference of Commissioners on Uniform State Laws (NCCUSL), Section 3, recognizes that something is a mediation if "the mediation parties use as a mediator an individual who holds himself or herself out as a mediator or the mediation is provided by a person that holds itself out as providing mediation." In essence, if I tell people that I'm mediating, then it's a mediation. My solution is: tell the client it's not mediation.

If clients are in conflict with each other and they ask me to mediate the conversation, I first obtain their informed consent to continue multiple representation in light of the conflict. I tell them that I can *assist* with or *facilitate* the conversation, but I must clarify that it is not officially mediation. I tell them that I cannot act as a mediator, since doing so would prevent me from continuing to act as their attorney. I also point out that in a typical mediation, clients could normally ask to speak with me alone and expect that I will keep the information confidential with regard to the other clients. This is not the case if I'm simultaneously representing two clients as their lawyer, so I tell clients that they should not expect me to keep any secrets from the other client.

After I have explained to clients that it is not officially mediation, I can still assist the clients by directing the conversation in ways that draw from my mediator's toolkit. For example, I might ask that clients take turns speaking, ask a client to restate what she has heard the other client say, restate and reframe what I hear clients saying, ask clarifying questions, and summarize issues and interests. Unlike a truly neutral mediator, I will continue to offer advice to both parties, when necessary.

It's important to acknowledge that assisting with conversations in this way calls into question whether I am still acting in my capacity as a legal advisor, which matters for the purpose of determining whether the attorney–client privilege applies to the communications. This is a question that an attorney should consider on a case-by-case basis, based on whether the lawyer's involvement in the conversation is sufficiently connected to the client's purpose of obtaining legal advice and services. Most of the time, the conversation will be so closely related to a matter on which the lawyer is advising the client, it will not be hard to argue that the communication was for the purpose of the representation, and therefore protected by privilege.

CHAPTER THREE

NEW KINDS OF AGREEMENTS

PART 1: AGREEMENTS AS THE BUILDING BLOCKS OF A SHARING ECONOMY

Building an Economy with Agreements

Agreements are the building blocks of a sharing economy. The sharing economy will not, for the most part, be brought to us by legislation or by solutions developed for us by large organizations and businesses. The sharing economy consists primarily of the millions of agreements that individuals make to share, form organizations, work together, and exchange with one another.

In many ways, this entire book is about agreements and the regulations that govern them. The chapters that follow are about the agreements we make to form organizations (Chapter 4), to exchange with each other (Chapter 5), to invest resources in each other's work (Chapter 6), to work together (Chapter 7), to provide for one another (Chapter 8), to share rights to land (Chapter 9), to share rights to intellectual property (Chapter 10), and to manage the risks we share (Chapter 11). Those chapters describe models for the formation of such agreements, the unique challenges involved, and the regulations that govern the relationships that people create by agreement. This chapter examines some of the basic components of agreements, best practices in negotiating and structuring them, and unique qualities of agreements we make in the sharing economy.

Agreements take many forms: they may be quick notes we exchange via email, spoken commitments, carefully crafted and detailed documents, and everything in between. Agreements are also the tacit and implicit understandings we have about the way we interact and transact with each other. As such, our lives already revolve around the making of agreements. As lawyer/mediator Stewart Levine puts it:

> We work and live in a "sea" (context) of agreements. You can view your life as a series of agreements. As you go through your day, try viewing your life through the "lens of agreement." From the moment you wake up to the moment you go to sleep, your life is governed by the set of expectations you have as a result of the explicit and implicit agreements between you and others.[1]

In the sharing economy, many of the common and implicit agreements of modern society will be replaced by new relationships that we actively form to provide for ourselves and others. Think about the implicit agreement most of us currently have with neighbors: we will all live independently, purchase our own food, purchase our own goods, and call on each other for help only when we are in a bind. We get what we need by going to stores, where there is an implicit agreement that we can select what we want off the shelf, stand in a checkout line, hand over dollars, and leave with our chosen items.

The sharing economy essentially offers us a new resource for meeting our needs: each other. This will bring us a much deeper involvement with the agreements we make. Instead of shopping to meet all of our needs, we will make agreements to borrow, lend, share ownership, collectively purchase, swap, barter, buy, sell, give, and receive from, to, and with one another. We will have written agreements to share a car, to share ownership of housing, to borrow a recreational vehicle, to share land for food growing, to share workspaces, and so on.

Agreements infuse a particular amount of certainty into our relationships. To the extent that the relationships of the sharing economy are meant to provide for our basic needs, we *need* some amount of certainty. For example, we need to be certain that sharing does not expose us to too much risk, we need to be certain that shared resources will be there when we need them, and we need to be certain that our sharing and cooperative arrangements can adapt when we need them to. We

---

1. Stewart Levine, The Book of Agreement: 10 Essential Elements for Getting the Results You Want 19 (Berrett-Koehler 2002).

will all soon be swimming in a sea of agreements designed to provide for us in new ways. As such, it is time that we all—sharing economy lawyers and lay people alike—become more fluent, facile, and dare I say, obsessed, with the skills of making agreements.

Agreements as Private Sharing Economy Laws

An important characteristic of agreements is that they are, in essence, privately created laws that are often publicly enforceable. When we exchange commitments with one another, each offering something of value to the other, our laws, with some exceptions, generally say that we have created a contract. If we do not carry through on our commitments to one another, parties that are harmed can seek redress through the court system. While most of what happens in the sharing economy will never go to court, our agreements are nevertheless built on this foundation. The solidity of contracts we make in the sharing economy will ultimately be backed by the legal system.

At the same time, not all agreements are contracts. For example, an agreement to give something without receiving something in return is a donative agreement, and it is generally not considered a contract. Such an agreement is said to lack "consideration." "Consideration," by the way, is an unfortunate word to use here because many non-lawyers do not know its legal meaning, and because giving something for nothing is, in another sense of the word, a considerate thing to do. Nevertheless, it's important to acknowledge here that the things we provide for one another in the spirit of generosity, nurturing, or gift economy are ultimately enforced by social expectation, not by legal contract.

Furthermore, not all contracts are enforceable. For example, contracts that contain illegal terms cannot be enforced.[2] This is actually quite common, since our legal system dictates many of the terms of our relationships, such as in areas of employment law, landlord/tenant law, securities law, consumer protection, and so on. As described throughout this book, many of the agreements we make in the sharing economy put us in legal gray areas. Some of these agreements will eventually be examined by the courts; until then, in some cases, we will only be able to make educated guesses about their enforceability.

---

2. In addition, certain contracts must be in writing in order to be enforced, such as contracts for the transfer of land, or contracts that cannot be carried out within one year. See the statute of frauds, which exists both in common law and statute.

The Unique Qualities of Agreements in the Sharing Economy

There are a few qualities that characterize agreements of the sharing economy. They are usually:

1. **Agreements that all parties have a hand in creating:** Many of the agreements we make in modern society have become quite standardized, and the majority of terms are not intended to be negotiable. Generally, one party (a store, service provider, employer, or landlord) offers a set of relatively fixed terms to the public, and we (as consumers, employees, or tenants) accept those terms. When we join a gym or rent a car, we generally accept the standard terms offered to all other customers. In contrast, the sharing economy is built on agreements we make with each other, uniquely tailored to our individual needs. In the case of four neighbors that invest in exercise equipment together or a neighbor that arranges to regularly lend her car to another neighbor, there are innumerable ways to work out the logistics and finances of such an arrangement, and all parties will need to give input to shape the agreement.
2. **Agreements that govern *ongoing* relationships:** Many of the agreements we make in the sharing economy are likely to establish ongoing relationships, rather than simply facilitate one-time transactions. For example, agreements to co-own a house, share use of a car, exchange child care, or cooperatively purchase food will require something more akin to an operating agreement, meant to govern various aspects of a long-term relationship and multiple transactions over time. Agreements are like roadmaps to relationships, and they are living documents that may be referenced throughout the relationship and adapted as relationships adapt.
3. **Agreements that are highly collaborative:** Many agreements of the sharing economy will be highly collaborative, meaning that the parties may *share* decisions, *share* responsibilities and costs, *share* the benefits and rights, and so on. In modern society, we have become accustomed to asymmetrical agreements, where parties divide rights and responsibilities between landlord and tenant, between service provider and customer, between employer and employee, and so on. Collaborative agreements call

for increased diligence in describing the more overlapping and intertwining roles and responsibilities of parties.

4. **Agreements governed by both social expectation and legal contract:** Many of the agreements people make in the sharing economy will derive from pre-existing personal and community connections. People will increasingly enter into agreements with housemates, neighbors, friends, and co-workers, and the success of the agreements will depend as much on the health of the relationships as on the thoroughness of legal documents. Trust and caring are powerful forces that bring parties together in the first place, and trust and caring will, therefore, be powerful forces in carrying out agreements. As a result, the parties will often wish for their agreements to be governed and enforced by a combination of social expectation and legal contract. Rather than reduce every contingency and condition to written contract, parties may wish for certain conditions or changed circumstances to be managed cooperatively when they arise. Legalese-filled contracts with adversarial language will not be appropriate to the relationships our clients envision. The tone and approach we take in writing agreements will seek to nourish clients' cooperative attitudes and human relationships.

Key Agreements for the Sharing Economy

Many of the agreements we use in the sharing economy will be created without the help of lawyers. However, lawyers will often be called on to draft agreements, especially when agreements implicate a set of regulations, when parties want to be sure their agreements will be legally enforceable contracts, and/or when something of great value is at stake. The following are examples of common agreements that sharing economy lawyers draft for clients:

- **Co-ownership agreements**
  - Tenancy-in-common (TIC) agreements for co-ownership of a house or multiplex
  - Car, truck, and van co-ownership agreements
  - Shared studio, workshop, and office agreements
  - Agreements for co-ownership of other items, such as work or recreational equipment and electronics

- **Leases**
  - Leases for urban farm space
  - Shared workspace agreements
  - Leases for shared housing
- **Licenses**
  - Licenses to share a yard for food-growing or recreation
  - Licenses for the use of coworking spaces
  - Licenses for short-term home stays (also known as peer-to-peer hotels)[3]
  - Licenses for the use of intellectual property
- **Borrow-lend agreements**
  - Agreements to regularly borrow a car or other equipment
- **Agreements for cooperative activity or mutual aid**
  - Childcare exchange agreements
  - Rideshare agreements
- **Operating agreements and bylaws for organizations**
  - Operating agreements for cohousing communities
  - Bylaws for cooperatives
- **Membership and use agreements**
  - Member agreements for cooperatives
  - Agreements that describe rights and responsibilities of members of community-supported agriculture (CSA) programs
  - Terms of use (TOU) and terms of service (TOS) for services that broker sharing relationships
- **Investment contracts and promissory notes**
  - Promissory notes for peer-to-peer loans to enterprises and homebuyers
  - Shareholder agreements and term sheets for local investing initiatives
- **Other**
  - Liability waivers for shared spaces or shared equipment
  - Agreements for barter transactions

---

3. Such as arrangements facilitated by CouchSurfing, http://www.couchsurfing.org, and AirBnB, http://www.airbnb.com.

Part 2: Key Considerations in the Creation of Agreements

Drafting agreements is some of the most interesting work I do, since, in many respects, I become involved in the creation and shaping of relationships. When I sit down to draft a co-ownership agreement or operating agreement for a client, I find that I do my best work if, rather than searching for a boilerplate form, I start by imagining that I'm telling a story. It's the story of how the parties' relationship will play out, what role each plays in the story, what happens when the plot thickens, twists, or turns, and so on. When clients read an agreement I've written, my hope is that they will nod (not nod off) as they witness the plan in their heads take shape on paper.

But the agreements I write are, by no means, page turners. Beyond telling a story, there are many other considerations to balance into the work. By the time I have factored in the need to be thorough, avoid ambiguity, adhere to legal requirements, and meet the standards of anyone (like a lender) that may need to approve an agreement, my agreements are often long and contain paragraphs that should only be read with a cup of coffee.

I recognize that I could make a lifelong study of the art and science of crafting and drafting agreements. This chapter is not an introductory guide to drafting agreements, since there are other wonderful sources for such training. I want to acknowledge that I have been inspired and helped by three lawyers/authors in particular—Stewart Levine,[4] Linda Alvarez,[5] and Tina Stark[6]—and I will mention their work and ideas at various points in this chapter. Nolo, the publisher of hundreds of do-it-yourself legal guides, including my first book, *The Sharing Solution*, has also helped me to see that contract language can be simple, elegant, and straightforward. The rest of this chapter examines some of the unique considerations to balance into drafting agreements for sharing economy clients.

---

4. Stewart Levine, Getting to Resolution (Berrett-Koehler, 2d ed. 2009).

5. See Linda Alvarez's work at Discovering Agreement, http://www.DiscoveringAgreement.com.

6. Tina Stark, Drafting Contracts: How and Why Lawyers Do What They Do (Aspen 2007).

The Many Functions of Written Agreements

Written agreements serve many purposes for clients. Beyond giving them an enforceable tool to take to court, written agreements have the following additional functions:

1. **To set a tone for a relationship:** Many agreements I write contain a few terms that will be difficult to enforce, but that I include to set a good tone for the relationship. Such terms, I hope, may prompt parties to act in good faith, even when they don't actually have to compromise with the each other. For example, in an agreement to co-own a duplex, I may state that each owner can take in housemates without the permission of the other owner, but then I will add:

    > If the other Owner feels resistant to or has worries about a proposed housemate, both Owners agree to sit down and discuss any worries, with the goal of making the arrangement workable and comfortable for everyone.

    Some clients have told me that they *love* that provision because it depicts the way they prefer to handle all issues. I've pointed out that it's vague and unenforceable, but this does not seem to matter. They usually just look at each other, eyes twinkling, as if to say "yes, we are going to be the best neighbors ever." Though it's hard to measure, I do believe that these attitudes go a long way in preventing conflict. And the fact is, there will always be occurrences not covered by the co-ownership agreement, at which point, parties *have to* sit down and discuss it. In small groups, most decisions will even need to be made unanimously, which means that an attitude of cooperation is a key thing to preserve.
2. **To provide fallback rules for relationships otherwise managed casually:** As described in Part 1, many clients envision that trust and good communication will be the driving forces behind their agreements. They may cringe when I suggest that they fill their agreements with rules and provisions they'd much rather, and likely will, sort out on their own. I will usually point out that the primary function of detailed rules serves to protect parties in the event that they truly cannot agree, or in the event that they find themselves unexpectedly sharing with someone

not currently a party to the agreement, like an heir of one party or a bankruptcy trustee. Using the "unless we agree otherwise" phrase brings great comfort as a reminder to clients that they do, in fact, have a great deal of flexibility, so long as they are all in agreement. Thus, I may include many sentences such as: "Unless owners unanimously agree otherwise and document such agreement in writing, the owners shall not allow recreational vehicles to be stored on the property."

3. **To communicate and keep track of information:** Agreements are also an excellent place to store information that parties might like to have on hand. For example, in co-ownership agreements, I may recite background information or even document payments that parties have made in the past (such as their contribution toward purchase price), even if the actual numbers are irrelevant to the contract. Parties may just like to have that information written down so they don't forget it. Such background information can also be incredibly helpful to people who become parties to the contract later on, and that need to be brought up to speed on the history of the agreement.

   It's important to note that sometimes the inclusion of such information in a contract has actual legal significance. According to Tina Stark, "a representation is a statement of a past or present fact, made as of a moment in time to induce a party to act."[7] Thus, if such parties are actually relying on such background information as necessary to their decision to enter into the agreement, such information could be distinguished by setting it apart with a phrase such as "Party A represents that ...."

   Another type of information that I like to "store" in written agreements is a list of alternative courses of action clients may choose if they do not wish to adhere to their default rule. For example, I might say, "If an Owner makes improvements to the common area, the Owners may choose to compensate the improving Owner in a variety of ways, including, but not limited to,..." after which I will give a few suggestions. However, I will likely indicate that, in absence of an agreement otherwise, there will be a default course of action. Thus, the inclusion of the list of

7. *Id.* at 9.

alternatives has no legal weight, but is meant to give clients ideas for alternatives. I look at this as an opportunity to include some handy "tips" within the agreement.

4. **To support development of a well-thought-out and well-communicated plan:** Imagined expectations have ways of obscuring gaps in the communication of a plan. Co-owners of a house may agree on a basic plan, such as: "We agree to build a deck." One owner may think this means "we shall build a gigantic deck sometime in the next few years," while the other owner thinks "just a small deck, and we should get started next week!" Such differences in expectations are, in my experience, one of the greatest sources of conflict. When people act on such unspoken expectations, other parties might interpret the behavior to be inconsiderate, impulsive, or inexplicable, after which anxieties, tensions, and judgment begin to weave the foundation of a stressful dispute. Putting an agreement into writing helps to bring expectations to the surface, as the writing process prompts parties to describe a plan step by step.
5. **To avoid application of legal default rules:** In absence of a contract, written or oral, our legal system imposes certain default rules on relationships we form. If two people are on the deed to a property, in absence of a co-ownership agreement, courts will assume that each party owns 50 percent and that each has the right to occupy the entire property. If three people form a business partnership, in absence of a detailed partnership agreement, courts will impose certain presumptions on how partners make decisions, share profits and losses, and so on. Written agreements, thus, help parties to overcome the application of such default rules and to set their own rules for the relationship.
6. **To demonstrate a group's legitimacy:** Written agreements sometimes serve to demonstrate a group's legitimacy and/or financial status to third parties. For example, a business may need to show its limited liability company (LLC) Operating Agreement to a bank prior to getting a loan. A bank offering fractional real estate loans for a co-owned multiplex building will likely want to see a TIC Agreement to ensure that the separate interests are fully described and protected. In such cases, it's important to write an agreement with those third parties in mind.

7. **To create a replicable model:** Many clients consider the bigger picture when they form cooperatives, co-ownership agreements, or other sharing arrangements; they often do so with the hope that their model will be replicated by others, thereby broadening the impact. A group's documents can therefore be a powerful tool for replication. Truthfully, while there are already many wonderful cohousing communities, local currencies, cooperatives, and other creative-sharing economy models throughout the country, I cringe when I read their legal documents, which are either pure legalese or the complete opposite. Throughout the country, there are groups that are poised to replicate such models, but the lack of clear documents makes this hard. Thus, many sharing economy lawyers that draft agreements will not only be creating a roadmap for their clients' relationships, but also creating a formula for replication.

Agreements That Foster Resilient Relationships

Conflict, Death, and Taxes

Conflict is as sure a thing as death and taxes. We've been taught to plan for death (estate planning) and to plan for taxes (tax planning and accounting), but we don't invest nearly enough time in planning for conflict. In fact, our conflict plans, if we have them at all, usually sit in a short dispute resolution paragraph at the end of a contract. But let's be honest: our *real* conflict plans, the ones we picture in our reptilian minds, probably involve either hiding under a rock or hissing and using our fangs. Conflict is scary, and it's even scarier when it involves (1) people we care about, (2) our livelihoods, and (3) our sustenance. Coincidentally, those are three things the sharing economy is *designed* to bring us, which means conflicts are inevitable.

The sharing economy is, for another reason, uniquely situated in a territory of high conflict. Conflict develops when reality doesn't measure up to expectation, and the sharing economy is founded on high expectations for ourselves and others. We expect our relationships to be rewarding, caring, accountable, reliable, and of high integrity. Contrast this to the low expectations we've become accustomed to in modern society. We may *expect* that we won't like our job and *expect* that we will be relatively powerless with regard to our employer. We *expect* impersonal service from our internet service providers, airlines, and megastores. We may despise such interactions and feel powerless, but none of this really surprises us. However, when we find ourselves feeling disrespected in the context of a worker cooperative or grocery cooperative, this will catch us off guard and hurt. When people come together to share and cooperate, even with the best of intentions and even with a thorough set of contracts, all hell does sometimes break loose.

Leaving Windows to Negotiation

Fostering "resilient" relationships sounds like a more realistic goal than fostering "harmonious" relationships, though we might as well strive for both. There are still two parts to this: conflict prevention and planning for conflict. Agreements, through their sheer clarity, thoroughness, and collaborative tone, can go a long way in preventing conflict. At the same time, not everything can and should be set in contractual stone. Sometimes, rather than making an agreement on how to handle an issue, our clients may simply want to make an "agreement to agree"—to say that if an issue arises, they will sit down and come up with a reasonable solution. Such a provision carries only a small amount of legal weight; it usually requires that clients negotiate in good faith,[8] but it doesn't actually mandate that they reach a resolution. Nevertheless, there are times when parties *choose* to leave an open window to future negotiation, and there are other times when renegotiation becomes necessary due to unforeseen circumstances. In such situations, what matters is the process clients agree to use in renegotiation and what purposes and values guide them.

To that end, attorney Linda Alvarez encourages contracting parties to make thoughtful use of mission, vision, values, intent, purpose, principles, and similar types of statements to clearly communicate the reasons that they have decided to work together and what matters to each party in their dealings. When such information is thoroughly communicated in combination with the adoption of a clear process for addressing conflict (a thorough mediation clause and/or consensus process), this gives parties a forum and a compass for finding resolution. Alvarez writes:

8. See below for a discussion of the "implied covenant of good faith and fair dealing" in contracts.

> The truth is that it is impossible to foresee every potential eventuality. Rather than subjecting our formative conversation to imagined stories of disaster or breach of trust, [we could] set out a structure together for how we will address unexpected change and times of disagreement.[9]

With such a structure in place, parties who are forced to adapt their agreements under changed circumstances will be reminded and guided by their original intent. Including statements of values and intent will also help parties to more clearly determine what "good faith" means in the context of their particular agreement. The implied covenant of good faith and fair dealing generally applies to the negotiation and interpretation of contracts, and the meaning of "good faith" is context-specific. One case[10] that summarized the implied covenant included the following description:

> The Uniform Commercial Code and the Restatement (Second) of Contracts state that every contract imposes an obligation of good faith in performance and enforcement. The term "good faith" is generally defined as "honesty in fact in the conduct or transaction concerned." This definition refers to "subjective" rather than "objective" good faith. According to the Restatement, good faith performance of a contract includes faithfulness to an *agreed common purpose and consistency with the justified expectations of the other party.*[11] (emphasis added)

Thus, if a contract includes a description of purpose, values, and expectations, it will be easier to determine what good faith looks like when it comes time to navigate a conflict. Furthermore, as Linda Alvarez puts it:

> Declaring purpose and values in the document also serves the parties by helping them move out of the "me-against-you" mindset that most of us fall into when we disagree or encounter a crisis. The declarations remind of *our* purpose and *our* values so that we can look at *our* situation and, together, come up with *our* plan to get things back on track.

---

9. Linda Alvarez, Discovering Agreement, http://www.DiscoveringAgreement.com.
10. White Stone Partners v. Piper Jaffray Cos., 978 F. Supp. 878, 880–881 (D. Minn. 1997).
11. *Id.* (citing U.C.C. § 1-203; RESTATEMENT (SECOND) OF CONTRACTS § 205; MINN. STAT. § 336.1-201(19) with comment; and U.C.C. § 1-201(19)).

> In my opinion, this re-orientation from "toe-to-toe" competition to "side-by-side" problem-solving is one of the most valuable things that a contract can offer.[12]

Deal Points

Even with clearly communicated intent and values, we will still spend a good amount of time ironing out the deal points and planning for eventualities. The tone and posture we take in this negotiation process matters tremendously. Attorney/mediator Stewart Levine differentiates between seeking "agreements for results" and "agreements for protection." He encourages parties to focus less on the "what ifs" and more on creating a strong vision for a successful relationship. Stewart writes:

> I was taught that a good lawyer is paid to become paranoid and worry about all the things that might go wrong. That was the mindset I was taught to step into when "protecting" clients. At some point I realized that it was just as important to focus on helping clients achieve results, and that if I was an overzealous protector, I was not serving my client.[13]

The phrase "zealous representation" has found its way into some state's rules of professional conduct for lawyers, and it also inhabits the Preamble of the ABA Model Rules as an ideal to which lawyers should strive in their advocacy. In the litigation context, zeal can sometimes be effective; but in transactional work, especially with highly collaborative clients, zeal might even get on everyone's nerves. Often, facilitating the growth of an open and trusting relationship among parties will be far more important than lobbying for favorable contract terms for a single party. The lawyers involved in the negotiation of such agreements will draw heavily on their skills as communicators, mediators, and facilitators. The important thing is that we give our clients the information they need to choose their own approach to the deal points—let them decide whether to play

---

12. This quote came directly from Linda Alvarez when she read and commented on this book chapter.

13. LEVINE, *supra* note 4, at 45.

hard ball and go for the best protection or implement a plan to preserve the spirit of cooperation.

Deciding on the Level of Detail

The level of detail we include in the agreement is another important consideration. Most of the time, when lawyers are called upon to draft an agreement, it is because the subject of the agreement is quite valuable—a van, a home, a business, or a 300-acre property. Each party wants to feel secure that they will get what they are envisioning and not set themselves up for a loss. Our clients want an unambiguous contract that will talk through the various twists and turns a relationship can take. A contract may contain step-by-step instructions on how parties will give notice that they want to withdraw, how other parties can exercise a right to buy them out, and so on. One might think that it's important to err on the side of detail, detail, detail.

The average TIC Agreement I write is 20 pages long, but I could easily turn one into 40 pages if I included all of the details I could think to add. Some of the those details are procedures, such as how *exactly* clients will keep records, how *exactly* they will go about searching for and deciding on insurance, and so on. The problems are: (1) clients may really prefer to sort out those details on their own; (2) if I include that level of detail, clients may disregard it; and (3) the longer the agreement gets, the less likely my clients are to actually read it all the way through. Most of the time, when I send a client a TIC Agreement, they take *weeks* to respond to me with feedback. One client has even, *five months* later, told me she is still reading and commenting on a 30-page TIC Agreement. Thus, it's worth weighing the pros and cons of including so much detail.

When I choose to spare my clients of certain details, it's because I think there is low risk that they will experience difficulty in filling in the gaps. For example, the agreement could require that they obtain liability insurance, and the agreement could even specify a minimum limit of liability; however, I will usually leave it to clients to choose an insurer and sort out the terms and coverage of the insurance policy. Clients do have an implied covenant to fill in the gaps and carry out the terms in good faith and fair dealing. If they do not fill in the gaps in a reasonable way, a court would ultimately do so for them.

Language [and Pictures]

Word Choice and Framing

The spirit of an agreement can be greatly influenced by word choice and voice. For example, I often prefer to use the word "agreement" over "contract" because contract sounds, to many people, like something with small print that they really hope they won't have to read. The framing of provisions can also make a huge difference. Compare, for example, this contract provision:

> If a member violates the requirement to pay monthly dues, the cooperative shall levy a fine of 1% per day on the amount of any unpaid dues, until the member pays all dues and fines in full. All membership privileges of the member shall be suspended if a member does not pay all dues and fines within 30 days of first failing to make a payment.

with this one:

> In the event that a member is unable to pay monthly dues on time, the member agrees to pay a late fee along with his/her dues payment. For each day that the member's fee is past due, the member agrees to pay an additional 1% of the dues amount. If a member is unable to make a dues and late fee payments within 30 days of first missing a payment, the member understands and agrees that his/her membership privileges shall be suspended by the cooperative.

The two contract provisions have the same legal outcome, but the tone of each is quite distinct. The second provision frames the member as an active collaborator in the payment of dues and fines, whereas the first provision frames the member as the passive recipient of a penalty. Also, the use of the word "violates" in the first provision has a tone of blaming or an implication of bad faith, whereas the second provision gives the benefit of the doubt by simply acknowledging that a member is unable to pay. One thing to acknowledge about these two provisions is that the second one is about 35 percent longer than the first. I think it is often the case that using friendlier language can result in longer contracts, and this is therefore another consideration to factor into the drafting process.

Will, Shall, or Agrees To?

One thing to weigh is when to use the words "will," "shall," and "agrees to." Tina Stark dedicates an entire chapter of her book *Drafting Contracts* to the question of when to use "will" versus "shall."[14] For the purpose of ensuring that a contract is clearly interpreted, the distinction could be important. Stark points out that it's always better to use the word "shall," rather than "will," to describe something that a party is agreeing to do (a covenant). The word "will," she says, should be used to describe a fact or speculation about something that may happen in the future. I often adhere to this rule, but I have noted that many sample contracts provided in Nolo books use the word "will" where Stark would say we should use "shall." I think that the reason for this is that "shall" sounds rather formal and somewhat intimidating. Using "will" may create a small risk of ambiguity, but a court would most likely know what the parties intended. My solution has often been to use the phrase "agrees to" in place of "shall," since I believe it sounds friendlier.

Party People

The way we refer to parties can also change the tone of the agreement (sort of like how the above subhead makes this paragraph sound festive). Using the parties' actual names sounds more personal than "Party A" and "Party B." Using the first names rather than last names can make it sound even friendlier. In the case of contracts that could be assigned to people who are not the original parties, I do usually opt to use "Party A" and "Party B." Thus, if one owner of a co-owned house transfers her share of the house to her daughter, the daughter simply assumes all rights of "Party A," and the co-owners do not need to create a new agreement to substitute in her name throughout. However, many agreements are very personal to parties, and first names, or even "I" and "you" will work just fine. Tina Stark acknowledged that "although the business world is more informal than it used to be (think business casual dress), it is hard to imagine a multimillion dollar contract between Dell and Intel in which Dell is referred to as *we* and Intel as *you*." Fortunately, most contracts of the sharing economy involve small groups of real people. If I make an agreement with a neighbor to let her borrow my car regularly,

14. Stark, *supra* note 6, at ch. 13.

I would probably draft an agreement where I refer to myself as "I" and refer to my neighbor as "you."

Heretofore, Theretofore, Blah, Blah, Blah

Finally, it goes without saying, that if agreements are truly to be roadmaps for relationships, we should use language that clients can actually understand. Needless to say, the contracts for the sharing economy will not be full of "heretofores" and "therefores." Use plain English. Or as performance artist Laurie Anderson advises: "Talk normal." Enough said.

Navigability

Navigability of a document is also critical, and tables of contents, clear organization, and descriptive subheads can go a long way. Many contracts include subheads that will be immediately uninteresting or even intimidating to clients. Take for example, a contract with a section entitled "Default; Breach; Remedies." Why not change this subhead to "What Happens If Parties Cannot Adhere to This Agreement?" I have given myself space to write highly descriptive and non-intimidating subheads and will usually include a provision in the contract that clarifies that the subheads are not meant to be a legally binding part of the agreement. For example, I might include the following:

> **Headings and Subheadings in This Agreement:** This Agreement contains many headings and subheadings (in bold), which are there to make the Agreement easier to read and navigate. The headings and subheadings are not intended to have any legal effect or limit the scope or meaning of the provisions contained in this Agreement.

Graphics and Annotations

In crafting documents that clients understand, we also have the option of taking it one or two steps further, by annotating or even illustrating contracts. I have been greatly inspired by the work of lawyer and visual artist Susanne Hoogwater,[15] who is pioneering models of expressing legal information in graphic form. She has created graphical maps to

15. See Susanne Hoogwater's work at Legal Visuals, http://www.legalvisuals.nl; Good Mood Law, http://goodmoodlaw.com; and Legal Sketchpad, http://www.legalsketchpad.com.

help clients navigate contracts,[16] images to help people more intuitively grasp the meaning of policies,[17] and graphics/animations that lend persuasion to legal arguments.[18]

Annotating a contract is another option. This could come in the form of explanations in sidebar comments, footnotes, or in bold brackets within the text. It would be important to clarify that the notes are not meant to be part of the contract nor meant to change the meaning of the terms. The notes would simply be used to give clients explanations and examples of how the terms may apply to the clients' particular situation.

Assisting Clients in Agreement Formation

Clients Who Draft Their Own Agreements

Because they tend to be independent and creative people, many of my clients will ask me if they could draft their own agreements and have me review them. In theory, I love the idea of clients empowering themselves and sorting out the details of their own relationship. However, in practice, when I receive an agreement that my clients draft from scratch, I'm faced with a quandary: Do I add in the same level of detail I would have included if I had drafted the agreement myself? Or do my clients merely want me to sign off and say that it's "good enough" and doesn't have any "serious problems"? And what is a "serious problem," when any ambiguous provision could conceivably develop into a serious problem? Truthfully, when my clients have drafted their own agreements for shared real estate ownership, I have had to add so much to the agreement that it truly would have been faster for me to draft the agreement myself.

One solution I have adopted, in the case of certain agreements, is to send clients a template that I feel comfortable with. For example, I may send them a set of nonprofit bylaws, cooperative bylaws, or a TIC Agreement, and offer a few hints about how they may need to adapt it to their purposes. When I give clients a template I like, things tend to go very well, and I don't find myself rewriting everything. I also usually encourage clients to have at least one consultation with me before

16. *See* Susanne Hoogwater, *Visual Wayfinding in Contracts*, Good Mood Law, Nov. 20, 2009, http://goodmoodlaw.com/2009/11/visual-wayfinding-in-contracts/.

17. *See* Susanne Hoogwater, *A Touchy Privacy Policy*, Good Mood Law (Feb. 9, 2011), http://goodmoodlaw.com/2011/02/a-touchy-privacy-policy/.

18. See examples of the litigation graphics by Susanne Hoogwater at Legal Visuals, http://www.legalvisuals.nl/index-en.html. Note that many of the examples are in Dutch.

they start drafting, to ensure that their plan will not be completely undermined by a regulation they are unaware of and to guide them on best practices.

Before Drafting

If I am to draft an agreement, I have a couple different ways of gathering information from clients. Often I will set up a consultation with them, and, in advance of the consultation, will send them a list of questions to discuss with each other prior to the meeting. At the meeting, I learn about everyone's needs, concerns, and goals. In the case of a multiple representation, I explain the benefits and risks for each person, explain the legal framework and requirements, and then guide clients in developing a plan that works for everyone. Often I will send them an email summarizing the conclusions we came to, to verify that the terms are correct before I begin drafting the full agreement. This is similar to the way a letter of intent (LOI) is used prior to entering into a commercial lease agreement.

Using Multiple Tiers of Agreements

In some sharing arrangements or organizations, it is common for parties to need multiple documents to manage their relationships and activities. Often, there is a document that governs major rights and responsibilities, financial provisions, and decision-making. For a cooperative, this is usually contained in the bylaws; for shared ownership of housing, this is usually contained in the TIC Agreement or LLC Operating Agreement. However, such documents are designed to remain in place and be altered infrequently. The members or co-owners may wish to adopt a second, third, or even fourth document to govern day-to-day matters or specific policies and procedures. For example, in shared housing, there may also be a document called "Rules," the "Community Agreement," or "Household Agreement" to govern day-to-day matters such as yard care responsibilities; such documents can be amended as often as necessary. In addition, there may be a "Consensus Policy and Process" that groups use to make decisions, outlining details of meeting procedures. There may also be a set of "Architectural Standards" or "Maintenance Standards," to govern the manner, standard, and style in which repairs, maintenance, and improvements are done on the property.

PART 3: KEY PROVISIONS OF AGREEMENTS

Different contract specialists have their own ways of breaking down the key parts of an agreement. I find such formulas very helpful, both in reminding me what needs to go into a contract, and in organizing and expressing the information.

For example, lawyer/mediator Stewart Levine manages to fit all kinds of agreements into a ten-part framework,[19] consisting of the following pieces:

1. Intent and vision
2. Roles
3. Promises
4. Time and value
5. Measurements of satisfaction
6. Concerns, risks, and fears
7. Renegotiation/dissolution
8. Consequences
9. Conflict resolution
10. Agreement?

I can imagine Stewart Levine's book, *The Book of Agreement*, could be incredibly useful to groups—such as cooperatives or cohousing communities—in which members make agreements for many purposes on a regular basis. Using a standardized framework for every agreement will likely empower members to become ever more skillful and confident in making agreements.

Tina Stark offers a different set of contract "building blocks," which are less welcoming to lay people, but which help a legal mind to analyze the purpose and place of various contract provisions. Stark's seven building blocks are (1) Representations, (2) Warranties, (3) Covenants, (4) Rights, (5) Conditions, (6) Discretionary authority, and (7) Declarations.[20]

In another list, Tina Stark helpfully names seven things that establish the terms of the parties' relationship, which could conceivably act as a checklist for someone drafting an agreement:

---

19. LEVINE, *supra* note 4, at 28–30.
20. STARK, *supra* note 6, at 9.

1. The statement of facts that each party made that induced the other to enter the transaction;
2. Each party's promises as to its future performance;
3. Each party's rights;
4. The events that must occur before each party is obligated to perform;
5. Each party's discretionary authority;
6. How the contract will end, including the events that constitute breach and the remedies for breach; and
7. The general policies that govern the parties' relationship.[21]

Two Frameworks for Sharing Agreements

I have adopted my own checklists, and these are tools that I share with clients as well. By the time they have answered the questions and discussed them with me, we generally have the foundation for the drafting of a sharing agreement. One of my frameworks is the set of 20 Questions that I can generally apply with any clients involved in sharing or collaboration. The other frameworks are checklists and questionnaires that apply to particular types of sharing arrangements and organizations, such as my Co-Ownership Questionnaire, provided below, which contains 58 questions specific to people who co-own real estate.

20 Questions for Sharing and Collaboration Arrangements[22]

1. **Why are we sharing?**
   - What are our personal, practical, financial, or environmental goals?
   - What do we each need or want to get out of the sharing arrangement?
2. **What are we sharing?**
   - And for that matter, what are we not sharing?

21. *Id.* at 3.

22. This list is adapted from Janelle Orsi & Emily Doskow, The Sharing Solution: How to Save Money, Simplify Your Life & Build Community (Nolo 2009).

3. **Whom are we sharing with?**
   - Do our co-sharers need to meet any particular qualifications?
4. **How many people are we sharing with?**
   - What are the pros and cons of having a large or small sharing group?
5. **How will the timing of our arrangement work?**
   - When will it stop and start?
   - Will it happen in phases?
6. **Who owns the shared item(s)?**
   - Will one person own it and let others use it?
   - Will we each own specific items or parts of the property?
   - Will we each own a percentage share of the whole property? If so, in what proportions?
7. **Should we form a separate legal entity, such as a nonprofit organization?**
8. **Should our group have a name, and what should we call ourselves?**
9. **What do we get to do?**
   - What benefits or services to we get from this sharing arrangement?
   - How much can we use the shared item(s) or services?
10. **How will we make decisions?**
    - Will we all take part in decision-making or delegate decisions to a small group?
    - Do we all have equal decision-making power?
    - Must all decisions be unanimous, made by majority vote, or by some other method?
11. **What responsibilities will each of us have?**
    - Will we assign roles and tasks?
    - Will we rotate responsibilities?
    - Will anyone receive extra benefits in return for extra responsibilities?
12. **What are the rules for using our shared property or meeting our shared responsibilities?**
13. **How will we handle administrative matters like scheduling, communication, and record keeping?**
14. **How will we divide expenses?**

- Will there be initial buy-in or start-up contributions? Will we need any loans?
- How will we divide overhead and variable costs?
- How will we collect money? Through regular dues or by reckoning expenses in some other way? Will we start a bank account?
- What kinds of unexpected costs could arise and how will we prepare for them?
- Who will keep track of our money?
- What happens if a member cannot pay?

15. **How will we manage risk and liability?**
    - What risks are involved in our sharing arrangement and how can we reduce them?
    - How is the risk distributed (i.e., who could suffer loss or be liable for damages)?
    - Do we want to redistribute risk by making agreements with each other or purchasing insurance?
16. **Are there legal requirements we need to follow?**
    - Are there any required licenses or permits?
    - Will this bring up any tax or employment law questions?
    - Are there any legal roadblocks arising from zoning laws or private land covenants?
    - What steps must we take to become a legal entity?
17. **How will we resolve conflicts or disputes?**
18. **How will we bring new people into the group?**
    - What procedures will new members follow?
    - How will new members be oriented?
    - What is our policy on guests?
19. **How can a member leave the group?**
    - What steps must be taken when a member leaves voluntarily?
    - What does a member get when they leave?
    - Can a member transfer their rights to third parties?
    - Under what circumstances can a member be asked to leave the group?
20. **How do we end the sharing arrangement?**
    - How will any shared assets be distributed?

Co-Ownership Questionnaire[23]

Use of this Questionnaire: This Questionnaire is a tool to help co-owners talk through the details of their shared property ownership. The answers to these questions could help lay the groundwork for a more detailed Co-ownership Agreement. Note that this Questionnaire assumes that the property in question contains multiple units, but many of the questions would also pertain to the co-ownership of a single unit property. Please do not rely on this as a thorough list of questions you should ask in connection with co-ownership, since there may be many other details to resolve or legal matters to sort through. It's a very good idea for co-owners to seek the advice of an attorney regarding the details of their co-ownership agreement.

Buying the Property

1. **Contribution to purchase price and costs:** Will each owner's contribution to the purchase price be based on financial ability, the value of the share of space they will receive, or other considerations? Are the units and/or private spaces substantially the same, or do they differ in value? If the units and private spaces differ in value, how will you determine the share of the total cost to be paid by the occupants of each unit? For example, would it make more sense to allocate the cost by square footage or to have each unit and its exclusive use common areas appraised? If the units are substantially similar, will you be able to come to an agreement after taking into consideration any unique attributes such as parking, decks, views, etc?
2. **Contribution toward down payment, monthly payments, and overall debt:** What will be the percent of the total paid by each co-owner for
    a. Down payment,
    b. Monthly payments, and
    c. Overall share of debt?
3. **Contribution of labor or property:** Will anyone be contributing goods or services in lieu of money payments for the purchase price or other costs? If so, what will those contributions be, and

23. The Co-Ownership Questionnaire was developed with an enormous amount of input and contribution from California cohousing attorney Cynthia Hawley.

how will you value them? What is the timeframe for completing this work? How will you manage the income tax consequences of "sweat equity"?

4. **Group ownership of units:** Will more than one person share the cost of one unit; that is, can a group of people buy into the property collectively as one co-owner to share one living space or unit?

Designation of Units, Exclusive Areas, and Common Areas

5. **Assignment of units and living areas:** Which unit or living area will each co-owner get to occupy?
6. **Common areas:** What common areas of the property will be shared by all owners?
7. **Exclusive use common areas:** What common areas of the property (outside of the units or living areas) will be reserved for the exclusive use of each owner, such as parking spaces, garages, yard and garden spaces, storage spaces, and decks? These areas are often referred to as "exclusive use common areas."

Who Lives at the Property

8. **Number of residents:** Do you want to limit the number of people who may live in each unit or living area?
9. **Housemates:** If a co-owner wants to have a housemate or roommates, should the co-owner get approval from the other co-owners?
10. **Renting units:** If a co-owner moves out and wants to rent out his or her unit or living space, should they have to get the other co-owner's approval of the prospective tenant? Typically, it's reasonable for the co-owner of the other unit to have the right to review a prospective renter's financial status and references and reject a renter on reasonable grounds.
11. **Rules for tenants:** Do you want potential tenants to sign a written agreement that includes all of the rules and use restrictions in the co-owners agreement?
12. **Eviction of tenants:** Do you want to restrict how a co-owner may evict a tenant in order to protect other co-owners from legal retaliation?
13. **Pets:** Do you want a pet policy in your TIC Agreement? You might want to consider how many pets per unit or living area

might be allowed, what kinds of pets might be allowed and specifically excluded, where pets are to be kept, what kind of pet behavior is unacceptable, and whether a co-owner has to get approval of other co-owners to have a new pet.

What May or May Not Be Done to or on the Property

14. **Alterations to units:** What kinds of alterations may a co-owner make to her or his unit or living area and which, if any, alterations would require the other co-owner's approval?
15. **Home business use:** May the property be used for a home business? If so, what kind of business? You may want to distinguish between businesses that involve visiting clients or customers versus a home office or studio with no visitors.
16. **Use of chemicals:** Do you want to limit the kinds of paints, pesticides, herbicides, cleaning chemicals, and the like that may be used on the property?
17. **Hazardous activities:** Do you want to limit or prohibit any hazardous activities—particularly things that could affect your ability to get proper insurance for the property?
18. **Risks to third parties:** Do you want to limit or prohibit any activities that create a risk to third parties and subject co-owners to liability such as, for example, teaching gymnastics on the property or building a tree house?
19. **Storage:** Do you want to limit what may or may not be stored on the property such as, for example, accumulated trash or clutter, discarded furniture or other personal items, or seldom used or unused vehicles? Do you want to limit storage of anything to certain areas of the property?

Property Related Costs and Accounting

20. **Budgeting:** Will you hold an annual meeting to adopt an annual budget?
21. **Bank account:** Will you open a joint bank account to manage collection of money and payment of bills?
22. **Utilities:** Are any utilities separately metered? If so, which ones? How will owners be reimbursed for the use of their separate utilities, such as water or lighting, in common areas? If any utility is not separately metered, on what basis will you share the

cost? An equal share per unit or living space? The number of people living in each unit or living space as a percentage of total residents?

23. **Other costs:** What other regular costs do you expect and on what basis will you allocate each co-owner's share of them?
24. **Process for collecting and making payments:** How will you collect money to pay for all shared monthly costs? Will each co-owner pay a fixed monthly amount into a joint or association bank account? In this case, an annual reckoning of the account would reimburse or charge co-owners as needed. Or will you get together every month to divide up expenses?
25. **Bookkeeper/treasurer:** Will one person be asked to manage accounting? If so, how long will that person be expected to provide the service? If not, will you hire an accountant or bookkeeper to manage accounting?
26. **Large expenses:** Are there foreseeable large expenses in the next 5–10 years such as, for example, roof replacement, painting, plumbing or sewer repairs or replacements, foundation work, or renovation?
27. **Reserve account:** Will you build a reserve account for foreseeable repairs and unanticipated expenses? If so, how much? How will you build the fund? Will each owner contribute a set monthly amount to the account until the goal is reached? What rules would you like to make about when the reserve fund can be used and how it must be reimbursed?
28. **Repairs:** If a repair is needed, how much may a co-owner spend before he/she needs to get the other co-owners' approval? If there are unforeseen expensive repairs, how will you manage payment for those?
29. **Insurance:** What minimum level of property and liability insurance will you maintain?
30. **Indemnification:** Do you want to agree to compensate and defend each other in situations in which one co-owner may cause liability that would extend to other co-owners?
31. **Record-keeping:** What records will you keep about the property and where will they be kept? What method will you use to account for co-owner contributions, expenses, and payments made?

Taking Care of and Developing the Property

32. **Maintenance standards for structures:** Do you want to have standards for the upkeep and maintenance of all structures on the property? If so, what are those standards? These standards are important to make sure the property is saleable, easier to insure, and more likely to get favorable financing.
33. **Maintenance standards for yards:** Do you want to have standards for the upkeep and maintenance of the yard and other common areas? If so, what are those standards?
34. **Architectural style:** Are there particular design or architectural features you would like to preserve, styles you want to follow, or materials you want to use or not use on the property?
35. **Maintenance responsibilities:** What parts of the property will each owner be responsible for maintaining?
36. **Shared maintenance:** For what areas will you share maintenance responsibilities? Typically, where a tenancy in common is all in one building, the owners will be jointly responsible for maintaining the entire structure of the building. Where the units are in separate buildings, each owner may take full responsibility for maintenance of his or her whole building or may be responsible only for the interior of the building.
37. **Alterations:** Should you need to get each other's consent to alter the interior of units or living spaces if it does not affect the structure of the building?
38. **Maintenance costs:** Do you want to have a monthly contribution from each co-owner to pay for upkeep and maintenance of common areas that will be maintained by all owners? If so, how do you want to allocate the costs?
39. **Property tax increases:** If property taxes are increased due to improvements made by a co-owner to his or her unit or living space, will that person be responsible for paying the added amount?
40. **Partial destruction:** If the property is partially destroyed, under what circumstances do you want to rebuild—is there a maximum out-of-pocket amount above which you would not rebuild? If you take an insurance payout, how will you divide the proceeds?
41. **Maintenance manager:** Will one person be responsible for managing the maintenance and repair of the property? If so, will

he/she be asked to serve as manager for a certain amount of time? If no co-owner will manage the maintenance and repair, will you hire someone to do that job?

42. **Improvements:** If a co-owner makes a significant improvement on the property that raises the value of the common area (such as installing a hot tub), how will co-owners compensate the owner who made the improvement? Will the improvement be appraised at the time the property is sold? Or will the owner have a right to reimbursement of costs from the sale proceeds? How will depreciation be taken into account?

Refinancing the Property

43. **Refinancing:** Under what circumstances may the co-owners refinance the property?
44. **Refinance costs:** Who will pay the refinancing costs?
45. **Borrowing against the property:** Under what circumstance, if any, may a co-owner take an equity line of credit or a second mortgage?

If One Co-Owner Has Financial Troubles

46. **Financial troubles:** What should happen if one co-owner runs into financial troubles and cannot make required payments?
47. **Default fund:** Do you want to set up a default fund to pay the costs due by a co-owner who runs into financial trouble? This would serve to protect the assets, equity, and credit ratings of the other co-owners.
48. **Advancing payments:** In lieu of a default fund, do you want to agree ahead of time to the terms under which co-owners would advance payment on behalf of another co-owner?
49. **Remedies for default:** How far behind on payments must a co-owner get before the other owner can demand that the property be sold, or demand to buy out or find a third-party purchaser for the defaulting owner's share?

Selling the Whole Property All at Once

50. **Timeline for selling the property:** If one owner finds it necessary to sell out, and if that owner is unable to sell his/her share separately to a third party after a reasonable amount of

marketing, should that owner be able to demand that the entire property be sold? If so, how might that owner compensate the other owner for the inconvenience of an untimely sale? Do you want to agree now to set a goal of selling the whole property in the future? If so, do you want to target a time to sell? Will the decision to sell be based on, for example, a number of years, the occurrence of a certain event, or conditions of the housing market?

51. **Division of sale proceeds:** How will you divide the proceeds if all co-owners decide to sell at once? For example:
    a. Will you split it on the basis of how much you each paid toward the purchase minus each owner's share of the outstanding debt on the property and other money owed?
    b. Will you base the split on the relative value of each owner's interest in the property? To do this, you would appraise each owner's interest (meaning their unit combined with their exclusive use common areas, their share of the common areas, and other rights with regard to the property), add the appraisals of all owners' interests together, and then divide sale proceeds based on each owner's percentage of the total. This method allows a co-owner to benefit from the increased value of improvements to his or her unit and provides an incentive to make improvements.

Selling Individual Interests in the Property

52. **Terms for sale of one owner's share:** Under what terms may a co-owner sell his or her interest in the property? For example:
    a. Do you want to make a sale to a third party (not a co-owner) contingent upon approval of the sale by your existing mortgage lender? If the sale is not approved by the lender, you may run the risk of the mortgage lender declaring the entire outstanding balance of the existing mortgage immediately due and payable—with potentially serious consequences to other co-owners.
    b. If sale of one owner's share requires a refinance of the property, who will pay for the costs of the refinance—the selling owner, the buyer, and remaining owner, or some combination?

c. Do you want to agree that each co-owner will notify the other co-owners when he or she intends to sell and that the other co-owners will have the first option of buying that seller's interest?
d. Do you want to agree ahead of time how you will determine the selling price for sale of a share to other co-owners?
e. Do you want to make the sale contingent on the prospective buyer signing your TIC Agreement so the agreement will bind all future co-owners? (Most TIC Agreements require this.)

53. **Approval of prospective buyers:** Should the non-selling co-owners be able to approve or reject a prospective buyer? If so, should the approval or rejection be on the basis of the financial status of the prospective buyer? Should approval or rejection be on the basis of personal reasons? While it is not clear whether personal reasons could be a legally enforceable basis on which to reject a prospective buyer, it's a good idea to talk about and consider in advance on what basis you might not want to share ownership and residency of a house with someone.

Making Decisions About the Property

54. **Meetings:** How often will you have regular meetings? What procedures do you want to adopt for meeting agendas, notice and scheduling, and so on?
55. **Decision-making process:** Will you use majority voting, supermajority voting, or a consensus process to make decisions about the property? What process will you use to consider and decide on proposals?
56. **Share of votes:** If each unit or living space will get one vote, are there any topics on which one co-owner will have a greater decision-making power or power to veto?
57. **Delegating decisions:** What kinds of decisions may co-owners make on their own, and what kinds of decisions must be made by all co-owners?
58. **Conflict resolution:** Will you rely on mediation or another process to resolve disputes? How will you choose a mediator? Who pays? How many mediations sessions must you attend before you turn to arbitration or litigation?

PART 4: SAMPLE CO-OWNERSHIP AGREEMENT

As a sample agreement, I have included a basic TIC Agreement for co-ownership of a two-unit property. This is an example of an agreement that could flow from the use of the above questionnaire. Co-ownership agreements are very useful for sharing economy lawyers, yet they can be very hard to come by, in comparison to other types of agreements. TIC Agreements, for example, rarely show up in legal practice guides.

Co-Ownership Agreements and the Spectrum of Sharing

Co-ownership agreements have a spectrum of different personalities, depending on the degree of sharing involved. Some co-ownership agreements seek to simulate separate ownership, by giving each owner his/her own exclusive unit and independent set of responsibilities, and by requiring that each owner obtain separate financing.[24] For example, on a two-unit property where each unit is contained within its own building, such as a house with a back cottage, each owner is likely solely responsible for maintaining his/her own building; this division may create a real feeling of separate ownership. In contrast, a co-ownership agreement for a single family home, for example, likely entails shared use of most spaces, shared financing, shared responsibilities for most maintenance tasks, and so on.

This agreement sits somewhere in the middle of the spectrum of sharing. The agreement is for co-ownership of a duplex where the units are housed under the same roof. When two units share a single structure, co-owners must usually be jointly responsible for maintaining the exterior, plumbing, foundation, roof, and weight-bearing walls of the building. This particular agreement is also written for co-owners who share a single mortgage, as opposed to each obtaining separate fractional financing. At the same time, rights and responsibilities under this agreement are divided to simulate separate ownership in other respects. Each owner is allocated a single living unit, the interior of which each owner is responsible for maintaining. Each owner may sell his/her unit to third parties on the open market, though only after providing the other owner the opportunity to buy the unit. If the entire property is

24. Fractional financing for TICs, however, can be somewhat difficult to come by, and the majority of TIC owners must share responsibility for a single home loan.

sold, the owners agree to divide the proceeds based on the appraised relative value of each unit, rather than based on a predetermined percentage. This method of dividing sale proceeds allows owners to benefit financially from careful upkeep and any improvements they make on their own unit; thus, it simulates separate ownership in that respect.

Working with This Agreement

Note that, although it is long, this TIC Agreement, in many ways, is somewhat bare bones. A significant amount of detail could potentially be added to nearly every provision, to give clients more thorough procedures for how to handle various matters. The decision to add details is up to you and your clients, balancing in various considerations, including many I named in Part 2 of this chapter.

Co-Ownership Agreement for [ADDRESS][25]

Background of this agreement: PERSON1 and PERSON2 share ownership of and responsibility for the duplex at ADDRESS. PERSON1 and PERSON2 have decided to co-own the property because they enjoy and respect each other, and they trust one another to be reliable and accountable. PERSON1 and PERSON2 value clear and open communication and expect to navigate any changes or challenges with a commitment to respectful communication. To ensure that expectations are clearly communicated and carried out, PERSON1 and PERSON2 want to clarify their rights and responsibilities with regard to the shared property and their shared debt and also want to ensure that any future co-owners and tenants adhere to any terms and conditions agreed upon now. Therefore, PERSON1 and PERSON2 now reduce their agreement to writing, and agree as follows:

---

25. Although I wrote this agreement largely from scratch, some provisions have been adapted from or inspired by TIC Agreements written by attorneys Andy Sirkin (http://www.andysirkin.com), John C. Gutierrez (from John E. Gutierrez, *Drafting and Reviewing Residential Cotenancy Ownership Agreements*, 20 CEB RPLR 153 (July 1997)), and Frederick C. Hertz (from Frederick C. Hertz, *A Model Home Purchase Cotenancy Contract*, 13(1) Practical Real Estate Law., Jan. 1997). I also would like to thank California cohousing attorney Cynthia Hawley for her extensive help and input on this agreement.

1. Tenants-in-Common Agreement in Relation to the Property

This is a Tenants-in-Common (TIC) Agreement ("Agreement"), and it governs the rights and obligations of any person or entity that has an ownership interest, under the terms of this Agreement, in the real property located at ADDRESS (the "Property"). The Property consists of one duplex building containing two legal units. By owning the Property as Tenants in Common, each Owner (defined in Paragraph 2) owns an undivided fractional interest in the entire Property. This means that none of the Owners has an individually deeded right to exclusive occupancy of any portion of the Property. However, through this Agreement, Owners intend to divide their rights and responsibilities with regard to the Property. The Owners do not intend to create a common interest development, partnership, or joint venture.

2. Owners and Parties to This Agreement

PERSON1 and PERSON2 are each a "Party" to this Agreement and an "Owner" of the Property; collectively they will be referred to as the "Parties" and/or "Owners." Anyone who later assumes the rights and obligations under this Agreement shall become a Party. By entering into this Agreement, PERSON1 assumes all rights and obligations of Owner A and PERSON2 assumes all rights and obligations of Owner B. An "Owner" may refer to an individual, an entity, or a group of people, depending on who owns the Property. For example, if the Cotenancy Interest of Owner A is later owned by two people, those two people will be referred to, together, as "Owner A."

3. How Owners Allocate Rights and Responsibilities

At the time this Agreement was entered into, Owner A and Owner B each took responsibility for a 50 percent share of the Property. However, this 50/50 allocation does not necessarily govern the way that decisions are made, that the Property is used, how much each owner should pay toward the mortgage, or how proceeds will be divided on sale, partition, destruction, or condemnation. The allocations of those and other rights and responsibilities allocated as set forth in this Agreement.

4. Cotenancy Interests

The total of an Owner's ownership share and rights and responsibilities with regard to the Property, as defined by this Agreement, is referred to as her "Cotenancy Interest." Each Owner's Cotenancy Interest includes, but is not limited to, her Unit, Exclusive Use Common Areas, and share of the Common Areas.

5. Units, Common Areas, and Exclusive Use Common Areas

a. **Units:**

   i. The Property consists of a duplex with two Units. Each Unit consists of the interior surfaces of the joists, studs, and beams within the perimeter walls, floors, ceilings, windows, window frames, doors, door frames, and trim of such Unit and the air-space bounded by and contained within those interior surfaces. Each Unit includes, without limitation, any appliances, hot water heaters, space heaters, air conditioning units, furnace, cabinetry, and lighting fixtures inside each unit. A Unit does not include those areas and those things that comprise the Common Area.

   ii. Owner A will have the right to exclusive use and possession of the Downstairs Unit, totaling 720 square feet, consisting of all rooms on the first floor, including __________ [more detailed description of what rooms it includes], not including the basement. Owner B will have the right to exclusive use and possession of the Upstairs Unit, totaling 750 square feet, consisting of all rooms on the top floor, including __________ [more detailed description of what rooms it includes].

b. **Common Areas:** The spaces of which both Owners have possession and use are referred to as "Common Areas." Owners shall be jointly responsible for maintaining all Common Areas. Each Owner may use these Common Areas in accordance with the purposes for which they are intended without hindering the exercise of or encroaching upon the rights of any other Owners to use the spaces for those purposes. Common Areas include all yards, driveways, the basement, decks, patios, walkways, roof, laundry room, foundation, all other exterior portions of the Property, and the entire building structure, minus the Units, described above.

c. **Exclusive Use Common Areas:** Certain portions of the Common Area, referred to as Exclusive Use Common Area, are set aside and allocated for the exclusive use of the Owner of the Unit to which they are either physically attached or assigned to a Unit, as described below. The Exclusive Use Common Area consists of:

   i. **Fixtures.** Shutters, awnings, window boxes, exterior stairways, porches, landings, doorsteps, exterior doors, doorframes and hardware incident thereto, screens and windows, skylights and other fixtures, all of which are designed to serve a single Unit, but located outside the boundaries of such Unit.
   ii. **Pipes and wiring.** The plumbing, pipes, conduits, wires, cables and all other electrical equipment or apparatus that are designed to serve a single Unit but located outside the boundaries of such Unit.
   iii. **Yards.** As owner of the downstairs unit, Owner A shall have exclusive use of the two-foot strip of garden that borders the front of the Downstairs Unit and runs the length of Unit A.
   iv. **Decks.** Owner A shall have exclusive use of the deck off the back door of Unit A and Owner B shall have exclusive use of the deck off the back door of Unit B.
   v. **Parking spaces.** Each Owner shall have the exclusive right to use and enjoy that parking space designated for the benefit of her Unit, described on the attached map.

6. Use of Property

a. **Residential use of Property:** Owners agree that the primary use of the Property shall be residential. Owners may operate a home business, so long as it complies with zoning rules pertaining to home businesses, and so long as it does not create a sound nuisance or clutter in the Common Areas.

b. **Pets:** Unless Owners agree otherwise, each Owner may keep no more than two dogs and two cats on the Property. Before adopting any pets, an Owner should consult with the other Owner to ensure that the other Owner does not have any serious concerns. The non-adopting Owner *may* block the adopting Owner from adopting a pet if the pet has a tendency to bite or attack, if the pet is loud and creates a sound nuisance, or if it is illegal to keep such an animal. An Owner with a dog agrees to clean up after any messes left by the dog in the Common Area and will not leave any dogs in the Common Area unattended, unless all Owners agree to it.

c. **Creating a clean and reasonably quiet environment:** Owners agree to keep all Common Areas clean and clutter-free, and shall respect one another's need for quiet.

d. **Prohibited activities:** No person living on the Property shall use hazardous chemicals in cleaning or caring for the Common Area.

7. Rental and Occupancy

a. **Housemates:** An Owner may allow others to live with her and does not need to receive the permission of the other Owner, so long as the number of people living in each unit does not exceed four. As a courtesy, an Owner bringing in housemates shall notify the other Owner before the proposed housemates move in. If the other Owner feels resistant to or has worries about a proposed housemate, both Owners agree to sit down and discuss any worries, with the goal of making the arrangement workable and comfortable for everyone.

b. **Leasing to third-party tenants:** Each Owner is entitled to lease her Unit to a Third-Party Tenant, and is entitled to all income derived from such a lease, provided that the following requirements are met:

   i. **Approval by nonleasing Owner:** Any prospective Third-Party Tenant is subject to approval by the nonleasing Owner. The nonleasing Owner may review a standard form rental application, credit report, and other information as the nonleasing Owner may reasonably request from the prospective Tenant or leasing Owner. The nonleasing Owner shall quickly respond to requests for approval of a Third-Party Tenant and shall not unreasonably withhold approval of a prospective tenant. A failure by the nonleasing Owner to respond within three days to a leasing Owner's request for approval of a Third-Party Tenant shall be treated as approval by the nonleasing Owner.

   ii. **Lease agreement:** Any lease agreement with a Third-Party Tenant shall be in writing, shall include this agreement and any written Rules as attachments, and must include an agreement that the Third-Party Tenants shall adhere to the terms of this TIC Agreement and to any written Rules regarding day-to-day management, use, and care of the Property as described below.

iii. **Agreement to avoid evicting a tenant:** If leasing a unit to a Third-Party Tenant, the leasing Owner agrees to not attempt an eviction without first consulting with the other Owner and receiving the other Owner's permission. This is because evicting a tenant could negatively affect the future applications for city approvals, such as for condo conversion.

8. Decision-Making and House Rules

a. **Meetings:** Owners agree to meet at least once per year to agree on an annual operating budget. There shall be no other requirement for regular and formal meetings. However, a meeting of the Owners may be called by any Owner provided she gives notice and a proposed agenda to the other Owner at least a week in advance. Owners agree to keep a written record of issues discussed and decisions made regarding the Property.

b. **Voting:** Regardless of the size and value of an Owner's Cotenancy Interest, and regardless of the number of people living at the Property, Owner A and Owner B each have one vote in decisions about the Property. Thus, except where this Agreement allows an Owner to take unilateral action, all decisions about the Property must be unanimous. In the event that Owners cannot agree about a Property-related issue, Owners shall discuss and adapt the proposal in order to find a solution that is agreeable to both Owners. If the issue cannot be resolved through discussion, Owners agree to attend mediation (described in greater detail below).

c. **Adopting Rules:** The Owners may, from time to time, adopt and amend written "Rules" regarding day-to-day management, use, and care of the Property. Such Rules may concern any subject or matter and shall be binding on all Owners, their household members, guests, and tenants.

9. Financial Arrangement for Purchase

PERSON1 and PERSON2 purchased the Property in January of 2013 for $460,000, of which each agreed to pay half. At the time of the purchase, PERSON2 paid an additional $10,000 toward the down payment, and PERSON1 and PERSON2 intend to treat this as a loan from

PERSON2 to PERSON1. PERSON1 agrees to repay this $10,000 to PERSON2 within one year of the execution of this Agreement.

10. Responsibility for Debt on the Property

Owners share responsibility for the Property-related debt as follows:

a. **Shared Mortgage:** The primary mortgage on the property is the Local Credit Union mortgage (the "Shared Mortgage") in the amount of $400,000. Owner A and Owner B shall share responsibility for the Shared Mortgage in the following proportions:

   i. Owner A: 50 percent
   ii. Owner B: 50 percent

   The portion of Shared Mortgage for which each Owner is responsible will be referred to in this Agreement as her "Share of the Outstanding Debt." An Owner's Share of the Outstanding Debt may be adjusted, as described below.

b. **Monthly payments on the Shared Mortgage:** Each Owner shall make a monthly payment toward the Shared Mortgage on the basis of her Share of the Outstanding Debt. At the time that this Agreement is entered into, the total required monthly payment on the Shared Mortgage is $2,300. In accordance with each Owner's Share of the Outstanding Debt, Owner A and Owner B shall make monthly payments as follows:

   i. Owner A: $1,150
   ii. Owner B: $1,150

c. **Adjustments due to prepayment:** An Owner may prepay all or a portion of her Share of Outstanding Debt, so long as the lender does not penalize prepayment. That Owner may arrange a reamortization, provided she pays the reamortization fee, so that the total monthly payment is reduced to reflect the prepayment. In such event, the Owners shall recalculate their Shares of Outstanding Debt, and the Owner making the prepayment will receive the full benefit of the monthly payment reduction.

11. Sharing Costs

a. **Costs shared on an equal basis:** Except as otherwise provided in this Agreement, regardless of the number of people living at the

Property, Owner A and Owner B shall each be responsible for one half of the following costs:

i. Maintenance and repairs of Common Areas
ii. Insurance
iii. Property taxes
iv. Trash

b. **Costs shared on the basis of the number of people living in a Unit:** Because gas, electric, and water costs are not separately metered, Owners will each pay 50 percent of the costs so long as each Unit has an equal number of occupants. If one Unit has one more occupant than the other Unit, the Owner of the Unit with the larger number of occupants shall pay an additional 7 percent of each bill, and the Unit with fewer occupants will pay 7 percent less. Thus, if the Downstairs Unit has two occupants and the Upstairs Unit has one occupant, Owner A shall pay 57 percent of all utilities bills and Owner B shall pay 43 percent. For each additional occupant, the bills shall be adjusted by an additional 7 percent.

12. Insurance

a. **Insurance coverage:** The Owners have agreed that they will jointly maintain an insurance policy that includes public liability and replacement coverage for damage to the Property. If an Owner wishes to do so, she may obtain a separate insurance policy covering personal property.

b. **Avoiding risky activities:** Owners agree not to engage in activities that could create a risk or hazard to property or persons or that would make the Property difficult or expensive to insure.

13. Creation of a Joint Bank Account and Payment of Expenses

a. Owners agree to open a joint bank account, and each Owner agrees to make a fixed monthly deposit into the account. Owners shall meet at least once a year to determine an operating budget for Property-related costs, taking into account foreseeable maintenance costs. Owners shall then determine how much each Owner should deposit into the joint bank account each month. Except when Owners front costs, all bills shall be paid from this bank account.

14. Creation of a Reserve Fund

a. **Creation and purpose of a Reserve:** Owners agree to keep at least $10,000 in the joint bank account to serve as a Reserve fund. The purpose of creating a Reserve is primarily to protect the credit and assets of Owners in the event that one Owner cannot make an obligatory payment related to the Property. In the event that one Owner does not make an obligatory payment, either Owner may use the Reserve to make necessary mortgage, tax, or insurance payments. The Reserve may also be used to make unforeseen and necessary repairs, so long as all Owners agree to such repairs.

b. **Contributions to and reimbursement of the Reserve:** Each Owner agrees to contribute $250 per month to the Reserve until the Reserve has reached $10,000. Owners will keep an accounting of how much each Owner has contributed to or drawn from the Reserve. When an Owner ceases to own the Property, she shall be reimbursed any contributions she made to the Reserve, minus her share of any payments that were made from the Reserve. Owners shall attempt to reimburse the Reserve fund as soon as possible after the Reserve is used to pay for an expense. If the Reserve fund is used to pay for an expense that would be divided on something other than an equal basis, Owners shall reimburse the Reserve fund accordingly.

15. Keeping Accounts and Records

a. **Maintaining an accounting spreadsheet:** Owners agree to maintain an accounting spreadsheet documenting the following:

    i. How much each Owner has contributed to the joint bank account,
    ii. All costs paid for directly by an Owner and whether that Owner was reimbursed by the joint bank account,
    iii. All payments made from the joint bank account, and
    iv. How each payment should be allocated among the Owners (for example, most costs shall be allocated on a 50/50 basis, but others may be unequal).

b. **Household record folder:** Each Owner agrees to deposit independent evidence of all her expenditures for the Property, such as canceled checks or receipts, in a household records folder to be jointly maintained by the Owners. To the extent possible, all records shall be kept current on a monthly basis.

c. **Annual reckoning of accounts:** Within one month of the end of each accounting year (ending December 31), Owners shall reckon the accounts by determining each Owner's total contributions to Property-related expenses and the total amount of Property-related expenses that should be allocated to each Owner. If an Owner's total contributions are less than that Owner's total allocation of expenses, that Owner shall reimburse the bank account for the difference. If an Owner's total contributions are more than that Owner's total allocation of expenses, that Owner shall be reimbursed by the bank account or by the other Owner.

16. Maintenance, Repair, Alterations, and Improvements

a. **Standards for maintenance, repair, alterations, and improvements:** Because the Owners desire to maintain a tidy and comfortable home environment, Owners agree that they will maintain the Property in good condition and will not allow any significant defects to remain unrepaired.

b. **Maintenance, repair, and improvement in Units:** Each Owner shall be solely responsible for maintaining and repairing the interior of her Unit, which includes ensuring that floors, walls, ceilings, light fixtures, and smoke detectors are kept in good condition. An Owner may make alterations to her Unit without the other Owner's approval; however, if the alteration might affect the structural or acoustic integrity of the building, the Owner must seek the other Owner's permission.

c. **Maintenance, repair, and improvements to Exclusive Use Common Areas:** Each Owner must maintain all parts of her Exclusive Use Common Areas, including utility lines, pipes, and conduits that serve her Unit exclusively. Each Owner must obtain permission from the Owner prior to making any substantial changes or improvements to her Exclusive Use Common Area, primarily to ensure that any changes or improvements fit in harmony with the design of the building and exterior. The other Owner shall not unreasonably withhold consent to any changes or improvements to an Exclusive Use Common Area.

d. **Maintenance and repair of Common Areas:** Owners are jointly responsible for maintenance and repair of Common Areas and agree to share the costs of such repairs on a 50/50 basis. The only exception to this is in the event that a negligent act or omission by one Owner or that Owner's guest or tenant causes damage to the Property, and that damage is not covered by insurance, then that Owner shall be responsible for making or paying for the repairs.

e. **Paying for necessary maintenance and repairs to Common Areas:** Unless an emergency repair is required, Owners agree to consult with each other prior to authorizing any repairs to the Common Area costing more than $200. If, at any time, the Owners determine that foreseeable and expensive repairs will become necessary within three years of such determination (such as roof or foundation replacement, exterior painting, or plumbing or wiring replacement), Owners agree to come up with a plan for paying for such repairs and will begin to make larger monthly payments into the joint bank account, in order to plan for that expense.

f. **Improvements to and alterations of Common Areas:** Owners, by mutual consent, may make improvements and alterations to the Common Areas. Prior to making an improvement or alteration, Owners shall come to an agreement about how to share the costs and labor. In the event that one Owner wishes to make an improvement, and the other Owner agrees to that improvement but does not want to contribute to the cost, then, recognizing that the other Owner could benefit financially from the improvement, Owners could agree in writing to handle the situation in a variety of ways, including, but not limited to:

   i. The Owner requesting the improvement could be reimbursed by the other Owner in monthly payments over time;
   ii. The Owner requesting the improvement could be reimbursed by the other Owner at the time the Property is sold, or at the time the other Owner sells her Cotenancy Interest;
   iii. The Owners could agree that, at the time the Property is sold in its entirety or at the time the non-improving Owner sells her Cotenancy Interest, the improvements shall be appraised to determine the amount by which the improvement has raised the fair market value of the Property or of the Cotenancy

Interest. The Owner that paid for the improvement shall then be paid that amount from the sale proceeds. Owners shall, at the time of sale, choose an appraiser together. Should Owners be unable to jointly agree to an appraiser, then each shall hire her own appraiser and the two appraisals shall be averaged. To assist in future appraisals, Owners should carefully document the condition of the Property prior to the improvement.

In the event that the Owners do not agree, in writing, to any of the above methods of handling an improvement to the Common Area, then the default rule will be that the Owner making improvement will be compensated according to the procedure described in Paragraph iii.

In a situation where one Owner makes an improvement to a Common Area without contribution by the other Owner, Owners should also discuss and come to an agreement about who should pay any property tax increases or insurance policy premium increases that could result from the improvement. In absence of an agreement otherwise, the default rule shall be that the Owner making the improvement shall be responsible for paying any increases to property taxes or insurance premiums.

g. **Effect of Unit improvements on property taxes and insurance:** Any Owner who alters her Unit agrees to be solely responsible for the payment of all property tax increases, insurance policy premium increases, and all other costs for any insurance policy or policies obtained and maintained by the Owners arising from such alteration or improvement of the Owner's Unit.

h. **Contributions of labor:** The Owners intend that there will be no monetary or additional ownership compensation for labor expended by an Owner for ordinary repair and maintenance of the Property, unless Owners agree to it in writing.

17. Failure to Make Payments

a. **Taking steps to avoid missed payments:** Owners recognize that there is significant risk involved with sharing ownership of a property, particularly when there are debts secured by the entire property, and when failure to pay bills and taxes could result in liens against the entire property. As a result, in order to avoid default on any loans secured by the Property and any Property-related bills and taxes, if one Owner has financial difficulties and becomes aware that she may not be able to make a full and timely payment, she shall notify the other Owner as soon as she becomes aware of her financial difficulties. This will allow the other Owner to plan for the possibility of making a substituted payment.

b. **Failure of an Owner to make payments:** If an Owner is unable to make any necessary payments because of illness, disability, prolonged unemployment, or other hardship, and if there are no funds in the Reserve to cover such payments, the other Owner may make those payments in the non-paying Owner's place, for as long as necessary or possible, or as long as the paying Owner is willing. The Owners agree that the Owner making the payments may choose the manner and time frame for reimbursement from among the following options:

   i. Treat the additional payments as a loan to the non-paying Owner, bearing interest at a rate of no more than 10 percent, and treat it as a lien in favor of the paying Owner upon the Cotenancy Interest of the non-paying Owner. The paying Owner may decide the time frame for repayment of this loan, and parties shall put the terms of the loan and lien into writing.
   ii. The Owners' Shares of the Outstanding Debt may be adjusted based on the amount of payments made by the paying Owner, thereby reducing the paying Owner's share of subsequent monthly mortgage payments.

c. **Forcing a sale or buyout as a remedy for non-payment:** If a paying Owner is unable or unwilling to cover a non-paying Owner's share of necessary payments, and the non-paying Owner is unable to resume regular payments within three months of first missing payments, the paying Owner may demand to buy the non-paying Owner's Cotenancy Interest at a price determined in accordance with Paragraph 20.b.ii of this Agreement. In the event of three months of missed payments by the other Owner, the paying Owner may also demand that the Property be sold in its entirety.

18. Encumbrances

Parties agree not to incur any obligations that would place a lien or any kind of encumbrance on the Property, unless all Owners agree to the encumbrance. In the event that a lien or encumbrance is placed on the Property as a result of one Party's obligations, that Party shall bear the cost of removing the encumbrance or shall compensate the other Owners for the resulting decrease in property value.

19. Transferring an Interest in the Property and First Right of Refusal

a. **Offering to sell to another Owner:** An Owner may, at any time, offer to sell her Cotenancy Interest to the other Owner.

b. **Transfer to a Third Party:** The Owners have agreed to co-own together because of their knowledge of and confidence in each other. Thus, an Owner may transfer her interest in the Property to a Third Party only in accordance with the guidelines provided in this section.

c. **Lender approval requirement:** All Parties understand and acknowledge that if a Cotenancy Interest in the Property is transferred to an individual who is not a signatory to the mortgage, and such transfer is not approved by the mortgage lender, the lender could declare the entire outstanding balance of the mortgage immediately due and payable (an "acceleration") and, in the event of non-payment, initiate foreclosure of the Property. Accordingly, notwithstanding anything to the contrary in this Agreement, no Party shall transfer any interest in the Property to an individual who is not already a signatory to the mortgage unless (i) the lender approves the transfer in writing, or (ii) all Parties agree, in writing, to allow the transfer without lender approval and assume the resulting risk of acceleration and foreclosure. In the event all Parties do not agree to allow the transfer without lender approval, each Party shall cooperate in good faith in securing such approval. Such cooperation shall include, but not be limited to, submitting all documentation required by the mortgage lender. All charges imposed by the mortgage lender shall be paid by the transferor and/or transferee.

d. **Unrestricted transfers of Cotenancy Interests:** Subject to the lender approval requirement noted above, an Owner may transfer a Cotenancy Interest without other restriction if the transferee is (i) a person who is already a Party or (ii) a revocable living trust of which a Party is a beneficiary.

e. **Restricted transfer of Cotenancy Interests:** Subject to the lender approval requirement noted above, an Owner may transfer a Cotenancy Interest as provided in this Section.

   i. **Notice of intended sale.** If a sale is intended, the transferring Owner shall provide to the other Owner a "Notice of Intended Partial Sale" stating (i) the expected sales price, terms, and conditions (including financing) and (ii) the amount of sales commission, if any, that shall be paid in the event of sale by a real estate agent.
   ii. **Initial right to purchase.** If a sale is intended, the non-transferring Owner shall have the right to purchase the transferring Owner's interest on the terms and conditions stated in the Notice of Intended Partial Sale, except that the price and the cash down payment required shall be reduced by the amount of the intended sales commission. The non-transferring Owner shall exercise this right (i) within 10 calendar days of receiving the Notice of Intended Partial Sale, by providing Notice to the transferring Owner of her tentative intent to purchase (a "Notice of Tentative Intent") and (ii) within 30 calendar days of the Effective Date of the Notice of Tentative Intent, by providing a second Notice to the transferring Owner reaffirming her intent to purchase (a "Notice of Final Intent"). The Notice of Final Intent shall be binding. If a non-transferring Owner fails to provide either Notice, she waives the Initial Right to Purchase.
   iii. **Additional right to purchase.** Before accepting any purchase offer, the transferring Owner shall provide a copy of the offer to the other Owner. If the offer is 2 percent or more lower than the original expected sales price, the non-transferring Owner shall have the right to purchase the transferring Owner's interest on the terms and conditions stated in the purchase offer (without deduction of the intended sales commission). A

non-transferring Owner shall exercise this right by promptly providing Notice to the transferring Owner of her intent to purchase. This Notice shall be binding. If a non-transferring Owner fails to provide the Notice within 48 hours of receiving a copy of the offer, she waives the Additional Right to Purchase with regard to that offer. No further purchase rights shall be created as a result of a good faith renegotiation of sale price or terms following inspections or other disclosures related to that particular offer.

iv. **Right to reject Transferee.** Before completing any sale, gift, or other voluntary transfer, the transferring Owner shall provide to the other Owner a statement of the financial qualifications of the prospective transferee including a loan application, credit report, and, in the case of a self-employed person, the two most recent years' federal tax returns. The non-transferring Owner shall have ten calendar days from delivery of this information to provide written notice of disapproval to the transferring Owner. During this period, each Party shall be entitled to contact the prospective transferee to arrange a personal or telephone interview. To be considered valid, the written notice of disapproval must (i) be delivered within the required time frame and (ii) state a reasonable basis not prohibited by law for the disapproval. A transfer shall be deemed approved unless the transferring Owner receives a valid notice of disapproval stating the basis for disapproval from the non-transferring Owner.

f. **Non-transferring Owner's right to demand sale of the entire Property.** In the event that one Owner would like to sell or transfer her Cotenancy Interest, and the non-transferring Owner would rather not end up co-owning the property with a Third-Party Transferee, the non-transferring Owner may then demand that the entire Property be sold and the proceeds divided in the manner described below.

g. **Allocating increased property taxes after a transfer.** The Owners understand and acknowledge that a transfer of any interest in the Property may trigger a reassessment of the Property. The Owners agree that the transferee should be solely liable for the amount by which property taxes increase as a result of the transfer.

20. Other Events Constituting Offers to Sell to the Other Owner

a. **Events triggering offer to sell:** Upon the occurrence of any of the events listed below, such event shall be deemed to constitute an offer by the affected Owner, or her executor, trustee, personal representative, or successor-in-interest, as the case may be, to sell her Cotenancy Interest to the other Owner at a specified purchase price, as described below:

   i. **Death:** The death of the Owner;
   ii. **Bankruptcy:** The voluntary or involuntary filing of a petition in bankruptcy or for the protection under similar insolvency laws or any general assignment of assets for the benefits of creditors; or
   iii. **Court-ordered transfer as a result of divorce:** The entry of a final decree of divorce or dissolution of marriage that transfers an Owner's Cotenancy Interest to any person not a party to this Agreement.

b. **Notice and appraisal.**

   i. **Giving notice of an event triggering offer to sell:** Upon an Owner's death, her personal representative or successor-in-interest or, in the event of an Owner's bankruptcy or proposed court-ordered sale of her interest pursuant to a final decree of marital dissolution, the Owner herself, shall give written notice to the remaining Owner of such Owner's demise, bankruptcy, or forced sale pursuant to a final decree of marital dissolution, as the case may be, and the remaining Owner shall have the right to purchase the Cotenancy Interest at a specified purchase price, as defined below, by giving written notice to the personal representative, successor-in-interest, Owner, or trustee in bankruptcy, as the case may be, within 30 days after their receipt of the notice.
   ii. **Determining price of sale:** The specified purchase price for occurrences in this section shall be the then current fair market value of the Cotenancy Interest, less the amount of the Selling Owner's or deceased Owner's Share of the Outstanding Debt and increased or decreased, as required, by the amount of any advances, credits, or excess contributions made

and not yet reimbursed. If the parties cannot agree on the fair market value, then parties shall either jointly appoint an appraiser for the purpose of determining the fair market value or, failing a joint action, each separately designate an appraiser. In the latter case, the average of the two appraisals shall serve as the specified purchase price.

21. Sharing of Losses Related to the Property

a. The Owners understand and acknowledge that as a result of fluctuating market circumstances, it is possible that the total indebtedness for the Property may exceed its market value at some point in time. In the event that the Owners are personally liable for any such obligation or if there is any loss incurred by the Owners with regard to the Property, the Owners agree that that obligation shall be borne by all Owners on the basis of the Owners' then current Shares of the Outstanding Debt, unless otherwise agreed upon in writing.

22. Refinancing the Property

a. **Agreement to refinance:** All Owners must consent to any refinance of a debt secured by a lien against the entire Property. For the Shared Mortgage, refinancing expenses shall be allocated to Owners in proportion to their then-existing Shares of Outstanding Debt.

b. **Assumable loans and fractional financing:** In connection with the refinancing of any loan secured by the entire Property, the Owners agree to make reasonable efforts to secure a loan that allows for substitution and may be assumable by subsequent purchasers of then-existing Owners' Cotenancy Interests. If fractional financing, in the form of TIC loans, is available, Owners agree to explore and weigh the pros and cons of obtaining such financing. Although it is generally more expensive, fractional financing will reduce risk exposure for each Owner and will make it simpler for each Owner to sell her Unit separately.

23. Events Triggering Distributions

a. **Distribution of proceeds upon sale, partition, destruction, or condemnation:** Proceeds from sale of the entire Property, condemnation, destruction, or partition will be distributed among the Owners based upon the Relative Value Percentage of each

Cotenancy Interest (the calculation process for which is described below). Each Owner's share of the distribution will be reduced by the amount of her Share of Outstanding Debt, and increased or decreased, as required, by the amount of any advances, credits, or excess contributions made and not yet reimbursed.

i. **Sale of entire Property:** Except as otherwise provided, sale of the entire Property would require the approval of all Owners. Owners shall distribute sale proceeds in accordance with Subparagraph (a.) of this Section.
ii. **Partition:** An Owner wishing to partition the Property shall first offer to sell her interest in the Property to the other Owner, according to the provisions of this Agreement, and agrees to participate in the mediation and arbitration procedures set forth in this Agreement. Owners shall distribute partition proceeds in accordance with Subparagraph (a.) of this Section.
iii. **Condemnation and eminent domain:** The proceeds of any condemnation or eminent domain proceeding shall be distributed in accordance with Subparagraph (a.) of this Section.
iv. **Destruction:** In the event that the house is destroyed and Owners choose not to rebuild, Owners shall share insurance proceeds in accordance with Subparagraph (a.) of this Section. Generally, Owners shall endeavor to repair any damage to the Property so long as the repairs do not incur any more than $10,000 in out-of-pocket expenses to any one Owner.

b. **Calculating the Relative Value Percentage of each Cotenancy Interest:** For the purpose of distributions listed above, Parties agree to use the Relative Value Percentage of each Cotenancy Interest; this is because the market value of each Cotenancy Interest may fluctuate based on improvements, maintenance, and other factors. The Relative Value Percentages will be determined by having each Cotenancy Interest appraised separately, then dividing each appraisal by total of the two appraised values. For example, if Owner A's Cotenancy Interest is appraised at $400,000 and Owner B's Cotenancy Interest is appraised at $350,000, then the Relative Value Percentages will be 53.33 percent and 46.66 percent, respectively. To ensure precision in this process, Owners may, at the request of either Owner, jointly hire two separate appraisers, each of whom will make a determination of the Relative Value Percentages. Owners will then average the two appraisals.

24. This Agreement Shall Bind Future Owners

a. Unless this Agreement is terminated, the terms of the Agreement shall be binding on each of the Owners and her heirs, assigns, transferees, and successors in interest and shall constitute a covenant and/or equitable servitude running with the Property. When a Cotenancy Interest in the Property is transferred, all rights and obligations under this Agreement must be accepted by the transferees. Any transfer of a Cotenancy Interest in this Property shall be void if the transferee does not accept all rights and obligations associated with the transferred share of the Property. Transferees must accept this Agreement by signing an addendum agreeing to be bound by the terms of this Agreement, or by entering into a new agreement with the non-transferring Owner, subject to approval by the non-transferring Owner.

25. Resolution of Disputes

a. **Mediation:** Any unresolvable disputes between the Owners regarding the use, management, ownership, or disposition of the Property shall be submitted to mediation. A mediator shall be chosen by both Owners, or if they cannot so agree, each Owner shall select one person and the two selected people shall, together, select a third person to act as mediator. The chosen mediator shall conduct at least one mediation session per week for three weeks, with both Owners present, unless the dispute can be resolved sooner. Each session must last up to two hours, unless the dispute is resolved sooner. Each Owner agrees to participate in the mediation in good faith and make reasonable efforts to resolve the dispute quickly. If no agreement is reached after three mediation sessions, the Owners agree to submit the dispute to arbitration as set forth in this Agreement.

b. **Arbitration:** If the Owners are unable to resolve their disputes by mediation, the issues in controversy shall be submitted to an arbitrator selected by the Owners. If the Owners cannot agree on an arbitrator, they shall each select one person, and the two people together shall choose an arbitrator. The arbitrator shall be competent to conduct arbitration proceedings in conformity to applicable provisions of California law. No Owners shall be awarded attorneys' fees incurred during arbitration of any dispute.

26. Indemnity

a. If a Party becomes subject to any claim, liability, obligation, or loss arising from or related to the willful or negligent act or omission of another Party, such other Party shall fully indemnify and defend the liable Party from all associated costs and expenses including attorneys' fees.

27. Effective Date, Term, and Termination

a. This Agreement is effective on the date it is signed and shall continue for 90 years from the effective date, unless parties terminate the Agreement sooner by mutual agreement, consolidation of the property under sole ownership, sale of the entire property, conversion of the property to a condominium, or partition.

28. Miscellaneous Provisions

a. **Headings and subheadings in this Agreement:** This Agreement contains many headings and subheadings (in bold), which are there to make the Agreement easier to read and navigate. The headings and subheadings are not intended to have any legal effect or limit the scope or meaning of the provisions contained in this Agreement.

b. **Pronouns:** For the sake of brevity and flow in this Agreement, the phrase "he or she" has been abbreviated by the word "she," and "his or her" has been abbreviated by the word "her."

c. **Agreement governed by the laws of California:** The validity and interpretation of this Agreement shall be governed by the laws of the State of California.

d. **Severability:** Should any provision of this Agreement be determined to be invalid, the remaining provisions shall remain in full force and effect.

e. **Consultation with attorneys:** This Agreement has been drafted with the assistance of attorney __________, who is representing PERSON1. Each Owner has been given the opportunity to consult with her own separate attorney, before executing this Agreement.

f. **Amending this Agreement:** This Agreement may be altered or amended only by written agreement signed by all Owners.

g. **Multiple originals of this Agreement:** This Agreement may be executed in multiple originals, each of which shall be considered an original.

In witness hereof, the Owners have signed this Agreement on the date and year set forth next to each signature.

Dated: ____________ ________________________________

PERSON1

Dated: ____________ ________________________________

PERSON2

Attachments:

Exhibit A: Attached as Exhibit A is a drawing of the property with buildings and features as described.

CHAPTER FOUR

NEW KINDS OF ORGANIZATIONS

By Jenny Kassan and Janelle Orsi*

Part 1: Organizations in the New Economy

The Mandate of Organizations in the New Economy

The last chapter began by saying that agreements are the building blocks of a sharing economy. Organizations are essentially agreements entered into by *groups* of people to govern how they will work together. Unlike simple agreements between two individuals, organizations are designed to endure even as people come and go from a group. In that

* Jenny Kassan is an attorney at Katovich & Kassan Law Group, a law firm that serves social enterprise. Her legal practice areas include small business start-up and financing, securities regulation, nonprofit law, and cooperatives. Jenny is CEO of Cutting Edge Capital, a consulting firm that helps small businesses raise community capital and pioneers tools for a more inclusive and values-driven economy.

Jenny earned a master's degree in City and Regional Planning from the University of California at Berkeley and earned her J.D. from Yale Law School. She worked for eleven years at the Unity Council, a nonprofit community development corporation in Oakland, where she served as staff attorney and managed community economic development projects including the formation and management of several social ventures designed to employ and create business ownership opportunities for low-income community residents.

Jenny is the president of Community Ventures, a nonprofit organization dedicated to promoting the economic and social development of communities. She also co-founded the Sustainable Economies Law Center, a nonprofit that provides legal information to support sustainable economies. She currently serves on the Board of Directors of Post Carbon Institute, Sustainable Business Alliance, HatchLab, Inc., and Local Ecology and Agriculture Fremont (LEAF).

respect, organizations become institutions in our communities, and they will lay the foundation for much of the sharing economy. The more we move our economic activities into organizations designed with equitable, social, and cooperative goals, the more we can transform our entire economy. The choices we make in structuring organizations are critical; the architecture of organizations will, essentially, be the architecture of a new economy.

The current state of the world has served us with a heavy mandate: we must change quickly, make use of very limited planetary resources, and provide for seven billion people. Our nonprofits cannot afford to sit around and wait for foundation grants to come through. Local enterprises cannot afford to die due to lack of cash flow or capitalization. We cannot afford to waste resources on endless layers of organizational administration and bureaucracy. We cannot continue to meet our needs through ever more concentrated commercial enterprises that ignore the needs of their stakeholders. Our patterns of work and consumption cannot continue to diminish the resources available to current and future generations. The situation demands radically different ways of organizing our economic activities.

Organizations in the new economy are, thus, driven at their core by new purposes and new resources:

1. **New purposes:** Material incentives will drive most organizations, but the material may not always be money. Participants in the sharing economy have diverse goals that likely do not include making the maximum amount of money in the shortest possible amount of time. High on our list of new priorities and purposes will tend to be creating rewarding livelihoods, providing for ourselves and our communities, regenerating damaged ecosystems and natural resources, and nourishing our local and global economies. A "payoff" in any of these categories will create wealth of a different kind and materially alter our world.

   A core purpose of the sharing economy is to *provide.* Many provisions we currently obtain from commercial enterprises will be obtained through cooperative arrangements. Instead of buying a car from a dealer, we might buy into a neighborhood car-sharing club. Instead of sending our children to a private day care, we might form a cooperative childcare arrangement with other families. Instead of forming businesses and competing in a cut-throat marketplace, we will actively create collaborative arrangements and marketplaces, like farmers markets, time banks, community-supported enterprises, and producer cooperatives to ensure that each entrepreneur can make a contribution and be sustained.

2. **New resources:** Organizations of a sharing economy will likely be driven and "financed" less by money and more by people and their needs, passions, concerns, time, and energy. Because these are such precious resources, organizations will necessarily mimic many qualities of natural ecosystems: they will create a place for and provide for an array of participants, they will work efficiently within the context of limited resources, and they will be unable to afford to waste energy and resources. Money will almost always be involved, in some way, with organizations in the new economy; however, again mimicking ecosystems, money will more likely be sourced from a broad cross-section of our communities, and it will intentionally be recirculated within such communities.

Designing Organizations for a Sharing Economy

Organizations will rise most fully to the needs of a sharing economy by integrating high levels of participation by and sharing with stakeholders. Here is a framework for considering the various ways that rights and responsibilities of an organization can be shared among its participants:

1. **Sharing decisions:** The best way to ensure that an organization will make decisions that benefit its stakeholders is to give stakeholders a legal right to participate in decision-making.
2. **Sharing information:** High levels of transparency are essential to the accountability of organizations and to the functioning of organizations with highly participatory decision-making.
3. **Sharing capitalization:** In conventional businesses, individuals and entities that provide capital to an entity tend to control that entity and benefit from its profits. In a sharing economy, the responsibility of capitalizing an organization (and the rewards, rights, and risks that flow from it) will ideally be spread among the stakeholders.
4. **Sharing profits/benefits:** The profits, products, and/or non-monetary benefits that are generated by the activities of an

organization will also, ideally, be spread and shared among stakeholders.

5. **Sharing equity:** Sharing equity in enterprises will help to keep such enterprises community-based and locally owned. In conventional businesses, owners often have an incentive to sell out to larger companies in order to receive a large payout. In the sharing economy, organizations can remove or weaken that incentive by requiring that proceeds from a sale be distributed to a large number of stakeholders. In this way, no single individual is likely to drive a sell-out.
6. **Sharing risk:** Founders and funders of enterprises tend to shoulder the risk that an enterprise will experience loss or liability. In the sharing economy, this risk can also be shared and spread among many stakeholders.
7. **Sharing work:** Organizations in the sharing economy are also likely to involve high levels of stakeholder participation in the actual work of an enterprise, rather than outsourcing and hiring others to do the work. A grocery cooperative, for example, is likely to be operated by its members. Community-supported farms are likely to involve customers in the actual work of the farm. (Note that this brings up employment law problems, which are discussed in Chapter 7.)

The work of sharing economy lawyers will often be to help clients form and structure entities that integrate, to varying degrees, the participation and sharing described above. There are three primary choices we tend to make in the formation of organizations:

1. **What entity to choose:** The entity we choose to form at the state level will dictate certain limits and possibilities for how the entity may operate.
2. **What tax status to obtain:** The tax status or tax exemption we choose will also confer certain constraints and benefits on the organization.
3. **How to structure governance, operations, and financial provisions:** Beyond the constraints imposed by choice of entity and tax status, most organizations have a vast amount of latitude to choose how to structure governance, operations, capitalization,

and management of an organization's resources. The choices we make are then reflected in how we draft bylaws, operating agreements, and other organizational policies.

These three sets of choices are pivotal in determining how our organizations are able to respond to the diverse members of our organizational ecosystems—the stakeholders. Truly responding to the needs of stakeholders necessarily mandates greater participation of such stakeholders in governance, operations, and the material incentives that drive the organization. The members, consumers, workers, suppliers, constituents, local communities, and other stakeholders of our organizations will increasingly have a role in understanding and deciding how the organization runs. Governance of larger organizations will necessarily become more dispersed, creating multiple avenues for stakeholders to give input, and for the organization to receive and adapt to such input. The profits, harvest, products, or other benefits created by the organization will be shared among a broader array of stakeholders, which ensures accountability to the stakeholders, and not to an absentee group of investors.

Not only must organizations respond to stakeholders, but stakeholders must respond to organizations. We will all have a civic/personal duty to *actually participate* thoughtfully and accountably in the various organizations that provide for us. Rather than simply purchasing food from a grocery store, we may become members of a cooperative that provides food for us, and our active participation in such organizations will determine whether it can actually respond to and provide for our needs.

Conventional organizations tend to fall into a few primary categories:

1. **Commercial:** Businesses that carry on commercial activities.
2. **Public and charitable:** Organizations that provide a benefit to the public.
3. **Mutual and cooperative:** Organizations that provide benefits to their members and patrons.

The sharing economy brings us a new take on all three categories, and we'll often see the lines between them blur. The blurring of these conventional categories is wonderful from the standpoint of creating organizations that are more effective at providing for us and our communities. But the blurring of categories means that sharing economy lawyers will often be forced to navigate uncharted waters when we help clients choose what entity to form, what tax status to seek, and how to structure the governance, operational, and financial aspects of an organization.

Most transactional lawyers are somewhat unfamiliar with legal structures for cooperatives and mutual benefit nonprofits, and most legal practice guides fail to discuss them in depth. Yet, this category of organization will become more common, as enterprises are increasingly driven by and designed to provide for their stakeholders. Mutual benefit organizations and cooperatives are designed to provide sustenance and services for their members, not to provide a profit to shareholders, or to benefit only a charitable class of people. As a result, many more of our clients will seek to form such organizations.

Transactional lawyers tend to be quite familiar with legal structures for commercial businesses and, to some extent, for charities, yet many lawyers struggle to serve clients that blur the lines between those traditional categories. In the new economy, our clients will often want to find ways to incorporate social and environmental goals into their business, to incorporate commercial activities into their charity, to implement models of cooperative ownership in their business, or to implement cooperative management into their nonprofit. Many of these proposals challenge conventional legal categories, and lawyers will often struggle to advise clients on how to form and structure organizations for such purposes.

This chapter reviews a variety of legal entity types and tax categories, examining their compatibility with the goals of the sharing economy, and offering proposals for ways to adapt and harness them for the needs of sharing and social enterprise. This chapter looks first at the limitations of traditional for-profit entities, creative ways that they have been structured to serve social purposes, and some of the new entity types that have recently been created under state laws. The chapter next addresses issues and considerations specific to cooperatives and then examines the unique challenges that arise when nonprofits engage in economic activity. The final section of this book examines governance models increasingly being adopted by organizations in a more collaborative and participatory economy.

THE DESIGN OF OWNERSHIP: THE ARCHITECTURE OF EXTRACTIVE VS. GENERATIVE OWNERSHIP

By Marjorie Kelly

Ownership is the underlying architecture of our economy. Since the dawn of the industrial age, a particular form of ownership has come to dominate our world—that of the publicly traded corporation, where ownership shares trade in public stock markets. The revenue of the largest of these corporations represents roughly 80 percent of global industrial output. Yet bubbling up today are alternative options that represent a new kind of ownership, private ownership for the common good. These alternatives include employee ownership, cooperatives, credit unions, community land trusts, co-housing communities, community wind, and other models. They also include large, mission-controlled corporations, such as family-owned businesses or the foundation-owned companies common in northern Europe.

As a class, these alternatives represent a coherent family of design. If industrial age ownership is based on a monoculture model, emerging designs are rich in biodiversity. They represent economic innovation not as it's usually meant, which is about better and better ways to make more and more money. This innovation is almost unimaginably more profound. It is a reinvention at the level of organizational purpose and structure. It is about creating economic architectures that are self-organized around serving the needs of life.

We might call this emerging school of design *generative.* In their animating intent and their living impact, these forms of ownership are aimed at generating the conditions for life. Should they one day spread to become a new norm, they might create a generative economy, which in its normal functioning tends to create fair and just outcomes, benefit the many rather than the few, and enable an enduring human presence on a flourishing Earth.

Adapted from *Owning Our Future: The Emerging Ownership Revolution*, by Marjorie Kelly (San Francisco: Berrett-Koehler. Copyright 2012 Marjorie Kelly)

Generative ownership designs are about generating and preserving real wealth, living wealth, rather than phantom wealth that can evaporate in the next quarter. They're about helping families enjoy secure homes, creating jobs, preserving a forest, generating nourishment out of waste, and generating broad well-being. These designs are in contrast to the dominant ownership design of today, which we might call *extractive*, for its focus is maximum physical and financial extraction. While the industrial age has been powered by fossil fuels extracted from the Earth, this physical extraction works in parallel with financial extraction—the extraction of financial wealth from the economy.

Five essential design elements work together to create these different kinds of ownership: purpose, membership, governance, capital, and networks. These elements can be used in *extractive* ways, aimed at extracting maximum financial wealth in the short term, or in *generative* ways, aimed at creating a world where all living beings can flourish for generations to come.

Extractive ownership has a *financial purpose*: maximizing profits. Generative ownership has a *living purpose*: creating the conditions for life. While public corporations generally have *absentee membership*, with owners disconnected from the life of enterprise, generative ownership has *rooted membership*, with ownership held in human hands. While extractive ownership involves *governance by markets*, control by capital markets on autopilot, generative designs have *mission-controlled governance*, control by those focused on social mission. Instead of investments that involve *capital as master*, new approaches involve *stakeholder finance*, where capital becomes a friend. Instead of *commodity networks*, where goods are traded based solely on price, generative enterprises are supported by *ethical networks*, which provide collective support for social and ecological norms.

Not every ownership model has every one of these design elements. But the more generative elements are employed, the more effective the design. Through grafting various pieces together to design still more models, we might together create the greenhouse of design experimentation where the future of our economy could be grown.

The Architecture of Extractive and Generative Ownership

Extractive Ownership	*Generative Ownership*
1. Financial purpose: maximizing profits in short term.	1. Living purpose: creating the conditions for life over long term.
2. Absentee membership: ownership disconnected from life of enterprise.	2. Rooted membership: ownership in human hands.
3. Governance by markets: control by capital markets on autopilot.	3. Mission-controlled governance: control by those dedicated to social mission.
4. Finance in charge: capital as master.	4. Stakeholder finance: capital as friend.
5. Ethical networks: collective support for focused ecological and social norms.	5. Commodity networks: trading solely on price and profits.

Part 2: Traditional For-Profit Legal Entities in the Sharing Economy

This section discusses corporations and, to some extent, limited liability companies (LLCs), as the primary, "traditional," for-profit legal entities that are used for businesses. There are a handful of issues that make general stock corporations, in particular, less than perfectly suited for mission-driven organizations. Note that a general choice-of-entity discussion is beyond the scope of this book. Guidance on entity selection issues like tax treatment and liability protection can be found in many general business law books.

Corporations and Shareholder Primacy

Ask a business lawyer or an MBA about the purpose of a corporation and you are likely to hear that it is to maximize shareholder return. A corporate board that chooses to consider the needs of stakeholders other than shareholders, according to this view, potentially violates its duties to the shareholders. A board that has the choice between destroying an irreplaceable ecosystem and foregoing the potential for profits MUST chop down that rainforest, so the story goes.

The reality of corporate law is much more complicated, and this section provides a general overview of the shareholder primacy issue.

First, it's important to note that corporations are governed by state law, so it is impossible to generalize about the law of corporations—each state has its own statutes and body of case law. Many generalizations that are made about corporations come from Delaware. Delaware is the jurisdiction of choice for big businesses to incorporate in, thanks in part to the large body of published opinions that provides a great deal of guidance to corporate lawyers. More than 50 percent of all publicly traded companies in the United States and 63 percent of the Fortune 500 are incorporated in Delaware.[1]

If a business incorporates under a different state's laws, different rules may apply. The location of the corporation's headquarters may also affect which laws are applicable. For example, a corporation that is formed under another state's law but that has significant ties to California is subject to several sections of the California Corporations Code, such as the sections governing election of directors and removal of directors, directors' standard of care, liability of directors and shareholders, and many more.[2] Given the great variability in state corporate law, it is important for the practitioner to research the laws applicable to a particular client, based on where the client is incorporated and where it is doing business.

The Business Judgment Rule

Despite the widespread belief that corporate boards must maximize shareholder returns, the fact is that, in most situations, corporate boards have broad discretion to make decisions based on many factors, including impacts on the community, the environment, and their employees, as well as shareholder return. No state has a statute that requires corporate boards, in all situations, to maximize shareholder return.[3] According to the American Law Institute,

1. State of Delaware, Div. of Corps., http://www.corp.delaware.gov/aboutagency.shtml.

2. CAL. CORP. CODE § 2115.

3. Einer Elhauge, *Sacrificing Corporate Profits in the Public Interest*, N.Y.U. L. REV. 733, 763 (June 2005).

> Even if corporate profit and shareholder gain are not thereby enhanced, the corporation, in the conduct of its business: (1) Is obliged, to the same extent as a natural person, to act within the boundaries set by law; (2) May take into account ethical considerations that are reasonably regarded as appropriate to the responsible conduct of business; and (3) May devote a reasonable amount of resources to public welfare, humanitarian, educational, and philanthropic purposes.[4]

The board's authority to make decisions regarding the management of a corporation is given extreme deference by the courts. This doctrine is known as the business judgment rule. The business judgment rule provides a rebuttable presumption "that in making a business decision the directors of a corporation acted on an informed basis, in good faith and in the honest belief that the action taken was in the best interests of the company."[5] Even in situations where a board's decision is certain to lead to reduced shareholder profit, the doctrine has been upheld.[6] This presumption protects against the risk that a court might "impos[e] itself unreasonably on the business and affairs of a corporation."[7]

A plaintiff must produce evidence that rebuts the business judgment presumption; for example, by "showing that the majority of directors who approved the action (1) had a personal interest in the subject matter of the action, (2) were not fully informed in approving the action, or (3) did not act in good faith in approving the action."[8] Only after the plaintiff successfully rebuts the business judgment presumption will the court then place the burden on the directors to prove that the action was entirely fair.[9]

---

4. *Id.* (quoting 1 Am. Law Inst., Principles of Corporate Governance: Analysis and Recommendations § 2.01(b)(2)–(3) & cmt. d (1994)).

5. *In re* Troll Commc'ns, 385 B.R. 110, 118 (Bankr. D. Del. 2008).

6. Elhauge, *supra* note 3, at 842–43. There are limits on the degree to which a board can sacrifice shareholder profits for the purpose of benefiting some other stakeholder. For example, if the board decided to give away half of its assets to charity, the shareholders could have a claim against the board for violation of the duty of care. *See* Mem'l Hosp. Ass'n v. Pac. Grape Prods., 290 P.2d 481 (Cal. 1955) (holding that there is "reasonable" limit to corporate manager's power to donate that depends on particular facts of each case).

7. eBay Domestic Holdings, Inc. v. Newmark, 16 A.3d 1, 36–37 (Del. Ch. 2010) (internal citations omitted).

8. *Id.* (internal citations omitted).

9. *Id.*

Higher Levels of Scrutiny

There are two exceptions to this general business judgment rule under Delaware law known as the *Unocal* and *Revlon* standards. The *Unocal* standard is applied when the board of a corporation adopts a measure to try to defend itself from a takeover. Under those circumstances, the burden shifts to the board to prove "(a) reasonable grounds for believing that a danger to corporate policy and effectiveness existed; and (b) that the defensive measure adopted was reasonable in relation to the threat posed. Directors satisfy the first part of the *Unocal* test by demonstrating good faith and reasonable investigation."[10]

Under the *Revlon* standard, when a controlling interest in a corporation is being sold, courts grant virtually no discretion to boards—the board is required to maximize the company's value for the stockholders' benefit.[11]

Whether these doctrines would apply in other states is not clear, but many business lawyers assume that they would. Even in Delaware there continues to be some lack of clarity on when this heightened scrutiny would apply. Few corporate boards or their lawyers want to take the chance of a shareholder lawsuit so they err on the side of caution.

Constituency Statutes

Since the 1980s, in response to a wave of hostile takeovers, about 30 states have adopted "constituency statutes" to protect corporate boards from liability for decisions that fail to maximize shareholder return even

10. Paramount Commc'ns, Inc. v. Time Inc., 571 A.2d 1140, 1152 (1989).

11. "The duty of the board had thus changed from the preservation of Revlon as a corporate entity to the maximization of the company's value at a sale for the stockholders' benefit. This significantly altered the board's responsibilities under the Unocal standards. It no longer faced threats to corporate policy and effectiveness, or to the stockholders' interests, from a grossly inadequate bid. The whole question of defensive measures became moot. The directors' role changed from defenders of the corporate bastion to auctioneers charged with getting the best price for the stockholders at a sale of the company. . . . A board may have regard for various constituencies in discharging its responsibilities, provided there are rationally related benefits accruing to the stockholders. However, such concern for non-stockholder interests is inappropriate when an auction among active bidders is in progress, and the object no longer is to protect or maintain the corporate enterprise but to sell it to the highest bidder." Revlon, Inc. v. MacAndrews & Forbes Holdings, Inc., 506 A.2d 173, 182 (Del. 1985).

in the context of a change in control.[12] The constituency statutes vary a great deal. In Connecticut, for example, directors must consider not only shareholder interests, but "the interests of the corporation's employees, customers, creditors, and suppliers"; "community and societal considerations"; and other factors.[13] In Arizona, directors must consider both the long-term and short-term interests of the corporation and its shareholders, "including the possibility that these interests may be best served by the continued independence of the corporation."[14]

The merits of constituency statutes have been hotly debated. Some argue that society benefits when directors are allowed (or required in the case of Connecticut) to consider constituencies other than shareholders. Others argue that constituency statutes entrench directors that may be serving nobody's interests but their own.

Also problematic is the fact that even in states with constituency statutes, there is little guidance for boards on the specific methods or degree to which they can consider other interests besides that of the shareholders. A recent article about benefit corporation statutes noted that "neither the constituency statutes themselves nor state case law address questions such as how directors should decide which parties fall within a protected constituency category, what weight the directors should assign to shareholder and non-shareholder interests and what standards a court should use in reviewing directors' decisions to consider (or not to consider) non-shareholder interests."[15] This lack of clear legal authority makes it difficult for directors of social or

---

12. When the California legislature voted to adopt a constituency statue, Governor Arnold Schwarzenegger vetoed the bill. The California Bar was firmly opposed to the bill, arguing that the bill would reduce director accountability by giving directors so much discretion that it would provide a means for directors to escape accountability by invoking one of the numerous interests listed in the bill and make it easier for them to escape liability for failure to meet fiduciary duties to shareholders. According to the California State Bar, "Institutional Shareholder Services, Inc., an influential proxy and corporate governance advisory firm, counts incorporation in a state with non-shareholder constituency provisions like those contained in the Bill as a negative factor when calculating its Corporate Governance Quotient, a well-known standard for measuring the quality of corporate governance." Corporations Committee, State Bar of California Business Law Section, Statement of Position on AB 2944, June 3, 2008.

13. Conn. Gen. Stat. § 33-756(d).

14. Ariz. Gen. Corp. Law § 10-2702.

15. William H. Clark, Jr. & Larry Vranka, The Need and Rationale for the Benefit Corporation: Why It Is the Legal Form That Best Addresses the Needs of Social Entrepreneurs, Investors, and, Ultimately, The Public (Oct. 31, 2011), at 10, http://benefitcorp.net/for-attorneys/benefit-corp-white-paper.

mission-driven organizations to pursue both profit and a company's social or environmental mission, because they may not feel that they are legally protected when considering the interests of constituencies other than the shareholders.[16]

What Does This Mean in Practice?

Let's say Sally has a dream of starting a social enterprise, the purpose of which is to provide clean water in rural African villages. She has invented a low-cost filter that will revolutionize people's ability to access clean water. She starts the business with the help of some friendly investors who believe in its mission and don't care so much about whether they will ever get any returns on their investment. She incorporates in Delaware because that's what her corporate lawyer friend advises.

The business grows little by little. Selling the filters to local governments, non-governmental organizations (NGOs), and others is generating more profits than Sally ever expected. She wants to expand to more villages and she needs more capital to do it. She finds more investors to fund the expansion.

Sally looks at her books and realizes that her profit margins are quite large. She's paying herself and her employees good salaries and the business expenses are pretty low. She decides that the right thing to do is to lower the price of the filters and the board agrees with her decision. A few months later she's happy to see that her profits are much lower and more people are benefiting from her invention.

But then she releases her annual report to her shareholders. She gets some angry calls demanding to know what happened to the profits? She calmly explains that the purpose of the company is not to make profits but to provide clean water. The shareholders call their lawyers. The lawyers threaten to sue Sally and her board.

In this situation, Sally is likely to prevail. The decision to lower the price would likely receive great deference from the court in Delaware because of the business judgment rule. However, Sally now has to contend with the time, energy, and legal fees necessary to respond to even the mere threat of a shareholder lawsuit.

Imagine that a few years later, all this is behind her and everything is still going well with the business. Imagine she has reincorporated in

16. *Id.*

Vermont, a state that has a constituency statute, so that she has a better chance of avoiding shareholder lawsuits in the future. Sally, happy with what she has created, is ready to move on to new adventures. She starts to talk to potential buyers for the company. She will only talk to socially responsible companies and investor groups that she feels confident will continue to make profits secondary to providing affordable clean water.

Word gets out that Sally is looking for a buyer. SuperMega Monolith Corporation (SMM), one of the world's largest multinational conglomerates, is interested. This filter could make them billions! SMM makes an offer to the board, which the board quickly rejects, fearing that, under SMM's control, the company's mission will be lost. SMM then makes an offer directly to Sally's shareholders—we'll buy your stock for $50 per share. Sally calls those other potential buyers she's been talking to but none of them can afford to pay that much. The company's lawyers advise the board that it has no choice but to let SMM buy the company.

"But, wait," Sally protests. "We are incorporated in Vermont, and Vermont has a constituency statute that protects us if we block SMM's offer." The lawyers shake their heads glumly—"Do you really want to take the chance that the courts will see it your way? Every member of the board could be held personally liable for not meeting their duties to the shareholders to maximize their return."[17]

Sound familiar? This is what happened to Ben and Jerry's. In 2000, a similar scenario led to the sale of Ben and Jerry's to Unilever.

The Take Away

Professor Michal Barzuza reviewed 108 antitakeover decisions in states other than Delaware. Every decision in the states with a strong constituency statute rejected the *Revlon* doctrine. Every case in a state without a constituency statute followed *Revlon*. But again, can social enterprises afford the time, energy, and legal fees necessary to find out whether *Revlon* would apply to them?[18]

---

17. Delaware, by case law, authorizes managers to reject a takeover bid based on "the impact on 'constituencies' other than shareholders (i.e., creditors, customers, employees, and perhaps even the community generally)." Unocal Corp. v. Mesa Petroleum Co., 493 A.2d 946, 955 (Del. 1985). *See also* Paramount Commc'ns v. Time, 571 A.2d 1140, 1153 (Del. 1990) ("[D]irectors may consider, when evaluating the threat posed by a takeover bid, . . . 'the impact on 'constituencies' other than shareholders . . . .'") (citations omitted).

18. Michal Barzuza, *The State of State Antitakeover Law*, 95(8) VA. L. REV. 1973–2052 (2010).

Given this concern, corporations may not be the best entity for an organization that wants to serve values that may conflict with shareholder profit maximization (see a discussion below for modifications that can be made to the standard corporate form that make it more friendly for sharing and social responsibility).

Other Corporate Design Flaws

An extensive discussion of the numerous critiques of the corporate form is beyond the scope of this book.[19] In summary, however, the current design of the corporation includes flaws that become more apparent as a corporation grows and especially if it is publicly traded.

Dilution of Ownership

While corporations are "owned" by their shareholders, this ownership is so diluted and changes so rapidly that it can hardly be considered ownership in the usual sense of the word. Shareholders (except for those few that own very large chunks of stock) have virtually none of the rights typically associated with ownership. They have no control or ability to influence management and they have no right to receive a share of profits. Thus the owners of the corporation have little control, while the board of directors has almost absolute control.

Short-Termism

Another flaw of large publicly traded corporations is "short-termism"—the pressure on managers to focus narrowly on quarterly profits. As Marjorie Kelly describes it,

> The financial meltdown of 2008 was a direct result of the pursuit of immediate profit by investment bankers and mortgage brokers that disregarded the impact of their actions on customers, on the larger economy, and indeed on stockholders and the company itself in the long term. Those that wanted to operate with integrity found it difficult. They were constrained by a corporate design that reinforced the need to 'make the numbers' by any means possible.[20]

---

19. A great resource on this topic is the website of Corporation 20/20, http://www.corporation2020.org.

20. Marjorie Kelly, *Not Just for Profit*, Strategy+Bus. (Spring 2009).

"SHARED OWNERSHIP"

By Marjorie Kelly

"Shared ownership" refers to economic entities where private ownership, in whole or in part, is blended with ownership that is shared among individuals, or between individuals and a community organization.

In emerging experiments nationwide—and in older alternative designs that may be under-appreciated—communities are demonstrating that powerful ways to own and control rural assets are through local and shared ownership.

While local ownership is broadly understood, shared ownership is an emerging, broad category of ownership designs that can take many forms. It can mean ownership is shared among individuals, as in cooperatives or employee-owned firms. It can mean ownership is shared between an individual and a collective entity like a land trust. Or it can mean a sharing of certain ownership duties—like marketing dairy goods or managing wind rights—while other aspects of property ownership remain in individual hands.

"Shared ownership" is a term beginning to gain traction in recent reports and conferences. See for example "Expanding Asset-Building Through Shared Ownership," 2008 report by Heather McCulloch and Beadsie Woo, for the Annie E. Casey Foundation. The Casey Foundation also in December 2008 sponsored a gathering for asset-building leaders to discuss innovative shared-ownership strategies.

From *Keeping Wealth Local: Shared Ownership and Wealth Control for Rural Communities* by Marjorie Kelly, Tellus Institute with Shanna Ratner, Yellow Wood Associates, a report for the Wealth Creation in Rural America project of the Ford Foundation

Corporations and Geographically Dispersed Ownership

One of the most admired qualities of the modern corporate form is the ease with which its ownership can spread to all corners of the earth. However, geographically dispersed ownership is inimical to the sharing economy. Local ownership is essential to the sharing economy because geographic closeness facilitates shared ownership and meaningful accountability. In their seminal report to the Ford Foundation on wealth creation in rural communities, Marjorie Kelly and Shanna Ratner describe the problem as follows:

> Absentee ownership is detached from the life of a community and its enterprises. By contrast, shared ownership means that the interests connected to the living fabric of an enterprise—employees, community members, the natural environment—are represented at the table of ownership and governance.[21]

An Environmental Protection Agency study found that the average amount of toxins released by absentee-owned facilities or those with out-of-state headquarters is nearly three times more than plants with in-state headquarters, and 15 times more than single location enterprises.[22]

Lack of "Siren Protection"

Traditional entity structures are quite flexible, which is a double-edged sword. Over the decades of the existence of corporations and LLCs, powerful interest groups have lobbied hard to increase flexibility and have been quite successful. Corporate charters and LLC articles of organization can easily be amended to alter the way that authority and profits are divided. On one hand, the flexibility allows groups, if they so choose, to implement high levels of accountability and creative governance structures. On the other hand, this can allow powerful interests to easily overtake an organization. Structures like partnerships, corporations, and LLCs have no built-in "siren protection."

What is siren protection? In Greek mythology, the Sirens were three women who lured sailors with their beauty and enchanting music to the rocky coast of their island where they would be shipwrecked. To protect themselves, sailors would tie themselves to the mast of their ships when navigating near the Sirens. The basic corporate and LLC forms do not provide any way to tie oneself to the mast. If a founder that is committed in the beginning to social responsibility and community

---

21. Marjorie Kelly & Shanna Ratner, Keeping Wealth Local: Shared Ownership and Wealth Control for Rural Communities (Tellus Inst. & Yellow Wood Assocs. 2009), http://www.yellowwood.org/Keeping%20Wealth%20Local.pdf.

22. Don Grant, EPA/NSP R828826, Organizational Structures, Citizen Participation, and Corporate Environmental Performance (2001), *available at* http://www.epa.gov.

well-being is lured by the promise of big profits away from this original mission, there is nothing to stop her.

Part 3: Adapting Traditional For-Profit Entities

While the traditional structures (corporations and LLCs) are not designed for the sharing economy, they can often be adapted to meet some or all of the sharing economy goals.

Modified Corporate Structure

Founders of organizations whose mission is to help build the sharing economy face a dilemma if they plan to operate a large capital-intensive business. Generally, a corporation is the most appropriate structure for a large business that needs to bring in many investors, but, as discussed above, it is not ideally suited to maintaining a mission that is inconsistent with shareholder profit maximization. This section discusses how to modify the corporate structure in order to mitigate potential shareholder pressure to choose profits over mission.

Super-Majority Voting Stock

Corporation statutes give a great deal of flexibility to boards in the design of their capital structure. Unlike the typical structure in which shareholders' votes are weighted based on the number of shares they own, some corporations are structured so that the founders have controlling voting rights even when they own only a small percentage of the company's stock. Examples of companies with this kind of capital structure include Google, the *New York Times*, and Interface, a flooring company with an admirable commitment to social and environmental responsibility.

The obvious flaw of this model is that it is completely dependent on the commitment of the founders. If the founders leave or start to drift from the original mission, the commitment to goals unrelated to profit maximization will be diminished.

Charter Provisions

Another innovation with a bit more teeth than the super-majority voting stock structure is to incorporate provisions into the company charter that make "mission drift" more difficult. For example, Portland,

Oregon–based Upstream 21 Corporation is a company that was set up for the purpose of buying other companies and helping them improve their financial, social, and environmental performance. Upstream's articles of incorporation include the following provisions (summarized here):

- Each director is required to sign an agreement stating that he/she shall discharge the duties of a director in a manner the director reasonably believes to be in the best interests of the Company, and the best interests of the Company are defined to include the Company's and its subsidiaries' social, legal and economic effects on their employees, customers, and suppliers and on the communities and geographic areas in which the Company and its subsidiaries operate; the long-term as well as short-term interests of the Company and its shareholders; and the Company's and its subsidiaries' effects on the environment.
- When evaluating any offer of another party to purchase the Company or merge, the directors are required to consider the following: the social, legal and economic effects on employees, customers and suppliers of the Company and its subsidiaries and on the communities and geographic areas in which the Company and its subsidiaries operate; the economy of the state and the nation; the environment; the long-term as well as short-term interests of the Company and its shareholders, including the possibility that these interests may be best served by the continued independence of the Company; and other relevant factors.
- There are four classes of voting stock:
    - The president and each member of the board of directors gets one share of Series 1 Class A Common Stock.
    - When outside investors invest in the Company, they get Series 2 Class A Common Stock.
    - Employees of the Company and its subsidiaries are issued Series 3 Class A Common Stock after 12 months of employment.
    - Class B Common Stock is sort of a catch-all class for any other types of shareholders. For example if a board member is voted off the board, his or her share of Series 1 Class A automatically converts to Class B, unless that person is an employee, in which

case the Series 1 Class A converts to Series 3 Class A. Series 2 Class A converts to Class B if the investor transfers his or her stock to someone else.

- When shareholders vote on any matter such as the election of the board, each share is entitled to one vote, but when the shareholders must vote on one of the following actions ("Extraordinary Actions"), different voting rules apply (described below):
  - Amendments to the articles of incorporation
  - Amendments to the bylaws
  - Conversion
  - Merger
  - Share exchange
  - Dissolution
  - The sale, lease, exchange, or other disposition of all or substantially all of the Company's property
  - Removal of a director
- An Extraordinary Action may only be approved if (1) a majority of all shares entitled to vote on the action, without regard to class or series, vote in favor of the action AND two-thirds of all shares of any two series of Class A Common Stock entitled to vote on the action, voting separately by series, shall not vote against the action; OR (2) two-thirds of all shares of any two series of Class A Common Stock entitled to vote on the action, voting separately by series, vote in favor of the action.

Upstream's complicated voting structure is designed to give greater control to employees and directors and to reduce the authority of outside investors, especially of those investors that acquire shares from other shareholders as opposed to directly from the company.

Note that most constituency statutes allow directors to consider interests other than shareholder profit maximization but do not require them to do so (Connecticut is an exception to this). Upstream 21 actually requires its directors to consider stakeholder interests.

Would such a structure be advisable under the law of a state that does not have a constituency statute, such as Delaware or California? In states without a constituency statute, many attorneys would advise clients against provisions that require consideration of interests of stakeholders like the environment, the economy, and the community. Such provisions arguably conflict with state law requiring, at least in a sale situation, that directors maximize shareholder profit.[23] However, the complicated structure of shares and voting rights would likely be permissible in any state.

Some attorneys would argue that as long as the provisions requiring directors to consider stakeholders other than shareholders were in the corporate charter before investors bought shares, shareholders would not have a valid cause of action even in a non-constituency statute state if directors failed to maximize shareholder profit. As one law professor put it, "Because shareholders would have bought their shares with the provision already in place, the price they paid for those shares would reflect any appropriate discount for that provision."[24]

Other Protections

Examples of other ways that corporations can be structured to protect their social or environmental mission include

- Bylaw or charter provisions that require one or more board members to have expertise in certain subject areas such as environmental conservation or corporate social responsibility;
- Bylaw or charter provisions that require the board to report on the company's performance in areas such as employee satisfaction and resource efficiency;
- Bylaw or charter provisions that require the company to maintain certain certifications or ratings with independent standards organizations such as the Global Impact Investing Rating System;
- Bylaw or charter provisions that require the company to buy only fair trade sourced inputs;
- Bylaw or charter provisions (or a separate buy/sell agreement) that prevent shareholders from transferring shares to third parties, that limit the return the shareholder gets from redeeming the stock with the corporation, and/or that give other shareholders the right of first refusal to buy the shares at a fixed price. This creates disincentives for shareholders to sell their shares at a profit.

---

23. Of course a corporation could always choose to form under one of the new statutes discussed below, which explicitly authorize consideration of stakeholders.

24. Elhauge, *supra* note 3, at 860.

Note that bylaws and articles can always be amended. When including such provisions in these documents, it is important to think carefully about additional provisions that reduce the ease with which these socially responsible commitments can be removed.

B Corporations

There is some confusion as to what it actually means to be a B Corp (as opposed to a Benefit Corporation, discussed below). A B Corp is not a statutory business form. B Lab, a nonprofit organization, gives B Corp certification to qualifying businesses, the same way that Fair Trade USA certifies Fair Trade coffee or USGBC certifies LEED buildings. There are more than 558 B Corps as of July 2012. Although the term implies that only a corporation can be a B Corp, a sole proprietorship, partnership, LLC, cooperative, or any other type of business can be a B Corp.

A business can apply for B Corp certification by completing a questionnaire about its business practices related to the environment, public service, community support, treatment of employees, diversity, etc. If the business earns sufficient points on the questionnaire, it is then eligible to become a B Corp. With the exception discussed in the next paragraph, a business must then add the following B Corp language to its organizational documents:

> In discharging his or her duties, and in determining what is in the best interests of the Company and its shareholders, a Director shall consider such factors as the Director deems relevant, including, but not limited to, the long-term prospects and interests of the Company and its shareholders, and the social, economic, legal, or other effects of any action on the current and retired employees, the suppliers and customers of the Company or its subsidiaries, and the communities and society in which the Company or its subsidiaries operate, (collectively, with the shareholders, the **"Stakeholders"**), together with the short-term, as well as long-term, interests of its shareholders and the effect of the Company's operations (and its subsidiaries' operations) on the environment and the economy of the state, the region and the nation.
>
> Nothing in this Article express or implied, is intended to create or shall create or grant any right in or for any person or any cause of action by or for any person.
>
> Notwithstanding the foregoing, any Director is entitled to rely upon the definition of "best interests" as set forth above in enforcing his or her rights hereunder and under state law, and such reliance shall not, absent another breach, be construed as a breach of a Director's fiduciary duty of care, even in the context of a Change in Control

> Transaction where, as a result of weighing other Stakeholders' interests, a Director determines to accept an offer, between two competing offers, with a lower price per share.[25]

B Lab, the nonprofit that created the B Corp certification, recognizes that adopting this language could be risky for a corporation organized in one of the approximately 20 states that do not have constituency statutes (as discussed in Part 2 of this chapter). Therefore, a corporation incorporated in one of those states is not required to add this language to its charter to become a B Corp. Instead, the corporation must sign an agreement that includes the following pledge:

> To the extent possible within the corporate law of the Company's state of incorporation, the Company shall consider the impact of its decisions not only on shareholders, but also on its employees, customers, suppliers, community, and the environment; and
>
> The Company will support B Lab's public policy objectives of passing legislation to create a new corporate form with higher standards of corporate purpose, accountability, and transparency, as well as incentives for certified sustainable businesses.[26]

A B Corp that is not a corporation, such as an LLC, can incorporate B Corp language into its founding documents (such as an operating agreement) regardless of what state it was formed in. B Corps must also pay an annual fee to B Lab.

LLC Modifications

LLCs are known for their flexibility. LLC operating agreements can include creative provisions regarding voting rights and profit sharing. While standard provisions confer voting rights and profit distributions based on percentage ownership, these can be altered if the founders so choose.

Many organizations that are committed to the values of a sharing economy have used the LLC structure as their entity of choice. For

25. Certified B Corporation, The Legal Requirement, http://www.bcorporation.net/become/legal.

26. Certified B Corporation, Term Sheet for Class of 2010 B Corporations: Corporations in States That Do *Not* Have Constituency Statutes (2010), http://www.bcorporation.net/resources/bcorp/documents/2010_Term_Sheet_Non-Constituency1.pdf.

example, Women's Action to Gain Economic Security, a nonprofit organization that helps low-income people organize and operate cooperatively structured businesses, uses the LLC form to set up the businesses it helps to launch. These businesses are identical in many respects to cooperatives. However, in some states, such as California, they may not use the word "cooperative" in their names because they are not formed under that state's cooperative statute.

Part 4: New Types of For-Profit Entities

In response to many shortcomings of traditional entities, activists have worked to create new entities specifically designed for enterprises that fall within that gray area between purely profit-driven businesses and purely charitable non-commercial organizations.

Converting from a traditional entity to one of these new kinds of entities is relatively simple, especially in the case of an LLC converting to a low-profit limited liability company (L3C) or a corporation converting to a benefit corporation or flexible purpose corporation. This can usually be accomplished with a members' or shareholders' vote and an amendment to the entity's charter.

Low-Profit Limited Liability Company (L3C)

To understand L3Cs, it is necessary to understand Program-Related Investments. Foundations are required to distribute 5 percent of the value of their net assets for charitable purposes each year. To meet this requirement, foundations primarily make grants to charitable organizations. However, foundations are also permitted, under the Internal Revenue Code, to invest this 5 percent of net assets in for-profit entities if the investment meets a three-pronged test:

- The investment is primarily for charitable or educational purposes;
- The production of income or the appreciation of property is not a significant purpose for the investment; and
- Attempting to influence legislation or taking part in political campaigns on behalf of candidates is not a purpose.[27]

27. I.R.C. § 4944(c), Treas. Reg. § 53.4944-3.

The investment (called a Program-Related Investment or PRI) may produce significant income or capital appreciation so long as the production of income or the appreciation of property is not a significant purpose. PRIs are relatively uncommon because foundations are unwilling to risk having the IRS determine that the investment does not in fact meet the statutory requirements, and thus be exposed to tax liability or risk losing its tax-exempt status.

L3Cs were created in response to this problem. L3C statutes contain language that requires entities formed under the statute to meet the three requirements of a PRI. In all other respects, an L3C is identical to an LLC. For example, Vermont's L3C statute provides:

> "L3C" or "Low-profit limited liability company" means a person organized under this chapter that is organized for a business purpose that satisfies and is at all times operated to satisfy each of the following requirements.
>
> (A) The Company (i) significantly furthers the accomplishment of one or more charitable or educational purposes within the meaning of Section 170(c)(2)(B) of the IRS Code of 1986, 26 U.S.C. Section 170 (c)(2)(B); and (ii) would not have been formed but for the company's relationship to the accomplishment of charitable or educational purposes.
>
> (B) No significant purpose of the company is the production of income or the appreciation of property; provided, however, that the fact that a person produces significant income or capital appreciation shall not, in the absence of other factors, be conclusive evidence of a significant purpose involving the production of income or the appreciation of property.
>
> (C) No purpose of the company is to accomplish one or more political or legislative purposes within the meaning of Section 170(c)(2)(D) of the IRS code of 1986, 26 U.S.C. Section 170(c)(2)(D).
>
> (D) If a company that met the definition of this subdivision (27) at its formation at any time ceases to satisfy any one of the requirements, it shall immediately cease to be a low-profit LLC, but by continuing to meet all the other requirements of this chapter, will continue to exist as a limited liability company. The name of the company must be changed to be in conformance with subsection 3005(a).

L3C statutes have been adopted in Illinois, Louisiana, Maine, Michigan, North Carolina, Rhode Island, Utah, Vermont, and Wyoming, and by the Oglala Sioux Tribe and the Crow Indian Nation of

Montana.[28] According to InterSector Partners, L3C, as of July 13, 2012, 596 L3Cs have been formed.[29] Some examples of L3Cs include Urban Worm Girl (worm composting education), Una Bella Vita (vitamin store), and Overflow Coffee Bar.

Because L3Cs are still new, several open questions remain. It is unclear what would happen if an L3C did not comply with the special L3C statutory language. It is also unclear whether the special L3C language will provide enough assurance to foundations to make program related investments in L3Cs. In the meantime, L3Cs can be a useful tool for a for-profit business that wants to demonstrate a strong commitment to charitable and/or educational purposes.

Benefit Corporation[30]

The Benefit Corporation is a new corporate form that has been adopted in several states. B Lab, the nonprofit organization that provides B Corp certification, advocates for its adoption. Maryland became the first state to pass Benefit Corp legislation in April 2010. Vermont followed in May 2010. As of July 2012, California, Hawaii, New Jersey, New York, and Virginia have also adopted legislation. A Benefit Corporation "ha[s] the purpose of creating general public benefit," which is defined as "a material positive impact on society and the environment . . . as measured by a third-party standard, through activities that promote some combination of specific public benefits."[31]

> "Specific public benefit" includes:
> (1) providing low-income or underserved individuals or communities with beneficial products or services;
> (2) promoting economic opportunity for individuals or communities beyond the creation of jobs in the normal course of business;
> (3) preserving the environment;
> (4) improving human health;

28. A list of jurisdictions that have adopted an L3C statute can be found at Americans for Community Development, http://www.americansforcommunitydevelopment.org/laws.php.

29. A list of L3Cs formed in each state can be found at interSector L3C, Latest L3C Tally, http://www.intersectorl3c.com/l3c_tally.html.

30. All quotations in this section are from Benefit Corporation, Model Legislation, http://www.benefitcorp.net/for-attorneys/model-legislation. Note that the details of each state's Benefit Corporation statute may vary.

31. *See id.*

> (5) promoting the arts, sciences or advancement of knowledge;
> (6) increasing the flow of capital to entities with a public benefit purpose; and
> (7) the accomplishment of any other particular benefit for society or the environment.[32]
>
> The articles of a benefit corporation may identify one or more specific public benefits that it is the purpose of the benefit corporation to create . . . . The identification of a specific public benefit under this subsection does not limit the obligation of a benefit corporation to create general public benefit.[33]

The model statute states that pursuing general and specific public benefit is in the best interests of the benefit corporation. This provision is designed to ensure that when the board of directors works to promote public benefit, that it is meeting its fiduciary duty to promote the best interest of the corporation. The statute requires

> [that the board and officers] in considering the best interests of the benefit corporation:
> (1) shall consider the effects of any action upon:
> (i) the shareholders of the benefit corporation;
> (ii) the employees and workforce of the benefit corporation and its subsidiaries and suppliers;
> (iii) the interests of customers as beneficiaries of the general or specific public benefit purposes of the benefit corporation;
> (iv) community and societal considerations, including those of any community in which offices or facilities of the benefit corporation or its subsidiaries or suppliers are located;
> (v) the local and global environment; and
> (vi) the short-term and long-term interests of the benefit corporation, including benefits that may accrue to the benefit corporation from its long-term plans and the possibility that these interests may be best served by the continued independence of the benefit corporation;
> (2) may consider:
> (i) the resources, intent and conduct (past, stated and potential) of any person seeking to acquire control of the corporation; and
> (ii) any other pertinent factors or the interests of any other group that they deem appropriate; and

---

32. *Id.*
33. *Id.*

> (3) shall not be required to give priority to the interests of any particular person or group referred to in paragraphs (1) and (2) over the interests of any other person or group unless the benefit corporation has stated its intention to give priority to interests related to a specific public benefit purpose identified in its articles."

The statute provides, in effect, that consideration of these factors will not result in liability under the *Revlon* or *Unocal* tests (discussed above).

The statute requires the board of a benefit corporation to have a "benefit director" that is independent (i.e., not an employee, shareholder, etc.). The benefit director is required to

> prepare . . . a statement whether, in the opinion of the benefit director, the benefit corporation acted in accordance with its general, and any specific, public benefit purpose in all material respects during the period covered by the report and whether the directors and officers complied with [the provisions] . . . relating to standard of conduct for directors . . . and . . . relating to standard of conduct for officers . . . . If in the opinion of the benefit director the benefit corporation or its directors or officers failed so to act, then the statement of the benefit director shall include a description of the ways in which the benefit corporation or its directors or officers failed so to act.

The duties of directors and officers under the statute and the general and any specific public benefit purpose of a benefit corporation may be enforced in a "benefit enforcement proceeding." This is

> a claim or action brought directly by a benefit corporation, or derivatively on behalf of a benefit corporation, against a director or officer for:
>
> > (1) failure to pursue the general public benefit purpose of the benefit corporation or any specific public benefit purpose set forth in its articles; or
> >
> > (2) violation of a duty or standard of conduct under [the benefit corporation statute].

Other than a benefit enforcement proceeding, the statute prohibits any person from bringing an action against a benefit corporation or its directors or officers regarding their duties under the statute or the general and any specific public benefit purpose.

A benefit corporation must deliver to each shareholder and post on its website an annual benefit report describing the ways in which the benefit corporation pursued public benefit and various other matters. Achievement of public benefit must be measured against a "third party standard."[34] According to the drafters of the legislation, "the requirement . . . that a benefit corporation prepare an annual benefit report that assesses its performance in creating general public benefit against a third-party standard provides an important protection against the abuse of benefit corporation status."

---

34. A recognized standard for defining, reporting and assessing corporate social and environmental performance that is:

- (1) Comprehensive in that it assesses the effect of the business and its operations upon the interests listed in [the statute].
- (2) Developed by an organization that is independent of the benefit corporation and satisfies the following requirements:
  - (i) Not more than one-third of the members of the governing body of the organization are representatives of any of the following:
    - (A) An association of businesses operating in a specific industry the performance of whose members is measured by the standard.
    - (B) Businesses from a specific industry or an association of businesses in that industry.
    - (C) Business whose performance is assessed against the standard.
  - (ii) The organization is not materially financed by an association or business described in subparagraph (i).
- (3) Credible because the standard is developed by a person that both:
  - (i) Has access to necessary expertise to assess overall corporate social and environmental performance.
  - (ii) Uses a balanced multi-stakeholder approach, including a public comment period of at least 30 days to develop the standard.
- (4) Transparent because the following information is publicly available:
  - (i) About the standard:
    - (A) The criteria considered when measuring the overall social and environmental performance of a business.
    - (B) The relative weightings of those criteria.
  - (ii) About the development and revision of the standard:
    - (A) The identity of the directors, officers, material owners and the governing body of the organization that developed and controls revisions to the standard.
    - (B) The process by which revisions to the standard and changes to the membership of the governing body are made.
    - (C) An accounting of the sources of financial support for the organization, with sufficient detail to disclose any relationships that could reasonably be considered to present a potential conflict of interest.

Flexible Purpose Corporation in California

In addition to the California Benefit Corporation statute, California has also adopted a Flexible Purpose Corporation statute, both of which were signed into law by the governor on the same day. After California Governor Schwarzenegger vetoed a constituency statute in 2008, a group of lawyers and advocates for socially responsible business got together to design a new corporate form, called, at the time, the H Corporation.

The working group spent about 18 months soliciting input from various stakeholders on the legislation. Eventually, they decided to name the new form the Flexible Purpose Corporation.

The ideas behind the California Benefit Corporation and Flexible Purpose Corporation statutes are similar, though the details differ. The founders of a flexible purpose corporation select (and identify in the articles) one or more special purposes from a list in the statute:

> (A) One or more charitable or public purpose activities that a non-profit public benefit corporation is authorized to carry out.
> (B) The purpose of promoting positive short-term or long-term effects of, or minimizing adverse short-term or long-term effects of, the flexible purpose corporation's activities upon any of the following:
>> (i) The flexible purpose corporation's employees, suppliers, customers, and creditors.
>> (ii) The community and society.
>> (iii) The environment.

Flexible purpose corporate directors must send annual reports to shareholders concerning the corporation's activities relating to its special purposes, but are not required to measure achievement of public benefit against a standard developed by third parties.

PART 5: COOPERATIVES

Cooperatives are, in one sense, a traditional entity form. They have been around for a long time. The first documented cooperatives were founded in the 18th century. However, cooperatives are not included in the section on traditional forms for two reasons: (1) cooperative statutes are very rarely used compared to standard corporations, LLCs, and nonprofits, and (2) unlike those three traditional structures, cooperatives can be very well suited to activities in the sharing economy.

ENABLING FOR-PROFIT CORPORATIONS TO SEEK SOCIAL GOOD

By Brian Howe, Vox Legal[1]

Washington State residents pride ourselves on being a "little different," and that holds true even for our corporate lawyers. So it's no surprise that when a Washington State Bar Association Committee began to study "Benefit Corporation" statutes enacted in other states, the 13-member Committee came up with a slightly different structure—the aptly named Social Purpose Corporation (SPC). Like many similarly envisioned structures, the vision behind the legislation is to enable businesses to boldly seek social or environmental impact alongside the primary objective of creating economic value.[2]

Traditional corporations are expected to prioritize the creation of shareholder profits above other considerations, such as employee benefits, environmental care, or community impact. By establishing Social Purpose Corporations, Washington State is signaling that companies should have the flexibility to make decisions based on the effects the company has on *all* stakeholders—that is, any person or entity affected by the corporation's decisions. Because the legislation[3] is permissive not proscriptive, SPCs are required to create general social benefit but are not told what that has to be or how to achieve it.[4]

---

1. Brian Howe is the founder of the law firm Vox Legal, PLLC, counsel with Apex Law Group, and an adjunct professor at Seattle University School of Law. Vox Legal, PLLC is the only certified B Corp law firm in Washington State and limits its practice to providing outside general counsel to other social enterprises. Reach Brian at bhowe@voxlegal.com.

2. Washington State Governor Christine Gregoire signed H.B. 2239 on March 30, 2012. On June 7, 2012, the State will begin to recognize Social Purpose Corporations.

3. H.B. 2239, 62d Legis., § 3 (proposed Jan. 10, 2012) (to amend Wash. Rev. Code §§ 23B.01.400, 23B.04.010).

4. Note that California's Flexible Purpose Corporation legislation requires a corporation either be dedicated to "charitable" activities such as would qualify a nonprofit public benefit corporation *or* be dedicated to the purpose of considering (1) employees, suppliers, customers, and creditors; (2) community and society; or (3) the environment. This second option is largely similar to the SPC's general purpose requirement except that the FPC includes creditors as a stakeholder group that may be considered, and the FPC permits "community and societal considerations," whereas the SPC would specify that such community/society considerations may be local, state, national, or global in scale.

SPCs have the additional flexibility to name a specific benefit, should the founders or initial shareholders desire to hold themselves to a higher standard.[5] Articulating a specific social purpose in conjunction with a general social purpose enables founders to ensure that future decisions of the corporation are in line with the founders' specific vision and not merely in line with the broad strokes of the general purpose requirement. For instance, founders of a local restaurant could conceivably structure as a social purpose corporation by naming the general purpose of promoting the long-term welfare of their employees and the specific purpose of primarily employing homeless and disadvantaged persons.

A third important aspect of the SPC, in addition to the general social purpose requirement and specific purpose option, is that, once established in the articles of incorporation, social purposes of the SPC may only be altered, amended, or eliminated by a two-thirds majority of the shareholders.[6] This requirement is intended to anchor the social purpose through sale, merger, or incorporation of the SPC. This will make it more difficult for investors to shift companies away from the original beneficial goals of the founders.

Supporters of the nonprofit B Labs, the entity behind the highly popular Benefit Corporation legislation (adopted in CA, HI, MD, NJ, NY, VT, and VA; learn more at benefitcorp.net), view the SPC as lacking teeth. Although an SPC is required to publish a report on its efforts to promote a social or environmental purpose or purposes,[7] the report is *not* required to meet third-party standards unless the company opts into that requirement. This differs from a Benefit Corporation, where outside review and approval is necessary to maintain its special designation. Further, under the proposed SPC statutes, directors and officers of a company are permitted—but not required—to consider one or more of the social purposes in making decisions.[8] This is unlike Benefit Corporations, which are mandated to consider the impact of their decisions

5. H.B. 2239, § 4 (proposed Jan. 10, 2012).
6. *Id.* § 10.
7. *Id.* § 16.
8. *Id.* § 6(2).

on stakeholders. Finally, whereas Benefit Corporation legislation allows shareholders to sue a company for failing to achieve a material positive impact on society and the environment (called a "benefit enforcement proceeding"), the proposed SPC legislation makes clear that directors are *not* liable for any "action taken as a director, or any failure to take any action" regarding achieving social purposes.[9]

Opinions vary on whether the Flexible/Social Purpose Corporation or the Benefit Corporation will result in greater good. Although a supporter of both forms of legislation as helpful experimentation, California attorney Todd Johnson believes that "The 'benefit corporation' form seeks to create accountability (beyond reporting) through a system of greater liability, whereas the 'flexible purpose corporation' [and the social purpose corporation] seeks to unleash directors from the risk of liability, permitting them to experiment more broadly with the right mix of doing well and doing good, without concerns of personal or corporate suits."[10] From the Benefit Corporation standpoint, Jay Coen Gilbert, co-founder of AND 1 and B Lab, responds that threat of litigation is "accountability to shareholders [...] not only to make them money, but to do so in a manner that creates a material positive impact on society and the environment [...] This doesn't seem very much to ask."[11]

The flexibility of a Social Purpose Corporation may reduce fears of conflict over future business plans while providing SPCs with greater access to capital markets. But while the possibility exists for founders to secure designated social purposes, there are few tangible requirements in the statute to give effect to that purpose. As our economy rebounds and we look for ways to promote companies that value long-term growth, sustainability, and positive value for all stakeholders, the Social Purpose Corporation could be

9. *Id.* § 6(4).

10. Todd Johnson, *The Benefit Corporation: A Step in the Right Direction, But...*, Bus. for Good (June 12, 2010), http://businessforgood.blogspot.com/2010/06/benefit-corporation-step-in-right.html.

11. Jay Coen Gilbert, comment posting to Johnson, *id.*, July 7, 2010. It is a live question as to whether a company that forms or converts to SPC status would be able to receive B Corp Certification. While founders of an SPC may elect to mandatory stakeholder consideration, the legislation specifically disclaims the expansion of a director's fiduciary duty (such as being subject to a benefit enforcement proceeding).

a powerful vehicle for Washington-based companies, but the Benefit Corporation should not be overlooked as an additional vehicle for the common good.

INTERNATIONAL COMPARISON: SOCIAL ENTERPRISE IN FRANCE AND THE LEGAL STRUCTURES THAT SUPPORT THEM

By Clementine Blazy, Senior Investment Officer at France Active-SIFA

The Mouvement des Entrepreneurs Sociaux[1] defines a social enterprise as an enterprise with a social or societal purpose, limited profit (reinvested profits, limited return on equity, regulated pay scale), and involvement of stakeholders in governance.

French social enterprises come in many legal forms, nonprofit, for-profit, cooperative, and hybrid (a nonprofit holding for-profit subsidiaries being the most common hybrid model).

France has a variety of cooperative statutes including Union d'Economie Sociale, Societe Coopérative Ouvrière de Production, Mutuelles, Coopératives d'Activités et d'Emplois, and Société Coopérative d'Intérêt Collectif. The Société Coopérative d'Intérêt Collectif (SCIC) was created recently to facilitate equity funding of cooperatives by local government. The SCIC has three classes of members: employees, community, and other stakeholders. Local governments participate by joining the "other stakeholder" category and may then provide equity to these businesses (up to 20 percent). SCICs have been formed in sectors such as environmental conservation, local green energy production, and mobility solutions. There are currently approximately 190 SCICs in France.

1. Mouvement des Entrepreneurs Sociaux, formed in February 2010, is dedicated to building, representing, and advocating for the social enterprises field. Together with le labo de l'ESS (the lab for a social and cooperative economy), it aims to improve the visibility, the cohesion and the development of this sector. The labo de l'ESS organizes the Etats Généraux de l'Economie Sociale et Solidaire, which in June 2011 assembled 5,000 attendees for its first convening.

Nonprofit social enterprises form under the Association Law of 1901. Nonprofits may not have distribution of profits as their purpose but they may earn revenues from commercial activities. As long as these revenues stay below €60,000 or are not a significant proportion of total earned income, these entities are exempt from tax on sales and net income. Many social enterprises simply adopt a regular for-profit status such as Société à Responsabilité Limitée or Société Anonyme.

As in the United States, social enterprises often create hybrids of the various possible structures. Typically, a nonprofit creates a wholly owned for-profit subsidiary to conduct commercial activities that support its mission.

Entreprise Solidaire

In France, a social enterprise can enter into a state-regulated agreement called an "agrément entreprise solidaire."[2] This is basically a two-year accreditation in which the social enterprise agrees to the following:

- 30 percent of its employees are people facing severe barriers to employment (lack of education, poverty, long term unemployment, disability) and they are hired with specific conditions, that is mostly fixed-term contracts, with expected social outcomes partly state-financed;[3] or
- Its governing body is elected by its employees/its stakeholders/its members, and the pay scale caps the highest wages at eight times the minimum wage.

Once accredited, the "enterprise solidaire" gets access to dedicated financial resources, from a pool of "solidarity savings" currently totaling €3.1 billion. These funds come from employee

2. Labour code, art. L3332-17-1 (2001).

3. Enterprises whose mission is to facilitate the employment of disadvantaged people are called *entreprise d'insertion* (workforce development enterprise/transitional jobs enterprise), *chantier d'insertion* (transitional jobs program for individuals with more significant barriers to employment), or *entreprise adaptée* (enterprises committed to employ people with mental or physical disabilities), depending on the nature of the barrier to employment their employees face. These enterprises compete with mainstream businesses but receive government funding. The activities of these businesses are regulated under the *loi d'orientation relative à la lutte contre les exclusions* (law to combat social exclusion), which was adopted in 1998.

savings plans and retirement plans of French employees. French employers are required to offer at least one "solidarity mutual fund" option for these plans. Thanks to the incentives created under French law, investments in solidarity mutual funds have skyrocketed in recent years. At least five, and up to ten, percent of these funds must be invested in accredited "entreprises solidaires."

Tax Incentives for Direct Investment in Social Enterprise

The loi en faveur du travail de l'emploi et du pouvoir d'achat (law to promote employment and purchasing power) adopted in 2008 provides a 75 percent tax deduction for investments in social enterprises with a five-year holding period. This has resulted in one pioneer private equity fund and many high net worth individuals investing in social enterprises.

What Is a Cooperative?

The definition of cooperative varies depending on whether you are looking at it from the perspective of a cooperative enthusiast, a corporate lawyer, or a tax lawyer. A cooperative enthusiast would probably say that ANY organization that is committed to and practices cooperative principles is a cooperative. However, a corporate lawyer would probably say that a cooperative must be formed under a cooperative statute. And a tax lawyer would say it doesn't matter what statute it's formed under as long as it "operates cooperatively" as that term is defined in tax law.

What are the basic (non-legal) cooperative principles? According to the International Cooperative Alliance, they are:

1. **Voluntary and open membership:** Cooperatives are voluntary organizations, open to all persons able to use their services and willing to accept the responsibilities of membership, without gender, social, racial, political, or religious discrimination.
2. **Democratic member control:** Cooperatives are democratic organizations controlled by their members, who actively participate in setting their policies and making decisions. Men and women serving as elected representatives are accountable to the membership. In primary cooperatives, members have equal voting rights

(one member, one vote), and cooperatives at other levels are also organized in a democratic manner.

3. **Member economic participation:** Members contribute equitably to, and democratically control, the capital of their cooperative. At least part of that capital is usually the common property of the cooperative. Members usually receive limited compensation, if any, on capital subscribed as a condition of membership. Members allocate surpluses for any or all of the following purposes: developing their cooperative, possibly by setting up reserves, part of which at least would be indivisible; benefiting members in proportion to their transactions with the cooperative; and supporting other activities approved by the membership.
4. **Autonomy and independence:** Cooperatives are autonomous, self-help organizations controlled by their members. If they enter into agreements with other organizations, including governments, or raise capital from external sources, they do so on terms that ensure democratic control by their members and maintain their cooperative autonomy.
5. **Education, training, and information:** Cooperatives provide education and training for their members, elected representatives, managers, and employees so they can contribute effectively to the development of their cooperatives. They inform the general public—particularly young people and opinion leaders—about the nature and benefits of co-operation.
6. **Co-operation among cooperatives:** Cooperatives serve their members most effectively and strengthen the cooperative movement by working together through local, national, regional, and international structures.
7. **Concern for community:** Cooperatives work for the sustainable development of their communities through policies approved by their members.[35]

It is clear that an organization may be formed under almost any kind of a state statute and still follow these principles. However, most states have one or more statutes specifically designed for cooperatives.

35. Available at the International Cooperative Alliance website: http://www.ica.coop/coop/principles.html.

In many states, an organization that is not formed under a cooperative statute may not use the word cooperative in its name.

From a tax law perspective, cooperatives are entitled to various beneficial tax treatments (under Subchapter T for regular cooperatives, Section 521 for agricultural cooperatives, and Section 501(c)(12) for tax-exempt cooperatives). To be eligible for these, it does not matter if the entity is formed under a particular statute but rather whether it meets the tax law definition of "operating on a cooperative basis."

The Internal Revenue Code and Regulations do not define what it means to "operate on a cooperative basis." This has been tested by the courts. The leading case is *Puget Sound Plywood v. Commissioner*,[36] in which the court said that "operating on a cooperative basis" means (1) democratic control by the members, (2) operation at cost, and (3) subordination of capital. "Democratic control" means that a cooperative is governed by its members on a one-member-one-vote basis. "Operation at cost" means that any money left over (beyond a reasonable reserve) after expenses are paid is returned back to the members. "Subordination of capital" means that returns to investors must be limited.

Cooperative Nuts and Bolts

Members and Patrons

The users of the services that the cooperative offers are known as "patrons." Cooperatives can be formed for many different purposes and by many different types of patrons. Cooperatives are formed by consumers, producers, workers, and sometimes by a combination of those groups. "Patronage" is the term that describes how the patrons use the cooperative. So, for example, the patronage of a consumer cooperative is the purchase of goods from the cooperative; patronage of a producer cooperative is the transfer of goods to the cooperative to be marketed by the cooperative; patronage of a worker cooperative is the work performed for the cooperative. There is a great deal of flexibility for cooperatives to define patronage and how it is measured. For example, one worker cooperative might define patronage as the number of hours worked in a fiscal year, whereas another might define patronage as the amount of money earned by a worker in a fiscal year.

---

36. *Puget Sound Plywood v. Commissioner*, 44 T.C. 305, 307–308 (1965).

EQUAL EXCHANGE'S RADICAL APPROACH TO CORPORATE SOCIAL RESPONSIBILITY

By Daniel Fireside, Capital Coordinator at Equal Exchange

Equal Exchange is about more than just changing the way people buy and sell what goes in their shopping basket. For more than 25 years, Equal Exchange has been turning a host of conventional business models and practices on their heads: entrusting complete control and ownership of the company to the people that work there, educating and engaging consumers, and supporting producers with credit, training, and above-market prices. And it's been working pretty well: over $40 million in annual sales, steady profits, growing product lines, and fanatically loyal customers and partners.

Long before Equal Exchange sold our first pound of coffee in 1986, the company's founders, Jonathan Rosenthal, Michael Rozyne, and our current co-president, Rink Dickinson, made decisions that continue to shape the nature of our company today. Should they incorporate as a nonprofit organization or a for-profit company? That's a question every social entrepreneur faces at the start. Jonathan, Michael, and Rink, having come from the world of cooperative groceries, chose a third path—they went co-op. For even the most progressive social enterprises, this remains a path rarely taken or even considered. Who wants to put in the crazy work of launching a start-up if you know that you'll be sharing ownership with everyone that works there? Yet they did, and today, we have over 100 "worker-owners" (as we call ourselves).

How do co-ops differ? For starters, by establishing an internal sense of fairness. For example, the average compensation range between the CEO and average paid workers in S&P 500 companies was 263-to-1 in 2009, the year that the federal government temporarily capped some executive pay as part of the TARP bill. At the height of the tech bubble, it was more than 500-to-1. At Equal Exchange, it's about 2-to-1. And the top-to-bottom ratio is by rule capped at 4-to-1. There are no executive perks or bonuses to offset this egalitarian arrangement. In fact, because the generous benefit package and profits are distributed equally across the cooperative, the real range in compensation is even flatter. And you'll find Rink on the kitchen-cleanup rotation just like every other worker-owner here.

When we say that the workers are the owners, we aren't talking about an Employee Stock Ownership Program (ESOP), or rank-and-file owning a few shares, or even token representation on the Board. We're talking one person, one share, one vote. The newest warehouse worker-owner has the same single share as the president. Every worker-owner gets an equal vote in co-op meetings. Only worker-owners are allowed to nominate and elect the nine members of our Board of Directors. Six of the seats are also reserved for worker-owners, with the remaining three reserved for outsiders. This employee-elected and employee-dominated Board hires and fires the executive directors, and approves budgets, major investments, and the like. Additionally, the entire worker-owner body meets regularly to vote on accepting new members, adopt changes to the company bylaws, and enact major policy decisions. The CEO and company managers run the day-to-day business, but they are ultimately held accountable to the people that work at the company.

When you give people shared, meaningful ownership, living wages and top-notch benefits, excellent products to market, sell, and distribute, enthusiastic suppliers and customers, plus weekly chocolate tastings—it makes for a loyal and motivated workforce. But if you also give everyone a vote in running the company, how do you ensure they will stay true to the company's founding mission? Our most surprising tool might strike some outsiders as a perk: every worker-owner has to visit a farming cooperative in their first two years here—paid for by the company. As an employee there's no way you can look at (or roast, pack, or invoice) our coffee the same way after you've spent time working and living alongside a coffee farmer in rural Nicaragua or Peru.

Ultimately, it's probably more helpful to think of the employee's ownership of Equal Exchange as a trusteeship. The worker-owners, the people that know Equal Exchange and its mission best, essentially hold the enterprise in trust for all its stakeholders, including future generations of farmers, workers, consumers, investors, and the Earth itself.

For social enterprises to claim the mantle of being socially responsible, you've got to do more than make a great product or treat your workers with respect. To make profound changes to the economy, you've also got to change the way you think of ownership, investment, and power.

It may be possible to put in these kinds of limits after a company is established and doing well, but it's like putting toothpaste back into the tube, and we've never heard of it being done. Many people would find it hard to give up power, control, or the potential for large financial gain once they have it. On the other hand, if you have the rules in place beforehand, everyone that comes to your business—investors, workers, suppliers, vendors—will have a shared set of expectations. And the people who are in it mainly for the money won't want to work or invest there in the first place. Rather than feeling like limits, these kinds of ground rules have been liberating. They free us to pursue our mission.

We don't claim to have figured out all the answers or discovered the only path forward. But we do believe that our example of success has helped create a new space for social entrepreneurs to create a truly different way of doing business.

Bread cooperative example: Here's an example to help explain what patronage is in different types of cooperatives. The phrase "bread cooperative" can mean many different things, depending on the relationship between the members and the cooperative. It can be

- **A consumer cooperative:** The member/owners are people who enjoy eating bread and have formed a cooperative to purchase bread collectively and obtain bulk discounts. A member's patronage is measured by how much bread he/she *buys from* the cooperative.
- **A producer cooperative:** The member/owners are individual home bread bakers who have formed a cooperative to jointly market their breads. The cooperative may, for example, operate stands at various farmers markets. A member's patronage is measured by how much bread he/she *sells to* the cooperative.
- **A worker cooperative:** The member/owners are workers in a single bakery. A member's patronage is measured by how much

❖❖❖❖

Helpful Resources and Additional Readings About Cooperatives

Although cooperatives have been around for a long time, there are few comprehensive legal resources about cooperatives. To learn more about the legal and business aspects of cooperatives, here are a few of the best resources:

- Charles T. Autry and Roland F. Hall, *The Law of Cooperatives* (American Bar Association 2009).
- Van P. Baldwin, *A Legal Sourcebook for California Cooperatives: Startup and Administration* (University of California-Davis Division of Agriculture and Natural Resources, Center for Cooperatives 2004), available at http://sfp.ucdavis.edu/cooperatives/reports/vanbaldwin/complete.pdf.
- United States Department of Agriculture Rural Development Library, available at http://www.rurdev.usda.gov/rbs/pub/NEWPUB.htm.
- California Center for Cooperative Development, available at http://cccd.coop.
- Ohio Cooperative Development Center, available at http://ocdc.osu.edu/.
- University of Wisconsin-Madison Center for Cooperatives, available at http://www.uwcc.wisc.edu/.

time he/she spends working for the cooperative or by the value of the work he/she contributes to the cooperative.

Not all of the cooperative's patrons are necessarily members. For example, REI, the cooperative recreational equipment retailer, is open to the public and anyone who shops there is a patron, but only some people who shop there are members. Generally, it is up to the cooperative members and/or board to decide which patrons will be admitted as members. Cooperative members get various benefits such as the right to share in excess revenues, discounts on products, invitations to member-only events, etc. The exact benefits of membership are generally up to the cooperative to decide. For example, most cooperatives distribute any excess revenues to their members at the end of a fiscal year. However, some cooperatives (mostly food cooperatives with hundreds or thousands of members) have decided that it would be too onerous to make cash distributions and therefore choose to provide other benefits such as product discounts.[37]

---

37. The National Cooperative Grocers Association (http://www.ncga.coop) is a great resource for cooperative grocery stores.

Governance

Generally, the co-op members elect a board of directors that has ultimate responsibility for governance. Elections happen regularly and each member has one vote. In some smaller cooperatives, the members may choose to have all of the members serve on the board. This model is sometimes referred to as a collective. Day-to-day decisions are generally made by staff; bigger decisions are made by the board; and major decisions such as bylaw amendments generally must be voted on by the members.

Contributions of Capital by the Members

When members join a co-op, they usually make an initial capital contribution and/or pay a fee. A fee is usually non-refundable, whereas a capital contribution (sometimes called a buy-in) becomes the member's capital in the cooperative. Not all cooperatives require a contribution to capital by members.

When members make a capital contribution, this amount of money becomes the starting balance in the member's capital account. The capital account is not literally a separate bank account, but it is accounted for separately on the books of the co-op. The members' capital accounts make up all or a part of the equity of the co-op. The co-op has rules about how and when the members can get the contents of their capital accounts back out of the co-op. Usually, a member does not get his or her capital back until he or she leaves the co-op. Often when the member leaves the co-op, the balance in the capital account converts to a loan from the departing member to the co-op, which the co-op then pays back over time.

Distribution of Surplus to the Members

At the end of each accounting period (usually the fiscal year), the cooperative's accountant determines whether there is any surplus (money left over after expenses). If there is any surplus, the board must decide what to do with it. The options are to (1) keep the money in reserve to cover unforeseen expenses or invest back into the business; (2) distribute the surplus to the members; or (3) do some combination of options 1 and 2.

Unlike in a regular corporation, the surplus is distributed not based on ownership interest but on patronage. So, for example, in a producer cooperative, if one member delivered 30 pounds of broccoli to be marketed through the cooperative and another member delivered 10 pounds of broccoli during the same period, the first member would receive three times as much of the surplus as the second member.

If some of the patronage is sourced from non-members, the cooperative will have to calculate what percentage of its total revenue is attributable to member patronage. Only surplus attributable to member patronage may be distributed to members if the cooperative wants to get the tax benefits related to patronage distributions (discussed below).

The co-op can choose to pay the entire patronage dividend in cash, or it may simply allocate all or a portion of the dividend to the members' capital accounts using a Written Notice of Allocation (WNA), which is defined in Subchapter T of the Internal Revenue Code.

The use of WNAs allows the co-op to retain more cash within the co-op. The co-op sets policy as to when members may withdraw these funds as cash from their accounts. One common practice is to redeem WNAs on a rolling basis to prevent long-time members from accumulating very large capital accounts. Some co-ops pay interest on the balance in the member capital accounts to prevent members from becoming frustrated by having capital accounts tied up in the cooperative without any financial return.

Tax Treatment

Earnings in a regular corporation are double-taxed—the corporation pays income tax on the net earnings, and then the shareholders pay income tax when they receive dividends on those earnings. In contrast, under Subchapter T of the Internal Revenue Code, a cooperative can avoid some of the traditional corporate double-tax. Assuming the cooperative meets all the requirements set forth in the Code, patronage dividends are generally tax-deductible for the cooperative if at least 20 percent of each patronage dividend is paid out in cash. Of course, the members must pay income tax on the total patronage dividend they receive regardless of whether it is paid in cash or as an allocation in the member's capital account.

Limiting Equity in a Cooperative

Many cooperatives intentionally limit the ways in which members may benefit from equity in a business. In a more conventional business, an owner who sells his/her share back to the company often has a right to be paid market value for that share. By contrast, when members leave a cooperative, they typically receive only what is in their capital account, without regard to the market value of the business. Furthermore, cooperative members are almost always prevented from selling their memberships to third parties.

The dissolution and sale provisions of cooperative bylaws also serve to limit equity of current members. If a worker cooperative starts an ice cream company that becomes wildly successful, it may be somewhat tempting for the worker-owners to sell the business and enjoy a windfall. To prevent the incentive to sell out, some cooperative bylaws require that, if the business is sold or dissolved, the proceeds must be divided among all current *and past* members, on the basis of their patronage. That way, a past member who put in years of service will be rewarded, even if that person is not a member at the time of the sale. Building in disincentives to sell the business helps the cooperative to maintain its purpose of providing livelihoods to its members, and it helps to keep businesses locally based and locally owned.

Furthermore, although there may not be enough precedent in tax court decisions to know this for sure, it is possible that this method of dividing sale proceeds is actually *necessary* to meeting the Subchapter T requirements. It follows that if regular earnings must be distributed on the basis of patronage, then so too must a payout of equity. Presumably, every member who has ever worked for a cooperative business contributed to its success and value and should therefore receive part of that payout.

Co-ops as an Exit Strategy for Retiring Business Owners

Section 1042 of the Internal Revenue Code allows a business owner to defer long-term gain from the sale of his or her business to an ESOP or a worker-owned cooperative. This is done frequently with ESOPs, but ESOPs can be prohibitively expensive to structure. Worker cooperatives, on the other hand, are relatively easy to set up.

The George and Gladys Dunlap Cooperative Leadership Program of the Nationwide Foundation, the Ohio Employee Ownership Center, and the Ohio Council of Cooperatives (now part of the Mid-America Cooperative Council) have developed a practical model for ownership succession in small businesses using the employee cooperative as an ownership structure. More information on the model and how it was used by an Ohio company called Select Machine can be found on the Ohio Employee Ownership Center website.[38]

38. John Logue, Ohio Emp. Ownership Ctr. The 1042 Roll-Over Cooperative in Practice: A Case Study of How Select Machine Became a Co-Op (2006), http://dept.kent.edu/oeoc/OEOClibrary/1042_rollover_co-ops_MN_case_study.htm.

Cooperatives That Are Not Cooperatives

When helping a client to start a cooperative, the first thing an attorney should do is review the cooperative statutes in the relevant state. This is always an interesting exercise because state laws governing cooperatives vary so much. You may find there is no cooperative statute at all, or you may find there are three or four different cooperative statutes for various purposes. For various reasons, you may end up deciding that your client would be better off forming under a non-cooperative statute.

For example, let's say a group of people approach you and they want to form a cooperative to develop software. They will be working on software for a while before they will have any real income. Let's say there is a cooperative statute in your state and, like most cooperative statutes, it defines cooperatives as corporations. As someone who is familiar with employment law, you know that if a group of people form a corporation and work for the corporation, there might be a presumption that these people are employees.[39] This means that the members of the cooperative would have to be paid at least minimum wage from day one, and all other employment law requirements would apply, such as the need to do payroll tax deductions, purchase workers compensation insurance, pay overtime, and so on. In this case you may suggest that your clients form an LLC structured like a cooperative. LLC owners are not generally considered employees[40] and therefore there would have more flexibility with respect to minimum wage, withholding, workers compensation, etc. Of course it would be essential to read Chapter 7 of this book and research these issues in your state before making a recommendation.

Another example: a group of parents come to you wanting to create a cooperative school for their children. It is very important to them that they control the school, and they also want to be able to apply for grant funding because the parents don't think they will charge enough tuition to cover costs. In this case, you may advise your client to form a membership nonprofit and apply for 501(c)(3) tax exemption. The parents would be entitled to elect the board on a one-member, one-vote basis just as they would in a cooperative, but the organization would be

39. However, this presumption may have been weakened by the U.S. Supreme Court in *Clackamas Gastroenterology Assocs., PC v. Wells*, 538 U.S. 440 (2003). This matter is discussed in much greater detail in Chapter 7.

40. Note that this matter is also discussed in greater detail in Chapter 7.

eligible to receive tax-deductible donations and grants that a cooperative would not be.

Some "cooperatives" can also form as nonprofit mutual benefit corporations. This type of entity is used by some cooperative housing groups, cooperative groceries, credit unions, and other consumer cooperatives. The important point is that a group of people that want to form an organization that follows cooperative principles may or may not end up forming an actual statutory cooperative.

Outside Investors and New Generation Cooperative Statutes

The issue of "outside investors" in cooperatives is the subject of a great deal of debate. Cooperatives must serve the interests of their members and must not subordinate member interests to outside investors. Most cooperatives avoid taking investments from non-members to avoid the potential for conflict between those two interests. However, it is becoming increasingly difficult for cooperatives to rely exclusively on member capital and bank loans, since bank loans for cooperatives are very scarce. Capital-intensive cooperatives such as agricultural processors or restaurants may find it impossible to start up and operate without outside capital. Although most cooperative statutes permit outside investors, they do not allow outside investors to have any voting rights, and they cap their returns. This is consistent with the principles laid out in *Puget Sound Plywood*.[41] Unfortunately, it is very difficult to attract outside investors without offering them any voting rights to protect their investment. Some cooperatives, like Organic Valley and Equal Exchange, have successfully sold non-voting preferred stock, but most cooperatives would have a hard time selling an investment like that because most investors would not feel comfortable making a large investment unless they have some right to influence major decisions, at least.

Because of this problem, some states, including Iowa, Minnesota, Tennessee, Wisconsin, and Wyoming, have adopted a statute called the Limited Cooperative Association (also known as a "new generation

---

41. *Puget Sound Plywood*, 44 T.C. 305 (1965).

cooperative").[42] This is a hybrid between a traditional cooperative corporation and an LLC. These statutes allow outside investors to have limited voting rights while still ensuring that members retain control and majority ownership. For example, Wisconsin's Chapter 193 authorizes the formation of Cooperative Associations. Investor-members' voting rights may not exceed 49 percent, but the bylaws may provide such members with the power to veto certain unusual decisions, such as merger or dissolution. In addition, the investors may not receive more than 70 percent of the profit allocations and distributions of the cooperative.

Because these cooperatives essentially are LLCs, they can elect to be taxed under Subchapter K, which has many of the same advantages as Subchapter T. It remains to be seen whether a cooperative that has a significant amount of outside investment and that provides limited voting rights to these investors would be deemed by the IRS as not "operating on a cooperative basis."

Types of Cooperatives and Examples

Producer/Marketing Cooperatives

A marketing cooperative, sometimes known as a producer cooperative, allows its members, who produce the same or similar products, to cooperatively market and sell the products. Producer/marketing cooperatives are most commonly found in the agriculture industry; 30 percent of total agricultural production is marketed by co-ops.[43]

Organic Valley in Wisconsin is a $528 million company owned by the 1,300 organic family farms that produce its milk, cheese, and meat. The company's mission is to save the family farm, which means paying as much as possible to farmers. "We don't have any need for profits much over 2 percent," said CEO George Siemon. "We'd just pay taxes on it. We'd rather give it to the farmers." Even though it is a national brand, the company organizes producers into regional pools, which limits the need to truck products over long distances. A customer buying milk in Boston is buying New England milk. The company capitalizes

42. The National Conference of Commissioners on Uniform State Laws adopted a Uniform Limited Cooperative Association Act that is the model legislation for the new generation cooperative statute.

43. Kelly & Ratner, *supra* note 21.

itself, in part, by selling preferred shares directly to the public, paying a 6 percent return to the investors annually.[44]

In Minnesota, farmers and community members came together to become energy producers by installing wind turbines on their land through the cooperatively owned MinWind. Out of state developers had been flocking to Minnesota to lease farmland for wind farms. The profits generated quickly left the state and landed in shareholders' pockets. MinWind allowed the community to keep wealth local. Owners of the wind turbines include two grocers and a newspaper editor, as well as farmers in the area.[45]

Purchasing Cooperatives

Purchasing cooperatives are made up of groups of businesses that wish to jointly purchase services or supplies. A purchasing cooperative helps its members lower their operating costs and in turn stay competitive with big-box stores on the retail prices for their goods or services. Ace Hardware, for example, is a cooperative of independent hardware stores that pool their buying power to purchase inventory. Another example is CCA Global Partners, one of the largest cooperatives in the United States. CCA Global Partners organizes independent businesses to pool resources for buying, marketing, insurance, and financing in industries including flooring, mortgage banking, lighting, and bicycles.

Consumer Cooperatives

Consumer cooperatives are organized by consumers who want to achieve better prices or quality in the goods or services they purchase. In contrast to traditional retail stores or service providers, a consumer cooperative exists to deliver goods or services rather than to maximize profit from selling those goods or services. Nationally, the most widely used co-op form is the credit union, with some 90 million members. Credit union assets have grown a hundredfold in three decades. Credit unions are essentially cooperatives of people that use banking services.[46]

---

44. *Id.*

45. *Id. See also* Paul Gipe, *MinWind: Farmer-Owned*, Wind-Works.org, 2004, http://www.wind-works.org/articles/minwind.html.

46. Kelly & Ratner, *supra* note 21.

Other common types of consumer cooperatives include grocery stores, energy-buying cooperatives, schools, and health care cooperatives.

Worker Cooperatives

Worker co-ops are the least common type of co-op in the United States, according to the National Cooperative Business Association, which estimates that there are fewer than 300 worker cooperatives in the country. In the more common types of cooperatives—marketing and consumer cooperatives—the patrons are producers, businesses, or consumers. In a worker cooperative, patrons are the worker-members, and its purpose is to provide employment for the members. A major difference between worker cooperatives and other cooperatives is that the members are generally very actively and intimately involved on a day-to-day basis with the business.

Examples of successful worker cooperatives include Equal Exchange, a fair trade importer of coffee, chocolate, and other goods; Arizmendi Bakery, which is actually a group of cooperatively owned bakeries in the San Francisco Bay Area; Rainbow Grocery, the nation's largest worker cooperative retail business; and Evergreen Cooperative Laundry in Cleveland, which was started by a partnership that included the Cleveland Foundation and the Ohio Employee Ownership Center to create opportunities for low-income Cleveland residents.

Multiple Stakeholder Cooperatives

Some cooperatives have multiple classes of members. For example, one food cooperative in Sonoma County, California, has three classes: workers, farmers, and customers. Having several classes of member can make the structuring of the cooperative complicated because it is necessary to determine how surplus and voting rights will be allocated among the classes.

These cooperatives are sometimes called hybrid co-ops or solidarity co-ops. Quebec, Canada, has over 300 solidarity cooperatives. One successful U.S. solidarity co-op is Weaver Street Market in Carrboro, North Carolina, where both consumers and workers are members.[47]

---

47. Coop. Dev. Ctr., Kent State Univ., Solidarity as a Business Model: A Multistakeholder Cooperatives Manual (2011).

ORGANIZING A COOPERATIVE FEDERAL CREDIT UNION

By Mike Leung, Founder of the Worker Cooperative Federal Credit Union

Since 2007, a group of worker cooperative advocates have been working on forming a credit union that would provide financing for worker cooperatives. The proposed Worker Cooperative Federal Credit Union (unchartered) is being organized in collaboration with the U.S. Federation of Worker Cooperatives (USFWC), Network of Bay Area Worker Cooperatives (NoBAWC), and North American Students of Cooperation (NASCO).

Credit unions are consumer cooperatives that provide financial services to their members. Organizing groups can choose between a state or federal charter. For federal credit unions that plan to operate in multiple states, the regulator is the National Credit Union Administration (NCUA), a federal government agency.

Whereas most credit unions are focused on serving individual consumer members, the primary mission of the proposed Worker Cooperative Federal Credit Union will be business lending to cooperatives that are worker-owned, democratically managed businesses. We will also lend to NASCO student housing cooperatives. Since our membership base is geographically diverse, we plan to be a virtual credit union where members transact primarily online, through a shared branch network, and ATMs.

Credit unions are required to have a field of membership or common bond that defines who can join the credit union. There are three field of membership categories: a business (employees of some company), a geographical region (city, county, etc.), or an association. The field of membership has to be approved early in the chartering process.

The proposed Worker Cooperative Federal Credit Union (unchartered) proposed a common bond with USFWC, NoBAWC, and NASCO. The NCUA approved our proposed common bond. This means that members of the three organizations will be allowed to join the credit union.

The chartering process requires potential members to make non-binding pledges to join the credit union to demonstrate there is sufficient support. The potential members must be part of the approved field of membership.

Fundraising will begin shortly. We need to raise a million dollars in grants and donations. These are not investments or deposits, but gifts that will be used to cover startup costs and expenses. Since credit unions are member-owned, they cannot issue equity to cover start-up costs the way banks can. We need to raise more than is typically required for most credit unions due to the higher amount of capital that has to be maintained in order to do business lending.

More info on the proposed Worker Cooperative Federal Credit Union can be found at www.WorkerCoopFCU.org. Those interested in starting a federal credit union should contact the National Credit Union Administration. The National Federation of Community Development Credit Unions also provides technical assistance to help low income credit unions get chartered.

Part 6: Nonprofit Organizations in the Sharing Economy

There are very few organizations in the world whose activities are solely nonprofit or for-profit—nonprofits generate revenue and for-profits do nonprofit-like activities on a daily basis. Founders of sharing organizations and social enterprises often struggle early on with the question: should we be a nonprofit or a for-profit?

What Is a Nonprofit?

Each state has its own statutes that govern "nonprofit" entities, but these statutes often do not clearly define what the word "nonprofit" means. Depending on the context, people understand nonprofits to be one or more of the following:

1. **"An organization that does not make a profit."** This understanding is inaccurate. Some nonprofits do not make profits and some do. There is nothing prohibiting a nonprofit from bringing in more revenues than expenses.

ABOUT THE PERMACULTURE CREDIT UNION

By William G. Sommers, CEO of PCU
Wesley Roe, Treasurer of PCU
Marjorie Lakin Erickson, Member of PCU (www.pcuonline.org)

The Permaculture Credit Union (PCU) was founded in 2000 by a group of permaculture designers and other like-minded people, with the goal of creating a financial institution that would effectuate the ethics of permaculture:

- Earth care
- People care
- Reinvesting the surplus for the betterment of both

The PCU was formed with the intention to create an ethical, replicable, grassroots, and ecological lending institution that is owned by its members. The Board, which is an active, volunteer Board, is elected by the member-owners in an annual democratic process.

The PCU members come from all over the United States. Requirement for membership is philosophically based as compared to geographically or organizationally based. Our members

1. Are members of an affiliated Permaculture Institute;
2. Have completed a recognized permaculture design course; and/or
3. Subscribe to permaculture ethics.

The organization and membership are dedicated to creating and maintaining a successful and dynamic financial institution that will contribute to the community at large and provide an important precedent in the financial world by developing the financial tools and capital dedicated to supporting environmentally sound practices, technologies, and businesses.

From its beginning in 2000 with no members or assets, the PCU has grown to 1,053 members from 44 different states and has total assets of $4,930,000. During that time, the PCU has originated a total of $14,000,000 in loans, and boasts an extraordinarily low portfolio default rate of 0.11 percent.

The Credit Union has developed several member-assisted micro-loan programs one of which is in conjunction with the Santa Fe Farmers Market Institute. The program allows members to pool their money in accounts, which then secure loans to small organic farmers in New Mexico.

Against the advice of its regulators, in order to further permaculture ethics, the PCU developed its discount loan program, pursuant to which it offers members a 0.75 percent discount for sustainable practices such as solar installation or rainwater harvesting. The PCU also offers vehicle loans at a 0.75 percent discount on rates for vehicles that get over 35 mpg and a 1.5 percent discount on rates for vehicles that get over 45 mpg. To our knowledge, we are the only financial institution that uses its rates as an incentive for members to do the "Earth friendly" thing.

Because the PCU understands sustainable building and projects, it can evaluate and successfully lend for such projects more readily than other, less knowledgeable institutions. As a result, the PCU has raised the bar for financial institutions, demonstrating that by concentrating on loans that benefit the environment, it is making an investment not only for the benefit of the Credit Union, but also for the benefit of generations to come. The PCU has helped and encouraged other institutions to develop similar programs.

All money for the operation of PCU comes from interest on loans, investments, and donations from various individuals and foundations. Although the PCU's IRS status as a 501(c)(14) does not allow for tax-deductible donations, it has a close working relationship with the Permaculture Guild, a 501(c)(3) tax-exempt organization in Santa Fe.

2. **"An organization that does not distribute profits to investors."** This is a much better candidate for a definition of a nonprofit. Federal tax laws governing tax-exempt organizations generally prohibit the distribution of profits to investors, and state laws governing nonprofits generally do the same.
3. **"An organization that is exempt from tax under Section 501(c)(3) of the Internal Revenue Code as a charitable and/or educational organization."** This is certainly one definition of

INTRODUCTION TO EMPLOYEE STOCK OWNERSHIP PLANS

By Loren Rodgers, Executive Director of the National Center for Employee Ownership

Over 11,000 companies in the United States have employee stock ownership plans (ESOPs), making them the primary vehicle for employee ownership of company stock. Most ESOPs are in closely held companies, often with 75 to 150 employees.

Since the Employee Retirement Income Security Act (ERISA) established a framework for ESOPs in the 1970s, analysis by diverse researchers has come to several points of consensus: ESOP companies tend to grow faster in terms of sales and employment, tend to have higher productivity, and tend to survive longer than comparable non-ESOP companies. ESOP participants have, on average, 2.5 times the assets in company-sponsored plans than do employees in comparable non-ESOP companies.

The Basics

ESOPs are retirement plans, subject to the same rules as other defined contribution plans, such as 401(k) plans. Two major differences between ESOPs and 401(k) plans are that ESOPs, by design, invest primarily in a single security, the stock of the employer, and that ESOPs may borrow money in order to purchase stock.

The ESOP trust, a separate legal entity from the company, is the legal owner of the shares, and as employees become participants in the plan, they become beneficiaries of the trust, which has an obligation under ERISA to operate the plan for the exclusive benefit of plan participants.

The most common uses for ESOPs are to allow business owners to sell their shares and to provide a competitive benefit that attracts and retains employees.

Setting Up an ESOP

A minority of ESOPs, roughly 15 percent, do not borrow money and are termed nonleveraged ESOPs. The company makes contributions at its own discretion to the plan. Contributions may be in the form of stock or in the form of cash, which would then be used to purchase stock.

Leveraged ESOPs borrow money and use that money to buy shares. A typical practice is to obtain external financing from a bank or other source. Rather than lending to the ESOP, lenders typically make their loan to the company (the external loan), and the company reloans the funds to the ESOP (the internal loan). Another common structure involves seller financing, where the owner of the shares sells those shares to the ESOP in exchange for a note. As the ESOP repays the loan, whether that means the internal loan from the company or the note from the seller, it releases shares into the accounts of participants.

ESOP Operations

ERISA establishes requirements for employees to become plan participants, for employees to become vested in their accounts, for the form and timing of distributions to those that leave the plan, and for diversification when employees meet age and years-of-participation requirements. Companies are free to be more generous than the requirements, but cannot be less generous.

ESOP participants have the right to direct the ESOP trustee how to vote their shares on specified shareholder issues, though in practice these voting rights tend to be of trivial importance in company operation.

Companies with ESOPs have a variety of tax benefits. The most important one in the current tax environment is for S corporations. S corporations pass taxes on to their shareholders, so if a non-tax-paying entity such as an ESOP is the sole shareholder, the company does not pay federal income tax. Also, most states will not impose state income tax in that situation. ESOPs first become allowable shareholders of S corporations in 1998, and since that time the number of 100 percent ESOP-owned companies has increased dramatically. The second major tax incentive is a tax deferral. People who sell C corporation shares and meet certain requirements can defer their capital gains tax.

a nonprofit, but it is too narrow. There are other sections of the Internal Revenue Code that grant tax exemption to other types of organizations (discussed in more detail below). Also, there are some organizations that meet the definition under definition 2 above, but do not seek federal tax-exempt status.[48]

4. **"An organization whose primary purpose is to benefit its constituency."** This definition is the reason why some people characterize cooperatives as nonprofits.

For the purpose of this particular section, we will limit our discussion to nonprofit organizations that are exempt from federal tax under Section 501(c)(3) of the Internal Revenue Code and are public charities (as opposed to private foundations). Other types of nonprofits will be discussed in the section below. The characteristics of public charities exempt under 501(c)(3) include the following:

1. **Incorporated at the state level:** They are formed under a state statute. For example, in California the entity of choice generally is a Nonprofit Public Benefit Corporation.
2. **Receive tax exemption from the IRS and state:** They apply for and receive exemption from federal income tax under Section 501(c)(3) of the Internal Revenue Code[49] and, if necessary, apply for and receive a comparable exemption from state income tax.
3. **Can receive tax-deductible donations:** Unlike organizations that are exempt from income tax under other sections of the Internal Revenue Code, 501(c)(3)s have an additional tax advantage: donations made to them are tax-deductible to the donor—this is why most nonprofits choose this designation if they can.

---

48. One example is nonprofit medical marijuana collectives formed under the laws of several states that permit such collectives but require them to be operated as nonprofits. These organizations do not seek federal tax-exempt status because their activities would not qualify for it; in fact, they are federally illegal.

49. Note, however, that IRS Publication 557 (Oct. 2011, at 25) indicates that an organization that normally receives less than $5,000 per year in gross income need not submit a Form 1023 application for tax exemption in order to be tax exempt. Such organizations are exempt automatically if they meet the requirements of section 501(c)(3).

4. **Regulated by the state:** They are usually subject to state regulations governing how they raise money and how they distribute money. For example, in California, they must register with the Attorney General and report on certain types of fundraising activities and transactions with interested parties such as board members.
5. **Required to receive broad public support:** They are required under federal tax law to have broad public support.[50]

This section is not intended to be a complete overview of the laws governing 501(c)(3) public charities. Rather, it is a summary of some of the issues that a sharing organization or social enterprise might need to consider if it is going to operate as a 501(c)(3).

Section 501(c)(3) of the Internal Revenue Code

Many social enterprises and organizations characteristic of the sharing economy will be attracted to the idea of forming a 501(c)(3) nonprofit. 501(c)(3)s benefit from the ability to receive grants and tax-deductible donations, exemption from taxes on net income, the ability to involve volunteers, and the public trust often conferred upon such organizations. Unfortunately, many social enterprises might fail to obtain tax exemption under 501(c)(3), since their activities and purposes may not meet the narrow list of purposes for which such organizations may operate. For example, some, but not all, farmers markets and car-sharing organizations have been found ineligible for 501(c)(3) status, because the IRS felt that their particular activities did not contribute primarily to a charitable or educational purpose. Social enterprises might also be denied tax exemption if their activities are too similar to regular commercial businesses.

In addition, a primary constraint of 501(c)(3)s is that they must be formed to benefit the public, and often to benefit a charitable class of people (poor, distressed, disadvantaged, and so on). Many people form sharing organizations—such as shared-housing arrangements, car-sharing organizations, and food cooperatives—to provide benefits to *themselves*, and not necessarily to the public at large. Even if such groups are not formed for the purpose of earning a profit, the types of benefits

50. I.R.C. § 170(b)(1)(A)(vi).

they confer upon themselves are sometimes legally inappropriate in the context of a 501(c)(3), which cannot operate to provide a private benefit to individuals. For this reason, many activities of the sharing economy are more easily fit into other types of nonprofits, discussed below.

To summarize the basic requirements of Section 501(c)(3) of the Internal Revenue Code, an organization:

- **Purposes:** Must be organized and operated exclusively[51] for religious, charitable, scientific, testing for public safety, literary, or educational purposes, or to foster national or international amateur sports competition [...], or for the prevention of cruelty to children or animals [...];
- **Prohibition against private benefit:** No part of the net earnings may inure to the benefit of any private shareholder or individual;
- **Rules against lobbying and supporting political candidates:** No substantial part of the activities may be carrying on propaganda or otherwise attempting to influence legislation, and the organization may not participate in, or intervene in any political campaign on behalf of (or in opposition to) any candidate for public office.

An organization that seeks tax-exempt status under Section 501(c)(3) must meet both the organizational and operational tests:

- **Organizational test (purposes):** The organizational test looks at whether the organization is organized exclusively for exempt purposes. The articles of incorporation must limit the organization's purposes to exempt purposes that are included in Section 501(c)(3). Also, the organizing documents must not expressly empower it to substantially engage in activities that are not in furtherance of one or more of those purposes.

---

51. IRS Regulations state that it must be operated *substantially*, not *exclusively*, for these purposes. Treasury Regulation § 1.501(c)(3)-1(c)(1) (as amended in 1990) states that an organization will be regarded as "operated exclusively" for one or more exempt purposes only if it engages primarily in activities which accomplish one or more of such exempt purposes specified in section 501(c)(3). An organization will not be so regarded if more than an insubstantial part of its activities is not in furtherance of an exempt purpose.

- **Operational test (activities):** The operational test looks at the activities of the organization. An organization must be operated *primarily* for exempt purposes, which means that it must engage primarily in activities that further exempt purposes. An "insubstantial part" of the charity's activities may be devoted to nonexempt purposes.

Examples of Exempt Purposes and Activities in Furtherance of Exempt Purposes

There are thousands of pages of IRS opinions and court decisions that attempt to differentiate between activities that the federal government considers related to exempt purposes and those that it considers unrelated. Unfortunately, they are at times seemingly contradictory and unclear. This section provides some examples, but further research is necessary when considering a specific activity. Activities that seem obviously "related" using the ordinary English language definition of the word are often seen by the IRS and the courts as unrelated for somewhat obscure reasons. For example, if you are an educational organization, it seems obvious that publishing books that are related to your educational mission would be a related activity, right? Maybe! For details, read on.

Relief of the Poor, Distressed, or Underprivileged

Examples of activities that generally contribute to this purpose include[52]

- Vocational training;
- Employment counseling and referral;
- Financial and technical assistance to disadvantaged businesses;
- Affordable housing;
- Legal services, child care, food, health care, or transportation for low-income people;
- Sale of handicrafts created by disadvantaged craftspeople or blind individuals.

---

52. Brad Caftel, Nat'l Econ. Dev. & Law Ctr., Legal Structure Issues in the Development of Business Ventures (Apr. 2001), http://www.insightcced.org/uploads/publications/legal/707.pdf (citing Rev. Rul. 76-37, 1976-1 C.B. 148 (1976); Rev. Rul. 66-257, 1966-2 C.B. 212 (1966); Rev. Rul. 74-587, 1974-2 C.B. 162 (1974); Rev. Rul. 68-167, 1968-1 C.B. 255 (1968); Rev. Rul. 78-428, 1978-2 C.B. 177 (1978)).

Many nonprofit organizations generate revenue by conducting these kinds of activities. One successful example is Rubicon Programs, which operated a successful bakery and a landscaping business with the purpose of providing vocational training to economically disadvantaged individuals.

These kinds of programs must be truly beneficial for the trainees to be considered exempt by the IRS. In a recent denial letter,[53] the IRS denied exemption under Section 501(c)(3) for a program that hired part-time workers to stuff envelopes. The letter stated that hiring low-income individuals "in and of itself, does not constitute an activity that furthers the charitable purpose of providing relief of the poor and distressed or of the underprivileged . . ." and the training and education activities are "negligible."[54]

Lessening Neighborhood Tensions, Eliminating Prejudice and Discrimination, Defending Human and Civil Rights Secured by Law, and Combating Community Deterioration and Juvenile Delinquency

Examples of activities that generally further these purposes include[55]

- Renovation of housing that is then rented or sold at affordable rates,
- Financial assistance to businesses unable to obtain conventional financing due to their location in a blighted community, and
- Development of commercial or industrial real estate that is rented to businesses that agree to train and employ low-income community residents.

Lessening the Burdens of Government

This category of exempt activity is difficult to qualify for. Generally, the applicant must provide evidence that it is conducting an activity that would otherwise be undertaken by government. As the IRS puts it, "One should be skeptical of letters from government officials that praise an organization's activities. The relevant determination is whether the activity engaged in by the organization is a burden of government,

---

53. IRS Release No. 200802036, *available at* http://www.irs.gov/pub/irs-wd/0802036.pdf.

54. *Id.*

55. Caftel, *supra* note 52 (citing Rev. Proc. 96-32, 1996-1 C.B. 717 (1996); Rev. Rul. 74-587, 1974-2 C.B. 162 (1974); Rev. Rul. 76-419, 1976-2 C.B. 146 (1976)).

not whether the government approves of the activity or of the people involved."[56]

The IRS will consider evidence including[57]

- Whether there is a statute or ordinance creating or authorizing the organization,
- The control exerted by governmental units over the organization's activities,
- The interrelationship between the governmental unit and the organization,
- The organization's funding,
- Whether the organization's activities defray general or specific expenses of the governmental unit,
- Whether the governmental unit has previously engaged in the same activity prior to the organization taking over such activity, and
- Whether the activity is one which the governmental unit may, under state or local law, conduct itself.

One activity that has had success securing 501(c)(3) status under this purpose is the Business Improvement District. This is a district created under state or local law that is created by a vote of the property or business owners for the purpose of assessing the property or business owners so that funds can be accumulated to conduct community improvement activities. Since such districts are created by local ordinance, the IRS can more clearly classify these activities as "lessening the burdens of government."

Education

Education is a category that encompasses a broad range of activities that are eligible for exemption under Section 501(c)(3). Education includes classroom instruction, providing scholarships, public education, museums, orchestras, art galleries, and zoos. The IRS may not deny exemption based on the beliefs and opinions advocated by an organization or

---

56. Robert Louthian & Amy Henchey, Lessening the Burdens of Government (IRS Exempt Organizations Topic 93, 1993), *available at* http://www.irs.gov/pub/irs-tege/eotopicb93.pdf.

57. *Id.*

the merits of the educational content presented. However, if an organization presents viewpoints unsupported by facts and uses inflammatory and disparaging rhetoric, the IRS may conclude that the organization is engaging in propaganda rather than education.

Educational Activities and the Sharing Economy

Some organizations that work to foster a sharing economy have obtained tax exemption on the grounds that they are educational. For example, many "time banks" obtain tax exemption under 501(c)(3), even though the primary activity of the time bank is to connect individuals for the purpose of exchanging favors without dollars. Time banks have obtained tax exemption, in part, by arguing that the operation of the time bank creates an educational laboratory where people can learn about and practice their skills of meetings their needs without dollars. It is not clear how many economic activities we could justify as "educational" under 501(c)(3). Given how much the world still needs to learn about and practice in the creation of new economies, perhaps a good number of activities could fall under an educational umbrella. However, the hope is that these activities will be less for the purpose of *teaching about* the new economy and more for the purpose of *becoming* the new economy. In that respect, the educational argument is limited.

Publishing

One area that has caused some consternation for educational nonprofits is publishing. Publishing books, articles, or other content as part of an educational purpose may not qualify as an educational purpose under the Internal Revenue Code. Publications must meet the following (highly unclear) criteria to be exempt:

- The content of the publication is educational;
- The preparation of material follows methods generally accepted as "educational" in character;
- The distribution of the materials is necessary or valuable in achieving the organization's educational and scientific purposes; and
- The manner in which the distribution is accomplished is distinguishable from ordinary commercial publishing practices.[58]

58. IRC 501(c)(3) ORGANIZATIONS AND PUBLISHING ACTIVITIES (IRS Exempt Organizations Topic 88, 1988), *available at* http://www.irs.gov/pub/irs-tege/eotopice88.pdf.

In one ruling,[59] the IRS reviewed the publication of an ethnic newspaper. It found that a nonprofit organization, whose only activities were preparing and publishing a newspaper of local, national, and international news articles with an ethnic emphasis and soliciting advertising and selling subscriptions to that newspaper in a manner indistinguishable from ordinary commercial publishing practices, was not operated exclusively for charitable and educational purposes and did not qualify for exemption.

In contrast, however, if a nonprofit selects what it publishes based on content, rather than financial considerations, and sells its publications through non-commercial channels, it will likely qualify for tax-exempt status.

Consulting Services

Can a nonprofit organization provide consulting as part of its educational activities? This question has also led many a nonprofit attorney to tear out her hair late at night!

The leading case on this topic is *BSW Group, Inc. v. Commissioner.*[60] In that case, BSW Group was formed for the purpose of providing consulting services primarily in the area of rural-related policy and program development, and planned to enter into consultant relationships with five or six nonprofit organizations involved with the fields of health, housing, vocational skills, and cooperative management. It planned to charge a fee based on its clients' ability to pay, well below market rate for such services and only slightly above cost.

The IRS denied exemption because it felt that BSW Group was "primarily engaged in an activity which is characteristic of a trade or business."

The Tax Court agreed with the IRS, stating:

> We must agree with the Commissioner that petitioner's activity constitutes the conduct of a consulting business of the sort which is ordinarily carried on by commercial ventures organized for profit . . . . Petitioner [BSW Group] has completely failed to demonstrate that its own services, or the services performed by its consultants, are not in competition with commercial businesses such as personnel agencies, consulting referral services, real estate agents, housing rental services,

59. Rev. Rul. 77-4, 1977-1 C.B. 141.
60. BSW Grp., Inc. v. Comm'r, 70 T.C. 352 (1978).

> banks, loan companies, trash disposal firms, or environmental consulting companies. [footnote omitted] Competition with commercial firms is strong evidence of the predominance of nonexempt commercial purposes.[61]

Several other factors weighed against BSW Group—consulting was its sole activity, there was no showing that the research conducted by the consultants furthered an exempt purpose, the organization did not plan to seek grants or donations, no services were provided for free or below cost, and not all of the prospective clients were tax-exempt.

It is hard to know, given the unusual facts of this case, to what extent and in what manner tax-exempt organizations may conduct consulting activities without jeopardizing their tax-exempt status. In more recent rulings, the IRS seems to focus on the fee charged. If the fee charged is not only below market rates but also below cost, requiring a subsidy from other charitable funds, the IRS is more likely to grant exemption.

In a more recent ruling,[62] the IRS considered an organization that proposed to conduct grant management and administrative services for other tax-exempt organizations. The IRS began its analysis by noting that there are

> dozens of for-profit companies that provide services similar to those you intend to sell. . . . Therefore, we find that the [services provided by for-profit companies] are nearly identical to those you propose to sell and that you are in direct competition with the for-profit foundation management industry. Nevertheless, the fact that commercial entities may also provide similar services, in and of itself is not determinative as to whether a particular service is or is not substantially related to exempt functions. If the provision of a service contributes importantly to benefiting the charitable class served by an organization's activities, the commercial nature of the service should not be controlling.

The IRS then went on to group the various services that the organization intended to sell into three categories: grant-making, administrative, and clerical. The IRS concluded that the grant-making group of services contributed importantly to the accomplishment of the organization's exempt purpose, which was to support charitable activities that benefit the local community. However, the administrative and clerical

61. *Id.*
62. I.R.S. Priv. Ltr. Rul. 2008-32-027 (Aug. 8, 2008).

group of services, according to the IRS, did not contribute importantly to accomplishing the exempt purpose:

> Although an argument may be made that these services assist charities [to] . . . conduct their charitable functions, this argument taken to its logical extreme would include any and all services that you could possibly provide to a charitable organization . . . . For example, providing janitorial services to maintain a charitable organization's physical place of operations would assist the charity accomplish its exempt purpose by removing the burdens associated with routine organizational administration, thereby, allowing the charity to focus solely on charitable activities. Naturally, providing janitorial services or a host of other services that a charitable organization routinely conducts as part of its internal management or administration functions cannot be claimed to be a narrowly tailored activity that is conducted to accomplish the exempt organization's purposes. Similarly, the administrative and clerical services you propose to sell are not narrowly tailored to be substantially related to your exempt purpose.

The IRS also noted that none of the services were being provided substantially below cost. The IRS concluded by stating that fees charged for the grant-making services would be considered related income, whereas fees charged for the clerical and administrative services would be treated as unrelated and therefore subject to unrelated business income tax (described in more detail below).

Retail Stores

What about the operation of retail stores? There are several rulings on museum gift shops that address this issue. In these rulings, the IRS looks at all of the items sold and determines that some items (such as reproductions of paintings in an art museum) are substantially related to the educational purpose of the museum, whereas others (such as children's toys) are not. Similar reasoning will be applied to web-based sales.

Efforts to Preserve and Protect the Environment[63]

Efforts to preserve and protect the natural environment for the benefit of the public will generally qualify for tax exemption. Examples of organizations found to be exempt for such activities include

---

63. Environmental and Historical Preservation Under IRC 501(c)(3) (IRS Exempt Organizations Topic 79, 1979), *available at* http://www.irs.gov/pub/irs-tege/eotopicb79.pdf.

- An organization formed to preserve a lake as a public recreational facility and to improve the condition of the water in the lake to enhance its recreational features;[64]
- An organization formed to promote and assist in city beautification projects and to educate the public in the advantages of street planting;[65]
- An organization formed by residents of a city to cooperate with municipal authorities in preserving, beautifying, and maintaining an urban public park;[66] and
- An organization formed to develop a sanctuary for wild birds and animals for the education of the public.[67]

One ruling recognized that efforts to preserve and protect the natural environment for the benefit of the public serve as a charitable purpose in itself, even if there is no educational component.[68]

However, in another ruling, an organization acquired real estate for the dual purpose of holding land for preservation of open space and farming.[69] However, the land contained no ecologically significant attributes. The ruling found that although there was some ecological preservation involved, the organization was not preserving land of any distinctive ecological significance and therefore was not eligible for exemption.

A nonprofit organization that owns farmland and restricts its use to farming or other uses the organization deems ecologically suitable, but is not operated for the purpose of preserving ecologically significant land, does not qualify for exemption under Section 501(c)(3).

If a property is designated as a "wilderness area" or a "wild and scenic river" or the like by federal, state, or local conservation agencies, this is one indication that the land is ecologically significant. The IRS may also consider whether the organization's governing body and membership are composed of scientists, educators, conservationists, and representatives of the community-at-large and whether the organization has

64. Rev. Rul. 70-186, 1970-1 C.B. 128.
65. Rev. Rul. 68-14, 1968-1 C.B. 243.
66. Rev. Rul. 78-85, 1978-1 C.B. 150.
67. Rev. Rul. 76-204, 1976-2 C.B. 152.
68. Rev. Rul. 76-204.
69. Rev. Rul. 78-384, 1978-43 I.R.B. 8.

close working relationships with appropriate private and governmental conservation organizations.

Unrelated Income

Even if an organization can describe its activities in a way that it will meet the operational test and receive its 501(c)(3) exemption status, the organization must be careful not to later conduct an activity that the IRS would consider unrelated to its exempt purpose. Unrelated business income is revenue from a trade or business, regularly carried on, that is not substantially related to the charitable, educational, or other purpose that is the basis of the organization's exemption. An exempt organization that has $1,000 or more of gross income from an unrelated business must file Form 990-T and pay tax on unrelated business income. An organization that receives a substantial portion of its revenues from unrelated business income risks losing its tax-exempt status.

Assets Dedicated to Exempt Purposes

A key characteristic of a 501(c)(3) is that it may not use its assets to benefit a private individual or entity. This means that it may not benefit private parties by doing things like paying excessive salaries, purchasing property at more than fair market value, paying dividends or paying assets remaining upon dissolution to private parties, or in any way allowing its earnings or assets to be used by private parties for private gain without reasonable compensation to the organization. This does not mean that private parties can't benefit in any way from the activities of the organization—but any benefit must be incidental to the organization's exempt activities.

Here is an example that illustrates this concept. An organization wishes to purchase a piece of property from a board member's son. If the son receives more than fair market value for the property, this would be an excess benefit transaction. Thus, the organization should secure an independent appraisal of the property to determine fair market value. The board member that is the father of the property owner should leave the room during the debate and vote on the purchase of the property. The meeting minutes should contain a discussion of how the board made its determination to purchase the property at the agreed-upon price. Excess benefit transactions can result in sanctions for board members, as well as loss of tax-exempt status.

Lobbying and Electioneering

There has been a great deal written on this topic, so suffice it to say that a 501(c)(3) may not support or oppose political candidates and may not engage in "substantial" lobbying. However, if the subject matter of the "lobbying" regards legislation that could affect the organization's "existence, powers, duties, tax-exempt status, or the deductibility of contributions" to the organization, then the 501(c)(3) is exempt, in that case, from such prohibitions on lobbying and attempting to influence legislation.[70] For example, a time bank that is exempt under 501(c)(3) could engage in lobbying if the topic of the legislation is one that would prevent the time bank from operating effectively. A great resource on the topic of lobbying by nonprofits is Alliance for Justice.[71]

Public Charity versus Private Foundation

There is another important consideration for 501(c)(3)s. A 501(c)(3) may be either a private foundation or a public charity. The default presumption is that it is a private foundation. However, most 501(c)(3)s would rather be a public charity because private foundations are somewhat more constrained in their activities. To be a public charity, the 501(c)(3) must have broad public support as opposed to receiving most of its funds from one or two private individuals, family foundations, or corporations. The tests for what is sufficient public support are very complicated and beyond the scope of this book, but it is yet one more thing that the managers of 501(c)(3)s must concern themselves with.

State Law Issues

In addition to the numerous complicated federal tax law rules that govern 501(c)(3)s, nonprofits are also governed by the laws of the states in which they are formed and operate. Most states regulate fundraising activities of charities, require charities to register with the state, and regulate charities to ensure they are serving public purposes.

---

70. IRM § 7.27.19.3.4 (Feb. 22, 1999).

71. Alliance for Justice, http://www.afj.org.

Pros and Cons of 501(c)(3)s

How They Can Raise Capital

501(c)(3)s have almost exclusive access to one source of capital: grants and donations. This is because grants and donations to 501(c)(3)s are tax-deductible to the donor and because most foundations only make grants to 501(c)(3)s (due to regulations governing foundations). This is a great advantage to an organization that thinks it might be attractive to donors.

On the other hand, unlike for-profit entities, 501(c)(3)s cannot raise equity capital from investors. 501(c)(3)s are not and cannot be "owned" by investors, so they have no equity to sell to investors, and they cannot pay returns to investors. 501(c)(3)s can raise money using loans, but they must not pay more than "market rate" interest (for reasons discussed above).

Limitations on Activities

As discussed in detail above, 501(c)(3)s are extremely limited in the activities they can conduct.

Limitations on Use of Funds

Funds cannot be used to reward investors. And they cannot be used to provide "excess benefit" to any private person or business. And (except on a very small scale), they cannot be used for lobbying or to conduct "unrelated activities."

Highly Regulated

In addition to all of the limitations described above, 501(c)(3)s generally have a fairly heavy burden in terms of reporting, record keeping, adopting, and implementing policies to ensure compliance, etc. This can all impede the ability of an organization to achieve its goals in helping to build the sharing economy.

Involvement of Volunteers

There is one major benefit of using a 501(c)(3) form. People are generally able to volunteer for charitable or humanitarian purposes without triggering the protections of employment law, thus it is much easier for 501(c)(3)s to utilize volunteers without running afoul of employment law. Chapter 7 provides detail about the labor and employment laws affecting an organization's abilities to involve volunteers.

Other Nonprofit Variations

Up until this point, we have focused on 501(c)(3)s. Now we turn our attention to other kinds of nonprofits and tax exemptions, of which there are many. We will not be able to discuss every kind of nonprofit, but we will touch on some of our favorites. Many of the forms discussed below will be more appropriate than 501(c)(3)s for activities characteristic of the sharing economy.

State Law Variations

Every state has at least one statute that authorizes the formation of a nonprofit organization. For example, in California, we have nonprofit unincorporated associations, nonprofit public benefit corporations, nonprofit mutual benefit corporations, nonprofit religious corporations, nonprofit corporations for medical services, nonprofit health care service plans, nonprofit legal services corporations, nonprofit hospital service plans, nonprofit cooperative agricultural marketing associations, and nonprofit medical associations.

And to make things even more complicated, some structures that are normally considered for-profit can be structured as nonprofits. For example, it is possible to form an LLC that has certain characteristics and then to apply to the IRS for tax exemption.[72]

Once an organization chooses a state statute to form under, the next step is to consider tax exemption. There is state and federal income tax exemption (not to mention state exemptions from sales and use tax, property tax, etc.), but generally it is a good idea to think about federal taxation first because most states follow the federal income tax exemption framework.

Other Federal Tax Exemption Categories

There are 28 categories of tax-exempt organizations listed in Section 501(c). A handful of these categories are also discussed in Chapter 9, specifically in relation to housing. Note that there are also other sections of the Internal Revenue Code that create other tax-exempt statuses, such as

72. For details, see Richard A. McCray & Ward L. Thomas, Limited Liability Companies as Exempt Organizations (IRS Exempt Organizations Topic 00, 2000), *available at* http://www.irs.gov/pub/irs-tege/eotopich00.pdf.

521 cooperatives (discussed below), 501(d) apostolic organizations, and 528 homeowners associations (discussed in Chapter 9).

The most commonly used exemption is 501(c)(3) because a 501(c)(3) is eligible to receive tax-deductible donations. However, some organizations that do not qualify under that exemption need to consider other options. An organization that wants to be able to participate in substantial lobbying activity should probably not apply for 501(c)(3) tax exemption—other exemptions do not impose the strict limitations on lobbying that Section 501(c)(3) does. Also, if an organization's activities don't fall within the activities that may be conducted by a 501(c)(3), the organization will need to consider other categories.

Section 501(c)(4)

Many organizations characteristic of a sharing economy could likely obtain tax exemption under 501(c)(4), even though they likely could not have under 501(c)(3). Examples of activities that are somewhat better suited to 501(c)(4) exemption include farmers markets, time banks, local currencies, and car-sharing organizations that offer membership to the public.

An organization exempt under 501(c)(4) is known as a civic league or social welfare organization. It operates primarily to further the common good and general welfare of the people of the community. Examples include community associations that work to improve public services, housing, and parking, that publish a free community newspaper, that sponsor community sports leagues, or that contract with a private security service to patrol the community.

Some practitioners call this exemption 501(c)(3) "light." In other words, an organization that looks a lot like a 501(c)(3) but does not quite meet the stringent requirements for exemption under that section may qualify for this exemption. The IRS has sought to explain the purpose of 501(c)(4)s as follows:

> There is no official Congressional or Service pronouncement construing the terms "civic league" or "social welfare" as embodied in section 501(c)(4). However, [the Sixth Circuit Court of Appeals] described [501(c)(4)s] as embodying "the ideas of citizens of a community cooperating to promote the common good and general welfare of the community." [The Fourth Circuit] described a civic organization as being "a movement of citizenry or the community," whereas the [the Third

> Circuit] while acknowledging the difficult task in arriving at a specific definition of "civic organization," stated that "the organization must be a community movement designed to accomplish community ends.[73]

For example, IRS Revenue Ruling 75-286 concluded that an organization formed by the residents of a city block to preserve and beautify that block may qualify for exemption under Section 501(c)(4), even though the element of private benefit is sufficient to disqualify it from exempt status under Section 501(c)(3).

An organization claiming exemption under Section 501(c)(4) must operate for the benefit of the community as a whole rather than for the benefit of a limited group:

> Compare Rev. Rul. 78-69, 1978-1 C.B. 156, which holds that an organization providing rush hour commuter bus service to all residents of a community qualifies for exemption under IRC 501(c)(4), with Rev. Rul. 55-311, 1955-1 C.B. 72, which holds that a local association of employees operating a bus primarily for the convenience of its members does not so qualify. Also compare Rev. Rul. 62-167, 1962-2 C.B. 142, which holds that an organization retransmitting television signals for the benefit of an entire community qualifies for exemption under IRC 501(c)(4), with Rev. Rul. 54-394, 1954-2 C.B. 131, which holds that an organization providing television on a cooperative basis does not qualify. See also GCM 39357 (May 3, 1985) which concluded that an employee health club in which membership is available only to salaried employees can qualify under section 501(c)(4), but as a local association of employees.[74]

Similarly, cooperative organizations formed to benefit their members, such as an organization to purchase food in bulk for its members, have been denied exemption under Section 501(c)(4).[75]

---

73. SOCIAL WELFARE: WHAT DOES IT MEAN? HOW MUCH PRIVATE BENEFIT IS PERMISSIBLE? WHAT IS A COMMUNITY? (IRS Exempt Organizations Topic 81, 1981), *available at* http://www.irs.gov/pub/irs-tege/eotopicg81.pdf.

74. VIRGINIA RICHARDSON, RODERICK DARLING & MARVIN FRIEDLANDER, HEALTH CLUBS 18–19 (IRS Exempt Organizations Topic 00, 2000), *available at* http://www.irs.gov/pub/irs-tege/eotopica00.pdf.

75. SOCIAL WELFARE, *supra* note 73, at 15.

Section 501(c)(5)

Organizations that work to better the conditions of agriculture or horticulture may be eligible for tax-exempt status under Section 501(c)(5).[76] The activities of these organizations may include raising livestock, managing forests, cultivating land, raising and harvesting crops or aquatic resources, cultivating useful or ornamental plants, and similar pursuits.

The primary purpose of exempt agricultural and horticultural organizations under Section 501(c)(5) must be to better the conditions of those engaged in agriculture or horticulture, develop more efficiency in agriculture or horticulture, or improve the products, for example:

- Promoting various cooperative agricultural, horticultural, and civic activities among rural residents by a state and county farm and home bureau;
- Exhibiting livestock, farm products, and other aspects of agriculture and horticulture;
- Testing soil for members and nonmembers of the farm bureau on a cost basis, the results of the tests and other recommendations being furnished to the community members to educate them in soil treatment;
- Guarding the purity of a specific breed of livestock;
- Encouraging improvements in the production of fish on privately owned fish farms;
- Negotiating with processors for the price to be paid to members for, but not acting as an agent to help members sell, their crops; and
- Operating an educational rodeo show promoting agriculture.

Section 501(c)(6)

An organization exempt under 501(c)(6) is known as a business league or chamber of commerce. The purpose of the organization must be to promote the common business interest of a group of persons. It may not engage in a regular business of a kind ordinarily carried on for profit. In addition, the organization must receive support from its members.

---

76. John Francis Reilly, Carter C. Hull, & Barbara A. Braig Allen, IRC 501(c)(5) Organizations (IRS Exempt Organizations, 2003).

An organization does not qualify for exemption under Section 501(c)(6) if any of its net earnings inures to the benefit of any member. Members may nevertheless receive some kinds of benefits from the organization, such as newsletters and similar material, and may benefit indirectly from the organization's activities (i.e., the successful promotion of a common business interest will indirectly benefit the members).

Many organizations that promote the interests of socially responsible, sustainable business use this exemption category. For example, most of the local chapters of Business Alliance for Local Living Economies and American Independent Business Alliance are exempt under 501(c)(6). These organizations conduct activities like promoting Shop Local First, member networking events, educational workshops, etc.

Section 501(c)(7)

Section 501(c)(7) is a category of exemption designed for social, recreational, and "other nonprofitable purposes."[77] Section 501(c)(7) is designed to provide tax exemption to organizations that groups form for their *own* benefit, rather than for a public benefit. In that respect, many activities of the sharing economy may fall within 501(c)(7). A community association whose primary function is to own and maintain recreational areas and facilities for its members can likely obtain exemption under 501(c)(7). A group of people that get together to share recreational equipment or facilities could seek tax exemption under this section. See Chapter 9 for additional discussion of 501(c)(7)s and the provision of amenities in relation to shared housing.

The rationale for granting tax exemption to a social club is that since individuals can participate in social and recreational activities without tax consequences, individuals that form a group to do such activities should be in the same position tax-wise as they would be if they did the activity on their own. Because of this reasoning, 501(c)(7) organizations must derive most of their income from their members and any income received from nonmember sources is taxed as unrelated business income.[78]

---

77. *See* Jim Langley & Conrad Rosenberg, Social Clubs—IRC 501(c)(7) (IRS Exempt Organizations-Technical Instruction Program 1996), *available at* http://www.irs.gov/pub/irs-tege/eotopicc96.pdf.

78. *See id.*

Note that even though the phrase "other nonprofitable purposes" may sound like a catch-all to include many types of activities, the IRS will generally deny exemption for activities that are not sufficiently connected to or in furtherance of social, recreational, or other pleasure activities.[79] It's easy to see how this can become a gray area in the sharing economy. Many things we do for the purpose of providing for ourselves will also, preferably, be enjoyable, like meal sharing, community gardening, neighborhood home repair groups, shared workshop spaces, tool-lending libraries, and so on. It's odd that the IRS has so clearly carved out a form of tax exemption to allow us to spend money and have fun together, but there is not a perfect category to allow us to spend money and share practical things.

Under 501(c)(7), a group could likely share a boat or recreational vehicle; however, if a group forms a nonprofit mutual benefit corporation simply to share one or a few cars for regular and practical use, the IRS might deny exemption, unless the group could prove that the purpose is truly social or recreational. The question is: how much fun do these activities have to be or how much socializing must happen in connection with such activities in order to obtain exemption under 501(c)(7)? Could the IRS be persuaded that we do all of this for social purposes? Could the IRS be persuaded that all of this is for the purpose of making life more enjoyable? It will be fun, at the very least, to have this conversation with the IRS.

Sections 501(c)(8) and 501(c)(10)

The IRS is aware of more than 100,000 fraternal organizations, which is evidence that they play a significant role in our society and economy.[80] It is worth further inquiry to determine the extent to which fraternal organizations, and their related tax-exemption categories, could serve as platforms for the sharing economy. Mutual aid societies—groups of people who come together to provide support to one another in times of need—are key institutions for the creation of a more sharing economy. Fraternal beneficiary societies that provide for the payment of life, sick, accident, or other related benefits are exempt from taxation under

---

79. *See* Rev. Rul. 75-494, 1975-2 C.B. 214.

80. For more information, see Sean M. Barnett & Ward L. Thomas, IRC 501(c)(8) Fraternal Beneficiary Societies and IRC 501(c)(10) Domestic Fraternal Societies (IRS Exempt Organizations Continuing Professional Education Topic 2004).

Section 501(c)(8). Fraternal societies exempt under Section 501(c)(10) are essentially the same as fraternal beneficiary societies except that no payments of benefits are offered. Both types of societies must engage in "fraternal activities," such as social activities, ceremonies, rituals, and so on, and an organization found to be lacking in such things will not be found to be tax-exempt.[81] For example, an organization formed simply to provide financial support and insurance to its members would not be found exempt under this category.

Fraternal beneficiary societies have been described as follows:

> A fraternal beneficiary society … would be one whose members have adopted the same, or a very similar calling, avocation, or profession, or who are working in union to accomplish some worthy object, and who for that reason have banded themselves together as an association or society to aid and assist one another, and to promote the common cause. The term "fraternal" can properly be applied to such an association for the reason that the pursuit of a common object, calling, or profession usually has a tendency to create a brotherly feeling among those who are thus engaged.[82]

An interesting and inconvenient characteristic of organizations seeking exemption under Section 501(c)(8) or Section 501(c)(10) is that they must operate under the "lodge system." Treasury Regulation 1.501(c)(8)-1 states that operating under the lodge system means "carrying on its activities under a form of organization that comprises local branches, chartered by a parent organization and largely self governing, called lodges, chapters, or the like."[83] The requirement to operate under a lodge system makes it somewhat difficult for minority groups to form new fraternal beneficiary societies, since they would need to, in theory, first form multiple organizations and then subsume them under a parent organization. By virtue of being part of a minority, it may be hard for such groups to find enough people to achieve a "lodge system." For example, if a group of Eritrean immigrants wished to form a society to provide "life, sick, accident or other related benefits" to one another,

---

81. Phila. & Reading Relief Ass'n, 4 B.T.A. 713 (1926).

82. See Barnett & Thomas *supra* note 80 (quoting Nat'l Union v. Marlow, 74 F. 775, 778–79 (8th Cir. 1896)).

83. Fraternal Beneficiary Societies and Fraternal Societies (IRS Exempt Organizations Topic 80, 1980), *available at* http://www.irs.gov/pub/irs-tege/eotopich80.pdf.

they might need to find or form a second group of Eritrean immigrants to do the same. Nevertheless, it is worth further inquiry to determine how 501(c)(8) and 501(c)(10) exempt organizations could be employed to serve the sharing economy.

Section 501(c)(12)

Section 501(c)(12) exemption is for benevolent life insurance associations, mutual ditch or irrigation companies, mutual or cooperative telephone companies, and "like organizations."[84] They are organized to provide these services to their members at the lowest possible cost. These organizations must use their income solely to cover losses and expenses, with any excess being returned to members or retained for future losses and expenses. They must collect at least 85 percent of their income from members for the sole purpose of meeting losses and expenses. "Like organizations" may sound like a catch-all, but it is somewhat narrowly defined and does not include organizations in most other sectors. For example, a housing cooperative applied for and was denied exemption under 501(c)(12).[85] However, funeral cooperatives,[86] cable television cooperatives,[87] and energy services[88] have been found to be "like organizations." This leaves open the question of what other kinds of modern communication cooperatives (like internet service providers), personal services, or renewable energy cooperatives might be found to be exempt under 501(c)(12).[89]

Sections 521 and 501(c)(16)

Section 521 provides favorable tax treatment (though not complete exemption) to farmer cooperatives that meet a list of requirements, which include that the "primary activity must be to market the products of members and other producers and/or purchase supplies and other equipment for members and other persons" and "[t]hey must pay patronage refunds to all patrons (members and nonmembers alike) on

---

84. For more information, see Organizations Exempt Under IRC 501(c)(12), IRM § 7.25.12.

85. Rev. Rul. 65-201, 1965-2 C.B. 170.

86. Thompson v. White River Burial Ass'n, 178 F.2d 954 (8th Cir. 1950).

87. Rev. Rul. 83-170, 1983-2 C.B. 97.

88. I.R.S. Priv. Ltr. Rul. 97-15-045 (Jan. 16, 1997).

89. For more information about 501(c)(12)s, see Michael Seto & Cheryl Chasin, General Survey of I.R.C. 501(c)(12) Cooperatives and Examination of Current Issues (IRS Exempt Organizations Continuing Professional Education Topic 2002).

the same basis."[90] Nonprofit organizations exempt from tax under Section 501(c)(16) are organized by Section 521 cooperatives for the purpose of financing the ordinary crop operations of members or other producers.

Nonprofits Without Tax Exemption

Some organizations form under a state nonprofit statute but do not apply for tax-exempt status for various reasons. For example, nonprofit corporations that primarily engage in social enterprise business activities may be happy to be taxed like normal corporations, since applying for tax exemption might put too many constraints on how they operate or might completely prevent them from engaging in business activities. If the entity is designed to operate at cost, it will likely have very little net income on which to pay taxes, though it may be subject to payment of minimum taxes in some states.

Even without tax exemption, there are benefits to operating a social enterprise as a nonprofit rather than a for-profit. In a nonprofit, no individual will be entitled to a share of the profits, which removes some of the incentives typical business owners have to steer away from the mission and focus only on profits. Being a nonprofit may also bring a business greater public trust than if the business were owned by private individuals.

State nonprofit corporations statutes may or may not specify the purposes for which the corporation may operate. In California, for example, nonprofit public benefit corporations must operate for "public or charitable purposes."[91] It's not entirely clear what can constitute a "public" purpose, but this could conceivably include many more social enterprises than would be permitted under 501(c)(3).

Some nonprofit statutes like the California nonprofit mutual benefit corporation statute do not restrict what types of activities may be done by organizations formed under them. In those cases, almost any type of business could form under such a statute and not apply for tax-exempt status. This would generally mean (depending on the details of the statute) that during the life of the organization, no distributions would be

90. DONALD A. FREDERICK, INCOME TAX TREATMENT OF COOPERATIVES: INTERNAL REVENUE CODE § 521, pt. 4 (2005 ed.), *available at* http://www.rurdev.usda.gov/rbs/pub/cir444.pdf.

91. CAL. CORP. CODE § 5111.

made to investors. Although they are generally prohibited from distributing profits, under some state laws, mutual benefit nonprofits may, upon dissolution, distribute assets to members.[92] This means that individual members may have some incentive to cash out by selling assets of the enterprise and dissolving the entity.

Another example of nonprofits that operate without tax exemption are medical marijuana collectives (legal under California law) formed as California nonprofit mutual benefit corporations. They do not apply for federal tax exemption because trafficking in marijuana is not legal under federal law.

Part 7: Nonprofit/For-Profit Hybrids

As discussed above, tax-exempt 501(c)(3) nonprofits are constrained in the kinds of activities they can do, how they can raise money, and how they can share profits. However, there are many successful models for social enterprises or entrepreneurial nonprofits. They differ from traditional nonprofits because their funding tends to come from a blend of traditional nonprofit sources (grants and donations) and entrepreneurial activities. This section provides some examples of these models as well as guidance on their legalities.

Fee for Service

Underwriters Laboratories (UL) generates a good portion of its revenue through fees received from a safety certification process. Others, such as Business for Social Responsibility (BSR), generate revenue from membership fees, conference fees, and a store that sells books and other materials on corporate social responsibility. Many nonprofit schools charge tuition. Generally, nonprofits may charge fees for the related services they provide so long as the fees are designed to cover costs.

Revenue-Generating Activities and Subsidiaries

Nonprofit organizations may generate revenue from their activities so long as the activities are related (see above regarding related versus unrelated activities). Nonprofits may also generate revenue from unrelated

92. *See, e.g.*, Cal. Corp. Code § 8717.

activities as long as these unrelated activities are not "substantial." If a nonprofit wishes to conduct a substantial activity that it fears the IRS will see as unrelated, the nonprofit will often create a for-profit subsidiary to conduct the activity. The nonprofit can receive profits from the subsidiary in the form of dividends or can collect other kinds of payments from the subsidiary such as rent or consulting fees. The for-profit can make donations to the nonprofit, but they would not be tax-deductible.[93] Income from rents, royalties, or interest that flows to the nonprofit will result in Unrelated Business Income Tax (or UBIT), if the nonprofit owns more than 50 percent of the subsidiary for-profit. The nonprofit does not pay tax on dividends received.[94]

Joint Ventures

Nonprofits may enter into "joint ventures" with for-profits. For example, a nonprofit could form an LLC and sell 99 percent of the ownership interest in the company to outside investors. There are strict rules governing these kinds of ventures. The venture must be set up to achieve one of the nonprofit's charitable purposes. Joint ventures are common in the affordable housing sector. A nonprofit whose purpose is to develop affordable housing can raise money to be able to complete a project by selling interests in the project (owned by an LLC) to investors. In a joint venture involving a pass-through entity like an LLC or limited partnership, the activities of the venture will be imputed to the nonprofit. To ensure that participation in the joint venture is not deemed unrelated activity, the nonprofit must maintain control of the venture to ensure that the charitable purpose (and not investor profit) remains primary. The nonprofit can maintain control in the venture by including certain provisions in the operating agreement, including provisions that require the nonprofit to approve certain decisions, or allow the nonprofit to appoint the governing body, etc. Investors' return should be reasonable and not excessive.[95]

---

93. Caftel, *supra* note 52 (citing Rev. Rul. 68-296, 1968-1 C.B., which provides that "[t]he subsidiary cannot make tax-deductible contributions to the Section 501(c)(3) organization because the organization controls the subsidiary").

94. IRS Publ'n 598, Tax on Unrelated Business Income of Exempt Organizations.

95. Caftel, *supra* note 52.

Sponsorships

Sponsorships are a method by which nonprofits can receive revenue without it being considered unrelated business income. If a business provides funds, goods, or services to the nonprofit and the nonprofit publicly acknowledges the sponsor by, for example, including its name and logo on the nonprofit's website, the funds are not considered unrelated business income. This is in contrast to a situation in which a business pays a nonprofit for advertising.

What is the difference between advertising and sponsorship? If the nonprofit merely acknowledges the business, then it is a sponsorship, but if it endorses or recommends the business, it is advertising. Also, if payment to the nonprofit is contingent on factors such as the number of eyeballs on a website or the number of attendees at an event, the payment will be treated as unrelated business income and therefore subject to UBIT.

Royalties

Another way that a 501(c)(3) can generate revenue that is not subject to UBIT is through royalties. A royalty is a payment related to the use of a right. Examples include payments for the use of trademarks, trade names, service marks, or copyrights. When you see a credit card with the logo of a nonprofit on it, this is an example of a royalty arrangement. When a nonprofit rents its mailing list to a for-profit, this is also considered a royalty arrangement. Royalty arrangements must be passive to be exempt from UBIT. So, if a nonprofit provides services in conjunction with the use of its mailing list or logo, the payment will likely be subject to UBIT.

Nonprofit Funds for For-Profits

In the preceding sections, we described ways that nonprofits can participate in economic activities that are usually associated with for-profits. This section describes ways that for-profits can participate in activities that are usually associated with nonprofits.

1. A nonprofit can pay a for-profit to do work as long as the payment is beneficial and fair to the nonprofit. For example, a nonprofit that receives a grant to build a model green home and does not have the expertise to build the home itself may contract with

a for-profit to build the home, as long as the payment to the for-profit is not above market rate and is negotiated at arms' length.

2. A nonprofit can conduct activities that directly benefit private businesses if those activities further the nonprofit's charitable purpose. So, for example, a nonprofit whose mission is to help disadvantaged small businesses can make low-interest loans to such businesses. And a nonprofit whose mission is to help low-income individuals find employment can provide free employee training services that benefit for-profit businesses.
3. Foundations can make loans to and invest in for-profit businesses to achieve their mission if the primary purpose of the loan or investment is charitable or educational. This is called a Program Related Investment (PRI) and is becoming increasingly popular (though still relatively rare) among foundations.
4. A for-profit business that conducts activities that would be eligible for tax-exemption can receive grant funds via a fiscal sponsorship arrangement. For example, let's say a for-profit acupuncture business would like to conduct free or low-cost community workshops about alternative medicine. The for-profit could find a nonprofit fiscal sponsor for the educational program it wants to conduct and could apply for grants under the fiscal sponsor's name. The nonprofit could contract with the for-profit to conduct the workshops at market rate.

LOCAL GOVERNMENT OWNERSHIP OF ENTERPRISE[1]

Municipal enterprises have different goals and time horizons than traditional companies. The aim is not to maximize profits but to develop a community asset that meets the needs of residents and benefits the community. As a number of experts have noted, a new strategy may be emerging: instead of offering incentives for businesses to relocate, municipalities are using their own investment capacity to start city-run businesses.

1. This section is adapted from Marjorie Kelly & Shanna Ratner, Keeping Wealth Local: Shared Ownership and Wealth Control for Rural Communities (Tellus Inst. & Yellow Wood Assocs. 2009).

City-owned enterprises operate in areas such as energy, telecommunications, solid waste services, convention centers, ports, airports, transit systems, hospitals, parking garages, golf courses, and even hotels and liquor stores.

Hutchinson, Minnesota, owns a recycling business that collects organic material for its *Creek Side Soils* brand of compost and colored mulch, which is sold to retailers, golf courses, and individuals. The city also owns a hospital, electric plant, liquor store, local cemetery, and airport.

When city leaders in Glasgow, Kentucky (pop. 14,000), became concerned about the high price of cable services, they decided to create a community-owned service that now charges just $27.50 a month. They are also one of the few cities to offer an alternative to the local commercial phone service.

Some two dozen rural towns in Vermont have joined together to create the East Central Vermont Community Fiber Network, to bring state-of-the-art broadband services to their residents.

Part 8: Organizational Governance Models

How does an organization manage activities and make decisions in a more collaborative economy? Traditional governance structures may have been adequate when applied to commercial businesses and charitable organizations. However, in a more sharing economy, businesses and organizations focus on providing for diverse stakeholders and participants. As the sharing economy grows, we will *all* likely be involved in more organizations that are designed to provide for our personal and community needs, such as cohousing communities, food cooperatives, car-sharing cooperatives, and childcare cooperatives. In all of these organizations, stakeholder participation is critical to ensure that the organization can provide for everyone's needs.

A well-thought-out decision-making process is also crucial to ensuring that a group can respond effectively to participating stakeholders. Leaving decisions to a small governing board will not necessarily be enough, even if that board is elected by stakeholders. Nor will it always be appropriate to allow decisions to be made by majority rule, which can sometimes result in alienation of a minority within the group. Hierarchies will often be ill-fitted to sharing organizations because there may not be owners or experts to whom governance should obviously be handed. In many such organizations, we are likely *all* the owners and *all* the experts about what needs to be done and how to meet our needs.

Governance in the sharing economy is, thus, highly participatory and inclusive and requires that all actions of a group are adequately considered and adapted to meet multiple needs. The new economy therefore demands that we all become fluent in participatory governance models.

Above, we spoke a great deal about how organizations *consider* or even *involve* multiple stakeholders in decision-making. The composition and selection of an organization's governing body is a key consideration in ensuring that decisions are truly representative of the needs of stakeholders. In addition, here are some other questions to consider in relation to organizational governance:

1. **In what way will stakeholders participate in decisions?** There is a broad spectrum of options for involving stakeholders in decision-making. In small worker-owned collectives, every worker-owner serves on the board of directors. In very large cooperatives where members are geographically spread out, the primary way that members participate in governance is by electing the board of directors. In that respect, participation in governance is minimal. The middle ground holds many promising options. Through governance and operational models like dynamic self governance (described below) and holacracy,[96] governance of an organization is often dispersed into multiple semi-autonomous spheres, which allows for high levels of participation even in large organizations.

---

96. *See* Brian J. Robertson, *Organization Evolved: Introducing Holacracy* (Aug. 6, 2009), http://holacracy.org/sites/default/files/resources/Organization_Evolved.pdf.

2. **What are the spheres of authority and management?** Even in cooperatives that are collectively governed by their members, innumerable decisions are delegated to individuals, committees, and management teams. How does an organization structure multiple spheres of authority and operations, and how do those spheres interact and remain accountable to the organization as a whole? This is where we feel that models like dynamic self governance and holacracy can be especially helpful.
3. **How are meetings conducted and proposals considered?** The ways in which meetings are conducted and proposals considered can greatly impact the extent to which an organization is meaningfully able to listen to the needs of stakeholders and respond to tensions that arise. Many organizations adopt specific procedures for ensuring that proposals and issues are adequately discussed. Traditional organizations often use Robert's Rules of Order to ensure that there is consistency in how a meeting is held and how items are discussed. Groups that require consensus to make decisions generally adopt a very different set of procedures, which are described below. Dynamic self-governance and holacracy models both tend to use carefully structured procedures for meetings and the consideration of proposals.
4. **What is the process for arriving at a decision?** Can a majority vote carry a decision? Would a two-thirds vote be more representative? Should the group seek consensus? How will the group handle disagreement and formal blocks to consensus?

Since we, the authors of this chapter, are not experts on the nuts and bolts of organizational governance models, we have asked two experts to profile two models and talk about how an organization may implement these governance models into its legal structure.

CONSENSUS DECISION-MAKING: WHAT, WHY, HOW?

By Tree Bressen

*Tree Bressen serves a wide variety of groups on a gift economy basis, offering skilled facilitation, dynamic workshops, and elegant process design.**

Every group makes decisions. A group of friends may decide what movie to watch, a car-sharing group decides how long someone can use a shared vehicle, a credit union decides what interest rate to offer its depositors. The larger and more formal the organization, the more formal their decision-making procedure is likely to be.

Every group faces a variety of decisions, sorted into categories that are handled differently. For example, in a group of friends, how to dress is probably a personal decision, whereas for employees at the credit union, how to dress is likely an organizational decision. Just because something is an organizational decision does not mean that everyone in the organization necessarily participates in the making of that decision; at the credit union, for example, the branch manager may have authority to set that policy, and then the tellers are expected to follow it. For any type of decision, the power to decide it may be given:

(a) to one person (may be someone in a leadership or managerial role, or may be any member acting autonomously);
(b) to a subgroup (for example, the board of a food co-op, or the media committee of an activist collective); or
(c) to the group as a whole.

The more clear a group is on which decisions get made by whom, the more easily their self-governance runs.

When a decision is being made by more than one person (either a subgroup or the group as a whole), then the group needs to have a way to do that. The two most well-known "decision rules" are

(1) **Consensus** (meaning all members must consent for a decision to move forward); and

* More information is available at www.treegroup.info.

(2) **Majority vote** (meaning agreement by a set majority of participants is sufficient to make a decision official).

In reality there is a spectrum of options, ranging from 51 percent vote through attempts at consensus with a super-majority voting fallback (typically 75 percent to 90 percent), through "consensus minus one," on to full consensus required. While voting may be faster, consensus offers a few key advantages:

- **More effective implementation:** When people's ideas and concerns are taken into account, then they are much more likely to actively participate in making something happen. If a participant with a minority position is overruled, they are naturally unlikely to help carry out the decision with enthusiasm.
- **Building connection among the members:** Using consensus as a decision rule means taking the time to find unity on how to proceed before moving forward. It is a synthesizing process. Voting creates winners and losers, thus it has an inherent polarizing effect.
- **Higher quality decisions:** Integrating the wisdom of more people into the decision generally results in better, smarter, more "co-intelligent" decisions that serve a group well into the future.

Humans have been making decisions together by consensus for millennia and carry innate knowledge of how to do that. At the same time, because English-speaking societies are currently immersed in a culture of separation, we need support, training, and models to help us. Every group's process is a little different according to its own organic development. In order for your group to write its own consensus policy, some questions you'll need to answer include the following.

If meeting agendas are formed in advance (usually a good idea), how does that happen, when, and by whom?

The planner role includes figuring out what items will be on the agenda, for how long, and in what order. If the agenda planner is not the facilitator of the meeting, they'll both need to work together to ensure that the agenda is realistic for the time available and that each person presenting an item is fully prepared, and to select formats. While our dominant image of a meeting is one person speaking at a time to an assembled group, many meetings can be improved by the creative use of alternative formats such as small group break-outs, fishbowls (where a subset of the group talks in the middle while others silently witness), spectrum line-ups (asking people to stand along a line that represents a spectrum of opinion on the issue at hand), and others.

Often people want to bring items to the meeting agenda that don't actually require full group involvement or should start first with a committee discussion—so the planner role includes aspects of gate-keeping (reserving full group time for the things that most need substantive interaction) and education (helping newer or forgetful members learn how to move items forward through appropriate means).

What process happens outside the official full-group meetings?

Every group has informal conversations on topics of mutual interest that naturally arise in the course of working together. Some groups deliberately acknowledge this as part of their process. If someone has strong feelings on an issue, seeking him/her out to talk it over outside the meeting may lead to a more effective conversation later in the official discussion.

Some groups use a log or decision board to decide smaller items that probably don't need full-group discussion. For example, new procedures proposed by an area manager or team may be announced or even discussed in writing, and unless someone says it needs to come to a meeting, then the written version is considered accepted. Be wary, obviously, of discussing anything emotionally charged in writing or via email, as those are generally not the most suitable venues for handling upsets.

Some groups hold separate gatherings in order to have time to discuss issues without any pressure to make a decision. For example, a committee may host a salon or "distillery" in order to get input from others on a matter of interest to the group. These kinds of sessions are often very useful, especially if those who disagree the most commit to being there.

For more complex proposals, there will almost certainly be some detailed work on them by one person or a committee, rather than hashing out every word on the fly in plenary (whole-group meeting). There is commonly an iterative back-and-forth between plenary and committee work, where ideas and drafts are brought forth, receive feedback, are revised and brought forth again. For example, a member or team broaches a subject by putting it onto the meeting agenda; then possible responses are discussed, and the team writes a specific proposal based on that discussion, which the plenary then considers.

What signals, if any, are used to let the facilitator and the group know participants' input?

The most common signal in any meeting is, of course, raising one's hand to indicate desire to speak. Larger groups often find it helpful to have additional visual cues, in order to help manage the speaking order and to let people know where others in the room are at. Some groups use hand signals, while others use colored cards. There are often two sets, depending on whether the meeting is in a *discussion* phase or a *decision* phase. A typical signal set might include a discussion phase and a decision phase.

Discussion Phase

1. **Process point:** Something in the process is off or can be improved.
2. **Question:** I have a question to help me understand or evaluate the proposal.
3. **Point of information:** I have an answer to a question that's been asked, or factual correction only.
4. **Comment:** I want to offer an idea/opinion/feeling/ concern.
5. **Vibes:** I have an emotional response to the topic that I need to share. (Groups that use this signal normally have

a procedure that happens following it, for example, someone automatically offers to reflect back what the speaker just said, before proceeding further.)

Decision Phase

1. Agreement
2. Consent with Reservations
3. Stand Aside
4. Block
5. Abstain (usually signified by not using any of the signals)

While in some groups silence might signify consent, this approach is not generally recommended. Having some active sign for consent (saying "yes," thumbs up, nodding head, etc.) prevents anyone from later ducking responsibility for the decision by saying, "I was in the room, but did not really agree, I just didn't speak up in time."

How will our group respond robustly to inappropriate blocks?

As explained below, the consensus process gives substantial power to individuals to make their own discernment as to whether a proposal is in the best interest of the group. That power needs to be balanced with limits and responsibilities. In other words, there needs to be some way to deal with a member who is blocking inappropriately. The most effective groups have both cultural and procedural means of doing this.

Cultural methods include

- Genuinely honoring dissenting viewpoints, including staying in relationship with those who disagree and not isolating them;
- Avoiding use of the word "block" prematurely by using the framing of "concerns" until after a thorough discussion has taken place and you are actually at the call for consensus; and

- Spreading the idea that if you've blocked an emerging consensus half a dozen times in your lifetime (for all the groups you are part of), you've used up your quota.

Procedural methods include

- Requiring anyone who is blocking to convene extra meetings in an effort to work out an alternative, within a time limit, or else their block is automatically lifted;
- Requiring group validation of a block in some form; for example, saying that a block does not count unless at least one other member agrees it is valid, or 75 percent of the group, or the executive team or steering council of the organization; and
- Using a fallback vote, as explained below.

Is there a voting fallback, and if so, how does it operate? Many groups using consensus choose to have a voting fallback in place in case there is an urgent need for a decision and no consensus has been found. Typically these fallbacks are not invoked frequently, but their existence serves as a reassurance and as a guard against tyranny of the minority. If you are going to have a fallback, you need to be clear on the circumstances under which it is invoked and what its procedures are. Often such a vote has a super-majority threshold, such as 75 percent or 90 percent rather than 51 percent, to avoid a complete split of the group.

There are also some non-policy questions worth considering, such as:

1. Are we clear on the purpose of our group and its meetings?
2. Aside from having a clear policy, what will the group do to make meetings fun and fulfilling, nurturing a positive spirit?
3. Groups run better when the people involved get along well together. How will our group's interpersonal relationships be nourished? What will help members feel appreciated?

4. How will incoming members get trained in the decision-making process?
5. How will facilitators (and minute-takers, agenda planners, etc.) be trained and supported?

* * *

SAMPLE CONSENSUS PROCESS POLICY

Here is one sample policy outlining a consensus decision-making process that may be useful to draw on. This level of detail would typically appear in a policy document rather than bylaws, so that it can be more easily modified as a group evolves. Often, an organization's bylaws will make reference to a separate consensus policy and require that decisions be made in accordance with the policy.

Introduction

Consensus is a cooperative process in which group members develop and agree to support a decision in the best interest of the whole. It embraces individual perspectives, honoring each person's piece of the truth, while emphasizing the sense of the meeting through a creative search for unity. By choosing to use consensus as our primary decision-making method, we recognize that we are pledging to do the hard, patient work of bringing our best selves forward and listening from the heart. We encourage participants to share ideas, feelings, needs, and concerns, in a spirit of honesty, kindness, and mutual respect, giving all viewpoints a fair hearing. We recognize we are sometimes called to accept with good grace a decision of the meeting with which we are not entirely in agreement. We affirm our willingness to listen with an open mind to the truths of others, and to work in good faith toward decisions that reflect the whole group intention and serve its greatest good.

Agenda Planning

Items to be considered for the monthly meeting agenda are expected to be received by the agenda planner(s) no later than ten days before the meeting, including any associated documentation. Agenda planners aim to publish the proposed agenda five to seven days before the meeting, along with the background materials (reports, research, survey results, proposals, etc.). Members are asked to please read this and come prepared to discuss the issues.

There are often more potential items for the agenda than time in the meeting. We support our agenda planners in prioritizing, recognizing that the group usually finds it more satisfying to do a thorough job on a few items than to take a quick pass at many. Agenda planners may also assist members in finding alternate ways to address issues without taking full-group time. The planner makes sure there are facilitators and minute-takers signed up for each meeting, as well as the next agenda planner.

Every plenary agenda includes time at the beginning for short personal check-ins and group confirmation and approval of the agenda; at least one break; and time at the end for evaluations and appreciations. Each item on the agenda is assigned a time allocation and labeled with a clear goal, such as: Information, Discussion, or Decision.

We use the following matrix in determining whether an item comes first as an issue discussion or an official proposal:

Is the issue...	*SIMPLE*	*COMPLEX*
SMALL	Proposal may pass with relative ease.	Likely send to committee for most of the work.
LARGE	Might be OK to start with proposal, and it might take a few more meetings, possibly with committee work in between.	Start with issue discussion, not proposal, and expect it to take a series of meetings, almost always with committee or individual work in between.

Facilitator Roles

We ask everyone present to share responsibility for creating a constructive conversation. Our facilitators take special responsibility to support us by managing our meeting process so the rest of us can focus on the content. The facilitator acts as a servant of the group. In order to do this, facilitators need to remain as neutral as possible—in word, deed, and appearance—and avoid stating or implying your opinion on the agenda items in the meeting. This includes not being the official presenter of any items at the meeting you are facilitating, and finding a replacement facilitator if something gets put onto the agenda that you have especially strong feelings about. If at any time your neutrality becomes an issue (for you personally or in someone else's perception), your co-facilitator and the rest of the team can support you by stepping in and giving you a break.

The facilitator job includes working with the agenda planner(s) beforehand. Each meeting has a lead facilitator and an assistant facilitator, who sign up ahead of time and together decide how to handle the job. They may recruit additional assistance if needed to cover all the work, which includes:

- Contacting presenters to discuss format and how the item may unfold at the meeting;
- Getting the room ready, including setting up chairs, flipchart, markers, and tape;
- Posting agenda clearly so everyone can read it;
- Welcoming the group and opening the meeting;
- Making it clear which step of the process we are on, and when;
- Keeping "stack" (a list of people desiring to speak) and deciding who speaks in what order, including ensuring that quieter voices are heard;
- Doing reflective listening to individual participants, especially those holding concerns;
- Weaving and summarizing input to the meeting;
- Scribing comments and lists onto the flipchart;
- Suggesting formats, "light & lively" exercises, or breaks to help improve the energy;
- Taking "temperature checks" if needed to get feedback from the group;
- "Vibes-watching," that is, keeping an eye out for emotional dynamics and responding appropriately;

- Running the call for consensus on each item that reaches the decision point;
- Ensuring that extraneous issues which arise mid-meeting and get put onto the "bike rack" (also known as a "parking lot," which is a list of matters that arise but which cannot be discussed in the present meeting) make it onto the agenda list afterward to get considered for future meetings; and
- Keeping track of time.

We try to have at least six facilitators on the team at any given time, serving staggered terms, and to pair up more and less experienced facilitators so that newcomers get support to step up.

Steps of the Consensus Process

Each item requiring a decision goes through the following steps. Some items may not need a decision, in which case they might not go through the full sequence. We expect substantive items to take multiple meetings, in which case we start each time with step #1, and then pick up where it makes sense based on what happened last time. Because we prefer to give power to people who are present in a meeting more than those who are absent, proposals can be modified on the floor and adopted; indeed, changing a proposal in response to new wisdom emerging is at the heart of the consensus process.

1. Introduction

Typically the introduction takes less than five minutes and covers the following:

- Why are we talking about this? Why does it matter?
- What is the history of the issue (including results of any previous meetings on it)?
- What is the goal for this item at this particular meeting (report, decision, committee to gather input, etc.)?

At the end of the initial presentation, others who have factual knowledge of the issue are sometimes invited to add in further bits about the history and so on, provided it doesn't go on for too long.

2. Clarifying Questions

These are simple questions just to make sure everyone in the room fully understands what has been presented or proposed.

3. Discussion

This is the exploratory phase, where people are invited to ask further questions, show the full diversity of perspectives, raise challenges and concerns, and so on. Agreements and disagreements on general direction are noticed, and the reasons for them examined—not just what the positions are, but why, and any underlying values conflicts brought out.

4. Establish Basic Direction

What is the sense of the meeting, in terms of basic direction on this issue? Here we seek general or philosophical agreement, an agreement in principle.

5. Synthesize or Modify Proposal (as needed)

Integrate what's been shared so far and make it as specific as needed, recognizing that some details will always be left to implementation and real-life experimentation. Again, we notice agreements and disagreements (this time on the specifics of the proposal) and work with the underlying reasons; then we generate ideas for addressing and resolving concerns, emerging with a proposal that has substantial group support. Periodically the facilitator may ask, "Are there any remaining unresolved concerns?"

6. Call for Consensus

The facilitator clearly restates the proposal and then asks people to indicate where they are, using the options listed below. Remember our bylaws require a 70 percent quorum for official decisions. Note that newcomers are required to attend an orientation from the facilitation team before they can be vested as fully empowered decision-making members.

7. Record

The note-taker reads back the decision to the group. In addition, they record any implementation information needed (tasks, who's responsible, timelines, etc.).

8. Revisiting the Decisions

Once a decision has been reached, it may be revisited if any of the following conditions apply:

(a) Something relevant and significant has changed since the decision was reached;
(b) More than two years have passed;
(c) Five or more members request a revisit.

Decision Point Options

At the point that the facilitator calls for consensus (step #6 above), participants have the following options:

1. **Agreement:** "I support this proposal, and am willing to abide by and implement it."
2. **Consent with reservations:** "I support the basic thrust of this proposal, and have one or more minor unresolved concerns."
3. **Stand aside:** "I have major concerns with the proposal, and agree to stand aside and let the group proceed with it." The choice to stand aside may be based on (but is not limited to) any of the following:
    - Disagreement with the proposal, or the process used to reach the decision;
    - Personal values or principles; or
    - Personal impact or need (e.g., "I can't afford this," or "I'd have to leave the group").

    If someone stands aside, their name and reason is recorded in the minutes. That person is relieved of any lead implementation responsibilities, yet is still bound to follow the decision.

4. **Blocking:** "I believe this proposal would be majorly detrimental to our group, because either it goes against our fundamental principles or it would lead to a disastrous outcome." Note that none of the following is an appropriate reason to block:
   - To get your way or because you prefer a different proposal, or no proposal;
   - To fulfill your unique personal preferences or how you want to live;
   - Tradition: because things have always been done this way;
   - Because the proposed action doesn't fit your personal needs (or finances); and
   - Because you'd have to leave the group if the proposal passed.

   In order to protect against inappropriate use of blocking, the group has the option to evaluate blocks: If 90 percent of the group present believes that a block is being applied inappropriately, then the block is invalidated. This power must be used carefully in order to avoid simply overruling those we disagree with.
5. **Abstain:** "I choose not to participate in the making of this decision." Typically used because a participant feels uninformed or not ready to participate.

If we've done a good job during the discussion period, there should not be any surprises at the call for consensus. If anyone consents with reservations, stands aside, or blocks, the group will pause to ensure that the reasons are clearly known and consider whether the proposal might be modified to address the concerns. If more than three people have minor reservations, or more than one person stands aside, we will ask whether or not the decision at hand requires higher support in order to fulfill the goals of our consensus process (high-quality decisions, effective implementation, and connection among the group), in which case we may hold the decision over to a future meeting. Most decisions don't need to be made in a rush; at the same time, we recognize that there is a cost to inaction, so we seek to move things along in order to respect people's time, energy, and morale.

If a decision is time-sensitive due to external factors and consensus is not reached, the group may elect to invoke a voting fallback. In order for that to happen, 95 percent of those present must agree it is called for. If a vote takes place, decisions may pass by 90 percent of those voting. Options at that decision point are: Yes, No, Abstain. (Abstentions don't count toward the total.)

* * *

Finally, here is a quotation from writer Mark Shepard:

> Consensus makes special demands on all. You must respect and consider each other. You must have a sense of common searching, instead of wanting to "win." You must be sensitive and open to each others' ideas and feelings, and honestly try to accommodate them. Finally, you must be dedicated to uncovering and pursuing truth—even if it leads where you never expected. Ignore these guidelines, and consensus can frustrate, divide, and fail. Follow them, and it can energize, unify, and succeed beyond your expectations.

Further Resources

- **Tree Bressen's website**, filled with free articles, handouts, and pointers to yet more resources; available at www.treegroup.info.
- **Group Works deck, published by the Group Pattern Language Project.** Distills the core wisdom of good meetings into an excellent hands-on tool; available at www.groupworksdeck.org.
- **Seeds for Change (UK)** has a wonderful website on consensus decision-making: their writing is straightforward, thorough, values-based, and includes a historical and multicultural

perspective; available at www.seedsforchange.org.uk/free/res#grp.

- **Starhawks's "Five-Fold Path of Productive Meetings,"** a free bonus chapter from her book *The Empowerment Manual: A Guide for Collaborative Groups*; available at www.starhawk.org/Empowerment_Five-Fold-Path.pdf.
- **Training for Change** has a great collection of tools and exercises on topics such as diversity, strategy, and team-building; available at www.trainingforchange.org.
- **Vernal Project.** Randy Schutt, long-time activist, has a dozen short papers on cooperative decision-making. See, for example, "Getting Unstuck: Common Problems in Meetings and Some Solutions"; available at www.vernalproject.org/papers/Process.html.

DYNAMIC SELF GOVERNANCE & SHARING LIVES

By Gaya Erlandson, PhD

Gaya Erlandson, PhD, is a psychologist and community consultant who teaches Dynamic Self Governance and who lives in a small cohousing-like community near Asheville, N.C.

Sharing is a vital aspect of community building. By uniting isolated neighbors into caring networks, sharing has the capacity to create communities of people who understand that their greatest source of abundance is in their shared, human assets. Parents who struggle alone to provide for their families, for example, can collaborate with neighbors for reliable, quality childcare, teen mentoring with local seniors, and meal and ride sharing.

Key to community building, however, is good governance and decision-making processes. Being a long-committed community-builder, I am excited to describe a highly effective governance system that enables communities to be thriving contexts of caring, collaborative relationships.

Dynamic Self Governance (DSG) is an innovative approach to governance that

- Streamlines decision-making while reducing tension around power;
- Maximizes decision-making effectiveness and efficiency;
- Kindles creativity, innovation, and entrepreneurial spirit;
- Decreases number of meetings and heightens productivity of meetings;
- Increases individual engagement, productivity, and commitment;
- Builds relationships and community belonging; and
- Provides a structure that assures ongoing progress, learning, and improvement.

In much of the world, Dynamic Self Governance is called "sociocracy" based on the Latin and Greek words *socius* meaning "social familiarity" and *kratei* meaning "governance." With roots dating back to 1851 when Auguste Comte coined the term, sociocracy has been developed extensively by Gerard Endenburg in the Netherlands, starting in 1970 when he began applying its principles to his electrical engineering corporation.

Sociocracy was brought to the United States by business consultant John Buck, who has studied with Endenburg since the 1980s. To date, sociocracy has been implemented in hundreds of organizations around the world—private and public schools and universities, professional groups, large and small businesses, government agencies, and intentional communities. In the United States, sociocracy is largely referred to as Dynamic Self Governance (DSG).

Structure and Principles

DSG can be pictured as a hierarchy of circles reflecting different levels of work, not control. Circles are groups of 2 to 40 people who know each other and who have a particular aim or job within a business or community organization. A simple three-tiered hierarchy includes the Top Circle, made up of those heading the organization (Board of Directors, CEO, CFO, etc.) and a representative from the next circle down called the General Circle. The General Circle is made up of representatives from the circles at the third level (sometimes referred to as departments, committees, etc.) and also has its own representative in each of the lowest level circles as well as in the Top Circle (see double-linking below).

The four principles of Dynamic Governance are simple, but have dramatic effects.

1. **Consent:** Policy decisions are made by consent. Consent means members must offer a well-reasoned "paramount objection" (relevant to stated aims) so it can be addressed. Rather than generating a negative turning point, paramount objections often result in the opposite. Discord and chaos are embraced as opportunities to improve the proposal—and as opportunities for the group to build trust and understanding. In articulating objections, for example, members learn about the needs, gifts, and ideas of the others. They also gain clarity on their own motivation, goals, and ideas.
2. **Circles of Equivalence:** Members within each circle are highly involved in determining meeting agendas, engaging in transparent elections, co-creating proposals for policies or projects, making decisions, etc. Decisions that are implemented are monitored and the outcomes are measured by members of the circle to further the group's learning and effectiveness.
3. **Double-Linking:** All the circles are "double-linked." Two people within each circle also are elected members of the next-higher circle. Because of this, ideas from the "lowest" circles can link upward and become implemented at any higher-level, or move laterally through the representatives. With a comprehensive feedback system that ensures communication up and down the organization, DSG's double-linking optimizes an organization's ability to respond to internal and external pressures. This self-optimization allows a business or community organization to be very resilient.

4. **Elections:** Although some people are elected for specific tasks and functions over time, everyone within each circle has an equal vote and can be elected for any function. The election process assures both that the elected person is accepted by the group as the best available one to do the task, and that s/he understands what the task requires.

DSG and Sharing Economy Law

Writing DSG governing documents into a new or existing legal structure can be done rather easily. In Appendix E of the book *We The People*, Buck and Villines offer an example of DSG operating agreements and bylaws for a limited liability company (LLC).

- Article 1 includes three sections entitled Organizational Model (describes the four principles), Structure (describes Top Circle, General Circle, Department Circles, etc.), and Investing and Working Partners.
- Article 2, entitled "Top Circle," gives details on its composition, roles, terms, meeting requirements, how to handle vacancies, etc.
- Article 3 focuses on "Executive Officers of the Top Circle." Significantly, the Board of Directors is part of the Top Circle and shall not meet separately from the Top Circle.
- Article 4, entitled "Circle Management," has several subsections. It is stated here, for example, that each circle shall be a separate organ of the LLC and shall be empowered to draft its own regulations (in agreement with Top Circle's vision, etc.); that the next-higher circle, through its representative, is responsible for ensuring that decision-making in a circle below functions according to the operating agreement; that recording circle minutes be done properly, etc.
- Article 5, entitled "Compensation and Profit Sharing," offers an ingenious way to compensate investing and working partners (workers), with both fixed and variable payments, depending on profitability.

Living Well Care Home

An excellent example of an organization that implemented DSG is Living Well, an award-winning, level III, residential care and assisted-living facility in Bristol, Vermont. Under John Buck's guidance in 2004, they adapted existing 501(c)(3) bylaws and other governing documents to implement the DSG principles and procedures described above.

Living Well is the first elder care facility in the United States to implement DSG. The Resident Circle, for example, meets regularly and actively discusses whatever is important to them—whether it be the menu, how services are provided, what activities to pursue, or how to measure outcomes. This circle also elects one of their members to represent them in the Staff Circle, and that person regularly checks in with all of the elders. Per Top Circle vision, Living Well removed toxic cleaning supplies as well as refined and artificial sugar. They started a community garden and hired a naturopathologist to see residents (in addition to the required medical staff). Within just six months, many residents showed noticeable improvements—physically, mentally, and socially. One woman thought to have severe dementia picked up the phone one day and had a lucid conversation with her family for the first time in years. Another who had previously just sat in her room started playing the piano in the living room. No one knew she had been a piano teacher. For further information on the Living Well Care Home, see http://LivingWellCareHome.org.

Implementing DSG from the Ground Up

DSG can also be implemented over time, from the ground up. For example, in a neighborhood with a Homeowners Association, a group of neighbors can begin with shared projects such as a garden. After experiencing success in sharing and making decisions together, members of this initial circle might seed new circles, such as one that creates a playground in a shared area or a food co-op. When several of these third-level circles exist, they could create a General Circle made up of representatives from each circle to better coordinate efforts. Eventually the Homeowners Association (or some other group) may adopt DSG and become the Top Circle and thus create a completely integrated (double-linked) DSG hierarchy. For an example of a cohousing community that has implemented DSG, see http://www.champlainvalleycohousing.org.

In short, DSG is a scalable, decision-making structure (from a few to countless, interlinked small groups) that guarantees the opportunity of self-directed contribution and optimal development for all within a sharing, caring context.

For a longer version of this article, along with a second article giving more of a description of the challenges and benefits of implementing DSG at Living Well, please go to http://www.livingnewstories.com.

References

- Buck, John & Sharon Villines, *We The People: Consenting to a Deeper Democracy, A Guide to Sociocratic Principles and Methods* (Sociocracy.info, 2007), available at http://GovernanceAlive.com/.
- Gerard Endenburg, *Sociocracy as Social Design: Its Characteristics and Course of Development, as Theoretical Design and Practical Project* (Translated, Eburon, 1997) (1998).
- Gerard Endenburg. 1981. *Sociocracy: The Organization of Decision-Making "No Objection" as the Principle of Sociocracy* (Translated, Eburon, 1998) (1981).
- John McKnight & Peter Block. *The Abundant Community* (Berrett-Koehler Publishers, 2010), available at http://ABCDinstitute.org/.
- John P. Kretzmann & John L. McKnight *Building Communities From the Inside Out: A Path Toward Finding and Mobilizing a Community's Assets* (ACTA Publications, 1993).

CHAPTER FIVE

NEW KINDS OF EXCHANGE

Part 1: I Can See Clearly Now the Money's Gone

A community without dollars is not a community without wealth—this basic understanding fuels the sharing economy. Every community, no matter how money-poor, has, at the very least, a wealth of human resources and the capacity to create material resources. Dollars give us a very organized means of sharing and exchanging those resources. However, when there is a scarcity of dollars, our economy need not grind to a frightening halt. We need only find additional ways to share and exchange. Our systems for exchange could be as organized as a local currency or online mutual credit system, or as casual as swapping and gift-based provision among friends and community members. This vast realm of economic possibility, of course, churns up new legal gray areas and unique challenges for attorneys working in this realm.

The Scarcity of Dollars

To the extent that people want them badly and use them often, dollars will always be in our lives. But today, U.S. society is plagued by foreclosures, business closures, and unemployment—these are both the causes and the effects of dollar scarcity. Even in better economic times, there have always been people who do not have enough money to meet their basic needs.

Scarcity is built into our money system itself. The majority of money in circulation today was issued by banks in the form of loans. Money is, essentially, lent into existence, with interest. Repaying a loan with interest means the borrowers must work hard to earn even *more* than they have spent. People end up competing with one another to earn that premium and to get ahead financially. Inevitably, some people do get ahead, and do so at the expense of others who fall behind, fall into default on credit cards, and fall into poverty. In such a system, money will always be scarce for some people. Today, in 2012, it is scarce for many.

If all dollars in existence were to simply disappear—evaporating from our wallets and our bank accounts—the sum total of all wealth in society would not be affected in the least. In fact, the disappearance of dollars would be our good fortune if it were to help us see that we have other reasons, incentives, and mechanisms for providing that wealth for one another. If dollars were out of the picture, humans would find innumerable and creative ways to exchange.

Even though dollars will not disappear entirely, their abundance is subject to wild fluctuation, and we would do very well to establish alternatives to our dependence on dollars. The more ways we find to exchange, the more resilient our economy will be in difficult times. For example, in 2011, the world watched as Greece suffered from a dramatic financial collapse, after which barter networks and local currencies gained strong traction, giving people means to continue transacting with each other.[1]

Also, in the 1930s, when Switzerland experienced a scarcity of the national currency, a complementary currency known as the WIR was created. The WIR is not a printed currency, but an exchange system that exists only in bookkeeping. Today, the WIR continues to play a strong role in the Swiss economy, with tens of thousands of people circulating the equivalent of $3 billion in WIR.[2] Use of the WIR grows in popularity when the Swiss Franc becomes scarce; because use of the WIR restores balance and enables transaction during times of scarcity, the Swiss economy is somewhat insulated from the extreme effects of recession.[3] A society that implements such complementary systems and habits of exchange can therefore be far more resilient during tough

1. Rachel Donadio, *Battered by Economic Crisis, Greeks Turn to Barter Networks*, N.Y. Times, Oct. 1, 2011.

2. For more information on the WIR Bank, see http://www.wir.ch.

3. *60 Years of the WIR Economic Circle Cooperative: Origins and Ideology of the Wirtschaftsring* (Thomas Greco trans. of article appearing in *WIR Magazin* (Sept. 1994)). http://projects.exeter.ac.uk/RDavies/arian/wir.html.

economic times and will also be far less likely to suffer from extreme ups and downs.

The Spectrum of Ways to Exchange

In the United States, there are already innumerable ways to exchange without money at the national, local, and personal levels. First of all, there are now systems to exchange with complete strangers all over the country. For example, last year, I "bought" and "sold" 18 DVDs using SwapaDVD.com, and the only currency I used consisted of "points" I earned after mailing free DVDs to total strangers. Many other websites have now been established to allow people to swap goods and services within a network and to pay one another with "points," "credits," or through other systems for tracking transactions.[4] The Green America Exchange[5] is an example of a barter exchange, where members, who are mostly green businesses, can offer their services and goods to other members, and receive "payment" in Exchange Dollars. In addition, Facebook has created its own currency called "Credits," which can be used to purchase apps, games, and other virtual goods. Credits are earned in a variety of ways—by playing games, watching ads, paying ten cents to Facebook, or buying an Arby's sandwich.[6]

At the level of local communities, there are now many time banks, which are communities of people who do favors for one another in exchange for "time dollars" that can be "spent" within the network to meet a variety of needs. Time banks are unique in that one person's hour is valued the same as someone else's hour, so there is no market-based valuation of people's services. In addition, people can spend time dollars and accumulate a negative account balance, and they are never legally obligated to "repay" them. It means that people who are in need can use a time bank to get assistance, without having to first accumulate a positive balance. In this respect, time banks aren't exactly facilitating barter; they are facilitating a culture of giving that could be an incredibly important tool for providing for people with diverse needs. Local currencies—both paper and digital—are also beginning to flow

---

4. Rachel Botsman & Roo Rogers, What's Mine Is Yours: How Collaborative Consumption Is Changing the Way We Live (Harper Collins 2010).

5. *See* http://www.greenamericaexchange.org.

6. Mark Hachman, *Buy an Arby's Sandwich, Get Facebook Credits with Plink*, PC Mag, Mar. 26, 2012, http://www.pcmag.com/article2/0,2817,2402151,00.asp.

in small communities around the country. Even *Time* has acknowledged that local currencies are gaining traction.[7]

Finally, on a person-to-person level, people may barter formally, swap casually, or simply adopt a habit of giving to one another. It is hard to measure how prevalent this has become in recent years. However, it is clear that when people do not have money to exchange with one another, gifting and bartering are often the first solutions people turn to.

When people transact using barter, swap networks, online currencies, local currencies, or time banks, this allows small-scale and local enterprises to gain an immediate advantage over multi-national businesses like Walmart, which only accepts dollars. Rather than struggling to compete with multimillion-dollar companies, a new generation of micro-entrepreneurs will thrive on new kinds of transactions.

Legal Gray Areas in the Spectrum

The spectrum of ways to exchange also means that there is a spectrum of legal reactions to those exchanges. On one end of the spectrum, there are highly formalized, contractual, and quantifiable exchanges, which are more likely to be subject to taxes, commercial regulations, employment laws, and so on. For example, if I pay $8 for a bowl of soup at a restaurant, I likely have a legal right to receive my soup (or my money back). I will pay sales tax on the $8, and the restaurant pays income tax on it. As an establishment that regularly provides soup for money, the restaurant is subject to all regulations of commercial food businesses.

At the other end of the spectrum are the casual and less quantifiable ways we provide for one another. If my neighbor brings me soup when I'm sick, I have no contractual right to demand my soup, and my neighbor has no contractual right to demand my gratitude. I'm not taxed on the value of the soup I receive and she's not taxed on my gratitude; as discussed further below, the Internal Revenue Service (IRS) generally does not consider gifts to be taxable income. Furthermore, my neighbor is not considered by the health department to be a restaurant. The gift of soup is a fairly simple transaction, free of legal headaches.

Between those two far ends of the spectrum, there are many ways to move soup around, and many gray areas in determining what regulations

7. Judith D. Schwartz, *Alternative Currencies Grow in Popularity*, Time, Dec. 14, 2008.

apply. Here are nine examples of ways that I might provide soup for others, moving from the casual to the formal end of the spectrum, and the legal questions that begin to arise along the way:[8]

1. **Soup parties:** Imagine, first of all, that I start throwing a monthly soup party for my friends. My friends may sometimes show their appreciation by inviting me over for dinner or by bringing dessert or drinks to my party. In that respect, I materially benefit in exchange for my soup, but in ways that are fairly unpredictable and unquantifiable. Most likely, the IRS and other regulatory agencies would not even bother with me. I haven't created a restaurant and the dessert my friends bring probably won't be taxable to me as "income."
2. **Gift economy soup:** Now what if I start having *weekly* soup parties and my friends start doing things for free too? As the spirit of giving and generosity grow, friends might offer free massage, gardening, computer help, handy work, or other favors. Other friends hold weekly salad nights, curry nights, or cookout nights, enough that all of us could get free dinners every day of the week. In this circle of giving, no one is *obligated* to give or receive anything, and no one is officially keeping track of who gives what and how it should be valued. Social expectation, not contract, governs this system of exchange.

   What are the legal implications in this scenario? Since the giving occurs among friends and comes largely from a place of generosity, it will all *probably* be tax-free. And because there are no contractual expectations of compensation and because people aren't bargaining for things at market prices, these activities *probably* wouldn't be considered commercial. The reason I say "*probably*" is that only slight variations in the above scenario could cause it to look more like example #3 (Barter soup) or #6 (Soup enterprises), which probably *are* taxed and regulated as businesses.
3. **Barter soup:** Now what if my accountant agrees to prepare my taxes in exchange for coming to five of my famous soup nights? This example differs from the above Gift Economy example

8. These soup examples are an expanded version of the examples I first published in *How to Barter, Give, and Get Stuff*, SHAREABLE.NET, Aug. 31, 2010.

because now we have a direct exchange that we've *bargained for*, and we have a binding verbal *contract* for barter. As discussed later in this chapter, although there are gray areas, this arrangement is quite possibly something the IRS would want us to report. My accountant would include the fair market value of my soup nights in her calculation of gross income. I would include the fair market value of the accounting services, and may suddenly even find myself paying self-employment taxes.

Another question to ask here is: am I now accidentally operating a soup business? Since I have a binding and bargained-for agreement to receive valuable services as "payment" for my soup, I've essentially *sold* soup to my accountant. Regulation of business comes from all kinds of agencies—such as health departments, planning departments, and state tax boards. In the eyes of these three types of agencies, selling soup even one time could technically be illegal without a health permit, zoning certificate, and seller's license, respectively.

4. **Time bank soup:** To continue expanding on the soup scenarios, my next project could be to go to the homes of elderly people to help by cooking soup. Because we are part of a local time bank similar to the Japanese Furaei Kippu ("Caring Relationship Tickets")[9] system, for each hour that I spend helping out, I get a "time dollar." Later on, I could redeem each "time dollar" for an hour of someone else's time, so long as someone is available and willing to do me a favor in exchange for a time dollar.

   In tax rulings described later in this chapter, the IRS has given some vague indication that they aren't interested in taxing exchange of services like this. They give at least two reasons: the exchanges are informal, meaning that I get no contractual right to have my favor returned, and the exchanges are non-commercial, meaning they aren't bargained for at market rates; whether I spend an hour cooking soup or an hour providing legal advice, my hour is valued at the same rate, and all transactions are an hour for an hour. Note, however, that I may, in fact, be subject to taxes and regulations for these time bank exchanges if my pri-

9. For more information, see the P2P Foundation wiki site on Fureai Kippu at http://p2pfoundation.net/Fureai_Kippu.

mary profession is as a personal chef and if normally I do cook for people in exchange for dollars.

5. **Soup for hire:** Next, my landlord, who lives downstairs from me, learns of my superb soup and asks me to become a personal chef for her family, in exchange for allowing me to live rent-free. I begin cooking two meals a day for her family, and at her pleading, learn to make things other than soup. The value of my free rent should be reported as income on my tax returns, and the value of my cooking services should be reported on her tax returns as rental income. It's also possible that I should now be classified as her employee, since I work for her regularly and take some direction from her about what and when to cook. Regular household workers often need to be classified as employees, which means they must be paid at least minimum wage in dollars. Our soup-in-exchange-for-rent arrangement may, therefore, be illegal under wage and hour laws.
6. **Soup enterprises:** Moving on with my soup scenario, now my soup has become so popular that I make multiple pots of soup every day, invite people over to share it, or put it in mason jars for people to pick up on my door step. No one ever pays me U.S. Dollars for my soup, but I have been able to use soup to "pay" for most of what I need. I now get "free" health care, bike repair, fresh produce, and many other necessities and perks in exchange for jars of soup. Even with no money changing hands, chances are that I've suddenly found myself in the soup business and should pay tax on the value of most of what I receive in return. Also, as bizarre as it sounds, when my friends come over to help me chop vegetables, the law says I may need to be paying them minimum wage and obtain a policy of workers compensation for them.[10]
7. **Soup bucks:** Next, I can take my soup operation one step further and start creating soup gift certificates. If I pay someone soup in exchange for a bicycle, it will be more convenient to give that person 50 soup certificates rather than 50 jars of soup. The recipient can redeem the certificates for soup when he or she needs it and could also give certificates to someone else. If my

10. As a general rule, employment laws prohibit people from volunteering for commercial enterprises. This is discussed in Chapter 7.

"Soup Bucks" start circulating within my local community, they essentially become a local currency. Each certificate has value not only because it can be exchanged for soup, but because it can be exchanged with anyone who is willing to accept it. (Interestingly, the U.S. Dollar came about in a similar way, except that it was backed by gold, not soup.)

Exchanges that take place with Soup Bucks will likely be taxed and regulated in the much the same way that dollar transactions are. When people transact with Soup Bucks, they likely need to assign a fair market value to the Bucks, which could be difficult. That value may be roughly the equivalent of the fair market value of a jar of my soup, which is $8 perhaps. However, if businesses begin accepting one Soup Buck for goods they would normally charge $10 for, then the fair market value of the Bucks rises. The value of the Bucks must be determined with reference to their value in the marketplace, not to the value of soup that backs them; if currency were valued on the basis of its backing, the U.S. Dollar would be worth absolutely nothing, now that it is no longer backed by gold. The legalities of issuing non-dollar currencies will be discussed further below.

8. **SoupExchange.com:** Next, to make the exchange of Soup Bucks somewhat simpler and streamlined, I create an online system for tracking exchanges. Many entrepreneurs in my community begin using digital Soup Bucks to buy and sell goods and services with one another. A lawyer offers services at a rate of ten Soup Bucks per hour, and uses her Soup Bucks to pay a house painter, who uses his Soup Bucks to pay a physical therapist, and so on. Because all of these exchanges take place through the online system I created and administer, the IRS could now consider me to be operating a "barter exchange"[11] and could require that I issue a 1099-B to participants for every exchange valued at more than $1.00.
9. **Soup credit union:** My final project is to issue 50,000 Soup Bucks and to donate them to a member-governed organization that I help to establish. People become members of the organization by depositing some of their Soup Bucks into accounts maintained by the organization, and the organization makes loans of

11. See Jenny Kassan's contribution to this chapter, discussing the IRS's definition of "barter exchange."

Soup Bucks to start-up businesses in my community. By making loans and receiving deposits, this organization is essentially a credit union, subject to banking regulations and charter requirements at the state or federal level.[12]

Areas of Law Implicated

There are multiple areas of law implicated by non-dollar exchanges, and many of these are the same areas of law implicated when dollars are in play. Non-dollar exchanges, however, do bring up unique questions in connection with the following areas of law, which comprise the remaining parts of this chapter:

- Tax law
- Regulations on issuance and administration of currencies
- Tax exemption for organizations administering currencies and exchange platforms
- Employment law

PART 2: TAX

Sharing economy lawyers will sometimes be called upon to advise clients on the taxation of their exchanges, and as described in the previous section, the answer to the tax question can sometimes be, well, soupy. In absence of clear guidance from statutes, the way a lawyer would normally advise a client is to compare a client's scenario to tax rulings and tax court cases that have addressed similar scenarios. The problem is that things don't usually go to court when there is not much value at stake. The jars of soup I may trade for guitar lessons, for example, would probably never be subject to a tax court decision or even an IRS private letter ruling (PLR).

We know the IRS doesn't intend to tax everything we give, swap, exchange, and trade with one another, but it's very hard to know where the IRS intends to draw the line. We can derive hints from a few things the IRS has stated and from rules in the Internal Revenue Code.

---

12. For a detailed blog on the process of starting a credit union, see the Internet Archive Credit Union description at http://creditunion.blog.archive.org.

BUILDING HEALTHY COMMUNITIES WITH TIME BANKS

By Edgar S. Cahn, Creator of Time Dollars, Founder of TimeBanks USA, and Co-founder of the National Legal Services Program and the Antioch School of Law (now the David A. Clarke School of Law) at the University of the District of Columbia

A time bank is simply an arrangement where people come together to give their time to help others. If you give an hour of help, you earn one time credit. The person receiving the help owes one time credit, and he or she pays back by helping someone else.

In 1986, time banking began as a vehicle to enlist older adults in community building, health promotion, and intergenerational support. Today, Mayor Bloomberg has launched TimeBanking for seniors in all five boroughs of New York. As baby boomers will turn 65 at the rate of 10,000 per day for the next 18 years, a paradigm shift will be needed to convert consumers of service into co-producers of health, well-being, and community. Time bank programs have tackled some of the toughest social problems and worked to address the needs of many different sectors of the population:

- In Montpelier, Vermont, the Administration on Aging has invested in a form of time banks called Carebanks. Seniors can get an assurance that informal care and support will be available if they or their families pay regular premiums—in time dollars earned helping build community or helping other seniors. In effect, the program uses time banking to create a new form of extended family. It is too early to project the cost savings associated with this program.
- In 27 of Chicago's lowest ranking elementary schools, fifth and sixth graders (many labeled Special Education or ADD) earned time credits as tutors of first and second graders. The need for special education and remediation went down; test scores and school attendance went up; fighting and truancy went down.
- In Oakland, California, the Alameda County Department of Public Health funded a time bank in a neighborhood beset by racial violence. African Americans are now teaching

English to Hispanics, who in turn are teaching Spanish to their neighbors.

- In upstate New York, the Youth Advocate program has incorporated a "pay-it-forward" element for youth on probation or subject to confinement at detention centers. Enrolled in a Red Cross–supervised restorative justice program, they earn credits teaching homeless people to use computers, working in soup kitchens, and collecting canned goods and toiletries.
- In Washington, D.C., for the past ten years, teenagers have earned time credits by serving as jurors in the Time Dollar Youth Court, which hears the cases of peers accused of nonviolent crimes. Offenders may be sentenced to community service, life skills classes, an apology, writing an essay, and duty on the jury. Recidivism rates are less than 10 percent; the Urban Institute estimates that the District saves $9,000 for every offender who goes to Youth Court instead of the traditional system.

Taxation of Barter, Swapping, and Gifts

First of all, here are some general rules about income, barter, and gifts:

- **Income:** With some exceptions, gross income is taxed, whether it comes in the form of money, property, or services.[13]
- **Barter:** The value of something received through barter is income and is therefore taxed, with some exceptions.[14]
- **Gifts:** Gifts are generally not counted as part of gross income and are therefore not taxed for the recipient, with some exceptions.[15]

In sum, the IRS considers bartered goods and services to be income, yet it considers gifted goods and services not to be income. There are, however, infinite ways to give and receive, and the line between barter and gifting could be unclear. Furthermore, it's hard to know how far the taxing of barter income actually extends. The IRS

13. Treas. Reg. § 1.61-1.
14. *See* IRS Publ'n 525.
15. I.R.C. § 102.

rule on barter, as written, appears to tax *any* good or service received in exchange for *any* other good or service. In practice, however, it is probably not such a blanket rule. The IRS doesn't seem to concern itself with casual and non-commercial exchanges of goods or property. Administratively, it would be a hassle both for the taxpayer and for the IRS to report the plums I gave my neighbor in exchange for his figs. Unfortunately, it's hard to say at what point a barter arrangement has become sufficiently formal or commercial to be something that should be reported.

A Middle Category: "Swapping"

Swapping is not a recognized category under the law, but I often use the word "swapping" to refer to the casual and non-commercial ways that people exchange things, such as: "I'll give you some of my home-grown zucchini in exchange for some of your basil." Swapping falls somewhere in between barter and gifting. Swapping is like gifting, to the extent that parties are likely to give to each other even without an agreed-upon exchange, and because the value of what is being exchanged may not be anywhere near equal. However, swapping is somewhat like barter to the extent that there is direct and immediate reciprocity.

I have begun to use the word "swapping" to distinguish certain exchange activities from those that the IRS or other regulators consider to be barter. For example, in 2011, at least one staff member at the City of Oakland, California, Planning Department declared it to be illegal for residents to barter with homegrown vegetables.[16] The staff person used the word "barter" to refer even to more casual swapping of home-grown food among friends. This misguided declaration was harmful, and even made its way into *The Atlantic*.[17] To the extent that commercial activities are generally prohibited in residential areas, it is true that *commercial* barter would also be prohibited. However, the casual swapping of vegetables among friends and neighbors is quite likely considered to be a customary accessory use of a residential property, and would, therefore, not be a violation of a zoning ordinance. Since the regula-

16. However, Oakland's Planning Code has since been amended to make it legal for Oakland residents to sell homegrown vegetables as a home occupation in most residential zones.

17. Marion Nestle, *Fighting for the Right to Farm*, Atlantic, May 11, 2011, http://www.theatlantic.com/health/archive/2011/05/fighting-for-the-right-to-farm/238690/.

tors in that case were unwilling to recognize the difference between commercial barter and casual barter, I have found it useful to use the word "swapping" instead of "barter," to call attention to the fact that it is generally legal for people to provide for one another casually and non-commercially.

Federal tax regulations and the IRS have even *hinted* that casual and non-commercial exchanges are not meant to be taxed, but we come to this conclusion in a somewhat roundabout way. The tax regulations state that a group that facilitates "informal exchange of similar services on a noncommercial basis" is not considered a "barter exchange" and is therefore not subject to the requirement to report transactions of its members. The regulations even contain an example of carpoolers swapping rides with one another:

> Example 3. A, B, and C belong to a carpool in which they commute to and from work. Every third day, each member of the carpool provides transportation for the other two members. Because the carpool arrangement provides solely for the informal exchange of similar services on a noncommercial basis, the carpool is not a barter exchange within the meaning of paragraph (a)(4).[18]

This regulation does not actually *say* that the carpoolers are not taxed on the value of their rides; it merely says that the group is not required to issue 1099-B forms to its members.

Similarly, one IRS private letter ruling examined a time bank and determined that it was not a barter exchange subject to the requirement of reporting every transaction. In determining this, the IRS acknowledged that the exchanges taking place were informal and non-commercial. It was significant that participants had *no contractual right* to receive services in exchange for the favors they do for others, and services were *not bargained for at market rate*, but were provided on an hour-for-hour basis, without regard to the market value of such services. Nevertheless, the IRS was unwilling to discuss whether participants would be taxed on the value of services they receive. The opinion ends with: "No opinion is expressed concerning whether a member earns income as a result of the member's participation in the program."[19]

---

18. 26 C.F.R. § 1.6045-1(b), "Returns of information of brokers and barter exchanges."

19. I.R.S. Priv. Ltr. Rul. 96-08-009 (Feb. 23, 1996).

I don't blame the IRS for not wanting to make rules about what exchanges are or are not taxable. However, this does leave taxpayers to make their own good-faith determinations. As a general rule, when we barter for something at market rate, provide goods and services we normally provide as a business, or make a contract to exchange goods and services, we will likely realize taxable barter income.

For example, I acknowledge that if I were to join a time bank and provide two hours of legal services in exchange for "time dollars," and if I spend those time dollars to receive two hours of services from an auto mechanic, I would likely pay taxes on the value of the auto mechanic's services. In spite of the fact that I had no contractual right to receive those services, and in spite of the fact that this is not a market-rate exchange, I recognize that, because I am in the business of being a lawyer, this is a more commercial-like transaction of the sort that the IRS would likely want to tax.

In contrast, if I join the time bank and spend two hours walking someone's dog, then I "pay" my neighbor "time dollars" to take me on a historical walking tour of the neighborhood, I would likely not report the value of the tour on my taxes. However, this is merely my own good-faith determination that the IRS doesn't intend to tax the value of the tour. There is no bright-line rule here, and it may turn out that I'm wrong.

What Is a Gift?[20]

It helps to further unwrap the legal definition of "gift" under federal tax law.[21] The U.S. Supreme Court, in *Commissioner v. Duberstein*,[22] has given us some guidance in this regard. Here are some quotes from the Supreme Court, along with my own summaries in bold:

1. **Gifts arise from generosity:** "A gift [...] proceeds from a detached and disinterested generosity, out of affection, respect, admiration, charity, or like impulses."
2. **Gifts don't come from a moral or legal obligation:** "If a payment proceeds primarily from the constraining force of any moral or legal duty, [...], it is not a gift."

20. This discussion of the legal definition of gift is partially adapted from my article *How to [Legally] Open Up a Gift [Economy,]* Shareable.net, Sept. 1, 2010.

21. I.R.C. § 102.

22. Comm'r v. Duberstein, 363 U.S. 278, 285 (1960).

3. **Gifts are not given with an anticipation of return:** "If a payment proceeds [...] from the incentive of an anticipated benefit of an economic nature, it is not a gift."
4. **Gifts are not given as a payment for something:** "Payment made in return for services rendered is not a gift."
5. **The intention of the giver is what matters:** "In determining whether a transfer of property is a gift, [...] the controlling factor is the intention with which the transfer [...] has been made."

Even with the clues the Court has given us, the concept of a "gift" is still somewhat unwieldy. If the IRS ever questions the authenticity of a gift, the judge or other ruling body must attempt to gain insight into the thoughts and feelings of the giver and to guess at his/her motives and intentions. They would have to rely on vague criteria, such as the existence of a friendship, the non-existence of a business relationship, and other quasi-objective factors to guess at what the giver was feeling.

Given the criteria, it's easy to see how a gift could transform into income, simply because of a slight change in motive. For example, imagine that, for years, I make soup for my elderly neighbor, simply as a kind gesture. Then, I go through a rough financial time after accidentally setting my kitchen on fire. My neighbor, who just received a large inheritance, gives me $1,000 to help me pay for the damage. These gestures do seem to arise from pure generosity and charity, so hopefully I wouldn't have to include the $1,000 in my income. But what if she gave me the check and said, "The soup has been so helpful to me over the years, but I've never been able to return the favor. I feel I should compensate you somehow!" Now there is a question: is she giving me money out of a feeling of obligation or in the spirit of compensating me? If so, does that mean the $1,000 is income to me?

Since the circumstances and intentions surrounding every gift could vary, the safest thing to do is to independently analyze every gift received to determine whether it should be included in taxable income. Considering the criteria listed above, the person receiving the item would want to consider the intentions of the person that gives. If it appears that a gift comes as payment for something the recipient has done or will do in the future, it may look more like income.

Paying Tax on Barter Income

First Rule: Do Not Send Soup to the IRS

An unfortunate fact about the taxation of non-dollar income is that the IRS requires that taxes be paid in dollars. If the IRS considers 50 jars of soup to be "income," it might, theoretically, follow that tax liability could be satisfied by sending eight jars of soup to the IRS. Unfortunately, we don't have that option at this time, and it requires everyone to keep enough of a toehold in the dollar economy to be able to pay taxes in dollars.

Note, however, that the idea of paying taxes in something other than cash is not an outrageous idea. As local currency expert Mira Luna has suggested, there should be a program that allows us to fulfill our tax liabilities by performing community service. Such a program could be like a time bank for paying taxes. In my hypothetical soup case, since I receive almost no cash for my soup, I could put in a few hours a week volunteering at a nonprofit soup kitchen to satisfy my tax liability.

Determining the Value of Barter Income

Determining the value of the barter income will also be a challenge. According to the IRS, "if services are paid for in property [or in exchange for other services], the fair market value of the property [or services] taken in payment must be included in income as compensation."[23] Fair market value is a dollar amount that is based on what people in society at large are willing to pay for something. The irony and difficulty of this requirement is that many barter transactions take place outside of the marketplace, and the elements of generosity, cooperation, and community skew the price.

Another tricky piece of this is that we must overcome the law's presumption that a barter transaction always entails an exchange of two things of equal value. The law states that "if the services are rendered at a stipulated price, such price will be presumed to be the fair market value of the compensation received *in the absence of evidence to the contrary*"[24] (emphasis added).

What this means is that if a lawyer advertises services at $200 per hour, but agrees to provide an hour-long consultation in exchange for a bag of homegrown vegetables, it is unlikely that the stipulated price

---

23. Treas. Reg. § 1.61-2(d)(1).
24. *Id.*

of $200 will be equaled by a bag of vegetables. The lawyer shouldn't have to report $200 of income, but the law presumes that she should, "*in the absence of evidence to the contrary*" (emphasis added). To maintain such evidence, she should make a reasonable determination of the fair market value of the vegetables she receives, keep a written record of what she received and how she determined the value, and then report that amount as income. That way, if she is ever audited, she has a record containing the required "evidence to the contrary."

Reporting Barter Income

There are generally three places on an individual tax return where barter income might be reported.[25] If the income is earned in connection with a sporadic activity or hobby, it would likely be reported along with "Other Income," and the type of income could be listed as "barter." If the income is earned in connection to a business, it would be calculated into business income on a Schedule C. If a good or service is received in lieu of receiving a rent payment, the value would be reported as rental income on Schedule E.

Note that if people barter and receive goods and services necessary to the operation of a business, the value of goods and services "paid" in the exchange could be deductible as a business expense. For example, if an accountant provides $1,000 worth of services to a web design business, and the web design business provides $1,000 worth of services to the accountant, they each report $1,000 of income, and deduct $1,000 of business expenses (since accounting fees and web design fees are presumably business expenses for each). The net effect is likely that no taxes are paid.

Part 3: Regulations on the Creation and Administration of Currencies

As a general rule, in most states it is legal for private individuals and groups to issue money.[26] Issuing money can be as easy as falling off a log, or, to be more precise, as easy as issuing a gift certificate. A gift

25. Thank you to Sustainable Economies Law Center Research Attorney Janelle J. Smith for elucidating the mechanics of reporting barter income.

26. "Private money is not prohibited if it complies with certain government regulations." Barbara A. Good, Fed. Reserve Bank of Cleveland, *Private Money: Everything Old is New Again* (Apr. 1, 1998), http://www.clevelandfed.org/research/commentary/1998/0401.pdf.

WHEN IS A LOCAL CURRENCY OR EXCHANGE NETWORK CONSIDERED A "BARTER EXCHANGE"?[1]

*By Jenny Kassan**

It is very important to determine whether the IRS would consider an online currency or other exchange network to be a "barter exchange." According to Treasury Regulation 1.6045-1, a "barter exchange" is

> any person[2] with members or clients that contract either with each other or with such person to trade or barter property or services either directly or through such person. The term does not include arrangements that provide solely for the informal exchange of similar services on a noncommercial basis.[3]

The regulation provides some examples to illustrate what is included in this definition of "barter exchange:"

> A, B, and C belong to a carpool in which they commute to and from work. Every third day, each member of the carpool provides transportation for the other two members. Because the carpool arrangement provides solely for the informal exchange of similar services on a noncommercial basis, the carpool is not a barter exchange . . . .
>
> X is an organization whose members include retail merchants, wholesale merchants, and persons in the trade or business of performing services. X's members exchange property and services among themselves using credits on the books of X as a medium of exchange. Each exchange through X is reflected on the books of X by crediting the account of the member providing property or services and debiting the

* Jenny Kassan's biography appears on page 151.

1. This section was written with the assistance of Jose Rivera, a student at Harvard Law School.

2. Note that by "person," the IRS also means corporation or association.

3. Treas. Reg. § 1.6045-1(a)(4).

> account of the member receiving such property or services. X also provides information to its members concerning property and services available for exchange through X. X charges its members a commission on each transaction in which credits on its books are used as a medium of exchange. X is a barter exchange . . .[4]

The IRS is concerned that barter exchanges provide an opportunity for tax avoidance, so an organization that falls within the definition of a barter exchange is required to report to the IRS regarding the transactions of its members.

Unfortunately, it is difficult to determine whether complementary currencies would be considered barter exchanges and therefore subject to these requirements. The IRS has determined in several private letter rulings that an informal, non-commercial time dollar program is not a barter exchange. These private letter rulings indicated that it was significant that the medium of exchange was not easily convertible to U.S. Dollars.[5] The IRS also considered the existence of contractual liabilities between members and the organization or among members. For example, the IRS has acknowledged that an exchange operated on a "noncommercial basis" because members did not have a "contractual right to receive any services from [the organization] or [the organization's] members," among other reasons.[6]

There is one example of a private letter ruling (PLR) that found a different kind of complementary currency system did not fall

---

4. Treas. Reg. § 1.6045-1(b).

5. *See* I.R.S. Priv. Ltr. Rul. 2007-24-006 (June 15, 2007) (holding that the exchange operated on a "noncommercial basis" because credits were valued "without regard to the type of service," among other reasons); I.R.S. Priv. Ltr. Rul. 96-08-009 (Feb. 23, 1996) (holding that the exchange operated on a "noncommercial basis" because credits were allocated "without regard to the type of service," credits were not freely transferable, and records showed "significant disparities" between the credits received and credits spent, among other reasons); I.R.S. Priv. Ltr. Rul. 85-36-060 (June 12, 1985) (holding that the exchange operated on a "noncommercial basis" because credits "have no monetary value," among other reasons).

6. I.R.S. Priv. Ltr. Rul. 96-08-009 (Feb. 23, 1996); *see also* I.R.S. Priv. Ltr. Rul. 85-36-060 (holding that the exchange operated on a "noncommercial basis" because "service recipients did not incur a contractual liability upon receipt of services under [the] program," among other reasons).

within the definition of a barter exchange. In a private letter ruling,[7] the IRS found that an "electronic cash exchange system" was not a barter exchange. The system involved the storing and transferring of electronic cash on a card. The stored value could be transferred from card to card by consumers and retailers in exchange for goods and services. One unit of value on the card is equal to one U.S. Dollar and is sold to participants in exchange for cash. The amount of money that may be stored on any card is expected initially to be limited to between $100 and $1,000. Members have the right to sell their cards back to the issuer at face value at any time.

Of course, PLRs cannot be relied upon as precedent. Local currency systems will be on the safe side if they assume that they fall within the definition of a barter exchange, or seek a letter ruling from the IRS to the contrary (a very expensive process).

Barter exchanges must report

> exchanges of personal property or services made through the exchange among its members or between these persons and the barter exchange. For this purpose, property or services are exchanged through a barter exchange if payment for property or services is made by means of a credit on the books of the barter exchange or scrip issued by the barter exchange or if the barter exchange arranges a direct exchange of property or services among its members or clients, or exchanges property or services with a member or client.[8]

There is an exemption from the reporting requirement if there are fewer than 100 exchanges during the calendar year.[9]

The barter exchange must report on Form 1099–B, "Proceeds From Broker and Barter Exchange Transactions," the following information: name, address, and taxpayer identification number of each member providing property or services in the exchange, the

7. I.R.S. Priv. Ltr. Rul. 97-43-047 (Oct. 24, 1997).
8. Treas. Reg. § 1.6045-1(e)(2)(i).
9. Treas. Reg. § 1.6045-1(e)(2)(ii).

property or services provided, the amount received by the member for the property or services, the date on which the exchange occurred, and other information required by the form.[10] Each transaction must be reported on a separate Form 1099-B.[11]

For members that are corporations, the exchange must report the name, address, and taxpayer identification number of the corporate member, the aggregate amount received by the corporate member during the reporting period for property or services provided by such corporate member, and such other information as may be required by the form.[12] Thus, for corporate members, transactions may be reported on an aggregate basis rather than reporting each individual transaction.

Exchanges involving property or services with a fair market value of less than $1.00 are not required to be reported.[13]

10. Treas. Reg. § 1.6045-1(f)(2)(i).
11. Form 1009-B instructions at 5.
12. Treas. Reg. § 1.6045-1(f)(2)(ii).
13. Form 1009-B instructions at 5.

certificate is essentially a note that allows the holder to redeem it for goods or services of a certain value or quantity. If someone issues many such notes, and if the notes begin to flow (like a current) from person to person as a medium of exchange, then they have become *current*, or, in other words, a *currency*. Rather than stop people from issuing their own currencies, the government has, for the most part, decided to go with the "flow."

At the same time, there are a handful of laws that restrict who may issue currency, how, and what it may look like. Many of these laws were put in place by the Founding Fathers, who had no idea what money would look like and how it would move around in the 21st century. This makes the laws somewhat mysterious or awkward in their application today. Courts have sometimes acknowledged that it may be unjust to enforce some of the early laws related to money and coinage, since the creators of those laws did not foresee the way that money would be created, used, and circulated today. In a case that involved charges of counterfeiting by defendants that made metal coins sometimes used in vending machines, the court noted that "[t]he difficulty is that this indictment seeks to charge the defendants with an offense under statutes which were enacted over one hundred years ago when vending machines probably did not exist."[27]

At least three states have laws that seem to go against the flow and may prevent the issuance of currencies. For example, in the California Corporations Code, which is not a logical place for a law about currencies, there is, nevertheless, a provision that states: "No corporation, flexible purpose corporation, association or individual shall issue or put in circulation, as money, anything but the lawful money of the United States." Such a provision leaves many open questions: What is money? What is *lawful* money? (There is something dizzyingly self-referential about a law that says it is illegal to do illegal things.) What is "of the United States"? What is circulation? It appears that California does not actively enforce this provision; otherwise, an enforcement agency could have a heyday in Silicon Valley, cracking down on every website that allows "points" or "credits" to be used as money. Arkansas[28] and Virginia[29] have laws similar to this statute in California.

Here is a handful of laws related to the issuance and administration of currencies:[30]

It Is Illegal to Make Coins That Will Circulate as Money

Federal law prohibits people from making metal coins "intended for use as current money."[31] Creation of souvenir coins not intended to act as currency, however, is not illegal. People have, in fact, recently created coins meant to be used in very small local communities in Marin

27. United States v. Gellman, 44 F. Supp. 360, 365–66 (D. Minn. 1942).

28. LEWIS D. SOLOMON, RETHINKING OUR CENTRALIZED MONEY SYSTEM 104–05 (Praeger 1996).

29. VA. CODE § 6.2-202 ("Issuance of currency and related prohibited acts. A. No individual or entity, unless authorized by law, shall: 1. Issue any note, bill, scrip, or other paper or thing with intent that the same be circulated as currency; or 2. Otherwise deal, trade, or carry on business as a bank of circulation.").

30. Note that there is a wonderful source of legal information about local currencies, found in Chapter 7 of *Rethinking Our Centralized Money System*, by Lewis D. Solomon, *supra* note 28.

31. 18 U.S.C. § 486 ("Uttering Coins of Gold, Silver or Other Metal: Whoever, except as authorized by law, makes or utters or passes, or attempts to utter or pass, any coins of gold or silver or other metal, or alloys of metals, intended for use as current money, whether in the resemblance of coins of the United States or of foreign countries, or of original design, shall be fined under this title or imprisoned not more than five years, or both."). Note that 18 U.S.C. § 491 addresses the creation of coins, but this particular code section prohibits the creation of coins or the use of similar metal objects for the purpose of inserting into parking meters, vending machines, and similar venues.

County, California.[32] Many people buy such coins as souvenirs, and others use them at a handful of local businesses that have agreed to accept them. Some have argued that such coins are not "intended for use as current money" because they can only be redeemed at a handful of local businesses. This may, in fact, be a valid argument, as described below.

How Much Flow Does It Take to Make a Current?

One court, examining the legalities of a souvenir-like coin issued in celebration of and for use at local businesses during the Alaska Centennial observance, summarized the meaning of "current money" as follows:[33]

> The expression "current money" has been defined as follows in *State v. Quackenbush*, 98 Minn. 515, 108 N.W. 953, 955 (1906): "Money includes 'whatever is lawfully and actually current in buying and selling, of the value and as the equivalent of coin.' [...] 'Current money' means money which passes from hand to hand and from person to person and circulates through the community. [...] Whatever is intended to, and does actually, circulate as money. [...] 'Current money,' that which is generally used as a medium of exchange. [...]"[34]

In that particular case, the court leaned heavily away from the idea that the coins were intended to circulate as current money. The court described the facts:

> The coins were, in part, to carry the following language: "Good for One Dollar in Trade at Any Cooperating Business Redeemable at Face Value at the Anchorage Centennial Exposition Site Until December 31, 1967." As finally stamped, the coins in part

---

32. See the Fairfax FairBuck (http://fairbuck.org/) and West Marin $3 Coin (http://www.coastalmarinfund.org/coins/index.php).

33. *See also* United States v. Monongahela Bridge Co., 26 F. Cas. 1292 (W.D. Pa. 1863) (finding that paper tickets that were issued for payment of a bridge toll were "not representatives of money, and therefore cannot be said to circulate, or be intended to circulate as money"); United States v. Van Auken, 96 U.S 366, 368–96 (1878) (where, in examining whether a certificate was meant to circulate, the Supreme Court looked at a certificate printed with the statement "The Bangor Furnace Company will pay the bearer, on demand, fifty cents, in goods, at their store, in Bangor, Mich." The Court explained that "Here the note is for 'goods,' to be paid at the store of the Furnace Company. It is not payable in money, but in goods, and in goods only.").

34. Anchorage Centennial Dev. Co. v. Van Wormer & Rodrigues, Inc., 443 P.2d 596, 600 n.2 (Alaska 1968).

> read, "Redeemable at Face Value at Anchorage the Air Crossroads of the World." There is nothing in either the proposed or final inscription which would indicate to Van Wormer that the Commission intended to use the coins as current money. [...] Additionally, there was no proof made as to the number of mercantile establishments in Anchorage at which the coins could be redeemed. Similarly, there was a lack of proof as to whether the coins were redeemable wholly or partially in cash. Finally, there was no evidence as to the number of business establishments at which the coins could be used in lieu of cash.[35]

If other courts follow the above precedent in analyzing the meaning of "current money," it is likely the two Marin County, California, coins would not be deemed to be in violation of the law. Because they are redeemable at only a fixed number of local businesses in very small communities, the coins are not likely to be considered "current money." This does, however, leave open the question of how the legal system might respond if the coins were to become widely accepted and achieve a high degree of flow.

The Liberty Dollars Case

In 2011, a man named Bernard van NotHaus was convicted of several federal charges in connection with a coin currency he created, called the Liberty Dollar. The prosecution of this case sent a wave of worry through local currency projects around the country. However, there were some important difference between van NotHaus's coins and other local currencies. The Liberty Dollar coins had a "$" symbol, used the words "dollar," "USA," "Liberty," "Trust in God" (instead of In God We Trust) and looked in design like coins of the national U.S. currency. According to the FBI, van NotHaus was found guilty on four counts: "making coins resembling U.S. coins; issuing, passing, selling, and possessing Liberty Dollar coins; issuing and passing Liberty Dollar coins intended for use as current money; and conspiring against the United States."[36]

---

35. *Id.* at 598.

36. Fed. Bureau of Investigation, Private Tender: Anti-Government Group Mints Its Own Coins (Apr. 5, 2011), http://www.fbi.gov/news/stories/2011/april/dollar_040511/dollar_040511. Mr. van NotHaus was charged with violations of 18 U.S.C. §§ 371, 485, 486, and 2.

It Is Illegal to Create Currency Worth Less Than $1.00

It is illegal to put into circulation a currency (or to write a check, for that matter), of a value of less than $1.00,[37] which leaves one to wonder whether a local currency or scrip could ever be used to purchase an apple or other inexpensive items. The purpose of this law was to prevent people from hoarding valuable coins and exchanging with notes valued at less than $1.00. This law is, of course, violated right and left; Facebook, for example, has created a virtual currency, called Facebook Credits, which are valued at only ten cents each.[38] In his article about alternative digital currencies, Reuben Grinberg points out that this law, enacted by the Stamp Payments Act, has not been interpreted in a court since 1899, which perhaps means that no one has cared to enforce it.[39]

It Is Illegal to Materially Alter the Dollar

To promote local recirculation of money, some groups and businesses have used special stickers and stamps attached to dollar bills. For example, my local bookstore puts a transparent purple ink stamp on money given to me as change, promising that the bills are worth double their face value if I return and spend the bills at that bookstore. Bernal Bucks, a neighborhood initiative in San Francisco, created a special sticker to put on $10 bills, which, if spent at participating businesses in the Bernal Heights neighborhood, would earn the spender a discount or other premium.

This brings up the question: Does stamping or putting stickers on U.S. Dollars violate laws against defacing money? Federal law makes it

---

37. 18 U.S.C. 336 ("Issuance of circulating obligations of less than $1. Whoever makes, issues, circulates, or pays out any note, check, memorandum, token, or other obligation for a less sum than $1, intended to circulate as money or to be received or used in lieu of lawful money of the United States, shall be fined under this title or imprisoned not more than six months, or both.").

38. Hachman, *supra* note 6.

39. "Perhaps the best argument against the application of the Act to Bitcoin is pragmatic. It is a 150-year-old statute that has outlived its usefulness. Courts began limiting its application almost immediately after it was passed. Although many academic works have noted that the Stamp Payments Act may be a problem for digital currencies, and digital currencies have existed for more than a decade, there has been no published court opinion interpreting the Act since 1899." Reuben Grinberg, *Bitcoin: An Innovative Alternative Digital Currency*, 4 HASTINGS SCI. & TECH. L.J. 160 (2011).

illegal to deface, mutilate, cut, or cement together dollar bills or other evidence of debt, "*with intent to render such bank bill, draft, note, or other evidence of debt unfit to be reissued*" (emphasis added).[40]

It is likely that if a sticker can be easily removed[41] or if a stamp has light and transparent ink, it would not be found to be in violation of the law. It is helpful to note that mutilation of a bill must be done with the intent to prevent it from being reissued or recirculated. Most people who stamp or put stickers on dollar bills intend the opposite, and hope that the bill will remain in circulation.

Furthermore what seems to matter is whether the mutilation causes a material change to the meaning of the words on the bill. In one case that examined this, the court held that "erasing words from an instrument or severing a portion thereof so that its effect is changed is a material alteration and constitutes forgery at common law."[42]

It Is Illegal to Make Things That Look Too Similar to the U.S. Dollar

Many local currencies have actively sought to avoid any claims that they are creating currency that is deceptively similar to the U.S. Dollar, as doing so would be illegal.[43] Burlington Bread, a now inactive currency project in Burlington Vermont, printed currency that was larger than the U.S. Dollar. The currency, however, fell into disuse, in part, because people had trouble fitting the currency into their wallets or cash registers. Other currencies have sought to differentiate themselves from the U.S. Dollar by using colorful graphics, words like "hour" or "bucks," instead of "dollars," and by explicitly writing on the bill that it is not a U.S. Dollar.

---

40. 18 U.S.C. § 333 ("Mutilation of national bank obligations. Whoever mutilates, cuts, defaces, disfigures, or perforates, or unites or cements together, or does any other thing to any bank bill, draft, note, or other evidence of debt issued by any national banking association, or Federal Reserve bank, or the Federal Reserve System, with intent to render such bank bill, draft, note, or other evidence of debt unfit to be reissued, shall be fined under this title or imprisoned not more than six months, or both.").

41. In the case of Bernal Bucks, the founders specifically chose to create a sticker with glue that allowed the sticker to be easily removed.

42. Keese v. Zerbst, 88 F.2d 795 (10th Cir. 1937).

43. *See, e.g.*, 18 U.S.C. § 485.

Bank Secrecy Act

Anyone forming an organization that will administer a local currency or similar program may want to delve into the question of what is a "money services business" under the Bank Secrecy Act (BSA) and accompanying regulations issued by the Financial Crimes Enforcement Network (FinCEN). The BSA was passed to prevent money from being laundered through money-transmitting businesses. The purpose is to prevent people from concealing the receipt and possession of money in connection with crimes. The regulations promulgated by FinCEN require that "money services businesses" register with FinCEN,[44] keep information about transactions, report certain transactions, and implement certain procedures to prevent money laundering.[45] The term "money services business" is "defined in regulations as "A person wherever located doing business . . . in one or more of the [following] capacities: (1) Dealer in foreign exchange . . . (2) Check casher . . . (3) Issuer or seller of traveler's checks or money orders . . . (4) Provider of prepaid access . . . (5) Money transmitter . . . (6) U.S. Postal Service . . . (7) Seller of prepaid access."[46]

Part 4: Tax Exemption for Organizations That Administer Time Banks, Barter Networks, or Currencies

Choice and structure of entity are major considerations for groups operating a local currency, barter network, or time bank. Many such groups may consider their mission to be non-profitable, and will often choose to form a nonprofit and seek tax exemption. Unfortunately, tax exemption under 501(c)(3) will be available only under limited circumstances, as described below. Many such organizations may, however, wish to explore the possibility of obtaining tax exemption under 501(c)(4).

---

44. 31 U.S.C. 5330(a)(1).

45. *See* Grinberg, *supra* note 39, at 204. *See also* Shawn Turner, *U.S. Anti-Money Laundering Regulations: An Economic Approach to Cyber-Laundering*, 54 Case W. Res. L. Rev. 1389, 1391 (2004).

46. Grinberg, *supra* note 39, at 205 n.211 (summarizing 31 C.F.R. § 1010.100(ff)).

THE U.S. CONSTITUTION AND CITIES THAT WISH TO ISSUE CURRENCIES

By Janelle Smith, Research Attorney, Sustainable Economies Law Center

When a city government wishes to issue a local currency, it must tread carefully so that it does not violate the U.S. Constitution. First, we must understand that Congress has the constitutional authority to provide a currency for the entire nation.[1] The basic intention behind the granting of that power was, reportedly, to promote solidarity, uniformity, and a strong central government.[2] To further this goal, the Constitution also prohibits "States" from "emit[ting] bills of credit."[3]

But what does that really mean? And, more importantly, what does that mean for a city that wants to create a local currency?

To start, we must determine if a city would be considered a "State." Sources seem to go both ways in answer to this question. There are several sources that indicate that a municipality would be considered a part of the "State;" at the same time, states like California do not themselves consider municipalities to be an arm of the state.[4] In absence of strong precedent and guidance on this

---

1. U.S. CONST. art. I, § 8, cl. 5 ("The Congress shall have Power To ... coin Money, regulate the Value thereof, and of foreign Coin, and fix the Standard of Weights and Measures").

2. *See* McCulloch v. Maryland, 17 U.S. 316 (1819); *see also* Legal Tender Cases, 110 U.S. 421 (1884).

3. U.S. CONST. art. I, § 10.

4. Lewis D. Soloman, *Local Currency: A Legal and Policy Analysis*, 5-WTR KAN. J.L. & PUB. POL'Y 59 (1995) ("The constitutional bar to emitting bills of credit appears to extend to other public bodies as well. The Court has held that a municipal corporation, 'a subordinate branch of the domestic government of a State' and with no 'purposes of private gain' has no power to issue 'paper clothed with all the attributes of negotiability.'" (citing The Mayor v. Ray, 86 U.S. 468, 474–75 (1873). *See also* Hitchcock v. Galveston, 96 U.S. 341, 350 (1877) (holding that even though a city illegally issued bonds to pay for sidewalk construction, the city must still honor the contract)). Notably, state law does not consider a city to be acting on behalf of the state as a state chartered entity. So, "while municipalities are institutions in the general sense that they are organized by state authority for state purposes, they do not come within that class of state institutions officially recognized as such by the California Constitution and statutes, and comprising prisons, hospitals, and similar establishments." CAJUR MUN § 1 (citing *In re* Houk's Estate, 186 Cal. 643 (1921).

question, a city wishing to play it safe may want to assume that it is, indeed, a "State" when looking toward the constitutionality of local currency issued by a city.

Next, we must consider whether local currency is a "bill of credit." In *Briscoe*, the Court had to define what exactly was a "bill of credit." The Court defined a bill of credit as an instrument of indebtedness: issued by the state; on the faith of the state; and designed to circulate as money.[5] A local currency quite possibly fits the bill (pun intended).

But *Briscoe* also addressed a second question: Is a *bank*, established by a state as a separate entity to issue "bills of credit," equivalent to the state itself issuing bills of credit? Three factors came to light to make sure the bank was not just a front for state issued bills of credit: (1) whether the bills of credit were issued by the state; (2) whether the bills of credit were issued on the faith of the state; and (3) whether the holder of the bill had a means of enforcing payment.

These factors should be considered carefully in conjunction with a close reading of the facts of *Briscoe*. Quite possibly, a city's local currency is not a "State" issued "bill of credit" if issued through a bank or other separate entity, instead of directly from the city.[6] This is true even if the city is the only stockholder of the entity, so long as the bill is not issued on the credit of the city, and instead backed by property of the entity giving holders of the bills a means of enforcing payment.[7]

One final "Thing": Just as the Constitution prohibits states from "emit[ting] bills of credit," it also prohibits states from "make[ing] any Thing but gold and silver Coin a Tender in Payment of Debts." So what if a city accepts local currency to tender a debt, such as in payment of local taxes and parking tickets? Today, in the age of cash, credit cards, and electronics accounts, we usually do not transact using gold and silver coin. In fact, the U.S. Dollar is no longer backed by gold or silver, making the antiquity of this

5. Briscoe v. Bank of Commonwealth of Ky., 36 U.S. 257 (1837).
6. *See id. See also* Darrington v. Bank of Ala., 54 U.S. 12, 13 (1851).
7. *Briscoe*, *supra* note 5.

provision of our Constitution evident.[8] Even if a city decided to accept the local currency in payment of taxes or similar "debts," the fact that electronic payments are widely accepted without being considered illegal greatly favors a city's ability to also accept a local currency. But it should be noted that the courts have not tested this exact scenario.

Additional research should be done to explore the possibility that a city may issue a currency, even without the creation of a separate bank or entity, and even without backing it with other property. In the meantime, a safer route would be for a city to create a local currency by using a separately chartered bank or other entity and backing the currency with sufficient property.

8. For an interesting petition placing a spotlight on how inconceivable this section of the Constitution is, see Leitch v. Bradbury, Petition for Writ of Certiorari, 2007 WL 776721 (Mar. 9, 2007). *See also* Radue v. Zanaty, 293 Ala. 585, 588 (1975).

501(c)(3) Tax Exemption

The IRS has weighed in a few times on the question of whether a time bank or barter network may be tax-exempt under 501(c)(3). The most helpful IRS letters and rulings are unpublished, which means they cannot be cited as precedent. They do, however, give us important clues about what the IRS considers to be charitable and educational.

The IRS has recognized *some* time banks as tax-exempt, but I believe it would be difficult to obtain exemption for a barter network or local currency. Time banks differ, in that the services people provide to one another are more like gifts, and the services aren't bargained for in a typical marketplace. The "time dollars" or "points" that people earn can be seen more like an incentive system that encourages people to help one another and be of service in their community. By contrast, with barter networks and local currencies, people may be motivated to exchange in order to be paid in something of more defined value. Thus, the IRS is far more likely to recognize time banks as a platform for charitable or educational activities and is more likely to look at barter networks and local currencies as platforms for private benefit.

In 2010, the IRS denied tax exemption to a "community barter organization,"[47] which operated very much like a time bank. This demonstrates that being a time bank, alone, does not enable an organization to obtain tax exemption under 501(c)(3). The time bank in that case was determined not to be operating for 501(c)(3) tax-exempt purposes because it was "a bartering exchange that coordinates the bartering services of [its] membership" and was therefore "operated for the private benefits of [its] members only."[48] In that case, the organization was not focused specifically on serving a charitable class of people or on serving educational purposes.

There are two primary grounds on which time banks have been able to obtain tax exemption under 501(c)(3).

Focusing on Relief of the "Poor, Distressed, and Underprivileged"

An organization that operates a time bank may be able to obtain tax exemption if it is designed solely to provide needed services to members of a charitable class of people, and/or to provide to such individuals opportunities and incentives to do work to for their own educational or therapeutic benefit. A charitable class of people includes those that are recognized by the IRS as "poor, distressed, or underprivileged." In 1985, the IRS wrote a letter to an organization operating a program very similar to a time bank, and the letter concluded (emphasis added):

> Based upon the information provided, we conclude that your exempt status under section 501(c)(3) of the Code will not be adversely affected by the operation of this computerized services exchange system, *provided, however, that those persons receiving services are or can be considered members of a charitable class of individuals which your general programs are designed to assist*, or your program itself is, or has been considered to be, a charitable activity.[49]

---

47. *See IRS Denied Tax-Exempt Status to Community Barter Organization*, 2010 Tax Notes Today 205–31 (discussing I.R.S. Priv. Ltr. Rul. 2010-42-040 (July 27, 2010)).

48. *Id.* (discussing I.R.S. Priv. Ltr. Rul. 2010-42-040 (July 27, 2010), at 6).

49. From a 1985 letter from the IRS to Consolidated Neighborhood Services, Inc., "Re: Member Organized Resource Exchange," drafted by E. L. Kennedy, Chief, Specialty Tax Branch. This ruling has not been published anywhere, but is circulated among time banks to provide guidance on obtaining 501(c)(3) status. Available at http://mketimeexchange.org/are-time-dollars-taxable/.

Thus, an exchange platform designed for use of the broader community, and not specifically for a charitable class, may not be considered a tax-exempt activity for a 501(c)(3) organization. As discussed by Dr. Edgar Cahn in his contributed section in this chapter, time banks have been established all over the country to serve underprivileged groups—focusing, for example, on at-risk youth, the homeless, seniors, and residents of high-violence neighborhoods. Such time banks, quite likely, could be recognized by the IRS as tax-exempt.

Note, however, that if, instead of a time bank, an organization operates a local currency or barter network, such an organization may be deemed to be operating for the private benefit of individuals, even if those individuals are members of a charitable class. This is because the nature of exchanges in a local currency or barter network may be driven more by the market and by a desire to earn a profit, and not necessarily by the desire to be of service to others.

Focusing on Educational Purposes

Some time banks have obtained 501(c)(3) tax exemption on the grounds that their primary purpose is education.[50] Such time banks provide an experiential learning opportunity for people, helping them learn how to trade and exchange without money. In other words, time banks provide people with a laboratory for learning about and adopting new economic practices, which may otherwise be difficult to learn and practice. In theory, if a time bank could obtain exemption on these grounds, so, too, could a local currency or barter network, perhaps. However, this approach to obtaining tax exemption has many limitations, and it limits the scale and scope of a time bank or exchange platform. In theory, if the time bank grew to provide for a lot of people on a regular basis, then the time bank could be deemed by the IRS to be larger than necessary to carrying out its educational purposes.

501(c)(4) Tax Exemption

Although this is less tested, when it comes to time banks, local currencies, and barter networks, the IRS may be far more willing to grant 501(c)(4) tax exemption than to grant 501(c)(3) tax exemption. To obtain tax exemption as a 501(c)(4) social welfare organization, a time bank,

50. Telephone Interview with Dr. Edgar Cahn of TimeBanks USA (July 2010).

barter network, or local currency must be designed to provide a broad benefit to a community, and not just to a limited group of members. As described in Chapter 4 of this book, tax exemption under 501(c)(4) is sometimes thought of as a "catch-all" exemption for organizations that do not quite fit into 501(c)(3) exemption, and organizations have a lot more latitude in their activities. The organization should demonstrate how the operation of the program promotes social welfare, and is not designed to confer private benefit to a limited group of people.

Part 5: Paying Employees with Something Other Than Dollars

Some employers, as an alternative to furloughs and layoffs, have recently begun to think creatively about how they compensate employees. To supplement wages and salaries paid in dollars, some employers have considered paying employees with gift certificates, store credits, food, goods, services, or a local currency. There are a few things to acknowledge with regard to the payment of employees in forms other than dollars.

First of all, minimum wage, at the very least, probably needs to be paid in U.S. Dollars, except under limited circumstances where board, lodging, and food can be credited against wages, as I'll describe below. Federal law provides that "payment of the prescribed wages" (which I take to mean the legally required minimum wages) must be "in cash or negotiable instrument payable at par"[51] (which I take to mean cash or something immediately convertible to cash, such as a check or direct deposit). The definition of "cash," however, is not clear, but I suspect that small-scale local and complementary currencies might not be acceptable. The regulations go on to say that "[s]crip, tokens, credit cards, 'dope checks,' coupons, and similar devices are not proper mediums of payment under the [Fair Labor Standards Act]."[52] One reason for the adoption of this law is that some employers have tried to pay their employees in coupons redeemable only at the "company store."

The irony of this, of course, is that dollars themselves were created to act as coupons redeemable in gold. President Nixon terminated that

51. 29 C.F.R. § 531.27(a).
52. 29 C.F.R. § 531.34.

practice in 1971, officially ending our right to redeem dollars for gold. Of course, today everyone uses dollars so much that, even without official backing, they are redeemable in practically anything. Nevertheless, there remains a need for more research into what is meant in labor codes by "cash" versus "scrip" or "coupon." I would argue that a local currency that reaches a high level of circulation—meaning it can be redeemed at hundreds or thousands of independent businesses, and not just at the "company store"—should be considered "cash" and allowed to be used for at least some portion of legally prescribed wages.

Not all minimum wages must be paid in cash, however, as the Fair Labor Standards Act does allow employers, under limited circumstances, to deduct from prescribed wages "the 'reasonable cost,' or 'fair value' [...] of furnishing such employee with board, lodging, or other facilities."[53] State and federal wage orders and regulations set limits on the value that an employer can claim for certain meals, and also set minimum standards for when, where, and how such lodging, food, and facilities are provided.

When an employer pays wages and salaries partially with something other than cash, such payments or benefits are generally taxable at their fair market value as employment income, unless they are excludable from taxation. IRS Publication 15-B[54] examines the varieties of fringe benefits employers commonly provide to employees, and lists the types of benefits that are excludable, which includes things like contributions toward health savings accounts, the use of on-site athletic facilities, certain meals, certain transportation credits, and "de minimis fringe benefits," such as donuts, occasional personal use of the office copier machine, and small non-cash "holiday gifts." (Note that it's not clear what a holiday is and how far an employer could go in declaring many occasions to be special.)

Non-cash benefits or local currency payments will need to be tracked and given a fair market value not only for the purposes of deducting payroll taxes, but also for the purpose of calculating overtime wages. If an employer pays an employee wages partially in the national currency and

53. 29 C.F.R. § 531.27(a).

54. IRS Publ'n 15-B, Employers Tax Guide to Fringe Benefits, http://www.irs.gov/publications/p15b/ar02.html.

partially in a local currency (as was done in the city of Wörgl, Austria, during the Depression[55]) all payments must be added together for the purposes of calculating overtime wages. It appears, although it's hard to be entirely certain, that overtime wages may be paid partially in a local currency, in the same way that they can also be paid partially in board, lodging, and other facilities. The Code of Federal Regulations provides:

> It should not be assumed that [...] all overtime compensation must be paid in cash and may not be paid in board, lodging, or other facilities. There appears to be no evidence in either the statute or its legislative history which demonstrates the intention to provide one rule for the payment of the minimum wage and another rule for the payment of overtime compensation.[56]

However, more research is necessary to determine how courts or departments of labor have treated situations where an employer sought to pay overtime wages with a benefit other than dollars.

55. *See* Thomas H. Greco, Jr., Comment on the Wörgl Experiment with Community Currency and Demurrage (May 9, 2002), http://www.reinventingmoney.com/documents/TGWoerglCommentDistributed.html.

56. 29 C.F.R. § 531.27(b).

CASE STUDY: THE SMOKEY MOUNTAIN HOLLERS, A LOCAL CURRENCY NETWORK

By Gordon Ng, Research Contributor, Sustainable Economies Law Center

Introduction

The Smokey Mountain Hollers (SMH) is an Asheville, N.C.-based cooperative founded by Amy Hamilton, John Robinson, and Julie Schantz. SMH is designed around a mutual credit clearinghouse, which is an old-world method for bartering without the use of traditional currencies. As Asheville has experienced one of the nation's highest unemployment rates recently, the SMH founders looked to the "Wörgl miracle" for their inspiration. The use of a mutual credit system and local currency helped insulate the city of Wörgl from the depression that ravaged the rest of Austria in 1932. Currently in its nascent period, SMH provides businesses and individuals in Western North Carolina with a trading platform that promotes economic sustainability. Their system consists of the Hollers Trade Exchange (HTE), an online barter network, and paper trade vouchers called Hollers.

How It Works

SMH does not run a direct barter system. Instead, members trade their goods and services for Hollers, which are used to purchase other goods and services. The online system keeps track of all trades. Cooperative members can exchange online trade credits for paper vouchers and vice versa. To join the HTE, one must join the cooperative. However, any individual or business may accept and spend paper Hollers in physical environments, regardless of cooperative membership status. SMH does not exchange Hollers for U.S. Dollars, although many of the local currency systems that SMH modeled itself after do.

The goods and services of the SMH members back the virtual and paper Hollers. Members guarantee that they will accept Hollers from the community in an amount that matches the amount they are able to spend, thus creating a cycle of reciprocity. The result is that no one is left without a place to spend Hollers. Members must also bring their balance back to zero before leaving the cooperative.

Design

The printed Hollers were specifically designed to not resemble U.S. Dollars, to avoid running afoul of counterfeit laws. SMH plans to use photocopy-resistant materials and quantum dots to help prevent the possibility that people can print their own Hollers.

Structure

The general membership of SMH consists of all exchange participants, and each member has an equal vote. SMH believes it should be owned and governed by all of its participants. This way, profits will be spread throughout the community rather than held by a few entities, and SMH will be operated for the benefit of a broad constituency. Any individual or locally owned independent business in Western North Carolina can join. The Articles of Incorporation and Bylaws provide for transparency and horizontal decision making via a day-to-day organizing committee. The committee consists of employees hired by the governing assembly (composed of a board of directors that rotate and are elected within the co-op membership), and a couple of positions for people who do not trade within the online system, for inclusiveness of those who do not use computers in the Asheville community.

Taxation

The tax treatment of transactions made in Hollers and in the online HTE system is the same as a transaction with U.S. Dollars. Individuals are responsible for reporting income earned in paper Hollers, and SMH, as a barter exchange, is responsible for reporting transactions made using the online HTE system. SMH employs open source software used by similar exchanges, and the software generates 1099-B statements for members annually.

Conclusion

SHM was developed as an alternative for people who believe the conventional economy has fallen short of the ideals of Asheville residents. SMH seeks to benefit a broad base of local participants by allowing them to turn surplus resources into value and increase cash flow, which confers advantages on local businesses. SMH seeks to help small businesses thrive even as the conventional economy tightens access to cash and capital. SMH facilitates local control and economic self-reliance, helping to insulate the community from boom and bust cycles, and creating a cooperative economy based on real value.

CASE STUDY: VBSR MARKETPLACE, A BARTER NETWORK

By Gordon Ng, Research Contributor, Sustainable Economies Law Center

Introduction

Amy Kirschner, who studied currency systems at the University of Vermont's Gund Institute, is the founder of Vermont Sustainable Exchange LLC (VSE), a social enterprise that aims to help businesses in Vermont operate sustainably through trade. Its primary function is to develop and operate an online business-to-business marketplace, called the VBSR Marketplace, to help organizations and individuals in the local economy trade their surplus resources with one another. VSE has partnered with an influential business organization, the Vermont Businesses for Social Responsibility (VBSR), to create and promote the VBSR Marketplace. By doing so, both organizations meet their mutual goals of stimulating the local economy and supporting responsible businesses in Vermont.

How It Works

The VBSR Marketplace is an online system that allows its members to exchange their surplus resources for the surplus resources of other members. Surplus resources are the goods and services that a business is *able to provide*, but that the business has been *unable to sell for dollars*. VBSR Marketplace functions by allowing its members to sell their goods or services for an alternate form of currency, called VBSR Trade Credits. The Trade Credits can then be used to buy goods or services listed on the Marketplace by other members. The transactions resemble cash sales, except that the electronic Trade Credits are used to facilitate the exchanges. Members are allowed to carry negative balances in their accounts, but are contractually bound to settle their accounts before they leave the exchange.

Design

The precursor to the VBSR Marketplace was Burlington Bread, which was a local paper currency. The currency was designed to not resemble U.S. Dollar currency, to avoid running afoul of counterfeit laws. To avoid the possibility of mistaking Burlington Bread with U.S. Dollars, designers made the bills larger than a U.S. Dollar bill. However this proved to be problematic, as businesses could not fit the currency into their cash register trays. As a result, cashiers placed the bills under the trays, where they were often forgotten and effectively put out of circulation. Learning from that experience, Kirschner bypassed these issues by using the virtual Trade Credit currency for the VBSR Marketplace.

Structure

VSE is a limited liability company (LLC). Kirschner considered alternative corporate structures and 501(c)(3) status, but ultimately chose an LLC for its flexibility. Utilizing this structure allows VSE to have fewer decision-making formalities as well as flexibility in choosing an ownership structure. In addition, Kirschner and other potential owners are shielded from personal liability. VSE administers the VBSR Marketplace and has essentially entered into a contract with the VBSR to help promote the VBSR Marketplace. VBSR is a membership-based nonprofit business league, tax exempt under 501(c)(6). VBSR gives each of its members access to the VBSR Marketplace.

Taxation

There is no tax advantage or disadvantage to exchanging via the Marketplace, as opposed to dollar transactions. There is no circumvention of tax requirements, and the tax deductibility of business expenses and capital purchases is also unaffected. VSE provides end-of-year 1099-B tax reports to every member. VSE does not collect sales tax, leaving that responsibility to the members.

Conclusion

The VBSR Marketplace greatly increases the ability of local businesses to exchange without dollars. The Marketplace created a larger market for surplus resources, allowing businesses to exchange and meet their needs, even when dollars are not available for every transaction. Consequently, the VBSR Marketplace continues to grow and realize the sustainability goals of its members and of the communities it serves.

CHAPTER SIX

NEW KINDS OF CAPITAL

*By Jenny Kassan**

PART 1: COMMUNITY CAPITAL IN THE SHARING ECONOMY

Introduction

As the sharing economy grows, participants look for creative and collaborative ways to finance their activities. Many of the things we do require that we aggregate large sums of dollars—much more than we have in our own bank accounts. Also, because many of the productive activities we undertake require an up-front investment of resources and only yield returns on that investment months or even years later, we need investment that is "patient"—able to wait for a return until the activity invested in yields fruit.

The traditional methods of financing are almost completely inadequate to meet the needs of the sharing economy. Bank loans and investments from wealthy individuals and investment funds are very hard to get—virtually impossible for a start-up social venture or cooperative enterprise. Start-up ventures usually have to turn to credit cards, second and third mortgages, or loans from family and friends. These options can lead to bankruptcy and strains on relationships. And even these are only available to the relatively privileged. It's incredibly unfortunate that many ventures that could create huge community benefits end up not happening due to lack of financing options.

* Jenny Kassan's biography appears on page 151.

Ideally, the diverse sources of wealth in our communities could be harnessed to fund community-based enterprises. However, the options for community-based capital raising are quite limited by state and federal securities laws and other laws that regulate finance and investing. This chapter will summarize those laws, along with a handful of creative options allowing communities to share in the financing of local ventures.

Why Is It So Hard to Raise Capital?

Is the difficulty of getting financing caused by a shortage of capital? Not at all! If you were to add up all the money that residents of your county have in banks, retirement accounts, mutual funds, and other investments, you would be amazed at how much wealth there is in your community. For example, the Employee Benefit Research Institute estimates that even in a tiny county like Trinity in California, there is over $325 million invested in retirement accounts. The problem is that virtually all of this money is invested in institutions that suck money right out of your community. For example, if I have a checking account at Bank of America, the chances that Bank of America is investing my money in my community are slim to none. If I have a 401(k) retirement plan at work, all of that money is likely invested in stocks and bonds and never touches my community.

If I woke up one morning and said "I want to move five percent of my money into my local community," how would I do it? It is amazing when you realize that in this age of highly complicated investment vehicles, there is virtually no investment vehicle that allows you to invest in your own community. This is largely due to securities laws that make it prohibitively expensive for a small business to offer securities to community residents and to create a local investment fund that is open to the general public. Right now, under current law, the only simple way to keep your investments local is to deposit them in a bank or credit union that focuses its lending in your community. If you walked into your favorite neighborhood bookstore tomorrow and said "I would like to invest in your business," the owner would have to turn you down or risk civil and criminal liability under state and federal securities laws.

In the sharing economy, community assets will be owned by broad cross-sections of the community. Community residents will pool resources, including money, to start new ventures. Wealth generated in our communities will stay within our communities and recirculate to create more wealth and income. Local institutions will be locally owned to ensure greater accountability to the community. What is the biggest barrier to these things happening? Securities law!

Here are some examples of things that may be illegal under state and/or federal securities law (unless extensive filings are completed):

- A group of people wants to start a car-sharing club and solicits members who must pay $100 to join the club so that the club can buy its first car.
- A farmer solicits $10 investments from her customers, promising to pay them back $12 in six months.
- A nonprofit 501(c)(3) organization sends a letter to all of its members asking for $1,000 loans to be paid back over five years with interest.

Most people have no idea that these ways of raising money are illegal. I like to tell people that it was not until 11 years after I passed the bar that I learned that there was such a thing as securities law that limits how money can be raised. The only reason I learned about it then was because I went to work for a law firm that specialized in securities law (I'm eternally grateful that John Katovich of Katovich Law Group hired me even though I knew so little!).

What This Chapter Covers

Most of this chapter is a primer on basic securities law, with a focus on the aspects of securities law that apply when a broad cross-section of a community is investing in a venture. The law governing investing by wealthy, sophisticated investors is not a focus, since information about that kind of investing can be easily found in any legal guide for working with start-up ventures.

This chapter addresses the following questions:

- What is the definition of a security—when does securities law apply?
- What has to be done before a security can be offered?
- What are the consequences of failing to comply with the securities laws?

- What does it mean to be a "public company"?
- How can securities be re-sold after the initial offering?
- Is it possible to create a "local exchange" where local securities could be bought and sold by community residents?
- Is it possible to create a community investment fund that is open to local residents to invest in?
- How do investment clubs work?
- Who can sell securities?
- What are models for creative capital raising?

Part 2: A Securities Law Primer

Before even thinking about raising capital for any type of venture, it is essential to understand the securities laws. Even some of the most experienced business attorneys make the mistake of assuming that securities laws don't apply to small isolated transactions, to loans, to investments by friends and family, or to nonprofits. But this could not be further from the truth! Securities laws apply in almost any situation involving funding for a venture.

The securities laws were passed early in the last century to protect investors from slick pitch artists who traveled across the country selling worthless investments. Kansas adopted the first securities law in 1911 to "keep 'Kansas money in Kansas' and help local farmers and small businesses rather than enriching 'New York Stock Exchange speculators and gamblers.'"[1] Ironically, these laws now make it almost impossible to invest in small businesses in our communities and pretty much compel us to invest in the New York Stock Exchange (which is where companies that can afford the millions of dollars required to do the compliance work to sell to the public are listed). In the name of protecting investors, securities laws now make it very difficult to raise community capital for small local independent business.

Any capital-raising activity will need to comply with both federal securities law AND the securities laws of any states in which capital-raising is taking place. So, for example, a venture in California that is soliciting investors in Oregon and Washington will have to be concerned

1. Amy Cortese, Locavesting: The Revolution in Local Investing and How to Profit from It 21 (Wiley 2011).

with four separate securities law regimes: California, Oregon, Washington, and federal.

What Is a Security?

Not every attempt by every venture to raise money will implicate securities laws. For example, a nonprofit 501(c)(3) soliciting donations is not subject to securities laws. But the definition of a security is incredibly broad, and attorneys must be able to spot a security from a mile away, since even the offering of a security (without any sale taking place) can be a securities law violation.

Securities Definition Under Federal Law

The term "security" is defined in the federal Securities Act of 1933[2] as follows:

> [A]ny note, stock, treasury stock, security future, bond, debenture, evidence of indebtedness, certificate of interest or participation in any profit-sharing agreement, collateral-trust certificate, preorganization certificate or subscription, transferable share, investment contract, voting-trust certificate, certificate of deposit for a security, fractional undivided interest in oil, gas, or other mineral rights, any put, call, straddle, option, or privilege on any security, certificate of deposit, or group or index of securities (including any interest therein or based on the value thereof), or any put, call, straddle, option, or privilege entered into on a national securities exchange relating to foreign currency, or, in general, any interest or instrument commonly known as a "security", or any certificate of interest or participation in, temporary or interim certificate for, receipt for, guarantee of, or warrant or right to subscribe to or purchase, any of the foregoing.[3]

This definition is not very helpful without more detailed definitions of each item listed. In determining what is a security under federal law, it is necessary to look to case law.

---

2. 15 U.S.C. § 77b(a)(1).

3. The Securities Exchange Act of 1934 (1934 Act) (15 U.S.C. §§ 78a–78pp) also contains a definition of "security." *See* 1934 Act § 3(a)(10), 15 U.S.C. § 78c(a)(10). Although it differs slightly from the 1933 Act definition above, in *Tcherepnin v. Knight*, 389 U.S. 332, 335 (1967), the Supreme Court called the two definitions "virtually identical."

Investment Contracts

Over the years, many schemes for raising capital have been devised in attempts to avoid application of the securities laws. These schemes have been analyzed by the courts to determine whether they are "investment contracts," and therefore "securities" under the Act.[4]

The Howey Test

The leading case on the definition of an investment contract is the U.S. Supreme Court case, *SEC v. W. J. Howey Co.*[5] In *Howey*, the "scheme" in question was the sale of land containing fruit trees as well as "service contracts" to cultivate and market the crops, with an allocation of the net profits going to the purchaser.

Under the *Howey* test, an investment contract is "a contract, transaction or scheme whereby a person invests his money in a common enterprise[6] and is led to expect profits solely from the efforts of the promoter or a third party."[7]

The "investment of money" prong of the *Howey* test requires that the investor commit his or her assets to the enterprise in such a manner as to subject the investor to financial loss.[8] The focus of the inquiry is on what the purchasers were offered or promised. "The test [for determining whether an instrument is a security] is what character the instrument is given in commerce by the terms of the offer, the plan of distribution, and the economic inducements held out to the prospect."[9]

The U.S. Supreme Court has defined "profits" as "either capital appreciation resulting from the development of the initial investment [...] or a participation in earnings resulting from the use of investors'

---

4. 15 U.S.C. § 77b(a)(1).

5. 328 U.S. 293 (1946).

6. "A common enterprise is a venture 'in which the "fortunes of the investor are interwoven with and dependent upon the efforts and success of those seeking the investment . . . ."' It is not necessary that the funds of investors are pooled; what must be shown is that the fortunes of the investors are linked with those of the promoters, thereby establishing the requisite element of vertical commonality. Thus, a common enterprise exists if a direct correlation has been established between success or failure of [the promoter's] efforts and success or failure of the investment." SEC v. Eurobond Exch., Ltd., 13 F.3d 1334, 1339 (9th Cir. 1994).

7. 328 U.S. at 298.

8. El Khadem v. Equity Secs. Corp., 494 F.2d 1224 (9th Cir.), *cert. denied*, 419 U.S. 900 (1974).

9. SEC v. C. M. Joiner Leasing Corp., 320 U.S. 344, 352–353 (1943).

funds."[10] The promised return may be fixed or variable and may be marketed as low-risk or "guaranteed."[11]

The *Howey* Court noted that its definition of a security "embodies a flexible rather than a static principle, one that is capable of adaptation to meet the countless and variable schemes devised by those who seek the use of the money of others on the promise of profits."[12] The courts have rejected attempts to narrow the definition of a security. As one opinion put it, "in searching for the meaning and scope of the word 'security' [...] form should be disregarded for substance and the emphasis should be on economic reality."[13]

Courts have frequently examined the promotional materials associated with an instrument in determining whether it is a security. If the materials promise things like great returns or guaranteed income, the court will almost certainly find the instrument to be a security, and therefore subject to federal securities regulations.

Other Characteristics of a Security Under Federal Law

The following are characteristics that will make it more likely that a court will consider an instrument to be a security, and therefore subject to securities regulations:[14]

1. The right to receive dividends contingent upon an apportionment of profits;
2. Negotiability (i.e., transferability);
3. The ability to be pledged or hypothecated (i.e., used as collateral);
4. The conferring of voting rights in proportion to the number of shares owned;
5. The capacity to appreciate in value;
6. The motivations of the seller and buyer—the seller's purpose is to raise capital and the buyer's purpose is to earn a profit;
7. The plan of distribution—there is "common trading for speculation of investment" and the instrument is offered and sold to a broad segment of the public;

10. United Hous. Found., Inc. v. Forman, 421 U.S. 837, 852 (1975).
11. SEC v. Edwards, 540 U.S. 389, 394 (2004).
12. 328 U.S. 293, 299.
13. Tcherepnin v. Knight, 389 U.S. 332, 336 (1967).
14. This list was developed from a review of federal cases regarding what is and is not a security.

8. Public perception—the public reasonably perceives the instrument as an investment;
9. The instrument poses a risk to the investing public.

When the Investor's Primary Motivation Is Consumption of a Commodity or Service

An important Supreme Court case for the sharing economy is *United Housing Foundation v. Forman*.[15] In that case, residents of a cooperative housing project sued the developer for, among other things, sale of unregistered securities (shares in the cooperative). To be able to rent an apartment, a prospective resident was required to buy 18 shares of stock for each room desired at $25 per share. Each apartment had one vote regardless of the number of shares purchased by the residents. Residents also paid monthly rent.

The Court in *Forman* noted that even though the instruments in question are called stock and the word "stock" is included in the definition of a security, the economic realities of the transaction are what need to be considered in light of the purposes of the securities laws. The Court stated:

> In holding that the name given to an instrument is not dispositive, we do not suggest that the name is wholly irrelevant to the decision whether it is a security. There may be occasions when the use of a traditional name such as "stocks" or "bonds" will lead a purchaser justifiably to assume that the federal securities laws apply. This would clearly be the case when the underlying transaction embodies some of the significant characteristics typically associated with the named instrument.[16]

The Court reasoned that

> people who intend to acquire only a residential apartment in a state-subsidized cooperative, for their personal use, are not likely to believe that, in reality they are purchasing investment securities simply because the transaction is evidenced by something called a share of stock. [...] [T]he inducement to purchase was solely to acquire subsidized low-cost living space; it was not to invest for profit.[17]

15. 421 U.S. 837 (1975).
16. *Id.* at 850–51.
17. *Id.* at 851.

Importantly, the Court concluded that "when a purchaser is motivated by a desire to use or consume the item purchased . . . the securities laws do not apply."[18]

Forman was very important for cooperatives and similar enterprises throughout the country. It clarified that the purchase of a membership in a cooperative, when the purchaser was motivated by a desire to use the goods and services of the cooperative, would not be considered a security. As we shall see, however, many states have rejected the *Forman* reasoning.

Notes: The Family Resemblance Test

The definition of a security includes "notes." Does this mean that all loans are covered by securities law? The Supreme Court has said that the phrase "any note" in the statutory definition of a security should not be interpreted to mean literally "any note" but must be understood against the backdrop of what Congress was attempting to accomplish in enacting the Securities Acts.

How does a court determine whether a note is a security? Federal courts apply the "family resemblance test." This is how the Supreme Court articulated the test in *Reves v. Ernst & Young:*

> First, we examine the transaction to assess the motivations that would prompt a reasonable seller and buyer to enter into it. If the seller's purpose is to raise money for the general use of a business enterprise or to finance substantial investments and the buyer is interested primarily in the profit the note is expected to generate, the instrument is likely to be a "security." If the note is exchanged to facilitate the purchase and sale of a minor asset or consumer good, to correct for the seller's cash-flow difficulties, or to advance some other commercial or consumer purpose, on the other hand, the note is less sensibly described as a "security."
>
> Second, we examine the "plan of distribution" of the instrument to determine whether it is an instrument in which there is "common trading for speculation or investment."
>
> Third, we examine the reasonable expectations of the investing public: The Court will consider instruments to be "securities" on the basis of such public expectations, even where an economic analysis of

18. *Id.* at 852–53.

> the circumstances of the particular transaction might suggest that the instruments are not "securities" as used in that transaction.
>
> Finally, we examine whether some factor such as the existence of another regulatory scheme significantly reduces the risk of the instrument, thereby rendering application of the Securities Acts unnecessary.[19]

To summarize the above test,

1. If the seller's purpose is to raise money for the general use of a business enterprise or to finance substantial investments and the buyer is interested primarily in the profit the note is expected to generate, the instrument is likely to be a "security."
2. If there is a plan to distribute the notes for trading and investment, the notes are likely to be considered securities.
3. If investors reasonably expect that the notes will be treated as securities, the courts are more likely to do so.
4. If some other regulatory scheme reduces the risk of the note, the courts are likely to find the application of the securities laws unnecessary.

The types of notes that are not "securities" include

> the note delivered in consumer financing, the note secured by a mortgage on a home, the short-term note secured by a lien on a small business or some of its assets, the note evidencing a character loan to a bank customer, short-term notes secured by an assignment of accounts receivable, or a note which simply formalizes an open-account debt incurred in the ordinary course of business (particularly if, as in the case of the customer of a broker, it is collateralized).[20]

Securities Definition Under State Law[21]

As noted above, it is necessary to comply with both state and federal securities law. So, let's say you want to raise money in Utah. You need to determine whether the instrument you are using is a security under

19. Reves v. Ernst & Young, 494 U.S. 56, 66–67 (1990).
20. *Id.* at 65.
21. This section is adapted from a research memorandum by Karan Singh Dhadialla, a law student at U.C. Berkeley and SELC intern during the summer of 2011.

federal law and under Utah law. It is possible that something that is not a security under federal law will be a security under state law.

The Risk Capital Test Used by a Minority of States

In 1959, some enterprising developers bought land in Marin County to develop a country club. To pay for some of the costs of building the club, they sold charter memberships in the club. The members would not share in the profits or ownership of the club but would have the right to use club facilities. Under the federal definition, these memberships would not be securities because the members joined the club to get the benefits of membership, not for a financial return. But the California Supreme Court, in a landmark case called *Silver Hills Country Club v. Sobieski*,[22] found that these memberships were securities.

The court formulated a new test for whether something is a security, called the risk capital test, which considers:

- Whether funds are being raised for a business venture or enterprise;
- Whether the transaction is offered indiscriminately to the public at large;
- Whether the investors are substantially powerless to effect [sic] the success of the enterprise; and
- Whether the investor's money is substantially at risk because it is inadequately secured.

In *Sobieski*, the court held that the sale of membership to a country club was a security because it fell under the purview of the regulatory intent of the California securities act.[23] On that point, the court held that courts have to look through form to substance to protect the public from schemes to attract "risk capital," which it found in this case.[24] The court found that the investors were risking their capital in expectation of receiving the benefits of club membership, which was in the control of the issuers of the membership.[25] Notably, the court stated the "act

22. 361 P.2d 906 (Cal. 1961).
23. *Id.* at 907.
24. *Id.*
25. *Id.*

extends even to transactions where capital is placed without expectation of any material benefits."[26]

Since *Sobieski*, the risk capital test has been applied by courts, with each case emphasizing different components of the test. The test is stated broadly as condemning a transaction that involves raising "funds for a business venture or enterprise; an indiscriminate offering to the public at large where the persons solicited are selected at random; a passive position on the part of the investor; and the conduct of the enterprise by the issuer with other people's money."[27] Most generally, the risk capital test "focuses retrospectively on what the investor stands to lose rather than prospectively on what he expects to gain."[28]

The broad formulation of the risk capital test emphasizes that the test eliminates the profit requirement of the federal *Howey* test.[29] "The risk capital test has two major advantages when contrasted with the federal test. First, it does not define a benefit as narrowly as the federal test defines a profit. The benefit need not be a material benefit."[30]

A couple of examples of fundraising schemes that were not found to be securities under the risk capital test might help clarify the test. First, in *Moreland v. Department of Corporations*, the court found that the sale of gold ore and a contract to refine the ore was not a security under the risk capital test even though "the promotional materials given to the public by appellant included the following statement: 'The reason for selling the gold at this price is to raise the capital for a new milling and refinery plant.'"[31] The Department of Corporations argued that the intended use of the proceeds demonstrated by this statement satisfied the requirement under the risk capital test that the funds "be used for a business venture or enterprise."[32] The court disagreed, stating,

---

26. *Id.*

27. Fox v. Ehrmantraut, 615 P.2d 1383, 1388 (Cal. 1980); People v. Coster, 199 Cal. Rptr. 253, 257 (Cal. Ct. App. 1984).

28. Wolf v. Banco Nacional De Mexico, 549 F. Supp. 841, 853 (N.D. Cal. 1982).

29. *Securities Adm'r v. College Assistance Plan (Guam)*, Inc., 533 F. Supp. 118, 122–23 (1981).

30. *Id.* at 122.

31. 194 Cal. App. 3d 506, 522 (1987).

32. *Id.*

> Superficially, this may be so since the construction of a mill and refinery is essential to the conduct of appellant's intended mining, milling and refining operations. However, it is equally true that every purchaser of a product from a seller, who reinvests the proceeds of the sale in his business operations, contributes to a seller's business capital. Notwithstanding, such a contribution is an investment in the purchased product and not a contribution of risk capital to a business enterprise within the normal scope of securities regulation.[33]

In *Hamilton Jewelers v. Department of Corporations*, the court held that the following offering did not constitute a security under the risk capital test:

> Hamilton Jewelers invites you to invest in a ONE CARAT DIAMOND for only $500, and if anytime [*sic*] within a three year period you elect to return the Stone, Hamilton will return to you the full purchase price *plus 5% interest* calculated daily from the date of purchase. A diamond investment of $500 will return $578.81 in cash at the end of a three year period.

The court reasoned that even though the offer to pay interest on an investment would normally fall within the definition of a security, in this case the investor's capital was not at risk because the investor had a diamond worth at least $500. The court stated, "[t]he customer, being adequately secured, would have placed no 'risk capital' with Hamilton; and, therefore, the transaction would not come within the regulatory purpose of the Corporate Securities Law even though 5 percent interest might ultimately be paid to the customer."[34]

The risk capital test has been adopted in some form in 16 jurisdictions (in addition to California):[35]

- By the Supreme Court of Hawaii (1971);
- By the Supreme Court of Arkansas (1987);
- By the District Court of Guam (Appellate Division, 1981);
- By the Court of Appeals of Ohio (10th District, 1975);

33. *Id.*
34. 37 Cal. App. 3d 330, 336 (1974).
35. *See* State v. Brewer, 932 S.W.2d 1, 28 (Tenn. Crim. App. 1996).

- By the Supreme Court of Oregon (1976);
- By statute in Alaska, Georgia, Michigan, North Dakota, Oklahoma, and Washington;
- Through regulatory rule in Illinois, New Mexico, North Carolina, Wisconsin, and Wyoming.

For example, Washington's statutory definition of a security includes "investment of money or other consideration in the risk capital of a venture with the expectation of some valuable benefit to the investor where the investor does not receive the right to exercise practical and actual control over the managerial decisions of the venture."[36]

The Hawaii Supreme Court devised a test that is a combination of the *Howey* test and the risk capital test established in *Sobieski.* This test states that an investment contract (and security) is formed when

> (1) An offeree furnishes initial value to an offeror, and
>
> (2) A portion of this initial value is subjected to the risks of the enterprise, and
>
> (3) The furnishing of the initial value is induced by the offeror's promises or representations which give rise to a reasonable understanding that a valuable benefit of some kind, over and above the initial value, will accrue to the offeree as a result of the operation of the enterprise, and
>
> (4) The offeree does not receive the right to exercise practical and actual control over the managerial decisions of the enterprise.[37]

The Hawaii test softens the harsh application of the risk capital test by specifying that the benefit has to be "over and above the initial value" and "as a result of the operation of the enterprise."[38]

Some jurisdictions have applied the risk capital test less broadly. For example,

---

36. Wash. Rev. Code § 21.20.005(12).
37. State by Comm'r of Sec. v. Haw. Mkt. Ctr., Inc., 485 P.2d 105, 109 (Haw. 1971).
38. *Id.* at 109.

- In *Hacker v. Goldberg*,[39] the court found that a sale of membership was not a security where "no financial profit or income could be derived under the charter."[40]
- In *Creasy Corp. v. Enz Bros. Co.*,[41] the court held that the state securities law was not enacted to protect against the sale of membership that would render a service available to them with no rights to the capital or profits of the company.[42]
- The New York Court of Appeals held that the sale of membership in recreational campgrounds is not a security where members acquire no legal interests in the company, no right to their business, any share of income, or any right to participate in management.[43] Rather than a financial interest, the court found that members acquired membership solely for their own personal enjoyment and not for resale or profit.[44] The court stated that the *Howey* test is the test of choice in New York; however, it also acknowledged the use of the risk capital test.[45] The court found application of the risk capital test irrelevant because the memberships were being sold for an established business instead of to raise capital for a new enterprise.[46] On this basis, the court failed to consider whether or not the risk capital test would be a useful addition to the *Howey* test in New York.[47]

---

39. 263 Ill. App. 73, 76–77 (Ill. App. Ct. 1931).

40. This case might be decided differently now since Illinois has subsequently adopted a version of the risk capital test in its statutory definition of an investment contract: "any enterprise or venture whereby the investor is solicited to transfer initial capital to an enterprise on the promise or inducement that a *value or benefit will accrue* to the investor from the enterprise where the investor's capital is placed at risk by the enterprise and the investor asserts no managerial or operational control over the enterprise." Ill. Admin. Code tit. 14, § 130.201 (emphasis added).

41. 187 N.W. 666 (Wis. 1922).

42. Again, this is an old case that might be decided differently today. Wisconsin has adopted a version of the *Howey*–risk capital test through regulatory rule. *Brewer*, 932 S.W.2d at 28.

43. All Seasons Resorts, Inc. v. Abrams, 497 N.E.2d 33, 35 (N.Y. 1986).

44. *Id.*

45. *Id.* at 40.

46. *Id.* This distinction was determinative in Oregon. *See* Jet Set Travel Club v. Corp. Comm'r, 535 P.2d 109 (Or. Ct. App. 1975). However, the distinction has also been criticized: "It is not clear why such a distinction should be made. An investment risk can exist regardless of whether an investor is asked to put capital at risk for an initial investment or for subsequent capital raising activities by an existing company." Thomas Lee Hazen, *The Basic Coverage of the Securities Laws*, ch. 1 *in* 1 The Law of Securities Regulation § 1.6(3) (6th ed. 2009).

47. *Id.*

- In *Dunwoody Country Club of Atlanta, Inc. v. Fortson*,[48] the court found that an investment in exchange for a membership certificate and use rights to social and recreational facilities was not the type of investment that the Securities Act meant to protect. Because the country club in question was a nonprofit organization, the court distinguished the present case from *Sobieski*.[49]

Even states that do not exclusively employ the risk capital test acknowledge its utility.[50]

There is some degree of judicial uncertainty regarding how the risk capital test should be applied.[51] In particular, California Appellate Courts, following the California Supreme Court, have avoided establishing an "all-inclusive formula" to test the facts of every case.[52] More specifically, the California Court of Appeals found that "[t]he 'risk capital' test is [...] not applicable in all situations," even though the parameters of its application are left unexplained.[53]

---

48. 253 S.E.2d 700 (Ga. 1979).

49. The court's reasoning was that "Where the promoter is engaged in a profit-making enterprise but the investor will receive no financial return (Silver Hills) or where the promoter is a non-profit corporation but the investor anticipates a financial return (e.g., sale of interest-bearing bonds), the Securities Act may apply. But where the promoter is not engaged in a profit-making enterprise and the investor cannot secure any financial advantage, the Securities Act does not apply." *Id.* at 704.

50. *See* State *ex rel.* Healy v. Consumer Bus. Sys., Inc., 482 P.2d 549, 552–54 (Or. Ct. App. 1971) ("[U]se of the Howey test should not foreclose the courts from using other methods of analysis when warranted . . . the risk-capital test is also to be used."); Jaciewicki v. Gordarl Assocs., Inc., 209 S.E.2d 693, 695–96 (Ga. Ct. App. 1974) ("The foregoing tests [the *Joiner* test, the *Howey* test, the capital-risk test, and the managerial-efforts test] are not exclusive of each other."); Artistic Door Corp. v. Rheney, 384 So. 2d 179, 181 (Fla. Dist. Ct. App. 1980) ("Whether or not the instant transaction falls within the definition set forth in either or both of these tests [the *Howey* test or the capital-risk test] is dependent upon the facts and circumstances of this individual case.").

51. *See* McLish v. Harris Farms, Inc., 507 F. Supp. 1075, 1086 (E.D. Cal. 1980):

> One can read hundreds, indeed, literally thousands of pages of commentary since the announcement of the Silver Hills case . . . as well as study intently the decisions of the California Appellate Courts since Silver Hills, and still not be able to state with any degree of certainty as to whether or not it was the purpose of the California Supreme Court to supplant the expectations of profit test with the risk of loss test, or merely to supplement the expectations of profit test with another test where . . . the purposes of the securities act would not be served because of the transactional bias contained in the expectations of profits test.

52. *See* People v. Figueroa, 715 P.2d 680, 695 (Cal. 1986) (quoting People v. Syde, 235 P.2d 601, 602 (Cal. 1951)); People v. Smith, 263 Cal. Rptr. 684, 688 (Cal. Ct. App. 1989); Moreland v. Dep't of Corps., 239 Cal. Rptr. 558, 561 (Cal. Ctp. App. 1987).

53. People v. Smith, 215 Cal. App. 3d 230, 237 (1989).

Is a Zero-Interest Loan a Security?

Now that you know about the two tests for what a security is, do you think a zero-interest loan would be considered a security? Under the *Howey* test, it would not be since there is no promise of a financial return, but what about under the risk capital test? If the lender's principal is at risk (i.e., unsecured), there is a very strong case to be made that the loan would be a security.

The only cases in which California courts find something not to be a security are those where the investments are sufficiently collateralized and/or where the investors are actively involved in the venture. For instance, in *Reiswig*, the court held that a CD-with-bonus package was not a security under the risk capital test, in part, because the CDs were FDIC insured, and there was therefore no substantial risk.[54]

Generally, courts in states that apply the risk capital test will use both the *Howey* test and the risk capital test to determine whether something is a security. If an instrument meets the definition under either test, the court will conclude that it is a security. States that do not apply the risk capital test will generally apply the *Howey* test only.

Requesting No Action Letters

Because the definition of a security can vary so much from state to state, it is essential to look at the relevant state's statutes, regulations, and judicial and regulatory opinions on the subject. When in doubt, it may be advisable to request a "no action letter" from the regulators. Such a request would describe the manner in which money is being raised, provide legal arguments about how the money-raising scheme is distinguishable from opinions where securities law was found to apply, and conclude with something like the following sentence:

> We respectfully request your confirmation that the [name of regulatory body] will not take enforcement action if [name of money-raising instrument] are offered and sold in the manner described herein without registration under [citation for law requiring registration of a securities offering].

54. Reiswig v. Department of Corporations, 50 Cal. Rptr. 3d 386, 391 (2006).

INVESTORS' PARTICIPATION IN THE ENTERPRISE

As we've seen, there are two tests for whether an investment scheme is a security, the *Howey* test and the risk capital test. They have in common one thing that is particularly relevant for the sharing economy: both of the tests require that the investor not be actively involved in the management of the venture for the investment to be considered a security.[1]

This means that if a group of ten people get together and start a business and all ten of them invest money in the business and actively participate in the management of the business, arguably their investment is not covered by securities law. This is a great "loophole" for participants in the sharing economy![2]

1. *See* Fox v. Ehrmantraut, 615 P.2d 1383, 1388 (Cal. 1980); *see also* People v. Graham, 210 Cal. Rptr. 318, 324 (Cal. Ct. App. 1985) (finding that a lack of managerial control on the part of an investor is implicit to identifying a security under the risk capital test).

2. Two caveats should be mentioned: first, active participation in management must be genuine and meaningful—for example, the investors should all be on the board of directors—it is not enough to name an investor VP of office décor to meet this requirement; and second, even when investors are actively participating in the management of the business, state securities filings still may be required when equity is issued to the investors.

Part 3: Registering Securities or Finding an Exemption

Registration Requirements

If something is a security, the default rule under federal and most state laws is that the issuer (the entity or individual offering the security) must do something called a registration (this is sometimes called a qualification under state law). For example, the 1933 Securities Act[55] states that

> Unless a registration statement is in effect as to a security, it shall be unlawful for any person, directly or indirectly—(1) to make use of any means or instruments of transportation or communication in interstate commerce or of the mails to sell such security through the use or medium of any prospectus or otherwise; or (2) to carry or cause to be carried through the mails or in interstate commerce, by any means or instruments of transportation, any such security for the purpose of sale or for delivery after sale.

55. § 5(a).

In other words, a registration statement must be filed before securities can be offered or sold. There are, however, several exemptions from this requirement contained in Sections 3 and 4 of the Act (discussed below).

Almost all states have a provision similar to the federal provision requiring registration of all securities offered in the state. For example, the Uniform Securities Act (adopted in some form by most states) states that "It is unlawful for a person to offer or sell a security in this State unless: (1) the security is a federal covered security (described below); (2) the security, transaction, or offer is exempted from registration . . .; or (3) the security is registered under this [Act]." One notable exception is New York, which does not generally require registration of securities offerings (though other filings are required).

What exactly is a registration? It is a very extensive set of filings that disclose all kinds of facts that would be relevant to an investor's decision about whether to invest in the offering. When a company does an Initial Public Offering (IPO), it does so pursuant to a registration. If you file a federal registration, you also have to register in the states where you plan to do your offering, but states generally have a streamlined process for federally registered securities (often called registration/qualification by coordination).

State and federal registrations must be approved by the relevant regulatory authorities.[56] Under federal law and in some states, all that is required for approval is sufficient disclosure of the material facts. This is called disclosure review. Some states, however, conduct merit review. In those states, even if the registration filing makes sufficient disclosures, the regulatory body may still reject the registration if it finds that the proposed offering imposes too great a risk for the investing public.

If you successfully complete the state and federal registration process, you will generally have the right to offer your securities to the public in the states where you have registered. Some states may require you to impose suitability standards on your investors so that you may not actually sell the securities to all members of the public but only those members of the public who meet the suitability standards. For example, in California, it is very common that the state securities regulators will

---

56. Note that this is not really an "approval"—you are usually required to include a statement in the offering document that says the securities regulators do not in any way endorse or recommend the offering.

require the following suitability standards unless the business making the offering has a track record of profitable operations:

> The investor (including any spouse) must have, *exclusive* of homes, home furnishings and cars, either: (1) a minimum net worth of at least $75,000 and minimum gross income of $50,000 during the last tax year and (based on a good faith estimate) minimum gross income of $50,000 during the current tax year, or (2) in the alternative, a minimum net worth of $150,000. In either case, the investment cannot exceed 10 percent of the net worth of the investor.

Very few companies attempt to do a full federal registration. The cost can be very high (hundreds of thousands of dollars). This is because audited financial statements are required (an audit can cost tens of thousands of dollars) and many hours of specialized legal work go into preparing the registration statement and related documents. Also, the federal government and each state charge filing fees that range from several hundred to several thousand dollars. This is one reason so few IPOs take place each year.

Exemptions from Registration

The good news, as noted above, is that there are exemptions from the general registration requirement. Almost all securities offerings will be completed under state and/or federal exemptions, which cost much less to comply with. It is always necessary to determine what state *and* federal exemptions can be used. The interplay between state and federal exemptions can be quite complicated!

For example, let's say a nonprofit public charity, exempt under Section 501(c)(3) of the Internal Revenue Code, is having a cash flow crisis. It's waiting for a big grant to come in, and it needs cash to meet payroll. The organization decides to solicit loans. It posts a plea on its website for lenders to provide $5,000 notes to be paid back in one year with five percent interest.

This nonprofit has just broken the securities laws! The offering of notes by a 501(c)(3) is exempt from federal securities registration, but it is not exempt in all states (it is exempt in most states, but even when exempt, certain filings and disclosures are required). By posting the offering on its website, which is visible to residents of all 50 states, it has violated the securities laws of several states (California and Pennsylvania, for example).

The following sections describe state and federal exemptions from the registration requirement and provide guidance on how the various exemptions can work together.

Summary of Federal Exemptions

Exempt Securities

The following securities are exempted from coverage of the 1933 Act (Section 3(a)—the numbers used below are the same as the section numbers in the Act; there is no number 1):[57]

> (2) **Any security issued or guaranteed by the United States** . . . or by any State of the United States, or by any political subdivision of a State or Territory, or by any public instrumentality of one or more States . . . or any security issued or guaranteed by any bank; or any security issued by or representing an interest in or a direct obligation of a Federal Reserve bank; . . . or any interest or participation in a single trust fund, or in a collective trust fund maintained by a bank, or any security arising out of a contract issued by an insurance company . . . .;
>
> (3) [**Short term notes**] Any note, draft, bill of exchange, or banker's acceptance . . . which has a maturity at the time of issuance of not exceeding nine months . . . .;
>
> (4) [**Charitable organizations**] Any security issued by a person organized and operated exclusively for religious, educational, benevolent, fraternal, charitable, or reformatory purposes and not for pecuniary profit, and no part of the net earnings of which inures to the benefit of any person, private stockholder, or individual, or any security of a fund that is excluded from the definition of an investment company under section 3(c)(10)(B) of the Investment Company Act of 1940 [a pooled income fund, collective trust fund, collective investment fund, or similar fund maintained by a charitable organization];
>
> (5) [**Savings and loans and farmers' co-ops**] Any security issued (A) by a savings and loan association, building and loan association,

57. Several provisions have been omitted in the interest of space. See the 1933 Act for a complete description of exempted securities.

cooperative bank, homestead association, or similar institution, which is supervised and examined by State or Federal authority having supervision over any such institution; or (B) by (i) a farmer's cooperative organization exempt from tax under section 521 of the Internal Revenue Code of 1954, (ii) a corporation described in section 501(c)(16) of such Code and exempt from tax under section 501(a) of such Code, or (iii) a corporation described in section 501(c)(2) of such Code which is exempt from tax under section 501(a) of such Code and is organized for the exclusive purpose of holding title to property, collecting income therefrom, and turning over the entire amount thereof, less expenses, to an organization or corporation described in clause (i) or (ii);

(6) **Any interest in a railroad equipment trust** [...].;

(7) **Certificates issued by a receiver or by a trustee in bankruptcy**, with the approval of the court;

(8) [**Insurance instruments**] Any insurance or endowment policy or annuity contract or optional annuity contract, issued by a corporation subject to the supervision of the insurance commissioner, bank commissioner, or any agency or officer performing like functions, of any State or Territory of the United States or the District of Columbia;

(9) [...] **any security exchanged by the issuer with its existing security holders** exclusively where no commission or other remuneration is paid or given directly or indirectly for soliciting such exchange;

(10) [**Exchanges**][...] any security which is issued in exchange for one or more bona fide outstanding securities, claims or property interests, or partly in such exchange and partly for cash, where the terms and conditions of such issuance and exchange are approved, after a hearing upon the fairness of such terms and conditions at which all persons to whom it is proposed to issue securities in such exchange shall have the right to appear, by any court, or by any official or agency of the United States, or by any State or Territorial banking or insurance commission or other governmental authority expressly authorized by law to grant such approval;

(11) [**Intrastate offerings**] Any security which is a part of an issue offered and sold only to persons resident within a single State or Territory, where the issuer of such security is a person resident and doing business within or, if a corporation, incorporated by and doing business within, such State or Territory;

(12) [**Bank holding company**] Any equity security issued in connection with the acquisition by a holding company of a bank [...];

(13) [**Church pension plan**] Any security issued by or any interest or participation in any church plan, company or account [...];

(14) **Any security futures product** that is—(A) cleared by a clearing agency [...]and (B) **traded on a national securities exchange** or a national securities association [...].

Exempt Transactions

What is the difference between an exempt security and an exempt transaction? An exempt security is always exempt, whereas a security that is exempt pursuant to a transaction exemption is only exempt for that particular transaction. If the security is offered or sold again, a new exemption must be identified. The following securities transactions are exempt according to Section 4 of the Act:

(1) transactions by any person other than an issuer, underwriter,[58] or dealer;[59]

(2) transactions by an issuer not involving any public offering;

(3) transactions by a dealer . . . ;

(4) brokers' transactions executed upon customers' orders on any exchange or in the over-the-counter market but not the solicitation of such orders;

(5) transactions involving offers or sales by an issuer solely to one or more accredited investors, if the aggregate offering price of an issue of securities offered in reliance on this paragraph does not exceed the

---

58. "The term 'underwriter' means any person who has purchased from an issuer with a view to, or offers or sells for an issuer in connection with, the distribution of any security, or participates or has a direct or indirect participation in any such undertaking, or participates or has a participation in the direct or indirect underwriting of any such undertaking; but such term shall not include a person whose interest is limited to a commission from an underwriter or dealer not in excess of the usual and customary distributors' or sellers' commission." The SEC has said that investors may be "underwriters" if "they act as links in a chain of transactions through which securities move from an issuer to the public." Preliminary Note 2 to Rule 144, 17 C.F.R. § 230.144 (2010).

59. The term "dealer" means any person who engages either for all or part of his time, directly or indirectly, as agent, broker, or principal, in the business of offering, buying, selling, or otherwise dealing or trading in securities issued by another person.

> amount allowed under section 3(b) of this title, if there is no advertising or public solicitation in connection with the transaction by the issuer or anyone acting on the issuer's behalf, and if the issuer files such notice with the Commission as the Commission shall prescribe.

A quick aside on the Section 4(1) exemption: It sounds quite broad because it exempts transactions by anyone other than an issuer, underwriter, or dealer. An issuer, of course, is the company that sells its own stock (or other securities) to raise money for itself. So the 4(1) exemption applies to secondary trading of securities. The reason it is rarely used is that the definition of underwriter is very broad (see footnote 58). You don't need to be a professional underwriter to be included in the definition—you simply must be someone with the intent to re-sell securities. More details about this exemption are contained in the section below on Resales of Restricted Securities.

Commonly Used Federal Exemptions

What are the most commonly used federal exemptions for initial offerings of securities by issuers (resales of securities following an initial offering are discussed below)?

Charitable Organizations

Section 3(a)(4) is used by religious, educational, benevolent, fraternal, charitable, or reformatory organizations. This allows nonprofit organizations to issue notes without having to worry about registration under federal securities laws. As mentioned above, not all of the states have a similar exemption.

Cooperatives

Section 3(a)(5) is used by farmers' cooperative organizations that meet the requirements of Section 521 of the Internal Revenue Code and by nonprofit organizations exempt from tax under Section 501(c)(16) (Cooperative Organizations to Finance Crop Operations). Section 521 provides favorable tax treatment to farmer co-ops that meet certain requirements (see Chapter 4 for a discussion of Section 521 co-ops). Nonprofit organizations exempt from tax under Section 501(c)(16) are organized by Section 521 cooperatives for the purpose of financing the ordinary crop operations of members or other producers.

In addition to the federal exemption for securities of these types of cooperatives, the federal Securities Act prohibits any state from requiring state level securities registration (see section below on the National Securities Markets Improvement Act (NSMIA)).

Intrastate Exemption

Section 3(a)(11) is known as the Intrastate Exemption. This exemption recognizes that an issuer that is only offering and selling securities within one state and doing most of its business within that state is best left alone by the federal securities laws and left to the regulatory authority of the state in which that issuer is located and offering securities.

The intrastate exemption is a godsend for the sharing economy! Sharing ventures are usually community-based and therefore focused within a single state. This is one of those rare securities laws that actually favors small local business as opposed to giant multinational corporations!

The Securities and Exchange Commission (SEC) has adopted a safe harbor rule to make it easier for an issuer to ensure that it is covered by the intrastate exemption. A safe harbor rule is one that contains requirements that, if complied with, ensure eligibility for the exemption. But non-compliance with the safe harbor requirements does not necessarily result in ineligibility for the exemption.

The intrastate exemption safe harbor is found in 17 CFR § 230.147 and is also known as Rule 147. It states, "This rule shall not raise any presumption that the exemption provided by Section 3(a)(11) of the Act is not available for transactions by an issuer which do not satisfy all of the provisions of the rule."

The rule's preliminary notes state that the intrastate exemption "was intended to apply only to issues genuinely local in character, which in reality represent local financing by local industries, carried out through local investment." The following items must be satisfied to comply with Rule 147:

- The issuer is incorporated or organized (or if an individual has his or her principal residence) in the state in which the offering is made.

- The issuer derived at least 80 percent of its gross revenues and those of its subsidiaries on a consolidated basis from that state.[60]
- The issuer had at the end of its most recent semi-annual fiscal period prior to the first offer of any part of the issue, at least 80 percent of its assets and those of its subsidiaries on a consolidated basis located within that state.
- The issuer intends to use and uses at least 80 percent of the net proceeds from sales made pursuant to the rule in connection with the operation of a business or of real property, the purchase of real property located in, or the rendering of services within such state.
- The principal office of the issuer is located within such state.
- No part of the issue may be offered or sold to non-residents for a period of nine months from the date of the last sale of an issue under the rule.[61]
- During that nine-month period, all resales of any part of the issue, by any person, shall be made only to persons resident within the state.
- The issuer shall, in connection with any securities sold by it pursuant to the rule: (i) place a legend on the certificate or other document evidencing the security stating that the securities have not been registered under the Act and setting forth the limitations on

60. Rule 147:

(1) For its most recent fiscal year, if the first offer of any part of the issue is made during the first six months of the issuer's current fiscal year; or (2) For the first six months of its current fiscal year or during the twelve-month fiscal period ending with such six-month period, if the first offer of any part of the issue is made during the last six months of the issuer's current fiscal year from the operation of a business or of real property located in or from the rendering of services within such state or territory; provided, however, that this provision does not apply to any issuer which has not had gross revenues in excess of $5,000 from the sale of products or services or other conduct of its business for its most recent twelve-month fiscal period.

61. Rule 147:

For purposes of determining the residence of offerees and purchasers: (1) A corporation, partnership, trust or other form of business organization shall be deemed to be a resident of a state or territory if, at the time of the offer and sale to it, it has its principal office within such state or territory. (2) An individual shall be deemed to be a resident of a state or territory if such individual has, at the time of the offer and sale to him, his principal residence in the state or territory. (3) A corporation, partnership, trust or other form of business organization which is organized for the specific purpose of acquiring part of an issue offered pursuant to this rule shall be deemed not to be a resident of a state or territory unless all of the beneficial owners of such organization are residents of such state or territory.

resale contained in the rule; (ii) issue stop transfer instructions to the issuer's transfer agent, if any, with respect to the securities, or, if the issuer transfers its own securities make a notation in the appropriate records of the issuer; and (iii) obtain a written representation from each purchaser as to his residence.

- The issuer shall, in connection with any offers, offers to sell, offers for sale or sales by it pursuant to this rule, disclose, in writing, the limitations on resale contained in the rule.

Finally, Rule 147 is not available if the offering, although in technical compliance with the rule, is part of a plan or scheme to make interstate offers or sales of securities.

Private Offerings

Section 4(2) exempts "transactions by an issuer not involving any public offering." This is obviously quite vague. As the Supreme Court said twenty years after the Securities Act was enacted, "[t]he Securities Act nowhere defines the scope of § 4([2])'s private offering exemption. Nor is the legislative history of much help in staking out its boundaries."[62]

Helpfully, the SEC has adopted a safe harbor rule to assist with compliance with this exemption. Before describing that rule, it is necessary to define "accredited investor."

Accredited Investors

What is the relevance of accredited investors? Companies that offer securities in a private offering only to accredited investors are subject to far simpler compliance requirements than companies that offer securities to even one unaccredited investor. Accredited investor includes the following:[63]

> (a) [**Savings and loans, brokers, public employee benefit plans**] Any savings and loan association or other institution . . .; any broker or dealer registered pursuant to section 15 of the Securities Exchange Act of 1934; any plan established and maintained by a state, its political subdivisions, or any agency or instrumentality of a state or its political subdivisions, for the benefit of its employees . . .;

62. SEC v. Ralston Purina Co., 346 U.S. 119, 122 (1953).

63. "Accredited investor" is defined in Section 2(a)(15) of the Act and 17 C.F.R. § 230.215.

(b) Any private **business development company** as defined in section 202(a)(22) of the Investment Advisers Act of 1940;

(c) [**Entity with at least $5 million in assets**] Any organization described in section 501(c)(3) of the Internal Revenue Code, corporation, . . . business trust, or partnership, not formed for the specific purpose of acquiring the securities offered, with total assets in excess of $5,000,000;

(d) [**Principal of the issuer**] Any director, executive officer, or general partner of the issuer of the securities being offered or sold, or any director, executive officer, or general partner of a general partner of that issuer;

(e) [**Person with at least $1 million in net worth**] Any natural person whose individual net worth, or joint net worth with that person's spouse, at the time of his purchase exceeds $1,000,000;[64]

(f) [**Person with at least $200,000 in annual income**] Any natural person who had an individual income in excess of $200,000 in each of the two most recent years or joint income with that person's spouse in excess of $300,000 in each of those years and has a reasonable expectation of reaching the same income level in the current year;

(g) [**Trust with at least $5 million in assets**] Any trust, with total assets in excess of $5,000,000, not formed for the specific purpose of acquiring the securities offered . . .; and

(h) [**Entity made up of accredited investors**] Any entity in which all of the equity owners are accredited investors.

Even before the definition of accredited investor was narrowed by the Dodd–Frank Act (discussed in footnote 64), it was estimated that only eight percent of the population meets the definition.[65] This is a source of great frustration to enterprises that would like to solicit a larger pool of potential investors.

64. This part of the definition was narrowed by the Dodd-Frank Wall Street Reform and Consumer Protection Act (Pub. L. No. 111-203, 124 Stat. 1376), which required that the value of an individual's primary residence must be excluded when determining net worth for accredited investor purposes.

65. SEC Release No. 33-8766; IA-2576; File No. S7-25-06, *available at* http://www.sec.gov/rules/proposed/2006/33-8766.pdf.

Conducting a Private Offering

To conduct an offering under the federal private offering exemption, there are two options: either conduct an offering that fits within the guidelines for private offerings that have been developed over the years by the courts, or use the private offering safe harbor known as Rule 506.

Relying on 4(2) is a bit risky since there are no hard and fast rules regarding what exactly is a private offering. The SEC has said that

> persons who offer or sell . . . securities without complying with [a safe harbor] are hereby put on notice by the Commission that in view of the broad remedial purposes of the [Securities] Act and of public policy which strongly supports registration, they will have a substantial burden of proof in establishing that an exemption from registration is available for such offers or sales and that such persons and the brokers and other persons who participate in the transactions do so at their risk.[66]

In the leading case interpreting Section 4(2), the Supreme Court stated that the availability of the exemption

> should turn on whether the particular class of persons affected need the protection of the [Securities] Act. An offering to those who are shown to be able to fend for themselves is a transaction "not involving any public offering."[67]

The Supreme Court also considered it important whether the offerees had "access to the same kind of information that the [Securities] [A]ct would make available in the form of a registration statement."[68]

According to the American Bar Association Committee on Federal Regulation of Securities,[69] the following factors are the most important in evaluating compliance with Section 4(2):

- **Manner of offering:** How the purchasers of the particular securities offered are found—whether through a public process (e.g.,

66. 37 Fed. Reg. at 592.

67. SEC v. Ralston Purina Corp., 346 U.S. 119, 125 (1953).

68. *Id.* at 125–26.

69. Law of Private Placements (Non-Public Offerings) Not Entitled to Benefits of Safe Harbors—A Report by Committee on Federal Regulation of Securities (ABA Section of Business Law, Apr. 2010).

general solicitation, advertising, seminars, etc.) or a non-public process.

- **Eligibility of the purchasers:** Whether each purchaser (not all offerees), either alone or with a qualified advisor, has such knowledge and experience in financial and business matters as to be capable of evaluating the merits and risks of the prospective investment.
- **Information:** Whether each purchaser (or its qualified advisor) receives, or has meaningful access to, such information as the particular purchaser needs to make an informed investment decision.
- **Resales:** Whether steps appropriate in the circumstances are taken to prevent resales that are not registered or exempt.

Notice that the inquiry focuses on actual purchasers, not offerees. So if an issuer were to accidentally make an offering to an investor that did not meet the requirements of Section 4(2), this would not defeat the exemption as long as that person did not ultimately purchase securities. The same is true under the private offering safe harbor (Rule 506).[70]

Rule 506 Safe Harbor

Rule 506 is part of Regulation D, which the SEC adopted in 1982. Regulation D (often called "Reg D") also includes Rules 504 and 505, which are discussed in the section on small offerings below. To meet the requirements of Rule 506, the offering must comply with the following:

- There are no more than 35 purchasers of securities. The following types of purchasers do not count toward this limit of 35:[71]
  - Any relative, spouse or relative of the spouse of a purchaser who has the same principal residence as the purchaser;
  - Any trust or estate in which a purchaser and his or her relatives collectively have more than 50 percent of the beneficial interest;

---

70. Proposed Revision of Certain Exemptions from the Registration Provisions of the Securities Act of 1933 for Transactions Involving Limited Offers and Sales, Securities Act Release No. 6339, 46 Fed. Reg. 41,791, 41,793, [1981–1982 Transfer Binder] Fed. Sec. L. Rep. (CCH) ¶ 83,014 (proposed Aug. 7, 1981).

71. A corporation, partnership, or other entity shall be counted as one purchaser. If, however, that entity is organized for the specific purpose of acquiring the securities offered and is not an accredited investor, then each beneficial owner of equity securities or equity interests in the entity shall count as a separate purchaser.

  - Any corporation or other organization of which a purchaser and his relatives collectively are beneficial owners of more than 50 percent of the equity interests; and
  - Accredited investors.
- Each purchaser who is not an accredited investor either alone or with his or her purchaser representative(s) has such knowledge and experience in financial and business matters that he/she/it is capable of evaluating the merits and risks of the prospective investment (or the issuer reasonably believes immediately prior to making any sale that such purchaser comes within this description).
- If the issuer sells securities to any purchaser that is not an accredited investor, the issuer is required to furnish certain information (specified in Reg D, 17 CFR 230.502(b)) to such purchaser a reasonable time prior to sale (this requirement can be quite onerous to comply with, which is why so few private placements are open to unaccredited investors).
- Neither the issuer nor any person acting on its behalf shall offer or sell the securities by any form of general solicitation or general advertising, including, but not limited to, the following:
  - Any advertisement, article, notice or other communication published in any newspaper, magazine, or similar media or broadcast over television or radio; and
  - Any seminar or meeting whose attendees have been invited by any general solicitation or general advertising.

How does the issuer determine who is and is not accredited? The issuer must have a reasonable belief that an investor is accredited. This can be accomplished by having the investor provide information and certifications related to wealth and income.

There is no maximum dollar amount that can be raised under Rule 506.

Securities sold under Rule 506 are "restricted securities." This means that they cannot be re-sold by the initial purchaser without some additional securities compliance. This is why securities purchased in a private placement come with a "legend" that says something like the following:

> THE SECURITIES REPRESENTED HEREBY HAVE NOT BEEN REGISTERED UNDER THE SECURITIES ACT OF 1933 (THE "*ACT*") AND MAY NOT BE OFFERED, SOLD, OR

> OTHERWISE TRANSFERRED, PLEDGED, OR HYPOTHECATED UNLESS AND UNTIL REGISTERED UNDER THE ACT OR, IN THE OPINION OF COUNSEL SATISFACTORY TO THE ISSUER OF THESE SECURITIES, SUCH OFFER, SALE OR TRANSFER, PLEDGE OR HYPOTHECATION OTHERWISE COMPLIES WITH THE ACT.

The issuer is required to

> exercise reasonable care to assure that the purchasers of the securities are not underwriters within the meaning of section 2(11) of the Act, which reasonable care may be demonstrated by the following: (1) Reasonable inquiry to determine if the purchaser is acquiring the securities for himself or for other persons; (2) Written disclosure to each purchaser prior to sale that the securities have not been registered under the Act and, therefore, cannot be resold unless they are registered under the Act or unless an exemption from registration is available; and (3) Placement of a legend on the certificate or other document that evidences the securities stating that the securities have not been registered under the Act and setting forth or referring to the restrictions on transferability and sale of the securities.[72]

As with all offerings under Reg D, the issuer must report the offering to the SEC using Form D.

One characteristic of Rule 506 that makes it very attractive to issuers is that the NSMIA preempts states from requiring registration of offerings made under Rule 506 (for more information, see the section on NSMIA below).

Small Offerings

Small offerings are not exempt under the 1933 Act. However, the Act says

> The [Securities and Exchange] Commission may from time to time by its rules and regulations, and subject to such terms and conditions as may be prescribed therein, add any class of securities to the securities exempted as provided in this section, if it finds that the enforcement of this title with respect to such securities is not necessary in the public interest and for the protection of investors by reason of the

72. This requirement also applies to Rule 505 and to Rule 504 when it is used for a private placement.

THE CROWDFUND ACT—NEW OPPORTUNITIES FOR RAISING COMMUNITY CAPITAL

In 2009, Sustainable Economies Law Center advisor Michael Shuman authored an article in the *Community Development Investment Review*, a publication of the Federal Reserve Bank of San Francisco. In the article, Michael pointed out that while locally owned, small businesses constitute about one-half of the private economy in terms of output and jobs, they receive almost no investment from the public.

The reason for this, Michael argued, is that securities laws essentially ban public investment in small, locally owned businesses. "The regulations prohibit the average American from investing in any small business, unless the firm is willing to spend $50,000 to $100,000 on lawyers . . . ." Michael pointed out that if you go to a casino, you're not required to attest that you are an accredited gambler and read a thick disclosure document about the risks of gambling. Yet this is what is required for investing, which is arguably less risky than gambling!

So Michael made a modest proposal in the article: "One easy reform would be for the SEC to exempt from its usual expensive disclosure requirements any low-risk public ownership of locally owned microbusinesses. By low-risk, I mean that no person can hold more than $100 worth of any one stock—which means that we're freeing up people to engage in the risk equivalent of a nice dinner for two. By local ownership, I mean that only residents within a state can buy, hold, and sell stock shares. And by microbusinesses, I mean any business with a total stock valuation on issuance of less than $250,000."

In the summer of 2010, law student interns at the Sustainable Economies Law Center, with support from Paul Spinrad of *Make* magazine, worked on a petition to the SEC to request a rule change that would implement Michael's proposal. Even though the SEC did not respond, news of this simple request spread. It seemed like a no-brainer—exempt $100 investments from the extremely onerous registration requirements. Amazingly, members of Congress and the President eventually expressed support for the idea of an exemption for small investments. This culminated in the passage of the CROWDFUND Act[1] (part of the JOBS Act, which includes several securities law reforms) on April 5, 2012.

The CROWDFUND Act, when it goes into effect, will allow organizations to raise capital from the public using an SEC-registered crowdfunding intermediary. The maximum amount that can be raised is $1 million, and each investor will be able to invest up to five percent of his or her annual income or net worth (ten percent if the investor has more than $100,000 in net worth or annual income).

The intermediaries will have to meet several requirements including

- Provide disclosures related to risks and other investor education materials;
- Ensure that each investor—
  - Reviews investor-education information;
  - Positively affirms that he/she understands that he/she is risking the loss of the entire investment, and that he/she could bear such a loss; and
  - Answers questions demonstrating an understanding of the level of risk generally applicable to investments in start-ups, emerging businesses, and small issuers and an understanding of the risk of illiquidity;
- Take measures to reduce the risk of fraud, including obtaining a background and securities enforcement regulatory history check on each officer, director, and person holding more than 20 percent of the outstanding equity of the issuer;
- Ensure that all offering proceeds are only provided to the issuer when the aggregate capital raised from all investors is equal to or greater than a target offering amount;
- Make efforts to ensure that no investor in a 12-month period has purchased securities offered pursuant to the crowdfunding exemption that, in the aggregate, from all issuers, exceed the investment limits of the exemption.

The intermediary will have to provide the following information:

- The name, legal status, physical address, and website address of the issuer;

1. H.R. 3606, 112th Cong. (2012).

- The names of the directors and officers (and any persons occupying a similar status or performing a similar function), and each person holding more than 20 percent of the shares of the issuer;
- A description of the business of the issuer and the anticipated business plan of the issuer;
- A description of the financial condition of the issuer, including, for offerings that, together with all other offerings of the issuer under the crowdfunding exemption within the preceding 12-month period, have, in the aggregate, target offering amounts of
  - $100,000 or less—the income tax returns filed by the issuer for the most recently completed year (if any) and financial statements of the issuer, which shall be certified by the principal executive officer of the issuer to be true and complete in all material respects;
  - More than $100,000, but not more than $500,000—financial statements reviewed by a public accountant who is independent of the issuer, using professional standards and procedures for such review or standards and procedures established by the SEC, by rule, for such purpose; and
  - More than $500,000 (or such other amount as the SEC may establish, by rule)—audited financial statements;
- A description of the stated purpose and intended use of the proceeds;
- The target offering amount, the deadline to reach the target offering amount, and regular updates regarding the progress of the issuer in meeting the target offering amount;
- The price to the public of the securities or the method for determining the price, provided that, prior to sale, each investor shall be provided in writing the final price and all required disclosures, with a reasonable opportunity to rescind the commitment to purchase the securities;
- A description of the ownership and capital structure of the issuer, including
  - Terms of the securities of the issuer being offered and each other class of security of the issuer, including how such terms

may be modified, and a summary of the differences between such securities, including how the rights of the securities being offered may be materially limited, diluted, or qualified by the rights of any other class of security of the issuer;

- A description of how the exercise of the rights held by the principal shareholders of the issuer could negatively impact the purchasers of the securities being offered;
- The name and ownership level of each existing shareholder who owns more than 20 percent of any class of the securities of the issuer;
- How the securities being offered are being valued, and examples of methods for how such securities may be valued by the issuer in the future, including during subsequent corporate actions; and
- The risks to purchasers of the securities relating to minority ownership in the issuer, the risks associated with corporate actions, including additional issuances of shares, a sale of the issuer or of assets of the issuer, or transactions with related parties.

The issuer may not advertise the terms of the offering, except for notices that direct investors to the intermediary's website. The issuer will also be required to provide regular reports to the SEC and investors.

There are two provisions of the CROWDFUND Act that will make it much easier to raise money from a large number of small investors:

1. Offerings under the CROWDFUND Act are exempt from the requirement that a company with more than 500 investors in a single equity class that has $10 million in assets automatically becomes a public reporting company (the SEC may impose conditions on this exemption in its rulemaking process).
2. The states are not allowed to require registration of offerings that are exempt under the CROWDFUND Act (however, they can require notice filings and fees in the state that is the issuer's principal place of business and in

any state in which purchasers of 50 percent or greater of the aggregate amount of the issue are residents).

Finally, the legislation requires that dollar amounts under the exemption will be adjusted not less frequently than once every five years to reflect any change in the Consumer Price Index.

The CROWDFUND Act has not yet gone into effect and will not go into effect until the SEC completes rulemaking under the Act. There are several places in the Act that require the SEC to make rules to flesh out the requirements. The Act gives the SEC nine months to complete the rulemaking process, but it is unclear whether the SEC will be able to meet this deadline.

> small amount involved or the limited character of the public offering; but no issue of securities shall be exempted under this subsection where the aggregate amount at which such issue is offered to the public exceeds $5,000,000.

Under this authority, the SEC has adopted rules that exempt small offerings. The three main exemptions under this provision are Regulation A, Rule 504, and Rule 505.

Regulation A[73]

Regulation A (Reg A) is an exemption that allows a public offering[74] that can be used to raise up to $5 million. It must meet the following conditions:

- The issuer of the securities must be
  - An entity organized under the laws of the United States or Canada, or any State, Province, Territory or possession thereof, or the District of Columbia, with its principal place of business in the United States or Canada;

73. 17 C.F.R. §§ 230.251 *et seq.*

74. What does the term "public offering" mean? It does not have a precise legal definition but it is generally used to refer to an offering in which the offeror is permitted to conduct general solicitation of the public through advertising. In a private offering, generally, advertising is not permitted.

  - Not subject to Section 13 or 15(d) of the Securities Exchange Act of 1934 (the "Exchange Act") (15 U.S.C. 78a *et seq.*) immediately before the offering (in other words not a public reporting company);
  - Not a development stage company that either has no specific business plan or purpose, or has indicated that its business plan is to merge with an unidentified company or companies;
  - Not an investment company registered or required to be registered under the Investment Company Act of 1940 (15 U.S.C. 80a-1 *et seq.*);
  - Not issuing fractional undivided interests in oil or gas rights or a similar interest in other mineral rights; and
  - Not disqualified because of Section 230.262 (these are called "bad boy" provisions that disqualify issuers that have been involved in fraud or other wrongdoing).
- Except as allowed by Section 230.254 (a section that allows a "testing of the waters" for interest in the offering prior to completion of the offering statement), no offer of securities shall be made unless a Form 1-A offering statement has been filed with the Commission.

The materials that must be filed are rather extensive and costly to prepare. Because they are considered almost as onerous as a full registration, offerings under Reg A are sometimes called "mini registrations." But, unlike a full registration, full state-level compliance is required. For these reasons, Reg A is not very commonly used.

The JOBS Act, passed on April 5, 2012, requires the SEC to either amend Reg A or adopt a new regulation similar to Reg A that increases the maximum amount that can be raised to $50 million, among other new provisions.

Rule 504

Rule 504 can be used for offerings of up to $1 million.[75] Rule 504 has two separate ways that it can be used: for a private offering and for a public offering.

75. The aggregate offering price for an offering of securities under Rule 504 shall not exceed $1,000,000, less the aggregate offering price for all securities sold within the twelve months before the start of and during the offering of securities under Rule 504. For example, if an issuer sold $4,100,000 in securities on December 1, 1987, under Rule 505, the issuer could not sell any of its securities under Rule 504 until December 1, 1988. Until then the issuer must count the December 1, 1987, sale towards the $1,000,000 limit within the preceding twelve months.

Rule 504 for Private Offerings

A private offering can be conducted under Rule 504 under the following conditions:

The issuer may not be

- Subject to the reporting requirements of Section 13 or 15(d) of the Exchange Act;
- An investment company; or
- A development stage company that either has no specific business plan or purpose or has indicated that its business plan is to engage in a merger or acquisition with an unidentified company or companies, or other entity or person.

The same rules regarding restricted securities and the prohibition on advertising that apply to Rule 506 also apply to Rule 504 when it is used to conduct a private offering.

Rule 504 for Public Offerings

The prohibition on advertising that generally applies under Rule 504 does not apply to offers and sales of securities that are made. From Rule 504:

> (i) Exclusively in one or more states that provide for the registration of the securities, and require the public filing and delivery to investors of a substantive disclosure document before sale, and are made in accordance with those state provisions;
>
> (ii) In one or more states that have no provision for the registration of the securities or the public filing or delivery of a disclosure document before sale, if the securities have been registered in at least one state that provides for such registration, public filing and delivery before sale, offers and sales are made in that state in accordance with such provisions, and the disclosure document is delivered before sale to all purchasers (including those in the states that have no such procedure); or
>
> (iii) Exclusively according to state law exemptions from registration that permit general solicitation and general advertising so long as sales are made only to accredited investors.

Here are some examples to illustrate what this means:

Julie lives in Spokane, Washington, and owns a business there. She would like to raise $1 million in a public offering from Washington residents. She doesn't qualify for the federal intrastate exemption because she sells products throughout the Pacific Northwest. As noted above, the ban on public advertising under Rule 504 does not apply to securities offerings made "exclusively in one or more states that provide for the registration of the securities, and require the public filing and delivery to investors of a substantive disclosure document before sale, and are made in accordance with those state provisions." Washington State *does* provide for the registration of securities and *does* require the public filing and delivery to investors of a substantive disclosure document before sale. So, as long as Julie complies with Washington's registration requirements, her offering is eligible for exemption under Rule 504, and there is no federal prohibition on public advertising.

Angelica lives in Buffalo, New York. She would like to raise $1 million in a public offering from New York residents. She doesn't qualify for the federal intrastate exemption because she sells products throughout the Mid Atlantic region. New York *does not* provide for the registration of the securities, and *does not* require the public filing and delivery to investors of a substantive disclosure document before sale. So Rule 504 would not allow Angelica to do a public offering. What should she do? Remember that the ban on public advertising under Rule 504 does not apply to securities offerings made in one or more states that have no provision for the registration of the securities or the public filing or delivery of a disclosure document before sale, if the securities have been registered in at least one state that provides for such registration, public filing and delivery before sale, offers and sales are made in that state in accordance with such provisions, and the disclosure document is delivered before sale to all purchasers (including those in the states that have no such procedure). This means that Angelica could register her public offering in another state (let's say Connecticut). Then, assuming she complies with New York's filing requirement as well as Connecticut's registration procedure and delivers the disclosure document she prepared for Connecticut to all purchasers in both Connecticut and New York, her public offering would be exempt under Rule 504.

If the conditions are met for conducting a public offering under Rule 504, the securities are not restricted which means they can be re-sold without registration.

Rule 505

Rule 505's requirements are very similar to Rule 506's except that no more than $5 million can be raised and the requirement that unaccredited investors have "such knowledge and experience in financial and business matters that he is capable of evaluating the merits and risks of the prospective investment" does not apply.

Offers and Sales That Occur Outside the United States—Regulation S[76]

Regulation S states that the federal registration requirements do not apply to offers and sales that occur outside the United States and provides safe harbors for those who are conducting securities offerings outside of the United States.

Exemption for Transactions Exempt from Qualification Under Section 25102(n) of the California Corporations Code[77]

This exemption was created specifically to coordinate with a California exemption that allows public solicitation and allows the purchase of securities by unaccredited investors as long as they meet wealth and income requirements that are less stringent than the accredited investor requirements. The total offering may not exceed $5 million.

State Exemptions

Once you have determined which federal exemption you can use for your offering, you still have to determine which state securities laws apply and what exemptions might be available under the applicable state laws.

State securities statutes vary quite a bit. This can create a huge hassle for an offeror that wants to offer securities in more than one state. For example, Pat is going to conduct a public offering under Rule 504 and would like to offer securities in both Louisiana and Texas. In addition to completing the required federal filing (Form D), it will be necessary to comply with the securities laws of both Louisiana and Texas, which may be quite different.

National Securities Markets Improvement Act

NSMIA, adopted in 1996, added Section 28 to the 1933 Securities Act in an attempt to partially alleviate this regulatory burden. NSMIA provides that certain securities offerings that are exempt under federal

76. 17 C.F.R. § 230.901–.905.
77. *Id.* at § 230.1001.

THE CONCEPT OF INTEGRATION

It is important to be familiar with the concept of integration when conducting securities offerings. The purpose of the integration requirements is to prevent someone from getting around the requirements of an exemption by doing more than one offering. For example, let's say Scott want to raise $6 million in a private offering. He does not want to use Rule 506 because he does not want to be limited to "sophisticated" investors. He decides to use Rule 505 and knowing that you cannot raise more than $5 million under Rule 505, he does two separate offerings under Rule 505 and raises $4 million in the first offering and then a couple of months later raises $2 million in the second offering. Obviously, the only reason he did two offerings was to evade the $5 million cap on a Rule 505 offering.

The SEC created the integration rules to prevent this kind of scheme. Similar requirements exist under state law. Generally, as long as two offerings are separated by at least six months, they will not be "integrated" (i.e., considered part of a single offering). Otherwise, the determination of whether separate sales of securities are part of the same offering generally depends on the particular facts and circumstances considering factors such as

> (a) Whether the sales are part of a single plan of financing; (b) Whether the sales involve issuance of the same class of securities; (c) Whether the sales have been made at or about the same time; (d) Whether the same type of consideration is being received; and (e) Whether the sales are made for the same general purpose.[1]

1. Rule 502(a).

law are also exempt from state registration requirements. The securities exempt from state registration requirements under NSMIA are called "covered securities." Covered securities include securities of farmers' cooperatives (exempt under Section 3(a)(5) of the Act) and securities issued under Rule 506.

States are still permitted to require notice filings and charge fees for offerings of covered securities. States also retain jurisdiction to investigate and bring enforcement actions in the case of fraud. Unfortunately,

❖❖❖❖

A Note About "Friends and Family" Offerings

Many entrepreneurs have heard of friends and family offerings and are under the mistaken impression that the securities laws don't apply as long as you only make your offering to close friends and family. The state and federal laws apply to all securities offerings!

It is true that there are often exemptions available when you keep your offering private and only solicit people with whom you have a pre-existing relationship. The federal private offering exemption would probably be available in this case, and most states have private offering exemptions as well. But it is still necessary to do the work required to meet the requirements of the exemption you plan to use. State private offering exemptions usually include limits on the number of unaccredited investors that can invest and may require filings with the securities regulators, specific information that must be provided to prospective investors, and so on.

NSMIA does not help Pat, in the example described above, because securities offered under Rule 504 are not covered securities.

Small Company Offering Registration (SCOR)

Another effort has been made, this one by the state securities regulators, to try to reduce the regulatory burden on people like Pat. The North American Securities Administrators Association (NASAA), the association of state securities regulators, created a form called SCOR (also known as U-7). The SCOR form was designed to be a generic form that would be accepted by all states to register a public offering. For example, in Pat's case, she could fill out one form and submit it to both the Texas and the Louisiana regulators.

In reality, not all states accept the SCOR form (though the vast majority do), and some states, even though they do accept the form, are considered "SCOR unfriendly." The best practice is to look at the options available in each state. Some states have their own requirements for registration and also accept the SCOR form. In those states it is worthwhile to compare the two options. Even though the SCOR form was designed for use by small businesses with limited resources, parts of it can be tricky to complete.

Whether you use the SCOR form or the state-specific registration process, it is likely that you will have to provide professionally prepared financial statements, your organizational documents, an opinion of counsel, and detailed information about the business. Once you complete the package, you submit it to the state regulators. They most likely will respond with various questions and requested changes to the document. There is a back-and-forth process until the state is satisfied with what has been provided. States will often require various protections for investors, such as an impound account where investment funds must be held until a pre-determined minimum has been raised. If you aren't able to raise the minimum within a specified period, all the money is returned to the investors.

If you do use the SCOR form, you may be able to use regional coordinated review. If you choose to request coordinated review, you will generally only have to work with one of the states, the lead jurisdiction, that will coordinate the review and comments of all states within the region in which you want to offer your securities.

The following is a list of the groups of states that do coordinated review:

- **CR-SCOR-Mid-Atlantic:** Delaware, Maryland, New Jersey, Pennsylvania, Virginia, and West Virginia;
- **CR-SCOR-Midwest:** Illinois, Indiana, Iowa, Kansas, Michigan, Minnesota, Missouri, Nebraska, North Dakota, South Dakota, and Wisconsin;
- **CR-SCOR-New England:** Connecticut, Maine, Massachusetts, New Hampshire, Rhode Island, and Vermont;
- **CR-SCOR-Southwest:** Arkansas, Oklahoma, and Texas;
- **CR-SCOR-West:** Alaska, Arizona, Colorado, Idaho, Montana, Nevada, New Mexico, Oregon, Utah, Washington, and Wyoming.

Anti-fraud Rules

Regardless of whether a securities offering is exempt from the federal or state registration requirements, anti-fraud provisions of the state and federal securities laws still apply. For example, Section 12 of the 1933 Act states that "any person who [...] offers or sells a security [...] by means of a prospectus or oral communication, which includes an untrue statement of a material fact or omits to state a material fact necessary in order to make the statements, in the light of the circumstances under which they were made, not misleading [...]shall be liable [...] to the person purchasing such security from him, who may sue either at law or in

❖❖❖❖

What If You Don't Comply with the State and Federal Registration Requirements?

Consequences that can result from non-compliance include the requirement to return all investor funds, fines, and civil and criminal liability. Generally the severity of the consequences increases with the level of malicious intent on the part of the offeror.

equity in any court of competent jurisdiction, to recover the consideration paid for such security with interest thereon [...]."

The anti-fraud provisions are the reason why offerors should prepare a prospectus for potential investors even when they are not required to do so under the applicable exemption from registration. This makes it less likely that an investor will sue, claiming that the offeror omitted to state a material fact.

Registration Under the 1934 Securities and Exchange Act

Under the 1933 Act, all securities offerings must be registered with the SEC unless exempt. In addition to this requirement, certain companies must file registrations under the 1934 Act. This registration establishes a public file containing financial and business information about the company. Because of this, a company that registers under the 1934 Act is known as a "public company." Public companies are required to make quarterly filings of reports on Forms 10-Q and 10-K, and on Form 8-K, as applicable. Public companies are also subject to certain regulations from which private companies are exempt such as the governance requirements of the Sarbanes–Oxley Act of 2002.

Under what circumstances does a company have to register under the 1934 Act? If a company wants to list a class of its securities on a national exchange (such as the New York Stock Exchange), it has to register under the 1934 Act.[78]

Also, any company that has at least 500 equity investors of record in any class of equity investment and has total assets of $10 million or more must register under the 1934 Act within 120 days after the end of the first fiscal year in which the both of those conditions are met.

78. 1934 Act § 12(a).

The term "class" includes all securities that are of substantially similar character and the holders of which enjoy substantially similar rights and privileges.[79]

There are some exemptions to the requirement to register under Section 12(g)(1):[80]

> (A) Any security listed and registered on a national securities exchange (which would be registered under Section 12(a)
>
> (B) Any security issued by an investment company registered pursuant to [...] the Investment Company Act of 1940
>
> (C) Most securities issued by banks and similar institutions
>
> (D) Any security of an issuer organized and operated exclusively for religious, educational, benevolent, fraternal, charitable, or reformatory purposes and not for pecuniary profit, and no part of the net earnings of which inures to the benefit of any private shareholder or individual [...].
>
> (E) Any security of an issuer which is a "cooperative association" as defined in the Agricultural Marketing Act, approved June 15, 1929, as amended, or a federation of such cooperative associations [...].
>
> (F) Any security issued by a mutual or cooperative organization which supplies a commodity or service primarily for the benefit of its members and operates not for pecuniary profit, but only if the security is part of a class issuable only to persons who purchase commodities or services from the issuer, the security is transferable only to a successor in interest or occupancy of premises serviced or to be served by the issuer, and no dividends are payable to the holder of the security
>
> (G) Any security issued by an insurance company (under certain conditions)
>
> (H) Any interest or participation in any collective trust funds maintained by a bank or in a separate account maintained by an insurance company [...].

The JOBS Act changed the requirements to register as a public company under 12(g)(1). You can now have up to 2,000 investors before the registration requirement is triggered, but no more than 500 unaccredited investors.

---

79. 1934 Act § 12(g)(1) & Rule 12g-1.
80. 1934 Act § 12(g)(2).

Resales of Restricted Securities

As noted above, securities sold by an issuer in a private placement are restricted and cannot be legally re-sold unless registered or unless an exemption applies. So let's say you're conducting a private placement to raise capital and your investors say to you, "I really want to invest in your business but I'm nervous. What if I have a family emergency and I want to sell my shares to someone else so I can get my money (or at least some of it) back? Or what if the company does really well and the demand for the securities goes up? Can I sell my securities to someone else at a profit in the same way that people can buy and sell securities on the public stock market?" Most investors like to have "liquidity," which means the ability to liquidate (sell) an investment whenever they choose.

Your investors need to understand the restrictions on resale of securities purchased in a private placement. The SEC does not want your investors buying shares in your company and then immediately turning around and selling them to someone else. That would make the private nature of the initial offering meaningless as your shares spread far and wide to people you have no relationship with. So before your investors can re-sell their securities, they need to find an exemption to the general rule that they cannot be re-sold.

The most commonly used exemption for the resale of restricted securities is Section 4(1) of the 1933 Act, which exempts a transaction "by a person other than an issuer, underwriter, or dealer."

Section 2(a)(11) of the 1933 Act states, "The term 'underwriter' means any person who has purchased from an issuer with a view to, or offers or sells for an issuer in connection with, the distribution of any security . . . ." This is why it is a good practice for issuers to have their investors sign a document that includes a representation like the following:

> I am purchasing the securities solely for investment purposes, and not for further distribution. I am not a party to, and do not presently intend to enter into, any contract or other arrangement with any other person or entity involving the resale, transfer, or other distribution of any of the securities. My investment intent is not limited to my present intention to hold the shares for the minimum capital gains period specified under any applicable tax law, for a deferred sale, for a specified increase or decrease in the market price of the shares, or for any other fixed period in the future.

If your investors did not invest in your company with the intent to further distribute the securities, your investors will not fall within the definition of an underwriter and therefore are exempt from the registration requirement under Section 4(1). Simply having your investors make the representation that they are not underwriters is not enough. Generally, courts will consider the length of time securities are held to determine whether a resale was permissible under Section 4(1). After several years have passed, it is difficult to claim that the person purchased with the intent to re-sell into the public market.

Rule 144

To decrease the uncertainty regarding when it is okay to re-sell a restricted security, the SEC adopted Rule 144, a safe harbor under Section 4(1). If securities are sold in compliance with Rule 144, they become unrestricted. Rule 144 is fairly complicated, especially when the person who wants to resell the security is an affiliate[81] of the issuer. The simplest way to comply with Rule 144 is to hold the securities for at least two years before re-selling them. The reasoning behind this is that if you hold the securities for two years, you must not have had the intention to re-sell them and therefore you are not an underwriter! But you have to be careful with this. If you purchase the securities and make it clear that your intention is to re-sell them as soon as you can possibly qualify under Rule 144, you are showing that you do have the intention to re-sell the securities and therefore you do meet the definition of an underwriter!

Secondary Trading

Let's say the securities in your company are unrestricted. This could be because you sold them pursuant to a registration/qualification that generally does not require you to restrict resales, or it could be because two years have passed since you completed the initial offering in a private placement. You would like your investors to have the opportunity to buy and sell your securities on a secondary market. What can you do?

---

81. An affiliate is "a person that directly, or indirectly through one or more intermediaries, controls, or is controlled by, or is under common control with, such issuer."

Unless you have restricted your investors' rights to buy and sell your securities in some way (some issuers impose restrictions for various reasons—see the discussion about Equal Exchange below), your investors already have the right to buy and sell. But how can you facilitate buyers and sellers finding each other? The largest companies list their securities on an exchange like NASDAQ or the New York Stock Exchange, but very few companies can meet the listing standards for these exchanges. Under some circumstances, you may be able to have your securities "listed" on something called a quotation service (OTCBB or pink sheets).

Exchanges

What if you want to create your own "exchange" platform? You need to be very careful that any platform or facility you create does not fall under the federal definition of an exchange. Exchanges are highly regulated under the 1934 Securities and Exchange Act. The legal definition of an exchange is an organization, association, or group of persons that

> (1) Brings together the orders for securities of multiple buyers and sellers; and (2) Uses established, non-discretionary methods (whether by providing a trading facility or by setting rules) under which such orders interact with each other, and the buyers and sellers entering such orders agree to the terms of a trade.[82]

This means that if you merely provide a platform for buyers and sellers to meet each other and to negotiate their own trades, you probably will not fall within the definition of an exchange. This was done by a company called Real Goods in California. Real Goods did the necessary compliance work to be able to sell securities to the public, advertising the investment opportunity in its product catalog. The owner of Real Goods wanted the purchasers of the securities to be able to buy and sell them conveniently, so he set up a bulletin board on his website to facilitate buyers and sellers funding each other. He was smart enough to run this by the Securities and Exchange Commission, and he actually got a no action letter for his "exchange" platform.[83] It is unclear whether the SEC would grant a no action letter for similar activities

82. Rule 3b-16.

83. The no action letter is available at http://www.sec.gov/divisions/investment/noaction/1996/realgoods062496.pdf.

today. That is why it is probably safer to set up an Alternative Trading System (described below).

How can you legally create something that looks more like an actual exchange? You could apply to the SEC for permission to create a new exchange. The application would have to describe the listing standards you would impose, i.e., what standards must be met by companies that want to be listed on your exchange, and you would need to clearly explain how the exchange will prevent fraud and abuse. This process is extremely difficult and would take several years and millions of dollars in legal fees. And there is no guarantee the SEC would grant permission for a new exchange.

Alternative Trading System

Another option is to set something up called an Alternative Trading System (ATS). The way this is done is that a company that is already a federally licensed broker-dealer applies to the SEC for designation as an ATS under Regulation ATS.

Under Regulation ATS, "Alternative trading system means any organization, association, person, group of persons, or system (1) That constitutes, maintains, or provides a market place or facilities for bringing together purchasers and sellers of securities or for otherwise performing with respect to securities the functions commonly performed by a stock exchange . . . ; and (2) That does not: (i) Set rules governing the conduct of subscribers other than the conduct of such subscribers' trading on such organization, association, person, group of persons, or system; or (ii) Discipline subscribers other than by exclusion from trading."[84]

Rule 301(b) of Regulation ATS contains detailed requirements for an Alternative Trading System.

Part 4: Funds, Investment Clubs, and Business Development Companies

Many people ask after learning about all the ways to raise capital legally under the 1933 Act, why can't I just set up a company whose purpose is to invest in other companies, raise enough money from investors

84. Regulation ATS Rule 300(a).

($5 million) so that my company itself becomes an accredited investor, and then invest that money in other businesses? This is a great idea but there is something that gets in the way: the 1940 Investment Company Act, which regulates companies that invest in other companies. Any company set up to invest in other companies is regulated not only under the 1933 Act but also under the 1940 Act.

The 1940 Investment Company Act

The 1940 Act regulates investment companies. The definition of an investment company is

> any issuer which (A) is or holds itself out as being engaged primarily, or proposes to engage primarily, in the business of investing, reinvesting, or trading in securities; (B) is engaged or proposes to engage in the business of issuing face-amount certificates of the installment type, or has been engaged in such business and has any such certificate outstanding; or (C) is engaged or proposes to engage in the business of investing, reinvesting, owning, holding, or trading in securities, and owns or proposes to acquire investment securities having a value exceeding 40 per centum of the value of such issuer's total assets (exclusive of Government securities and cash items) on an unconsolidated basis.[85]

To simplify, an investment company is a company whose primary activity is to invest in other companies or 40 percent of whose total assets consist of investment securities.[86] If something falls within the definition of an investment company, it will be subject to numerous regulations under the Act that are extremely costly and onerous to comply with—generally the same regulations that mutual funds are subject to.

The following are exemptions from the definition of an investment company (Sections 3(b) and (c)) (note that Section 3(c)(8) has been repealed):

---

85. 1940 Act § 3(a)(1).

86. "[All] securities except (A) Government securities, (B) securities issued by employees' securities companies, and (C) securities issued by majority-owned subsidiaries of the owner which (i) are not investment companies, and (ii) are not relying on the exception from the definition of investment company in paragraph (1) or (7) of subsection (c)." *Id.* at § 3(a)(2).

(b)(1) Any issuer primarily engaged, directly or through a wholly-owned subsidiary or subsidiaries, in a business or businesses other than that of investing, reinvesting, owning, holding, or trading in securities.

(2) Any issuer which the Commission, upon application by such issuer, finds and by order declares to be primarily engaged in a business or businesses other than that of investing, reinvesting, owning, holding, or trading in securities [...].[87]

(3) Any issuer all the outstanding securities of which (other than short-term paper and directors' qualifying shares) are directly or indirectly owned by a company excepted from the definition of investment company [...].

(c)(1) Any issuer whose outstanding securities (other than short- term paper) are beneficially owned by not more than one hundred persons and which is not making and does not presently propose to make a public offering of its securities[...].

(2)(A) Any person primarily engaged in the business of underwriting and distributing securities issued by other persons, selling securities to customers, acting as broker, and acting as market intermediary, or any one or more of such activities, whose gross income normally is derived principally from such business and related activities[...].

(3) Any bank or insurance company; any savings and loan association, building and loan association, cooperative bank, homestead association, or similar institution, or any receiver, conservator, liquidator, liquidating agent, or similar official or person thereof or therefore [...].

(4) Any person substantially all of whose business is confined to making small loans, industrial banking, or similar businesses.

(5) Any person who is not engaged in the business of issuing redeemable securities, face-amount certificates of the installment type or

87. "The filing of an application under this paragraph in good faith by an issuer other than a registered investment company shall exempt the applicant for a period of sixty days from all provisions of this title applicable to investment companies as such. For cause shown, the Commission by order may extend such period of exemption for an additional period or periods. Whenever the Commission, upon its own motion or upon application, finds that the circumstances which gave rise to the issuance of an order granting an application under this paragraph no longer exist, the Commission shall by order revoke such order."

periodic payment plan certificates, and who is primarily engaged in one or more of the following businesses: (A) Purchasing or otherwise acquiring notes, drafts, acceptances, open accounts receivable, and other obligations representing part or all of the sales price of merchandise, insurance, and services; (B) making loans to manufacturers, wholesalers, and retailers of, and to prospective purchasers of, specified merchandise, insurance, and services; and (C) purchasing or otherwise acquiring mortgages and other liens on and interests in real estate.

(6) Any company primarily engaged, directly or through majority-owned subsidiaries, in one or more of the businesses described in paragraphs (3), (4), and (5), or in one or more of such businesses (from which not less than 25 centum of such company's gross income during its last fiscal year was derived) together with an additional business or businesses other than investing, reinvesting, owning, holding, or trading in securities.

(7)(A) Any issuer, the outstanding securities of which are owned exclusively by persons who, at the time of acquisition of such securities, are qualified purchasers,[88] and which is not making and does not at that time propose to make a public offering of such securities [...].

(9) Any person substantially all of whose business consists of owning or holding oil, gas, or other mineral royalties or leases, or fractional interests therein, or certificates of interest or participation in or investment contracts relative to such royalties, leases, or fractional interests.

(10)(A) Any company organized and operated exclusively for religious, educational, benevolent, fraternal, charitable, or reformatory purposes [...].

---

88. "(i) any natural person . . . who owns not less than $5,000,000 in investments . . . (ii) any company that owns not less than $5,000,000 in investments and that is owned directly or indirectly by or for 2 or more natural persons who are related as siblings or spouse (including former spouses), or direct lineal descendants by birth or adoption, spouses of such persons, the estates of such persons, or foundations, charitable organizations, or trusts established by or for the benefit of such persons; (iii) any trust that is not covered by clause (ii) and that was not formed for the specific purpose of acquiring the securities offered, as to which the trustee or other person authorized to make decisions with respect to the trust, and each settlor or other person who has contributed assets to the trust, is a person described in clause (i), (ii), or (iv); or (iv) any person, acting for its own account or the accounts of other qualified purchasers, who in the aggregate owns and invests on a discretionary basis, not less than $25,000,000 in investments. . . ." 1940 Act § 2(a)(51).

(11) Any employee's stock bonus, pension, or profit-sharing trust [...].

(12) Any voting trust the assets of which consist exclusively of securities of a single issuer which is not an investment company.

(13) Any security holders' protective committee or similar issuer having outstanding and issuing no securities other than certificates of deposit and short-term paper.

(14) Any church plan described in section 414(e) of the Internal Revenue Code of 1986 [...].

Private funds most commonly use the 3(c)(1) and 3(c)(7) exemptions. Under Section 3(c)(1), private funds with no more than 100 investors are exempt from coverage under the Investment Company Act. If a fund wants to have more than 100 investors, it generally uses the 3(c)(7) exemption, which requires that investors be "qualified purchasers" (high net worth individuals and institutional investors—see footnote 88 for a more detailed definition).

Business Development Company

Business development companies (BDCs) are a category of investment funds under the 1940 Investment Company Act that are operated for the purpose of making investments in small and developing businesses and financially troubled businesses. BDCs are required to make available significant managerial assistance to those portfolio companies. BDCs are provided greater flexibility under the 1940 Investment Company Act than are other investment companies in dealing with their portfolio companies, issuing securities, and compensating their managers.

Generally, to be eligible to elect BDC status, a company must engage in the business of furnishing capital and offering significant managerial assistance to companies that do not have ready access to capital through conventional financial channels. More specifically, in order to qualify as a BDC, a company must: (a) be a domestic company; (b) have registered a class of its securities or have filed a registration statement with the SEC pursuant to the Exchange Act; (c) operate for the purpose of investing in the securities of certain types of eligible portfolio companies, namely less seasoned or emerging companies and businesses suffering or recovering from financial distress; and (d) extend significant managerial assistance to such eligible portfolio companies.

The BDC may register itself under the Investment Company Act as a BDC by filing a notice with the SEC. It must also file a registration under the 1934 Securities Exchange Act.

A BDC is required to have at least 70 percent of its investments in eligible assets. These assets generally consist of

- Securities purchased in transactions not involving a public offering;
- Securities of any eligible portfolio company (EPC) cannot include: securities purchased in transactions not involving any public offering from a person who is, or who within the preceding 13 months has been, an affiliated person of such issuer;
- Cash, government securities, or high-quality debt securities maturing in one year or less from the time of investment; and
- Office furniture and equipment, interests in real estate and leasehold improvements and facilities maintained to conduct the business operations of the BDC, deferred organization and operating expenses, and other noninvestment assets necessary and appropriate to its operations, including notes of indebtedness of directors, officers, and employees as payment for securities of such company issued in connection with an executive compensation plan—or purposes of the 70 percent basket, the assets set forth in this subsection are considered to be neutral assets and would not be included in the asset numerator or denominator.

BDCs are required to make available significant managerial assistance to their portfolio companies. Significant managerial assistance refers to any arrangement whereby a BDC provides significant guidance and counsel concerning the management, operations, or business objectives and policies of a portfolio company. Examples of such activities include arranging financing, managing relationships with financing sources, recruiting management personnel, and evaluating acquisition and divestiture opportunities.

❖❖❖❖

Who Can Sell Your Securities?

So let's say you go through the process necessary to allow you to legally solicit investors. Who can actually go out and sell those securities on your behalf? "Any person engaged in the business of effecting transactions in securities for the account of others" must register as a broker. So if someone offers to help you find investors and is paid a success fee or a commission, chances are that person will need to be a licensed broker. It is not always clear who will be considered a broker under state and federal law.

The factors that are considered by the regulators and the courts when determining whether someone meets the definition of a broker include whether the person provides investment advice, whether the person participates in negotiations, and whether the person is compensated based on a percentage of the transaction amount.

A majority of the directors of a BDC must be persons who are not "interested persons" of the BDC. The 1940 Act defines interested persons to include, among others: (i) officers, directors, and employees (however, no person is deemed to be interested solely by reason of being a member of the board of directors); (ii) a five percent or more voting shareholder of the company; (iii) a person who is a member of the immediate family of an affiliate of the company; (iv) legal counsel for the company; and (v) any natural person whom the SEC determines to have had a material business relationship in the past two completed fiscal years with the company or its chief executive officer.

A BDC could register its securities with the relevant state and/or federal regulators and would then be able to sell securities to the public, including unaccredited investors.

State-Regulated Funds

There is an exemption to the Investment Company Act's coverage that allows states to adopt legislation that authorizes the creation of state-regulated funds that are exempt from coverage under the 1940 Act. Section 6(a)(5)(A) of the 1940 Act exempts "Any company . . . the operations of which are subject to regulation by the State in which the company is organized under a statute governing entities that provide financial or managerial assistance to enterprises doing business, or proposing to do business, in that State" provided a number of conditions are satisfied.[89] Unfortunately, these funds can only sell securities to accredited investors under the provisions of the 1940 Act.

California is the only state that has adopted a statute that takes advantage of this provision. The California Capital Access Company Law was adopted more than a decade ago but apparently no one has ever set up a Capital Access Company (CAC). Recently SB 1155, a bill that attempted to address the shortcomings of the CAC Law, was passed.

A CAC can apply for a qualification to do a public offering of its securities, but the CAC's securities can only be sold to accredited investors. The California Department of Corporations has indicated its willingness to allow a coordinated filing for a CAC permit and a public offering permit.

A CAC can also file with the federal Small Business Administration to become a Small Business Investment Company (SBIC) and obtain 2:1 leverage of up to $150 million—this means that in addition to its equity capital, the CAC will have low-interest debt securities to invest in local business.

---

89. (5)(A) Any company that is not engaged in the business of issuing redeemable securities, the operations of which are subject to regulation by the State in which the company is organized under a statute governing entities that provide financial or managerial assistance to enterprises doing business, or proposing to do business, in that State if—

(i) the organizational documents of the company state that the activities of the company are limited to the promotion of economic, business, or industrial development in the State through the provision of financial or managerial assistance to enterprises doing business, or proposing to do business, in that State, and such other activities that are incidental or necessary to carry out that purpose;

(ii) immediately following each sale of the securities of the company by the company or any underwriter for the company, not less than 80 percent of the securities of the company being offered in such sale, on a class-by-class basis, are held by persons who reside or who have a substantial business presence in that State;

(iii) the securities of the company are sold, or proposed to be sold, by the company or by any underwriter for the company, solely to accredited investors, as that term is defined in § 2(a)(15) of the Securities Act of 1933, or to such other persons that the Commission, as necessary or appropriate in the public interest and consistent with the protection of investors, may permit by rule, regulation, or order; and

(iv) the company does not purchase any security issued by an investment company . . . .

Investment Clubs

An investment club is a group of people who pool their money to make investments. Yet unlike a regulated investment fund, all of the investors actively participate in the investment decisions. Because of this, investment clubs generally do not have to register the offering of memberships to the public (because memberships do not fall within the definition of a security since the return is not made through the efforts of others (see definition of a security discussed at the beginning of this chapter)). To ensure that the club's memberships do not need to be registered, it is essential that every member of the club actively participates in deciding what investments to make. As long as the memberships are not securities, the club is not required to register as an investment company under the 1940 Act.

Note that an investment club needs to be aware of how the companies it is investing in have complied with securities law. Unless the club has over $5 million in assets, it is not an accredited investor. The companies that the club invests in must ensure they comply with applicable securities laws.

The No Small Potatoes Investment Club of Maine was formed out of the Maine chapter of Slow Money to invest in Maine's food system. The goal was for regular Maine residents to be able to pool their funds and move their money out of Wall Street and into the local food system. The founders explored several options and decided to use the investment club model because the SEC guidelines are clear, the costs are low, and thousands of successful investment clubs already exist in the United States (though these mostly invest in publicly traded securities, not small local businesses). The Club decided to limit its membership to 20 people, each of whom would contribute $5,000 to the pool, and to offer loans of up to $5,000. Club members do extensive due diligence on potential borrowers, including visits to their farms. The entire Club votes on each investment decision.

Part 5: Models for Creative Capital Raising and Shared Equity

Community-Supported Enterprise Models

The Supreme Court has said, "What distinguishes a security transaction [...] is an investment where one parts with his money in the hope of receiving profits from the efforts of others, and not where he purchases a commodity for personal consumption [...] ."

So what if a business sells something to its customers and there is a separation in time between the customer making the purchase and the business delivering the commodity? That can be a way to raise funds that falls outside of securities law!

For example, let's say a café (this is a true story) wants to expand to a larger space. The café needs to raise $50,000 to cover the costs of this expansion. The café can sell gift cards to its customers in large denominations. Let's say the café sells 50 $1,000 gift cards to its 50 most loyal customers. The customers will use the cards over time but the café has the $50,000 now to complete its expansion.

This model is used quite a bit by small farms and is sometimes referred to as community supported agriculture (CSA). In these models, customers pay up front for a whole year's worth of produce, which provides the farmer with enough money to cover the costs of the planting season.

One restaurant in Oakland sold the right to be a "seatholder" for $500. Seatholders receive 20 percent off their tab, priority reservations, and invitations to special events.

There are some caveats with this model. Remember that some states have adopted the risk capital test for the definition of a security. Under this definition, an arrangement like this could be seen as a security if the purchasers' money is "at risk." In the states that apply the risk capital test, it is not advisable to use this method for raising capital.

Also, what if you sell the pre-purchased gift card at a discount? For example, you sell a gift card worth $1,000 for $800. There is a possibility that could be considered a security since there is a financial return on the "investment." When in doubt, it is best to contact the relevant securities regulators and request a no action letter (described earlier in this chapter).

Crowdfunding

The term "crowdfunding" can mean different things to different people. For purposes of this section, I am using the term to mean the solicitation of lots of small donations that can add up to what you need for your business. For example, let's say I need $2,000 to buy a special piece of equipment for my landscaping business. If I go out to my friends and customers and ask them to invest, I need to deal with the onerous securities regulations described in this chapter. But if, instead, I ask them to make small donations, this almost certainly would be exempt from securities law since the donors do not expect anything in return for their donation. It may seem strange for a business to solicit donations, but it is perfectly legal! It is a good idea to make sure your donors know that their donation is not tax-deductible the way it would be if they were donating to a 501(c)(3) nonprofit.

Several websites have sprung up that provide a platform for crowdfunding, though of course it is not necessary to use a web-based platform. The two most well-know are IndieGoGo and Kickstarter, but there are many more. Each one has different policies regarding what kinds of projects can list, what percentage the platform takes, etc. There have been some very successful campaigns on these websites. The person raising the funds often will offer "perks" to reward donors.

For example, New Parkway Theater in Oakland offered the following:

- Pledge $25 or more: Five free showings at the New Parkway Theater.
- Pledge $50 or more: Two tickets to the theater, a pitcher of beer, a pizza, and a RESERVED loveseat.
- Pledge $100 or more: Ten free showings at the New Parkway Theater and a +1 pass to the Grand Reopening Party.
- Pledge $500 or more: Annual movie pass for free movies for an entire year AND a +1 pass to the Grand Reopening Party.
- Pledge $1,000 or more: One screening room at the theater is yours for the night with 10 pitchers of beer and 10 pizzas.
- Pledge $2,500 or more: Lifetime movie pass for the New Parkway and a +1 pass to the Grand Reopening Party.
- Pledge $5,000 or more: Two lifetime movie passes for the New Parkway (including 2 passes to the Grand Reopening Party) and a reserved loveseat for you every time you'd like to come to the movies.

This campaign raised $56,832.

As discussed in the section on community supported models, it is possible that perks could be so valuable that the campaign would start to look like a securities offering.

The courts have held that the "investment" prong of the *Howey* test may be satisfied by the investment of something other than cash, such as goods or services.

However, payment of the "profits" in something other than cash has not been addressed by the courts. Dicta in the *United Housing Foundation, Inc. v. Forman* case imply that non-cash "rewards" could be excluded from the definition of profits if they are not easily convertible into cash:

> The Court of Appeals also found support for its concept of profits in the fact that Co-op City offered space at a cost substantially below the going rental charges for comparable housing. Again, this is an inappropriate theory of "profits" that we cannot accept. . . . This benefit cannot be liquidated into cash . . . .[90]

Direct Public Offerings

A Direct Public Offering (DPO) is like an Initial Public Offering (IPO), except that the company sells its securities directly to the public rather than using an investment bank as an intermediary.

The cost to do an IPO (legal, accounting, filing, and listing fees; printing costs; etc.) can easily exceed $1 million, so IPOs make sense only for companies seeking to raise large sums, usually $25 million or more. The median IPO size 20 years ago was $10 million; by 2009, it was $140 million.

A DPO is a generic term that can involve several different legal compliance strategies, some of which are surprisingly simple and easy to do! For example, let's say your company is based in Washington State and pretty much all of your customers are in Washington State. You are incorporated under Washington State law, and you want to raise capital from Washington State residents. You could conduct a DPO without doing any federal filings because you would be eligible for the federal intrastate exemption. All you would have to do is register your offering with the state securities regulators. How do you do that? You need to complete an application that includes an offering document that describes your company, the investment you're offering, the risk factors that potential investors need to be aware of, and so on. You file this with the state and then the state will either grant you permission

---

90. 421 U.S. 837, 855 (1975).

to conduct your offering or will ask you to clarify some things in your application. Once the state is satisfied that your offering documents disclose enough information for investors to make an informed decision, you should be granted the right to offer your securities to the public in Washington.

Even though this is a fairly simple process, it is not well known and not very common. There are, however, quite a few examples of successful DPOs. Some recent ones include Saranac Lake Community Store in New York, which recently raised $500,000 from community residents using a DPO and FarmPower, a manure digester manufacturer in Washington, which recently raised $750,000 in a DPO.

A COMMUNITY-BASED DPO

By Attorney Janelle Smith

In 1998 the Jacobs Center for Neighborhood Innovation (JCNI) recognized a need for revitalization of an area in San Diego known as the Diamond Neighborhoods. In an effort to bring business to and make a positive impact on the area, JCNI developed the idea of Market Creek Plaza—a shopping plaza that would cater to the needs of the neighborhood residents. The Diamond Neighborhood residents were actively engaged in the planning of the project.[1] JCNI formed Market Creek Partners LLC to offer community members the opportunity to invest in the shopping center.[2]

In 2006, after years of planning and negotiations with the California securities regulators, Market Creek Partners received a permit from the state and initiated a securities offering to the community in the Diamond Neighborhoods (the offering was exempt from federal securities registration requirements under the intrastate exemption). They dubbed this offering a "Community Development Initial Public Offering."

JCNI owns (directly or through subsidiaries) 80 percent of Market Creek Partners. The remaining 20 percent was offered to

1. Market Creek Partners, LLC Offering Circular, at 29.
2. *Id.* at 17.

local residents through the DPO in the form of "Diamond Community Investor Units" (DCI Units). Holders of these units get preferred returns on their investment and elect eight of the nine-member "Diamond Community Advisory Council," which gives input on management.[3] JCNI kept the number of investors below 500 and therefore did not have to do a registration under the 1934 Securities Exchange Act.

Only investors that met one of the following criteria were allowed to purchase DCI Units: (1) currently live or previously lived in the Diamond Neighborhoods; (2) currently own a business located in the Diamond Neighborhoods; (3) member, director, trustee, or staff member of an organization located or providing services in the Diamond Neighborhoods; (4) family member of a person that meets criteria 1, 2, or 3; (5) a stakeholder in the Diamond Neighborhoods (e.g., someone who attends church in one of the neighborhoods); (6) nonprofit organization in the Diamond Neighborhoods; or (7) business, organization, or group controlled by any of the persons in the first six categories.[4]

Market Creek Partners offered 50,000 DCI Units at $10 each, with a minimum investment of $200. The following limitations were imposed (among others):

> If the proposed investor is an individual (or husband and wife investing together), the amount invested may be no more than the greater of A or B:
> A. 5% of reported taxable income, or
> B. 10% of current net worth, excluding the investor's home, home furnishings, automobiles, and retirement or pension accounts and benefits.
>
> If the proposed investor is a business, the amount invested may be no more than the greater of A or B:
> A. 5% of adjusted gross income, or
> B. 10% of current net assets.[5]

---

3. *Id.* at 2.
4. *Id.* at IV.
5. *Id.* at 4.

EQUAL EXCHANGE'S FINANCING MODEL

By Daniel Fireside, Capital Coordinator at Equal Exchange

Equal Exchange, the pioneering Fair Trade coffee company, chose a radically democratic and accountable governance structure for itself (see sidebar in Chapter 4). To go along with that structure, how it chooses to raise capital is equally radical. The primary principle is this: make sure there is no exit strategy.

There have been countless social enterprises that make a splash, take off, and then ... cash out. To get the capital to go big, you're told that you need to open up to outside investors, or sell the company to a global conglomerate that's looking for a socially responsible branding opportunity, or maybe just reward the visionary entrepreneurs and early investors who got the venture off the ground. That's the story with Burt's Bees (Clorox), Ben & Jerry's (Unilever), Tom's of Maine (Colgate-Palmolive), The Body Shop (L'Oréal), Green & Black (Kraft), Stonyfield Farm (Groupe Danone), Dagoba Chocolate (Hershey's), Honest Tea (Coke), and countless others. That's how the system works, right?

In the world of social enterprises and mission investing, we're told that the job of entrepreneurs and investors is to turn an exciting, idealistic vision into reality. Hopefully, you won't have to compromise your initial social vision when you're faced with the harsh realities of the marketplace. And when you do relinquish the reins to outside investors or the new corporate owner, you just have to have faith that they're still in it for the right reasons, and will do the right thing no matter what signals they get from Wall Street.

Equal Exchange is trying to show that there is a different way to raise capital, that doesn't put your social mission at risk. We hope that our success will inspire others in this still evolving field of social entrepreneurship.

Like any growing business, social or otherwise, Equal Exchange needs equity and loans, investors and lenders, but the company founders realized that it's essential not to let the capital drive the mission.

Equal Exchange's Fair Trade business model means that the company is more capital intensive than similar-sized competitors.

For example, while a conventional coffee company buys its green (unroasted) coffee as needed off the market to keep down their inventory costs, Equal Exchange intentionally takes delivery of the coffee from the farmer co-ops soon after harvesting—many months before we expect to sell it. This shifts millions of pounds of inventory, and its capital burden, to us. We also help the co-ops get affordable financing so they get cash before the harvest—which is when they need it most. These are two critical, but behind-the-scenes, practices that complement our Fair Trade policies of developing long-term relationships and always paying above-market prices. But it all takes financing.

As a profitable business with a long track record of growth and sound management, we don't have a problem getting conventional bank loans or private capital from people who want a piece of the action if we make it into the big leagues. But that kind of money comes with a lot of strings, and a lot of pressure to put profits ahead of all other values. We're not about to let that happen.

In the early days, Equal Exchange had to scramble for cash just like every other social enterprise start-up. Rink Dickinson, one of our founders and current co-president, likes to talk about how he used to practically guarantee to our earliest outside investors that they shouldn't expect to see their money again. It probably helped that, as part of the co-operative model, everyone here was putting up some of their own money, too. In the beginning we also received some key financing from sympathetic faith-based organizations (back then we needed their prayers as much as their loans).

In some ways, the real challenges to a mission-driven company come when you start making a profit. Early on, Equal Exchange set a policy that invited outside investors to be a vital part of the company, but under our terms. The key elements included a fixed stock price, a five-year minimum holding period, no voting rights (which are reserved for workers), and a modest dividend, targeted—but not guaranteed—at five percent. The essential philosophy is that we are for profits, but against capital gains. There have been a few dips and rises in the rate, but we've paid a dividend every year since 1989. To the amazement of those early investors who were promised a goose egg, we've often outperformed their other conventional investments.

Today, we don't guarantee that we'll lose our investors' money—although, the financial crisis has reminded us that no business is immune from disaster. We do assure them, however, that we won't make anyone rich. It's an odd sales pitch to potential investors, but it's been compelling enough to have brought in over $10 million in preferred stock sales through private placements. A growing number of people are drawn by a mix of connection to our social mission and business model.

What usually seals the deal, though, is perhaps the most unusual item in our bylaws—what we call the no-exit clause. If a Starbucks, Nestle, or other deep-pocketed competitor ever dangled a large check in front of us to sell, our bylaws would require us to give back the money our lenders and investors put in and to give away all net proceeds to another Fair Trade organization. Simply put, we wouldn't get to keep the money—and would probably lose our jobs after the sale—so there's no incentive to sell out.

Preemptively taking this little devil off our shoulder has several effects. First, it assures outside investors that they aren't being taken for suckers by agreeing to forgo the potential of windfall profits. Second, it frees us from worrying about making decisions based on how we're viewed by speculators with no connection to our mission. Without this clause, the worker-owners might not have voted to invest in developing a Fair Trade organic banana business, where we find ourselves fighting it out in an industry with razor-thin margins competing with global oligopolies that overthrow governments in their spare time. Our investors give us full backing to expand our Fair Trade model into other ventures like olive oil from co-ops in the West Bank of Palestine, and sugar from small farmers in Paraguay.

The rationale of the no-exit clause is rooted in Equal Exchange's raison d'etre and in a different conception of ownership. Equal Exchange exists to change how trade is conducted and how it's perceived—to promote egalitarian and democratic workplaces, the cooperative business model, and more. The no-exit clause helps to ensure that Equal Exchange will not stray from its mission. Conversely, Equal Exchange does not exist to maximize capital appreciation—neither for investors nor even for the workers themselves.

But we also see "ownership" differently and do not equate it with capital. While investors provide most of the equity, those funds are just one of the many ingredients Equal Exchange requires, and investors are not granted special privileges. We also need farmers to commit their best coffee, tea, and cacao; workers to give their time, their skills, and to invest their careers with us. We need land, buildings, equipment, packaging, electricity, and gas to roast the coffee. We're happy to pay for all of these inputs—especially the ones that come from our farmer partners. Ultimately, it's probably more helpful to think of the employee's ownership of Equal Exchange as a trusteeship. The worker-owners, the people who know Equal Exchange and its mission best, essentially hold the enterprise in trust for all its stakeholders, including future generations of farmers, workers, consumers, investors, and the Earth itself.

Our latest innovation has been a partnership with Eastern Bank, a mutual bank that's owned by its depositors, to create a unique, branded certificate of deposit. With a conventional CD, you have no idea what the bank is doing with your money. With the Equal Exchange CD, Eastern Bank pools all the funds and makes up to 90 percent of it available to us as a line of credit at a below-market interest rate. The Equal Exchange CD pays the same rate as the bank's standard CD, yet creates a new socially responsible financial product that supports the operation of a leading Fair Trade, organic business. Eastern Bank is FIDC insured, so if they were to go out of business, depositors would be covered up to the legal limit. However, since the bank is using the deposits as collateral for the line of credit, depositors risk losing their money if Equal Exchange were to default on the loan. Yet a growing number of depositors seem eager to take on this additional risk in exchange for the social return.

The program recently hit a milestone when the Seward Food Co-op of Minneapolis chose to put $100,000 into an Equal Exchange CD. That was a striking example of one mission-driven organization channeling its own investments in order to support another like-minded enterprise. Seward's investment also pushed total deposits in the CD program to the $1 million mark. This innovative product is now a significant part of Equal Exchange's unorthodox financial model.

The company has also been building partnerships with other non-traditional lenders, including the Calvert Foundation and with religious institutions that are working to align their financial assets with their social mission.

With financing from the stock, worker-owner investments, the Eastern Bank CD, and alternative loans, Equal Exchange is able to fund almost all its growth from people and institutions that share its commitment to Fair Trade and small farmer and worker cooperatives. And we're doing it without ever having to risk selling out our company or our values.

CHAPTER SEVEN

EMPLOYMENT LAWS AND NEW WAYS OF WORKING TOGETHER

Part 1: New Ways of Working Together

A primary goal of the sharing economy is to give individuals and communities control over their livelihoods and economic well-being. This creates an immediate legal conundrum: most of our employment and labor laws are designed to protect workers that lack control over their livelihoods. The reach and coverage of such laws has grown to the extent that they now cover even the collaborative, democratic, participatory, self-sufficient, and accountable economic relationships we are creating in a sharing economy. In fact, our employment law framework may be one of the greatest barriers to the creation of more cooperative and sustainable economies.

This chapter will provide an overview of the common employment law puzzles that come up in contexts such as social enterprise, worker cooperatives, food cooperatives, shared housing, collaborative farming arrangements, and other activities common to the sharing economy. Lawyers must be empowered to spot issues, learn the intricacies of the legal gray areas, and help clients implement legal solutions that balance the protection of individuals and preservation of clients' cooperative visions.

From Working for *Others ... to Working* with *Others*

Working *for* others is how the vast majority (roughly 92 percent[1]) of working adults in the United States earn their livelihoods. Having a job is an attractive option to the extent that it provides us with a predictable source of income.[2] Unfortunately, widespread reliance on jobs creates a vulnerable economy. The inherent flaw in relying on *other* people to create the opportunities for our livelihoods is that the system is designed to ensure that employers have enough workers, not to ensure that workers have just enough jobs. Individual workers have little or no control over the availability and diversity of job options.

Searching for a job becomes like a game of musical chairs,[3] where players, with great urgency, vie for a scarce number of seats. The people that find a seat will not necessarily find it fitting or comfortable, but they likely feel relieved to at least *have* a seat. These days, the game has a larger number of people and a smaller number of chairs. Musical chairs was fun as a kindergarten game. But as a way to sustain ourselves, our families, and our communities? Not so much.

The solution, of course, is to stop waiting for chairs to appear and to make our own. Even though jobs can disappear, our abilities to be productive and provide for one another will never disappear. When we learn how to harness this powerful capacity and create stable opportunities to be productive, the game will always involve more than enough chairs. The new economy is characterized by many new opportunities and arrangements to work, spend our time, and contribute productively to society. Microenterprise, cooperative enterprise, community-supported enterprise, and sharing enterprise are likely to become the norm, since they put control of livelihoods back into the hands of communities.

---

1. Dep't of Labor, Entrepreneurship: A Flexible Route to Economic Independence for People with Disabilities (Aug. 2005), http://www.dol.gov/odep/pubs/misc/entrepre.htm.

2. Jobs have also become the primary way in which people access health care, which is rather odd, if you think about it. Why should our ability to access health care be almost entirely determined by how we choose to make our livelihood? Why should access to this part of the social safety net be managed by employers?

3. I am grateful to Charles Eisenstein (author of *Sacred Economics*) for using the musical chairs metaphor and inspiring me to start using it in talking about many aspects of the economy. He told me he's grateful to Lynne Twist (founder of the Pachamama Alliance) for inspiring him to use that metaphor.

Working *with* others is how we will make it happen. We won't succeed if we each create our *own* businesses and compete with each other for a share of the market; that would just result in different game of musical chairs. Rather, we will succeed if we form relationships and organizations that allow us to cooperate. Everyone can be and needs to be productive, and everyone can be and needs to be provided for, and we can achieve both through a variety of agreements with each other:

- **Agreements to cooperatively work for our mutual benefit:** A grocery cooperative is, essentially, a group of people who provide for themselves by means of their own food aggregation and distribution center. Many grocery cooperatives are operated entirely by the efforts of members, who order food and divvy it among themselves, thereby obtaining food at cost and removing the need for a commercial grocery store to serve as an intermediary.
- **Agreements by a group of people to "adopt" an enterprise:** This is another way of saying "community-supported enterprise." In the example of community-supported agriculture, a group of people agrees to adopt and support a farmer by purchasing a share of the farmer's harvest in advance.
- **Agreements to work separately in multiple enterprises and provide reciprocal support:** Controlling workload can be quite difficult in some industries, and this creates a particular strain on very small businesses. A group of small-scale farmers or a group of caterers may, formally or informally, agree to chip in and help each other out when things get busy. One farmer may get help from another at harvest time, and reciprocate later. A caterer may help out another during a big event and receive the same in return later.
- **Agreements to work separately and market together:** A producer cooperative allows multiple independent enterprises to benefit and thrive through cooperation. For example, a group of home bakers may form an agreement to cooperatively sell their breads at a joint farmers market stand or under a single brand, thus reducing competition and the high cost of each entrepreneur marketing products alone.
- **Agreements to work together in an enterprise:** Worker cooperatives are groups of people who have chosen to work together in the creation and operation of an enterprise. Worker cooperatives

are particularly useful as a structure for enterprises that would be highly difficult and expensive to start and operate as a solo entrepreneur, such as a construction business, a café, or many of the "blue collar" industries of modern society.

- **Agreements to engage in activities that bring together work and life:** People long to engage in productive work for a variety of reasons—to learn, to connect with other people, to get exercise, to provide for others, to build skills and credentials, to gain the respect of others, to have fun, and so on. Any of these motivations may lead a person to volunteer in the kitchen of a local café or help a friend on her organic farm. The motivations often outweigh the need or desire to spend that time working for money. Cooking and growing food are things people do for sustenance and enjoyment—they are part of *life*. In other contexts, they are *work*. There is no reason that work and life must stay separate, and we are seeing a growing number of community-based activities—like community farms and cafés—where the two merge and become somewhat indistinguishable.
- **Agreements to provide for each other without using dollars:** In modern society, people have a tendency to not do work for others if there is no one with dollars to pay for the work; other people suffer from a lack of access to goods and services when they lack dollars to purchase them. But there is no reason that lack of access to dollars should make us unproductive and impoverished, when we need only turn to one another and exchange without dollars. Working in exchange for housing, trading one product for another, providing and receiving services through a time bank—these are ways that our work can provide for us, even without dollars acting as an intermediary. Within a close-knit community, people simply provide for each other on a gift basis; such communities can thrive and flourish even when their dollar income is very low (this, by the way, is how many people of the world do thrive even with $1 of monetary income per day).

In essence, cooperation, not competition, becomes the key to success of "enterprise" and productive activity in the new economy. A consumer cooperative is unlikely to fail from lack of "customers"; entrepreneurs that frequently barter are unlikely to fail from lack of customers with money; through relationships of reciprocal support, a farmer is unlikely to fail from lack of support during a busy harvest. In sum, the agreements we make with each other ensure something important: that we will have enough. What does "enough" mean for the game of musical chairs? It means that when the music stops, we can take our time, help others to find a seat, let others help us find a seat, and, in the end, we all have a seat.

Part 2: Employment Laws Get an Economic Reality Check

The arrangements I listed above sound quite doable from a practical standpoint; from a legal standpoint, some are incredibly challenging. I have never seen clients' eyes so wide as when I tell them that their idea for a food cooperative, work exchange system, or farm volunteer program violates employment laws. The highly collaborative, egalitarian, or community-oriented reality of their project may have so little in common with the impersonal, unequal, and often exploitative reality of the employment relationships that our laws were designed to protect.

Our labor and employment laws recognize that a basic reality pervades most employment relationships: Employers *control* the work *of* an employee and *benefit* economically from work of the employee. If you are in control of someone's work *and* you are benefiting from it, chances are you will make decisions to maximize your gain. A perverse incentive system is embedded into this relationship: for example, the less an employee is paid, the more an employer makes. The less an employer invests into the health and well-being of employees, the more the employer will have available to invest in growing the business and profits. It's a system of competing interests where one side is primarily in control.

Employers will do right by employees to the extent that they care about their workers. Unfortunately, caring is not a sure thing in a world full of large and impersonal companies controlled by absentee shareholders. Employers will also do right by employees to the extent that they are dependent on finding and retaining good workers. But in an economy where there is a scarcity of job opportunities and few alternative ways to make a livelihood, the reality is that workers are far more dependent on an employer than the employer is on them. The result is that employees have far less bargaining power than the employer. In the late 1800s and early 1900s, there was an enormous number of labor unions, which gave bargaining power to workers. However, by the 1930s, unions were disappearing, and legislators were seeing more clearly the harsh effects of the imbalance. Thus began the adoption of a long line of laws to give rights and protections to workers, beginning with the Fair Labor Standards Act.[4]

Employment Laws and Our Relationship "Issues"

Regulation is the government's way of saying: "If you can't balance your own relationship, we will have to balance it for you!" And we have a long history of worker exploitation to show that employers and workers have serious relationship "issues." In that respect, it's enormously important that we have implemented minimum wage laws, limits on work hours, occupational health and safety protections, mandatory workers compensation insurance, wrongful termination laws, whistleblower protections, anti-discrimination laws, mandatory employer contributions to unemployment and disability funds, and so on.

It's a funny story how we got to our current regulatory framework, though. In the early 1900s, courts were initially quite reluctant to let the government regulate our work relationships, since the Contracts Clause of the U.S. Constitution says that the government should not intervene in our right to set the terms of our economic relationships.[5] The Supreme Court broke with this trend in 1937 when it upheld Washington State's minimum wage law.[6] It's revealing to see how the Court explained itself:

> Deprivation of liberty to contract is forbidden by the Constitution if without due process of law, but restraint or regulation of this liberty, if reasonable in relation to its subject and if adopted for the protection of the community against evils menacing the health, safety, morals and welfare of the people, is due process.[7] […]
>
> In dealing with the relation of employer and employed, the legislature has necessarily a wide field of discretion in order that there

4. *See* United States v. Silk, 331 U.S. 704, 713 (1947) ("the aim of the [Fair Labor Standards] Act was to remedy the inequality of bargaining power in controversies over wages, hours and working conditions").

5. Lochner v. New York, 198 U.S. 45 (1905).

6. W. Coast Hotel Co. v. Parrish, 300 U.S. 379 (1937).

7. *Id.* at 391.

> may be suitable protection of health and safety, and that peace and good order may be promoted through regulations designed to insure wholesome conditions of work and freedom from oppression.[8]

In other words, the Court was saying: the government can limit your freedom of contract and impose regulations, because your relationship "issues" are causing harm to people. But this leaves us to wonder whether those regulations can be upheld in application to a very different kind of relationship—one of cooperative work and mutual support. That's a hard question, and it's one that may not be answered until we ask the Court in a more official manner and bring them a case.

In 1983, the Supreme Court further elucidated the circumstances under which laws may restrict the private right of contract. First of all, the state "must have a significant and legitimate public purpose behind the regulation, [...] such as remedying of a broad and general social or economic problem."[9] The next inquiry is whether "the adjustment of 'the rights and responsibilities of contracting parties [is based] upon reasonable conditions and [is] of a character appropriate to the public purpose justifying [the legislation's] adoption.'"[10]

The Court has potentially left us a window to renew our inquiry. Are the conditions still appropriate to the public purpose of the regulation if their impact is to limit society's ability to create an alternative to the worker/employer relationship?

The sad irony about all of the regulation is that it still hasn't led to balanced employer/worker relationships and that it contributes to another kind of social and economic imbalance: even though the laws are designed to protect employees, the laws also force some people to *become and remain* employees by making it prohibitive for them to operate a small enterprise, a cooperative, or a project designed to generate a non-monetary income. In contrast, large businesses can afford the cost of complying with employment laws because the reliance on the work of employees generates a surplus of monetary income. In essence, the situation leaves two kinds of people in the game: (1) people who work for others and (2) people who make a lot of money by having others

---

8. *Id.* at 393.

9. Energy Reserves Grp., Inc. v. Kan. Power & Light Co., 459 U.S. 400, 411–13 (1983).

10. *Id.* (quoting U.S. Trust Co. v. New Jersey, 431 U.S. 1 (1977)).

work for them. The challenge now is to maintain those critical legal protections for workers, while carving out a space for them to join a third category of people: (3) people who thrive by working together for mutual, cooperative, nonprofit, low-profit, and/or non-monetary benefit.

Employment Laws and the Relationships of the Sharing Economy

Many clients in the sharing economy will create relationships that they do not intend to be subject to employment laws. It will sometimes devastate them to learn from their lawyer that their voluntary, enjoyable, and collaborative relationships are subject to minimum wage requirements and other employment laws. The task of sharing economy lawyers, in the case of many cooperatives and community-based activities, is to find a way for clients to restructure their relationships and to legitimately argue that there is no master–servant relationship.

The legal system has carved out categories of work that are not subject to the normal regulations on employers and employees. The threshold question tends to be: "Is the worker an employee?" The Fair Labor Standards Act (FLSA) states that an employee is "any individual employed by an employer."[11] The primary thing this definition achieves is to inspire some occasional sarcasm: "Thank you, FLSA—that was very helpful."

FLSA gives us another hint in the definition of "employ," which is "to suffer or permit to work."[12] But such a broad definition leaves us assuming that if anyone gives you permission to lift a finger under any circumstance, you are an employee. Thus, we almost have to start with an assumption that all working people are employees, and work backward from there.

Statutes and case law have given us tests for determining who is not an employee, and there are five primary categories I'll discuss here, and in much greater detail in the next section. Note that I'm using my own words here, not the law's words, to encapsulate the categories:

1. People who do work for their own or mutual benefit = Proprietors/Partners/Principals

11. 29 U.S.C. § 203(e)(1).
12. *Id.* at § 203(g).

2. People who do work for public/charitable/humanitarian benefit = Volunteers
3. People who do work for their own educational benefit = Interns
4. People who do work for others in an independent manner = Independent Contractors
5. People who do "work" for others that is not legally classified as work

The work arrangements of the sharing economy *sometimes* fit into the above categories. For example, the sharing economy is characterized by relationships where people:

1. Work together as equals to benefit themselves (which can sometimes meet the definition of "partners").
2. Do work motivated by generosity or mutually supportive relationships (which can occasionally meet the definition of "volunteer").
3. Do work motivated by non-monetary reward (which can sometimes meet the definition of "intern").
4. Work independently and collaborate with each other on a limited basis (which can sometimes meet the definition of "independent contractors").
5. Lend a hand to others in their homes or in other personal projects (which is not necessarily seen as "work").

The work that people are doing under many of these circumstances is designed to generate a benefit of some kind, but may not always be designed to generate a monetary income. In that respect, doing work under the legal framework usually applied to employers and employees is not practical because it's too expensive. Paying even minimum wage, paying for workers compensation, and paying payroll taxes are often out of the question. However, most regulations on employers and employees are automatic, and they cannot be waived. For example, a volunteer on a farm cannot simply sign a document waiving his or her right to be paid minimum wage. The justification for this legal fact is that ability to waive a protection would likely result in more vulnerable workers doing so under coercion.

Many of the tests of who is an employee look at the "economic realities" of the situation—usually asking whether the worker is economically dependent on the person or entity for whom they appear to be working (the principal), asking whether the principal is in control over the work of the worker, and a variety of other related factors.[13]

But it is time for an economic reality check. The point of the sharing economy is that we are creating new relationships that give us more control over our livelihoods. It should be an imperative for our legal system to allow us to do so. The biggest difficulty we will face is that many relationships in a sharing economy appear, even with five categories of exemption listed above, to be employment relationships.

Illegal Grocery Cooperative Example

> **Example:** A group of 300 low-income people form a grocery-buying cooperative. They rent a small warehouse, where they receive regular orders from a range of nearby farmers, food producers, and food distributors. They put the food on shelves so that members can come in and "shop." The purpose of the cooperative is not to make money, since the 300 members are the only customers. The purpose is to get affordable access to good food and to support the local food producers. Each member is required to spend three hours per month volunteering at the warehouse, receiving and organizing food shipments, helping to check out members, and handling other administrative tasks. Each 3-hour shift has a leader that assigns tasks to the volunteer members, and the co-op is managed by a board of directors elected by the members.

It pains me to say it, but a court could quite possibly find that the volunteers in this situation should be paid minimum wage and that all other regulations on employers and employees apply. The members are not independent contractors because they aren't working independently. They are not likely partners because most members have very

13. Courts have actually acknowledged that there is no single "economic realities" test, and that it's a different test depending on whether you are looking at partners or independent contractors. For example, the court in *Wheeler v. Hurdman*, 825 F.2d 257, 271 (10th Cir. 1987), examined a range of tests applied by courts, and ultimately said, "The foregoing survey of tests and factors offered by the proponents has been set forth in detail partly for purposes of our analysis, and partly to show the absence, rather than the presence, of any coherent standard of 'economic reality' for supposed application to partners."

little control over the day-to-day operation of the cooperative. They are not interns because they are not doing it for the purpose of learning a skill. They are not volunteers because the legal definition of volunteers generally requires that they be working for charitable/humanitarian purposes.

In this example, people are working under the direction of others, albeit only for three hours per month. They are also working for an economic benefit—the benefit of receiving inexpensive food. How can a court distinguish this from a situation where a migrant farm worker is coerced into working on a farm for a few hours in exchange for a meal and water? Unfortunately, courts haven't really *tried* to distinguish the two; to play it safe, they have generally created a blanket prohibition on allowing people work under supervision, voluntarily, for a for-profit business. Our labor laws have, in that respect, taken the cooperation out of cooperative—making it impossible for people to work for their own cooperatives.

The state of Hawaii recognized this problem and passed a law making it legal for people to volunteer up to 25 hours per month for their own cooperatives or mutual benefit associations.[14] This offers a wonderful precedent for other states to follow, though this law may, unfortunately, conflict with federal employment laws. In fact, a 1997 federal Department of Labor opinion, though not addressing the Hawaii law specifically, did address the role of volunteers in a consumer cooperative. The opinion stated:

> In this case, the cooperative members do not appear to be "volunteers" within the meaning of the FLSA. This is so because the services volunteered are not for public service, religious, or humanitarian

---

14. *See* Haw. Rev. Stat. Ann. § 421C-33, which provides:

Volunteers exempted:

(a) For the purposes of this section, "volunteer" means an individual who:

(1) Is a member of an association;

(2) Is not an employee of the association; and

(3) Who volunteers and donates up to twenty-five hours of labor and services per month to the association.

(b) Associations may accept labor and services from volunteers.

(c) In addition to any exemptions granted to nonpaid labor, volunteers who acknowledge in writing that they are volunteers shall be construed not to be in the employ of the association, their labor and services shall be construed to not be employment, and they shall not be construed to be employees of the association, under title 21 or any other labor law.

> objectives as required by the FLSA; rather, the services are being donated for commercial business purposes. It is, therefore, our opinion that the cooperative members would be considered "employees" within the meaning of the FLSA, and would be subject to the minimum wage and overtime provisions of the Act. This determination would not change even if member employees were not given discounts, or if they performed tasks of their own choosing and worked anytime they chose.[15]

Thus, it may be necessary to change both federal and state labor laws in order to allow people to volunteer on a limited basis for their own cooperatives. Note that, in conjunction with changing the law, it will be important to address the requirement or the option to carry something like workers' compensation insurance for member/volunteers under certain circumstances. A cooperative like the one described above could likely not afford to carry regular workers' compensation insurance for each of its 300 volunteers. Ideally, however, states could offer more tailored and economically feasible insurance options to enable cooperation and compensate injured parties under such circumstances.

Why the Cooperative Example Should Give Us Pause

It may be tempting to dismiss the grocery co-op example as a single anomaly—an isolated example of labor laws preventing a beneficial activity. But our communities would be wonderful if *many* more of our "businesses" were run in this way. Laundromats or gyms owned by their patrons, requiring members to do a little work when they come in to wash clothes or work out; housing cooperatives that allow residents to volunteer for the co-op in exchange for lower rent; cafés operated partially by their patrons; and so on. Such arrangements allow goods, services, and housing to be put back into hands of our communities, and not "outsourced" to chain stores and absentee business and housing owners. Many non-chain restaurants and other businesses close down soon after opening, usually because the owners found that the expenses of operating the business are too great in comparison to the income it generates. They cannot compete with

15. U.S. Dep't of Labor, 1997 DOLWH LEXIS 1 (Jan. 21, 1997), Judge: Maria Echaveste, Administrator.

larger chains that have benefited from economies of scale and access to large amounts of capital, which drive prices down.

But what if a restaurant could operate by some of the agreements I listed in Part 1? A community-supported café, for example, could have members that agree to buy a certain number of meals per month and participate in some of the governance of the café. They would receive periodic free meals in exchange for putting in a few work hours per week or per month. Members would be motivated to work not just for the free food, but also for the experience of working alongside friends and learning about food. A café like this is very likely to thrive and not go out of business as many new cafés do. Our local economies would benefit immensely if there were a legal space for such arrangements.

Community Farmer Example

Let's look at another example of how employment laws limit collaborative work relationships. The Sustainable Economies Law Center has been working on this issue.

> **Example:** In and around Fresno, California, there are more than 1,300 Hmong and Lao refugee farmers. Most of these farmers cultivate between 1 and 10 acres, and each farm is usually worked by a single household. Most of these families live very humble lives—growing food for themselves and their community and selling enough vegetables to earn a very modest income. In that respect, many Hmong farmers are semi-subsistence farmers.[16] All told, many do not ultimately make the equivalent of minimum wage in dollars. Many of the crops they grow have special labor requirements: green beans, for example, generally cannot be mechanically harvested, and they must not be allowed to stay on the plant for a day or two after they are ready to be picked. This means that many hands are needed on the harvest day in particular. The family from one farm is likely to show up on a friend's farm to help out, and vice versa. There is a culture of reciprocity, lending a hand here and there because it means receiving a hand when needed.

16. *See* European Network for Rural Development, *Semi-Subsistence Farming in Europe: Concepts and Key Issues* (background paper prepared for a conference in Sibiu, Romania, Apr. 21–31, 2010), at 5 (defining semi-subsistence farms as "agricultural holdings which produce primarily for their own consumption and also market a proportion of their output").

In the case of the Hmong and Lao farmers, there is no exemption to allow them to perform these reciprocal favors for one another, and regulators repeatedly tell farmers that anyone helping in their fields must be treated as an employee. The farmers can't even quietly get away with it; the California Department of Labor Standards Enforcement regularly shows up and issues citations when they see groups of people working in a field. For example, there is a $1,500 per worker fine in California for failure to provide workers' compensation for a worker. However, given that the cost of workers' compensation insurance can run between $0.50 and $2.00 per hour for a farm worker, and given that it's hard to get a policy for less than three months, carrying such insurance is impossible for a farmer who only needs outside help a few days per season. Since the Hmong and Lao farmers earn a very small monetary income, asking them to jump through such legal hoops would simply put them out of business and destroy the livelihoods of 1,300 farmers and their families.

In a world where it is hard enough for micro-entrepreneurs to get by, we should make legal space for them to "get by with a little help from [their] friends."[17] In the refugee farmer case, a solution within the current legal framework may be for farmers to form small cooperatives to harvest and sell vegetables together under the same business umbrella. However, this solution will not work for many of the farmers for practical reasons, and it actually removes an incredibly valuable factor of the economic equation: generosity and gift. These practices and sentiments exist in every culture and act as a form of social glue. If I have a neighbor over for dinner, she does not offer me money at the end of the meal. In fact, this would be bizarre behavior, as bringing money into the picture would make me feel more like a business and less like a giving friend. I have to imagine that many neighboring farmers who help each other out do so with similar feelings, and formalizing the relationship—either through payment of wages or through business co-ownership—removes the important role of gift and generosity in their economy. If we force Hmong and Lao farmers to stop farming in this way, we destroy not only their livelihoods but also an important part of their community and humanity.

---

17. If only the Beatles made the laws.

The Difficulty of Distinguishing Between Work and Life

Because they are semi-subsistence farmers, another difficulty the Hmong and Lao farmers face is demonstrating a distinction between the work of growing food for sale and for personal consumption. Generally, if family members all work together in a garden to grow food for themselves, they are not seen as employees. However, the fact that the Hmong and Lao farmers also grow food for sale means that an assumption of employment exists any time people are working in the field. One farmer I met was fined $1,000 for not obtaining workers compensation insurance for his live-in uncle. When the Department of Industrial Relationships (DIR) visited the farm, the uncle was helping out in the garden, tending to food that the family planned to eat. On appeal, the farmer was unsuccessful in persuading the DIR commissioner that the uncle was not working for the enterprise.

Why the Hmong Farmer Example Should Give Us Pause

It may be tempting to dismiss the example of the Hmong and Lao farmers as another isolated case of employment laws interfering in a single enterprise. But if those 1,300 farmers are put out of business by employment laws, then the rest of us should have little hope that we can ever take control of our livelihoods and survival. A "semi-subsistence" livelihood is not the ideal to which modern society has taught us to strive, but it is, in fact, how an enormous number of people on this planet already thrive. As we watch industrialized economies around the world stumble (such as in the United States) and even crumble (such as in Greece), we *need* to find other ways to ensure that we can meet our sustenance needs. It won't work if we live in the woods and forage for ourselves, and it won't work if we each get our own little house on the prairie and farm for ourselves. But it will work if we *produce* some of what we need, allow other members of the community to *give* us what we need, and then sell, buy, exchange, and barter for everything else. The sharing economy *allows* us to make rewarding and abundant livelihoods through semi-subsistence enterprises. Such livelihoods necessarily involve *people working together* and *fewer dollars changing hands*. Such livelihoods cannot afford to pay minimum wage, but they *can* provide the sustenance that seven billion people will need to survive in a world of increasingly limited resources.

The Unfair Competition Argument
Note that prevention of worker exploitation is not the only thing leading to the across-the-board application of employment laws. The other justification often put forth is the idea that carving out special exemptions would create circumstances of unfair competition. Some argue that if one farm receives volunteer help from friends, then it is unfairly competing with a farm that pays workers minimum wage. We should abandon this consideration in the labor law context because the circumstances of businesses are far too variable to compare. If we are worried about unfair competition, we should point out that a farmer who purchases large machines to do harvesting is unfairly competing with small subsistence farmers who harvest by hand. Or a farm that uses chemical pesticides is unfairly competing with a farm that uses organic methods. Large businesses with access to large amounts of capital do not operate on an even playing field with humble "mom and pop" businesses and small cooperatives. Any reconsideration of employment laws should focus on the need to protect individuals and the need to enable small and cooperative enterprise, and not on the need to preserve some guise of fair competition.

A Few More Examples
Here are a few more examples of situations where clients are prone to violating employment laws through their work arrangements:

a. **Volunteering for a social enterprise:** When a privately owned business does work aimed at helping people or making the world a better place, people feel drawn to volunteer. Sometimes people volunteer at private nursing homes, for example, or they feel drawn to volunteer for companies that work in the realm of sustainability. As a general rule, people cannot volunteer for a for-profit business, and I will examine this more below, and explore the possible arguments that will allow someone to volunteer for a for-profit business.
b. **Worker collectives:** In the case of a 15-member worker-owned collective, it may be difficult to determine whether the workers should be treated as employees. In a collective, decisions are made as a group, often by consensus, which gives each member a great deal of power to influence decisions about the business and about the day-to-day work. This might lend credence to the argument

that the workers are not employees and points to the fact that the collective is in a gray area. For a new worker cooperative that does not yet have significant cash flow, paying minimum wages to workers can be a huge financial burden, and it may require that the cooperative raise start-up capital, rather than bootstrap the business. Many cooperatives will not have access to outside start-up capital, which means that payment of minimum wage from day one would be impossible.

c. **Housing cooperatives:** In housing cooperatives owned by a nonprofit or cooperative corporation, many residents are assigned chores, maintenance duties, or other tasks to lower the cost of operating the cooperative. Depending on the size and management structure of the cooperative, this could be seen as creating an employment relationship between the residents and the entity that owns the housing.

d. **Compensating people in forms other than dollars:** Although dollars are useful and in high demand, many people are willing and excited to work in exchange for other forms of compensation, such as food, housing, or credits that can be redeemed for goods and services. For example, many groups have proposed the creation of food currencies, which are points that people accumulate by volunteering at a food business, and which can be spent within a network of food businesses to purchase food. Unfortunately, law requires that minimum wage be paid in cash (which most likely means dollars), and under only very limited circumstances, in lodging, board, and other facilities.[18] This makes the food currency described here illegal under current law, since the participants could not volunteer at food businesses. The payment of employees and volunteers in non-dollar currencies and benefits is discussed in Chapter 5 of this book.

Enabling Cooperation and Managing Risks

Employment laws are designed to prevent harm to vulnerable individuals, and it's important to recognize that harm is still possible even in many of the arrangements described above. People could get injured while volunteering for their cooperative, or unequal power dynamics within a group

18. 29 C.F.R. § 531.27(a).

could leave certain individuals with less control over the way they work or benefit from the arrangement. In carving out a legal space for cooperative work arrangements, we must be mindful of those risks. As a general rule, there will be far less risk of exploitation or harm when

- No single individual or group is benefiting from a significantly greater share of the profits of an activity;
- Members of a group have an equal vote on decisions about the activity;
- Decision-making processes allow everyone to have a voice, bring up tensions, and make proposals;
- Each individual has a large amount of choice in how and when he/she works;
- Members of a group have close pre-existing relationships with one another, through family ties or friendship;
- Members of the group have an agreement about how to share risks and compensate members that are injured;
- People work on a project for less than 10 hours per week, which indicates that the activity is not their sole source of sustenance; and/or
- People work primarily with the intent to earn non-material benefit, such as socializing, fun, or learning.

Wait, What If Jobs Disappear?

When 92 percent of working adults currently choose employment as their primary source of livelihood, it can be hard to even picture what will happen if the various enterprises described above begin to replace those commercial businesses that provide conventional employment. A member-owned grocery cooperative, for example, takes business away from a large grocery chain, which means that chain will offer fewer jobs. If we rely less on conventional commercial businesses to meet our needs, there will also be fewer conventional job opportunities. This fact points to something quite powerful: if consumers have the ultimate power to remove jobs from the marketplace, then we also have the ultimate power to create a marketplace of new livelihoods. We have the power to direct our resources—monetary or otherwise—to directly support ourselves, others, and our community.

Think about the life of a dollar bill. A dollar we previously would have spent at a grocery chain will now be available to give *directly* to a local farmer or food producer. That dollar will not line the pocket of a rich company and its executives, and it is unlikely to even leave our community. In a localized sharing economy, that same dollar will likely be spent to purchase another good or service, likely from another community member. If that dollar keeps circulating in the community and changes hands 100 times in a year, it is actually worth $100 to the community. If we had spent it at a large grocery chain, only a fraction of it would have stayed in the community to pay the wages of a grocery store employee. In sum, the transition to a sharing economy may diminish traditional employment opportunities, but it multiplies the wealth we have to create livelihoods in our communities.

Part 3: Working Together Outside of Employment Relationships

Short of changing the laws, there are still many things that sharing economy lawyers do to help clients reshape their work relationships in ways that fall outside of employer/employee relationships. I will primarily examine five ways here.

The most important thing to remember about the rest of the information in this chapter is that employment laws show up not just in the FLSA but in a variety of different statutes at the federal and state levels. Each statute has its own case history and its own interpretation of who is an employee. Some courts have indicated that the definition of employee as determined under one statute will be persuasive in determining who is an employee under another statute.[19] At the same time, each statute was enacted with a somewhat different purpose, and it can be unsafe to rely on a court's definition of employee under one statute and assume it will apply in the same way under another statute. In fact, you may have cases where you ultimately conclude that, for the purpose of one set of statutes, there is an employer/employee relationship, and for the purpose of other

19. *See, e.g.*, Wheeler v. Hurdman, 825 F.2d 257, 263 (10th Cir. 1987) (noting that interpretations of the FLSA could be used in interpreting the definition of employee under the Age Discrimination and Employment Act (ADEA): "All parties acknowledge that nothing in the legislative history of these Acts explicitly addresses the definition of employee. In general, cases construing definitions of one of the Acts are to be viewed as persuasive authority when interpreting the others."). *See also* Hyland v. New Haven Radiology Assocs., 794 F.2d 793, 796 (2d Cir. 1986) ("cases construing the definitional provisions of [the FLSA, Title VII or the ADEA] are persuasive authorities when interpreting the others").

statutes, there is not.[20] The moral to the story is that you need to know the laws and court interpretations under your jurisdiction and for all categories of employment regulations (wage and hour, workers compensation, payroll taxes, the Occupational Safety and Health Administration (OSHA), discrimination statutes, and so on).

Partners/Proprietors

It is widely accepted that if you start a sole proprietorship and work for yourself, you are not your own employee. The fact that you are solely in control of your work and solely benefiting from the revenue it generates means that you are not vulnerable to the perverse incentives built into an employer/employee relationship. Now how does that apply when two people own, manage, and work for their own business? How about when 500 people own, manage, and work for their own business? Business owners can certainly be considered employees of their own business,[21] so the question is: what are the qualities of a co-ownership relationship that create or do not create an employer/employee relationship? How do you prove that there is no master–servant relationship between a group and its members?

As sharing economy lawyers, our task will often be to help clients restructure their relationships and activities such that they are, for employment law purposes, considered partners to an enterprise they are working for.[22] Consider, for example, the two cases studies I

20. *See, e.g.*, Clackamas Gastroenterology Assocs., PC v. Wells, 538 U.S. 440, 453 (2003) (holding that though the business in question treated shareholders as employees for the purpose of the Employee Retirement Income Security Act (ERISA) and state workers compensation law, the shareholders were not employees for the purposes of applying anti-discrimination statutes).

21. *See* Goldberg v. Whitaker House Coop., Inc., 366 U.S. 28, 33 (1961) ("There is nothing inherently inconsistent between the coexistence of a proprietary and an employment relationship. If members of a trade union bought stock in their corporate employer, they would not cease to be employees within the conception of this Act. For the corporation would 'suffer or permit' them to work whether or not they owned one share of stock or none or many.").

22. *See* Godoy v. Rest. Opportunity Ctr. of N.Y., Inc., 615 F. Supp. 2d 186, 194 (S.D.N.Y. 2009) ("[S]tatus as a general partner carries important economic reality as well. Employees do not assume the risks of loss and liabilities of their employers; partners do. . . . Other common characteristics of partnerships are profit sharing; contributions to capital; part ownership of partnership assets, including a share of assets in dissolution of the enterprise; and the right to share in management subject to an agreement among the partners. These are economic realities, and no definition of 'employee' is co-extensive. . . When individuals combine to carry on a business as partners all these factors introduce complexities and economic realities which are not consonant with employee status.").

gave above—that of the cooperative grocery and the family farmers. If the cooperative grocery were structured in such a way that everyone has meaningful control over the cooperative and their own realm of work, then they might succeed in arguing that an employment relationship does not exist. In the case of extended family members that farm together, there would likely be no employer/employee relationship if the family members adopt an agreement that demonstrates that everyone participates meaningfully in ownership, management, profits, and losses of the farm. In the case of friends helping friends harvest crops, there would likely be no employer/employee relationship if the farmers form a business partnership for the purposes of jointly harvesting and marketing the vegetables from multiple farms.

What Is a Master-Servant Relationship?

A lawyer who grapples with this issue must become familiar with the various factors courts consider in determining whether a master–servant relationship exists, and with how each factor has been examined. Again, this varies from jurisdiction to jurisdiction, and from statute to statute within a single jurisdiction. What follows is a relatively short examination of this question. The sharing economy movement could benefit from a much more detailed analysis of cases that have examined this question nationally.

Strong precedent was created in answer to the question when the U.S. Supreme Court decided the case of *Clackamas Gastroenterology Associates, P.C. v. Wells* in 2003.[23] There, the Court was asked to decide whether the Americans with Disabilities Act (ADA) applies to working shareholders of a small professional corporation. The Court in *Clackamas* cited a prior case in explaining that "'when Congress has used the term "employee" without defining it, we have concluded that Congress intended to describe the conventional master–servant relationship as understood by common-law agency doctrine.'"[24] The Court then adopted the Equal Employment Opportunity Commission's (EEOC) guidelines for determining when a master–servant relationship exists (numbers added):

23. Clackamas Gastroenterology Assocs., PC v. Wells, 538 U.S. 440 (2003).

24. *Id.* at 452 (citing Nationwide Mut. Ins. Co. v. Darden, 503 U.S. 318, 322–23 (1992)).

> We are persuaded by the EEOC's focus on the common-law touchstone of control, see *Skidmore* v. *Swift & Co.*, 323 U. S. 134, 140 (1944), and specifically by its submission that each of the following six factors is relevant to the inquiry whether a shareholder–director is an employee:
>
> [1.] Whether the organization can hire or fire the individual or set the rules and regulations of the individual's work
>
> [2.] Whether and, if so, to what extent the organization supervises the individual's work
>
> [3.] Whether the individual reports to someone higher in the organization
>
> [4.] Whether and, if so, to what extent the individual is able to influence the organization
>
> [5.] Whether the parties intended that the individual be an employee, as expressed in written agreements or contracts
>
> [6.] Whether the individual shares in the profits, losses, and liabilities of the organization.[25]

It remains to be fully seen whether *Clackamas* can or will always be relied upon to make similar arguments under state employment laws and under other types of employment statutes, such as FLSA. Hundreds of cases have now cited or relied on *Clackamas* in making determinations of who is an employee, and many cases prior to *Clackamas* examine the status of partners in enterprises of all sizes.

The list of criteria weighed in the determination of partner status varies from case to case, and some courts place heavy weight on factors that other courts ignore. Another case that summarized the factors courts consider is *Simpson v. Ernst & Young*, decided by the Sixth Circuit in 1996. The court looked at the application of ADEA and ERISA to a partner in large accounting firm, and named the following factors as relevant to the determination:

1. The right and duty to participate in management,
2. The right and duty to act as an agent of other partners,
3. Exposure to liability,
4. The fiduciary relationship among partners,

---

25. *Id.* at 449–50 (2003) (citing EQUAL EMPLOYMENT OPPORTUNITY COMM'N, COMPLIANCE MANUAL §§ 605:0008–605:00010 (2000)).

5. Use of the term "co-owners" to indicate each partner's "power of ultimate control,"
6. Participation in profits and losses,
7. Investment in the firm,
8. Partial ownership of firm assets,
9. Voting rights,
10. The aggrieved individual's ability to control and operate the business,
11. The extent to which the aggrieved individual's compensation was calculated as a percentage of the firm's profits,
12. The extent of that individual's employment security, and
13. Other similar indicia of ownership.[26]

Does It Matter How You Remove a Partner?

The question of "whether the organization can hire or fire the individual," named as a factor in *Clackamas*, is somewhat odd, if you think about it. Almost no organization or partnership would tie its own hands in such a way to make it impossible to remove someone. Thus, it appears that courts are not so much interested in "*whether* the organization can hire or fire the individual" but *how* the organization can hire and fire the individual. It seems that courts are primarily looking to see whether the organization can hire and fire people at will and whether there are barriers to simply firing someone.

For example, in a Seventh Circuit case that examined a four-member partnership, the court thought it was significant that the "partnership agreement allowed for [the partner's] involuntary termination only by a two-thirds vote of the general partners, meaning that the other three had to agree unanimously to remove him."[27] Thus, the fact that a vote of a significant number of partners is required seems to help satisfy courts in examining this factor. Most co-owned business entities are structured in such a way as to require a super-majority vote prior to removing any member, shareholder, or partner. Typically, there is not one person empowered with the right to hire and fire co-owners, which adds to the argument that there is no employment relationship.

---

26. Simpson v. Ernst & Young, 100 F.3d 436, 443–44 (6th Cir. 1996).
27. Solon v. Kaplan, 398 F.3d 629, 633 (7th Cir. 2005).

Does Size of the Group Make a Difference?

It appears that size of a group will matter to the extent that, under some courts' analyses, the group size affects whether partners take part meaningfully in management. However, a case that has acted as very strong precedent in the partnership question is *Wheeler v. Hurdman*,[28] decided by the Tenth Circuit in 1987. There, the court held that a 502-member accounting firm was a partnership for employment law purposes. The court even acknowledged that size shouldn't be a determining factor because "large partnerships may operate more democratically overall than small partnerships, which are frequently vulnerable to domination by a single partner or a small group of partners."[29]

How Much Control Must Each Partner Have?

The *Wheeler* court examined application of FLSA, Title VII, and ADEA (Age Discrimination in Employment Act) to a partner in the firm, and ultimately relied on these factors in making the decision that she was a bona fide partner:

1. Participation in profits and losses,
2. Exposure to liability,
3. Investment in the firm,
4. Partial ownership of firm assets,
5. Voting rights,
6. Position under the partnership agreement, and
7. Position under partnership laws.[30]

Note that the *Wheeler* court placed very little emphasis on the factor of management and whether the partner is actually able to control the workings of the firm. The court even noted that the practical needs of the business may result in partners giving up a certain amount of control over day-to-day activities, and abdicating such control to managers, teams, or committees. The court essentially recognized the following practical reality: any time a group of people voluntarily works together, each individual gives up a certain amount of control to the group or to

28. Wheeler v. Hurdman, 825 F.2d 257 (10th Cir. 1987).
29. *Id.* at 273.
30. *Id.* at 276.

members of the group, and that this would be true in all cases but "sole proprietors and a limited number of dominant partners."[31]

In *Fountain v. Metcalf, Zima & Co.*, the court focused on certain voting rights as the indicator of control, and not on the actual realities of management in the firm. There the court ignored the argument that a managing partner was running the firm autocratically and focused instead on the fact that the plaintiff partner "had a right to vote his thirty-one percent ownership on member/shareholders' amendments to the agreement, on admission of new member/shareholders, on termination of relationship with member/shareholders, on draws, and on distribution of profits and income."[32]

In contrast to *Wheeler* and *Fountain*, however, other courts have focused heavily on the issue of control, and found that factor to be a deal breaker. For example, the court in *Caruso v. Peat, Marwick, Mitchell & Co.*[33] examined the employment status of a partner in a 1,350-member accounting firm, and the court looked at three primary factors:

1. The extent of ability to control and operate the business,
2. The extent to which compensation is calculated as a percentage of the firm's profits, and
3. The extent of employment security.

On the question of "ability to control and operate the business" in the Caruso case, it was significant that the firm was "managed by a board of directors separated from plaintiff by six levels of hierarchy" and that the plaintiff tended to seek approval of management-level partners in decisions about his own work.[34] The court held that the plaintiff was, indeed, an employee.

The Court in *Clackamas* also focused heavily on the question of control and common law definitions of the master–servant relationship:

> At common law the relevant factors defining the master–servant relationship focus on the master's control over the servant. The general definition of the term "servant" in the Restatement (Second) of Agency

31. *Id.* at 273.

32. Fountain v. Metcalf, Zima & Co., PA, 925 F.2d 1398, 1401 (11th Cir. 1991).

33. Caruso v. Peat, Marwick, Mitchell & Co., 664 F. Supp. 144, 149–50 (S.D.N.Y. 1987).

34. *Id.* at 150.

> § 2(2) (1957), for example, refers to a person whose work is "controlled or is subject to the right to control by the master." See also *id.*, § 220(1) ("A servant is a person employed to perform services in the affairs of another and who with respect to the physical conduct in the performance of the services is subject to the other's control or right to control"). [...] We think that the common-law element of control is the principal guidepost that should be followed in this case. [...] A court should examine "whether shareholder-directors operate independently and manage the business or instead are subject to the firm's control." [...] "[i]f the shareholder-directors operate independently and manage the business, they are proprietors and not employees; if they are subject to the firm's control, they are employees."[35]

These cases beg the question: how does this apply in situations where neither the worker controls the business nor the business controls the worker? What if a firm were divided into distributed and semi-autonomous circles of governance and operation, applying a governance model such as holacracy[36] or dynamic self governance?[37] In such a case, each individual may have only a small amount of control over the entire firm, but may have a great deal of control and voice in the particular realm of that individual's work. In the example of a large consumer-owned grocery cooperative, such a governance model could lend strongly to the argument that each member does indeed have a large amount of control in management—not necessarily control over the cooperative as a whole, but over the member's own work.

These cases also beg the question: how does this apply in situations where each member has a significant amount of control by virtue of a decision-making process that mandates the use of a consensus process or super-majority voting?[38] In some worker collectives, decisions are made by unanimous consent, which means that every member has an enormous amount of control. Even in the absence of a unanimity requirement, each member still has a large amount of control if the organization uses a decision-making process that requires that proposals

35. Clackamas Gastroenterology Assocs., PC v. Wells, 538 U.S. 440, 448 (2003) (quoting the EEOC's amicus brief).

36. *See* Brian J. Robertson, Organization Evolved: Introducing Holacracy (Aug. 6, 2009), http://www.holacracy.org/sites/default/files/resources/organization_evolved.pdf.

37. For more information about dynamic governance, see Dynamic Self Governance & Sharing Lives in Chapter 4.

38. See Chapter 4 for a description of consensus processes.

be considered and modified until they are satisfactory to each member. In such a process, everyone has the opportunity to be heard, and may even have the power to block proposals. Arguably, every member still has a large amount of power even if the organization can take a super-majority vote as a fallback plan in the case of a deadlock. Even without a consensus process, organizations that require major decisions be made by super-majorities, arguably, give every member a large amount of control over what happens, in that joining with a large enough minority can overturn a decision.

Does Choice of Entity Matter?

In some jurisdictions and under some statutes, courts have leaned toward the assumption that shareholders of corporations are employees when they work for the corporation they co-own.[39] This assumption has actually caused a great deal of stress for California worker cooperatives,[40] which are generally formed as cooperative corporations. If there is an assumption of an employer/employee relationship from the moment of incorporation, this means that cooperatives must have enough start-up

---

39. For an examination of this issue, see Ann C. McGinley, *Functionality or Formalism—Partners and Shareholders as Employees under the Anti-Discrimination Laws*, 57 S.M.U. L. Rev. 3 (2004).

40. *See* Neil A. Helfman, The Application of Labor Laws to Workers' Cooperatives (Dec. 1992), at 3, *available at* http://sfp.ucdavis.edu/cooperatives/reports/LaborLawWorkerCoops.pdf (citing Interview at California Employment Development Department, Nov. 4, 1991, with David Johnson (Senior Tax Counsel), Terry Savage (Section Chief Auditor and attorney), and Noreen Vincent (tax auditor)).

"As the law presently stands, it looks at form over function. The fact of incorporation may have more bearing upon the determination of an employment relationship than the actual relationship between the parties. A worker in an incorporated cooperative who has managerial authority, for example, may be considered an employee just because the business is incorporated; while a junior partner of a thousand-partner accounting firm, who is under the control of others, is not. The rationale for this distinction is not entirely clear; one explanation is that in the former, worker members are providing services to an entity. For example, in the Matter of Construction Survey Cooperative (Case No. T-62-3) (1962)) before the California Unemployment Insurance Appeals Board, members of a workers' cooperative were held not to be employees. In that case, member workers received compensation on the basis of their contributed labor. By common consent, the activities of the cooperative were directed by a manager, although ultimate authority for managerial decisions rested with the membership. The appeals board found the workers to be principals of the cooperative, and held that under California law that it was incompatible for them to be employees of their own organization. When presented to the Employment Development Department, EDD representatives took the position that if the entity were incorporated, workers should be considered employees even if no other facts had changed."

capital to pay members minimum wage, obtain workers compensation, and so on. The Catch-22 is that most worker cooperatives have great difficulty raising start-up capital, due to the reluctance of banks to loan or of individuals to invest. This means that most worker cooperatives must bootstrap their business, and work for little or no pay in the beginning, like most partners to a start-up business do. Some worker "cooperatives" choose to act as partnerships or limited liability companies (LLCs)[41] in order to avoid application of employment law to members.

The simple fact of incorporation, in the eyes of some courts, is enough to establish a presumption that the shareholder is separate from the entity, and therefore cannot be considered a partner. The court in *Wheeler* seemed to imply that formation of an actual partnership under a state's partnership statute was a significant factor. That court also acknowledged that ERISA does not apply to partners in a business partnership but indicated that it may apply to them if they form a corporation, thus indicating that the simple act of incorporating can make all the difference as far as determining an employment relationship. The court explained:

> In *United States v. Empey*, 406 F.2d 157 (10th Cir.1969), this court found that a partner was not an employee for the purpose of certain tax statutes; therefore, it was necessary under the tax laws for professionals to incorporate in order to obtain retirement plan benefits available to corporate employees.[42]

However, other courts, including the Supreme Court in *Clackamas*, have rejected the de facto assumption that the formation of a corporation should determine employment status. In *Clackamas*, the Court rejected the Ninth Circuit's reliance on a Second Circuit decision that held that

> the use of any corporation, including a professional corporation, "precludes any examination designed to determine whether the entity is in fact a partnership." 271 F. 3d 903, 905 (2001) (quoting *Hyland* v. *New*

41. Note that for employment law purposes, LLCs and partnerships are generally treated the same.

42. Wheeler v. Hurdman, 825 F.2d 257, 268 (10th Cir. 1987); *see also* Yates v. Hendon, 541 U.S. 1 (2004) (holding that a doctor that was the sole shareholder of a professional corporation could qualify as participant/employee for purposes of ERISA, as the plan also covered one of his employees).

> *Haven Radiology Associates, P. C.*, 794 F. 2d 793, 798 (CA2 1986)). It saw "no reason to permit a professional corporation to secure the 'best of both possible worlds' by allowing it both to assert its corporate status in order to reap the tax and civil liability advantages and to argue that it is like a partnership in order to avoid liability for unlawful employment discrimination." 271 F. 3d, at 905.[43]

The *Clackamas* Court's rejection of the presumption serves as powerful precedent, which may even serve to relieve California worker cooperatives of the automatic presumption of employment relationships. Many lower courts have also found that a "partnership" relationship exists even when the entity is a corporation.[44] The court in *Godoy v. Restaurant Opportunity Center of New York, Inc.* also held that the members of a worker-owned cooperative were "partners," in spite of the fact that they were working under a corporation.[45] Many courts may ultimately consider the incorporation status of an entity as relevant, but as only one factor among many in determining whether an employment relationship exists.

The lesson here is: if your clients are planning to work for their own corporation without treating themselves as employees, tread very carefully. Look up the cases in your own jurisdiction to see if they have applied the presumption of employment to people who work for their own corporations. Also look to whether cases in your jurisdiction have relied on *Clackamas.* Thanks to *Clackamas*, we now have a very strong argument that the fact of incorporation should not matter, or, at the very least, that it is only one of many factors to be weighed.

Does It Matter Whether You Are a Business?

Employment relationships can be found even when there is no enterprise involved. For example, nannies and full-time housekeepers for individual households typically need to be treated as employees. How would employment law apply if a group of people rents a house together and calculates each tenant's share of the rent with consideration to the number of hours each tenant contributes to household chores, child care, maintenance work, and so on? If one household member gets a

---

43. Clackamas Gastroenterology Assocs., PC v. Wells, 538 U.S. 440, 443 (2003).
44. *See* EEOC v. Dowd & Dowd, Ltd., 736 F.2d 1177 (7th Cir. 1984).
45. Godoy v. Rest. Opportunity Ctr. of N.Y., Inc., 615 F. Supp. 2d 186, 195 (S.D.N.Y. 2009).

large break on rent in exchange for taking on a large share of the work, should that household member be treated as an employee of the others? This is, in fact, an incredibly important question relevant to student housing cooperatives and other shared housing arrangements all over the country.[46]

Even when no entity exists and even when there is no actual enterprise involved, I would argue that the cases that examine partnerships are highly relevant to this question. The cases are essentially asking the question of whether a master–servant relationship exists, and the relationships of tenants in a housing cooperative can be examined with the same criteria. I would argue that if the tenants enter into a co-tenants' agreement that provides for collective decision-making, and so long as all tenants are involved in and mutually benefiting from the household work, then there is no master–servant relationship.

Volunteers

Social enterprises, cooperative groceries, nonprofit businesses, organic farms, and ecovillages are the wave of the future, so it pains me to say that the law often prevents us from volunteering our time to create and sustain them. Many people feel moved to volunteer for enterprises of all kinds, especially if they make our communities a better place. But our labor laws allow us to be moved only so far, and limit volunteering to government entities and nonprofit organizations conventionally recognized as charitable, religious, civic, and humanitarian.[47]

Here is the federal law on volunteering, as summed up by one Department of Labor Opinion Letter (numbering added):

> Individuals may work for charitable, civic or religious nonprofit enterprises without expectation of compensation and be considered a "volunteer" not included in the definition of "employee" subject to the requirements of the Act. Such activities have been described as "ordinary volunteerism." *Tony and Susan Alamo Foundation v. Secretary of Labor*, 471 U.S. 290, 303 (1985). In determining whether a particular

46. By the way, there are other questions related to this example, including: Must the working tenant report the value of the rent discount as income? Must the tenant group report the value of the labor as rental income? Is the value of the work considered part of rent for the purposes of rent control ordinances?

47. The word "humanitarian" is only sometimes included in the list of purposes for which someone may volunteer. *See* Dep't of Labor Op. Letter, FLSA2008-13 (Dec. 18, 2008).

> activity involves "ordinary volunteerism," the Department considers a variety of factors, including
> [1.] the nature of the entity receiving the services,
> [2.] the receipt by the worker (or expectation thereof) of any benefits from those for whom the services are performed,
> [3.] whether the activity is less than a full-time occupation,
> [4.] whether regular employees are displaced,
> [5.] whether the services are offered freely without pressure or coercion, and
> [6.] whether the services are of the kind typically associated with volunteer work.[48]

It's also important to emphasize that someone can be determined to be an employee, even if they "vehemently" feel that they are volunteers. In the case of *Tony & Susan Alamo Foundation*, where volunteer associates helped operate commercial businesses in support of a nonprofit religious foundation, the Supreme Court stated:

> That the associates themselves vehemently protest coverage under the Act makes this case unusual, but the purposes of the Act require that it be applied even to those who would decline its protections. If an exception to the Act were carved out for employees willing to testify that they performed work "voluntarily," employers might be able to use superior bargaining power to coerce employees to make such assertions, or to waive their protections under the Act.[49]

The Nature of the Entity

One question to ponder is how choice of entity makes a difference for the purposes of applying employment law to volunteers. Laws that govern the formation, operation, and taxation of entities are entirely separate bodies of law from employment law, and the two bodies of law have yet to get together and discuss how employment law applies in new hybrid entities, such as low-profit limited liability companies (L3Cs) and benefit corporations, or in regular for-profit businesses that operate charitable projects separate from their business activities.

---

48. Dep't of Labor Op. Letter, Nurses and Volunteer Hours/Training Time, FLSA2001-18 (July 31, 2001).

49. Tony & Susan Alamo Found. v. Sec'y of Labor, 471 U.S. 290, 302 (1985).

FLSA specifically allows people to volunteer for governmental agencies under certain circumstances,[50] and the ability to volunteer for nonprofit charities and religious organizations has been clearly established by courts along the way. As a general rule, people cannot volunteer for "ordinary commercial activities," even if those activities are operated by and for the benefit of charities and religious organizations.[51]

Protecting workers is also not the only motivation behind FLSA, as acknowledged in *Tony & Susan Alamo Foundation*. Another purpose is to prevent unfair competition between businesses, by ensuring that some businesses do not gain an edge by using volunteer labor. The Court noted in *Tony & Susan Alamo Foundation* that "the Foundation's businesses serve the general public in competition with ordinary commercial enterprises," and allowing people to volunteer would "give petitioners and similar organizations an advantage over their competitors." The Court declared:

> It is exactly this kind of "unfair method of competition" that the Act was intended to prevent, see 29 U. S. C. § 202(a)(3), and the admixture of religious motivations does not alter a business' effect on commerce.[52]

As I've explained above in connection to the Hmong and Lao farmer example, business practices and market conditions tip the scales of competition so far in favor of large companies that it's simply not practical to try to compare businesses for the purposes of the "unfair competition" argument. In the meantime, it is worth doing more research to understand what courts mean by "ordinary commercial enterprise," and to question whether people may volunteer for a somewhat *unordinary* commercial enterprises, if those enterprises are designed to directly serve charitable purposes.

---

50. The FLSA provides that "[t]he term 'employee' does not include any individual who volunteers to perform services for a public agency . . . if—(i) the individual receives no compensation or is paid expenses, reasonable benefits, or a nominal fee to perform the services for which the individual volunteered; and (ii) such services are not the same type of services which the individual is employed to perform for such public agency." 29 U.S.C. § 203(e)(4)(A) (2006).

51. *Tony & Susan Alamo Found.*, 471 U.S. at 302.

52. *Id.* at 299.

For example, imagine that a cooperative of 100 low-income people is formed and each member pays, on a sliding scale, to have rotating teams of members install energy-saving retrofits in each other's homes. The income is used to purchase supplies, teach classes on sustainable living, and to expand the cooperative's purposes to serve members in other ways. Even if this cooperative is not structured as a nonprofit corporation, because it does not distribute profits to members, this entity might be considered nonprofitable under some definitions, and it is arguably serving charitable aims by serving low-income members. At the same time, it *might* be considered an enterprise operating in competition with similar businesses. Part of this last determination may turn on whether the services are offered to the general public. One California Division of Labor Standards Enforcement (DLSE) Opinion Letter states that people cannot volunteer for a nonprofit if that nonprofit is operating a business that serves the general public:

> [W]hen religious, charitable, or nonprofit organizations operate commercial enterprises which serve the general public, such as restaurants or thrift stores, or when they contract to provide personal services to businesses, such enterprises are subject to the Industrial Welfare Commission Orders and volunteers may not be utilized.[53]

Such a rule would seem to make it illegal for Girl Scouts to sell cookies, so it's not entirely clear how far this rule is actually intended to extend. However, it is significant that this prohibition applies only to enterprises that serve the "general public," which might indicate that people could sometimes volunteer for charitable enterprises that are serving a limited group of disadvantaged people, such in the energy retrofit example I gave above.

While it is generally not permissible for people to volunteer for commercial activities operated by charities, what is the rule for charitable activities operated by commercial businesses? Under what circumstances people may volunteer under the umbrella of a for-profit to engage in a project that is primarily charitable? Some courts have

---

53. *See* Cal. Div. of Labor Standards Enforcement Op. Letter (Oct. 27, 1988), *available at* http://www.dir.ca.gov/dlse/opinions/1988-10-27.pdf.

hinted that incorporation as a nonprofit is important,[54] but there otherwise does not seem to be strong precedent *requiring* this. For example, if a restaurant converts to a charitable "soup kitchen" once per month and offers meals for free to the public, can individuals volunteer their time for that project? Granted, the "soup kitchen" event brings good PR to the restaurant, but the primary purpose of the restaurant and the primary motivation of people volunteering is likely charitable. In my opinion, volunteering should be allowed under these circumstances, but more case law research is necessary to flesh out the exact limits and possibilities for this. Note, however, that if the café has regular employees, those employees probably could not volunteer on "soup kitchen" day because the work may be too similar to the work they normally do for pay.

Can Volunteers Receive Benefits?

Another interesting question is: what kinds of incentives and material gratitude can you offer people when they volunteer? Many nonprofit community gardens "pay" their volunteers in food, for example. Does such compensation lend to the argument that they are actually economically dependent on the garden and therefore should be treated as employees?

The rule expressed by the Department of Labor and in FLSA is that people are allowed to volunteer so long as it is "without promise, expectation, or receipt of compensation for the services rendered, although a volunteer can be paid expenses, reasonable benefits, or a nominal fee to perform such services."[55] The FLSA does explicitly allow people to volunteer for a private nonprofit food bank, even if the volunteer receives groceries in return.[56] It is hard to know whether that is a narrow rule applicable only to food banks, or whether that rule can be extrapolated to similar types of organizations, like community gardens.

---

54. *See* Isaacson v. Penn Cmty. Servs., Inc., 450 F.2d 1306, 1310 (4th Cir. 1971) ("Penn Community is a non-profit corporation and its corporate purposes are the public good in the community in which it operates. In the broad sense, therefore, any benefit to Penn Community was benefit to the public at large—a benefit of a different nature than that of a for-profit enterprise.").

55. *See* Dep't of Labor Op. Letter, Volunteer Emergency Crew as Separate and Independent Agency under Section 3(e)(4)(A)," FLSA 2008-13 (Dec. 18, 2008), and FLSA, which notes that volunteers may receive "nominal fees" and "reasonable benefits" (29 U.S.C. § 203(e)(4)(A)).

56. 29 U.S.C. § 203(e)(5).

One interesting case on this is *Hoste v. Shanty Creek Management, Inc.*,[57] where a volunteer ski patroller was injured and made a claim for workers' compensation. The court decided that he was a volunteer, not an employee, even though he received free lift tickets, skiing privileges for family members, free hot beverages, and discounts on meals and merchandise. The court found that these benefits were "an accommodation" to the claimant rather than a payment intended as wages.

In one Opinion Letter, the Department of Labor (DOL) employed a "20 percent test" to determine the acceptability of fees paid to volunteers in a public agency.[58] In that case, high school sports coaches were paid small stipends, and the DOL decided that such stipends may be paid to volunteers, as long as the amount is no more than 20 percent of what would normally be paid to a person employed in the same position. The irony of this rule is that it acknowledges that employees might normally fill such a position, and seems to go against the rule that volunteers should not replace regular employees. Note also that this opinion applied to a public agency, and not to a nonprofit organization. Nevertheless, the 20 percent test offers helpful guidance in determining what is or is not considered nominal.

Interns

Interns work for the primary purpose of their own learning or therapeutic benefit. Many of my business clients eventually find themselves grappling with the question of how they may have interns. My clients are organic farms, gourmet cafes, and other businesses that attract people that want to lend a hand and learn skills. They are often displeased with what I have to tell them about the law on internships, and many find that the laws inflexibly prohibit what they feel would be a wonderful opportunity to teach and work with others.

In the same way that minimum wage laws serve to ensure that workers get paid a reasonable amount of money for their work, internships laws are, you might say, designed to ensure that interns get enough learning from their work. The primary case setting a standard for internships and training programs is *Walling v. Portland Terminal*, where the Court

57. Hoste v. Shanty Creek Mgmt., Inc., 592 N.E.2d 360 (Mich. 1999).

58. Dep't of Labor Op. Letter, Nonexempt Employees Who Volunteer as Coaches/Advisors and Nominal Fees under Section 3(e)(4)(A), FLSA 2005-51 (Nov. 10, 2005).

recognized that money is not the only thing that may motivate someone to work. The Court admitted that the FLSA was

> obviously not intended to stamp out all persons as employees who, without any express or implied compensation agreement, might work for their own advantage on the premises of another. Otherwise, all students would be employees of the school or college they attended, and as such entitled to receive minimum wages.[59]

Who Is an Intern?

Using the *Walling* decision, the Department of Labor has clarified a six-criteria test for determining whether someone is an intern (also referred to as trainee or student) exempt from coverage under the FLSA. To ensure that employers don't find sneaky ways around compliance with employment laws, the exemption for interns has been quite narrowly defined:

1. The training, even though it includes actual operation of the employer's facilities, is similar to that which would be given in a vocational school;
2. The training is for the benefit of the trainees or students;
3. The trainees or students do not displace regular employees, but work under their close observation;
4. The employer derives no immediate advantage from the activities of trainees or students, and on occasion the employer's operations may be actually impeded;
5. The trainees or students are not necessarily entitled to a job at the conclusion of the training period; and
6. The employer and the trainees or students understand that the trainees or students are not entitled to wages for the time spent in training.[60]

This definition of intern is narrow enough that most employers that want to hire "interns" will have a difficult time meeting the standards. I will discuss this more below, after noting a few important things about these six criteria. First, these six criteria are the Department of Labor's and some courts' *interpretation* of the *Walling* case, and not every court has been willing to interpret the test in quite the same way. For example,

---

59. Walling v. Portland Terminal Co., 330 U.S. 148, 152 (1947).

60. Dep't of Labor Non-Administrator Letter, Internship Program and Employment Relationship under FLSA, FLSA 2004-5NA (May 17, 2004).

the Fourth Circuit has applied a much simpler test, which asks whether the intern or the employer is the primary beneficiary of the intern's work.[61] Second, courts that do use the test are divided as to whether the six criteria constitute an "all or nothing" test or a "totality of circumstances" test. For example, the Fifth Circuit[62] has ruled that every one of the six criteria must be met, whereas the Tenth Circuit[63] looked at the criteria as guidance in assessing the full picture of the internship (in the same way that various factors may be weighed and considered in determination of who is an independent contractor).[64] The Sixth Circuit has similarly affirmed a decision that held that "the entire fabric of plaintiffs' relationship to the companies must be considered."[65]

Each state may adopt its own more restrictive test for the determination of who is an intern, so it's important to check state laws to see if they match or go beyond these six criteria. For example, California used to apply an 11-criteria test to the determination of who is an intern,[66] until the Department of Labor Standards Enforcement realized that [oops!] many of the criteria seemed to have no basis in statute or case law, and returned to the six-criteria test. In sum, you may have more or less wiggle room with internship tests, depending on which state and which federal district you are in.

---

61. McLaughlin v. Ensley, 877 F.2d 1207, 1209 n.2 (4th Cir. 1989).

62. Donovan v. Am. Airlines, Inc., 686 F.2d 267, 273 (5th Cir. 1982).

63. Reich v. Parker Fire Prot. Dist., 992 F.2d 1023, 1026–27 (10th Cir. 1993).

64. For additional discussion on the variations in interpretation of "intern," see Jessica L. Curiale, *America's New Glass Ceiling: Unpaid Internships, the Fair Labor Standards Act, and the Urgent Need for Change*, 61 Hastings L.J. 1531 (July 2010).

65. Sims v. Parke Davis & Co., 344 F. Supp. 774, 786 (E.D. Mich. 1971), *aff'd*, 453 F.2d 1259 (6th Cir. 1971).

66. Cal. Div. of Labor Standards Enforcement Op. Letter, Re: Educational Internship Programs (Apr. 7, 2010):

> The additional factors to be met under the historical 11-factor test by DLSE are as follows: (7) Any clinical training is part of an educational curriculum, (8) the trainees or students do not receive employee benefits, (9) the training is general, so as to qualify the trainees or students for work in any similar business, rather than designed specifically for a job with the employer offering the program, i.e. upon completion of the program, the trainees or students must not be fully trained to work specifically for only the employer offering the program, (10) the screening process for the program is not the same as for employment, and does not appear to be for that purpose, but involves only criteria relevant for admission to an independent educational program, and (11) advertisements for the program are couched clearly in terms of education or training, rather than employment, although the employer may indicate that qualified graduates will be considered for employment.

Note also that it's not always necessary to adhere to the six-part test in the case of "interns" in nonprofits. Such "interns" are also likely to be exempt from coverage under FLSA due to the fact that they motivated to volunteer for the nonprofit to serve humanitarian or charitable purposes. Things get sticky primarily in cases of interns working for for-profit businesses and for commercial enterprises of nonprofits.

The Importance of Being Unhelpful

Most businesses struggle especially with fourth criteria in the internship test, which is the requirement that "the employer derives no immediate advantage from the activities of trainees or students, and on occasion the employer's operations may be actually impeded."[67] Some businesses do seek interns for the sole purpose of providing an educational experience, but let's be real: Most employers hope that interns will also be helpful to the enterprise, and the framing of this law makes it very hard to have both. Conceivably, and I've seen this happen, an intern who works hard and benefits a business could later bring a wage claim and argue that they actually should have been treated and paid as an employee. Disgruntled interns do often have the law on their side, should they choose to exercise it. My advice to businesses is often: "Just don't let the intern be too helpful to the business."

Some courts have been quite strict in finding an employment relationship any time a business benefits *at all* from an intern or other worker. For example, in *Souder v. Brennan*, a D.C. district court held that "[s]o long as the institution derives any consequential economic benefit, the economic reality test would indicate an employment relationship rather than mere therapeutic exercise. To hold otherwise would be to make therapy the sole justification for thousands of positions as dishwashers, kitchen helpers, messengers and the like."[68] The First Circuit has also clarified that "courts faced with scenarios not clearly anticipated by Congress have looked primarily to whether the *employer* was benefitted to determine if particular hours are covered under FLSA."[69]

At the same time, other courts have demonstrated greater flexibility around the question of whether a business can benefit from an intern's

67. Dep't of Labor Non-Administrator Letter, Internship Program and Employment Relationship under FLSA, FLSA2004-5NA (May 17, 2004).

68. Souder v. Brennan, 367 F. Supp. 808, 813 (D.D.C. 1973).

69. Plumley v. S. Container, Inc., 303 F.3d 364, 371 (2d Cir. 2002).

work. As noted above, the Fourth Circuit looks at the question of who is *primarily* benefiting, and will uphold a finding that someone is an intern even when the business received a benefit.[70] In *Williams v. Strickland*, the Ninth Circuit looked at a case involving a man who volunteered for a long time for a Salvation Army store, primarily for the purpose of his rehabilitation. Even though he participated in and benefited a business activity, and even though he may have done work typically done by employees, the court *still* decided that he wasn't an employee, arguing that he was a *beneficiary* of the opportunities Salvation Army offered him for his rehabilitation.[71]

I'm particularly fond of one quote by a Hawaii district court that examined the question of whether school children are employees when they volunteer in the school cafeteria: "[I]t would be absurd for this Court to rule that any educational activity would be placed within the requirements of the FLSA simply because there may be an economic benefit to the institution involved. This would throw the baby out with the bath water."[72] Throwing the baby out with the bath water is, essentially, what employment laws do when they prevent people from engaging in activities that are beneficial to themselves and our communities. In the case of internships, I think that it's important to allow some amount of mutual benefit, so that an intern doesn't simply become a drain on a business, and so that businesses have incentives to educate people about their work.

How to Have an Intern

Given the limitations on how interns can work in enterprises, I have often given clients a set of recommendations for how they could legitimately operate an internship program. My recommendations usually include

a. **Create a curriculum to accompany the work:** This helps to meet the requirement that the training be "similar to that which would be given in a vocational school."[73]

70. McLaughlin v. Ensley, 877 F.2d 1207, 1209 n.2 (4th Cir. 1989).

71. Williams v. Strickland, 87 F.3d 1064 (9th Cir. 1996).

72. Bobilin v. Bd. of Educ., State of Haw., 403 F. Supp. 1095, 1108 (D. Haw. 1975).

73. Dep't of Labor Non-Administrator Letter, "Internship Program and Employment Relationship under FLSA," FLSA2004-5NA (May 17, 2004).

b. **Implement a systematic training program whereby interns will be exposed to nearly every aspect of running the business:** If an intern is exposed to multiple aspects of running the business, it means that he/she will not spend a significant amount of time repeatedly doing one task. This helps to undermine any argument that the employer is benefiting from the intern's work, since the intern never has the opportunity to be that helpful on any one task, and the employer is constantly training the intern in a different facet of the business. I have recommended that clients create a checklist of tasks that each intern will engage in during the internship. In the case of a business with many interns, I have also suggested that interns help to train other interns on each task, since people tend to learn more when they teach others, and since this relieves some burden on the business.
c. **Limit the amount of time that interns spend doing rote tasks or work normally done by employees:** In the case of a farm, an intern should not spend a significant amount of time planting, weeding, or harvesting a field, but may do this work on a limited basis, for the purpose of developing basic skills. It is better to engage the intern in projects somewhat separate from the day-to-day work of the farm, such as installing a new demonstration project or building a rain water catchment system. This helps to prevent any argument that the intern is displacing an employee.
d. **Create an affiliation with an educational institution or nonprofit:** If a business serves as an educational laboratory for school or university students, this helps to create a clearer educational purpose to the work an intern does with the enterprise.

Internship Program Laws

In at least one state that I know of, there is now a special internship program law that, in theory, opens up doors for people to do more internships. The state of Washington has recognized that the restrictiveness of internship laws makes it very difficult for people to learn about certain industries, such as farming. Washington passed SB 6349[74] in 2009 to create a special program to allow for and oversee farm internships, and

74. See Wash. State Legislature, Bill Information: SB 6349, http://apps.leg.wa.gov/billinfo/summary.aspx?year=2009&bill=6349.

to provide a special workers' compensation program that farmers can use to cover farm interns.[75] The program was piloted with small farms in two counties and, at the time of this writing, is being considered for expansion. My impression of SB 6349 is that it does not change any employment laws, but simply creates an oversight program that the Washington Department of Labor and Industry (L&I) feels comfortable with, which allows farmers to relax and know they are unlikely to be cited and fined by L&I. At the same time, the program doesn't actually prevent the interns from bringing wage claims or other actions under employment laws. An intern could still conceivably win a case if he/she succeed in arguing that the internship didn't meet the federal criteria, particularly if that intern does a significant amount of day-to-day farm work. Thus, the Washington law is helpful, but it does not remedy the general problem that businesses are not allowed to benefit from the help of interns.

Apprenticeship Laws

Note that interns and trainees are not, for employment law definitions and purposes, the same thing as apprentices. Federal law defines and allows for special treatment of "apprentices,"[76] "learners,"[77] and "student learners,"[78] but this does not include a policy allowing them to work

75. Thank you to SELC Legal Intern Julie Pennington for her research on Washington's program and SB 6349.

76. 29 C.F.R. § 520.300 provides: "*Apprentice* means a worker, at least sixteen years of age unless a higher minimum age standard is otherwise fixed by law, who is employed to learn a skilled trade through a registered apprenticeship program. Training is provided through structured on-the-job training combined with supplemental related theoretical and technical instruction. This term excludes pre-apprentices, trainees, learners, and student-learners. The terms learner and student-learner are defined in this subpart."

77. 29 C.F.R. § 520.300 provides: "*Learner* means a worker who is being trained for an occupation, which is not customarily recognized as an apprenticeable trade, for which skill, dexterity and judgment must be learned and who, when initially employed produces little or nothing of value. Except in extraordinary circumstances, an employee cannot be considered a 'learner' once he/she has acquired a total of 240 hours of job-related and/or vocational training with the same or other employer(s) or training facility(ies) during the past three years. An individual qualifying as a 'learner' may only be trained in two qualifying occupations."

78. 29 C.F.R. § 520.300 provides: "*Student-learner* means a student who is at least sixteen years of age, or at least eighteen years of age if employed in an occupation which the Secretary has declared to be particularly hazardous, who is receiving instruction in an accredited school, college or university and who is employed by an establishment on a part-time basis, pursuant to a bona fide vocational training program."

without pay. Employers that register their apprenticeship programs can become eligible for certain tax benefits or workforce development grants, and may be able to pay apprentices less than minimum wage (though not likely less than 75 percent of minimum wage) or less than the prevailing wage rates set in certain industries, such as construction. Apprenticeship programs must be registered with the Department of Labor's Office of Apprenticeship or with a state agency overseeing apprenticeships.

Independent Contractors

Independence and cooperation sound somewhat like opposites, but they are actually closely intertwined in the sharing economy. Through cooperative production, cooperative marketing, cooperative ownership of equipment, and cooperative purchasing of supplies and services, many small-scale and independent enterprises can access economies of scale usually only harnessed by big businesses. For example, now that 30 U.S. states have adopted cottage food laws,[79] allowing for sale of certain homemade food items, tens of thousands of people are likely to operate small enterprises to bake bread, dry fruit, make jam, and so on. Each cottage food producer will likely benefit from connections to other cottage food producers—to purchase sugar and flour in bulk, to share farmers' market stands, to sell products under the same label, to share advertising, and so on. This kind of cooperation makes independent micro-entrepreneurship economically viable.

When multiple independent entrepreneurs come together and form a producer, marketing, and/or purchasing cooperative, the relationship between the entrepreneurs and the cooperative is *usually* one of independent contractors. In the cottage bread baker example, each bread baker has his/her own home business. After joining a cooperative, a baker may agree to sell a certain amount of bread to the cooperative each week and may also purchase ingredients through the cooperative. It is possible, however, that such a relationship could creep into a gray area and move more toward an employment relationship. This all depends on the

79. *See* Sustainable Economies Law Center, Summary of Cottage Food Laws in the U.S., http://www.theselc.org/wp-content/uploads/2011/05/Table-of-Cottage-Food-Laws-in-US1.pdf.

agreement between the cooperative and the baker, and on the circumstances of the baker's work.

The test for who is an independent contractor has been articulated by many courts. One Supreme Court opinion helpfully summed them up as follows (for the sake of brevity, I have omitted the court's many helpful footnotes, and, for the sake of readability, I have added numbers):

> In determining whether a hired party is an employee under the general common law of agency, we consider:
>
> [1.] the hiring party's right to control the manner and means by which the product is accomplished.
>
> Among the other factors relevant to this inquiry are:
>
> [2.] the skill required;
> [3.] the source of the instrumentalities and tools;
> [4.] the location of the work;
> [5.] the duration of the relationship between the parties;
> [6.] whether the hiring party has the right to assign additional projects to the hired party;
> [7.] the extent of the hired party's discretion over when and how long to work;
> [8.] the method of payment;
> [9.] the hired party's role in hiring and paying assistants;
> [10.] whether the work is part of the regular business of the hiring party;
> [11.] whether the hiring party is in business;
> [12.] the provision of employee benefits; and
> [13.] the tax treatment of the hired party.
>
> [...] No one of these factors is determinative.[80]

Weighing the factors named above, a court would likely find that bread bakers are not employees of a cooperative through which they sell their breads; this is so long as the bakers work in their own homes, use their own appliances, hire their own assistants, set their own hours, decide on the manner in which they bake, and have the freedom to sell bread elsewhere.

However, if an autocratic manager or board of the cooperative began to exert more control over each baker, the relationship might

80. Cmty. for Creative Non-Violence v. Reid, 490 U.S. 730, 751–52 (1989).

change. If the cooperative dictates how much each baker must produce, sets specifications for ingredients, and fixes prices on the breads of all bakers, and if one manager has the power to hire and fire bakers, this could potentially be ruled to be an employment relationship. This was essentially the outcome of the Supreme Court's 1961 ruling in *Goldberg v. Whitaker House Cooperative, Inc.*,[81] where 200 home-based clothing manufacturers (primarily women engaged in knitting and embroidery) joined a cooperative and sold clothing items to the cooperative. The Court determined that an employment relationship existed, due to the level of control the cooperative had over each member's work (dictating design, order size, timing, payment, and other terms of work).[82]

The ruling likely dealt a hard blow to the 200 women in the cooperative, since it would not have been legal for them to work as *employees* either, given the strict regulations on employment of people doing industrial homework.[83] They would have had to begin working outside of the home.

Three Justices dissented in the *Whitaker House Cooperative* case, arguing that the women were truly independent in the way that they worked. The dissent argued that

> each member worked for herself—in her own home when and as she chose—toward the production of knitted articles which she marketed through her cooperative, receiving immediately "an advance" thereon, and ultimately—after payment of her portion of the cooperative's "expenses" and setting up its "necessary depreciation [and capital] reserves"—the balance of the proceeds of sale would "be distributed [to her] according to the percentage of work [she] submitted to the Cooperative for sale." Like the two courts below, I fail to see in this any element of employment by the cooperative of its members.[84]

Given the strong dissent in *Whitaker House Cooperative*, it's likely that the cooperative fell very close to a gray area and could have avoided the

81. Goldberg v. Whitaker House Coop., Inc., 366 U.S. 28 (1961).

82. *Id.* at 33.

83. As a general rule, it is not legal, without a special license, to employ people to engage in manufacturing activities in their homes. *See* 29 C.F.R. §§ 530.1–530.12 and Fair Labor Standards Act § 211(d).

84. *Whitaker House Coop.*, 366 U.S. at 34 (Whittaker, J., dissenting).

ruling by altering the relationship between the manufacturers and the cooperative in a way that met more of the criteria for determination of an independent contractor relationship.[85] Note also that the cooperative could have argued that all members were partners, though to have succeeded with this, the co-op may have needed a different legal entity and a much more collective and participatory management structure.

In the same way that many independent entrepreneurs form cooperatives to leverage economies of scale, many separate nonprofit projects often come together under the umbrella of a single nonprofit corporation, in a model known as fiscal sponsorship.[86] By operating under a single umbrella, each project is free from the burden of managing its own accounting, tax reporting, tax exemption, and other administrative matters. It's important to learn how to navigate the difference between independent contractors and employers in this realm as well. In many cases, the coordinators of a project may be sufficiently independent in the operation of the project and an employment relationship may be avoided. However, if a project grows to involve multiple people working under the control of the project coordinator or nonprofit, an employment relationship may exist.

Work That Is Not Actually Work

In some situations, it may be possible to argue that an employer/employee relationship does not exist because the activity or exertion in question is not actually "work." For example, any of the following activities are, arguably, not "work:"

- **Exercise:** Working out at the gym does not make you the gym's employee. Is this still true even if your work on the equipment is generating electricity used to power the gym or sold to others?
- **Leisure/play/socializing:** Organizing a "crop mob" party to help a farm harvest is arguably seen by the mob as a form of play, not work; the Department of Labor may not see it that way, however.

85. For a similar case looking at this issue, see *Brock v. Superior Care, Inc.*, 840 F.2d 1054 (2d Cir. 1988).

86. *See* Gregory L. Colvin, Fiscal Sponsorship (handout prepared for the Western Conference on Tax Exempt Organizations, Nov. 17, 2006, San Francisco), http://www.fiscalsponsorship.com/images/WCTEO_Gregory-Colvin.pdf.

- **U-Pick:** Picking berries for *yourself* on someone else's farm generally does not make you the farm's employee.
- **Caring:** Making food for your neighbor when she is sick or helping a friend move into a new apartment are arguably not work, but activities inspired by caring.
- **Being on reality TV:** Imagine that a TV producer approached you about the possibility of making a reality TV show about your home life. Your job would be to carry on life as usual with the presence of TV cameras. But are you now working for the show? A surprising number of law review articles have addressed this question.[87]
- **Household chores:** Doing dishes for yourself and your family is arguably not work; as my mom would have said, "that's *life*, kid."

There are simply not enough cases examining the definition of "work," so it's hard to know how to handle this question. The 1944 Supreme Court case *Tennessee Coal*, examined the question of whether travel time to and from a coal mine is "work."[88] The Court explained that

> in the absence of a contrary legislative expression, we cannot assume that Congress here was referring to work or employment other than as those words are commonly used—as meaning physical or mental exertion (whether burdensome or not) controlled or required by the employer and pursued necessarily and primarily for the benefit of the employer and his business.[89]

The key, according to the Court, is that the activity it is "controlled," "required," and "pursued […] for the benefit" of someone else. How do you apply this to a case of an exuberant "crop mob" that shows up for a harvest party on a farm? These are groups of energetic, earth-loving, farm-friendly people who descend upon a farm for a few hours to get their hands dirty and help with planting, weeding, or harvest. The fact that they are volunteering and being helpful to a farm enterprise may, however, make them employees. This is because an agent of the

87. *See* Adam P. Greenberg, *Note: Reality's Kids: Are Children Who Participate on Reality Television Shows Covered under the Fair Labor Standards Act?*, 82 S. CAL. L. REV. 59; Kimberlianne Podlas, *Does Exploiting a Child Amount to Employing a Child? The FLSA's Child Labor Provisions and Children on Reality Television*, 17 UCLA ENT. L. REV. 39.

88. Tenn. Coal, Iron & R. Co. v. Muscoda Local No. 123, 321 U.S. 590 (1944).

89. *Id.* at 598.

Department of Labor may, on the surface, not be able to tell the difference between a crop mob and exploited farm laborers.

But how might this change if the crop mob *paid* the farmer for the privilege of helping pick veggies? Then this becomes more similar to the gym example, where people pay for the privilege of using exercise equipment. Sure, the farmer still benefits, but this now makes it similar to the example where the gym members generate electricity for the gym while they work out. It is easy to see how work and life can merge in certain activities, and it truly is a legal gray area.

What About Being a Responsible Human Being, Participating In Society, and Doing Our Share?

Using the *Tennessee Coal* description of work and trying to argue that work we do doesn't benefit others will often be impossible. The reality is that many ways we choose to spend our time *do* benefit others, and that is often why we do them. It's worth again quoting the Hawaii court that examined the question of whether children are employees of a school when they help out in the cafeteria:

> [T]his Court notes the widespread and common practice of requiring elementary school children to perform small tasks such as erasing blackboards, putting their chairs on their desks after school, and serving as crosswalk monitors. These experiences teach not only neatness and responsibility but also civic attitudes fundamental in a collective society where a citizen is often called upon to "do his share" without economic compensation.
>
> Such small tasks admittedly do have economic value to the state in that they save the cost of hiring adults to perform these same tasks. Nevertheless, looking to the "economic reality" of the entire situation, it is obvious to this Court that such economically valuable activities could not reasonably be considered employment under the FLSA, which would require the payment of minimum wages to students.[90]

In the sharing economy, I believe we will do many more things simply because we live in a "collective society" and we are expected to "do [our] share." Sometimes this will look like work; sometimes not. Sometimes it will benefit others; sometimes it will benefit just us. In many cases it will be impossible to sort out the difference, and that is, in fact, what makes it so wonderful.

---

90. Bobilin v. Bd. of Educ., 403 F. Supp. 1095, 1107 (D. Haw. 1975).

CHAPTER EIGHT

NEW FORMS OF PRODUCTION AND COMMERCE

Part 1: Collaborative Production/ Collaborative Consumption

New Modes of Production and Consumption

The sharing economy offers us interesting new ways to meet our needs. Put simply, we will turn less frequently to big businesses to meet our needs, and turn more frequently to ourselves and each other. Turning to ourselves means taking a DIY (do-it-yourself) approach to making, growing, building, repairing, and doing other things that we previously "outsourced" to conventional commercial businesses. However, since we can't actually do everything *ourselves*, we fortunately have *each other*. That also happens to be the primary resource fueling a sharing economy: *each other*.

Turning to one another means connecting with others to meet our needs, and cooperating to do the many things we cannot easily do on our own. It means forming babysitting cooperatives, tool lending libraries, food-buying cooperatives, community gardens, car-sharing clubs, community renewable energy projects, and health care cooperatives. It means borrowing someone's car when you might normally have rented one. It means staying in someone's home when you might normally have stayed in a hotel. It means going to a community dinner gathering, when you might normally have gone to a restaurant. When people come together to provide for one another in these ways, these activities are sometimes called collaborative consumption, collaborative production, or just plain sharing. The phrase "peer-to-peer" or "P2P" is also frequently used to describe ways that individuals borrow, lend, give, buy, sell, and share with their peers, rather than meeting needs solely at stores or commercial businesses.

When Sharing Becomes Commerce

The challenging question to answer with many of these activities is: Are they regulated in the same ways that typical commercial businesses are regulated? The answer will often be elusive. For example, if you go to a buffet restaurant or salad bar, you will notice that the restaurant is required, by law, to install a protective "sneeze guard" over the food. Compare that to the potluck you host at home, where there are no mandatory sneeze guards. Now how do health regulations apply in circumstances where larger communities gather to share meals, where people turn their home into a "restaurant for the night," or where a group organizes a public potluck event? These are phenomena of the sharing economy, and the sharing economy is nothing to be sneezed at. We'll increasingly find ourselves asking questions like: will our car-sharing club be subject to the same regulations as a car rental company? Will our babysitting cooperative need to be licensed as a childcare provider?

Every way that people provide for each other can be put somewhere on a spectrum between the private/personal realm and the public/commercial realm. On one end of the spectrum, we find people cooking meals for their families; at the other end of the spectrum, we find fast food restaurants that sell mass-produced food items to massive numbers of people via drive-thru windows. Somewhere in the middle of that spectrum is a point at which regulations kick in. Where does that point lie, exactly? That is one of the most intriguing questions for the sharing economy.

Because much of what we do in the sharing economy lies in a gray area of that spectrum, the job of a sharing economy lawyer will be to advise people on how to shape their activities and relationships to either come into compliance or move out of the scope of regulation. Most of the time, clients will prefer to move out of the scope of regulation and will likely be surprised to find themselves there in the first place. Many activities and enterprises in the sharing economy are not commercial to begin with; but when they start to get organized and scale up, they begin to adopt qualities and practices more similar to commercial businesses.

Purposes of Regulation

It is helpful to think about the purposes behind the regulation of commercial and productive activities, in order to think more clearly about the applicability of those laws to sharing activities. The purposes fall into a handful of categories, including

- **Laws that protect consumers:** A large number of commercial regulations exist to protect consumers from the stores, services, and companies they patronize. We have regulations related to food safety, product safety, public health, and many more. These are the laws that tell us how to label products, how to operate safely, what licenses we need, what inspections we are subject to, what warnings and disclosures we must give, what standards we must meet, what records we must keep, when we can operate, what warranties we must make, what insurance we must carry, what consumer information we must keep private, and so on.

  These laws recognize that large businesses driven by profit motives may not always be fully accountable to the people they serve. In that respect, the regulations are somewhat out of place when applied to small-scale, cooperative, and/or community-based activities, where there are high levels of accountability and involvement and much lower levels of risk. In essence, laws that protect consumers from producers do not apply well when the consumer IS the producer, or when the consumer has a very close or collaborative relationship with the producer.
- **Laws that protect a marketplace:** Some regulations are targeted less at the protection of consumers and aimed more at regulating the availability of goods and services in a marketplace or at ensuring the ability of certain entrepreneurs to make a secure livelihood. Such regulations may seek to prevent flooding of a marketplace by capping the number of enterprises operating within an area. For example, cities may grant only a limited number of taxi cab permits because an oversupply of cabs in a city might make it more difficult for each cab driver to make a living. Cities might also cap the number of mobile food vendors operating in the streets. On the flip side of preventing the flooding of marketplaces, laws may also seek to prevent a single business from dominating an industry. However, due to the highly dispersed and decentralized nature of commerce in the sharing economy, antitrust law will not be discussed here.

- **Laws that regulate a profession:** Many professions require licensure and oversight by a licensing body. This serves a dual role of protecting consumers/clients and of regulating competition within the profession. This begs the question: when we provide and care for one another in a more casual and sharing economy, when might we step over the line and engage in activities that require licensure? If we regularly help people prune their fruit trees, offer to give haircuts to people at a shelter, offer massages to members of our timebank, or help our friends fix and retrofit their water heaters, is it possible that we are engaging in activity that normally requires a license?
- **Laws that protect communities and ecosystems:** Regulations such as land use and environmental laws seek to protect communities and ecosystems by regulating where and how certain activities take place. Laws that control *where* commercial and productive activities take place turn out to be a significant consideration for the sharing economy, as many small-scale commercial and productive activities are returning to our residential neighborhoods. The 20th-century zoning frameworks that sought to keep large-scale, noisy, dusty, polluting industries and agriculture out of our quiet neighborhoods simply don't fit well as we return to cottage-scale, sustainable, localized production.
- **Laws that protect a resource or necessity for the public:** Other regulations seek to control and ensure proper provision of important resources to communities. Companies that provide energy, water, transportation, and communication, for example, are often regulated under public utilities laws, which may dictate rates or service areas, for example. How do such laws apply when people cooperatively provide for such needs, as by operating a small local renewable energy cooperative, or a shuttle serving area ecovillages?
- **Laws that protect workers and contractors in a particular industry:** Certain industries are subject to heightened oversight and regulation due to the unique vulnerability of workers in those industries. For example, people who work in garment manufacturing often need to register with a state agency that monitors clothing manufacturing contractors, particularly when it involves people working from home.[1] In the sharing economy, some small-

1. *See, e.g.*, Cal. Code Regs. tit. 8, § 13630; Cal. Lab. Code § 2671(b).

scale sewing, tailoring, and knitting cooperatives have already found such laws awkward in application to their own activities.

- **Laws that ensure equitable access to public accommodations:** Private companies and organizations that provide public accommodations—like hotels, private schools, and recreation centers—are mandated by civil rights laws to allow equal access to such accommodations without regard to race, sex, and other protected characteristics, and to make reasonable accommodations for people with disabilities. The sharing economy is characterized by increased numbers of quasi-public gathering spaces, events, and activities, and there will sometimes be a gray area in determining which of them are legally "public accommodations," such as in the case of a community garden operated by a homeowners' association for use by people in a neighborhood, or in the case of a large network of carpoolers.
- **Laws that impose additional taxes on certain industries:** Certain industries are subject to special taxes and fees, often levied at the local or state level. San Francisco's 14 percent hotel tax is an example. In the sharing economy, we will often face the question: should such taxes apply to similar activities that generate income, such as hosting a short-term guest at your house and charging $15 per day?
- **Laws that require consumers to purchase a particular good or service:** Many states mandate that car owners purchase liability insurance, for example. In addition, starting in 2014, with the implementation of the Patient Protection and Affordable Care Act,[2] individuals will be required to purchase health coverage for themselves when it is not available to them through an employer or other means. The Act and administrating agencies will set certain requirements for the types of services provided and the scope of the coverage. This Act and potential sharing economy exemptions are discussed on page 432.

PART 2: APPROACHING THE GRAY AREAS

This chapter is not meant to survey all commercial and productive activities that are regulated or to describe the details of any particular

2. Patient Protection and Affordable Care Act, H.R. 3590, 111th Cong. (2009–2010), *available at* http://www.govtrack.us/congress/bills/111/hr3590/text.

regulation. The primary goal here is to call attention to the gray areas that arise in the context of collaborative production and consumption and to equip lawyers and communities with tools and arguments for navigating those gray areas.

Examples of Gray Areas

Here are examples of situations where collaborative activities could begin to creep toward the realm of regulated activities, along with examples of the types of regulations to which they would potentially be subject, if found to be commercial.

Personal Activities	***Sharing Activities: The Gray Area Between Personal and Commercial***	***Commercial Activities and Their Related Regulations***
Giving a friend a ride	*Ridesharing:* Giving friends or strangers a ride in exchange for money or points that can be redeemed in other ways.	*Taxi, limousine, and shuttle services:* Usually subject to licensing requirements, safety laws, and rate-setting rules. Limousine, shuttle, and taxi services are also sometimes regulated under public utilities laws.
Lending your car to a friend	*Car sharing:* A neighborhood car sharing club where everyone pays into the club on the basis of how much they use the cars.	*Car rental companies:* Usually subject to safety laws and insurance requirements.
Having a dinner party for friends	*Meal sharing and peer-to-peer restaurants:* Having a dinner party at your house for friends or strangers, and charging admission.	*Restaurants:* Usually subject to health and safety laws, heightened fire codes, rules governing public accommodations, zoning restrictions, and special taxes.

Personal Activities	*Sharing Activities: The Gray Area Between Personal and Commercial*	*Commercial Activities and Their Related Regulations*
Swapping babysitting with another parent	*Childcare cooperatives:* 15 parents form a babysitting group to exchange child care cooperatively.	*Childcare businesses:* Usually subject to licensing requirements and health and safety laws.
Having an overnight guest	*Peer-to-peer hotels:* Swapping homes with strangers or charging money to an overnight guest.	*Hotels:* Usually subject to health and safety laws, zoning restrictions, special taxes, rules governing public accommodations, rules on advertising rates.
Buying groceries	*Consumer cooperatives:* Collectively buying groceries with 50 people and selling homemade food items to one another.	*Grocery stores:* Usually subject to health and safety laws, higher local business taxes, and zoning restrictions.
Putting solar panels on your house	*Shared energy project:* Sharing a solar array with neighbors in a condominium complex.	*Energy companies:* Usually subject to public utilities regulation.
Installing your own drip irrigation system or your own solar panels	*Cooperative work groups:* A cooperative of 12 households that take turns doing construction or repair projects on each other's homes.	*Professional builders, electricians, and plumbers:* Often subject to a requirement to obtain a license prior to building, installing, or repairing projects of a certain value.*

* For information about each state's contractor's license requirements, see Contractor's License Reference Site, http://www.contractors-license.org/.

Personal Activities	***Sharing Activities: The Gray Area Between Personal and Commercial***	***Commercial Activities and Their Related Regulations***
Knitting a hat for a friend	*Clothing cooperatives:* A cooperative of individuals that work together and share skills and equipment to collect, repair, alter and make clothing for themselves and other cooperative members.	*Garment manufacturers:* Often subject to registration requirements, restrictions on home manufacture, and labeling requirements.
Gardening at home	*Community garden:* A space shared by neighbors or members of a particular group or community for the purpose of growing food for participants.	*Public parks or commercial farms:* Public parks are subject to rules governing public accommodations; commercial farms are subject to food and agriculture regulations.
Keeping a goat for milk	*Herdsharing:* A group of 40 people sharing a herd of 15 goats and consuming their milk.	*Dairies:* Subject to strict health, safety, food, and agricultural regulations.
Drinking water filtered at home	*Drinking water cooperatives:* In an area with contaminated drinking water, a group of 100 people share an advanced water filtration and purification system to bottle safe drinking water for themselves.	*Bottled water companies:* May be subject to water bottling plant licenses, drinking water haulers' permits, and, depending on the source of the water, private water source operator permits.

Personal Activities	*Sharing Activities: The Gray Area Between Personal and Commercial*	*Commercial Activities and Their Related Regulations*
Sharing "hand-me-downs"	*Used item swap meets and cooperatives:* An event where people bring used and unwanted items to swap with and sell to others. May also be a cooperative that takes members' unwanted items and sells them to other members.	*Used merchandise stores:* Often subject to secondhand dealer registration requirements. May also be prohibited from resale of certain used items, such as children's car seats.
Caring for an aging family member	*Cooperative and community-based care:* A group of ten aging adults purchase and live in a property together and make agreements to cooperatively care for one another and to share the services of in-home care providers.	*Residential care facilities:* Required to be licensed, adhere to health and safety rules, and restricted by zoning.

Steps to Approaching a Gray Area

In most cases where clients have organized one of the activities listed in the middle column above, clients will prefer to manage the terms of their own activities and not be subject to regulation. Here is a process a sharing economy lawyer could use to advise a client on the application of regulations:

1. **Determine what areas of regulation might apply if this were a public or commercial activity.** There's no single source to find the answer to the various ways that an industry or activity is regulated. In California, I often rely on the Governor's Office of Business and Economic Development website CalGOLD,[3]

3. http://www.CalGOLD.ca.gov.

which lists the local, state, and federal agencies that regulate 147 different industries. General familiarity with the topic headings of state and local codes can also be very helpful, not to mention intriguing. In Oakland, for example, the topic headings under the business regulation section of the municipal code include things like "cabarets," "mattresses," "trampoline centers," and other things you might not have imagined would have their own dedicated section of code.

2. **Determine whether that realm of regulation designates explicit exemptions for small-scale, community-based, or cooperative activities.** Where legislators have had the foresight to consider or respond to the needs of certain small-scale and community activities, there are explicit exemptions in the laws. For example, in California, the state has an exemption from childcare center licensing requirements where the parents create a cooperative arrangement to provide child care.[4] In the realm of food safety, there may be other explicit exemptions where the food being produced is "non-potentially hazardous," where transactions take place directly between producer and consumer, or where food is sold in the context of a private club or charity event. Common types of exemptions are discussed in Part 3.
3. **If there is no explicit exemption, determine whether the activity legitimately falls outside of the realm of regulation.** The law has not and cannot foresee all of the ways people may come together and provide for one another. In the absence of specific exemptions, it's important to recognize that regulations, in many cases, simply were not intended to apply to many of our activities. If I regularly give friends rides to the airport, the public utilities commission does not require me to register my shuttle service. When I have a dinner party with friends, the health department does not inspect my kitchen. When activities are truly private and non-commercial, they are usually unregulated. The trick then, is to argue that the ways people share and provide for one another are also private and non-commercial, and therefore fall outside of the scope of the regulation. These arguments are described in Part 4.

---

4. *See* Cal. Health & Safety Code § 1596.792(e); for the full text of the exemption, see note 8 *infra*.

4. **If the activity is truly in a gray area, help clients alter the activity so that it falls into a much safer end of the gray area.** If an activity falls squarely into a gray area, there are many ways to help clients change the characteristics of their arrangement so that it is far less likely to be deemed public or commercial in nature. Many of these characteristics are described in Part 4 in relation to determining what is or isn't public or commercial.
5. **If there's no way to find an exemption to regulation, in what ways might compliance be made less burdensome?** Sharing and cooperation come in very handy in answer to this question, as the expenses, hurdles, and burden of regulatory compliance can be shared among multiple people or groups. Shared commercial kitchen spaces, shared farmers market stands, shared retail spaces, shared equipment, and/or the formation of producer and consumer cooperatives help to create economies of scale and reduce the regulatory hurdles that people might otherwise be unable to face alone.

Part 3: When the Sharing Economy Is Exempt from Regulation

Although it will be somewhat unusual to find an explicit place in the law allowing for activities listed in the above table, certain types of activities are specifically exempted from regulation. Listed here are some common categories of exemption to look for in relation to the sharing economy. I also consider this list to be a helpful framework for legislative advocacy, and believe we should lobby to create exemptions from regulation under many of the circumstances listed below:

1. **Exemptions for low-risk activities:** Cottage food laws, now passed in more than 30 states,[5] allow people to sell certain foods they produce at home, exempting the producers from the usual health and safety regulations imposed on food producers. Under cottage food laws, the class of foods that can be sold is typically known as "non-potentially hazardous" and consists of foods that

5. *See* Sustainable Economies Law Center, Summary of Cottage Food Laws in the U.S., http://www.theselc.org/wp-content/uploads/2011/05/Table-of-Cottage-Food-Laws-in-US1.pdf.

are not prone to developing harmful bacteria (such as breads, dried fruit, jams, and granola).

2. **Exemptions for small-scale and low-impact activities:** In many cities, it is illegal to operate most businesses out of the home, due to zoning laws that seek to preserve the quiet residential character of neighborhoods. However, cities do allow some small businesses to operate in a home, usually so long as there are no employees and so long as the impact on neighbors will be low. For example, in many places people can offer tutoring out of their home, but there will likely be a limit on the number of students who can be there at a time, and a limit on the hours of operation.
3. **Exemptions for infrequent activities:** California's health and safety code exempts from regulation certain private or charitable food sales activities if they take place no more than three times within a 90-day period.[6] In addition, many cities allow people to hold garage sales, but often no more than once or twice per month. I would argue that many activities of the sharing economy should be allowed so long as they happen infrequently. In the zoning context, for example, I would suggest that cities allow residents to host paying houseguests, so long as it happens no more than, say, 50 nights per year. This prevents neighbors from feeling the impact of strangers *constantly* coming and going from the property, but still allows the homeowner or renter to offset the cost of living by periodically hosting paid guests.
4. **Exemptions for activities designed for cost sharing:** Money will often change hands in a sharing economy, but not always for the purpose of earning a profit. If I pay my neighbor 20 cents per mile to borrow her car, the payment is really designed as a way for the two of us to share the costs of operating her car, not for my neighbor to earn a profit. In one limited piece of legislation, California has recognized the important distinction between cost-sharing activities and profit-earning activities.[7] The legislation essentially provides that car insurance companies may not terminate policies for customers that participate in certain car-

6. *See* Cal. Health & Safety Code § 113789.

7. For more information about California's AB 1871, see Janelle Orsi, *Car Sharing Laws for Everyone*, Shareable.net (Mar. 9, 2011), http://www.shareable.net/blog/car-sharing-laws-for-everyone.

sharing programs, as long as the car owner is not earning more money than it costs him/her to own the car.

5. **Exemptions where there is a small cooperative group:** California will not require a parent group that cooperatively provides child care for a group of children to obtain childcare provider licenses.[8] This law requires that no more than 12 children are involved, that no money is paid for the care, that parents rotate responsibilities, and that the care take place in one or more of the members' homes. Another section of the same code exempts from health and safety regulations food provided through "a cooperative arrangement wherein no permanent facilities are used for storing or handling food." It's hard to know what a "cooperative arrangement" means in the food context, except, perhaps with reference to the example of the cooperative arrangement among parents for childcare. In the food context, a cooperative arrangement could potentially mean a small group of people that buys or prepares food together, divvies it up in their own homes, and does not pay any one person for the service of providing food to others.

   Even where there are no explicit exemptions in statutes, I discuss below that many small-scale cooperative activities are naturally exempt by virtue of the fact that they are truly private and

8. Cal. Health & Safety Code § 1596.792(e) provides an exemption from licensure for

> Any cooperative arrangement between parents for the care of their children when no payment is involved and the arrangement meets all of the following conditions:
>
> (1) In a cooperative arrangement, parents shall combine their efforts so that each parent, or set of parents, rotates as the responsible caregiver with respect to all the children in the cooperative.
>
> (2) Any person caring for children shall be a parent, legal guardian, stepparent, grandparent, aunt, uncle, or adult sibling of at least one of the children in the cooperative.
>
> (3) There can be no payment of money or receipt of in-kind income in exchange for the provision of care. This does not prohibit in-kind contributions of snacks, games, toys, blankets for napping, pillows, and other materials parents deem appropriate for their children. It is not the intent of this paragraph to prohibit payment for outside activities, the amount of which may not exceed the actual cost of the activity.
>
> (4) No more than 12 children are receiving care in the same place at the same time.

non-commercial, or by virtue of the fact that there is no separation between producer and consumer.

6. **Exemptions where there is a direct or face-to-face transaction between producer and consumer:** When there is a direct or face-to-face transaction between producer and consumer, sometimes regulations are less burdensome. In many states, farmers that sell unprocessed products directly to the consumers are subject to fewer regulations than third-party retail food facilities. Presumably, in a direct transaction, the consumers are protected by the fact that they can communicate directly with the producers and ask questions necessary to protect themselves. In a direct transaction, the producer is also much more likely to act with integrity, as compared to a situation where the customers are faceless and unknown to the producer. Direct transactions need not always be face-to-face, as many goods are delivered to consumers by mail or other means. For example, community-supported agriculture (CSA) programs are often framed as direct sales, even if the produce is put into a box and delivered by a third party to a member's home.
7. **Exemptions where there are pre-existing relationships between producer and consumer:** In the context of securities laws, there are sometimes exemptions from regulation where someone receives a loan or investment from someone with whom he/she has a pre-existing relationship.[9] The idea here is that the investors, through the relationship, presumably have enough information to know what they are getting into, and the relationship also helps to ensure accountability between parties. Although I cannot think of a perfectly comparable example in the realm of consumer/producer relations, this concept could easily be extrapolated to allow producers to sell things to consumers with whom they have a sufficiently close pre-existing relationship. For the same reason that face-to-face sales transactions are sometimes exempted from regulation, as in the example above, I believe a transaction should be exempt when goods are shipped or delivered by third parties, as long as the producer and consumer know one another.

9. *See* Cal. Corp. Code § 25102(f).

8. **Exemptions where consumers have access to information necessary to protect themselves:** Many consumer protection regulations are aimed primarily at ensuring that consumers are informed of the risks involved in a purchase. Product labeling requirements are an example of this. If a business has high levels of transparency or consumer participation in production or decision making, consumers will generally be far better informed of the risks they assume in patronizing the business. For example, in a cooperative grocery run entirely by the work and decisions of members, there is arguably less urgent need for application of conventional health and safety standards because the members are fully informed of how food is handled.
9. **Exemptions for charitable activities:** Some health and safety codes will exempt from regulation food sales activities that are done for the purpose of raising charitable funds.
10. **Exemptions for private clubs:** Some health and safety laws will exempt from regulation food that is sold by or within the context of a private club. I have included information about the legal meaning of "private club" in the next section.
11. **Exemptions for activities in private home:** According to the California Health and Safety Code, a private home is not a "food facility" subject to health and safety regulation.[10]
12. **Regulations that are absent until harm arises:** Nuisance laws are an example of how our law can allow people to engage in a wide variety of activities, so long as those activities do not cause harm in the form of a nuisance. A nuisance law type of framework could be employed in other situations where a regulation is primarily aimed at preventing slow-developing or low-grade harm. "Harm," of course, is highly subjective, which means such laws could be unequally enforced. However, such a framework could work well when the goal is to enable a beneficial activity of a sort that manifests in a wide variety of ways. For example, many cities belabor the question of how to regulate the keeping of urban livestock; cities might set limits on numbers and species of animals per property, require specific size and placement of animal enclosures, and so on. However, given the difficulty of

10. *See* Cal. Health & Safety Code § 113789.

> regulating such a variable activity, some have argued that cities should simply use a nuisance law framework—allowing people to have animals unless and until they create a sound, smell, dust, or visual nuisance.[11] If a nuisance does develop, people who are impacted will have access to a complaint process.

As regulators are made more aware of collaborative consumption and collaborative production, some have been hospitable to carving out exemptions to allow people to engage in such activities without fear of crack-down. The recent widespread adoption of cottage food laws and urban agriculture laws is an example of how states and cities are creating a space for localized production.

By the same token, as regulators become aware of sharing economy activities, they have also taken the liberty to impose special taxes and increase regulation on such activities. For example, the City of San Francisco has declared that residents will be subject to a hotel tax if they host paying guests on a short-term basis,[12] and city officials have generally acknowledged that they want to find a way to impose special taxes on cottage-scale sharing activities where money changes hands.[13] This news was not pleasing to many of the people that use online services to rent out their rooms to visitors or that rent out their cars to strangers; however, it does bode well in one respect: At least San Francisco is going to let the sharing economy move forward, and is even doing so with enthusiasm. In March of 2012, the Mayor of San Francisco, Edwin Lee, broke new ground by announcing the creation of a "Sharing Economy

---

11. Mary Wood, Jeremy Pyle, Naomi Rowden & Katy Irwin, *Promoting the Urban Homestead: Reform of Local Land Use Laws to Allow Microlivestock on Residential Lots*, 37 Ecology Law Currents 68 (2010).

12. *See* Andrew S. Ross, *Airbnb's Argument Against Tax Doesn't Fly*, S.F. Chronicle, Apr. 6, 2012; John Coté, *S.F. Eyes Tax on Cottage Services Offered Online*, S.F. Chronicle, Apr. 8, 2012.

13. Note that income generated through sharing activities will often be subject to income tax, regardless of the imposition of other special taxes. For example, people do receive 1099-MISC forms after they participate in peer-to-peer carsharing programs and make their cars available for strangers to rent. This likely creates an interesting dilemma for the car owner: Can they file a Schedule C and deduct any expenses of car ownership as a business expense? Had the car owner instead chosen to share ownership of a car with a neighbor and split the costs, the neighbor's payments would not be considered income to the co-owner; however, in the peer-to-peer rental situation, a car owner has to pay taxes on the payments received from people using the car.

Working Group" for the city,[14] which will, among other things, work to create a legal space for sharing in the city.

Part 4: Navigating Out of Gray Areas

Until laws change and make more *explicit* categories of regulatory exemption for sharing economy activities, many activities are nevertheless *implicitly* exempt, by virtue of being truly private and non-commercial, or by virtue of the fact that there is no separation between producer and consumer. In cases where clients fall into gray areas, sharing economy lawyers can draw from the tools and arguments below to help clients move to safer parts of the gray areas, or to assert that the nature of the activity or relationship is such that regulations truly do not apply.

Below, I will address four approaches to arguing that regulations do not apply to sharing activities. These are

a. When there is no separation between consumer and producer;
b. When an economic activity is private;
c. When an economic activity is non-commercial; and
d. In the context of zoning, when an economic activity is an "accessory use."

When the Consumer, by Means of Collaborative Agreements, IS the Producer[15]

It's a fun irony that Prohibition-era "criminals"[16] may have laid important legal groundwork for collaborative production in the sharing economy. During Prohibition, individuals who collaborated in the production of liquor were often found guilty of "constructive possession" of that liquor, even when the production took place at someone else's house and was operated on a day-to-day basis by someone else. Anyone exercising control and dominion over a liquor production operation was

14. Neal Gorenflo, *San Francisco Announces Sharing Economy Working Group*, Shareable.net (Mar. 27, 2012), http://www.shareable.net/blog/breaking-san-francisco-announces-sharing-economy-working-group.

15. Thank you to SELC Volunteer Researcher Nicole Bartolomucci for her amazing research into the issues of milk production and "possession."

16. *See* People v. Helt, 100 Cal. App. 279 (1929); People v. Stine, 110 Cal. App. 156 (1930).

HEALTH CARE SHARING AND HEALTH CARE REFORM[1]

The health care industry is highly regulated, and it's interesting to consider the role of the sharing economy in such a regulated field. Sharing and health naturally go together. Human beings can provide for one another's health in a variety of ways—through conventional medicine, healing practices of all kinds, better nourishment, fitness programs, preventative care, caring relationships, and so on. Care is often more effective when provided in a community context, by and among people who know each other, as opposed to by enormous systems administered via many layers of administration and bureaucracy.

The Patient Protection and Affordable Care Act[2] is set to take effect in 2014 and essentially mandates that every individual purchase health insurance. Much of the care required to be purchased under the Act will be provided through conventional channels and dominant health care providers, and will often not include options that cover complementary, alternative, community-based, holistic, or nature-based health care practices. Individuals seeking to purchase such non-conventional health care may, as a result, be forced to shoulder the cost of *two* systems of care—the mandatory conventional health care and their alternative care of choice. In order to ensure the adequacy of choices of coverage under the Act's requirements, communities may wish to begin forming cooperatives for the provision of services more tailored to communities' needs and preferences.

It's significant to note that the Act provides two relevant exemptions to mandatory coverage, including a "religious conscience exemption,"[3] and membership in a pre-existing "health care sharing ministry," which is a 501(c)(3) tax-exempt nonprofit, "members of which share a common set of ethical or religious beliefs and share medical expenses among members in accordance with those

---

1. I am grateful to change agent and lawyer Cheryl Connor for sharing with me her insights into the role of community-organized health care under the Patient Protection and Affordable Care Act.

2. Patient Protection and Affordable Care Act, H.R. 3590, 111th Cong. (2009–2010), http://www.govtrack.us/congress/bills/111/hr3590/text.

3. Patient Protection and Affordable Care Act § 1500A.

beliefs."[4] It appears from the definition (included in a footnote here) that the Act gives this exemption only to health care–sharing ministries in existence prior to 1999, which seems unfortunate and unfair. It would be worth additional inquiry and advocacy to carve out an exemption for new groups to form "ministries"—whether based on religious creed or simply a common set of ethics—to provide for one another's health needs.

4. Patient Protection and Affordable Care Act §§ 1411(d)(5), 1500A(d)(B)(ii), defining Health Care Sharing Ministry as follows:

> The term "health care sharing ministry" means an organization—
>
> (I) which is described in section 501(c)(3) and is exempt from taxation under section 501(a),
>
> (II) members of which share a common set of ethical or religious beliefs and share medical expenses among members in accordance with those beliefs and without regard to the State in which a member resides or is employed,
>
> (III) members of which retain membership even after they develop a medical condition,
>
> (IV) which (or a predecessor of which) has been in existence at all times since December 31, 1999, and medical expenses of its members have been shared continuously and without interruption since at least December 31, 1999, and
>
> (V) which conducts an annual audit which is performed by an independent certified public accounting firm in accordance with generally accepted accounting principles and which is made available to the public upon request.

found to be in possession of it, even when operation was delegated to certain members of the group.

We can derive an important concept from these cases and from the innumerable other cases[17] that address the concept of possession: if a consumer is in possession of a good while it is being produced, there really is no change of hands of that good, and therefore no producer/consumer relationship. In that respect, the many laws that are designed to protect consumers from producers may not apply to a group of people that has made an agreement to produce things for themselves in a truly cooperative way.

Let's use milk as an example. If you own a cow, the law generally says that you cannot even give that cow's milk away to a neighbor, unless the

17. *See, e.g.*, People v. Showers, 68 Cal. 2d 639 (1968); People v. Barnes, 57 Cal. App. 4th 552 (1997); Armstrong v. Superior Court, 217 Cal. App. 3d 535 (1990).

milk has been certified. Milk is a rare example where even private and non-commercial sharing is illegal. This is a difficult situation because cows produce a lot of milk, and sharing is simply a smart and practical way to manage extra milk. It generally costs thousands or even tens of thousands of dollars to certify a facility that produces milk. It entails using highly specialized equipment, obtaining expensive licenses, and undergoing expensive inspections. The burden of certification has essentially stamped out the feasibility of micro-dairy operations.

Laws specifically state that it is illegal to sell, buy, *deliver*, *give away*, or knowingly *receive* milk that has not been certified.[18] The United States Department of Agriculture (USDA) and state departments of agriculture have cracked down heavily on uncertified milk operations.[19] To get access to milk produced locally and on a small scale, many people have turned to "cowpooling" and "herdsharing" as solutions. They argue that a group of people that shares ownership of a cow or a herd of cows should be allowed to drink the milk from those cows. To prove ownership, groups even execute documents granting people partial title to animals. Unfortunately, ownership alone may not help groups exempt themselves from the application of milk certification requirements. The reason for this is that it's possible to *own* something without actually *possessing* it, as in the example of a landowner who leases property to tenants—the tenants are considered to be in possession of the property. If you are not in possession of something, the only way to get it in your hands is by delivery and receipt.

Even though it's illegal to deliver, give, or receive uncertified milk, it is not illegal to *possess* and *consume* uncertified milk. Furthermore, it is impossible to *receive* something if you have been in possession of it all along. This is where the Prohibition-era cases are helpful, yet ironic. Defendants during Prohibition were let off the hook if they argued that they were *not* in possession of a liquor production operation. A group of "cowpoolers," if prosecuted for delivery and receipt of milk, should be let off the hook if they establish that they *are* in possession of their own milk production operation.

---

18. *See, e.g.*, Cal. Food & Agric. Code § 32901.

19. For more information about the crack-down on milk producers, see the Farm-to-Consumer Legal Defense Fund, http://www.farmtoconsumer.org/.

So the question is: what is required to legally establish possession? Physical possession usually means that the item in question is on or near a person, and under that person's knowing control. "Constructive possession," however, can be established when the item in question is nowhere near the person. The primary element of constructive possession is control, and constructive possession can be found when a person "maintained some control *or right to control* over contraband [or other items] in the physical possession of another."[20] Courts will look at the "totality of the circumstances," examining the "degree of intentional direction over"[21] the activity or item in question, considering whether the item was "immediately and exclusively accessible to" the people in question.[22]

This concept could potentially apply to negate the existence of producer/consumer relationships in many of the cooperative activities listed in the table in Part 2 of this chapter. In the case of laws that regulate the provision and transfer of goods and services, one can simply argue that no transfer has taken place, so long as cooperative members are truly in control of the operation. The result is that the more cooperative and participatory a group is, and the more involved each individual is in the work and decision-making of the group, and the more power each person has to bring or block a proposal of the group, then the more likely it is a group can establish that each individual is in possession of the products in question.

It is likely that larger groups will have a more difficult time making this argument, but even large groups could conceivably establish governance systems that ensure that each member has a powerful voice in decisions and a strong hand in activities of the group. I used to be part of a food cooperative in Emeryville, California, that closed down, due, in part, to difficulties the co-op had with getting health permits for the warehouse it occupied. Although the cooperative was large (around 200 active members at any given time), I think it would have been worth making an argument to the local health department that the cooperative was essentially a large group of people purchasing bulk foods together.

20. People v. Rogers, 5 Cal. 3d 129, 134 (1971).
21. Armstrong v. Superior Court, 217 Cal. App. 3d 535, 539 (1990).
22. People v. Showers, 68 Cal. 2d 639, 643–44 (1968).

If we could have established that individual members were in collective possession of groceries when they were delivered to the warehouse, then we could perhaps have avoided the necessity of certifying the warehouse as a retail food facility. Unfortunately, I wasn't equipped with such an argument at the time, and it's a tragedy that the health and safety requirements contributed to the dissolution of a wonderful community.

However, note that if a group of people forms a corporation, such as a cooperative corporation, to carry out collaborative production activities, it may be harder to argue that producer and consumer are one and the same. In the food cooperative example, the corporation purchased large quantities of food, and members purchased that food from the corporation. Even if members are all owners of the cooperative and participate in its management, there's a possibility that the members would be considered "customers" of the corporation (which is, after all, a "person" separate from its owners and members).

Production and Exchange in a Private Context

In situations where it's not possible to argue that the producer and consumer are one and the same, another argument to make is that an activity should be unregulated because it takes place in a private context. Many regulations are designed to apply only to public activities, and some regulations even specifically exempt activities in "private homes" and private activities that take place outside of homes, such in the context of "private clubs."

The Sharing Economy and Private Association

When people choose to associate with and provide for one another in highly personal contexts, their ability to do so is often protected by the U.S. Constitution, which grants citizens a right to "freedom of association." The types of regulations imposed on commercial businesses generally do not extend their reach into our private homes and more intimate associations; if they did, such regulations would potentially interfere with our relationships. Many laws, implicitly or explicitly, simply do not apply to economic provision within the context of families.

For many people, the sharing economy means adopting a much broader notion of "family," or, to put it in a less "touchy-feely" way, a more expansive list of people with whom we have mutually supportive relationships. Many ways we provide for one another simulate provisioning within a private family. In a cohousing community, members of 30 neighboring households may regularly share meals, share household goods, share cars, and engage in many collective activities. Presumably, or preferably anyway, laws will not interfere to tell us that we may not make a large pot of soup for our family, or even for our 30 neighbors. Laws do, however, sometimes prevent people without permits from making large pots of soups for strangers.[23] As usual, we don't know exactly where the legal line is drawn, but we can get clues from the courts.

In *Roberts v. United States Jaycees*,[24] the U.S. Supreme Court addressed the question of whether the "private" organization in question could exclude women. The Court ultimately concluded that members of the organization lacked the necessary characteristics of private relationships that might otherwise afford them the constitutional protection and freedom from interference by the state. Although the Court did not define a clear line between private and public, the Court described some of the factors relevant to this determination and also acknowledged that there is a "broad range of human relationships" that would fall into a gray area:

> Family relationships, by their nature, involve deep attachments and commitments to the necessarily few other individuals with whom one shares not only a special community of thoughts, experiences, and beliefs but also distinctively personal aspects of one's life. Among other things, therefore, they are distinguished by such attributes as relative smallness, a high degree of selectivity in decisions to begin and maintain the affiliation, and seclusion from others in critical aspects of the relationship. As a general matter, only relationships with these sorts of qualities are likely to reflect the considerations that have led to an understanding of freedom of association as an intrinsic element of personal liberty. Conversely, an association lacking these qualities—such as a large business enterprise—seems remote from the concerns giving rise to this constitutional protection. Accordingly, the Constitution undoubtedly imposes constraints on the State's

23. *See generally* Nat'l Coalition for the Homeless & Nat'l Law Center on Homelessness & Poverty, A Place at the Table: Prohibitions on Sharing Food with People Experiencing Homelessness (July 2010), http://www.nlchp.org/content/pubs/A_Place_at_the_Table.pdf.

24. Roberts v. U.S. Jaycees, 468 U.S. 609, 619–20 (1984).

> power to control the selection of one's spouse that would not apply to regulations affecting the choice of one's fellow employees. Compare *Loving v. Virginia*, 388 U.S. 1, 12 (1967), with *Railway Mail Assn. v. Corsi*, 326 U.S. 88, 93–94 (1945).
>
> Between these poles, of course, lies a broad range of human relationships that may make greater or lesser claims to constitutional protection from particular incursions by the State. Determining the limits of state authority over an individual's freedom to enter into a particular association therefore unavoidably entails a careful assessment of where that relationship's objective characteristics locate it on a spectrum from the most intimate to the most attenuated of personal attachments. See generally *Runyon v. McCrary*, 427 U.S. 160, 187–189 (1976) (POWELL, J., concurring). We need not mark the potentially significant points on this terrain with any precision. We note only that factors that may be relevant include size, purpose, policies, selectivity, congeniality, and other characteristics that in a particular case may be pertinent.

Note that every category of regulation will apply differently, and some regulations reach more deeply into our private lives than others. The applicability of a regulation will depend, in part, on its purpose. When a regulation is designed to remedy a broad or serious social ill, courts are generally more willing to let such regulations interfere with our freedom to choose the nature and terms of our associations.

What Is a Private Club?[25]

"Private club" may sometimes act as a magic password to the sharing economy, for legal purposes, anyway. At first, it might conjure up images of an exclusive place where people smoke cigars. But, to the extent that private clubs are exempt from burdensome legal regulations normally applied to public activities, such exemptions will also benefit groups of people that come together for their own mutual benefit, for collaboration, and for sharing.

We can derive guidance from a handful of cases that examine the issue in the context of civil rights laws, the Americans with Disabilities Act (ADA), smoking laws, and employment laws. The cases that provide

---

25. Thank you to Sustainable Economies Law Center 2011 summer Legal Intern Kelly Densmore for her extensive research into case law exploring the definition of "private club." In addition, some of the material in this section has been adapted from Janelle Orsi & Kelly Densmore, *The Shareable Food Movement Meets the Law*, Shareable.net (July 1, 2011).

the strongest guidance also lack certain charm—most of the time they involve private clubs that want to exclude women, gays, people of color, or people with disabilities. Nevertheless, these cases are helpful, in that they show us how courts make the determination of whether a group is sufficiently private to claim an exemption from regulation.

The cases vary, but, generally, courts have weighed a handful of factors to decide whether a club is truly private.[26] Factors that courts tend to weigh include

- Whether the club applies meaningful selection criteria to the admission of new members,
- The size of the membership,
- The degree of member control of club operations,
- Whether substantial membership fees are charged,
- Whether the entity is operated on a nonprofit basis,
- Whether members know each other and whether there is personal interaction among members,
- Whether the primary purpose served by the club is social or business,
- The extent to which the facilities are open to the public,
- The extent to which the club advertises to the public and/or publicly solicits new members,
- The degree to which club facilities are available for use by non-members,
- The degree of public funding, and
- Whether the club was created specifically to avoid compliance with the Civil Rights Act or other laws.

---

26. *See, e.g.*, City of Wausau v. Jusufi, 315 Wis. 2d 780 (2008); Nicholls v. Holiday Panay Marina, L.P., 173 Cal. App. 4th 966 (2009); Tillman v. Wheaton-Haven Recreation Ass'n, Inc., 410 U.S. 431 (1973); EEOC v. Chi. Club, 86 F.3d 1423 (7th Cir. 1996); Moose Lodge No. 107 v. Irvis, 407 U.S. 163 (1972); Daniel v. Paul, 395 U.S. 298 (1969); Hurley v. Irish-American Gay, Lesbian, Bisexual Group of Bos., 515 U.S. 557 (1995); Nesmith v. Young Men's Christian Ass'n of Raleigh, N.C., 397 F.2d 96 (4th Cir. 1968); Warfield v. Peninsula Golf & Country Club, 10 Cal. 4th 594 (1995); Nat'l Org. for Women, Essex Cnty. Chapter v. Little League Baseball, Inc., 127 N.J. Super. 522 (1974); Isbister v. Boys' Club of Santa Cruz, 707 P.2d 212 (Cal. 1985); Martin v. PGA Tour, Inc., 204 F.3d 994 (9th Cir. 2000); Found. for Indep. Living, Inc. v. Cabell-Huntington Bd. of Health, 214 W. Va. 818 (2003); Players, Inc. v. City of New York, 371 F. Supp. 2d 522 (S.D.N.Y. 2005). *See also* Americans with Disabilities Act of 1990, § 307, 42 U.S.C. § 12187.

Although no single factor is controlling when determining whether a club is private, most courts have considered the selectivity of the membership to be of great importance. Preferably, private clubs will have meaningful criteria on which people are chosen to be accepted as members, rather than allowing anyone to join at any time. Here are some cases that illustrate how courts look at the issue.

In *Nicholls v. Holiday Panay Marina*,[27] a tenant brought an ADA lawsuit against a marina for not making the marina accessible to wheelchairs. The marina argued that the facilities were "private," since only member tenants could enter and must use a key card to access docks and boats. The court ruled that, although the marina was restricted only to members, it was not private, since it provides leases on a first-come, first-served basis to the general public, without setting any member selection criteria.

In *City of Wausau v. Jusufi*,[28] the operator of the Red Apple Social Club restaurant was found to have violated a ban on smoking. Red Apple's operator asserted that the restaurant was a private club, pointing to the fact that only members could patronize the restaurant and members must pay a one-time membership fee of one dollar. The court ruled that Red Apple was not private because the small one-time fee was not a sufficient barrier to patronizing the club. Another factor that weighed against the "club" was that members exercised very little control over the restaurant. The court warned that, without meaningful membership criteria and member involvement, "[r]estaurants could create the illusion of private clubs by creating memberships with no meaningful membership criteria. The memberships would essentially be shams, with members having no control over, or stake in, the restaurant's operations."

In the next example, the court argued, fervently, to uphold a group's private club status: In *Equal Employment Opportunity Commission v. The Chicago Club*,[29] the court ruled that the social/recreational club in question was, indeed, private, and therefore exempt from certain employment reporting requirements because

27. Nicholls v. Holiday Panay Marina, L.P., 173 Cal. App. 4th 966 (2009).
28. City of Wausau v. Jusufi, 315 Wis. 2d 780 (2008).
29. EEOC v. Chi. Club, 86 F.3d 1423 (1996).

- Club candidates go through an extensive screening process that involves the approval of the board as well as interaction between the candidate and club members;
- Members elect their own board of directors, which oversees the club's operations and appoints a general manager; and
- The club was not open to the public, there is a limited use of facilities by non-members, and guests must be invited to the club by a member.

Of particular note in this case, the court took no issue with the fact that the club was rather large: 1,247 members, and even stated that size of an organization is not necessarily "probative of its privateness."

Example of Private Economic Activity

Given the factors that courts have considered in the private club context, it's interesting to contemplate what kinds of economic activities could be considered private and therefore exempt from certain regulations. Even where money changes hands within a group, I would argue that certain exchanges and collective provisioning activities should be exempt from certain commercial regulations.

For example, imagine that you and ten of your close friends jointly concoct a plan for a "Quiche Café," which is essentially a weekly dinner party at your house. You buy the ingredients and make the quiche. Your ten friends, the core members of the Café, bring the drinks and plan fun activities. Most importantly, everyone helps out with the dishes. Each core member of Quiche Café is encouraged to bring a friend or two, so each dinner is attended by an average of 25 people. Everyone chips in around $8, even though you've calculated the per-person cost of ingredients to be around $4. Everyone feels that any surplus could be seen as a modest stipend for you or your thank-you gift for hosting.

Is Quiche Cafe private enough to avoid health and safety regulation? Based on the guidelines gleaned from the court decisions, I would argue that that it is. Participation is restricted to the original ten friends and the friends that they personally invite. Quiche Café is not advertised and is not open to the public. The members jointly manage the club for their own benefit. Although the quiche chef is making a small stipend, the core purpose of the activity is to provide social and edible sustenance to friends.

Note that tax and zoning are separate issues. The chef will most likely owe taxes on any income generated. In addition, a neighbor could still complain to the local planning department about the operation of a social club or business in violation of the residential zoning of the neighborhood. As discussed below, arguing that you are a private dining club might not help here, but you could argue that this is a dinner party, which is generally accepted as a residential use of a home.

Non-Commercial Production and Exchange

Even when a group of people would fail to argue that their activity is private, and even when they would fail to argue that the producer and consumer are one and the same, it may still be possible to argue that an activity is exempt from regulation because it is not commercial.

Regulators tend to perk up anytime they see money move. But money, in many ways, is just a glorified way to track people's contributions to a group or to society. As discussed below, the exchange of money does not necessarily signify a commercial activity, nor does the absence of money signify the absence of a commercial activity. When no money changes hands, it's usually easiest to argue that something is not commercial, as the economic benefits exchanged tend to be less tangible or measurable. Yet, the distinction between monetary and non-monetary exchanges is an artificial one, and I believe that a *commercial* exchange can take place in either case. Likewise, when movement of money is solely designed for the purposes of *sharing costs*, such as when one person pays an electrical bill and gets reimbursed for half the bill by her housemate, there is arguably no commercial exchange.

Non-Commercial Economic Benefits

Even when people provide and receive material economic benefits, they will not necessarily be regulated as commercial enterprises. People who use Couchsurfing.org, to "participate in creating a better world, one couch at a time," are not doing so for commercial purposes, and they are highly unlikely to be regulated as hotels. A member might host another member—a complete stranger—at his/her home, with no expectation of compensation. There is a spirit of generosity and adventure that drives literally millions of people to take part in this network of no-cost home stays.

Even though it may lack a *commercial* spirit or motivation, there is still an element of *economic* exchange, in that people are giving and receiving something of material value. There is a strong culture of reciprocity among Couchsurfers—a person that travels is expected to return home and host others. The peer-rating system on Couchsurfing .org becomes a currency of sorts, as people that host others gain a stronger reputation and are more likely to be hosted when they travel. To the extent that Couchsurfing.org enables people to travel inexpensively, there is certainly a material economic benefit. Yet, that I know of, no city planning department, health department, or regulator of the hotel industry has tried to impose regulations on Couchsurfing.

By contrast, when people use a service such as airbnb.com to host travelers *for money*, regulators are far more likely to step in and impose regulations and taxes.[30] Some might argue that the distinction between Couchsurfing and Airbnb is fictitious because both involve elements of economic exchange. However, there is, I would argue, a key distinction: even though it confers economic benefits, exchange in the Couchsurfing context is, nevertheless, not commercial.

What makes something commercial? This question could take vast amounts of research to answer, and the definition of commercial will vary depending on the area of regulation or body of law. In law school Constitutional Law classes, we learned that "commerce" is another word for "pretty much everything,"[31] as far as determining the scope of Congress's authority to regulate an incredibly broad range of activities. Fortunately, when it comes to determining the application of various categories of commercial regulation, "commerce" is likely to be defined much more narrowly. Although definitions will vary, I have derived key insight into the issue from the IRS in looking at how they decide the difference between taxable income and gifts/casual exchange.[32] Chapter 5 discusses this matter in greater detail. I would argue that a commercial transaction generally involves

---

30. *See* Janelle Orsi, *Airbnb Debacle Uncovers Collaborative Consumption's Legal Paradox*, Shareable.net (Aug. 10, 2011).

31. *See* Robert G. Natelson, *The Legal Meaning of "Commerce" in the Commerce Clause*, 80 St. John's L. Rev. 789, 793 ("[I]t would seem that 'commerce[ ]' . . . is used [...] to mean the whole economy, the whole system of exchange, the whole congeries of interrelated gainful activities, which the American nation is to carry on") (quoting William Winslow Crosskey, Politics and the Constitution in the History of the United States 95 (1953)).

32. *See* I.R.S. Priv. Ltr. Rul. 96-08-009 (Feb. 23, 1996).

- **A bargained-for exchange:** When people bargain, they are generally trying to get something of equal value to or greater value than what they give. When an exchange is not bargained for, people give or receive with much less regard to measuring value and evening the score. Therefore, to varying degrees, they may give with generosity, and may receive with gratitude.
- **A contractual right to payment:** Hosts that use Airbnb have a contractual right to be paid by people that stay with them. By contrast, hosts that use Couchsurfing have no contractual right to "payment"; in other words, they have no contractual right to stay at anyone else's home. A Couchsufing host could conceivably host many people and never travel and stay with someone else. Or they could travel extensively and never host a single person.

Given the above considerations, it is also, of course, entirely possible that commercial exchanges can occur in the absence of money. If people replaced dollars with clam shells, and if they bargained for exchanges and made agreements for payment in clams, this would, nevertheless, be commercial activity.

Cost-Sharing versus Commerce

Even when money does change hands, there are many situations where activities are, nevertheless, not commercial. I know of a group of about 20 carpoolers who gather in a park 'n ride lot every morning and consolidate themselves into four or five cars for their commute to University of California, Berkeley. One member of the group created tokens using a metal stamping machine to imprint a bunch of metal washers. Each time someone is a passenger, he/she "pays" the driver with one token. If the driver collects four tokens, he/she will be able to use the tokens to be a passenger on four other days.

The exchange of tokens, instead of dollars, prevents any one person from earning a profit in the system, and it is designed to ensure equal cost sharing. This group is highly unlikely to be subject to the same regulations applied to taxis and shuttles. The exchange of rides is not for commercial purpose; rather, it is for *cost-sharing* purposes. This distinction is key to the sharing economy, and it also means that *even when dollars do change hands*, there is no commercial transaction, so long as the exchange is truly for *cost sharing* and not for profit. The same carpooling group could use dollars instead of tokens, so long as the exchange of dollars is monitored or designed to ensure that no one is profiting, but that the *actual costs* of driving are being shared.

Zoning and the Sharing Economy

The re-localization of commerce and production in the sharing economy brings up interesting considerations related to zoning. Twentieth-century zoning laws have separated home life from work life by dividing cities into separate residential, commercial, industrial, and agricultural zones. We have done this to prevent the impacts of *large*-scale agriculture, *large*-scale industry, and *large* commercial activities from causing a nuisance and encroaching on our quiet home lives. But this means our entire zoning framework has been built on the assumption that things tend to happen on a *large* scale, and this framework now makes it difficult to engage in small-scale, localized production, such as urban agriculture and cottage industries. Simply put, land use laws have not created an ideal space for small, sustainable, localized livelihoods.

Zoning serves a distinct set of purposes from many of the regulations discussed in this chapter. The other regulations are generally designed to protect individual consumers or professionals, whereas zoning is designed to protect resources and communities. In that respect, what matters is not whether an activity has the potential to harm an individual, but whether the activity is likely to generate an undesirable atmosphere or nuisance. For ease of categorization, many planning codes prohibit most or all commercial, industrial, or agricultural activities in residential neighborhoods, under the assumption that the impact will *likely* be undesirable. This blanket prohibition on certain categories of activities can also stamp out necessary and desirable sharing activities. When our sharing activities begin to creep into the gray areas and move toward the commercial and public ends of the spectrum, it's quite possible that zoning regulations could block the activities. For example, many zoning codes prohibit the operation of hotels in most residential neighborhoods; the definition of hotel often is so broad that it includes *any* situation where a person pays to stay in another person's home for fewer than 30 days.

However, given the underlying goals of zoning, what matters is not *whether* an activity is commercial, but the *actual impact* of the activity. In coming years, it's important for citizens all over the country to begin lobbying local governments to change zoning laws and to create a more friendly space for sharing economies. This will often involve creating exemptions for activities that meet some of the criteria listed in Part 3 of this chapter. For a much longer list of policy recommendations, see my 20-part article series on Shareable.net entitled "Policies for a Shareable City."[33]

Sharing as an "Accessory Use"[34]

Even without changing the laws, there's room to argue that we have a *right* to share in our residential neighborhoods. "Accessory use" is a term that we should all get comfortable with, since it's a window to arguing that we have a protected right to engage in certain sharing activities. "Accessory use" is a zoning term that, in the residential context, refers to the ways that we customarily and incidentally make use of our homes. For example, there is rarely anything in our zoning ordinances that explicitly allows us to have visitors, but our right to do so is protected by the fact that such an activity is a *customary* use of our home. Sharing, under many circumstances, is an accessory use. Having a dinner party, having a houseguest, lending a tool to your neighbor—these are natural and *customary* things we all do as part of making a home.

In addition to being customary, an accessory use must be *incidental* to the primary use of the property as a home. The activity of receiving visitors should never become so frequent or large in scale that it overtakes the primary residential use. Furthermore, having visitors must be *related* to one's own residential use of the property. Many court cases examine what is or is not related, incidental, customary, and so on. For example, in a 1958 New York case, *Facci v. City of Schenectady*,[35] a homeowner was denied the ability to park a commercial vehicle at his house since parking the vehicle was not related to his residential use of the property. At the same time, it might have been fine for that vehicle to park there if the driver was there for a social visit, which *is* related to the residential use. That's just one example of the way courts think about the issue.

---

33. The Policies for a Shareable City article series is available at http://www.shareable.net/blog/policies-for-a-shareable-city#index.

34. This short section has been adapted from Orsi, *supra* note 30.

35. Facci v. City of Schenectady, 13 Misc. 2d 247 (Sup. Ct. Schenectady Cnty., NY 1958).

Having social guests is *related* to a resident's enjoyment of the home. But what about having a series of total strangers pay to rent your room—is that an accessory use? I have to imagine that the sharing movement will be aided, somewhat, by the fact that definitions of accessory use developed during times when people really did share a lot more. After all, where DID travelers stay in the days before hotels? They often stayed with complete strangers, and usually offered *some* form of compensation. It would be worthwhile to comb through accessory use cases to determine how various sharing activities fit in to courts' and planning departments' interpretations of accessory use.

The Moral to This Story

Enthusiasts of the sharing economy get starry-eyed when they talk about the revolutionary potential for centralized systems and web-based tools to transform the way we produce and consume. They see a world where conventional hotels and restaurants are given a run for their money by home-based peer-to-peer hotels and restaurants. They see a world where people share, borrow, and "swap-trade" all kinds of goods and services online. They see a world where peer-to-peer car rental services replace car ownership for many people. I admit, the sharing economy is mind blowing and its potential to transform commerce is amazing. I am also delighted to see that the transformation is fast on its way.

At the same, the lawyer in me hears all this and thinks: "Oh boy...." What many enthusiasts will emphasize is that the sharing economy allows people to "make money by sharing with total strangers!"[36] That statement contains two things likely to trigger regulation: making money and strangers. To add one more layer of complication: when sharing or exchange is facilitated by third-party services, this often removes the direct nature of the exchange and triggers heighted levels of regulation. The fact that such activities are highly regulated does not mean that we shouldn't do them; it simply means they will be difficult and sometimes risky, which is a barrier to scaling the movement.

The sharing economy needs to scale up quickly, for obvious reasons: ice caps are melting and economies are crumbling around the globe. Scaling up could happen in at least a couple different ways: it could mean that enormous numbers of people begin using large and

36. *See* Orsi, *supra* note 30.

centralized systems for collaborative consumption and production, and it could mean that people everywhere create an infinite number of small and dispersed sharing arrangements. I advocate for both approaches, and particularly for the second. The latter will encounter fewer barriers, and it is also, technically speaking, a glorious way to build a society.

As discussed above, regulations are far less likely to apply when sharing (1) occurs among friends, neighbors, and acquaintances; (2) is accomplished by direct and face-to-face transactions; (3) involves groups of people working together and making decisions together; (4) is not aimed at making a profit, but rather at sharing costs; (5) is casual, not contractual; and (6) is driven, at least in part, by generosity. It is not necessary for all of these characteristics to be present, but these qualities do define the circumstances under which we are likely to be free to share. Put simply, if kindness, cooperation, and the bonds of our relationships drive our economic activity, almost anything is possible. More importantly, sharing economy lawyers will have the pleasure of telling their clients: "Your plan sounds wonderful! Go for it!"

HERE COMES THE SUN: HARNESSING SOLAR POWER IN OUR COMMUNITIES

By Linda Barrera, Volunteer Research Attorney, Sustainable Economies Law Center

Linda Barrera is a passionate advocate for solar power, including distributed generation. She has navigated the realm of environmental law and policy and utilities regulations through her past work for the California Public Utilities Commission and various nonprofit organizations. Linda has also worked on the installation of solar power systems in Nicaragua and Northern California.

Increasing energy costs and an unsustainable reliance on fossil fuels are prompting people to consider community-based renewable sources of energy to reduce their electric bills and their carbon footprint. While the cost of a rooftop solar photovoltaic (PV) system often pays for itself over the long run, the up-front investment necessary to purchase solar panels remains cost prohibitive for most households. For those seeking less expensive options to produce and use renewable energy, the good news is that an increasing number of people and communities are coming together in a variety of ways to gain access to solar energy at a more affordable cost. Some of these models and related legal considerations will be examined here.

Community Solar Projects

One common trend is that communities are beginning to develop distributed solar electric facilities, known as community solar projects.[1] A community solar project is a solar energy system (generally a PV system of less than 2 megawatts)[2] that provides power to multiple community members who live in proximity to the solar project. Organizing a community solar project allows community members to share the costs and benefits of ownership from the electricity generated by a single solar energy system. In addition, community solar provides renters and other community members who are unable to install a PV system on their own property access to cost-effective models for investing in a clean, renewable source of energy.

Community solar projects are much smaller than the solar projects developed by large electric utilities and private companies, and generally have only a single connection to the local electric utility's distribution grid. Unlike the centralized system needed to supply power from large-scale power plants that require an extensive network of transmission and distribution lines, community solar projects lend themselves to a decentralized system of power generation and ownership. This decentralized approach to generating solar power in a community is an excellent way to provide clean energy locally and efficiently. From a sharing economy law perspective, community solar is also important because income from the community solar project is more likely to be kept in the community.

---

1. Community solar is one form of distributed generation, which is a decentralized approach to generating electric power.

2. A megawatt (MW) is a standard measure of electrical power plant generating capacity equal to 1,000 kilowatts. A kilowatt is a standard unit of electrical power equal to 1,000 watts. A common unit of measuring energy is a kilowatt-hour (kWh), which is a unit of energy equal to 1,000 watts used over the course of an hour. One kWh is enough energy to run a 100 watt light bulb for 10 hours.

Because community solar projects are small power production facilities, federal law generally exempts them from the Federal Power Act[3] and certain state regulations governing the rates of electric utilities and the financial and organizational regulation of electric utilities.[4] This means that an entity created by project organizers to develop a community solar project and share the electricity generated by the project is not considered an "electric utility," and is therefore not subject to the oversight of federal and state regulatory authorities which govern electric utilities. However, in order to link the community solar project to the grid, project organizers must make sure they comply with notice requirements necessary to arrange interconnection agreements with their local utility.[5]

If you are interested in helping your community organize a community solar project, your first step should be to contact the local utility to investigate options for installing a community solar energy system. The following are two models people are using to organize and participate in community solar projects:

- **Utility-sponsored model:** Several communities are participating in community solar projects sponsored by publicly owned utilities such as municipal utilities[6] and not-for-profit

3. *See* Federal Power Act as amended, 16 U.S.C. §§ 792 *et seq.*

4. *See* 18 C.F.R. §§ 292.601, 292.602. Federal law considers renewable energy (hydro, wind, and solar) facilities that are 80 MW and smaller to be "qualified facilities." To be considered a qualified facility, a small power producer's primary source of energy must be renewable and must meet all of the requirements of 18 C.F.R. §§ 292.203(a), 292.203(c), and 292.204 for size and fuel use, and be certified as a qualifying facility pursuant to 18 C.F.R. § 292.207. Federal law exempts renewable energy facilities that are 1 MW and smaller from the need to file a form (Form No. 556) with the Federal Energy Regulatory Commission (FERC) in order to certify the facility as a "qualified facility." *See* Revisions to Form, Procedures, and Criteria for Certification of Qualifying Facility Status for a Small Power Production or Cogeneration Facility, Order No. 732, 130 FERC ¶ 61,214 (2010).

5. A small power production facility has the right to sell energy to a utility if the purchasing utility has not been relieved from its qualified facility purchase obligation. *See* 18 C.F.R. §§ 304, 309–311. However, facilities with a net production capacity of 500 kW or greater are required to provide notification of their qualified facility status to the local utility to which they connect. *See* 18 C.F.R. § 292.207(c)(2).

6. Municipal utilities' service areas may include territories outside of city limits or may not serve the entire city.

cooperatives.[7] Although a solar project under this model is owned by the utility or a third party, rather than individual community members, this is an attractive model because utilities often have experience developing energy projects and dealing with the financial and legal aspects of those projects. Since cooperatives and municipal utilities are governed by their customers, they can be directed to invest in community solar projects on behalf of the communities they serve.[8] To help finance a project, customers voluntarily pay a monthly fee based on the amount of solar energy they want to subscribe to and receive a credit on their electric utility bill that is proportional to the output of electricity from their solar subscription.

A good example of this type of arrangement is the Sacramento Municipal Utility District's (SMUD) SolarShares program in California, which is 1 MW in size and the nation's largest community solar project.[9] Other examples of utility-sponsored model projects include the City of Ellensburg Community Renewable Park in Washington, a 36-kW community solar pilot project completed in 2006,[10] and United Power's Sol Partners Cooperative Solar Farm in Colorado, a 10-kW community solar program launched in 2009.[11] Customers participating in these utility-sponsored projects lease one or more solar panels and receive credit for the energy produced by their solar panels. The utility-sponsored model helps communities that cannot directly invest in solar themselves

---

7. Cooperatives are usually formed for the purpose of delivering electricity to rural communities. Rural utility cooperatives are owned by the customers they serve and financed by federal loans. They are distinct from business cooperatives, which are formed to produce power to sell to a utility. Under the utility-sponsored model, members of a cooperative do not provide financing for the project, and instead only purchase electricity.

8. The utility-sponsored model could also apply to customers of investor-owned utilities (IOUs). However, customers of IOUs have no control over an IOU's decision to develop or invest in community solar projects.

9. For more information about SMUD's SolarShare program, see https://www.smud.org/en/residential/environment/solar-for-your-home/solarshares/.

10. For information on the City of Ellensburg Community Renewable Energy Park, see http://www.ci.ellensburg.wa.us/index.aspx?NID=310.

11. More information on United Power's Cooperative Solar Farm is available at http://www.unitedpower.com/mainNav/greenPower/solPartners.aspx.

and reduces the cost to participate in community solar projects, but this model may be less attractive when compared to the financial benefits of project ownership.

- **Community ownership model:** Several solar project organizers have created business ownership structures, such as limited liability companies (LLCs), to share the costs and benefits among the owners of a community solar project. One example is the Clean Energy Collective LLC in Colorado, which is pioneering the community ownership model by delivering clean power generation through medium-scale facilities that are collectively owned by participating utility customers.[12] To participate in the community solar project, customers of the local utility can purchase and own solar panels that are installed in the project. The Clean Energy Collective operates and maintains the community solar project and sells the energy produced by the project directly to the local utility through purchase power agreements (PPAs). Owners of the project receive a credit on their utility bill for the energy produced by their solar panels while also obtaining a credit comparable to the tax benefits of an individually owned solar project.

  Another example of this model is the University Park Solar, LLC community solar project in Maryland.[13] The organizers of this project created a private membership LLC that is owned and financed by its members. This project benefits from the federal tax credits that come with project ownership. Compared with the utility-sponsored model, the community ownership model provides owners more control over the project and access to tax benefits. However, this model requires jumping over many legal and financial hurdles, including compliance with securities and tax laws, and should be approached with a full understanding of the challenges of creating a business entity and raising capital. Furthermore, in

12. For more information about the Clean Energy Collective LLC, visit http://www.easycleanenergy.com.

13. For more information about University Park Solar, see http://universityparksolar.com/.

pursuing the community ownership model, project organizers must establish and maintain production partnerships between project owners and the local utility and are required to operate and maintain the solar project themselves.

Other Common Models

Three additional models are helping people come together to increase access to solar energy at reduced up-front cost. While not exactly "community solar" in that a community does not collectively own or participate in a small to mid-sized solar energy project, these models can be thought of as community-based models because they provide a framework that people can use to join together to make it more affordable for individuals and organizations to install solar panels.

- **Bargaining group model:** People who could fit their homes with solar panels, but do not have enough money to purchase a solar PV system, are forming bargaining groups to help reduce the cost of individual ownership. Under this model, a community does not share a common solar PV system. Instead, this model brings together a group of people who want to install solar panels on their homes and helps them negotiate a lower price for the purchase and installation of their solar panels. Several communities have formed cooperatives to use their buying power to secure discounted prices. Cooperative Community Energy[14] in California and Mount Pleasant Solar Cooperative[15] in Washington, D.C., are examples of communities using the bargaining group model to facilitate access to solar energy. The bargaining group model is also being used in programs such as Solarize Portland,[16] led by the City of Portland in Oregon, and by companies like One

14. For information about Cooperative Community Energy, see http://www.ccenergy.com.

15. For information about Mount Pleasant Solar Cooperative, see http://www.mtpleasantsolarcoop.org/.

16. For information about Solarize Portland, see http://www.portlandonline.com/bps/index.cfm?c=51902.

Block Off the Grid, Inc.,[17] a business based in San Francisco that is offering group discounts on solar installations to individuals who sign up to form neighborhood groups.

- **Nonprofit ownership model:** Many people who do not own homes and/or do not have enough money to invest in their own solar PV system have elected to go solar by raising money to install solar panels on the rooftops of organizations that are unable to go solar on their own. Under the nonprofit ownership model, supporters of an organization, such as a school, community center, or church, are joining together to donate money to help the organization go solar at reduced or no cost. An example of an organization using this model is Community Energy Solutions, a nonprofit organization located on Bainbridge Island, Washington, which led the "Solar for Sakai" effort to fund a solar installation at a local school.[18] Although donors under this model do not share the financial benefit of project ownership or direct savings in energy cost, they can help their favorite nonprofit benefit from lower energy bills and share in the environmental benefits of reducing the use of fossil fuel–generated electricity.
- **Crowdfunding model:** The latest model used to finance and promote community solar projects is crowdfunding, where people pool their money together, usually through an Internet-based platform, to support the efforts of an organization developing small- to mid-sized solar energy projects in their communities. Solar Mosaic, LLC, an organization based in Berkeley, California, pioneered a crowdfunding Internet-based platform that allowed people to support solar energy projects in their communities.[19] This platform enabled people to invest $100 each for a "tile" of a solar panel to be installed on the rooftop of a nonprofit or government building. In 2011,

---

17. Information about One Block Off the Grid is available at http://1bog.org/.
18. Information about Community Energy Solutions can be found at http://www.cenergysolutions.org/.
19. For more information about Solar Mosaic, LLC, see http://solarmosaic.com.

Solar Mosaic's crowdfunding platform was used to install a 28.8-kW solar energy system on the rooftop of the Asian Resource Center in Oakland, California. Under this model, project supporters can earn back their investment in the form of lease payments from the project host once the solar panels have been installed. When done in compliance with securities laws, the crowdfunding model has the potential of increasing the financing of and participation in community solar projects by allowing organizations to access the capital necessary to tap into local, clean, renewable sources of energy, like solar.

Most communities can implement at least one of these models. A community's choice of which model best suits its needs will depend on the community's visions and goals, the location of the project, whether the community is currently served by a publicly owned or an investor-owned utility, and the community's ability to raise capital to finance the project. In making this choice, you should also be aware that a community must consider numerous complex financial, legal, and policy issues.

Legal Issues to Consider When Organizing Community Solar

The following is not a comprehensive discussion of the legal issues communities should consider, but only a brief overview of some of the challenges involved when people join together to organize a community solar project.

- **Compliance with securities laws**
  In choosing a community solar project model, project organizers must be careful to ensure the project complies with Securities and Exchange Commission (SEC) regulations[20] and state securities laws. Under the utility-sponsored model, close attention must be paid to the type of benefits people receive from investing in community solar projects. In most utility-sponsored projects, members or customers of the utility pay

20. A summary of laws governing securities, including federal statutes and SEC regulations, is available at http://www.sec.gov/about/laws.shtml.

a monthly fee or lease solar panels, and in exchange only receive a credit on their electric bills that is proportional to the output of electricity from their solar subscription in the project. This structure helps the utility avoid the appearance of selling securities.

If project organizers choose to pursue the community ownership model, they will embark on the difficult road of having to form a business entity and raise capital, which may require compliance with securities regulations. As described in Chapter 6, because complying with securities regulations can be costly and time consuming, project organizers often seek a private offering exemption to the registration requirements of the securities regulations. To keep the offering private, project organizers can only seek participants (or investors) without publicly advertising and must limit the number of "unaccredited" (i.e., not wealthy) investors to 35 or fewer investors. Securities regulations are meant to protect people from fraudulent or overly risky investment opportunities, but these restrictions pose serious challenges to the concept of community solar, which is intended to allow ordinary people to join together to contribute small amounts of money to collectively fund a solar project in their community.

The regulatory restrictions challenging community solar projects developed under the community ownership model are also significantly affecting community solar projects financed under the crowdfunding model. Project organizers using Internet-based platforms or other public solicitation methods to raise funds for community solar projects have been faced with a costly securities registration process, unless they qualify for an exemption. In the absence of an exemption to current securities laws or compliance with registration requirements, it is illegal to offer a financial return to investors on this type of investment. However, this restriction may soon no longer be a challenge. In April of 2012, President Obama signed the Capital Raising Online While Deterring

Fraud and Unethical Non-Disclosure Act of 2012 (CROWDFUND Act),[21] which has made significant changes to the securities laws governing the raising of capital.

The CROWDFUND Act exempts crowdfunded investments from federal registration requirements and permits the raising of small amounts of money (based on an investor's income or net worth) from an unlimited number of unaccredited (non-wealthy) investors. Furthermore, states are not allowed to require registration of offerings that are exempt under the crowdfunding exemption. When the SEC completes the rulemaking to implement the new law, organizers of community solar projects will be able to use the crowdfunding exemption to facilitate raising capital to develop community solar projects under the community-owned model and/or crowdfunding model.

Moreover, a crowdfunding exemption will provide project organizers access to capital from the type of investors that would be most inclined to invest in community solar projects intended to serve their community: local utility customers, neighbors, and other community members who are mostly unaccredited and therefore generally restricted from investing in these types of projects. This means that project organizers using crowdfunding Internet-platforms will be able to offer a financial return to people who pool their money together to finance the installation of solar panels on the rooftops of organizations that are serving their communities. For an update on the progress of the SEC's rulemaking to implement the CROWDFUND Act, visit http://crowdfundinglaw.com/. This new law is also discussed in Chapter 6, where Jenny Kassan describes the JOBS Act.

- **Access to financial incentives**

  Since installing a solar PV system requires an up-front investment, communities often seek access to tax credits, grants, and

---

21. The CROWDFUND Act was passed as Title III of the Jumpstart Our Business Startups Act (JOBS Act), H.R. 3606, 112th Cong. (2012), http://www.gpo.gov/fdsys/pkg/BILLS-112hr3606pcs/pdf/BILLS-112hr3606pcs.pdf.

other incentives to switch from or reduce reliance on conventional sources of energy. The most valuable incentive is the federal solar incentive tax credit (ITC), equivalent to 30 percent of the installed cost of the solar energy system, which was initially intended for commercial scale solar projects owned by business- or investor-owned utilities. Under the community ownership model, project organizers can form business entities to take advantage of the ITC. However, this can be challenging because most people that want to participate in a community solar project do not have significant taxable income to make full use of the ITC.

Utility-sponsored projects owned by publicly owned utilities or by not-for-profit cooperatives do not qualify for the ITC because they do not pay federal taxes. To make the utility-sponsored model economically viable, project organizers must seek federal or state grants or make use of tax credit bonds, such as Clean Renewable Energy Bonds (CREBs), which help non-taxed entities lower the cost of financing debt. Alternatively, municipal utilities can partner with third-party businesses, which can build and own the PV system and take advantage of the tax benefits. This arrangement was used in SMUD's SolarShare program. Instead of owning the solar project, SMUD contracted with a solar developer to build and own the solar energy system and the developer took advantage of the ITC. The developer may then pass on these tax benefits to project participants by reducing the overall cost to participate in the community solar project.

Project organizers considering other types of community solar project models should also consider the financial incentives and disincentives of such models. For instance, under the bargaining group model, people who participate in the group and install solar PV systems on their own residences can take advantage of the ITC available to individual homeowners. This credit is not available to people who participate in a community solar project developed under the utility-sponsored or the community ownership models.

Community solar projects developed under the nonprofit ownership model are not eligible for the ITC. Since nonprofit organizations generally do not pay taxes, they are usually ineligible for tax incentives. However, these projects may be eligible for grants and other sources of funding not available to for-profit entities. In addition, people who donate money to a community solar project can claim a deduction for their contribution if the project sponsor is a charitable organization under the Internal Revenue Code, 26 U.S.C. § 501(c)(3). To maximize access to financial incentives, nonprofits have altered this model by partnering with a third-party for-profit entity, which can own and install the system and take advantage of tax benefits. This type of partnership has been implemented in the California Public Utilities Commission's Multifamily Affordable Solar Housing (MASH) program.[22]

One related federal legislative effort is the Solar Uniting Neighborhoods Act (SUN Act) re-introduced by Senator Udall (D-Colo.) in 2011. The SUN Act is designed to help people who jointly install a community solar energy system take advantage of the 30 percent ITC, even if the community solar energy system is hosted on an off-site property or does not directly power their home. If this legislation is passed, renters and homeowners with shading or other home restrictions who come together to participate in a community solar project under the community ownership model will be able to take advantage of the 30 percent ITC. This legislation would allow any community member to participate in his/her community's efforts to own and produce solar energy, locally and efficiently, at a more affordable cost. If you would like to learn more about this legislative effort, visit http://votesolar.org/communitysolar/sun-act-2011/.

- **Net metering policies**

  A community solar project may be hindered by barriers imposed by net metering policies, which require a utility to

22. For more information on California's Multifamily Affordable Solar Housing program, see http://www.cpuc.ca.gov/puc/energy/solar/mash.htm.

provide a bill credit and/or payment for the net excess electricity produced by a residential or commercial on-site solar PV system. The net metering laws of many states do not allow multiple owners to receive credits from community solar projects. Without net metering policy changes, it will continue to be difficult to share the electricity credits with each of the owners or participants of a community solar project, even if they all live in proximity to the project.

Some states have implemented community net metering (also known as virtual net metering) programs that allow utilities to allocate credits for energy production from community solar projects to multiple participants or owners of the project.[23] For example, in California, virtual net metering is a component of the MASH program. By using virtual net metering, the community solar project developer and the utility can take an entire solar array, feed it into one meter, and then allocate energy use and credits to several virtual meters.[24]

- **Policies that enable and promote community solar** Changes to the legal and regulatory framework necessary to broaden participation in community solar are finally taking place at the state level. For example, in 2010, Colorado enacted House Bill 1342, the Community Solar Gardens Act, to provide customers of investor-owned utilities the opportunity to participate in solar generation.[25] The Act allows people, including renters and low-income customers, to own interests in solar-generating facilities that are not on their property.[26] A community solar garden must have at least ten customers of a local utility, called "subscribers," who own subscriptions in the solar electric–generating facility and live in the same municipality or county.[27] The Act was designed to allow all

23. A review of state net metering policies is included in the report Freeing the Grid, Best Practices in Net Metering Policies and Interconnection Procedures, http://www.freeingthegrid.org.

24. Additional information on California's virtual net metering policies can be found at http://www.cpuc.ca.gov/PUC/energy/DistGen/vnm.htm.

25. *See* COLO. REV. STAT. § 40-2-127(1)(b) (2011).

26. *See id.* § 40-2-127(1)(b)(II).

27. *See id.* § 40-2-127(2)(b)(I)(A) & (b)(II).

customers who purchase subscriptions to a solar garden access to the same benefits as homeowners, such as state rebates and tax incentives.

Under the Act, a community solar garden is a solar energy system of 2 MW or less which is located in or near a community served by a local utility.[28] A community solar garden can be partly owned by the local utility or any for-profit or nonprofit entity or organization, including a "subscriber organization," whose sole purpose is to operate the solar garden and sell the output of the community solar garden to the local utility.[29] Colorado also joins other states in allowing virtual net metering. A local utility's purchase of the power output of a community solar garden takes the form of a net metering credit against a subscriber's electric bill which is proportionate to the output of electricity from their solar subscription.[30] If you want to learn more about the Act and similar solar garden laws recently passed and pending in other states, see http://www.solargardens.org/. For additional information, see the Colorado Public Utilities Commission's Solar Garden rulemaking, available at https://www.dora.state.co.us/pls/efi/EFI.Show_Docket?p_session_id=&p_docket_id=10R-674E.

Conclusion

There are many different models in which people can come together to harness and share the power of the sun. Community solar allows for innovative ways in which communities across the country can participate in or directly own systems that create clean, renewable energy. However, there remains room and need for improving laws and policies to increase participation in community solar projects, improve access to financing, and reduce costs of these projects. As described above, several states have implemented policies to help remove some of the barriers to community solar. Much more could be done at the state and federal levels to spur the development of

28. *See id.* § 40-2-127(2)(b)(I)(A).
29. *See id.* § 40-2-127(2)(b)(I)(A) & (3)(a).
30. *See id.* § 40-2-127(5)(b)(II).

community solar projects, including (1) enacting more laws that promote participation in community solar, (2) removing securities law barriers to community-financed solar projects, and (3) ensuring equal access to federal incentive tax credits for solar.

If you are interested in learning more about Community Solar, see U.S. Department of Energy, *A Guide to Community Solar: Utility, Private, and Non-profit Development* (2010), available at http://www.nrel.gov/docs/fy11osti/49930.pdf. Additional useful information is provided by Community Power Network, available at http://communitypowernetwork.com/.

CHAPTER NINE

NEW RELATIONSHIPS WITH LAND AND HOUSING

Part 1: Building Economically Sustainable Relationships with Land

The practice of real property law is largely about managing the bundle of rights and responsibilities traditionally attached to land ownership. This chapter unpacks that bundle, exploring the possibility for agreements and organizations that allow us to *share* and more wisely manage those rights and responsibilities. This chapter is not specifically about sharing housing and land; rather, it is about how shared use arrangements, shared financing, shared management, and other cooperative arrangements can help us to establish economically sustainable ways of managing land and housing ourselves.

Each of us needs to have a secure relationship with land because we all require a place to physically exist, to be sheltered, to make a livelihood, and to be nourished by land's resources. The goal of a sharing economy lawyer is straightforward: to build legal relationships and legal frameworks to ensure that everyone and everything alive will be nourished by their relationships with land, and that future generations will be, too. I said the goal was *straightforward*; I didn't say it was *modest.*

Whether by necessity, by choice, or by inspiration, most of us will soon have to make new and different choices about how we house ourselves and how we use land. As this happens, innumerable sharing lawyers will need to develop the requisite expertise in real property law so that we can guide citizens in creating the agreements and organizations that will govern our new relationships with land.

Unpacking the Bundle of Rights

Ownership of land is generally thought to come with a "bundle of rights," such as the right to possess and occupy the land, the right to build on it, the right to use its resources, the right to set terms for the transfer of land, and the right to decide how it is used, by whom, and for how much money. Those rights, however, are tempered in two primary ways:

1. **Private "laws":** Private individuals and groups can make agreements to set limitations and directives on how land is used, transferred, and so on. These limitations typically come in the form of covenants that run with the land, equitable servitudes, lease agreements, co-ownership agreements, and other contracts and rules that are enforced by homeowners' associations (HOAs), co-owners, neighbors, mortgage holders, landlords, tenants, and easement holders.
2. **Public laws:** There are local, state, and federal laws that place limits on what we do with land. These include land use laws, environmental protection laws, inclusionary housing laws, rent control laws, regulations on the subdivision of land, regulations on the powers of HOAs, taxation of property, anti-discrimination laws, and so on.

The role of a sharing economy lawyer, then, is twofold:

1. **Creating private agreements and organizations:** A sharing economy lawyer helps clients choose from and structure the large number of tools for the private management of land rights and responsibilities. This work entails drafting covenants and contracts, choosing entities, structuring organizations, choosing tax statuses, structuring relationships between entities and individuals, and much more. The options vary from state to state, and the choices must be made while weighing a wide variety of factors, such as the goals and needs of clients, sources of financing, limitations imposed by lenders, tax implications of the arrangement, and limitations imposed by public laws.

2. **Navigating public laws:** The legal relationships that clients wish to create for the management of land are often limited by laws that dictate how such relationships may be created and how land can be used. These laws are particularly awkward to apply when clients have created systems that involve shared use, shared management, and/or shared financing of land. It conjures up a theme reiterated throughout this book: Sharing economy lawyers often find that their clients fall squarely within legal gray areas. For example, it is difficult to apply landlord/tenant laws to situations where the landlord *is* the tenant, such as in a housing cooperative. It is awkward to apply laws that govern transactions between a developer and homebuyer when the homebuyer *is* the developer, such as in many cohousing communities. Furthermore, land use laws that have sought to prevent the mixing of residential, commercial, industrial, and agricultural uses prove awkward when clients wish to bring production back to their neighborhoods, such as by forming a residential community that engages in collective food production activities.

Because of the multitude of ways to manage private land rights and the variety of public laws affecting our relationships with land, being a sharing economy lawyer focused on land and housing requires learning a lot about real estate law. This chapter is not a full overview of the knowledge and skills required of such a lawyer, but it provides a framework for thinking about the unique tools used and challenges faced by lawyers working with clients in a sharing economy.

When Land Is Not Shared

Creating more economically and ecologically sustainable relationships with land should perhaps not be a *goal*, but rather an *imperative*. It's not simply due to the fact that we must begin the future with a severely degraded planetary ecosystem. We also face a crisis in housing. Landless people's movements throughout the world are vocalizing the essential unfairness of the fact that so many people must struggle to simply secure a place to physically exist, much less make a livelihood, on the planet. The struggle is not confined to the poor. Middle-income people in the United States are floundering to determine how their current housing arrangements will be financially sustainable into the future.

The burden of housing ourselves is heavy, and the currently available options are limiting.

Sharing and the lack of sharing have an interesting effect on the whole situation. When land is shared, it becomes more valuable to the cause of securing the long-term sustainability of our economy and building the wealth of our communities. When land is *not shared*, land prices rise and land becomes more "valuable" in a speculative marketplace. The latter is an incentive hard for most individuals to resist, at least not without a more attractive alternative.

In this way, the speculative marketplace drives most of society's decisions about land and housing. Rather than simply regard our home as a *home*, we also treat it as a speculative investment. We strive to buy in a buyers' market and sell in a sellers' market, and to maximize short-term monetary gains. People who own land benefit from scarcities of affordable land because the market value of their own land rises. With their profits, they can acquire larger or additional properties, which exacerbates scarcity. Most homeowners are advised to play this speculative game. The winners of the game tend to keep winning, and this game-like marketplace begins to feel far too reminiscent of Monopoly.

Land and housing resources have also been made artificially scarce because we have parceled them into ever larger and more expensive single-family boxes. The average size of the American home has more than doubled since the 1950s.[1] Individual families take on increasingly heavy burdens when they purchase and maintain large properties. Widespread foreclosure crises have now demonstrated to us that such burdens were not within the means of many households. We now have an incredible number of housing units that sit empty and provide for no one, whereas other parcels of land are over-exploited and degraded, and millions of people lack homes. The fragmentation of land and the failure to implement systems of sharing have resulted in what Columbia law professor Michael Heller has referred to as a simultaneous tragedy

---

1. Margot Adler, *Behind the Ever-Expanding American Dream House*, NPR, July 4, 2006, http://www.npr.org/templates/story/story.php?storyId=5525283.

of the commons and tragedy of the anti-commons.[2] In sum, the entire situation pleads urgently for solutions.

Solutions Addressed Here

This chapter explores some solutions, along with some legal tools for implementing them. The solutions described here are of a particular kind and focus.

1. **Solutions applicable to *every person*:** The solutions that most interest me are ones that can be implemented by individuals and groups, rather than by government programs or large-scale developers. In that respect, I intend this chapter to be relevant to the land needs of *every person*, since I also believe that it is the economic choices of *every person* that will ultimately reshape our economy.
2. **Solutions possible within the *current* legal framework:** The solutions described here are mostly possible within the current legal framework; they are not solutions that must wait for laws to change. Truthfully, I think that great strides would be made if local, state, and federal governments were to make new rules about how we own, manage, use, and transfer land. We should all *advocate* for changes to our laws, but we must not *rely* on changes that may or may not happen as soon as we need them to. In the meantime, the agreements and organizations we form with each other will change how we own, manage, use, and transfer land. That, alone, will have a huge impact and may eventually influence the legal framework.
3. **Solutions focused on *economic* sustainability:** The solutions described here focus largely on the *economic* sustainability of our relationships with land, and not so much on the *ecological* sustainability, although the two are, of course, interdependent.

---

2. M. A. Heller, *The Boundaries of Private Property*, 108 YALE L.J. at 1165–66 (1999): The danger with fragmentation is that it may operate as a one-way ratchet: Because of high transaction costs, strategic behaviors, and cognitive biases, people may find it easier to divide property than to recombine it. If too many people gain rights to use or exclude, then bargaining among owners may break down. With too many owners of property fragments, resources become prone to waste either through over use in a commons or underuse in an anticommons.

Economic motivations are at the root of our tendencies to exploit ecosystems; exhausted ecosystems are fueling our growing economic desperation. Financial concerns are also at the forefront of people's minds at a time when economies are crumbling. The relationships and organizations we form in a sharing economy can address the root economic concerns. Our new relationships and organizations will be aimed at removing incentives to exploit and ensuring that every human feels a sense of economic security and material abundance.

4. **Solutions focused on *housing*:** The solutions here look primarily at models for management of the land *where we live* (i.e., how we house ourselves) and less at the how we manage land for the purposes of agriculture, open space, commercial and industrial use, and so on. Housing is the primary way in which every person develops a legal relationship with land—generally either as an owner or as a renter. Housing also makes up the largest part of each person's interaction with the economy. In 2010, housing made up 34 percent of the average consumer's expenditures.[3] All told, housing is a big deal and a huge piece of the economic puzzle.

In sum, the primary focus of this chapter is immediately relevant to every human being—the need to find an economically sustainable housing solution for oneself.

Common Goals of Clients

Sharing economy lawyers will encounter clients with varying needs and goals, but there are some common goals we will begin to see expressed by many clients:

1. **To be more than just a renter:** Society generally offers us two options for obtaining our housing—we own or we rent. Another way to put it is that we either assume a large bundle of rights and responsibilities, including the right to benefit from equity in the property (owning), or we assume a small sack of rights and responsibilities (renting). This two-option system contributes

3. News Release, Bureau of Labor Statistics, Consumer Expenditures—2010 (Sept. 27, 2011), http://www.bls.gov/news.release/cesan.nr0.htm.

to society's overall economic divide, in the sense that it creates a class of landlords that are positioned to continually grow their land holdings. As land becomes more concentrated into the hands of few, the owners have decreased connection and accountability to the lands that they own. Decisions that absentee landlords make tend to be driven more by the desire for a financial return than by a desire to care for land or make it a wonderful place to live. This system, therefore, does not tend to build in incentives that contribute to the long-term economic and ecological sustainability of land. Resident ownership, or, at the very least, resident control, aligns the interest of those in charge with the residents, creating a greater chance of land stewardship and investment in the community. Clients will increasingly look for solutions that fall in between renting and owning, since assuming the full burden of ownership is not going to be affordable or ideal for many, for some of the reasons stated further below.

2. **To avoid stressful financial burdens:** Most people aspire to find housing that will not create a stressful financial burden. Another way of saying this is: people want housing they can afford. I began to shy away from using the word "affordable" after I got some strange reactions from using it. One woman, who complained that she could not afford to live in San Francisco, turned slightly defensive when I commiserated and said that the city sure does need more affordable housing. "Oh no, I'm not looking to live in *affordable housing*," she quickly clarified. The phrase "affordable housing," unfortunately, makes many people think of "the projects." But affordability is, after all, what everyone is looking for, no matter their income levels. To me, affordability simply means that we can access it without a stressful financial burden.
3. **To avoid inflexible, long-term debt:** Clients are increasingly looking for ways to finance land purchases without taking out large bank mortgages. Committing to a 30-year mortgage means committing to 30 years of a stable and predictable income, which is something that none of us can rely on in times of rapid economic change. And fear of foreclosure is what prevents many people from quitting bad jobs and creating healthier and more rewarding livelihoods. Long-term loans can also be expensive: most home purchases are financed by bank loans, which, taking

into account the accumulation of interest over the life of the loan, add an enormous premium onto the cost of the home. Finally, the large bank financing machine, as it stands now, is intricately and dangerously tied to the health of our economy. Relying on bank mortgages to provide our home financing means relying on banks to secure our society's future economic stability. There is a growing consensus on this: it doesn't work.

4. **To live in housing that facilitates local economy, sharing, and sustainability:** Social and economic isolation is another byproduct of subdividing our land into so many single-family boxes. In the latter half of the 20th century, each household in the United States became increasingly pressured to take on, *alone*, the burden of all aspects of household sustenance, including food, goods, and services. We got by this way, in large part through unsustainable shortcuts like TV dinners, packaged foods, and cheap, disposable consumer goods. Now, we as a society cannot afford that disposable lifestyle. Our imperative is to reduce material resource use, reduce waste, reduce energy use, reduce water use, reduce the amount of space we take up, and localize production. And the growing consensus is: it's too hard to do this alone. We need to cooperate and share, and the physical arrangement of our housing will make a huge difference in our ability to do this. Thus, many people have begun to picture themselves in housing arrangements that, to varying degrees, entail shared spaces in addition to private spaces.
5. **To foster a non-speculative housing system:** More and more, clients are seeing themselves in the bigger picture of our housing market, and do not want to contribute to its long-term unsustainability. A client of means could easily choose the common option of buying a property of his/her own, but doing so does not remove their property from the speculative game, as the property may one day go back onto the market. Clients, therefore, are increasingly looking for mechanisms that remove properties from the speculative game and place them into a system of management and governance that ensures that they will benefit the long-term housing and land needs of the community. Clients are thus interested in legal structures that limit equity and/or that put land into ownership by entities like nonprofit land trusts.

6. **To foster a thriving ecosystem:** The rights to extract resources, mine, deforest, and develop land are generally packaged within the bundle of rights that come with land ownership, and those rights are tempered primarily by land use and environmental laws that have sadly fallen short in protecting our ecosystems. Ownership of land, unfortunately, comes with a small bundle of responsibilities, relative to the size of its bundle of rights. As a result, many clients seek legal structures that create privately imposed limits on the exercise of rights to extract resources and develop land. Clients may even seek to create affirmative responsibilities to steward and regenerate damaged land. This may entail conservation easements, obtaining approval for developments that incorporate open space preservation, nonprofit ownership or stewardship, and other mechanisms for preserving land and regenerating ecosystems.

Part 2: Solutions: Sharing Use, Management, and/or Financing

That Bundle Is Toooo Large, This Bundle Is Toooo Small

As discussed above, society typically gives us two options for housing ourselves: we own our home and assume the large bundle of rights associated with ownership, or we rent our home and assume a very small bundle of rights, the primary of which is the right to occupy it. The bundle that is "juuust right" and that meets the above goals of clients likely falls somewhere in between the large and small bundles of rights.

Our relationship with land in a sharing economy therefore looks like this: we allocate important rights to individuals and other key rights to cooperatives, nonprofits, and other group-managed and community-managed entities. There is nothing new about this model. Common interest developments (CIDs), also called common interest communities, do exactly that. A condo community allocates some rights of ownership to individuals, while allocating other rights and common property management to a condo owners' association. Sharing economy lawyers can therefore draw on many of the legal frameworks developed in CID law, but taking the shared property and community-managed elements to new levels.

Importantly, putting more *rights* into the hands of groups means putting more *responsibilities* into the hands of groups, thereby relieving some of the burdens that previously made ownership inaccessible and unaffordable to many people. The responsibility for financing purchases and the responsibility of maintaining land and buildings, for example, can be shared.

I will address three primary things that can be shared in relation to real estate: (1) the use of physical spaces; (2) the management and control of how properties are used, maintained, and transferred; and (3) the capitalization of land purchases. Any group of people can choose to share some or all of these things to varying degrees, depending on the goals of their housing arrangement.

Sharing Space

The housing solution that many people are beginning to envision for themselves can be summed up as follows: more humble abodes in combination with more robust shared spaces. Home is where we engage in many activities, including sleeping, cooking, bathing, recreation, lounging, and socializing. There is no reason why all of those functions must be crammed into every single-family home. In fact, if we had access to shared social gathering spaces, shared recreation spaces, shared lounges, shared outdoor areas, and so on, each of us could probably be content to live in a more simple dwelling unit. There is already a movement of tiny house dwellers—people living in 100- to 300-square foot dwellings. However, such tiny homes will not likely be a viable solution for most people unless they are clustered in communities where people also share additional living spaces and amenities.

The degree of space sharing will vary, and one way of envisioning the different models of space sharing is to break it down as follows:

1. **Intentional villages/neighborhoods:** Housing units are intentionally clustered around some shared amenities, such as roads, parking, outdoor areas, recreational facilities, and/or renewable energy facilities. The word "village" may sound misleading, since such intentional villages can be as small as two units, as many duplexes and other small multiplexes are essentially designed for this kind of sharing.
2. **Cohousing:** Smaller housing units are clustered in combination with a significant amount of shared space and amenities that supplement the intentionally small size of units. This usu-

ally includes a large social/recreational space, a commercial scale kitchen where residents gather and share meals, and common outdoor areas.

3. **Shared homes:** Multiple individuals or households share a legal unit, such as a large home. In contrast to the cohousing or village model, each household does not necessarily have its own legal unit including a kitchen and bathroom.

Note that the degree of space sharing will shape, but not necessarily dictate, how much day-to-day cooperation and sharing take place among the individuals. Each of the configurations described above could involve households that are largely independent from each other, or they could entail a significant amount of community activity, depending on the choice of residents. In communities with higher degrees of community activity, a sharing economy lawyer, in addition to creating the legal framework for property rights, may also help shape the agreements or organizational structure under which the community activities take place.

Sharing Management

Whether or not physical spaces are shared, groups may choose to share management of certain property rights and responsibilities. An HOA is an example of a shared management structure to which individual homeowners submit themselves when they purchase a home in a planned community.

When communities manage property rights collectively, a somewhat different mindset guides decisions—one that focuses on the longer-term health, comfort, viability, and/or sustainability of the entire community, rather than on benefits to individual homeowners. HOAs can, for example, prohibit a homeowner from drilling an oil well in his front yard, since such a well could detract from the charm and design scheme of the neighborhood. HOAs have become widespread because of the recognition that the benefits conferred by community management often outweigh the costs (monthly dues) and inconveniences of being part of an HOA.

While community management can be used for the well-being of communities, the structure and goals of HOAs do not necessarily strike the balance needed for more sustainable communities. HOAs tend to provoke a certain amount of eye-rolling among people that have dealt with them because they have often been known to protect speculative investments rather than fostering community. For example, HOAs have been known to prohibit homeowners from installing drought-tolerant landscapes or vegetable gardens instead of grass, installing solar panels that obscure charming Spanish-style roofs, or other activities the HOAs perceive to diminish the property values in the neighborhood. State laws have even had to intervene on behalf of homeowners, limiting the authority of HOAs to make rules against public policy,[4] and also limiting the authority of HOAs to make decisions, raise assessments, or use enforcement liens without due process.[5]

HOAs can and should be used to promote sustainable communities. The structures we create to share management of land and housing in a more sustainable economy should factor in needs beyond that of maintaining property market values. Whether rights are allocated to an HOA, condo owners' association, cooperative, land trust, or simply to a group of co-owners, such associations may, more and more, be charged with goals that include promoting economic and ecological sustainability, cultivating a sense of community and sharing, and/or preserving affordability. A key right that is increasingly being handed over to group management is the right to control how a property is sold, to whom, and for how much.[6] Partially removing this right from the control of individuals means that a community can better decide how a property interacts in the larger marketplace and, to some extent, removes it from full play in the game of Monopoly.

The governance structure of management entities will play a key role in its accountability. For example, most community land trusts are governed by a board of directors, one-third of which is comprised of people who live in the trust's housing units. This structure ensures that residents have a strong voice in decisions but also ensures that residents cannot make controlling decisions that prioritize their financial gain over the provision of long-term affordable housing in a community.

---

4. *See* A.B. 1061 (Cal. 2009).

5. *See* Unif. Planned Community Act and Unif. Condo Act (National Conference of Commissioners on Uniform State Laws (NCCUSL), 1980), and state laws such as California's Davis-Stirling Act, Cal. Civil Code § 1350 *et seq.*

6. Limited equity housing is an example of a model that removes an individual's right to set the terms of sale for his/her housing unit.

Sharing Financing

The financial burden of purchasing or developing housing is enormous, and it is a burden that we have most commonly shared with risk-loving developers who require a high return on investment and large banks that supply the financing. But banks are usually beholden to the financial bottom line of their shareholders, and not to the financial well-being of our communities. It just makes more sense to share the financing burden with individuals and organizations that are more interested in and committed to the economic health of our communities. Government and nonprofit grants and subsidies are sometimes available, but there are rarely enough. That leaves us with an important task: to develop more ways for community members to share in the financing of housing purchases and development.

Our communities are full of capital that could be harnessed to finance housing, but a good amount of that capital is used to finance companies traded on Wall Street, by means of typical individual investments and retirement funds. The question becomes: what incentives and legal structures will lead individuals, local businesses, and organizations to move their money and invest in, lend to, and donate to support housing purchases and developments in their communities?

Resident Financing

In some cases, housing could simply be financed by the residents themselves—if a group of people pools funds to buy an unsubdivided multiplex, the cost is generally much lower than if they each purchased their own homes. Purchase of raw land is similarly much cheaper, and residents have the option to "finance" their housing with "sweat equity" if they build dwellings themselves. Furthermore, individual residents who have greater access to capital than other residents can finance a larger share of the purchase and either own a greater share or be compensated over time by co-owners.

Non-resident Financing

Resident financing, however, will not always be an option, so it's necessary to create structures for bringing in outside capital. As they say, "you can't get somethin' for nothin'," which requires that we create legal relationships that reward the people and organizations that share in the financing of our housing. The reward could be a share of the management, a share of the monetary appreciation, a share of the rental income, a commitment to serving a social or environmental purpose, or other financial or social returns. Here are some common arrangements.

1. **Loans:** The most common type of exchange is one where people receive a loan and agree to repay it with interest. The widespread use of such a financing arrangement, particularly without significant regulation of lenders, can result in real estate bubbles and undermine efforts to stabilize economies. Purchasers are bound to repay loan principal along with substantial interest, regardless of fluctuations in the market value. There are bound to be losers in this system, as not every borrower will be able to earn enough to repay principal plus interest.

   Nevertheless, loans are and will continue to be an important piece of the financing picture, and it's important to ensure that they are designed so that both lender and borrower succeed and thrive. This could mean setting more dynamic repayment terms, establishing more flexible default remedies, and/or structuring a more reasonable return for the lender. Most importantly, the financial return on loans should ideally be poured back into the community. If we create local loan funds and credit unions, the interest we pay on loans will simply be reinvested into our communities, which builds wealth within the local market.
2. **Investments:** Ideally, a financing arrangement will allow residents and financers to *share* both the risks and benefits of property ownership. When people invest in housing, the incentive is usually a share of the appreciated value, a share of the rental income, and/or a share of the control. Of course, there need to be boundaries constructed around the control by and returns to non-resident investors, to ensure that decisions about the property are not solely driven by a financial bottom line. Equity sharing[7] and shared-appreciation mortgages are common arrangements for investment; through either arrangement, a lender or co-owner is granted the right to share in some portion of the property's appreciation [or depreciation], usually realized at the time the property is sold or refinanced.

7. *See* ANDY SIRKIN, THE HOME EQUITY SHARING MANUAL (Wiley 1994).

3. **Donations:** Housing arrangements that build in strong commitments to social and environmental purposes will also be able to access grants and donations as a source of funding. Housing or land that is purchased or supported by nonprofits generally comes with strings attached. In the case of housing, the mandate may be to use a legal structure that ensures that the housing remains affordable for future residents. In the case of open space, funders may mandate a commitment that land be preserved and stewarded for the benefit of ecosystems. In the case of agricultural land, funders may mandate that land be perpetually used for agricultural purposes and not sold to developers.

Note that community financing of housing often implicates securities laws, and anyone seeking to create an avenue to lend or invest in housing should thoroughly read Chapter 6 of this book. However, when a loan or investment is adequately secured by an interest in the real property or by a deed of trust, such an arrangement may not be considered a security.

Part 3: Agreements and Organizations to Share Property Rights

Common Configurations

The shared use, management, and financing of property can be accomplished through a range of different agreements and organizational relationships. Although it's impossible to describe the full range of legal arrangements for the reallocation of rights, below are some common configurations that sharing economy lawyers will assist clients in developing, along with descriptions of situations in which they may be used. This section considers clients who lease property, clients who directly own property, clients who own property through an entity, and clients who combine entity ownership with direct ownership.

Clients Who Lease Property

Some clients' relationship with a property may be as renters, and a role of a sharing economy lawyer is to allocate rights among co-tenants and/or between the landlord and tenant. Although renting generally confers a much smaller bundle of rights than ownership, this bundle can be enlarged by means of a lease that confers a significant number of rights and responsibilities to the tenant. Here are some common scenarios where a lawyer may help clients to configure a relationship that is more than just a typical landlord/renter relationship.

a. **Lease + co-tenants agreements:** When a group of tenants leases a property, they sometimes enter into a second agreement to govern their intratenant relationship, allocating rights and responsibilities among themselves. This is common in cooperative houses where the tenants are all renters, but where they wish to create a resident-governed community. Note that in some cases, one tenant may sign the lease and act as a master tenant, entering into separate sublease agreements with subtenants. In some respects, this is administratively easier because the tenant group does not need to involve the landlord in removing or adding parties to the primary lease every time tenants come and go. Larger tenant groups may also wish to form an entity, such as a cooperative corporation or limited liability company (LLC), to serve as the primary tenant.
b. **Lease + purchase option:** A lease combined with a purchase option agreement is what many clients will refer to as a "lease-to-own" arrangement. Clients who seek to establish a longer-term connection with land, but who are not yet able to finance a purchase, may enter into an additional agreement with the landlord to allow the tenants the right to exercise an option to purchase the property within a period of time. The option agreement details the price and terms under which the tenants can purchase the property if they choose to exercise the option. In exchange for holding the right to purchase, tenants may pay an additional monthly or yearly fee to the landlord. However, this fee and some portion of rent payments may later be credited toward the purchase price if the tenants choose to exercise the option. To protect the rights of the option holder, it is generally a good idea to record a Memorandum of Option to provide notice to potential buyers that someone holds an option.[8]

8. However, note that purchase options can sometimes be construed to trigger the "due on sale" clause of a mortgage.

c. **Capital lease:** A capital lease is an agreement that generally confers most rights of ownership and that ultimately ends with the tenant taking title to the property. This is similar to a Contract of Sale, whereby a buyer makes payments to a seller over a period of time, and title transfers at the end of the period. Under some laws and interpretations, a capital lease may be considered a change of ownership when the agreement is made. In the case of a lease that confers a significant number of rights, it may be necessary to record the lease to ensure that rights under the lease remain in place even if there is a change of property ownership.

   The owners of a large house in Maryland have used a capital lease to transfer a significant number of rights to a limited liability company owned by a tenant group known as Maitri House. Through the capital lease, the tenants have agreed to pay off the loan on the property by making payments to owners.

d. **Ground lease:** A ground lease is usually a long-term lease (30–99 years) that gives the tenant the right to occupy *land* and to make improvements, which are generally owned by the tenant. Land trusts that hold title to property for the purpose of conservation or community development often use a long-term ground lease to give occupants the feeling of ownership. At the same time, the terms of the ground lease set standards for how the property is used, developed, or transferred. As with capital leases, ground leases create a significant and long-term relationship with land, and are often recorded.

e. **Triple net lease:** A triple net lease is a phrase more commonly used in commercial real estate, but the concept applies similarly in the residential context. A triple net lease allocates extra responsibilities to a tenant, including the obligation to pay for property taxes, insurance, utilities, and maintenance costs of the property. Such a lease generally also confers additional rights to improve the property, use it for flexible purposes, sublet it, and so on. It also generally comes with a longer lease term, which creates more of a sense of ownership by tenants.

f. **Life lease:** A life lease creates a lifelong relationship with land usually by giving tenants the right to live on a property for the duration of their lives. A group of people I know formed an entity to purchase land that they currently use as a vacation spot, and they gave themselves life leases to create a more permanent relationship with the land.

Clients Who Directly Own Property

When property is directly owned by clients, a variety of agreements can be used to share the bundle of rights and responsibilities. Here are some common ways that agreements can reallocate the rights of ownership:

a. **Co-ownership agreements with shared use:** One of the most common agreements I write is a Tenancy in Common (TIC) Agreement to allocate the property rights and responsibilities among co-owners. (A sample TIC Agreement is included in Chapter 3 of this book.) Most commonly, the TIC Agreements I write are for two families jointly purchasing and living on a property with two units (often a house with a cottage or mother-in-law unit). The default legal presumption with a co-owned property is that owners each own an equal share of the property and that everyone has use of all parts of the property.[9] TIC Agreements overcome this presumption by means of a contract delineating which parts of the property each owner may use, what each contributes to the purchase and ongoing costs, what each gets when they sell out, and so on.[10]

   Be aware, however, that if title is held as joint tenants (which *requires* shared possession and equal interests), it's possible that an agreement dividing interests and possession into separate unequal shares could sever the joint tenancy, causing the title to transform

9. Peter M. Carrozzo, *Tenancies in Antiquity: A Transformation of Concurrent Ownership for Modern Relationships*, 85 MARQUETTE L. REV. 423, 427–28:

> A tenancy in common is an estate held by two or more persons whereby each tenant has several separate interests in the land but an undivided possession of the entire estate. As a result of these several separate interests, and unlike the joint tenancy, there is no right of survivorship between or among tenants in common. When one tenant in common dies, his or her interest is administered as part of his or her estate and will either devise by will or descend by the laws of intestacy. The four unities are not necessary to create a tenancy in common. Tenants may acquire by different conveyances at different times and be in possession of unequal shares. . . .The sole unity required is that of possession.

10. Note that while tenancies in common require a unity of possession, courts will nevertheless enforce agreements to divide possession, giving each owner the right to exclusive occupancy of certain parts of the property. *See, e.g.*, *In re* Whiting, 311 B.R. 539 (Bankr. N.D. Cal. 2004) (examining whether a bankruptcy trustee would be bound by a TIC Agreement made between co-owners).

into a TIC, and removing the automatic right of one owner to take title to the other owner's interest at death.[11] This remains a question for further research: what kinds of agreements *can* joint tenants make with regard to how they share or divide use, responsibilities, financing, or proceeds of a property? At what point could division of rights result in a severance of the joint tenancy? If and to the extent that this is somewhat legally uncertain, if clients want to divide their interests in and possession of the property *and* create a right of survivorship for their co-owners, they may not be able to do so with a joint tenancy, but may instead need to use other estate planning tools to control the transfer of interests at death.

b. **Co-ownership agreements *without* shared use:** To financially support friends or family in purchasing properties, sometimes people become co-owners of a property and act primarily as passive investors. For example, it is common for the non-resident to make the down payment and have the resident make regular mortgage payments. Often, the parties agree that the non-resident investor will receive a share of the appreciated value when they cash out. In such an equity-sharing arrangement, a TIC Agreement would lay out the differing rights and responsibilities of residents and non-residents, and usually provides for an exit plan for the non-resident, including a plan for the possibility of property depreciation.

c. **Ownership + lease:** Many property owners seek to bring in housemates/co-tenants in the spirit of building community and reducing costs, and many intentional communities are structured in this way: one person owns the property and enters into leases with people that will share property with her. Generally, the terms of the lease will give the tenant the power to make certain decisions together with the owner, such as the decision to accept or reject new tenants.

---

11. Carrozzo, *supra* note 9, at 425:

> Inevitably, the existence of a joint tenancy requires determining whether the four unities—time, title, interest and possession—are present. For the four unities to be present, it is necessary for the joint tenants' interests to accrue at the same moment (unity of time); by the same deed or conveyance (unity of title); each joint tenant must possess an equal undivided share of the entire estate (unity of possession); and their interests must be equal in length and quality (unity of interest). At common law, if one of the four unities was not present, a joint tenancy could not exist. An ineffectual attempt to create a joint tenancy results in the creation of a tenancy in common.

d. **Ownership + co-owner purchase option:** Many property owners are in a particularly difficult place right now—their property may be "under water," they have difficulty making payments, and there is no chance of a refinance. The due-on-sale clause of mortgage loans makes it difficult to enter into a shared ownership arrangement to relieve the financial burden, so one solution we can help clients with is creating a purchase option agreement for tenants.[12] If the tenant takes over some or all of the monthly mortgage payments, those payments will be credited to the tenant when they later exercise the option to buy in as a co-owner. To compensate the tenant for buying into a property that is under water, the agreement could even provide that the tenant will take a larger share of ownership for a smaller financial contribution.

e. **Ownership + affordability deed restriction:** Cities and nonprofit housing developers often sell affordable housing units subject to a deed restriction, which requires that the owner of the property re-sell the property at an affordable rate to an individual or family meeting a specified definition of low income. Deed restrictions generally must designate a person or entity, like a city or nonprofit, to enforce the restriction.

f. **Ownership + easement:** Easements can be a very useful tool in reallocating land rights and promoting shared use and shared management. An easement gives an easement-holder the right to use someone else's property in a certain way, or to prevent a certain type of use. Here are four examples.

   1) **Easements for shared spaces:** Any existing suburban neighborhood, for example, could become a cohousing community by building or designating a building to be used as a common house by multiple neighbors and by granting each neighbor an easement to access the common house. The Temescal Creek cohousing community in Oakland did this.

      Easements could also be used for the sharing of gray water systems, for example. If one neighbor successfully builds a certified gray water recycling wetland in her yard, she could grant and record an easement to her adjacent neighbors to pipe gray wastewater into the wetland, and to use recycled water in irrigating their gardens.

12. Note, however, that a purchase option agreement could *potentially* be construed as a transfer to trigger the due on sale clause.

2) **Easement for public spaces:** Easements can be used to preserve the public's access to open space, trails, beach access, and so on. Through a common law doctrine of dedication or related statutory framework, owners of land may dedicate land or a right-of-way to public use, or may, in some cases, be forced to do so through an implied doctrine of dedication, on principles similar to that of a prescriptive easement.[13]
3) **Easements for conservation:** Conservation easements give the easement holder the right to prevent a property from being developed, mined, or used in a way that destroys the ecosystem or open space. Conservation easements can be crafted in a variety of ways, since there are many ways to define what conservation looks like for different properties. Usually conservation easements are held and enforced by conservation land trusts. Property owners typically sell easements to trusts or donate them, which may entitle the owner to an income tax deduction or credit.
4) **Affordability easements:** In the same way that conservation easements preserve natural ecosystems, it is conceivable to create an easement that preserves the affordability of land. An "affordability easement" could be donated or sold to a nonprofit community land trust that would step in during a sale to ensure that the property is sold at a price determined by a formula set in the easement. It is possible that such an "easement" would simply be treated like and called a "deed restriction." However, I like the idea of characterizing it as an easement similar to a conservation easement; if people could get income tax deductions and property tax deductions for the donation of an affordability easement on their property, many more people might voluntarily remove their home from the speculative market in this way. Typical mortgage lenders might object to such an easement encumbering the property, but it seems feasible that smaller local banks could be persuaded to lend if they feel sufficiently protected under the arrangement.

---

13. Richard E. Llewellyn II, *The Common Law Doctrine of Implied Dedication and Its Effect on the California Coastline Property Owner:* Gion v. City of Santa Cruz, 4 Loy. L.A. L. Rev. 438 (1971).

g. **Ownership + lien:** Liens are essentially agreements that create an interest in property that secures the payment of loans or the performance of other obligations. Sharing economy lawyers should get into the practice of drafting down-to-earth and plain-English mortgages or deed of trust documents, which can be used when an individual or entity lends money to support the purchase or improvement of a property. Instead of using legalese-filled deeds of trust that large banks hand to us, we will preferably prepare much more thoughtful documents that clients understand and that are enforceable, and that will thereby encourage community members to put their money into local real estate loans.
    1) **Affordability liens:** Liens could be used to preserve the affordability of properties. Such a lien could require that if the property is sold, a percentage of the appreciated value will be paid to a nonprofit organization that holds the lien, and the funds could be used to subsidize purchases by other low-income homebuyers. This is similar to the concept of a shared-appreciation mortgage, where the lenders agree to a lower interest rate or waive the down payment, in exchange for a share of the appreciated value when the property is sold.

h. **Ownership + license:** Generally, when you stay in a hotel, camp on someone's property, or use private land for recreational purposes, your right to use the land is considered a license, not a lease (since a lease usually gives exclusive possession to the lessee) or an easement (which is long-term or permanent). Property owners can defray ownership costs by granting licenses for short-term use of their homes or land. This has even become a common practice with the help of websites like Airbnb, which connect travelers and hosts to enable "couchsurfing" for money. The host is essentially granting a license to the guest. As this practice grows and becomes a substantial peer-to-peer alternative to hotels, it is likely that lawyers will be more often called upon to draft clear license agreements for short-term property uses. Licenses can also be used to grant short-term use of commercial spaces, such as for "pop-up" stores.

i. **Ownership + possibility of reverter:** Another way to control how a property is used is to grant ownership to a person or entity, but to require that title be returned to the original grantor if the land is used or not used in a certain way. For example, Raines could execute a deed and gift property "to Such and Such Homeowners' Association, as long as the property is used as a common house and recreational facility for the Association members until the year 2030."[14] This clause would require that ownership of the property be returned to Raines in the event that the HOA ceases to provide the property as a common house. This prevents the HOA from simply selling the property and using the proceeds for other purposes.[15]

j. **Ownership + agreement for common management and improvement:** Even when neighbors share little or no property, they may still benefit from forming or joining an entity that is charged with making certain rules about how properties are used and that engages in neighborhood improvement projects. This is essentially what an HOA does. Most HOAs are put into place when a neighborhood is built. Even in the absence of an HOA, homeowners may still agree, after the fact, to form an HOA and legally bind their property and future owners of their property to take part.

A somewhat more likely scenario is for neighbors to form a neighborhood association that residents may opt in and out of at will. The association could provide certain benefits to members (such as buy-in to a neighborhood solar array or assistance with preservation of historical home features), and members may, in exchange, agree to engage or not engage in certain activities. For example, neighbors may agree to refrain from using chemical fertilizers or from creating excessive smoke or other emissions, in order to care for the neighborhood air, water, and soil quality.

If a city or state provided the legal means to do so, a neighborhood could also take initiative and vote to impose a tax on property owners, the proceeds of which would go to form

---

14. Note that the use of a possibility of reverter may require inquiry into the applicability of the rules against perpetuities, which will not be explained here, since it was, after all, everyone's favorite subject in law school.

15. Note that courts might consider such a possibility of reverter to be an unreasonable restraint on alienation, discussed later in this chapter. However, courts are more likely to uphold such a restraint when property is gifted, perhaps under a recognition that you get what you pay for!

and operate a "Community Benefit District" or a "Residential Improvement District" that engages in projects to enhance and improve the community.[16] This is a model similar to the much more common Business Improvement Districts, which are created when a certain percentage of businesses owners in a neighborhood vote to create such an entity.[17]

k. **Ownership + co-ownership + agreement for common management:** In the case of a community where neighbors own their own units or homes and also share ownership of common spaces, the legal arrangement will be much like a condominium or planned unit development (PUD). A large number of cohousing communities use such a legal arrangement: each neighbor is deeded ownership of parcel or unit, and granted a share of ownership of common areas. Conditions, Covenants, and Restrictions (CC&Rs) are recorded along with each deed, requiring that owners of units be members of a community association that manages the commonly owned spaces. Note that, in some cases, ownership of the common areas is actually deeded to the community association, rather than jointly owned by residents.

l. **Ownership + community-supported reverse mortgages:** Even though I do not know of an example of communities or individuals creating their own reverse mortgage programs, I believe that such an arrangement could be beneficial in many ways. For example, a cohousing condo community could make regular payments to support elderly residents in exchange for a reverse mortgage. When the resident passes on, the community would receive the money back (plus interest, if they choose) from the sale proceeds of the condo unit. Such an arrangement could also give the community a purchase option or right of first refusal to buy the unit by simply paying the remaining balance of the

16. A few legal writers have called for the creation of a legal framework allowing a certain number of neighbors (perhaps two-thirds) within an area to vote to bring the neighborhood under the governance of such an association. *See* Robert H. Nelson, *New Community Associations for Established Neighborhoods*, 23(6) Rev. Pol'y Res. (2006). *See also* G. W. Liebmann, *Devolution of Power to Community and Block Associations*, 25 Urb. Law. 335, 382–83 (1993).

17. *See* Rebecca J. Olson & Lacey Keys, *Business Improvement Districts and Proposition 218: After* Silicon Valley Taxpayers Association v. Santa Clara County Open Space Authority, 31(4) Pub. L.J., Fall 2008, http://publiclaw.calbar.ca.gov/Publications/Journal.aspx. *See also* Pennsylvania Neighborhood Improvement District (NID) Act of 2000, Pub. L. 949, No. 130, Section 5.

condo value. This could be a win for both the resident, who is financially supported to age in her home, and for the community, which could earn interest income, or, at the very least, can regain ownership and control over the unit.

Clients Who Own Property Through an Entity

All of the scenarios in the above section involved clients who own property directly. However, in many cases, clients will find it beneficial to form an entity to own property, particularly if it involves a large number of people or a large property. The reasons for forming an entity to own and manage land may include the following:

- Most entities limit the liability of individuals for property-related debts; this is especially important to individuals if there is a large loan on the property, or if there is a large number of people involved.
- Ownership by an entity prevents title from transferring when people come and go; transfer of title not only is inconvenient but could also have implications for financing, property tax, and transfer taxes.
- Entities usually have bylaws or operating agreements that create clear governance structures and procedures.
- The formation of an entity imposes certain limitations on how it may operate and for what purposes, which can play an important role in preserving the founders' vision for a property.
- Forming an entity may attract other sources of financing for a property, such as individual investors that are more comfortable lending to a clearly structured entity governed by state law than to a group of individuals.
- Ownership by an entity can provide a way to control who may rent or buy into the community.
- Ownership by an entity can provide a structure for low income or affordable housing by limiting the ways in which the entity's owners can extract equity from the property.

Here are some common arrangements by which individuals create an entity to own property:

a. **Ownership by a private entity + proprietary leases:** Clients seeking to develop their own housing opportunities often form LLCs, regular corporations, or cooperative corporations to purchase residential properties. Usually, some or all of the members or shareholders of the entity are given the right to live on the property. Unlike direct ownership of land, membership in an entity that owns land does not, under any laws that I know of,[18] come with a presumption that the members have a right to occupy the land; otherwise, Disney shareholders could claim a right to live in the Magic Kingdom. Each member's right to occupy the property needs to be specified by the entity. This can sometimes be done by means of the entity's operating agreement,[19] but this is more often accomplished by means of a separate lease document, often referred to as a "proprietary lease" or "occupancy agreement."

Entities that give their members/shareholders a right to live on the property may meet one or more legal definitions of "housing cooperative" or "stock cooperative."[20] This is our legal system's way of recognizing that ownership of housing through an entity can, for many practical purposes, be made to look and feel a good deal like direct ownership, similar to condos. One job of a sharing economy lawyer is to help clients decide whether it is beneficial to be classified as a cooperative, then to help clients shape their organization and agreements to fall within or outside the definition.

---

18. However, I would be interested to know whether a landowning entity has ever been "disregarded" to create a presumption that members have a right to possession.

19. Many clients in this situation would prefer not to think of themselves as "tenants," and may also want to avoid the application of landlord/tenant law. Note, however, that granting possession by means of an operating agreement, rather than a lease, probably still makes the resident a "tenant," since the interest they hold is a leasehold interest. *See, e.g.*, Susskind v. 1136 Tenants Corp., 43 Misc. 2d 588 (N.Y.C. Civ. Ct. 1964); Suarez v. Rivercross, 107 Misc. 2d 135 (N.Y. App. Div. 1981); Matter of State Tax Comm. v. Shor, 84 Misc. 2d 161 (N.Y. Sup. Ct. 1975); Hauptman v. 222 E 80 St. Corp., 100 Misc. 2d 153 (N.Y.C. Civ. Ct. 1979); Frisch v. Bellmarc Mgt., 190 A.D. 2d 383 (N.Y. App. Div. 1993); Prosnitz v. Augustus, 175 Misc. 2d 582 (N.Y.C. Civ. Ct. 1998); Ostrovsky v. Cartier Apartments Owners Corp., 247 A.D.2d 598 (N.Y. App. Div. 1998).

20. Note that the use of the word "cooperative" here does not necessarily imply or require that a cooperative corporation be the entity of choice, nor that the entity operate "on a cooperative basis" under Subchapter T of the Internal Revenue Code, nor that the cooperative be managed democratically, nor that the cooperative follow the Rochedale Principles for cooperatives. The moral to the story is: the word "cooperative" has way too many meanings, and it's no wonder that it's hard to get a straight answer about what a cooperative is.

Being a cooperative has certain tax benefits. Communities that meet the IRS definition of "cooperative housing corporation"[21] provide tenant-shareholders the opportunity to use many of the same tax deductions and credits that a typical homeowner would have, under the recognition that this is simply an alternative means to homeownership. The IRS's definition requires that *all* members/shareholders be entitled to occupy a dwelling on the property, and that 90 percent of the property be put to residential use or purposes ancillary to residential use.[22]

At the state level, the definition of cooperative has other purposes—usually to determine whether the community will be subject to the same regulations as a subdivision and common interest community. For many resident-developed communities, this treatment is not ideal since it presents burdensome legal hurdles and administrative hassles. Meeting California's definition

---

21. I.R.C. § 216(b), Definitions:

For purposes of this section—

(1) Cooperative housing corporation

The term "cooperative housing corporation" means a corporation—

(A) having one and only one class of stock outstanding,

(B) each of the stockholders of which is entitled, solely by reason of his ownership of stock in the corporation, to occupy for dwelling purposes a house, or an apartment in a building, owned or leased by such corporation,

(C) no stockholder of which is entitled (either conditionally or unconditionally) to receive any distribution not out of earnings and profits of the corporation except on a complete or partial liquidation of the corporation, and

(D) meeting 1 or more of the following requirements for the taxable year in which the taxes and interest described in subsection (a) are paid or incurred:

(i) 80 percent or more of the corporation's gross income for such taxable year is derived from tenant-stockholders.

(ii) At all times during such taxable year, 80 percent or more of the total square footage of the corporation's property is used or available for use by the tenant-stockholders for residential purposes or purposes ancillary to such residential use.

(iii) 90 percent or more of the expenditures of the corporation paid or incurred during such taxable year are paid or incurred for the acquisition, construction, management, maintenance, or care of the corporation's property for the benefit of the tenant-stockholders.

22. For a case interpreting the I.R.S. definition of "tenant-stockholder" under I.R.C. § 216, see *United States v. Evans*, 375 F.2d 730 (9th Cir. 1967) (finding that a tenant's membership in a nonprofit corporation and life lease to a portion of the nonprofit's property did not constitute "stock" under the I.R.S. definition).

of "stock cooperative"[23] requires that *substantially all* members/shareholders be entitled to live at the property. This allows for one or possibly more non-resident owners; but any significant number of non-resident owners will, therefore, bring the community outside the definition of "stock cooperative," which some clients actually prefer, if they want to avoid jumping through legal hoops normally applied to subdivisions.

b. **Ownership by a public benefit nonprofit + leases:** Nonprofit public benefit corporations[24] are the entities most often used to hold residential properties when the goal is to create some form of affordable housing, supportive housing, religious community, or housing for a group with distinct housing needs, such as students. Being a nonprofit public benefit corporation comes with a key restraint: the profits and the assets of the corporation cannot be distributed to private individuals. This is a critical control that removes individual incentives to buy, sell, develop, or extract resources from the land for profit-making purposes. Widespread ownership of land by public benefit nonprofit corporations could, therefore, significantly change the dynamics of the land market and reduce incentives to exploit or speculate on land.

When most people use the phrase "land trust," they are usually not referring to the type of trust that has a trustee and beneficiary; the phrase most often refers to a nonprofit public benefit corporation that owns land and/or easements, usually for the purpose of preserving ecosystems, agricultural land, or affordable housing in the long term.

Not all nonprofits that own land necessarily think of or refer to themselves as "trusts." For example, many of the housing "cooperatives" occupied by University of California, Berkeley

---

23. Cal. Civ. Code § 1351(m):

"Stock cooperative" means a development in which a corporation is formed or availed of, primarily for the purpose of holding title to, either in fee simple or for a term of years, improved real property, and all or substantially all of the shareholders of the corporation receive a right of exclusive occupancy in a portion of the real property, title to which is held by the corporation. The owners' interest in the corporation, whether evidenced by a share of stock, a certificate of membership, or otherwise, shall be deemed to be an interest in a common interest development and a real estate development for purposes of subdivision (f) of Section 25100 of the Corporations Code.

24. The actual name of the corporation type actually varies from state to state, but most states classify nonprofit corporations roughly in this manner: some are for public benefit and some are for the mutual benefit of members.

students are actually owned by the umbrella nonprofit, the Berkeley Student Cooperative.

Note that in most, but not all cases, a nonprofit public benefit corporation will likely seek tax exemption under Section 501(c)(3) or Section 501(c)(4) of the Internal Revenue Code.

c. **Ownership by a mutual benefit nonprofit + proprietary leases:** For housing that does not necessarily serve a special charitable class of individuals or purpose, a mutual benefit nonprofit form is sometimes used to hold title to property. Mutual benefit nonprofits provide a good, service, or benefit to a group of members, and HOAs generally form as mutual benefit corporations. The ownership of land at Earthaven Ecovillage in North Carolina is by a mutual benefit type of nonprofit. Mutual benefit nonprofit corporations are subject to an important constraint, which is that they may not distribute profits to individuals during the life of the organization; this prevents the corporation's land from being developed or mined to serve profit-making goals of individuals. At the same time, mutual benefit corporations are generally allowed to distribute assets to individuals upon dissolution, which means that profit-making goals are not completely prevented from driving the decisions of such an organization.

d. **Ownership by a trust:** Owning land through a trust essentially means designating a trustee who will hold title to and manage land for the benefit or use of one or more beneficiaries. The manner in which the property is to be used will be designated by the written instrument that creates the trust and usually directed by the beneficiaries. Note that this is different from the "land trusts" described above. Many people use trusts as estate planning tools, to reduce taxes, to protect from property-related liability, and/or to hide ownership of a property. Except where estate planning has been involved, in my work as an attorney for shared housing communities, I have yet to find a situation where I thought that it would be ideal to use a trust, over an LLC or other entity, to hold title to land. This remains an open question in my mind, and is worth further research.

Clients Who Combine Entity Ownership with Direct Ownership

Here are two common arrangements through which ownership by an entity might be combined with direct property ownership.

a. **Ownership by entity + ground lease + individually-owned improvements:** Community land trusts typically operate under this model: The nonprofit trust holds title to a piece of land and grants two things to each resident household: a very long term lease (known as a "ground lease") to occupy the land and ownership of certain improvements on that land (usually a housing unit). This model gives residents the feel of ownership, while the land trust's ownership of the underlying land gives the trust the power to set limitations on the use and transfer of the property. In particular, the terms of the ground lease generally limit the residents' ability to sell their unit at market rate, thereby preserving the affordability of the unit and creating what is usually called "limited equity housing." Limited equity housing models use a variety of formulas to determine what kind of return a resident may get when he/she sells the unit. The formula is typically the purchase price multiplied by the change in the consumer price index or the change in area median income, plus the value of any improvements added by the resident.
b. **Ownership of units + ownership of an entity that owns common areas:** Many condominium communities grant individual owners an undivided interest in the common areas and grant *management* to a condo owners' association. However, other condo communities actually give common area *title and management* to a condo owners' association. The practical differences between the two methods are very few. However, conceivably, the latter method of allocating ownership does more to protect individual owners from liability resulting from injuries in common areas. Particularly in communities that make their common areas frequently open to the public or visitors, this arrangement may be ideal.

A Few Considerations in Drafting Agreements and Forming Organizations

The first section of Part 3 provided a long list of agreements and organizations that can be used to help clients share the bundle of property ownership rights and responsibilities. In crafting any arrangement for the allocation of such rights, there are certain challenges and considerations that a sharing economy lawyer will frequently grapple with. One is how the choice, structure, and tax status of an entity will affect the arrangement, which will be covered later. In the meantime, here is a handful of other considerations that come up regardless of whether an entity is involved in the ownership or management of land.

1. **Will the agreement remain even when the people do not?** Agreements are meant to create a framework for stability and predictability in what is otherwise a rather changeable world. Property rights are often transferred at death, divorce, dissolution, or foreclosure; yet the remaining parties to an agreement about land will likely desire that the agreement be kept in place, to preserve the rights allocated to them. Thus, a question to ask about any agreement is whether it is only personal to the parties or whether it will bind successors to the parties.

   When it comes to real property, our legal framework leans in favor of the idea that a person taking title to land should receive the full bundle of property rights. If they meet certain requirements,[25] agreements to reallocate land rights can "run

25. One case that has helpfully summarized the common law and statutory requirements for a covenant that burdens a property to run with the land is *In re Snow*, which explained:

> Under the traditional United States law of covenants running with the land, the following requirements must be met for the burden of a covenant to run with the land: (1) intent by the contracting parties that the burden bind subsequent owners of the servient estate; (2) horizontal privity (mutual interest in the same land) at the time of creation; (3) vertical privity (the successor to the servient estate holds the same interest as that held by the original promisor); (4) a promise that "touches and concerns" the land; and (5) notice, usually given by the recordation of the covenant. For the running of the benefit with the dominant estate, the elements of intent, vertical privity and touch and concern must be met. *See generally* 1 Arthur R. Gaudio, The American Law of Real Property § 6.04 (1994).
>
> California law on covenants is slightly different. The California statute, as amended in 1968 and 1969, requires the following elements for a covenant to run with the land: (1) the instrument containing the covenant must describe both the dominant estate and the servient estate; (2) the instrument must expressly provide that all successive owners of the servient estate are to be bound by the covenant, and the deed must refer to the recorded restrictions to show the intent of the parties that the covenant run with the land; (3) each act required by the covenant must relate to the use, repair, maintenance, or improvement of, or payment of taxes and assessments on, the land described; (4) the instrument containing the covenant must be recorded in the office of the county recorder of the county where the land is situated. Cal. Civ. Code § 1468 (West 1996).

In re Snow, 201 B.R. 968, 972–73 (Bankr. C.D. Cal. 1996).

with the land" and thereby bind all future owners. However, many of the agreements described in the above section will not meet either the common law or the state statutory requirements for the creation of a covenant that runs with the land, particularly those agreements that are not or cannot be recorded in property records. Instead, if they meet the requirements, many agreements will be enforced as equitable servitudes, which courts will enforce by means of injunction. Equitable servitudes generally require that successors have some notice that such an agreement exists, and that the original parties intended that successors be bound.[26]

For example, an unrecorded Tenancy in Common (TIC) Agreement between two co-owners is unlikely to be deemed a covenant running with the land. Most people do not record TIC Agreements for fear that doing so could subject the co-ownership arrangement to laws applicable to subdivisions. But this leaves the question: will the agreement bind heirs if they inherit one co-owner's interest?

Here are a few practices that a lawyer can use to improve the likelihood that an agreement about land will be enforceable as an equitable servitude: (1) including clear language in the agreement that it is meant to bind successors; (2) recording in public records a Memorandum of Agreement, which is a brief statement to put

---

26. *In re Snow* also provides a helpful explanation of the legal requirements for the creation of an equitable servitude:

> An equitable servitude arises where one or more of the requirements of a [covenant] running with the land are not met, but the following conditions are met: (1) the subsequent owner of the servient estate has notice of the covenant; (2) the holder of the servitude is seeking equitable relief only (as opposed to a remedy at law); and (3) it is inequitable to deny the enforcement of the servitude. *See, e.g.*, Restatement of Property § 539 cmt. b (1944); 7 Harry D. Miller & Marvin B. Starr, Current Law of California Real Estate §§ 22:5–22:26 (2d ed. 1990).
>
> The California Supreme Court has recently described equitable servitudes as follows:
>
> > Under the law of equitable servitudes, courts may enforce a promise about the use of land even though the person who made the promise has transferred the land to another. . . . [E]quitable servitudes permit courts to enforce promises restricting land use when there is no privity of contract between the party seeking to enforce the promise and the party resisting enforcement.
>
> Nahrstedt v. Lakeside Village Condominium Association, 8 Cal. 4th 361, 33 Cal. Rptr. 2d 63, 73–74, 878 P.2d 1275, 1285–86 (1994) (citations omitted).

In re Snow, 201 B.R. at 973.

the public on notice that such an agreement reallocating property rights exists; (3) advising parties to provide a copy or information about such an agreement to likely successors; (4) ensuring that the terms of the agreement would be fair in the eyes of a "reasonable person" (because courts have some discretion and will decline to enforce an agreement that appears unfair or inequitable); and (5) crafting the agreement in a way that will not create an unreasonable restraint on alienation (described below).

2. **Does the arrangement create unenforceable restrictions on transfer of the property?** This is only a slightly less lawyerly way of saying: does it create unreasonable restraints on alienation? As a general and long-standing rule, courts will not enforce agreements that, without useful justification, prevent an owner from gifting, leasing, or selling the property in a reasonable and typical way.

    The way that courts decide what is an unreasonable restraint on alienation has important implications for many of the solutions proposed in this chapter, since many of the agreements people make to share use, management, and financing of land could also put some constraints on the way the land is transferred, and/or that detract from the marketability of the property.

    Over time and case by case, courts have broadened the number of ways that people can lawfully create restraints on alienation, and my hope is that they will continue to broaden in light of the land access crisis that society is facing. A sharing economy lawyer focusing on real property should become familiar with the ways that courts make this decision,[27] and also be prepared to make arguments that restraints are reasonable. It is helpful here to quote directly from the Restatement (Third) of Property, regarding how courts generally determine the reasonableness of a restraint.[28] I have added emphasis in italics:

    > **Determining reasonableness.** Determining reasonableness of a restraint on alienation requires balancing the utility of the

27. *See generally* George Lefcoe, *Should We Ban or Welcome "Spec" Home Buyers?*, U.S.C. Legal Studies Research Paper No. 09-33, 36 J. Legis. 1 (2010) (summarizing courts' approaches).

28. Restatement (Third) of Property § 3.4, Direct Restraints on Alienation, cmt. C at 442 (2000).

purpose served by the restraint against the harm that is likely to flow from its enforcement. Restraints on alienation of land are used to accomplish a wide variety of purposes of differing utility. They are used to retain land in families and to *preserve affordable housing.* They are used to control entry into cooperative, condominium, and subsidized housing developments that require particular financial qualifications. They are also used to *control entry into communities, like retirement communities, developed for specialized purposes.* Entry controls may be used for legitimate purposes or for the purpose of effecting illegal discrimination. *Restraints on alienation are used to further the conservation, preservation, and charitable purposes to which land is devoted.* They are also imposed to facilitate land development and create investment opportunities. Restraints on renting or leasing property may also be imposed to ensure that a certain percentage of a development be owner occupied to meet requirements for financing imposed by institutional lenders.

The harmful effects that may flow from restraints on alienation include impediments to the operation of a free market in land, limiting the prospects for improvement, development, and redevelopment of land, and limiting the mobility of landowners and would-be purchasers. Other harmful consequences include the demoralization costs associated with subordinating the desires of current landowners to the desires of past owners, and frustrating the expectations that normally flow from land ownership. Harmful consequences also may flow from enforcement of restraints on alienation that place one person in a position to take unfair advantage of another's need or desire to transfer property.

In determining the injurious consequences likely to flow from enforcement of a restraint on alienation, *the nature, extent, and duration of the restraint are important considerations. The standard against which the impact of a restraint is to be measured is that of the property owner free to transfer property at his/her convenience at a price determined by the market.* Common types of restraints include prohibitions on transfers without consent of another, rights of first refusal, requirements that transfers be made only to persons meeting certain eligibility requirements, and options that require transfer to a particular person at a time selected by that person. The restraint may extend to all types of transfers, or only to certain types, like leases and subleases. It may require transfer at a fixed price, a price determined by

> a formula, by an appraisal, or by an offer received from a third party. The duration may be a fixed period, long or short, it may be limited by the occurrence of some event, or it may be unlimited. *The greater the practical interference with the owner's ability to transfer, the stronger the purpose that is required to justify a direct restraint on alienation.*

The irony of the legal framework on unreasonable restraints on alienation is that it begins with the assumption that, ideally, we could all transfer land freely in the open market.[29] Yet, many restraints allowable by courts are designed for charitable or conservation purposes—in other words, to *counteract* the harmful impacts of a land marketplace left to its own devices. Courts are empowered to perform a highly subjective balancing act, one that is subject to judges' personal opinions about the needs of society, people, and the environment. At the same time, empowering courts to perform this balancing act potentially turns the courtroom into a forum for the discussion of society's land access crisis. It should force courts to examine the harmful impact that the marketplace has had on people, communities, and ecosystems, and to recognize that remedying those harms is, indeed, a "strong purpose" justifying the creation of restraints.

Courts have, in essence, already begun to do this, as demonstrated by their willingness to uphold restraints on the ways that subsidized affordable housing units are transferred or leased to tenants,[30] for example. We can draw on this precedent if and when we are forced to argue that our agreements for managing shared property rights are reasonable and important.

In drafting agreements, a lawyer could help to preserve the enforceability of the restraint by (1) explicitly describing the purpose and social/environmental/personal needs for such a restraint, (2) describing the way in which the owners will benefit

---

29. *See also* Alby v. Banc One Fin., 128 P.3d 81 (Wash. 2006) (Chambers, J., dissenting) (arguing that a restraint on the ability to mortgage a property should be deemed unreasonable, since this has become the primary way in which people effect transfers of property).

30. City of Oceanside v. McKenna, 264 Cal. Rptr. 275, 279 (Cal. Ct. App. 1989) (upholding a restriction preventing owners of subsidized affordable condo units from moving out and renting to a tenant of the owner's choice).

from or benefit "in consideration of" the restraint, and (3) building in a sufficient number of exit options for property owners and co-owners, along with clear procedures and timelines for how to exercise them.

Building in exit options is what, for example, causes many co-ownership agreements to become quite lengthy. Co-owners usually make agreements to waive their right to seek partition of the property,[31] but a court will only uphold this if it feels that the owners have sufficient other options for exit. If a co-owner wants out, the remaining co-owners are often then given a specified period of time in which to exercise options to buy out the departing owner, to search for and choose new co-owners, or to decide to allow the co-owner to put his/her share on the open market. Thereafter, co-owners might still exercise a right of first refusal on an offer, they might refuse a prospective buyer on specified reasonable grounds, and the agreement will ultimately set the terms under which a departing co-owner could simply force a sale of the entire property. Clients may go cross-eyed when I give them an agreement with *pages* of procedures for how an exit will play out; yet, such provisions protect co-owners and the enforceability of the agreement by giving them both a reasonable opportunity to stay and a reasonable opportunity to leave.

Note that, as a general rule, courts are less willing to enforce restraints on alienation as applied to condos, since those are legally divided interests that were *designed* to be easily transferred. Unlike in a TIC or cooperative, the units in a condo have been legally divided out from the total ownership of the building, which, in theory, makes them easier to transfer without affecting other units. Some states may even have explicit rules prohibiting condo owners' associations from putting restraints on the transferability of a condo.

Ownership of land by means of an entity such as an LLC brings up another question with regard to the issue of restraints on alienation. An ownership interest in an LLC may be considered ownership of *personal* property, not *real* property, which

31. Although the word "partition" connotes the physical division of land parcels, the vast majority of partitions actually involve the sale of the property and division of the proceeds among co-owners.

means that the entity may have greater freedom to impose restraints on alienation of the membership interests.[32]

3. **What are the individual tax implications of the arrangement?** Property ownership, and particularly ownership of one's primary residence, generally comes with tax benefits to the individual. Reallocating property rights in some of the ways described above may affect the availability of certain tax benefits, which include:
   a. **The capital gains exclusion:** The IRS currently allows homeowners to exclude from taxation the first $250,000 (or $500,000 for a married couple) of capital gains on the sale of a primary residence.[33] Unfortunately, individuals that own their property through an entity that does not meet the IRS definition of a "cooperative housing corporation"[34] or that is a disregarded entity, such as a single-member LLC,[35] will not be eligible to use this exclusion if they sell their share of a landholding entity and realize a gain.
   b. **The mortgage interest tax deduction:** Payment of interest on home mortgages is generally a tax deduction for an individual.[36] This is a substantial tax benefit, since a significant portion of mortgage payments consist of interest during the first years of payment, and the deduction could reduce an individual's taxable income by tens of thousands of dollars. This tax deduction is available to tenant-shareholders of housing that meets the IRS's definition of "cooperative housing corporation," and it allows the tenant to deduct his/her share of the interest on the cooperative blanket mortgage.

      The availability of the mortgage interest tax deduction is a major consideration when a group of people is contemplating

32. Business interests are also sometimes found by courts to be subject to unreasonable restraints on alienation. *See* Peter A. Mahler, *Beware Unreasonable Restraints on Alienation When Drafting Shareholder and Operating Agreements*, N.Y. Bus. Divorce, Nov. 23, 2009, http://www.nybusinessdivorce.com (summarizing case law).

33. *See* I.R.S. Publ'n 523, Selling Your Home, http://www.irs.gov/pub/irs-pdf/p523.pdf.

34. *See* I.R.C. § 216(b), *supra* note 21.

35. *See* I.R.S. Publ'n 3402, Taxation of Limited Liability Companies (Mar. 2010), at 3 (explaining when a single-member LLC may be considered a disregarded entity).

36. *See* I.R.S. Publ'n 530, Tax Information for Homeowners, http://www.irs.gov/pub/irs-pdf/p530.pdf.

purchasing a multi-unit residential property together and choosing between ownership as a TIC or an LLC. Although the members of the LLC cannot claim the deduction in the same way direct homeowners may, an LLC passes the mortgage interest through to members as a business expense, which usually results in a business loss shown on the member's K-1 (the statement of a member's share of profits, losses, deductions, and credits in the LLC).

c. **The property tax deduction:** Homeowners can generally deduct from income amounts paid toward local real property taxes. This benefit is available to direct homeowners and tenant-shareholders of cooperatives, but must be passed through to members as a business expense in the case of ownership by an LLC that does not meet the IRS definition of "cooperative housing corporation."

4. **Are there other tax issues?**
   a. **Sweat equity:** Another tax issue to consider is the effect of an agreement to grant a property interest to a person in exchange for work they do on a property. Clients are frequently shocked when I tell them that such a "sweat equity" arrangement generates taxable income to the person contributing work, as measured by the value of the land interest that they are granted.
   b. **Property taxes:** In California, where property tax assessors generally do not reappraise a property unless there has been a change of ownership, a group of co-owners may want to find a way to prevent frequent changes of ownership. For example, if a California property is owned by eight people as a TIC, chances are that every several years an owner may wish to leave and relocate. If that person sells his/her share, this could trigger partial reappraisal of the property and, if the property value has risen, higher property taxes. One way to avoid frequent reappraisal is to own the property through an entity, such as a partnership, corporation, or LLC. Under California law, a change of ownership may not take place unless there is a transfer of more than 50 percent of the interests in the entity.[37]

37. Cal. Rev. & Tax. Code § 64.

5. **What are the implications for the financing of the property?** Large institutional lenders make loans with a variety of strings attached and can sometimes prevent groups from managing property in the way they desire. Some examples follow:
   a. **Due on sale clause:** Most mortgages come with a "due on transfer" or "due on sale" clause, which accelerates the loan and requires payment in full upon the transfer of an interest in the property. The Garn-St. Germain Federal Depository Institutions Act[38] lays out a list of transfers that are allowed and that may not trigger the loan acceleration. This includes transfers to living trusts, transfers to joint tenants upon the death of one tenant, and a transfer to make a spouse or child an owner. One listed exemption is "the granting of a leasehold interest of three years or less not containing an option to purchase,"[39] which begs the question of whether a lease for longer than three years or a lease with purchase option *could* trigger the clause. As mentioned earlier, notices of long-term leases and purchase options should generally be recorded in public records to provide notice to the public of such a right. Recordation, however, could result in notice to the lender, who *may* choose to accelerate the loan. Whether the lender actually accelerates it is another question, as many lenders are content to let things like that slide.
   b. **Access to fractional finance:** Co-owners of multi-unit properties are sometimes able to obtain fractional loans, which means that each co-owner is responsible for a separate loan that is secured by that owner's interest in the property. Most lenders are hesitant to make such loans, and when they do, they typically must review and approve a co-ownership agreement to ensure that the rights and responsibilities are sufficiently described and divided, to ensure that the lender is protected in the event that it must foreclose on one owner's fractional interest. These loans may incur higher interest rates than conventional loans.

      When fractional financing is not available, TIC co-owners often share responsibility for a single mortgage,

38. 12 U.S.C. § 1701J-3, Preemption of Due-on-Sale Prohibitions.
39. 12 U.S.C. § 1701J-3(d)(4).

which means that TIC Agreements must contain a significant number of provisions to ensure that one owner's financial troubles do not put everyone else's interest at risk.

c. **Residential versus commercial finance:** A downside to purchasing a property as an LLC or corporation, as opposed to a TIC, is that the financing available for such a purchase is more likely a commercial loan than a residential mortgage, which generally requires that the purchasers make a significant down payment (often 30 percent). Lack of access to optimal financing leads some clients to avoid formation of an LLC or other entity, even when most other factors indicate that it would advantageous to do so.

6. **When might you use multiple tiers of agreements?** The creation of any of the legal configurations listed above could potentially entail multiple tiers of documents. Oftentimes, a lawyer will draft an agreement to allocate property rights (e.g., lease, CC&R, TIC Agreement), and work with clients to create a second or third level of agreements of the sort that are likely to change more often in response to the evolving needs of the arrangement.

   For example, in a cohousing community, in addition to deeds that confer ownership, CC&Rs that allocate property rights, and bylaws that provide for the governance of the Community Association, the community may wish to adopt policies and procedures for various matters related to the operation of community, such as how maintenance or other projects are managed, how committees operate, how supplies purchases are made, how reimbursements are handled, and so on. They may also wish to adopt rules related to noise, pets, drugs, gatherings, and chemical use. Some communities execute a document called Architectural Guidelines or something similar to set rules on how each unit owner can make exterior alterations to the unit in order to ensure a common design scheme. Many communities also have an extensive document-detailing procedure for the management of meetings and consensus decision-making; sometimes this is included in the bylaws and other times the bylaws incorporate this document by reference. Likewise, parties to a TIC Agreement in a co-owned property may wish to adopt a second-tier document called the

"Community Agreement" or "House Policies," to govern day-to-day matters such as maintenance, purchases, and chores.

Forming and Structuring Organizations

There are three primary layers of considerations in the design of organizations for the ownership and management of land:

- **What entity we choose:** The entity we choose and form at the state level comes with a set of built-in parameters for how the entity can operate, manage funds, make decisions, and engage in activities.
- **What tax status the entity chooses:** The choice of tax status adds another layer of parameters that guide how an entity can operate, and also affects the financial status of the entity and individuals involved.
- **How we structure the entity:** Once we have chosen and formed an entity, the next consideration is how to structure it, including how to manage governance, capitalization, allocation of profits/losses, etc. This is done through the choices we make in drafting bylaws, operating agreements, and policies.

Sometimes multiple entities will be involved in the creation of a housing arrangement. For example, there may be one for the ownership of land, one for the management of a development project, and one for management of shared activities. Sometimes, holding title to land under a separate entity protects it from liability incurred by an entity that operates programs on and develops the property. In addition, each entity may have different purposes or activities that mandate different legal structures and tax exemptions.

The formation, structure, and taxation of entities is the focus of Chapter 4 of this book, so this section focuses primarily on the considerations related to the formation of entities to hold and manage land and housing.

Choice of Entity

Every state offers a large handful of entity types to choose from, and each entity comes with a set of legal requirements and constraints. The rules governing entities vary from state to state, so it's important to read the statute governing the entity types. The most common entity types available at the state level and used for the ownership of land are

- Partnerships (general and limited);
- Limited liability companies (LLC);
- Low-profit limited liability companies (L3C);[40]
- General stock corporations,[41] which include new corporation types, such as benefit corporations and flexible purpose corporations;[42]
- Cooperative corporations;
- Nonprofit public benefit corporations;
- Nonprofit mutual benefit corporations; and
- Nonprofit religious corporations.

There are usually many considerations to weigh in the choice of entity; these are discussed generally in transactional law practice guides, and also in Chapter 4 of this book. Here are some considerations relevant to the ownership and management of land:

a. **Does the choice of entity limit liability of individual members/shareholders?** If managed properly, LLCs and corporations of all kinds generally shield individual members/shareholders from liability for the entity's debts, acts, and omissions. If multiple people come together to purchase and develop land together, particularly if they plan to take out large loans, a entity with limited liability will likely be optimal to ensure that no one individual is left holding the bag if things go wrong. All entities listed above, except partnerships, offer limited liability. In many states, the primary reason that some groups may choose to form a partnership to own land is to save money on the costs otherwise required in forming and operating a limited liability entity.

40. These are available in only a handful of states. See Chapter 4 for more information.

41. I use the phrase "general stock corporations" to refer to run-of-the mill for-profit corporations, to differentiate between those corporations and cooperatives and nonprofits.

42. These are available in only a small handful of states. See Chapter 4 for more information.

In California, for example, partnerships are not required to pay the $800 annual minimum franchise tax required of LLCs and corporations.

b. **Does the choice of entity limit individuals' abilities to derive profit from the entity?** The ability to profit from the equity or income of land offers a strong incentive for people to buy land, but this incentive also drives people to exploit land and buy/sell/own in ways that drive up prices for others. Many clients will want to limit individuals' ability to profit from land and will thus choose to form a nonprofit public benefit corporation or a nonprofit religious corporation. Whereas the exact name of the corporation type and the legal restrictions vary from state to state, such nonprofits are generally prohibited from distributing their profits and assets to individuals, and may only distribute profits and assets to other nonprofits.

   There are at least two other entity types that tend to impose *some* restrictions on the distribution of profits and assets. A nonprofit mutual benefit corporation, under some state laws, is prohibited from distributing profits to members, but may purchase or redeem memberships from the members.[43] Thus, if a member buys a membership in a land-owning nonprofit mutual benefit corporation for $10,000, the corporation can pay that amount back to the member when he/she leaves. Most likely, however, no dividend, interest, or appreciation could be paid along with the redemption. Although they are prohibited from distributing profits, under some state laws, mutual benefit nonprofits may, upon dissolution only, distribute assets to members or to a person or entity of its choosing.[44] This means that individual members may have some incentive to cash out by selling the entire property and dissolving the entity.

   Often, cooperative corporations are limited by state laws in the ways that they can distribute profits to individuals. For example, in California, a cooperative cannot distribute more than a 15 percent return per year on individuals' capital contributions.[45] Cooperatives are generally required to distribute earnings on the

43. *See, e.g.*, Cal. Corp. Code § 7411.
44. *See, e.g.*, Cal. Corp. Code § 8717.
45. Cal. Corp. Code § 12451.

basis of patronage, rather than on the basis of capital contributed.[46] This means that earnings are distributed to individuals, but that one individual cannot make a large profit on his/her capital investment.

c. **Does the choice of entity mandate democratic or accountable governance?** If an entity mandates a certain type of governance structure, this can contribute to the protection of land, by helping to ensure that private interests cannot control an entity for their personal benefit. Cooperative corporations, nonprofit mutual benefit corporations, and nonprofit public benefit corporations with members are typically mandated, by law, to have elections and major decisions be made on a one-member/one-vote basis. This helps to ensure that an organization operates with its members' interests or the original purpose of the organization in mind. In addition, even when they do not obtain tax exemption under 501(c)(3), nonprofit public benefit corporations are often subject to certain rules that help to maintain the integrity of the board. For example, state statutes may limit the number of financially interested directors that may serve on a board and require that self-dealing transactions be approved by a disinterested panel of directors or by a government entity, such as the state attorney general.[47]

d. **Does choice of entity mandate a certain tax treatment?** As described below, an entity can choose between two or more tax statuses or exemptions, but the IRS will also impose certain other rules on an entity depending on whether it is a corporation, LLC, or partnership. Tax law is vast, and it's impossible to summarize it all here. However, I'll describe one major consideration briefly, which is that in the real estate context, most of the time it will be optimal to own land as an LLC (or partnership, if partners are willing to assume personal liability for debts). Most commonly, my clients choose to form an LLC over a corporation because an LLC member's adjusted basis in the LLC is raised by the member's allocable share of the entity's debt. Because each member's adjusted basis is much higher than the amount of cash the mem-

46. *See* Cal. Corp. Code § 12201 and Chapter 4 of this book for a description of patronage in cooperatives.

47. *See, e.g.*, Cal. Corp. Code § 5233.

ber has actually contributed to the entity, each member is able to deduct greater losses in an LLC than they would through a corporation (where the entity's debt is not included in determination of a shareholder's basis). The loss deducted by an LLC member may, therefore, be greater than the amount of cash the individual member has actually contributed to the LLC. Many LLCs formed for the purposes of holding real estate will be able to pass significant losses through to individual members, as a result of payment of mortgage interest, property taxes, insurance and other expenses, and by allocating a share of the property depreciation to members.[48] By passing through deductible losses to members in this way, LLCs are able to simulate some of the tax advantages of individual home ownership (such as tax deductions for mortgage interest and property tax payments).

Choice of Tax Status

The question of an entity's tax status is answered somewhat separately from the choice of entity formation at the state level. Most entities, once formed, will then be able to choose from two or more tax statuses or exemptions.

a. **Entity-level taxation versus pass-through taxation:** Some entities (C Corporations and LLCs that elect to be taxed like C Corporations) are subject to "double taxation"—the entity pays tax on its net earnings, and individual members/shareholders pay tax on those earnings when they are distributed to individuals. By contrast, pass-through entities (S Corporations, most LLCs, and partnerships) are not taxed until profits are distributed or allocated to members and shareholders. Pass-through status is especially important in housing ownership because, often more importantly, *losses* can be passed through to individuals to offset other sources of individual income.
b. **Cooperative taxation:** As described in Chapter 4, entities that distribute income to members on a cooperative basis (on the basis of how much each "patronized" the cooperative) can be taxed under Subchapter T of the Internal Revenue Code, which pro-

48. For more information, see I.R.S. Publications 541 and 925.

vides for a type of pass-through taxation. Under Subchapter T, cooperative earnings that are distributed as patronage dividends are taxable to individual, but not to the entity.

c. **Forms of tax exemption:** Most nonprofit corporations will seek some form of tax exemption from the IRS. The section of the Internal Revenue Code under which an entity obtains tax exemption may dictate many things about how the entity operates, for what purposes, how it is governed, what sources of income it may have, and how it may spend or distribute its funds. Here is a brief summary of the categories of tax exemption land-owning organizations may contemplate:

    i. **Section 501(c)(2) Title holding corporations:** An entity "organized for the exclusive purpose of holding title to property, collecting income therefrom, and turning over the entire amount thereof, less expenses, to [another tax-exempt nonprofit]" may obtain exemption under section 501(c)(2) of the Internal Revenue Code.[49] There are a variety reasons that a nonprofit might want to create a separate entity to hold title to and manage income-producing properties, some of which are named by the IRS in one publication on 501(c)(2):

    > These factors would include limitation of liability from potential damage suits; enhancement of ability to borrow; limitations imposed in gifts and bequests to exempt organizations that effectively require such gifts to be kept in separate entities; clarity of title; accounting simplification; and limitations imposed by various state laws on organizations that would be recognized as exempt under the federal revenue laws.[50]

    ii. **Section 501(c)(3) Charitable, religious, educational, and scientific organizations:** Unless it is in furtherance of a recognized charitable, educational, religious, or scientific purpose, developing and providing housing, alone, is generally not considered a purpose that is tax-exempt under 501(c)(3). Providing housing to people who are poor, distressed,

---

49. *See* C. IRC 501(c)(2)—Title Holding Corporations (IRS Exempt Organizations 1986), *available at* http://www.irs.gov/pub/irs-tege/eotopicc86.pdf.

50. *See id.* at 2.

or underprivileged is considered a charitable purpose.[51] Through various rulings and guidance documents, the IRS has provided guidance on the circumstances under which provision of housing to low-income individuals,[52] people with disabilities,[53] and the elderly[54] will be tax-exempt. Providing housing in furtherance of another tax-exempt purpose can also, itself, be a tax-exempt activity. For example, providing housing to students (whether or not students are part of an underprivileged group) may be tax-exempt because provision of housing advances the school's educational purpose. Housing provided in connection with a religious center or other educational center will also likely be found to be a tax-exempt purpose, if the provision of such housing is necessary to achieving the religious or educational purposes. Organizations formed to preserve ecologically significant land[55] or, in some cases, historically significant buildings[56] may also obtain tax exemption under 501(c)(3).

Many of my clients who form groups with the intent of developing housing for themselves will ask me about the possibility of obtaining 501(c)(3) status and using grant money or tax-deductible donations in the purchase or development of their housing. Unfortunately, many of these groups would fail to meet the requirements necessary to 501(c)(3) tax exemption, primarily because their organization is designed to meet the housing needs of a fixed and defined group of people, and is not necessarily formed for the purpose of creating broader

---

51. *See* I.R.S. Publ'n 557 (Oct. 2011), at 30.

52. *See* Robert Louthian & Marvin Friedlander, Low-Income Housing as a Charitable Activity (IRS Exempt Organizations 1992), *available at* http://www.irs.gov/pub/irs-tege/eotopicd92.pdf. *See also* Rev. Rul. 70-585, 1970-2 C.B. 115; Rev. Rul. 67-138, 1967-1 C.B. 129; I.R.S. Low Income Housing Guidelines Revenue Procedure, Rev. Proc. 96-32, 1996-1 C.B. 717, 1996-20 I.R.B. 14, *available at* http://www.irs.gov/pub/irs-tege/rp_1996-32.pdf.

53. *See* Rev. Rul. 79-19, 1979-1 C.B. 195.

54. Rental Housing for the Elderly Under IRC 501(c)(3) (IRS Exempt Organizations 1979), *available at* http://www.irs.gov/pub/irs-tege/eotopich79.pdf. *See also* Rev. Rul. 72-124, 1972-1 C.B. 145; Rev. Rul. 79-18, 1979-1 C.B. 194; and Rev. Rul. 79-18, 1979-2 C.B. 194.

55. Rev. Rul. 76-204, 1976-2 C.B. 15.

56. *See* Rev. Rul. 75-470, 1975-2 C.B. 207; Rev. Rul. 67-6, 1967-1 C.B. 135; Rev. Rul. 76-147, 1976-1 C.B. 151.

public benefit. However, such groups may benefit from creating a separate 501(c)(3) corporation for the operation of specific activities that are tax-exempt, such as educational or charitable programs provided on the property. Groups may also sell or give title, a conservation easement, or other rights to a 501(c)(3) organization to empower that organization to enforce the preservation of ecosystems on the land or the affordability of some of the housing on the land.

iii. **Section 501(c)(4) Social welfare organizations:** 501(c)(4) tax exemption is generally available to organizations engaging in activities that benefit the public or a broad sector of the community.[57] Many activities can fall under 501(c)(4) tax exemption, so long as they don't look a good deal like commercial activities and so long as they are not designed to benefit only a fixed group of people. A group that wants to develop housing for itself will likely fail to meet the requirements of 501(c)(4) for some of the same reasons that it might fail under 501(c)(3), since the group's efforts are often aimed primarily to benefit the group, as opposed to a broad community. Some HOAs, however, obtain 501(c)(4) status if they operate primarily to provide facilities to the public[58] or if they operate to provide benefit to a large community (as opposed to a small geographic area).[59] If the organization works to improve individually owned properties, it will likely fail to qualify for exemption under 501(c)(4).[60] Donations to 501(c)(4)s are not tax deductible to donors and most foundations do not make grants to 501(c)(4)s; this means that 501(c)(4) status generally does not help an organization to fundraise.

iv. **Section 501(c)(7) Social and recreational organizations:** In contrast to 501(c)(3) and 501(c)(4) organizations, which are required to provide benefits to the public, 501(c)(7) tax exemption is designed specifically for groups that provide a private benefit *to themselves*. In that respect, 501(c)(7)s may be

---

57. *See* John Francis Reilly, Carter C. Hull & Barbara A. Braig Allen, IRC 501(c)(4) Organizations (IRS Exempt Organizations 2003), *available at* http://www.irs.gov/pub/irs-tege/eotopici03.pdf.

58. *See* Rev. Rul. 80-63, 1980-1 C.B. 116.

59. *See* Rev. Rul. 74-99, 1974-1 C.B. 131.

60. *See* Rev. Rul. 74-17, 1974-1 C.B. 130.

fitting for groups seeking to provide certain housing amenities to themselves, like a country club, swimming pool, or possibly a cohousing common house. 501(c)(7) is a category of exemption designed for social, recreational, and "other nonprofitable purposes."[61] A question for further inquiry is: what kinds of activities can be included under 501(c)(7)'s "other nonprofitable purposes" category? It is not a perfect "catch-all" because the IRS has already said that maintaining roads in a neighborhood is not a proper activity for a 501(c)(7) because is not related to social or pleasurable purposes.[62] Apparently the IRS has appointed itself the arbiter of "pleasure" in deciding what does and does not further social and pleasurable purposes. Maintaining roads, to the IRS, must sound like all work and no play. 501(c)(7) may be a fine tax category for a group that wants to share a private vacation home or campground (which sounds like fun), but it will not likely work for a group that simply wants to provide itself with primary residences (which sounds too normal and boring).[63]

Note that 501(c)(7)s may not receive more than 35 percent of their income from non-member sources, and no more than 15 percent of the income may come from the use of the club's facilities by the general public. This rule *requires* that the organization provide only for a limited group of people. The income derived from members must also be of a sort "traditionally" associated with "normal and usual" activities of a social club (member fees, entrance fees, and so on).[64] The IRS seems to have also appointed itself arbiter of "tradition," in deciding what groups can provide for themselves and on what terms. A cohousing community could likely own a common house as a 501(c)(7) and could charge members dues and fees for involvement in community meals and social activities. But could that entity also operate a grocery-buying club for

61. *See* Jim Langley & Conrad Rosenberg, Social Clubs—IRC 501(c)(7) (IRS Exempt Organizations 1996), *available at* http://www.irs.gov/pub/irs-tege/eotopicc96.pdf.

62. *See* Rev. Rul. 75-494, 1975-2 C.B. 214.

63. *Id.*

64. *See* Langley & Rosenberg, *supra* note 61.

the members, an equipment rental service, a shared Internet service, a guest house, or other amenity that the members must pay for? This is an area for further inquiry, and it may require that we seek guidance from the U.S. Department of Pleasure and Tradition (the IRS).

v. **Section 501(d) Apostolic associations:** A group of people that wishes to develop and own housing communally may want to consider seeking tax exemption under 501(d)[65] if that group is bound together by a set of common beliefs and values. To obtain exemption under this section, a group must meet requirements of the statute, which are summarized by the Ninth Circuit as follows: "that there be a common treasury, that the members of the organization include pro-rata shares when reporting taxable income, and implicitly, that the organization have a religious or apostolic character."[66] The phrase "common treasury" generally means that members share income and property.

    Twin Oaks is an intentional community in Virginia that has tax exemption under 501(d). Twin Oaks was also the subject of a Tax Court decision that held that members of a 501(d) community need not surrender their personal property and take a vow of poverty upon joining.[67] In determining what is a proper religious or apostolic "character," 501(d) organizations appear to be subject to far less scrutiny than are churches that seek tax exemption under 501(c)(3). A 501(d) organization need not hold religious services or engage in activities characteristic of traditional religions, such as songs, adoption of symbols, or rituals. The community may simply create "an environment for the daily practice of its beliefs," as the Tax Court observed in the *Twin Oaks* case.[68]

vi. **Section 528 "Homeowners' associations":** A homeowners' association (HOA) may sound like something you'd find managing common areas and property use in a run-of-the mill subdivision, but the tax category that the IRS has created

---

65. *See* IRM § 4.76.29 (June 4, 2010).
66. Kleinsasser v. United States, 707 F.2d 1024 (9th Cir. 1983).
67. Twin Oaks Cmty., Inc. v. Comm'r, 87 T.C. 1233 (1986).
68. *Id.*

for HOA could also be used to purchase, develop, and own entire properties for the creation of intentional communities. Earthhaven Ecovillage in North Carolina, for example, owns a 320-acre property as an HOA and files taxes under Section 528.[69] Earthhaven leases plots of land to members, who construct residences on those plots. HOAs are defined by the IRS to include condominium management associations, residential real estate management associations, and timeshare associations.[70] Such organizations are usually formed under state law as mutual benefit nonprofits. To qualify for tax status under Section 528, 90 percent of the entity's expenditures must be made to acquire, construct, manage, and maintain property.[71] In addition, 60 percent of the organization's income must be derived from member fees, dues, and assessments.[72] Income from other sources is generally taxable. An organization need not apply for tax exemption under Section 528, but need only meet the requirements of the statute and file its tax return using Form 1120 or 1120-H.

Considerations When Structuring the Entity

Choice of entity and tax status are important considerations in designing an organization to own and manage land; however, the real "teeth" of an organization can sometimes be found in the choices the members/owners make in designing its structure, governance, and financial terms. These terms can greatly influence an organization's accountability to its members and to the purposes it was designed to serve.

Some entities, like LLCs, afford a vast amount of flexibility to members to structure and manage the entity however they wish. Even in corporations, which, by statute, require specific structural and procedural formalities, there is flexibility to build in the structural "teeth" to sustain the organization's purposes and ensure accountability. Chapter 4 discusses some of these choices, but here are some of the important considerations to be made in structuring an entity to own land:

---

69. Diana Leafe Christian, Creating a Life Together: Practical Tools to Grow Ecovillages and Intentional Communities 179 (New Society 2003).
70. I.R.C. § 528(c)(1).
71. I.R.C. § 528(c)(1)(C).
72. I.R.C. § 528(c)(1)(B).

a. **Composition of membership:** Who may join and/or buy in to the entity?
b. **Voting rights:** Do members receive one vote each, or are voting rights allocated in proportion to a member's investment, share of land ownership, or on some other basis?
c. **Governing body:** Will there be a governing board of directors or will members manage the entity directly?
d. **Election and appointment procedures:** If the entity has a governing body, how will members of the governing body be elected or appointed? How will officers be elected or appointed?
e. **Composition of governing body:** Will the governing body be comprised of people who live on the property, people who do not live there, or some balance? (For example, many community land trusts require that one-third of the board be comprised of residents of the trust's housing, that one-third be comprised of experts, professionals, and public officials helpful to the trust, and that one-third be comprised of concerned and committed community members.)
f. **Spheres of decision-making, management, and operations:** What decisions must be put to all members of the entity and what are decisions that will be made by governing bodies? Are some decisions allocated to certain committees within the organization? Will certain officers of the organization be empowered to make some decisions? How will the activities of the organization be managed?
g. **Procedures for meetings and decision-making:** What procedures will be used to hold meetings? What procedures are used to consider and decide on proposals?
h. **Financial provisions:** How will members buy in and sell out? How will profits and losses of the entity be allocated and distributed to members, if applicable? What fees may members be required to pay regularly?
i. **Conflict of interest policies:** How will the organization preserve the integrity of its governing body and ensure that it is not steered to serve the interest of certain individuals or certain profit interests? Under what circumstances might a member or director be deemed financially interested in a transaction or issue, and how will the organization handle this?

j. **Procedures for amending governing documents:** If governing documents can be amended simply (such as by a majority vote of the board), this means that many of the safeguards built into legal structure could be easily undermined. Many organizations may want to build in greater safeguards, such as by requiring approval by a super-majority of the board or members, unanimous approval, or approval by a third party (such as a designated nonprofit) to change certain key provisions of the governing documents.
k. **Dissolution of the entity:** Under what circumstances might the entity dissolve and sell its assets? How will the proceeds be distributed? To a nonprofit, to current members, or to both current and past members?

Part 4: Navigating Public Laws

There are many areas of public regulation that real estate–focused sharing economy lawyers should learn about, since these laws may constrain the use of land or how land rights can be shared. These regulations include those that control what we can do with the land (such as land use and inclusionary zoning laws) and regulations on the relationships we create with each other to share or transfer land rights (such as subdivision regulations and landlord/tenant laws). This section will look briefly at nine categories of regulations: (1) land use and zoning; (2) landlord/tenant; (3) inclusionary housing laws; (4) laws governing hotels, hostels, boarding houses, and temporary stays; (5) regulations on subdividing land; (6) regulations on community associations; (7) fair housing laws; (8) building codes; and (9) property taxes.

As mentioned above, attorneys should also learn about securities laws, discussed in Chapter 6, for situations where a group of people forms and puts money into an entity for the purpose of developing or purchasing a property. For housing arrangements where people work in exchange for housing, it's important to know the employment law implications, discussed in Chapter 7. And although they are not discussed in this book, it's also a good idea for real estate–focused sharing economy lawyers to know the basics of marital property laws and estate planning.

Land Use and Zoning

The topic of zoning was discussed in Chapter 8, with regard to productive and commercial activities characteristic of the sharing economy. Here zoning is discussed in relation to housing. Zoning laws have carved up cities and suburbs into single-family homes and units, largely separating household units into isolated spaces. Because they challenge this framework, housing solutions that involve shared spaces often encounter zoning barriers. Julie Pennington's piece below will examine how some cohousing communities and ecovillages have overcome zoning barriers and even changed local zoning laws. Here is a brief summary of the types of barriers clients may face:

1. **Restrictions on the number of units on a parcel:** Most cities restrict residential land uses by capping or setting a minimum number of units that must be put on a parcel. While the purposes of density capping are often rooted in management and protection of limited resources such as water, clean air, healthy ecosystems, and the capacity and upkeep of infrastructure such sewage treatment systems, transportation, and schools, density caps can present obstacles to groups wishing to create community-oriented housing with shared spaces.

   Many people wishing to create semi-shared housing arrangements have worked around such restrictions by, for example, building an addition onto a house and including a shared kitchen in between two otherwise separate living spaces. This is because a dwelling constructed without a kitchen sometimes does not meet the legal definition of a dwelling unit.[73]

   In some places, states have passed laws mandating that cities allow residents to build accessory dwelling units (ADUs), granny flats, in-law units, second units, accessory apartments. For example, recognizing that ADUs may provide the most important means by which we will house our growing population, the Cali-

73. For example, the International Residential Code (2009) defines "Dwelling Unit" as "[a] single unit providing complete independent living facilities for one or more persons, including permanent provisions for living, sleeping, eating, cooking and sanitation."

fornia legislature passed AB 1866 in 2003, requiring that cities adopt more streamlined policies for the permitting of ADUs.

Where possible, cities could increase allowable density, even in single-family residential areas, if the land will be used in a way that mitigates the typical impacts of density. For example, if a cohousing community or ecovillage is built with systems to capture, purify, and recycle water, to manage its own waste and wastewater, to produce its own energy, and to provide residents with a car-sharing program and easy access to public transit, this would mitigate the impact on the surrounding community, local ecosystems, and city infrastructure.

Form-based zoning codes,[74] already implemented in cities around the United States, may offer groups a unique opportunity for shared housing. Such codes focus on urban planning based on, among other things, the form, shape, size, and impact of buildings on parcels. This model may provide groups with the opportunity to participate in the planning and development of compact urban multi-use communities that accommodate the needs of shared living.

2. **Restrictions on the relationships of or number of occupants per unit:** In many cities throughout the county, zoning laws still restrict the number of unrelated individuals that may live together in a unit. Such laws have presented barriers to groups that intentionally seek to live in a shared and/or supportive living arrangement. Mental Health Advocacy Services, Inc., has issued a set of recommendations for how cities can redefine household and occupancy standards.[75]

   Other laws require that unrelated individuals in a unit be part of a "household unit" or "single housekeeping unit," meaning that they share financial responsibilities and chores, and act, in some respects, like a family. Such a law prevents a single owner of a

74. For more information on form-based codes, see the Form Based Codes Institute: http://www.formbasedcodes.org.

75. Mental Health Advocacy Servs., Fair Housing Issues Land Use and Zoning: Definitions of Family and Occupancy Standards (Sept. 1998), http://www.housingrights.org/pdfs/def_family.pdf.

three-bedroom house from renting out her other two bedrooms to students or other people found on Craigslist.[76]

3. **Mandatory parking spaces:** Mandatory parking requirements can be a significant barrier to shared housing. In Mountain View, California, the cost of one cohousing development significantly increased, due to the city's inflexible requirement that the development provide 2.3 parking spaces per new unit.[77] This is unfortunate, because cities could actually incentivize shared housing, car sharing, ride sharing, and public transit use by loosening requirements that each new unit be accompanied by off-street parking, and by finding other ways to ensure that street parking doesn't become scarce. For example, a city could require that new unit developments be accompanied by a car-sharing plan or program, transit passes for residents, bicycle parking, and other infrastructure that enables residents to not own a car. Cities could also require residents of new units to pay higher fees for street-parking permits, since those residents would normally have incurred the expense of installing a new parking spot on the property.

Landlord/Tenant Laws

Landlord/tenant laws are designed primarily to protect tenants in what is seen as an economically dependent relationship. Landlords control a valuable resource, and landlord/tenant laws generally ensure that people who do not own land will be able to have a stable relationship with the land they occupy. Such laws may give tenants the assurances that they will not be arbitrarily evicted, that their dwelling will be habitable, and that their rent will not be raised to unreasonable rates. Landlord/tenant laws are a constraint on the freedom to contract, justified by the unequal bargaining power between landlords and tenants.

---

76. See, for example, a proposed Los Angeles law called the State Licensed Facilities ordinance, Council File 11-0262, which defines a boarding house as "[a] one-family dwelling where lodging is provided to individuals with or without meals, for monetary or non-monetary consideration under two or more separate agreements or leases, either written or oral."

77. Neal Gorenflo, *Cohousing and Carsharing: A Great Opportunity*, SHAREABLE.NET (Oct. 11, 2009), http://shareable.net/blog/cohousing-and-car-sharing-a-great-opportunity.

ZONING FOR SHARING

By Julie Pennington, Legal Intern, Sustainable Economies Law Center

Zoning codes set out regulations for the use of land and buildings within cities and counties, in order to protect the public health and welfare, protect natural and public resources, support economic vitality, and develop and maintain public infrastructure. Contemporary zoning ordinances evolved from the early 20th-century need to separate land uses to protect the public health and safety by, for example, separating pollution-spewing or noisy industrial mills from residential neighborhoods. Today, with growing human populations, zoning ordinances are also used to protect public natural resources such as water and waterways, agricultural land, and open space, and to provide land for expanding public infrastructure and cultural needs.

Density restrictions imposed by zoning codes can pose a barrier to cohousing and ecovillages, as the density restrictions limit the number of units on a parcel or the number of unrelated persons permitted to live in a given space. However, shared housing arrangements are often designed with the intention of lessening human impact on the environment, and they therefore potentially mitigate some of the negative effects of density. For example, some cohousing communities and ecovillages adopt measures to reduce waste, share cars, use renewable energy systems, collect rainwater, recycle wastewater, and grow food.

Those who attempt to make a smaller footprint on the earth by living close together and sharing resources are wise to become familiar with laws that govern zoning in their area. Many codes have become outdated or excessively complex as they are amended piecemeal in response to, among other things, growing human populations, expanding resource demands, and a shrinking resource base. To make matters even more challenging, most land use decision-makers are unfamiliar with contemporary shared housing models and with the economic, social, and environmental values of shared housing. Groups and individuals who want to create and live in intentional shared housing will need to look closely at the purposes and effects of zoning codes to distinguish between unnecessary or discriminatory barriers to environmentally and socially beneficial housing solutions and codes that are needed to protect resources and infrastructure.

The good news is that citizens can participate in public local decision-making processes to directly introduce zoning changes that provide for and support creative and sustainable shared housing communities.

Zoning reform may be slow to catch up to trends in the ways people are living, but committed people all over the country are encouraging their cities to think outside the boundaries of traditional zoning and develop new standards for greener development. The learning processes that these groups experience through research and dialogue with officials and neighbors offer excellent models of ways that higher-density living can work with zoning codes to allow for a reduction in environmental impact and protection of resource and infrastructure systems.

Yarrow Ecovillage and O.U.R. Ecovillage, both in British Columbia, have successfully petitioned their respective municipalities to create distinct zoning categories for their projects. In 2004 the Chilliwack City Council unanimously approved Yarrow Ecovillage's proposal to create an "Ecovillage Zone," the first of its kind. Yarrow was redesignated from its former "rural residential" zone to an Ecovillage Zone, which made it possible for the community to offer 40 individual residences, a community building with extensive amenities, an organic farm, an education center, and small cottage industries. Chilliwack residents identified these offerings as needed improvements to the entire city, yet they would not have been permitted within the confines of the previous rural residential zoning.

The land that O.U.R. Ecovillage in Cowichan Valley, British Columbia, occupied was previously designated as a "secondary agricultural" zone, which meant that its likely use might be pasture grazing or hay production. The group entered a full comprehensive development rezoning process, which transformed the limitations of the space to allow a variety of land uses in a single zone and involved multiple public meetings and hearings, as well as an amendment to the local official community plan. At the conclusion of this process, O.U.R. Ecovillage was designated as a Rural Community Residential "Ecovillage" in 2003. The successful rezoning of the space allowed the group much more flexibility in the use of their land. Because of the rezoning, barriers were removed to allow O.U.R. Ecovillage to create multiple dwellings to house a larger number of people, a food production facility and related businesses, ecological restoration and education programs, and an eco–bed & breakfast. As an extension of their commitment to protecting sensitive ecosystems, the group also chose to preserve one-third of the land as park space.

Founding members of Dandelion Village began meeting in 2009 to design and build an ecovillage and cohousing community in Bloomington, Indiana, that would utilize alternative energies, creative transportation methods, ecological agriculture, and natural construction. Because the group knew that their ecovillage design didn't quite fit into any of the established zones in Bloomington's zoning portfolio, they worked closely with the City Planning Department to consider properties where rezoning would attract the least possible resistance. They settled on 2.23 acres of land situated between two railroad tracks and just south of a junkyard, yet only a few blocks from one of the city's most thriving neighborhoods. Dandelion members understood that, if each new ecovillage or cohousing community had to reinvent the process of seeking variances or rezoning in the unique municipality where they operate, the sustainability of the ecovillage as a larger concept would be lost in the laborious process. Their work expanded beyond simply finding a way to make their creative vision fit what existed, to creating a framework and precedent that could be replicated widely. To move toward this goal, and with the blessing of city officials, the group entered the planned unit development (PUD) process that developers go through to define the look and location of homes in traditional new developments like apartment complexes or gated communities. Dandelion Village creatively reinterpreted the acronym in their proposal to reflect their purpose, "permaculture urban demonstration." Their PUD proposal offered in-depth plans for how the Village intends to take natural forces like water, wind, sun, and sound into account and harness those elements for optimal integration into the design of the community. To craft the proposal, members sought input from architects, engineers, and permaculture experts, and surveyed other successful ecovillages and cohousing communities. Their design weaves in goals and recommendations already established by local conservation taskforces and planning bodies, and the proposal was reviewed by city officials regularly.

Through the PUD process, Dandelion Village members' attitude of flexibility and cooperation undoubtedly played a major role in the success of passing their proposal. After meeting with their planning committee and neighbors for several months, the group voluntarily amended their original vision several times to adapt to the concerns and desires of their community. For example, after processing input from officials, they voluntarily reduced the proposed number of homes from 25 to 10, reduced the number of adults from 75 to 30, refined their drainage plan, and reduced the number of square feet that they asked to build on. Like Yarrow Ecovillage and O.U.R. Ecovillage, Dandelion Village recognized the crucial role that neighbors play in the success or struggle of a project like this one. They organized a meeting to gather input from neighbors and individually visited over 100 homes to field concerns while inviting neighbors to join the Planning Commission dialogue. Soon after purchasing the land, members of Dandelion Village worked with neighbors to revive the defunct neighborhood association, thereby instigating a positive forum for dialogue and relationship building. This combination of thoughtfulness for community needs and smart design ideas reflects an excellent strategy based in cooperative principles. In October 2011, Dandelion Village obtained the significant rezoning needed to allow the development of a mixed cooperative housing community that will house up to 30 unrelated adults, plus children, while utilizing natural energy sources, preserving and restoring native habitats, and promoting values of cooperative living.

As demographics change and the need for resource conservation and available housing grows, the ways that people live must change and are changing. Zoning may likewise adapt to meet these needs and reflect shareable solutions. The thoroughly documented proposals and the successes of these projects have the potential to serve as models for establishing shared housing zoning ordinances in cities around the country.

At the same time, landlord/tenant laws do not necessarily apply helpfully in situations where the landlord *is* the tenant, where the tenant is part of a cooperative that serves as "landlord," or where parties seek to collaboratively create unique agreements for the sharing of land. Many clients form entities to purchase land and proceed to lease parts of the land to themselves. Although the tenants are, indirectly, owners of the property, the creation of a leasehold interest may trigger the application of landlord/tenant laws. Many of my clients find the application of landlord/tenant laws counterintuitive, since they think of themselves as owners and want the flexibility to set the terms of their agreements for the use of the land. A question remains for further research: under what circumstances, if at all, have courts declined to apply landlord/tenant laws to a situation where the tenant owns a significant share of the entity that is the landlord?

In the meantime, here are some of the primary ways that landlord/tenant laws may restrict the kinds of agreements clients can form to occupy land as both owners and tenants:

1. **Tenantability laws and the warranty of habitability:** If clients form an entity to purchase land and then grant leases to themselves to occupy self-constructed units, this brings up the question of whether the entity is responsible for ensuring the "tenantability" or "habitability" of the spaces occupied by the member-tenants. This is especially important to consider when clients are living "off the grid" and using composting toilets, captured rainwater, and other alternatives to regular plumbing or other common amenities. Many state laws prohibit a property owner from renting a residential unit to a tenant if the unit

has certain defects that could affect the health and safety of the tenant. Even if no requirements exist in statutes, courts may impose certain requirements on landlords to provide a space that is habitable to a tenant. Over time, courts have even adapted the definition of habitable to include modern amenities, such as flush toilets and running water.[78] The fact that courts have used their discretion in determining what is a reasonable way to live means that courts could probably also recognize that some people consciously choose to live off the grid. Courts would hopefully allow for tenants to voluntarily assume this way of life. Now, however, some courts have also held that the warranty of habitability cannot be waived.[79] Other courts have allowed the warranty to be waived under circumstances where it is demonstrated that the tenant or homebuyer is fully informed of the condition of the property.[80]

Note that states have also likely adopted statutes that define what is or is not a "tenantable" dwelling, but these laws may allow for a landlord and tenant to waive the laws. For example, in California Civil Code Section 1941 provides that a landlord "of a building intended for the occupation of human beings must, *in the absence of an agreement to the contrary*, put it into a condition fit for such occupation, and repair all subsequent dilapidations thereof, which render it untenantable" (emphasis added). The

---

78. A leading California Supreme Court case on the warranty of habitability, *Green v. Superior Court*, 517 P.2d 1168 (Cal. 1974), provides the following summary of habitability standards:

> The recent case of *Academy Spires, Inc.* v. *Brown* (1970) 111 N.J. Super. 477 [268 A.2d 556] gives a good indication of the general scope of the warranty of habitability. In that case, a tenant in a multi-story apartment building complained of a series of defects, including (1) the periodic failure to supply heat and water, (2) the malfunctioning of an incinerator, (3) the failure in hot water supply, (4) several leaks in the bathroom, (5) defective venetian blinds, (6) cracks in plaster walls, (7) unpainted condition of walls and (8) a nonfunctioning elevator. The *Academy Spires* court held: "Some of these clearly go to bare living requirements. In a modern society one cannot be expected to live in a multi-storied apartment building without heat, hot water, garbage disposal or elevator service. Failure to supply such things is a breach of the implied covenant of habitability.

517 P.2d at 640 n.22.

79. *See, e.g.*, Centex Homes v. Buecher, 95 S.W.3d 266 (Tex. 2002) (holding that the implied warranty of habitability cannot be waived except under very specific circumstances, and examining the approach taken by other state courts).

80. *See* Crowder v. Vandendeale, 564 S.W.2d 879, 881 (Mo. 1978).

definition of tenantable in Section 1941.1 includes requirements for running hot and cold water and connection to a "sewage disposal system."

In sum, if clients wish to live in such modest, off-the-grid, and/or experimental dwellings, and if clients have formed an entity for the ownership of properties, it may be important to ensure that there is an adequate written waiver of habitability and tenantability between the individual occupants and the entity. Attorneys should also research state statutes on tenantability/habitability and common law cases on the implied warranty of habitability, in order to know if, when, and how the requirements can be waived.

2. **Just-cause eviction laws:** When clients form intentional communities, they may envision that community members will cooperate in various activities and make agreements to engage in or withhold from engaging in certain activities. However, in jurisdictions with just-cause eviction ordinances, it may be difficult to use eviction as a means of upholding such agreements. This is because the law leans heavily in favor of protecting the tenure of renters. For example, a community may, for health reasons, wish to adhere to some of the 25 Principles of Building Biology,[81] and agree to create a community free of certain chemicals, noises, vibrations, radiation, synthetic materials, and so on. If a community member repeatedly violates lease provisions related to chemical use, the community *may* not be able to evict the tenant on the grounds that the tenant is in default under the lease. This is because a court may consider such provisions unreasonable as grounds for eviction. The community must instead seek other legal remedies, such as obtaining an injunction mandating that the tenant comply with the no-chemical rule.
3. **Rights of tenants in condo conversion:** When a property is converted into resident-owned housing, such as a stock cooperative or condominium, local laws sometimes require that tenants present at the time of conversion be given additional rights, such as the first right to purchase the condo unit, or the right to lease the property and not be evicted, but for just cause.

81. *See* Institute of Building Biology & Ecology, The 25 Principles of Building Biology, http://www.baubiologie.de/site/english/principles.php.

4. **Rent control laws:** Rent control laws cap the rates at which landlords may raise rents, thereby ensuring that a tenant can continue to afford living in a unit. In the case of resident-owned housing, residents may want to vote to raise rents in order to cover operation costs. If rent control laws prevent this, however, it may be possible for the tenants to demand that everyone make additional payments as *owners* of a business entity, rather than as the entity's renters.

Inclusionary Housing Laws

Inclusionary zoning is a tool used by cities to ensure a supply of affordable housing units. Such laws often require that new developments contain a certain number of affordable units and/or rental units, or they impose fees when multi-unit buildings are converted from rental properties to resident-owned condos. At the same time, such laws sometimes present barriers to the creation of cohousing units. For example, in Oakland, California, if a group of 10 people were to buy a 10-unit building for the purpose of creating cohousing for themselves, they might be required to create a certain number of replacement rental units in their building or elsewhere in the city.[82] Such laws add significant costs to a project and can negatively impact the feasibility of resident-developed cohousing projects. Cities should make special exemptions for owner-occupied units that are cooperatively developed by the people intending to live in the units.

Note that it may be possible to structure the cohousing entity in such a way that it avoids meeting the definition of a stock cooperative or condominium. For example, if clients form an entity to purchase a multi-unit building to rent to themselves, and if there are some non-resident owners of that entity, this becomes, in effect, a hybrid between a rental property and a resident-owned property, and it may not be restricted by inclusionary zoning rules.

Regulations on Hotels, Hostels, Boarding Houses, and Temporary Stays

For various reasons related to their livelihoods or personal preferences, some people choose to live semi-nomadic lifestyles, requiring temporary and flexible housing arrangements. Most people, at the very least,

82. Oakland [Cal.] Mun. Code § 16.36.070.

travel and vacation away from home. Bloomberg News reports that 70 percent of the hotel market in the United States is dominated by large chains,[83] the vast majority of which fall under the ownership of about 12 hotel groups. Local economies, nomads, and travelers will all benefit greatly from the creation of locally owned, community-owned, small-scale, and/or peer-to-peer solutions for the provision of temporary housing, including hotels, B&Bs, hostels, boarding houses, rooming houses, campgrounds, RV parks, and guest houses.

The provision of temporary housing tends to be subject to a different set of regulations than the provision of leasehold interests. First of all, although definitions vary by jurisdiction, the right to stay in a place for fewer than 30 days is generally seen as the granting of a license, not a lease. Housing provided for longer periods under other special circumstances may also be treated as a license, not a lease; for example, provision of college dorm rooms to students and provision of housing in connection with employment, such as for lighthouse keepers, are sometimes treated as licenses, not leases; this makes them easier to terminate at the conclusion of an academic year or at termination of employment.

The provider of a license is often seen as the operator of a business, subject to local business tax, sales tax, special hotel tax rates, and local business regulations. Because the person staying in the space is generally not considered to have full possession and control of the space, the owner/provider has a higher threshold of responsibility to provide a healthy and safe environment. Regulations may require the posting of exit signs, adherence to heightened fire codes (which may mandate the installation of sprinklers), prohibitions on smoking, and so on.

Hotels, boarding houses, and other temporary housing providers are generally not allowed to operate in certain residential zones of a city, particularly in single-family residential zones. I have discussed this issue and some of its gray areas in Chapter 8, and have called for more flexible laws for the allowance of temporary housing.

Laws Governing the Sale of Subdivided Properties

In many states, there are laws that are designed to regulate the sale of subdivided lands by developers to purchasers. In the same way that securities laws were meant to protect investors from losing money in investment

83. Nadja Brandt & Armorel Kenna, *Big Hotel Chains Aim to Dominate Europe After Conquering U.S.*, Bloomberg News, Apr. 29, 2010.

schemes, subdivision regulations are meant to protect purchasers from losing money through the purchase of a property in a common interest development that has been improperly managed, fiscally or otherwise.

Laws designed to protect the purchasers of subdivided properties are somewhat awkward to apply when the purchaser is part of a group of people that also developed and is selling the land. The legal hoops that such groups have to jump through may feel incredibly high, considering that the hoops were designed for a relationship where the developer may not even know the purchaser.

In California, where there are five or more units in a condominium project, cooperative, planned unit development, community apartment project, or TIC, the project must undergo a long and expensive approval process with the state Department of Real Estate (DRE) before the units in the project can be sold or, in the case of cooperatives and community apartment projects, leased. In approving a project, the DRE examines the planned division of the property, ensures clear title to the land, examines proposed governing documents, and must feel satisfied that all necessary services (utilities, roads, etc.) are provided for each unit. The DRE also looks at budgets and considers whether the financing structure for the project will put buyers at too much risk, in the event that another buyer can't make mortgage payments. The DRE ultimately produces something called a Public Report on a project, which serves as a set of disclosures that will be provided to anyone who buys a unit.[84]

Laws Governing Community Associations

Many states[85] have laws that govern the operation of associations, such as HOAs and condo owners' associations, formed for the management of property rights and undivided interests in land. In a community where the ownership or lease of a unit is coupled with an undivided interest in property, such as in a condo community or cooperative, and/or where the Conditions, Covenants, and Restrictions (CC&Rs) provide for a common management scheme for property rights in a neighborhood, it may be necessary to adhere to certain regulations pertaining to the structure and operation of the community association. Such statutes tend to set minimum standards for meeting procedures, notice requirements,

84. CAL. BUS. & PROF. CODE § 11018.

85. California and Florida, for example, both impose extensive regulations on the operation of community associations.

quorum, number of votes required to pass certain proposals, election procedures, requirements for the adoption of increased assessments or special assessments, remedies for nonpayment, use of liens as a mechanism for enforcement, and so on. Such statutes may also impose limits on the rights of associations to dictate how a property may or may not be used. For example, California[86] and Florida[87] have both passed laws prohibiting a community association from making grass lawns mandatory, and allowing residents to install drought tolerant landscapes. Colorado state law prohibits HOAs from banning clotheslines and solar panels.[88]

The Uniform Condominium Act (UCA)[89] and the Uniform Planned Community Act (UPCA)[90] are examples of regulations on community associations, and these acts have been adopted in some states. In California, the applicable law is called the Davis-Stirling Act. These laws set mandatory procedures or mandatory minimums, which can override rules placed in an association's governing documents. Other times, these laws set default rules that will apply when an association's governing documents are silent.

Building and Fire Codes

Building codes can sometimes present a barrier to the "outside of the box" ways that clients wish to house themselves, or "inside the box" ways, for that matter, in the case of people living in very tiny dwellings. The documentary film *Garbage Warrior*,[91] for example, documented the plight of New Mexico eco-architect Michael Reynolds in his attempts to build experimental housing ("earthships") out of recycled materials. He was repeatedly cited for building code violations until he, at last, successfully lobbied the New Mexico legislature to pass a bill creating limited circumstances under which people may construct and live in experimental buildings.

The clustering of tiny houses in combination with shared spaces may offer an affordable and sustainable housing option, yet building

---

86. A.B. 1061 (Cal. 2009), amending CAL. CIV. CODE § 1353.8.

87. S.B. 2080 (Fla. 2009).

88. COLO. REV. STAT. § 38-30-168, Unreasonable Restrictions on Renewable Energy Generation Devices.

89. Unif. Condominium Act, *available at* http://www.law.upenn.edu/bll/archives/ulc/fnact99/1980s/uca80.htm.

90. Unif. Planned Community Act, *available at* http://www.law.upenn.edu/bll/archives/ulc/fnact99/1980s/upca80.pdf.

91. http://www.garbagewarrior.com/.

codes may act as a barrier. Owners of such units may encounter difficulty in getting legal clearance for the occupancy of such tiny homes, since many cities have adopted International Residential Code requirements that a dwelling unit include a minimum of one room that is at least 120 square feet in area,[92] and other minimum area and height requirements for rooms within a dwelling unit.

Fire codes sometimes apply more strict requirements in multi-unit buildings or other shared housing arrangements. For example, in Colorado, some cohousing communities have been required to include expensive fire protections in their common house kitchens, including a $10,000 exhaust system installed over the stove.

Fair Housing Laws

Some clients may wish to form residential communities of a certain composition—all senior citizens, all women, or all Buddhists, for example. Title VIII of the Civil Rights Act, also known as the Fair Housing Act, prohibits discrimination on the basis of race, color, religion, sex, national origin, disability, or familial status in the sale or rental of real estate. States that have adopted similar laws may have added to the list of prohibited bases of discrimination. For example, California's Fair Employment and Housing Act also prohibits discrimination on the basis of sexual orientation, source of income, ancestry, mental disability, and HIV status.[93]

Certain exemptions have been made to the law to allow, for example, the creation of senior housing. The 1988 Amendments and the adoption of the Housing for Older Persons Act (HOPA) of 1995 allow for the exclusion of families with children in communities designed for seniors, so long as those communities meet certain requirements.[94]

The Federal Fair Housing Act also exempts some small owner-occupied communities, renting of single-family homes, and "housing operated by organizations and private clubs that limit occupancy to members,"[95] which is what allows, under certain circumstances, frater-

92. *See* Cal. Code Regs. § R304.1 ("Every *dwelling* unit shall have at least one habitable room that shall have not less than 120 square feet (11 m^2) of gross floor area.").

93. Cal. Gov't Code §§ 12900–12996.

94. U.S. Dep't of Hous. & Urban Dev., *Fair Housing—It's Your Right*, http://portal.hud.gov/hudportal/HUD?src=/program_offices/fair_housing_equal_opp/FHLaws/yourrights.

95. *Id.*

nity houses to provide housing only to men or sorority houses to provide housing only to women.

However, the Act's advertising restrictions may apply even to the advertising of a room rental in a single-family home or the sale of a unit in a small owner-occupied community. In those cases, it is still likely illegal to "advertise or make any statement that indicates a limitation or preference based on race, color, national origin, religion, sex, familial status, or handicap."[96] A client who wants to create a community of a certain character may still communicate such a vision in advertising without expressing a preference for a certain protected class of people. For example, the community may state that part of its mission is to create a safe and welcoming place for lesbian and gay parents and their children, but the community should not express a preference that prospective renter or purchaser *be* lesbian and gay parents.

Property Taxes and Property Tax Exemption

Property tax considerations may sometimes influence a decision about how to structure ownership or use of land, particularly in California where, as a result of Proposition 13, a property is generally not re-appraised and taxed at current market value until there is a change of ownership. My California clients try very hard to structure shared ownership relationships in ways that will not result in frequent changes of ownership. For example, owning property through an entity such as an LLC means that a member may join or leave the LLC without triggering a "change of ownership" and reassessment, so long as the member does not own more than 50 percent of the interests in the LLC.[97]

Sometimes the use of a property may entitle the owners to a property tax break. For example, in California, the Williamson Act provides reduced property tax assessments for land that is used for agricultural purposes for an extended period of time. The Williamson Act does, however, limit the number of dwelling units that can be constructed on a parcel. Even when clients intend to build very humble dwellings and

---

96. *Id.*

97. The California Board of Equalization regulations provide very clear and detailed explanations of what constitutes a change of ownership. The regulations are contained in the Property Tax Law Guide, art. 4., Change in Ownership and New Construction (§§ 460–500).

live in ways that will have a low ecological impact, the Williamson Act may prove to be too limiting.

Property Tax Exemption

As communities rethink their relationships to land, the role of property tax exemption will be interesting to consider. In *Walz v. Tax Commission*,[98] the U.S. Supreme Court acknowledged the public purposes behind property tax exemption: "[states have] determined that certain entities that exist in a harmonious relationship to the community at large, and that foster its 'moral or mental improvement,' should not be inhibited in their activities by property taxation or the hazard of loss of those properties for nonpayment of taxes."

Every state has a different framework for deciding when to grant property tax exemption. Some states will grant exemption for properties used for affordable housing or land conservation, and other states may not. Generally, states grant property tax exemption to charitable, scientific, religious, and hospital organizations, depending on the actual use of the property. The way the property tax exemptions are administered in California, for example, is that the state makes a determination of whether an *organization* is eligible to receive a property tax exemption on the property it owns. Then the county tax assessors make a determination of whether the *property* owned by the organization qualifies for the exemption, based on how the property is being used.[99]

Property Tax Exemption for Housing Connected with Nonprofit Activities

Providing living quarters to people involved in a nonprofit's work might qualify an organization for property tax exemption, but you may need to demonstrate that the provision of those living quarters is reasonably necessary to achieving the nonprofit's purposes. For example, in the case of a farm education center, you could show that the housing is provided only to staff, volunteers, and students of the nonprofit education center, and only because living on-site is necessary to full participation in the

98. Walz v. Tax Comm'n of City of New York, 397 U.S. 664 (1970).

99. Cal. State Bd. of Equalization, Publ'n 149: Property Tax Welfare Exemption (Mar. 2008).

program. A nonprofit that offers housing to staff as an optional benefit may or may not be able to receive property tax exemption for the housing.

Note that some states limit the types of educational activities for which an organization may receive property tax exemption. In California for example, land used for educational purposes must be aimed at providing education to the general public and a broad community, as opposed to a specified group of people.[100]

Property Tax Exemption for Affordable Housing

Some, but not all, states offer property tax exemption to nonprofit organizations that own properties for the purpose of creating affordable housing, which is considered a charitable activity. If your client is a nonprofit that has created affordable housing, the state may require that you meet additional requirements and provide detailed documentation about tenants and their incomes. For example, in California, you must demonstrate that:

> "The property use is restricted to low-income housing by a regulatory agreement, recorded deed restriction, or other legal document if the property is owned by a nonprofit corporation.
>
> "The funds that would have been necessary to pay property taxes are used to maintain the affordability of the housing or to reduce the rents for the units occupied by lower income households.
>
> "The property receives either federal low-income housing tax credits or government financing, or 90 percent or more of the tenants are qualified low-income tenants within the prescribed rent levels, if the property is owned by an eligible nonprofit corporation."[101]

Property Tax Exemption for Conservation Land

Some states provide property tax exemption to nonprofits that own land for conservation purposes, usually on the grounds that the land conservation meets a charitable or scientific purpose. Other states grant tax exemption for properties under conservation easement, whether or not the property is owned by a nonprofit.[102] For example, Florida gives

---

100. *Id.*

101. *Id.*

102. *See* Land Trust Alliance, State and Local Tax Incentives, http://www.landtrustalliance.org/policy/tax-matters/campaigns/state-tax-incentives (listing local, state, and federal incentives for conservation easements).

all property owners tax exemption if the property is under a conservation easement owned by a nonprofit, and if the easement and land meet certain criteria, roughly mirroring the requirements of the IRS tax deduction for conservation easements.[103] Other states, such as Maryland, take a different approach, offering a property tax *credit* rather than a property tax exemption.[104]

103. H.B. 7157, ch. 2009-157 (Fla. 2009), *available at* http://laws.flrules.org/files/Ch_2009-157.pdf.

104. *See* Maryland Conservation Property Tax Credit Application.

CHAPTER TEN

NEW APPROACHES TO INTELLECTUAL PROPERTY

By D. Inder Comar, Esq.*

A philosophy of sharing has made tremendous strides in all areas of law, including intellectual property. Due to its intangible nature, intellectual property is more easily shared than other types of property. Yet, traditional copyright and patent protection frameworks have offered very little on the spectrum between sharing with everyone and sharing with no one.

Today, new licensing frameworks increasingly abound for creative people to share on their own terms, by controlling the ways ideas and works are used and shared. This dynamic framework for sharing intellectual property is broadening everyone's access to information, stimulating creativity and collaboration, spurring rapid innovation as people build upon the creations of others, and allowing important ideas to simultaneously benefit the public good and reward innovators.

* D. Inder Comar is an attorney in San Francisco who helps companies and individuals promote change—technological, social, and legal change. His practice spans intellectual property, Internet, employment and civil and human rights concerns. Mr. Comar has worked on projects with start-ups, nonprofits, Fortune 100 companies, and governments related to creative approaches to intellectual property protection, licensing, and management.

Part 1: Intellectual Property and Sharing

What Is Intellectual Property?

Intellectual property is a special form of property that is produced by the human mind. Ideas, creative works, business secrets, and brands have no physical reality, but they nonetheless possess value even in an intangible form.

Four Major Forms of Intellectual Property

Intellectual property is created either by federal statute or recognized by state law. In the United States, four forms of intellectual property are generally recognized:

- A **patent** is a federal government–issued monopoly on an invention, giving the inventor the exclusive right to use and monetize the invention for a certain amount of time (20 years in the case of utility and plant patents).
- A **copyright** is a federal government–issued protection over any creative expression fixed in tangible form, generally giving the author the exclusive right to display, distribute, reproduce, and create derivatives of that expressive work for his/her entire life, plus another 70 years.
- A **trademark** is a government-issued acknowledgment that a person or company has the exclusive right to use a specific mark—such as a name or logo—to distinguish goods or services in the marketplace. Federal trademark registration protects a mark in the national market.
- And finally, a **trade secret** is any business secret that gives a company an edge in the marketplace.

There are other forms of intellectual property (trade dress, for example, protects the way a product is packaged), but patents, copyrights, trademarks and trade secrets are ones that are well recognized across numerous jurisdictions.

Why Does Intellectual Property Exist?

Whereas the reasons for government recognition and protection of intellectual property in the United States could occupy several large treatises, a primary goal that can be quickly mentioned is social policy. Specifically, governments want to encourage their citizens to innovate. The theory is that by permitting people to control their intangible assets—and giving them the right to exclude others from using those assets—it will encourage people to take time to invent new ideas, compose new creative works, and create new consumer brands.

On the flip side, building so many restrictions around the use of an asset can also stifle derivative innovations, and lead to underuse and waste of an asset. New frameworks for sharing intellectual property seek to balance these effects—to simultaneously motivate creators and ensure that a work or asset can be put to broader creative use.

Sharing in the World of Intellectual Property

Copyright law has the most well-developed culture of sharing, in large part due to sharing in the software industry. But sharing is making inroads in the context of patent and trademark law as well.

Because they have to remain secret in order to remain valuable, trade secrets are rarely (if ever) shared, and if they are, they are kept under strict forms of confidentiality. Consequently, trade secrets will not be discussed in this chapter.

The License Agreement

Intellectual property is typically shared through a license agreement. A license agreement is a contract that allows an owner of intellectual property to share it with others, so long as certain conditions are followed.

In the commercial setting, license agreements may be provided for a share of royalties or a one-time license fee. In the sharing context, however, a party can forego payment and instead permit sharing of the intellectual property subject to specific terms and conditions.

A Word About the Public Domain

The term "public domain" refers to forms of intellectual property that are open to public use without restriction. As wonderful as this idea is, it is a more limited concept than most people realize. A "public domain" of intellectual property really only exists for copyrights and patents and mostly describes works and ideas for which a copyright or patent has expired. As discussed further below, strong inroads are being made to create larger "commons" and a bigger public domain through innovative license agreements, including agreements that "gift" a copyright or patent into the public domain.

PART 2: SHARING AND COPYRIGHT LAW

Copyright Law Basics

Copyright law protects creative expression by giving authors of creative works the ability to control the distribution, display, and performance of the work. Copyright law also gives authors the right to control so-called "derivative" works, which are new creations derived from the protected work.

In earlier times, a work was only protected by copyright if it complied with formal notice requirements. These notice requirements have been removed to make copyright law automatic: under current law, copyright protection attaches to a work the moment it is created and fixed "in any tangible medium of expression," without any notice or registration requirements.[1]

Copyright protection is also significantly longer today than it used to be. In earlier times, copyright protection lasted 28 years from the date of first publication, with an option to renew for an additional length of time. Today, for most works, copyright protection endures for the life of the author plus another 70 years.[2] A work created in 2010 by an author who lives until 2050 will thus be protected by copyright until 2120.

Infringement and Damages

People who use a protected work without permission are called "infringers." Current copyright law essentially makes infringement a strict liability offense—if a person uses a work without permission, even innocently, he/she can still be held liable for damages.[3]

A person who "innocently" infringes can have statutory damages reduced to $200 per infringement. On the other hand, a showing of willful infringement may entitle a copyright holder to up to $150,000 in damages per infringement.[4]

---

1. 17 U.S.C. § 102(a).
2. *Id.* at § 302(a). Time frames differ for works of corporate authorship, anonymous works, or works made for hire.
3. *Id.* at §§ 106, 501.
4. *Id.* at § 504(c)(2).

In light of this legal framework, promoting the sharing of copyrighted works can be tricky: an error in determining copyright validity or applicability could possibly subject an infringer to tens of thousands (or even hundreds of thousands) of dollars in damages.

Sharing becomes even more challenging in light of common misperceptions about copyright law. For example, people sometimes assume that it is permissible to use a copyrighted image as long as attribution is given. *This is not the case*: even with attribution, use of a copyrighted work without explicit permission from the copyright holder can result in liability for copyright infringement.

Despite these hurdles, tremendous strides have been made in creating a sharing regime with respect to copyrighted works. Specifically, sharing within the context of copyright law has focused on creating effective licenses that permit people to share without fear of facing a copyright infringement suit and creating a "public domain commons" whereby individuals can gift works into the commons or take and use works from the commons without any copyright restriction.

Innovations in Open Sourcing

One significant form of sharing in the context of copyright law comes from the software industry. Anyone who has ever been involved in the coding and development of software will be familiar with "open source" software: code that is freely available in source form for modification and redistribution. Indeed, the success of open source licenses in promoting sharing in the software industry is a potentially powerful template for other industries relying on creative development.

One of the most common open source licenses (partly because it is the license governing the Linux kernel) is the GNU General Public License or GPL. In broad strokes, the GPL requires any new works based on GPL-licensed code (or which uses GPL-licensed code) to be open source as well.[5]

GPLv3, released in 2007, includes provisions that limit the patentability of software that relies on GPL-protected code, including limitations on the right to initiate patent litigation.[6]

The GPL is not the only open source license arrangement in the software world. Other open source licenses include the Berkeley

5. GPL § 2.
6. GPLv3 pmbl., § 10.

Software Distribution license (otherwise known as the BSD license, and used to distribute the source code of AT&T's UNIX operating system), the Apache license, and the Mozilla Public License (otherwise known as the MPL license, and used to distribute the Firefox browser and Thunderbird mail client).

The GPL and other open source licenses are just as "legal" as other types of licenses. In 2008, the U.S. Court of Appeals for the Federal Circuit held that an engineer who made code available through an "artistic license" could bring suit against a defendant for violating its terms.[7] The Federal Circuit wrote that the terms of the artistic license were "vital" to the copyright holder and the license "expressly stated the terms" governing "the right to modify and distribute the material."[8] The court concluded: "Copyright holders who engage in open source licensing have the right to control the modification and distribution of copyrighted material."[9]

This kind of licensing permits creators of works to impose a philosophy of sharing—if you want to use my software, you have to share your software. For software that is exceptionally useful or popular, the effect could very well be the dominance of open source or freely given software that can successfully compete with proprietary or commercial alternatives.

Creative Commons Licenses

Some of the most popular forms of copyright sharing derive from the licenses developed by Creative Commons, a nonprofit founded in 2001, dedicated to maximizing digital creativity, sharing, and innovation. Any person can stamp his/her work with a Creative Commons license and put the world on notice that the work can be shared, within certain limitations, without fear of copyright infringement.

Creative Commons has developed several licensing arrangements that permit various degrees of sharing. The most open Creative Commons license lets others distribute, remix, tweak, and build upon the work, even commercially, so long as credit is given to the author for the original creation. On the other end of the spectrum, the most restrictive Creative Commons license only permits others to download

---

7. Jacobsen v. Katzer, 535 F.3d 1373 (Fed. Cir. 2008).
8. *Id.* at 1381.
9. *Id.*

and share the works, with attribution to the author, but changes cannot be made to the original work and commercial use is prohibited.

Name of Creative Commons License	***Permissions Granted***	***Most permissive***
Attribution ("CC BY")	Lets others distribute, remix, tweak, and build upon the work, even commercially, so long as attribution is given to the author.	
Attribution-ShareAlike ("CC BY-SA")	Lets others remix, tweak, and build upon the work, even commercially, as long as attribution is given to the author and new creations are licensed under the identical terms.	
Attribution-NoDerivs ("CC BY-ND")	Lets others redistribute for commercial and non-commercial purposes, as long as no changes are made and attribution is given to the author.	
Attribution-NonCommercial ("CC BY-NC")	Lets others remix, tweak, and build upon work non-commercially, as long as attribution is given to the author; however, there is no need to license new creations under these same terms.	
Attribution-NonCommercial-ShareAlike ("CC BY-NC-SA")	Lets other remix, tweak, and build upon work non-commercially, as long as attribution is given to the author and as long as new creations are licensed under these identical terms.	
Attribution-NonCommercial-NoDerivs ("CC BY-NC-ND")	Lets others only download works and share them with others, as long as attribution is given to the author; no commercial use and no changes to the work are permitted.	***Least permissive***

Source: Information in the above table is provided courtesy of Creative Commons.

Many websites (including the online encyclopedia Wikipedia) incorporate Creative Commons licenses as part of their services. Because of the variety of Creative Commons licensing arrangements, make sure to understand what is and what is not permitted when using any work stamped with a Creative Commons license.

Other Approaches with Licenses—Crowdsourcing

The GNU and Creative Commons licenses are some of the most popular ways to share copyrights, but they are by no means the only way to structure a copyright license. For example, neither set of licenses really addresses the challenge of a creative project that may encompass different and simultaneous contributions from other people. Such "crowdsourced" projects may involve a licensing arrangement where contributors agree that any copyrightable material they create belongs to the project itself and can be openly shared without restriction. A license or assignment may be needed to ensure that control over the contributed materials belongs to a single entity or person, to avoid disputes over potential infringement down the road. This "clearinghouse" can then license out the copyrights or other intellectual property rights to third parties on an as-needed basis.

Less formal solutions can also work well, however. Wikipedia, a free online encyclopedia operated by the Wikimedia Foundation, mandates that all user contributions be licensed under a CC-BY-SA copyright license. Copyrights are never transferred to Wikipedia, so a contributor can later republish and relicense any contributed materials in another format. However, the license provided to Wikipedia is permanent and cannot be retracted or altered.[10]

Public Domain Commons

Numerous websites and nonprofits are attempting to establish public domain commons, which are repositories of works that are freely available for any purpose.

In theory, this should be relatively straightforward, but the nature of copyright law makes this challenging. In earlier times, when copyright law was governed by more formal requirements, a person could affirmatively place a work in the public domain by simply removing a copyright notice from the work, or not renewing the copyright at the end of its life. However, laws have changed to make copyright protection automatic: once a work is created and fixed in a tangible medium of

---

10. Wikipedia, http://en.wikipedia.org/wiki/Wikipedia:Copyrights (last accessed June 12, 2012).

expression, it is protected without any need for registration or notice requirements.

Thus, current law is unclear whether a person can affirmatively place something in the public domain and strip it of copyright protection. Someone that declares a work to be freely available without copyright may, however, be prevented from later suing for infringement under an equitable defense, such as waiver, laches, or estoppel.

Despite this lack of clarity, public domain commons make two types of works publicly available: works for which copyright protection has expired, and works that the authors have declared to be freely available.

A Few Public Domain Commons	***Works Offered***
Wikimedia Commons (commons.wikimedia.org)	Repository that makes available public domain and freely licensed educational media content (images, sound, and video clips).
Internet Archive (web.archive.org)	Repository of moving images, texts, audio, and software, much of which is in the public domain and available for free download.
Flikr: The Commons (www.flikr.com/commons/)	Repository of images provided by various collections and libraries, with "no known copyright restrictions."
Project Gutenberg (www.gutenberg.org)	Repository of over 36,000 free ebooks, the vast majority of which are free of copyright restrictions.

Creative Commons is also experimenting with tools that will "mark" works as part of the public domain. As of the date of this writing, Creative Commons offers a CC0 mark for authors to release works into the public domain, which in many respects is simply a CC-BY license without the requirement of attribution. The CC0 mark permits a party to dedicate a work to the public domain by waiving all rights under copyright law as well as associated claims and causes of action, known or unknown, to the greatest extent permitted by law. Should the waiver be declared invalid by any court, the CC0 states that the waiver shall be construed to provide a royalty-free, non-transferable, non-exclusive, irrevocable license to use the work under applicable copyright law.

Creative Commons also provides a "Public Domain Mark" that anyone can use to mark older works for which a copyright has expired. By providing such a tool, Creative Commons hopes that works free of copyright can be easily discoverable and available to others. Because some jurisdictions have unusually long copyright terms, a work that may be freely available in one country can still be protected by copyright in another, thus making it difficult to correctly identify a work that is truly in the public domain. Thus, the Public Domain Mark is recommended only for very old works.

Part 3: Sharing and Patent Law

Patent Law Basics

A patent provides one of the broadest forms of intellectual property protection, as it actually protects any idea that constitutes an invention. Federal law gives a patent holder a monopoly over use of the invention for some length of time, generally 20 years.[11] Anyone who wants to use the invention during this time must receive a license from the patent holder.

Unlike copyrights, patent protection is *not* automatic. A person who wants a monopoly on the use of an invention must "prosecute" the patent before the U.S. Patent and Trademark Office. An application is submitted for review to a patent examiner, who reviews the invention within the context of prior works. If the invention described in the patent application is useful, novel, and non-obvious, a patent will be granted.[12]

Patent law is similar to copyright law with regard to the rules of infringement. A person who "makes, uses, offers to sell, or sells any patented invention" without permission of the patent holder can be liable for infringement.[13] A court may award lost profits or a reasonable royalty and, in instances of willful infringement, has the authority to award triple damages.[14]

Because patents offer a broad form of intellectual property protection, they are closely guarded by their owners. In recent years, companies have found it extremely profitable to seek damages for patent infringement.

11. 35 U.S.C. § 154(a).
12. *Id.* at §§ 101, 102, 103.
13. *Id.* at § 271.
14. *Id.* at § 284.

In 2006, Research in Motion Ltd. (which makes the popular BlackBerry device) agreed to pay $612.5 million in patent infringement damages as part of a settlement to a patent holding company called NTP, Inc. A court-ordered shutdown of BlackBerry services was only averted through the intervention of the U.S. Department of Defense!

But as with copyrights, a philosophy of sharing is taking root in the world of patent law. Patent holders interested in sharing their inventions have looked to creative licensing approaches as well as the creation of "patent commons."

Humanitarian Licenses

A relatively new development in the world of patent licenses is the "humanitarian license." A humanitarian license permits a patent holder to share a humanitarian or life-saving invention in places where it would otherwise be prohibitively expensive to sell at market rate, while also preserving the ability of the patent holder to sell or license the invention at normal cost in mature markets.

Humanitarian licenses are important for a number of reasons. First, they permit the spread of potentially life-saving ideas and technologies to places that could otherwise not afford to license or purchase them. This has obvious application in a variety of industries and technologies but particularly with regard to energy, clean water, and medical inventions.

Second, humanitarian licenses help patent holders avoid the tough decision of whether to turn a blind eye to patent infringement of a life-saving invention or to vigorously protect their rights in order to preserve the legitimacy of a patent. If a patent holder knows of infringement but fails to take steps to stop that infringement, it can later be prevented from filing infringement actions under equitable doctrines such as estoppel and laches. Thus, a humanitarian license provides a legal mechanism whereby a patent holder can permit use of the patent for humanitarian or life-saving purpose without waiving its ability to prosecute infringement actions against parties that can afford to pay a normal licensing rate.

Sample Clauses from a Template Humanitarian License

On behalf of Natural Innovation.org (NI), Comar Law has drafted a template humanitarian license that is available at www.comarlaw .com and www.naturalinnovation.org under a Creative Commons license. NI has already been able to use the humanitarian license on several occasions.

Reprinted here are key sections, with commentary:

Defining the Humanitarian Domain (Section 1.2)—This section defines the appropriate scope of the license. The default definition broadly includes not only developing countries, but also poor areas in developed countries. The definition can be further refined as an attachment to the back of the license (called Schedule A in this clause).

> 1.2 "**Humanitarian Domain**" shall mean geographic locations and populations in which it is possible to alleviate suffering through the use of Intellectual Property, Technology, and Products related to clean-energy technology, and where the population is typically too poor to afford such technologies. In particular, the Humanitarian Domain refers to people who are usually poor, usually rural, and usually in developing countries. But it also explicitly includes indigenous peoples in developed countries such as Australia and the United States. The geographic locations and populations constituting the Humanitarian Domain shall be listed and/or determined by the formulae contained in Schedule A attached to this Agreement.

Defining the license (Section 2.1)—This section is the heart of the humanitarian license and provides that the recipient of the license can use the intellectual property and technology to sell products in the Humanitarian Domain.

> 2.1 OWNER hereby grants to LICENSEE a non-exclusive, worldwide, royalty free license to use the Technology and Intellectual Property to make, have made, use, import, export, offer for sale and sell Products in the Humanitarian Domain.

Defining the ability to manufacture products (Section 5.1)—This section permits the recipient of rights to arrange for the manufacture of products using the licensed intellectual property and technology. The license permits manufacture if the finished product can be sold at a price of 70% or less than what could otherwise be obtained through normal market channels. This number can be modified depending on the circumstances; it is primarily designed to ensure that the humanitarian-based products will not compete with normal-market products in the Humanitarian Domain.

> 5.1 LICENSEE shall have the non-exclusive, worldwide right to arrange for the manufacture and/or assembly of Products when any such arrangement permits the delivery of Products to customers in the Humanitarian Domain at a price of 70% or less than is otherwise obtainable through other licensed manufacturers.

Ownership of intellectual property (Section 7.1)—This section affirms that the owner of the intellectual property and technology retains ownership under the license arrangement.

> 7.1 OWNER shall retain sole and exclusive ownership of all rights, title and interest in and to the Intellectual Property and the Technology, subject to the licenses granted to LICENSEE under this agreement. OWNER shall also retain all rights under and to the Intellectual Property and Technology that are not expressly granted to LICENSEE and shall have the right to grant further licenses to third parties with respect to such retained rights.

Ownership of improvements (Section 8.1)—This section permits the owner to retain the rights to all improvements and discoveries made by agents or employees of the owner after the license is granted. Other related sections permit the recipient of the license to use these "owner improvements," and also provide the owner with an irrevocable license to use improvements and discoveries made or uncovered by the licensee.

> 8.1 OWNER shall own all rights, title and interest in or to any Improvements made or discovered on or after the Effective Date of this Agreement by employees or agents of OWNER in connection with the development, manufacture or commercialization of Products ("Owner Improvements"). Owner Improvements constituting intellectual property shall include, without limitation, copyrightable material,

trademarks, trade secrets, and any and all patent applications covering Owner Improvements that are filed anywhere in the world by or on behalf of OWNER at any time after the Effective Date of this Agreement, and any and all granted patents that directly or indirectly result from such patent applications, or any divisions, continuations or continuations-in-part or other patent applications claiming priority thereto (collectively, "Owner IP").

Termination (Section 9)—This section, not included in the template humanitarian license, could nevertheless be included where a rights-holder is concerned about preserving its ability to sell a product with the licensed intellectual property and technology at normal market rates.

9.3 This Agreement, and any licenses and rights provided hereunder, will terminate when OWNER, at its sole discretion, determines that the product can be sold through normal production channels at market rates. Upon such determination, OWNER will notify LICENSEE and provide thirty (30) days for LICENSEE to cease manufacture and use of the Product as defined in Section 9.2.

Indemnity (Section 12.5)—Because of the global scope of the Humanitarian Domain, the licensee should take responsibility for any problems that arise from manufacture and use. This section requires the licensee to indemnify the rights-holder based on any breach by the licensee. As part of this indemnity, the licensee is required to obtain products liability insurance.

12.5 In addition to any other indemnifications provided for herein, LICENSEE shall indemnify and hold harmless OWNER and its affiliates and their respective employees, agents, partners, officers and directors from and against any claims, losses, liabilities or damages (including reasonable attorneys' fees and expenses) incurred or sustained by OWNER arising out of or in connection with any breach of any representation, covenant, warranty or obligation by LICENSEE hereunder. As part of this indemnity, LICENSEE shall obtain products liability insurance in the

> countries where it distributes the Products and shall name OWNER as a beneficiary of said insurance. LICENSEE shall be responsible for paying all deductibles of insurance.

Other Efforts Related to Humanitarian Licenses

PIPRA (Public Intellectual Property Resource for Agriculture), a nonprofit based out of the University of California at Davis, manages resources related to open access of intellectual property in the context of agriculture and biotechnology, among other things. More information can be found at: www.pipra.org.

The Central Advisory Service on Intellectual Property, out of the Consultative Group of International Agricultural Research (CGIAR) is also developing a template humanitarian use license. Concepts for a draft can be found on its website at www.cas-ip.org.

Patent Commons

As in the world of copyrights, attempts have been made to formulate repositories of patents that are freely available for use without restriction—"patent commons." Two of the more well-known attempts are the Eco-Patent Commons (organized by the World Business Counsel for Sustainable Development) and the Patent Commons Project (organized by the Linux Foundation). The Eco-Patent Commons serves as a repository for patents, donated into the public by universities and businesses, that relate to solutions to environmental problems such as pollution, global warming, energy needs, and waste. The Linux Foundation's Patent Commons Project provides a repository of a wide variety of patents and lists those patents that include covenants not to sue third parties for specified activities.

Freeing an Invention Completely

Increasingly, rather than seeking patents, inventors are simply seeking ways to ensure that their inventions can be shared freely and not patented by others. Is it possible to somehow ensure that an invention can always be shared freely and can never be patented? Without actually first patenting the invention and then making it freely available through some type of license or donation, the answer is probably no. However, a person can take important steps toward protection by openly describing and publishing information about his/her invention as much as possible. This makes it more difficult for another party to successfully obtain a patent for a similar idea. If a person takes an openly accessible invention and somehow successfully patents it, the patent may later be held invalid through a re-examination proceeding, on the basis that the invention was not novel, as demonstrated by the fact that it was openly accessible prior to obtaining a patent. The Leahy–Smith America Invents Act, signed into law on September 16, 2011, has also expanded procedures for challenging a patent post-grant.

Part 4: Sharing and Trademark Law

Trademarks are a form of intellectual property that protect brand names. Under current law, a trademark can include any word, name, symbol, or device used to identify and distinguish goods and services from those manufactured or sold by others.[15] This broad definition can include words, personal names, trade names, symbols, abbreviations, fragrances, colors, sounds, or any combination of these things.

Sharing is not as developed in the world of trademarks, but in many ways this is consequence of trademark law: by definition, a trademark serves to specifically identify a particular good or service. However, trademark law does provide mechanisms whereby parties working in common can use a trademark for a common or shared purpose. This is possible through the use of a collective mark or a certification mark.

Collective Marks

Federal trademark law permits "collective marks," which designate membership in an organization.[16] Collective marks indicate that the person or party providing a good or service is a member of a certain group and meets the standards for admission of the organization.[17] A collective mark could be the name of a fraternity or a sorority, the name of an umbrella group for a professional or religious society, or the name of a volunteer organization with chapters in several parts of the country.

If a group of people wanted to come together under one organization for a common purpose, they could obtain a collective mark and thus

15. 15 U.S.C. § 1127.
16. *Id.*
17. Trademark Manual of Examination Procedures (TMEP) § 1303.

differentiate themselves from other people who may be involved in similar activities. For example, a group of urban farmers in California could form a group and give it the trademark of "THE AMERICAN COLLEGE OF URBAN FARMERS" and open chapters all over the United States. Farms that are part of the group could then use this mark to indicate membership in the group (perhaps as part of identification or marketing materials) and be united with other members across the country through shared activities and vision—just like a university fraternity, a professional association.

Certification Marks

A certification mark is a trademark that is used to indicate that a particular good or service meets an independent standard. Certification marks can certify that (1) goods or services originate in a particular geographic area; (2) they meet certain quality standards; or (3) the work was performed by a certain qualified worker (such as a specialist or a union member).[18]

The essential message conveyed by a certification mark is that the goods or services "have been examined, tested, inspected, or in some way checked by a person who is not their producer, using methods determined by the certifier/owner."[19] Think of labels you may have seen that include words such as "approved by," "inspected," "conforming to," or "certified," which all serve to tell the world that the goods have met some standard.[20]

The owner of the certification mark is the party responsible for determining the requirements for the certification.[21] Thus, sharing within the context of a certification mark can permit an independent body to issue a certifying standard that may be of interest to the public. Using our urban farmer example again, a group of farmers may decide that it is in their best interest to come up with a standard by which consumers of urban produce can feel assured about the way in which the produce was grown and harvested. A certifying mark—say, "CERTIFIED PRODUCT OF URBAN AGRICULTURE"—could be created that would indicate that the produce was cultivated within

18. 15 U.S.C. § 1127.
19. TMEP § 1306.01(b).
20. *Id.* at 1306.05.
21. *Id.* at 1306.04.

five miles of an urban area without pesticides, for example. In the absence of a national standard regarding what is or is not considered "urban agriculture," the market and consumers are given the ability to determine which standards they prefer.

Avoiding the "Naked License" When Sharing Trademarks

Groups interested in licensing their trademarks to other entities or forming collective or certification marks must be careful to follow trademark formalities. Sharing the mark, but failing to police how it is used, can lead to a finding of "naked licensing" and abandonment of the trademark.

The U.S. Court of Appeals for the Ninth Circuit recently found naked licensing in a lawsuit between two organizations using terms related to "freecycling." As described by the Ninth Circuit, the term "freecycling" combines the words "free" and "recycling" and refers to the practice of giving an unwanted item to a stranger so that it can continue to be used for its intended purpose.

In 2003, an Arizona nonprofit named "The Freecycle Network" permitted a Sunnyvale, California group named "FreecycleSunnyvale" to use its three trademarks: "FREECYCLE," "THE FREECYCLE NETWORK," and a special logo. In 2005, a dispute broke out between FreecycleSunnyvale and The Freecycle Network regarding use of the trademarks. On appeal, the Ninth Circuit ruled that The Freecycle Network had abandoned its trademarks by engaging in naked licensing because it "fail[ed] to exercise adequate quality control."[22] Adequate quality control requires a trademark owner to possess an express contractual right to inspect and supervise the operations of the person using the trademark or, at least, to actually control through inspection or supervision the use of the trademark.[23]

In the absence of these two things, a trademark owner may rely on its member-groups' quality control measures only if there is a "close working relationship."[24] After reviewing the record, the Ninth Circuit held that The Freecycle Network had abandoned its trademarks because (1) it did not retain express contractual control over FreecycleSunnyvale's quality control measures, (2) did not have actual

22. FreecycleSunnyvale v. Freecycle Network, 626 F.3d 509, 515–16 (9th Cir. 2010).
23. *Id.* at 516–18.
24. *Id.* at 518.

control over FreecycleSunnyvale's quality control measures, and (3) did not have a close enough working relationship with FreecycleSunnyvale to justify a lack of quality control.

The result of FreecycleSunnyvale is that groups interested in sharing their trademarks must include express contractual control over quality control measures or must *actually* control quality control measures, or else they risk losing any rights over the trademark at all. And even where there is a close working relationship, the Ninth Circuit wrote that it may be inappropriate for a trademark owner to rely on a licensee's own quality control measures "without other indicia of control."[25]

In seeking to avoid a naked license, trademark owners should also be wary of giving themselves *too much* control over the licensee and inadvertently creating a franchise or parent/subsidiary relationship. Any arrangement for use of a trademark should be affirmatively spelled out in writing, with an eye toward factors that could contribute to a finding of a franchise relationship under state or federal law. Otherwise, a contract providing that a trademark licensor can control aspects of the licensing company could lead to disputes over the scope of the relationship between the parties.

25. *Id.* at 519.

CHAPTER ELEVEN

NEW APPROACHES TO RISK AND LIABILITY

PART 1: SHARING ECONOMY/SHARING RISK/SHARING RESPONSIBILITY

Loss Is Scary, but Uncertainty Is Scarier

Sharing is society's most promising form of social security. Sharing reduces burdens on individuals and spreads risks and responsibilities among many. On the flip side, however, sharing triggers some of our greatest insecurities. A basic fact about the sharing economy is that the more people share, the more we expose each other to risk. Fears about loss and liability often dominate people's thoughts as they contemplate the formation of agreements and organizations to share.

However, loss and liability are, themselves, probably not what scare people the most. What is really scary is the *uncertainty* about how we will respond to them. *Time* magazine once started an article by saying: "The brain loathes uncertainty. In laboratory experiments, humans actually fear uncertainty more than physical pain."[1] Although the article didn't actually cite the studies (leaving us, ironically, uncertain about their reliability), there is something that rings quite true about this statement.

For example, I've learned that fender benders are a breeze. This is not to say that they are pleasant or cheap; they are, however, somewhat predictable because car insurance companies have plans and procedures in place for responding to then. Social custom also dictates our

1. Amanda Ripley, *Learning to Live with the Fear of the Flu*, TIME, Sept. 22, 2009.

response—we get out of our vehicles, make sure everyone is all right, and trade contact and insurance information. Many people handle all of it with confidence and grace.

In the sharing economy, what are the plans, procedures, and customs that will dictate how we respond to loss? Further, how will we manage it with the same confidence and grace we've learned to apply elsewhere? These questions have yet to be answered thoroughly for many things we'll do in the sharing economy, since so much of it is new to us. For example, if we are paying a neighbor to regularly borrow her car, how do we handle a situation where we cause a fender bender and how will insurance companies handle it?

The sharing economy demands thoughtful and creative risk management. First, this means taking steps to decrease risk of loss and to mitigate its impact. Second, and importantly, thorough planning can dramatically reduce the uncertainty of how we will respond and how we will restore what is lost. By eliminating a large amount of uncertainty, thoughtful risk management will open up doors and open up minds to a more sharing society.

It's important to acknowledge, however, that risk management in the sharing economy is still largely uncharted territory. The primary purpose of this chapter is to highlight some of the unique challenges sharing economy lawyers may face and to provide some guidance in thinking through the issues. Nevertheless, there remains a vast field to explore and many best practices to develop.

Taking Risks in a Sharing Economy

Here are some examples of ways that we commonly expose ourselves to risk in the sharing economy, along with some of the questions that come up in connection:

1. **Lending our things:** By borrowing and lending things like cars, electronics, equipment, and tools, people make optimal use of resources we have, and greatly reduce our needs to buy and own consumer goods. Instead of letting our car sit in the driveway all day, we might let a neighbor regularly borrow it. However, this brings up uncertainties: What happens if there's an accident? Is the neighbor covered by our insurance? Who should be responsible for out-of pocket costs? Should fault matter?

2. **Sharing our space:** In cities, people with yards are increasingly inviting people without yards—be they friends or strangers—to come regularly to the yard and grow food. This movement is aided by the large number of websites designed to connect people to share yards.[2] This brings up uncertainties: what happens if a gardener gets injured? What happens if she damages the property? Does homeowners' insurance cover these things? Would that change if the gardener were using the space for business purposes and selling the veggies at a farm stand?
3. **Sharing ownership:** Co-ownership is also becoming more common, and there are many questions to answer about dividing and sharing risk. For example, if we co-own a property with a few cottages on it, what happens if a tree falls and damages one person's cottage? Will the group be responsible for repair, or will responsibility lie only with the person who lives in that cottage? What out-of-pocket costs might the group be asked to contribute if insurance doesn't cover the full cost?
4. **Membership in groups and organizations:** In the sharing economy, we will all likely be members or co-owners in more organizations, which has the potential to expose us to liability for the actions of others. For example, if we purchase our groceries through a buying club formed with 30 others, what happens if someone in our group drives recklessly and causes an accident while picking up our food order? Could the whole group be liable?
5. **Sharing decision-making:** As more people become trustees, directors, and officers of organizations (like cohousing communities, car-sharing clubs, and cooperatives), such individuals assume a heightened duty of care and responsibility to a group and to the group's assets. Such individuals may, as such, expose themselves to greater risks than others, and groups may wish to manage and reallocate that risk accordingly, such as by purchasing liability insurance for directors and officers (D&O insurance).

---

2. *See, e.g.*, http://www.landshare.net; http://www.sharingbackyards.com; http://www.sharedearth.com; http://www.urbangardenshare.org; http://www.wepatch.org; http://www.y2g.org; http://www.yardsharing.org.

The Role of Sharing Economy Lawyers

Risk management is largely about recognizing risks, reducing them where possible, and making agreements to manage and reallocate the risks that remain. Key risk management considerations, detailed in the rest of this chapter, include

1. **Implementing practices that reduce risk:** Being careful is an obvious and excellent way to reduce risk, and the sharing economy is beginning to adopt a set of best practices for care, particularly when strangers or large groups share. Some of these practices will be described in the next section.
2. **Making agreements and forming limited liability entities:** Sharing economy lawyers play a very important role in helping clients manage risk, as we will draft many agreements about how groups will respond to loss, allocate responsibility, and much more. We will also form and structure entities, such as corporations and LLCs, which limit individuals' liability for a group's actions. These will be described in Part 2.
3. **Interpreting and tailoring insurance policies:** Sharing economy lawyers will also spend a lot of time interpreting insurance policies. For example, we will need to *actually read* homeowners' and car insurance policies with a fine-toothed comb and to advise people about what sharing activities are or are not covered. As with many things in the sharing economy, there will be gray areas, particularly when sharing activities begin to adopt qualities of commercial activity. Sharing economy lawyers will also advise people on what insurance to get, and often, we may need to advise insurers on how to tailor their policies to the unique needs of the sharing economy. In some cases, we may even need to lobby for new rules governing the insurance industry, as happened in the case of car-sharing laws. Insurance will be discussed in Part 3.

Being Careful in the Sharing Economy

In the sharing economy, we will more often rely on others to meet our needs. Putting this kind of trust in and reliance on others imposes a higher duty of care for everyone. When others put their well-being in our hands, our carelessness could have a deeper impact.

Common sense already gives us a long list of practices for being careful—like, tie your shoelaces, don't leave the stove burning, and don't run with scissors. But common sense may not yet tell us how to behave in sharing relationships that are innovative and that were, until very recently, rather uncommon. Sharing is nothing new in human history, but the information age offers us many new ways to connect for, communicate about, and coordinate sharing. Thanks to websites that act as match makers of sharing relationships and brokers of peer-to-peer transactions, we can share more than ever, even with total strangers.

When we share with strangers, our transactions may initially lack one of the most effective risk mitigation tools of all: relationships. In contrast, when we have pre-existing relationships with people and when we are part of common social circles, there is an automatic level of care and accountability in place to protect people. Social expectations within a group may be one of the most effective mechanisms to keep people honest and considerate. When there are pre-existing relationships, we also have information about the other person's past behaviors, which tells us how careful we may need to be in sharing with them.

The Internet also allows us to share with strangers without even meeting them. We might use a peer-to-peer car-sharing service, like Relay Rides[3], to access and drive another person's car, and we might swap homes with strangers when we travel. Face-to-face interactions tend to keep people responsible and accountable to one another, but such interactions will not be present for some of the ways that we share.

The question then becomes: when strangers share, how do you reproduce the level of care and accountability people might use in the context of personal relationships and direct interactions? To reduce risk and foster accountability, many sharing economy organizations are implementing practices such as

1. **Background checks:** The small town of Geronimo in Marin County, California, implemented a "safe hitchhiking" program, which offered community members and school children a way to catch rides with strangers in and out of the town.[4] Although the program no longer exists, Go Geronimo had 275 members at one point, and conducted background checks on each member through

3. For more information, see http://www.relayrides.com.
4. For more information, see http://www.gogeronimo.org.

the county Sheriff's Department. After completing background checks, members were given special ID cards, which let drivers and riders know that the person in the car with them had passed muster under the program.

2. **Reputation, peer review, and peer-rating systems:** Conventional background checks tell you very little about a person, but reputation within a community can tell a great deal. Today, there are thousands of websites designed to connect people for sharing,[5] and most of those websites have implemented peer-review systems to allow users to build reputations. For example, if I use a service like Rentalic.com to lend someone a projector, then I may begin to develop a good reputation if the borrower posts a positive review. Later, if I ask to borrow something from someone else, the lender of the item may be especially welcoming of me if they see that others have had good interactions with me. Reputation systems allow us to quickly learn from the bad experiences of others. Seeing that others have had a bad interaction with someone will alert us to be extra careful with that person. Many websites use a five-star rating system, which allows people to quickly spot potential problems if they are contemplating sharing with someone that has a low rating.
3. **Identity verification:** Verifying the identity of online sharing service participants helps to prevent the use of such services in committing fraud or crime. Participants' identities can be verified in a variety of ways and through a variety of online services that cross-check a person's answers to questions with information in public records.
4. **Address verification:** Some sharing networks are highly localized to specific neighborhoods, and such networks may wish to verify the addresses of members that take part. This helps to ensure that outsiders do not monitor activities of neighbors and do not plan, for example, to burglarize a home while the neighbors are gathered elsewhere at a potluck. The neighborhood social network platform, Nextdoor.com, creates networks of people living only on a certain block or within a larger defined

5. *See* Mesh Directory, http://meshing.it. As of April 2012, the Mesh Directory lists over 6,000 companies operating within or to create the sharing economy.

area. To join an online community, each Nextdoor user must verify his/her address, either by making a charge to a credit card with his/her home billing address, or by entering a code from a postcard sent to the user's home address.

5. **Third-party facilitators, brokers, and escrows:** Many peer-to-peer transactions now take place through third-party services, such as the thousands of sharing websites now operating throughout the world. Some of these sites act simply as match makers, whereas other services actively facilitate and broker transactions. If one party is to pay another for the use of a shared item, and the third-party service keeps that money pending a successful transaction, this could greatly help to reduce fraudulent or irresponsible use of the system. Note, however, that sharing services that broker transactions in this way may be deemed, by law, to be escrow services. In California, for example, this means that sharing services may need to review the state escrow law,[6] register as an escrow service, possibly obtain a bond or special insurance, and keep records of transactions.[7]

Advocating for Laws That Encourage Sharing

Policy-makers have already recognized that fear of litigation sometimes prevents people from doing the right thing. The high cost of litigation and astronomical damages sometimes awarded by courts have not only raised fears, but raised the cost of insurance, which also has a chilling effect on people's desire and ability to engage in certain activities. Good Samaritan laws[8] are an example of ways that policy has restored a little balance in a world dominated by fears of expensive litigation.

Relevant to the sharing of land and food, respectively, are two additional types of laws already implemented in most or all states: recreational use statutes and good Samaritan food donation acts.

---

6. Cal. Fin. Code § 17000; Cal. Code Regs. tit. 10, § 1700.

7. *See* Cal. Dep't of Corps., Escrow Law, http://www.corp.ca.gov/Laws/Escrow_Law/Default.asp.

8. Good Samaritan laws vary greatly in their application and by jurisdiction, but they generally provide protection from liability to a person that aids a sick or injured person in need.

1. **Recreational use statutes:** Every state in the United States has a recreational use statute,[9] which is a law that protects landowners from liability if they open up their land for others to use for recreational purposes. California's recreational use statute, for example, provides:

> An owner of any estate or any other interest in real property, whether possessory or nonpossessory, who gives permission to another for entry or use for [a recreational] purpose upon the premises does not thereby (a) extend any assurance that the premises are safe for such purpose, or (b) constitute the person to whom permission has been granted the legal status of an invitee or licensee to whom a duty of care is owed, or (c) assume responsibility for or incur liability for any injury to person or property caused by any act of such person to whom permission has been granted except as provided in this section.[10]

Recreational use statutes list the types of activities that are considered "recreational,"[11] and also typically require that the landowner receive no payment for the recreational use. Another interesting thing to note, in at least some statutes, is that the recreational use should be by *mere permission*, not *express invitation*.[12] There could easily be a gray area between those two concepts,

---

9. *See* Elizabeth R. Springsteen and Rusty W. Rumley, Nat'l Agric. Law Ctr., States' Recreational Use Statutes, http://www.nationalaglawcenter.org/assets/recreationaluse/index.html.

10. Cal. Civ. Code § 846.

11. A "recreational purpose," as defined in California's recreational use statute (Cal. Civ. Code § 846), includes "such activities as fishing, hunting, camping, water sports, hiking, spelunking, sport parachuting, riding, including animal riding, snowmobiling, and all other types of vehicular riding, rock collecting, sightseeing, picnicking, nature study, nature contacting, recreational gardening, gleaning, hang gliding, winter sports, and viewing or enjoying historical, archaeological, scenic, natural, or scientific sites."

12. Cal. Civ. Code § 846 provides: "This section does not limit the liability which otherwise exists (a) for willful or malicious failure to guard or warn against a dangerous condition, use, structure or activity; or (b) for injury suffered in any case where permission to enter for the above purpose was granted for a consideration other than the consideration, if any, paid to said landowner by the state, or where consideration has been received from others for the same purpose; or (c) to any persons who are expressly invited rather than merely permitted to come upon the premises by the landowner."

but the difference can perhaps be seen in comparing these two statements: "Sure, you can walk your dogs here," and "Come over tomorrow and let's take the dogs for a walk." The latter statement imposes a higher duty of care on the landowner to ensure that the land is relatively free of hazards.

2. **Good Samaritan food donation laws:** In 1996, Bill Clinton signed the Bill Emerson Good Samaritan Food Donation Act,[13] which created a federal law to protect individuals, businesses, and organizations from potential liability when they donate food to nonprofit organizations that distribute food to needy individuals.[14] This law leaves "needy individuals" undefined, and also does not fully clarify whether food can be given directly to a needy individual or whether it must go through a nonprofit organization.[15] Note that nonprofit organizations, under the act, need not be incorporated, which means that any association or informal project with charitable goals could potentially be covered by the act. It is nevertheless somewhat unclear whether the Act would cover a group of neighbors that collaborates to bring food to another neighbor while he is sick and unable to cook for himself. Note, also, that states have adopted their own acts, which may provide additional protection to food donors.

Recreational use statutes and good Samaritan food donation acts are good models for other laws that could be proposed to facilitate a more sharing society. For example, similar laws could be passed to protect people from liability when they allow others to grow food on their land or borrow tools and equipment.

13. Pub. L. No. 104-210, 110 Stat. 3011 (Oct. 1, 1996).

14. *See* USDA, A Citizen's Guide to Food Recovery, pt. VII, Legal Issues, The Emerson Good Samaritan Food Donation Act, http://www.usda.gov/news/pubs/gleaning/seven.htm.

15. See, for example, the law's definition of "gleaner," which is "a person who harvests for free distribution to the needy, or for donation to a nonprofit organization for ultimate distribution to the needy, an agricultural crop that has been donated by the owner." This definition was codified in the National Community Services Act, Pub. L. No. 101-610, 104 Stat. 3183 (codified at 42 U.S.C. §§ 12671–12673).

Part 2: Making Agreements

Ingredients of Risk Management Agreements

In absence of agreements otherwise, legal defaults will generally dictate where loss and liability fall. A sharing economy lawyer can help clients understand these defaults, and then draft agreements tailored to clients' *own* plans for risk management. Such agreements may be integrated into governing documents of a group, or into a contract for shared ownership, borrowing/lending, or of a peer-to-peer transaction. The agreements will memorialize clients' answers to questions such as

1. **Reducing risk:** How can we reduce risk? What precautions will we take?
2. **Procedures:** What specific steps will be taken in the event of loss or liability?
3. **What is lost:** What are the types of things that can go wrong? How might our response vary depending on what is lost?
4. **Cause:** How might we respond differently to loss depending on *how* it happened? How will the response differ if damage is caused by negligence, recklessness, crime, acts of nature, bad luck, and so on?
5. **Fault:** How might we respond differently to loss depending on who is at fault? How will fault be determined? What if multiple people are fault?
6. **Insurance:** How can we insure against loss? How much coverage should we seek?
7. **Who shoulders the burden:** Should responsibility be allocated to anyone in particular? Is risk currently falling disproportionately on one person? Should that person be indemnified? Should everyone in a group share risk equally?
8. **Waivers:** Should anyone waive their right to seek damages from others in the event of a loss?
9. **Minimum and maximum contributions:** Is there a minimum that each individual should be required to contribute? Is there a maximum contribution, after which an individual may refuse to contribute?
10. **Agreeing in advance to damage amounts:** Should parties, in advance, agree to pay specific damage amounts in the event of a

loss? For example, if one person lends a kayak to the other, should the parties agree on a dollar amount for the replacement of the kayak if it is lost or severely damaged by the borrower?

11. **Guaranteeing compensation:** Will anyone offer collateral or a personal guaranty to ensure compensation in the event of loss? Would it make sense to use a security interest to ensure compensation, such as using a property lien in the event that someone does not pay? Should a reserve fund be used to ensure availability of funds for restoring a loss?
12. **Responding to intangible harm:** How will we respond and make whole damages that are less tangible or measurable, such as emotional distress, damage to reputation, or damage to businesses?
13. **Standards:** What are our standards of repair and replacement? Will we restore damaged property only to the level of repair reflected immediately prior to damage? Or will the property be replaced entirely? What materials may or may not be used?
14. **Timelines:** How soon must we restore that which is lost? What will be done in the interim?
15. **Decisions:** Is any one person designated to make decisions unilaterally? When loss requires that we make a decision as a group, by what process will that decision be made?
16. **Disputes:** What dispute resolution process should we use?

Note that the enforceability of clients' risk management agreements will sometimes be undermined by precedents established by case law, which means that a sharing economy lawyer should become familiar with the types of agreements courts are prone to upholding or rejecting. For example, as discussed further below, courts often give very little weight to liability waivers, since public policy favors the idea that everyone should have a duty to be careful, and that use of waivers may cause people to shirk that duty. As such, we will be guided by case law in drafting liability waivers to imitate those that courts have upheld, and we'll avoid the fine-print waivers that courts tend to throw out.

Common Agreements for Sharing Economy Clients

The following describe agreements that sharing economy lawyers will commonly be called on to write for sharing economy clients:

1. **"Everyone chips in" agreements:** When the impact of loss will fall disproportionately on one person, or where members of a group want to insulate one another from the distressing financial burdens, groups may make agreements that everyone will chip in to cover a loss or financial burden. Such agreements can also act as a form of community insurance. Groups may even wish to maintain bank accounts for the creation of reserve funds, to ensure that funds will be available as soon as they are needed. Such agreements may resemble what is also referred to as "tandas" or "rotating credit associations," where members of a group pool funds in order to help individual members when they have urgent needs for cash.[16]
2. **Indemnity agreements:** Certain parties to a sharing arrangement or certain members of a group may sometimes, by legal default, be disproportionately subject to liability in a lawsuit brought by outside parties. For example, the owner of a shared vehicle is the party most likely to be sued in a car accident, even if someone else was driving the car and caused the accident. In cases where liability would be unfairly distributed, parties may wish to indemnify the potentially liable party, by agreeing to fully or partially compensate that party in the event that they are held liable for a loss or injury. At the very least, parties may wish to indemnify one another for any amounts not covered by insurance.
3. **Liability waivers:** No one wants to be sued, especially if a lawsuit arises from an act of sharing. When a homeowner lets someone else use her yard to grow food, when an ecovillage allows visitors to camp on the property, or when one person lends a bicycle to another, the hosting/lending party will often want the visiting/borrowing party to agree not to sue in the event of an injury or other loss.

Sharing economy lawyers will find it useful to learn the art and science of drafting liability releases, and also the art of explaining their utility to clients. Generally, the law does not lean

16. Rosalba Gama, Delma Medrano & Luis Medrano, Tandas and Cundinas: Mexican-American and Latino-American Rotating Credit Associations in Southern California (Anthropology of Money in Southern California online exhibit), http://www.anthropology.uci.edu/~wmmaurer/courses/anthro_money_2004/Tandas.htm.

in favor of organizations and individuals that use liability releases, since such releases could provide an easy way for organizations or individuals to avoid taking proper care in their activities or carrying proper insurance, and because they eliminate a source of compensation for injured parties. Courts always strictly construe release forms *against* the party seeking to be released from liability.

For example, if a visiting camper steps in a hole at an ecovillage and is injured, the visitor might sue the ecovillage. As a defense in court, the ecovillage would present the liability release form that the visitor signed. The visitor's attorney would analyze the release with a fine-toothed comb and point out all the reasons why the visitor couldn't have known that he was signing away his ability to sue for all injuries. The court will listen to the visitor's attorney and may rule in favor of the visitor if the court encounters anything questionable about the release.

That said, there are plenty of cases where individuals and organizations (including outdoor recreational organizations, ski resorts, skydiving companies, and indoor gyms) have been sued and successfully defended against the claim because they had a well-drafted release form that was clear, had no contradictions, informed the client of the risks involved, and had broad enough language to cover many different injury scenarios.[17] Even though courts are somewhat hostile to liability release forms, courts also understand that many organizations would not be able to engage in certain activities or invite others onto their premises, if they were subject to liability. Likewise, courts think that it is often reasonable to expect participants who sign a release form to give up that right to sue, in exchange for the benefit of participating in an activity.

One California court has given a particularly colorful description of the balancing act required in drafting a release (internal citations, although very useful, have been removed for the sake of brevity):

> Drafters of releases always face the problem of steering between the Scylla of simplicity and the Charybdis of

17. Susan M. Heinrich-Wells, *Practice Tips: The Enforceability of Liability Releases in High-Risk Sports*, 21 L.A. LAW. 26 (June 1998).

> completeness. Apparently no release is immune from attack. If short and to the point, a release will be challenged as failing to mention the particular risk which caused a plaintiff's injury [...] or as insufficiently comprehensive [...]. It will be attacked as totally ineffective if a key word is placed in the caption for emphasis but not repeated in the text [...]. or if, despite unambiguous language, the word "negligence" is not used [...]. If the drafter avoids these shortcomings by adding details and illustrations, the plaintiff invokes the doctrine *expressio unius exclusio alterius est* and characterizes the causative hazard as one not found among those listed in the release, but if the list ends with an inclusive term—"and all other risks not specifically enumerated"—it will be argued, under the principle *ejusdem generis*, that the risk encountered is nonetheless not assumed, because its nature is different from those listed. If the drafter strives to be comprehensive, the release is attacked as unduly lengthy [...], but if he fits it onto a single page, the type size will be criticized as inadequate [...]. If the significance of the release is emphasized by its repetition in two documents, any variation in wording fuels a challenge. [...][18]

Note, in addition, that court generally won't uphold a liability release in the event of gross negligence by a defendant. Only liability for ordinary negligence may be released.[19]

When I draft liability releases, I employ some of the following key practices:

- Use at least 12-point font;
- Disclose every risk involved, which, although it sounds dramatic, "may include death";
- Make it as clear as possible that the person signing is waiving his/her right to sue (using bold or underlined language);
- Draft the document in plain English; and
- Make the agreement short enough that the signor will actually read it.

18. Nat'l & Int'l Bhd. of St. Racers, Inc., v. Superior Court of L.A. Cnty., 215 Cal. App. 3d 934 (1989).

19. *See also* City of Santa Barbara v. Superior Court, 41 Cal. 4th 747 (2007).

I also generally advise my clients to

- Verbally explain to people the purpose of the release before they sign it;
- Make sure that both parties keep a copy;
- In the case of long-term arrangements, revisit the release from time to time and have the signor execute a new one every year; and
- Post a copy on a wall of the premises, if appropriate.

Even when they may not be upheld in court, liability releases can go a long way in two other regards: they can create and communicate clear expectations that signor should be careful, and they can set a good tone and discourage parties from suing each other.

4. **Alternative dispute resolution agreements:** The cost of litigation, and even, in some cases, arbitration, may discourage people from entering into sharing relationships where conflict, loss, or injury is possible or foreseeable. When parties make detailed agreements for the use of mediation and/or inexpensive arbitration, this can greatly alleviate fears. Such agreements should provide detail about how the process will be initiated, how parties will choose a mediator or arbitrator, how the process will be managed, how parties will share the costs of the process, and so on.

Forming Limited Liability Entities

Contracts can go a long way in managing and reallocating risk; however, in many cases, the formation of a limited liability entity, like an LLC or corporation, will nevertheless be key to easing clients' worries. In the sharing economy, people will often come together for joint and collaborative projects, and a significant barrier to such collaborations is the fear that people will be liable for the mistakes of their collaborators.

For example, if ten neighbors decide to share ownership and use of three cars, they may be well served by the formation of an LLC or nonprofit mutual benefit corporation. In this way, individual members will be protected in the event that another member negligently causes an accident. In that case, the LLC may be liable, and the negligent driver may be liable, but other members of the group are likely shielded from liability.

To preserve the liability shield, however, such groups, however small, will want to adhere carefully to corporate formalities or to formalities dictated by their operating agreement. This includes maintaining separate bank accounts for the entity, providing formal notice of meetings, setting clear procedures for decision-making, and keeping minutes and other records of the entity's transactions. Failure to adhere to such formalities allows courts to "pierce the corporate veil" and hold individuals liable.

Part 3: Insurance

Whereas making agreements with one another goes a long way toward quelling fears, sharing economy clients will nevertheless often turn to insurance to cover the risks they cannot shoulder. However, our current insurance options do not fully provide for the insurance needs of the sharing economy. The sharing economy is characterized by a larger number of diverse enterprises, some of which resemble public and commercial enterprises and some of which do not. Because of the difficulty in classifying them and predicting the risk involved, the cost of insurance for relatively simple activities can be prohibitively high. There will also be many gray areas when it comes to determining what activities will be covered by our current insurance policies.

Insurance companies have not evolved policies that are tailored to the range of small-scale localized economic activities, and there are two common activities that insurance companies will react negatively to: regular sharing of things we normally only use ourselves and commercial activity in the context of our personal lives. Here are a couple of examples:

> **Example 1:** Let's say that you want to regularly lend your car to your neighbor. Your neighbor pays you 40 cents a mile when he borrows it. If you have regular car insurance and the neighbor gets in an accident, the insurance company might refuse to cover the damage on two grounds. They will say:
>
> 1. "We didn't know you were sharing. Your neighbor isn't covered if he is more than an occasional driver."
> 2. "You were charging money to your neighbor. You are not covered to operate a car rental business."

> **Example 2:** Let's say you hold twice-weekly dinner parties at your house and people make a "suggested donation" of $10 each time they come. If someone is injured, the homeowners' insurance company may refuse to cover you on two grounds. They will say:
>
> 1. "Regular and frequent gathering activities were not included in the scope of use for which your home is covered."
> 2. "Commercial activities were not covered by your homeowners' policy."

The example of car sharing illustrates the need both to create specialized insurance policies and to create laws that make certain that sharing activities will be insurable. Most car insurance policies allow for a small amount of sharing. Most of the time, our friends are covered if we lend them our car *occasionally*. This leaves a gray area, first and foremost between, *occasionally* and *regularly*. How often is too often? If we lend someone our car every Sunday, is that routine enough to be considered more than occasional?

Some car insurance companies leave us no option to regularly share with people who do not live in our household and do not co-own the car. If we try to add a friend to our insurance policy, we may encounter a barrier, which is that the insurance company will not consider the friend to have an "insurable interest" in the vehicle. The reasoning goes that if the friend does not own the vehicle, he should not be compensated for damage caused to it.

At the same time, it is possible to purchase a type of policy called non-owner's car insurance, which provides liability coverage to the person borrowing another's car. Non-owner's insurance is generally cheaper than regular car insurance, and many car sharers may feel greater ease knowing that there are two potential sources of coverage in the event of an accident by the non-owner.

In the cases of car sharing clubs where title to the vehicle is held by an entity such as an LLC, insurance may be somewhat more expensive, but potentially more straightforward, since the *entity* has the insurable interest. In such cases, the entity may still be required to provide info about every driver to the car insurance company, and the insurance company may reserve the right to reject members with a tarnished driving history.

Both California[20] and Oregon[21] have now passed peer-to-peer car-sharing laws, which force insurance companies to adapt somewhat to the car-sharing times. California's law, for example, makes it illegal for car insurance companies to classify a car as a "vehicle for-hire" or "commercial vehicle" when the owner places the car in a program meeting the requirements of a Personal Vehicle Sharing Program (PVSP). This prevents insurance companies from denying, terminating, or raising the rates of coverage for the car owner. The law requires that the car-sharing program carry insurance to cover any drivers using the car and provides that the owner and his/her insurance should not be held liable, and that they should be indemnified, in the event of an accident by the borrowing driver.

A basic idea behind the car-sharing laws is that if you share your car and get money in return, so long as you don't make more money than it costs to own your car, then you should not be treated by your insurer as a car rental business. The law was an important step forward in recognizing the difference between sharing for commercial purposes and sharing for the sake of offsetting costs.

Another basic premise behind the laws is that people who share, and their insurance companies, should not be subjected to additional risk if the people with whom they are sharing are not adequately covered to provide for injured parties. Sharing should not always result in a broader pool of people who are potentially liable. Rather, sharing, under certain circumstances, should shift responsibility and liability from one party to another.

Whereas the laws add fuel to the car-sharing movement, the laws were also limited, and require that people manage the car-sharing arrangement through third-party personal vehicle–sharing programs (PVSPs). I believe it would be worth revisiting and questioning the necessity of all of the provisions of the two laws, including, particularly, the requirement that third-party PVSP be involved. PVSPs are not yet available in most parts of the country and may just add an unnecessary layer of administrative hassle. I believe that it should be enough to allow people to share their cars with others, so long as they aren't making a

20. *See* A.B. 1871 (Cal.; effective Jan. 1, 2011) (codified at Cal. Ins. Code § 11580.24).
21. *See* H.B. 3149 (Or.; effective Jan. 1, 2012).

profit and so long as the other drivers carry their own insurance policies. The law in that case could provide that the owner may not be held liable for accidents caused by someone borrowing the vehicle, so long as the driver has his/her own insurance policy in place.[22]

In states without car-sharing laws, and even perhaps in California and Oregon, there remain unanswered questions about who will be liable for accidents in cases of car sharing. Even with a car-sharing law in place, or even with strong waivers of liability and indemnity agreements, it is not clear when and whether courts will be willing to shield car owners from liability for the acts of people borrowing their vehicles.[23]

Adapting Insurance to the Sharing Economy

Formation of cooperatively owned insurance companies is one solution to meeting the unique insurance needs of the sharing economy. An even simpler option is to create bargaining collectives for certain types of sharing economy activities. For example, if 100 car-sharing enthusiasts formed a group to approach car insurance companies to bargain for 100 insurance policies, the insurance companies would have an incentive to develop competitive policies tailored to the sharing needs of the group. For example, the insurance company could draft a policy that allows for the regular sharing of a vehicle. The formation of such bargaining coalitions is a solution that leverages the power of cooperation in furtherance of an economy built on sharing.

---

22. *See generally* Janelle Orsi, *DIY Car Sharing: How to Start Your Own Car-Sharing Program*, SHAREABLE.NET (Mar. 1, 2011); Janelle Orsi, *Car Sharing Laws for Everyone*, SHAREABLE.NET (Mar. 9, 2011).

23. *See, e.g.*, Ron Lieber, *Share a Car, Risk Your Insurance*, N.Y. TIMES, Mar. 16, 2012; Ron Lieber, *Fatal Collision Makes Car-Sharing Worries No Longer Theoretical*, N.Y. TIMES, Apr. 13, 2012.

INDEX

S

ABOUT THE AUTHOR

Janelle Orsi is the director of the national nonprofit Sustainable Economies Law Center, and she is a "sharing economy lawyer" in private law practice in Oakland, CA. Her work is focused on helping communities share, barter, and create cooperatives, social enterprises, cohousing communities, urban farms, local currencies, and community-supported enterprises. In 2010, Janelle was profiled by the American Bar Association as a "Legal Rebel," an attorney who is "remaking the legal profession through the power of innovation."

Janelle is co-author of *The Sharing Solution: How to Save Money, Simplify Your Life & Build Community* (Nolo 2009), a legal and practical guide to shared ownership and cooperative activity. Janelle earned her J.D. from the University of California, Berkeley School of Law.